McGraw
Graw
Hill
Education

Also Available from McGraw-Hill Education

Cover: Nathan Love, Erwin Madrid

mheducation.com/prek-12

Send all inquiries to:
McGraw-Hill Education
Two Penn Plaza
New York, New York 10121

ISBN: 978-0-07-901678-2
MHID: 0-07-901678-2

Printed in the United States of America

2 3 4 5 6 7 QVS 23 22 21 20 19

B

Welcome to
Wonders

Developed for today's students—grounded in research

⭐ Building firm foundations for literacy

⭐ Integrating science, social studies, and powerful literature

⭐ Supporting English Language Learners

⭐ Teaching the whole child

> **❝** My hope for our students is that they develop competence and confidence in their literacy skills. Literacy is key to all other learning, so I hope our collective efforts result in exceptional levels of achievement in reading, writing, speaking, listening, and thinking. **❞**
>
> Dr. Douglas Fisher

Mc
Graw
Hill
Education

Authors

Dr. Diane August
American Institute for Research

Dr. Donald R. Bear
Iowa State University
University of Nevada, Reno
Professor Emeritus

Kathy R. Bumgardner, M.Ed., Ed.S.
Strategies Unlimited, Inc.
National Literacy Consultant
School Improvement Specialist

Dr. Jana Echevarria
California State University,
Long Beach
Professor Emerita

Dr. Douglas Fisher
San Diego State University

Dr. David J. Francis
University of Houston

Dr. Vicki Gibson
Gibson Hasbrouck and Associates

Dr. Jan Hasbrouck
University of Oregon
Gibson Hasbrouck and Associates

Dr. Timothy Shanahan
University of Illinois at Chicago
Professor Emeritus

Dr. Josefina V. Tinajero
University of Texas at El Paso

> **"** My hope for our students is that their teachers can help every student become a skillful and motivated reader and writer. **"**
>
> Dr. Jan Hasbrouck

Program Advisor

Sesame Workshop
Nonprofit educational organization behind Sesame Street, The Electric Company, and so much more.

> **"** My hope for our students, including English Learners, is that they will receive outstanding English language arts and reading instruction to allow them to reach their full academic potential and excel in school and in life. **"**

Dr. Josefina V. Tinajero

Consulting Authors

Peggy Cerna
Dual Language Training Institute

Sheila Collazo, M.Ed.
Educational Consultant

Jay McTighe
Jay McTighe and Associates

Dr. Tracy Spinrad
Arizona State University

Dr. Doris Walker-Dalhouse
Marquette University

Dinah Zike
Dinah-Might Activities, Inc.

TEACH IT YOUR WAY

Are you workshop-focused? Committed to blended learning? Project-based? All about authentic literature?

You know what your students need, drawing on the connections you make every day. **Wonders** makes it easy to integrate your own favorite resources in both print and digital formats.

Lots of classroom tech, or just getting started? 100% print, 100% digital, or somewhere in between? **Wonders** resources and tools will meet you where you are, and take you where you want to be, in both print and digital formats.

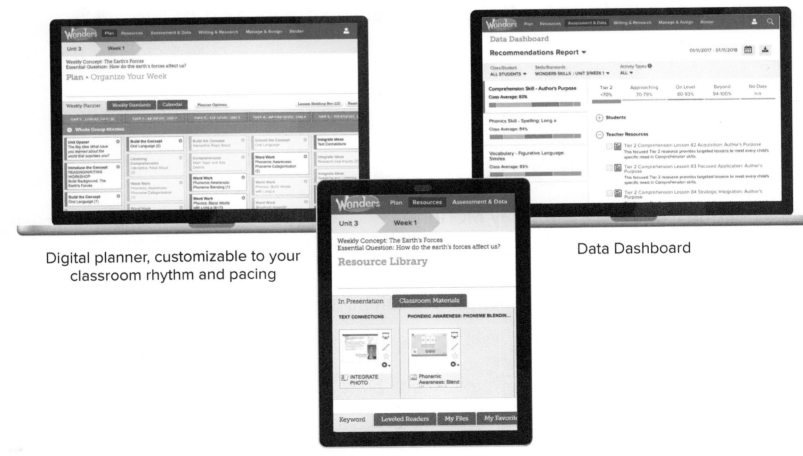

Digital planner, customizable to your classroom rhythm and pacing

Data Dashboard

Ready-to-go presentations

Have your students already mastered core objectives? Adapt your instruction with confidence, freeing you to go further. Look for the Teach It Your Way features throughout.

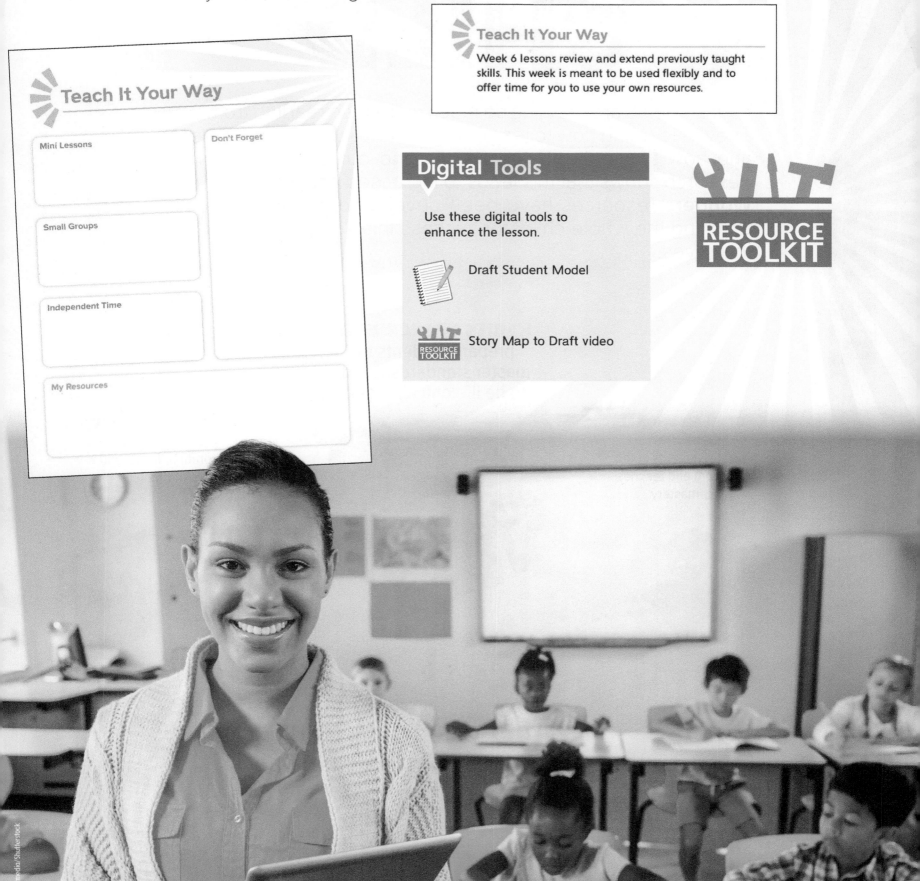

Teach It Your Way

Mini Lessons	Don't Forget
Small Groups	
Independent Time	
My Resources	

Teach It Your Way

Week 6 lessons review and extend previously taught skills. This week is meant to be used flexibly and to offer time for you to use your own resources.

Digital Tools

Use these digital tools to enhance the lesson.

Draft Student Model

Story Map to Draft video

RESOURCE TOOLKIT

Teaching the WHOLE CHILD

Your students are learning so much more than reading from you. They're learning how to learn, how to master new content areas, and how to handle themselves in and out of the classroom. Research shows that this leads to increased academic success. **Wonders** resources have been developed to support you in teaching the whole child, for success this year and throughout their lives.

HABITS OF LEARNING prepare students to master standards... and to be lifelong learners.

SOCIAL EMOTIONAL LEARNING grounds students in the classroom and teaches self-mastery.

CLASSROOM CULTURE sets the stage for collaboration, focus, and a love of reading.

DEVELOPING CRITICAL THINKERS

- Mastery of reading, writing, speaking, and listening
- Knowledge that spans content areas
- College and career readiness
- Strong results this year and beyond

HABITS of Learning

To master reading and writing, speaking and listening is to master thinking. These six habits of learning, reinforced throughout the year and across the grades, teach children how to learn. Each unit focuses on one habit that will set students up for success.

I use a variety of strategies to understand.

make predictions

take notes

think about how a piece is organized

visualize

I think critically about what I read.

ask questions

look for text evidence

think across domains

make inferences

I write to communicate.

think about my message

think about my audience

talk with my peers

use rubrics

I am part of a community of learners.

listen actively

build on others' thoughts

share what I know

choose the right words

gather information before I act or speak

I believe I can succeed.

challenge myself

stay on task

I am a problem solver.

analyze the problem

try different ways

AUTHOR INSIGHT

> " My hope for our students is that they are encouraged to collaborate and talk more to develop their oral language, in ways that will enhance reading comprehension and written expression. "

Dr. Vicki Gibson

SOCIAL EMOTIONAL LEARNING

Social emotional learning is one of the most important factors in predicting school success. **Wonders** is developed to support students in mastering themselves and how they interact with the world.

As students grow through the grades, while building literacy they develop:

+ Social Problem-Solving

+ Self-Confidence

+ Maintained Focus

+ Sustained Attention

+ Working Memory

+ Task Persistence

+ Planning and Problem-Solving

+ Flexible Thinking

+ Self-Control

+ Rules and Routines

+ Curiosity

+ Creativity

+ Initiative

+ Logical Reasoning

+ Care and Empathy

+ Managing Emotions

+ Identity and Belonging

+ Executive Function

+ Emotional Self-Regulation

+ Behavioral Self-Regulation

+ Relationships and Pro-Social Behavior with Adults

+ Relationships and Pro-Social Behavior with Other Children

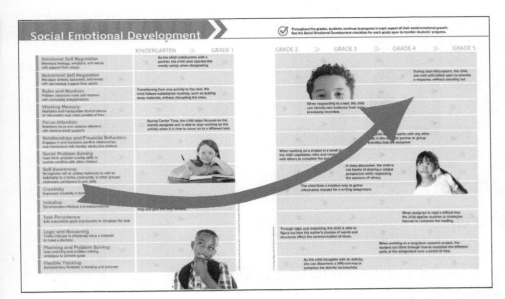

Lessons are carefully shaped to bolster targeted literacy skills, supporting children's learning and social emotional development throughout the year.

Weekly school-to-home family communication letters, ready to send in multiple languages, encourage parents to log on and share resources with their children, including listening to audio summaries of all main selections so they can ask questions. This deepens the connection between community and classroom, supporting social emotional development. This helps ensure that each and every child comes to school engaged, motivated, and eager to learn!

- English
- Spanish
- Hmong
- Chinese
- Korean
- Tagalog
- Vietnamese
- Urdu
- Arabic

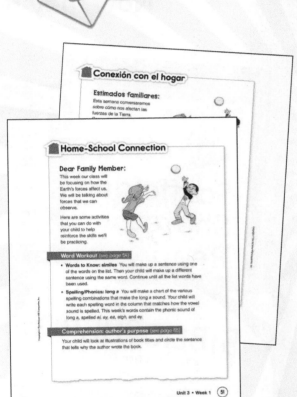

E-books for all main selections include audio summaries in the same languages.

AUTHOR INSIGHT

My hope for our students is that those who are developing literacy in a new language will, through meaningful, scaffolded instruction, accelerate their language proficiency and develop the knowledge and skills necessary to reach their full academic potential.

Dr. Jana Echevarria

©Michael Grover_Heinemann, Portsmouth, NH

Teaching through
GENRE

Wonders is grounded throughout in a firm understanding of **genre**.

Students read widely across a connected text set, speak and listen about what they've noted, and write in the genre from an expert model or mentor text.

Now they're ready for independent reading.

FOLKTALE

Persuasive Text

Poetry

Realistic Fiction

Informational Text Nonfiction

BIOGRAPHY

Fantasy

DRAMA

By mastering the key features of each genre, students are better prepared to understand subject matter, and read more broadly and deeply.

Leveled Reader Library Online

Genre · Personal Narrative

Compare Texts
Read about how a girl helped her dad, the gymnastics coach.

Landing on Your Feet

Before I wake up for school, Dad is already at work. He is an ironworker in the city. Ironworkers build tall buildings and repair giant bridges. They build with heavy metal beams made of iron. When Dad comes home, he likes to cook or do things for our house. He also teaches his favorite sport to kids. Dad is a gymnastics coach at a community center. He teaches girls like me at the same gym where he learned gymnastics as a boy.

Gymnastics is fun but hard to learn. Dad encourages us to practice to get better. He teaches older kids amazing skills like backflips and handstands. We all feel proud after we work hard and learn a cool new skill.

ONE PLASTIC BAG

ISATOU CEESAY AND THE RECYCLING WOMEN OF THE GAMBIA

MIRANDA PAUL

ILLUSTRATED BY ELIZABETH ZUNON

Debby drives her truck from place to place. It is **lonely** with no one riding along. Then she thinks about how exciting it was to use electricity for the first time. Now families can do the things you do without thinking about them. They can heat their homes or turn on a light! Debby says she is "lighting up people's lives."

NARRATIVE NONFICTION

FIND TEXT EVIDENCE

Genre
Author's Purpose
Circle the description of what it is like when Debby drives from place to place. **Underline** what Debby thinks about.

Summarize

Use the most important details from "Lighting Lives" to orally summarize how Debby Tewa helps her community get electricity.

Fluency

With a partner, read aloud page 7. Use the author's ideas and end punctuation to guide your expression.

Author's Craft

What does Debby mean when she says she is "lighting up people's lives"? Why does the author include this quote?

Integrate DOK 4

• Integrate knowledge and ideas.
• Make text-to-text connections.
• Use the Integrate lesson.
• Inspire action.

Foundations of RIGOR

LITERACY BEGINS WITH FIRM FOUNDATIONS.

Wonders offers a thorough grounding in foundational skills, from the first steps in phonemic awareness and concepts of print, through sophisticated academic vocabulary and advanced morphological analysis. All along the way, integrated Tier 2 lessons fill any gaps quickly.

As they deepen understanding, students are encouraged to listen before speaking, speak before writing, and think critically all along.

With integrated grammar, spelling, and handwriting instruction, students build their capabilities every day.

Foundational Skills K–5

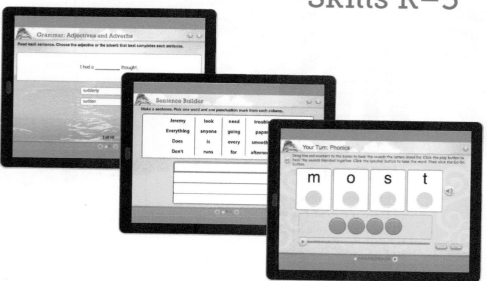

Foundational Skills Kit also available

Every year, as students progress in fluency, they are also deepening their knowledge of science and social studies topics, and plunging into a world of authentic literature.

🌐 **Content Area Learning**
- Research ways that people help in their communities

 Content Area Learning
- Research patterns of objects that can be observed in the sky

Integrate   DOK 4

- Integrate knowledge and ideas.
- Make text-to-text connections.
- Use the Integrate lesson.
- Inspire action.

DOK Level **4** questions throughout inspire learning at the highest levels.

A C T   Access Complex Text

Connection of Ideas

Children may need help connecting to the idea that Debby is motivated to help her own community because of her own experience growing up.

- Make sure children understand that because Debby grew up without electricity, there were many things she could not do.

- Discuss how growing up without electricity would motivate Debby to help bring electricity to others in her community.

- Help children identify photos, captions, and other text evidence that illustrates how Debby lived as a child and how her work is changing the community in which she grew up.

AUTHOR INSIGHT

❝ My hope for our students is that they will come to see themselves as able to make sense of even difficult texts—that their reading determination and perseverance can be keys to their academic success. ❞

Dr. Timothy Shanahan

DIFFERENTIATED
for **EVERY** Student

Wonders gives you resources and instruction to move students ahead as soon as they're ready. With your digital Data Dashboard, you can see proficiency at a glance, offering you instructional flexibility with confidence—freeing you to teach your way.

STRUGGLING READERS find targeted support including Tier 2 resources.

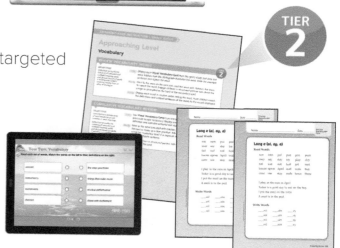

TIER 2

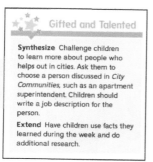

Gifted and Talented

Synthesize Challenge children to learn more about people who helps out in cities. Ask them to choose a person discussed in *City Communities*, such as an apartment superintendent. Children should write a job description for the person.

Extend Have children use facts they learned during the week and do additional research.

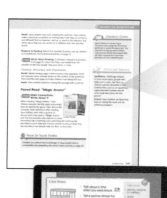

GIFTED AND TALENTED students will find additional choices to extend their reading, research areas of interest, and write about everything they've learned.

ENGLISH LANGUAGE LEARNERS are supported in both content and language acquisition, from newcomers to those of advanced proficiency.

Scaffolded Shared Read

Wonders

Language Transfers Handbook

English Learner Benchmark Assessments also available online

lisegagne/Getty Images

Wonders brings the best in blended learning to your classroom. Every print resource is also available digitally . . . as well as thousands more readers, hundreds more games, and a myriad of optional resources to extend every lesson. You'll find just the right additional resources for all kinds of learners.

In Grades 2–5, students can practice responsible use of social media, in a controlled setting focused on core academic content. This prepares them for StudySync, available for grades 6–12.

Maravillas offers equity of academic content, as well as deep instruction of Spanish foundational skills and a wealth of authentic Spanish literature.

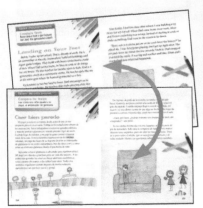

Academic content with deep equity

Authentic literature in English and Spanish

For additional information about how to differentiate for English language learners, students with special needs, and gifted and talented students, see the Instructional Routines Handbook.

RESOURCES

Minilesson Resources

Reading/Writing Companion

Visual Vocabulary Cards

High-Frequency Word Cards

Collaborative Conversations student models

Word-Building Cards

Authentic Literature

Sound-Spelling Cards

Interactive Read-Aloud Cards

Decodable Readers

Foundational Skills Activities

Teacher Resources

Teacher's Edition

Professional Development

Instructional Routines Handbook

School-to-Home Support

Assessments

Unit Assessments

Progress Monitoring Assessments

Benchmark Assessments

Online Assessments

Data Dashboard

Small Group and Guided Reading Resources

(A) → Written to Guided Reading Levels → (Z)

Leveled Readers

Leveled Reader Lesson Cards

K–8 Leveled Reader Library Online

Workstation Activity Cards at four levels

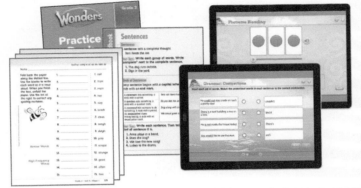

Word Work, Grammar, Spelling, Vocabulary practice

Classroom Library Trade Books with Lessons

Decodable Passages

Independent Practice

Writer's Notebook

Differentiated Genre Passages

More Resources for English Language Learners

Newcomer Teacher's Guide

Newcomer Cards

Differentiated Texts at three proficiency levels

Language Development Cards

Language Development Practice

Language Transfers Handbook

ELL Scaffolded Shared Read

**TEACH IT YOUR WAY**

Contents

Unit Planning

Genre Study 1 **Narrative Nonfiction**   T10

Genre Study 2 **Fiction**   T166

Genre Study 3 **Expository Text**   T322

Review, Extend, and Assess   T440

Unit Overview

	GENRE STUDY 1	**GENRE STUDY 2**
	NARRATIVE NONFICTION	**FICTION**

READING

GENRE STUDY 1 — NARRATIVE NONFICTION

ESSENTIAL QUESTION
How can people help out their community?

Vocabulary
across, borrow, countryside, ideas, insists, lonely, solution, villages
Strategy: Synonyms
Comprehension
Strategy: Ask and Answer Questions
Skill: Author's Purpose
Text Features: Photos and Captions
Author's Craft: Time Words
Word Work
Phonological/Phonemic Awareness: Identify and Generate Rhyme; Phoneme Categorization, Blending, Isolation, Substitution
Phonics: Long *a*, Long *i*
Structural Analysis: Contractions, Open Syllables
High-Frequency Words
Fluency
Expression, Phrasing

GENRE STUDY 2 — FICTION

ESSENTIAL QUESTION
What can we see in the sky?

Vocabulary
adventure, delighted, dreamed, enjoyed, grumbled, moonlight, neighbor, nighttime
Strategy: Compound Words
Comprehension
Strategy: Reread
Skill: Plot: Sequence
Literary Elements: Point of View
Author's Craft: Heads
Word Work
Phonological/Phonemic Awareness: Identify Syllables Phonemic Deletion, Substitution, Addition, Blending, Categorization
Phonics: Long *o*, Long *e*
Structural Analysis: Contractions with *not*, Plurals
High-Frequency Words
Fluency
Intonation, Expression

LANGUAGE ARTS

GENRE STUDY 1

Writing
Personal Narrative: Expert Model, Plan, Draft
Grammar
Action Verbs, Present-Tense Verbs
Spelling
Long *a*, Long *i*
Vocabulary
Expand Vocabulary

GENRE STUDY 2

Writing
Personal Narrative: Revise, Edit and Proofread, Publish
Grammar
Past- and Future-Tense Verbs, Subject-Verb Agreement
Spelling
Long *o*, Long *e*
Vocabulary
Expand Vocabulary

KEY SKILLS TRACE

PHONICS

··· > Short Vowels; Consonant Blends; **Long Vowels** > Soft *c* and *g*; Consonant Digraphs > 3-Letter Consonant Blends > Silent Letters > *r*-Controlled Vowels > ···

COMPREHENSION

Author's Purpose
Introduce Unit 3: Genre Study 1
Review Unit 3, Week 6, Unit 5: Genre Study 3
Assess Unit 3, Unit 5

Character, Setting, Events/Plot
Introduce Unit 1: Genre Study 1
Review Unit 2: Genre Study 2, Week 6, Unit 3: Genre Study 2, Week 6, Unit 4: Genre Study 1, Week 6
Assess Unit 1, Unit 2, Unit 3, Unit 4

Main Topic/Idea and Key Details
Introduce Unit 2: Genre Study 1
Review Unit 2, Week 6, Unit 3: Genre Study 3, Week 6
Assess Unit 2, Unit 3

VOCABULARY

Synonyms
Introduce Unit 1: Genre Study 3
Review Unit 1, Week 6, Unit 3: Genre Study 1, Unit 5: Genre Study 1
Assess Unit 1, Unit 3, Unit 5

Homographs, Compound Words
Introduce Unit 2: Genre Study 1
Review Unit 3: Genre Study 2
Assess Unit 2, Unit 3

Root Words, Suffixes, and Prefixes
Introduce Unit 1: Genre Study 1
Review Unit 1: Genre Study 2, Unit 2: Genre Study 3, Unit 3: Genre Study 3, Week 6, Unit 5: Genre Study 2
Assess Unit 1, Unit 2, Unit 3, Unit 5

GENRE STUDY 3

EXPOSITORY TEXT

ESSENTIAL QUESTION

How do you express yourself?

Vocabulary

cheered, concert, instrument, movements, music, rhythm, sounds, understand
Strategy: Prefixes

Comprehension

Strategy: Ask and Answer Questions
Skill: Main Idea and Key Details
Text Features: Bar Graphs
Author's Craft: Graphic Features

Word Work

Phonological/Phonemic Awareness: Identify, Generate Alliteration; Phoneme Addition, Deletion, Blending
Phonics: Long *u*
Structural Analysis: Comparative Endings *-er, -est*
High-Frequency Words

Fluency

Intonation

Writing

Expository Essay: Expert Model, Plan, Draft

Grammar

The verb *have*

Spelling

Long *u*

Vocabulary

Expand Vocabulary

WEEK 6

REVIEW, EXTEND, AND ASSESS

Reading Digitally
Notetaking
Navigating Links

Reader's Theater
Focus on Vocabulary
Fluency: Phrasing and Expression

Unit Wrap Up
Show What You Learned
Extend Your Learning
Track Your Progress
Wrap Up the Unit

Presentation Options
Research and Inquiry
Writing

Unit 3 Assessment
Unit Assessment Book
Fluency Assessment pages 82–91

Writing

Expository Essay: Revise, Edit and Proofread, Publish
Portfolio Choice

| Diphthongs | Variant Vowels | Vowel Digraphs | Syllables |

GRAMMAR

Verbs

Introduce Unit 3: Genre Study 1
Review Unit 3: Genre Study 2, Genre Study 3, Unit 4: Genre Study 1, Genre Study 2, Grammar Handbook and Writing Process lessons, Unit 5, Unit 6
Assess Unit 3, Unit 4

WRITING PROCESS

Unit 1 Realistic Fiction, Expository Essay
Unit 2 Expository Essay, Rhyming Poem
Unit 3 Personal Narrative, Expository Essay
Unit 4 Realistic Fiction, Free Verse
Unit 5 Biography, Persuasive Essay
Unit 6 Research Report, Rhyming Poem

Social Emotional Learning

You may wish to foster the social emotional development of children by connecting the Essential Questions for your genre studies to these skills.

Unit 3 Genre Study 1: Initiative
Unit 3 Genre Study 2: Curiosity
Unit 3 Genre Study 3: Creativity

Develop Critical Thinkers

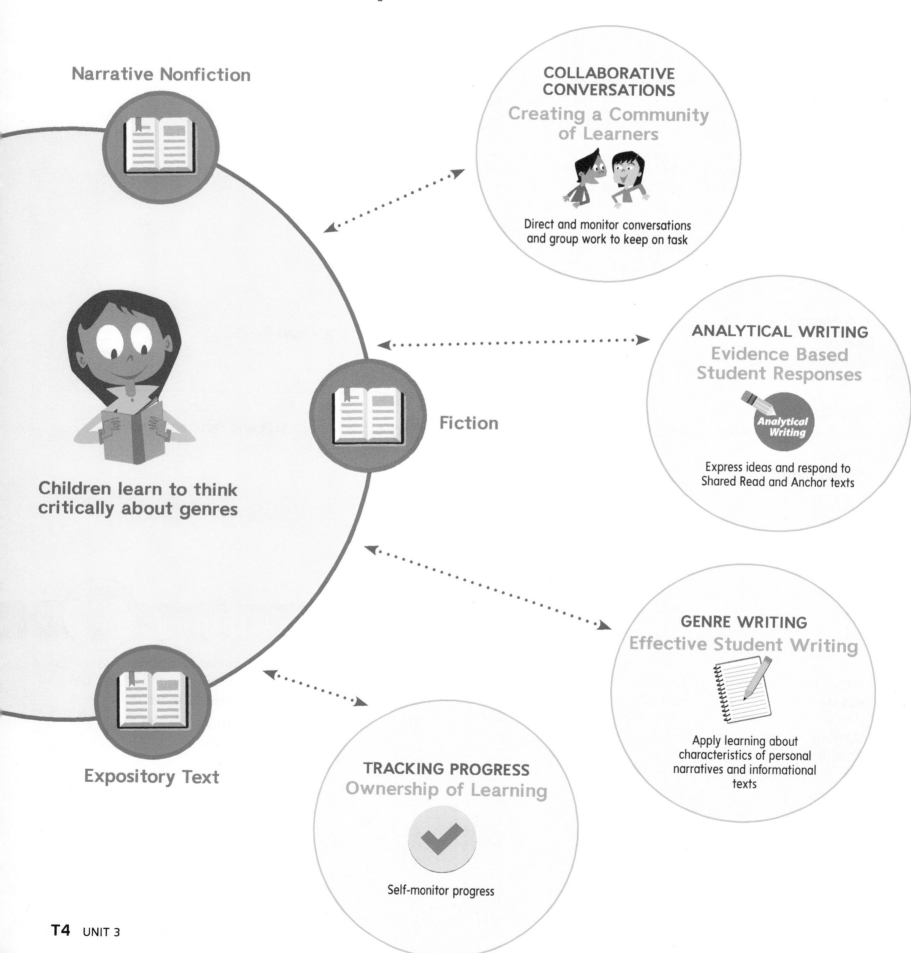

Narrative Nonfiction

Children learn to think critically about genres

Fiction

Expository Text

COLLABORATIVE CONVERSATIONS
Creating a Community of Learners

Direct and monitor conversations and group work to keep on task

ANALYTICAL WRITING
Evidence Based Student Responses

Analytical Writing

Express ideas and respond to Shared Read and Anchor texts

GENRE WRITING
Effective Student Writing

Apply learning about characteristics of personal narratives and informational texts

TRACKING PROGRESS
Ownership of Learning

Self-monitor progress

Encourage Independent Learners

PROJECT-BASED LEARNING
Research and Inquiry

Genre Study 1
Create a history picture book using primary and secondary resources

Genre Study 2
Describe a phase of the moon

Genre Study 3
Create a patriotic song collage

STEP 1	STEP 2	STEP 3	STEP 4	STEP 5
Set Research Goals	Identify Sources	Find and Record Information	Organize	Synthesize and Present

Children learn to research online and use a variety of sources to complete their projects.

Speaking and listening rubrics and checklists for evaluating children's work are provided at the end of Step 5.

INDEPENDENT READING

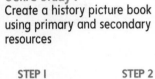

Read critically
Write analytically

Engage in academic discourse
Read books in the genre being studied and self-selected texts

Independent Reading routines help students:

Choose just the right book

Engage in partner discussions and activities to share what they are learning

Make connections from what they are learning to what they read independently

Develop the confidence to read different types of texts and reflect on the texts as critical thinkers

See the Instructional Routine Handbook online.

DIGITAL LITERACY
StudySync Blasts

Safe way for children to respond to topics in a social-media like tweet form

▶ Genre Study 1: **Making Our Lives Better...Together**
▶ Genre Study 2: **When the Night Sky Dances**
▶ Genre Study 3: **Show Yourself Through Art**

Teach It Your Way

Resources for Minilessons

Use Wonders resources for effective instruction and practice to enhance student outcomes in Reading, Writing, and Word Work.

Narrative Nonfiction Text Set

Interactive Read Aloud
"Color Your Community,"
T26–T27

Shared Read
"Lighting Lives,"
Reading/Writing Companion
pp. 2–7

Anchor Text
Biblioburro: A True Story from Colombia,
Literature Anthology pp. 231–233

Classroom Library Trade Books
Fire Fighter!
Lexile 500L
One Plastic Bag
Lexile 480L
See Unit Bibliography online

Self-Selected from Classroom Resources

with minilessons for Reading, Writing, and Word Work

Fiction Text Set

Interactive Read Aloud
"The Hidden Sun,"
T182–T183

Shared Read
"Starry Night,"
Reading/Writing Companion
pp. 38–43

Anchor Text
Mr. Putter & Tabby See the Stars,
Literature Anthology pp. 255–257

Classroom Library Trade Books
Henry and Mudge and the Starry Night
Lexile 440L
How Many Stars in the Sky?
Lexile 500L
See Unit Bibliography online

Self-Selected from Classroom Resources

with minilessons for Reading, Writing, and Word Work

Expository Text Set

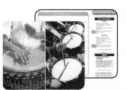

Interactive Read Aloud
"Why People Drum," T336–T337

Shared Read
"They've Got the Beat!"
Reading/Writing Companion
pp. 64–67

Anchor Text
Many Ways to Enjoy Music,
Literature Anthology pp. 262–265

Student's CHOICE

Self Selected from Classroom Resources

with minilessons for Reading, Writing, and Word Work

Resources for Small Group Instruction

Differentiate Instruction and Accelerate Learning using these leveled text resources for targeted instruction in Comprehension, Vocabulary, Phonics/Word Study, and Fluency.

Leveled Readers
City Communities
Approaching **GR** G **Lexile** 290L
On Level **GR** K **Lexile** 470L
Beyond **GR** O **Lexile** 620L
ELL **GR** J **Lexile** 400L

Genre Passages
"Helping Out in the Community"
Approaching **Lexile** 420L
On Level **Lexile** 510L
Beyond **Lexile** 610L
ELL **Lexile** 480L

ELL Scaffolded Shared Read
"Lighting Lives"

MORE TITLES TO CHOOSE FROM!

Leveled Reader Library
my.mheducation.com

Bonus Leveled Readers

Leveled Readers
A Special Sunset
Approaching **GR** G **Lexile** 200L
A Different Set of Stars
On Level **GR** K **Lexile** 390L
Shadows in the Sky
Beyond **GR** N **Lexile** 540L
A Different Set of Stars
ELL **GR** J **Lexile** 330L

Genre Passages
"A Shooting Star"
Approaching **Lexile** 350L
On Level **Lexile** 440L
Beyond **Lexile** 540L
ELL **Lexile** 390L

ELL Scaffolded Shared Read
"Starry Night"

MORE TITLES TO CHOOSE FROM!

Leveled Reader Library
my.mheducation.com

Bonus Leveled Readers

Leveled Readers
The Sounds of Trash
Approaching **GR** G **Lexile** 410L
On Level **GR** L **Lexile** 530L
Beyond **GR** O **Lexile** 590L
ELL **GR** J **Lexile** 380L

Genre Passages
"Musical Expression"
Approaching **Lexile** 450L
On Level **Lexile** 560L
Beyond **Lexile** 670L
ELL **Lexile** 510L

ELL Scaffolded Shared Read
"They've Got the Beat!"

MORE TITLES TO CHOOSE FROM!

Leveled Reader Library
my.mheducation.com

Bonus Leveled Readers

Teach the Whole Child

These suggestions will help you nurture children's confidence in their ability to succeed both academically and socially.

AUTHOR INSIGHT

"It is essential that students have a high level of motivation if they are going to succeed with particularly demanding texts. . . .""

—Dr. Timothy Shanahan

CLASSROOM CULTURE

Unit Focus: We promote ownership of learning.

Post the "we" statement and explain that every child is responsible for his or her own learning. As such, children need to think about what they need to learn and how they can best learn it. Encourage them to ask questions, try different strategies, find resources, seek help, record their efforts, and discover what tools and strategies help them learn best. Explain that self-evaluation is key to this process, and peer reviews, checklists, and rubrics will help them monitor their learning. Reassure children that you are there to help them, but that they are ultimately in charge of their learning.

HABITS OF LEARNING

Unit Focus: I believe I can succeed.

The goal of this Habit of Learning is to help children develop a positive attitude about learning. It goes hand in hand with the Classroom Culture focus. When children are encouraged to find the learning strategies and tools that work best for them, they develop a sense of agency and see that their actions make a difference. Share the following statements and discuss with children.

- I try different ways to learn things that are difficult for me.
- I challenge myself to do better.
- I stay on task until it is completed.

Courtesy of Timothy Shanahan

SOCIAL EMOTIONAL LEARNING

Unit Skills: Initiative, Curiosity, Creativity

The concept, Essential Question, and literature of each genre study in the unit allow you to focus on a key social emotional learning skill.

Genre Study 1

Concept: Ways People Help

Essential Question: **How can people help out their community?**

Initiative Children should have the confidence to take action when they see a chance to solve a problem or make a difference.

Before children read the texts in the genre study, discuss the concept of initiative. Ask: *What can you do when you a see a problem that you know how to solve?*

Genre Study 2

Concept: Look at the Sky

Essential Question: **What can we see in the sky?**

Curiosity Children should have a sense of wonder and curiosity about the world around them.

Before beginning the genre study, explain that curiosity is wondering about something and wanting to find out more about it. Ask: *What are you curious about? How can curiosity help you learn?*

Genre Study 3

Concept: Express Yourself

Essential Question: **How do you express yourself?**

Creativity Children should show creativity in their thinking and communication.

Before the genre study, ask children to share different ways they can express creativity. Tell them that creativity in thinking can lead to new and interesting ideas. Ask: *What are some creative solutions you have found to problems?*

Look for the Collaborate icons throughout the lessons. These indicate opportunities for children to practice and develop their SEL skills as they discuss and work together.

TEACH IT YOUR WAY

You know your children, so take a flexible approach to how you integrate Social Emotional Learning and address Habits of Learning and Classroom Culture in your classroom. For example, you may choose to emphasize one Habits of Learning "I" statement per genre study.

Genre Study
Narrative Nonfiction

Key Features

- Tells a story about a real person or people and real events

- Has a text structure that includes the order in which things happen, and may be based on problem and solution

- May have text features including photos and captions to give additional information

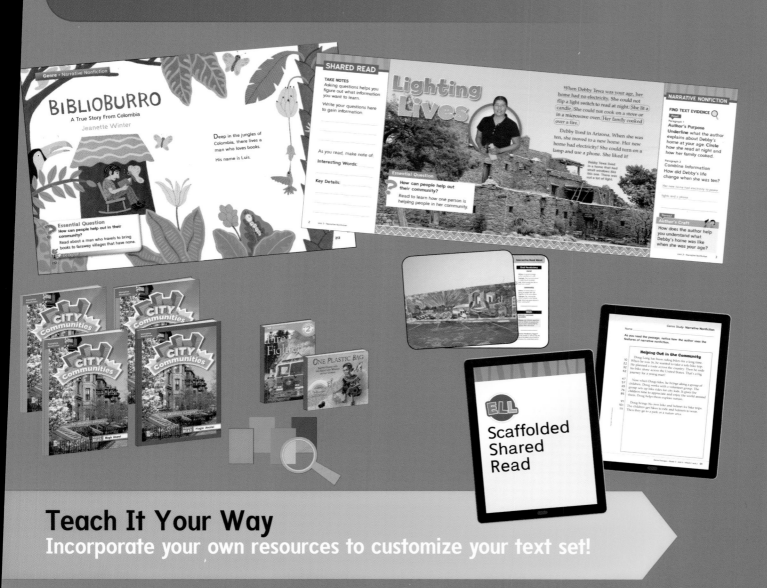

Teach It Your Way

Incorporate your own resources to customize your text set!

Make Learning Visible

Genre Study - Narrative Nonfiction

Students learn to think critically as they explore the narrative nonfiction genre and apply new knowledge and skills encompassing the four domains of language.

Active Engagement in Learning

Students Know What They Are Learning

Students review the Learning Goals for the Narrative Nonfiction Genre Study. The Home/School Family Letter includes a list of the Learning Goals and activities related to student outcomes.

Model Anchor Chart

Students Document Their Learning

Students will create the following Anchor Charts:

Anchor
Chart

- Narrative Nonfiction Genre Features
- Author's Purpose
- Ask and Answer Questions
- Synonyms
- Personal Narrative

Students Learn From Each Other

- Collaborative conversations
- Talk About It digital message board
- Blasts

COLLABORATE

Genre: Narrative Nonfiction

- Tells a story about a real person or people.
- May have a beginning, middle, and end, but the people and events are real.
- May include text features such as
  - Photos
  - Captions

✓ Tested in *Wonders* assessments

Student Outcomes

Comprehension/Genre/Author's Craft

- ✓ Cite relevant evidence from text
- ✓ Make inferences to support understanding
- ✓ Understand author's purpose
- Ask and answer questions about text
- Demonstrate understanding of time words
- ✓ Identify and use text features

Writing

Writing Process
- ✓ Plan and draft a personal narrative

Analytical Writing
- ✓ Write responses that demonstrate understanding.

Speaking and Listening

- Engage in collaborative discussions
- Retell "Color Your Community"
- Present information about an important person or event in history

Language Development

Oral Vocabulary Acquisition
artist   celebration   commented
community   mural

Vocabulary Acquisition
- Acquire and use academic vocabulary
across borrow countryside ideas insists
lonely solution villages

Vocabulary Strategy
- ✓ Identify, explain, and use synonyms

Grammar
- ✓ Understand and use action verbs
- ✓ Understand and use present tense verbs

Foundational Skills

Word Work
- Phonological Awareness: Identify and Generate Rhyme; Phonemic Awareness: categorization, blending, isolation
- ✓ Phonics: Words with long *a* and long *i*
- Structural Analysis: Contractions, Open Syllables
- High-Frequency Words
- Handwriting: Cursive *h, k, g, q, j, p, r, s*

Spelling Words

Week 1

nail   train main hay   stay break steak weigh
sleigh prey scrape strange good often two

Week 2

light sight mind cry   tie high wild dry try lie
hay   steak begin those apart

- Differentiated Spelling Lists, pages T68 and T70

Fluency
- Read with Expression and Phrasing

Research and Inquiry
- Identify and use primary and secondary sources
- Research and create a history picture book

🌐 Content Area Learning
- Research ways that people help in their communities

ELL Scaffolded supports for English Language Learners are embedded throughout the instruction.

Use the Data Dashboard to filter class, group, or individual student data to guide group placement decisions. It provides recommendations to enhance learning for gifted and talented children and offers extra support for children needing remediation.

Focus on Word Work

Support Foundational Skills

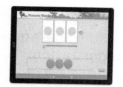
Phonological/Phonemic Awareness Activities

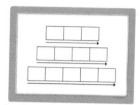
Response Board

Sound-Spelling Cards

Word-Building Cards online

Phonics Activities

Practice Book

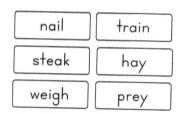
Spelling Word Cards online

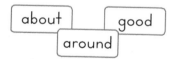
High-Frequency Word Cards

High-Frequency Word Activities

Decodable Readers

Decodable Passages

Phonological/Phonemic Awareness

- Identify and Generate Rhyme, Categorization, Blending
- Phoneme Isolation, Substitution, Blending, Categorization

Phonics: Words with Long *a*, Words with Long *i*

- Introduce and blend words
- Use manipulatives for sound-spelling review
- Structural Analysis: Contractions with *'s, 're, 'll, 've*; Open Syllables

Spelling: Words with Long *a*, Words with Long *i*

- Differentiated spelling instruction
- Encode with sound-spellings
- Explore relationships with word sorts
- Apply spelling to writing

High-Frequency Words

- Read/Spell/Write routine

See Word Work, pages T76–T131

Apply Skills to Read

- Reads are designed to incorporate foundational skills

Short Vowels; Consonant Blends; Long Vowels › Soft *c* and *g*; Consonant Digraphs › 3-Letter Consonant Blends › Silent Letters › *r*-Controlled Vowels › Diphthongs › Variant Vowels › Vowel Digraphs › Syllables

Explicit Systematic Instruction

Word Work instruction expands foundational skills to enable students to become proficient readers.

Daily Review

Review prior sound-spellings to build fluency.

Explicit Minilessons

Use daily instruction in both whole and small groups to model, practice, and apply key foundational skills. Provide corrective feedback. ELL support is provided in all lessons.

Check for Success

Check that students are on track and ready to move forward. Follow up with:

Differentiated Instruction

To strengthen skills, provide targeted review and reteaching lessons to meet students' specific needs.

Approaching

- Includes Tier 2

On Level

Beyond

- Includes Gifted and Talented

ELL

Independent Practice

Students who have the key skills can work independently or with partners.

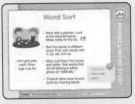

Workstation Activity Cards

Digital Activities

Word-Building Cards online

Decodable Readers

Practice Book

Foster a Love of Reading

Narrative Nonfiction Text Set

 Key Concept
Ways People Help

 Essential Question
How can people help out their community?

Students read and write about ways people can help each other and help their community.

"Color Your Community"
Interactive Read-Aloud Cards
Genre Realistic Fiction

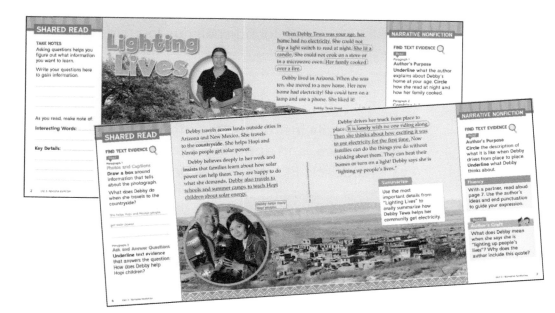

"Lighting Lives"
Reading/Writing Companion pp. 2–7
Genre Narrative Nonfiction • **Lexile** 650L

Biblioburro: A True Story from Colombia
Literature Anthology pp. 212–231
Genre Narrative Nonfiction • **Lexile** 700L

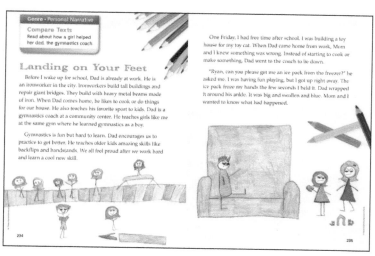

"Landing on Your Feet"
Literature Anthology pp. 234–237
Genre Personal Narrative • **Lexile** 610

Scaffolded Shared Read

"Lighting Lives"
Available online

ELL Scaffolded Shared Read

Lexile 290L
GR G
Approaching

Lexile 470L
GR K
On Level

Lexile 620L
GR O
Beyond

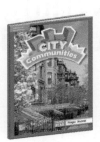

Lexile 400L
GR J
ELL

Leveled Readers with Paired Reads

Approaching Lexile 420L
On Level Lexile 510L
Beyond Lexile 610L
ELL Lexile 480L

Genre Passages

Independent Reading Focus

Classroom Library

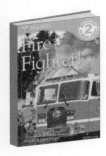

Fire Fighter!
Lexile 500L

One Plastic Bag
Lexile 480L

More Leveled Readers to Explore

Bonus Leveled Readers

Leveled Reader Library Online

Lessons available online

Bibliography

Have students self-select independent reading texts about ways people can help each other and help their community. Share the online **Unit Bibliography**.

Reading Across Genres

Rathmann, Peggy. *Ruby the Copycat.* Scholastic, 2006. Fiction **Lexile** 500L

Desmimini, Lisa. *Policeman Lou and Policewoman Sue.* Blue Sky Press, 2003. Fiction **Lexile** AD460L

More Narrative Nonfiction Texts

Winter, Jeanette. *Wangari's Trees of Peace: A True Story from Africa.* Harcourt Children's Books, 2008. Narrative Nonfiction **Lexile** AD600L

Rendon, Marcie. *Farmer's Market.* Carolrhoda Books, 2001. Narrative Nonfiction **Lexile** AD390L

Inspire Confident Writers

Analytical Writing: Narrative Nonfiction

Develop student habits of writing while reading.

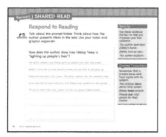

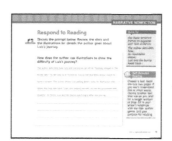

Notetaking Video

Take Notes to monitor comprehension

Shared Read - Model
"Lighting Lives"
Reading/Writing Companion pp. 2–7

Anchor Text - Practice and Apply
Biblioburro: A True Story from Columbia
Literature Anthology pp. 212–231
Reading/Writing Companion pp. 16–18

Summarize using important details

Shared Read - Model
"Lighting Lives"
Reading/Writing Companion p. 7

Anchor Text - Practice and Apply
Biblioburro: A True Story from Columbia
Literature Anthology p. 233

Respond using text evidence

Shared Read - Model
"Lighting Lives"
Reading/Writing Companion p. 14

Anchor Text - Practice and Apply
Biblioburro: A True Story from Columbia
Literature Anthology p. 233
Reading/Writing Companion p. 19

Genre Writing:
Write Your Own Personal Narrative

PROCESS WRITING

| Expert Model | Plan | Draft | Revise | Edit and Proofread | Publish |

WEEKS 1 AND 2   WEEKS 3 AND 4

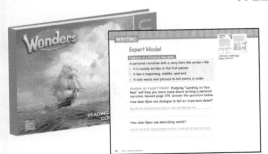

Study the Expert Model
Reading/Writing Companion p. 26

- Discuss features of personal narrative
- Discuss the mentor text (Literature Anthology, p. 233)

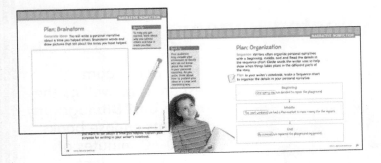

Plan the Story
Reading/Writing Companion pp. 27–29

- Choose the topic
- Discuss purpose and audience
- Identify Sequence: Beginning, Middle, End
- Take notes

Write a Draft
Reading/Writing Companion p. 30

- Discuss how to focus on an event
- Write the draft

Grammar, Spelling, and Handwriting Resources

Practice Book, pp. 179–187, 196–204

Assign practice pages online for auto-grading.

Grammar Handbook

Digital Activities

Develop self-directed, critical thinkers.

Independent Reading

Classroom Library

Fire Fighter!
Genre Narrative Nonfiction
Lexile 500L

One Plastic Bag
Genre Narrative Nonfiction
Lexile 480L

Leveled Readers

Leveled Reader Library Online
Additional Leveled Readers allow for flexibility.

Bonus Leveled Readers
Students can read more nonfiction texts.

Reading Across Genres

Literature Anthology
Wild Weather p. 288
Genre Expository Text

"Can You Predict the Weather"
p. 300, **Genre** Expository Text

Differentiated Genre Passages
Six leveled sets of passages are available on diverse genres.

Self-Selected Reading

Share book room resources as well as the online **Unit Bibliography.** Students choose books for 30–40 minutes of daily independent reading and respond in their writer's notebooks.

Differentiated Workstation Activities

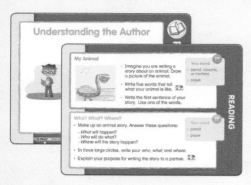

Reading 8

Reading 25

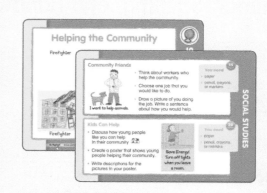

Social Studies 13

Independent Writing

ONLINE Writer's Notebook

Self-Selected Writing

Have students plan and draft their personal narrative or use these suggestions and choose the form they write in.

RESOURCE TOOLKIT

Resource Toolkit

Write about one way you can help at your school.

What is one invention you would like to create to help make people's lives better?

Write a letter to the mayor of your city. Tell the mayor one thing you think should be done to help your community.

Who is your hero? Describe this person and explain what he or she does that inspires you.

If you could speak with any famous person, living or dead, who would it be? What questions would you ask this person?

Research and Inquiry Project

Students conduct research about a local leader or event that has impacted their community and choose how to present their work.

Digital Activities

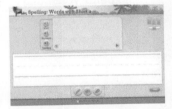

Grammar:
Action Verbs
Present Tense Verbs

Spelling:
Words with Long *a*
Words with Long *i*

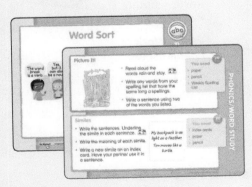

Phonics/Word Study 11

Phonics/Word Study 12

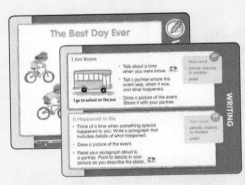

Writing 1

Suggested Lesson Plan

KEY

 Writing activity

Can be taught in small groups

DAY 1

Introduce the Concept T24–T25

Oral Vocabulary/Listening Comprehension T26–T27

Word Work T76–T83
• Phonological Awareness: Identify and Generate Rhyme • Phonics: Introduce, Blend words with Long *a* • High-Frequency Words • Decodable Reader: "Ray Saves the Play" • Handwriting

Read the Shared Read "Lighting Lives," T28–T33

Summarize Quick Write, T33

Vocabulary Words in Context, Synonyms, T34–T35

Grammar Action Verbs, T64–65

Spelling Words with Long *a*, T68–T69

Word Work T80
• Structural Analysis: Contractions with *'s, 're, 'll, 've*

Preteach Vocabulary T34–T35

Grammar Talk About It, T64

Expand Vocabulary T72

DAY 2

Strategy Ask and Answer Questions, T36–T37

Text Features Photos and Captions, T38–T39

Skill Author's Purpose, T40–41

Word Work T86–T89
• Phonics: Blend, Build Words with Long *a* • Structural Analysis: Contractions with *'s, 're, 'll, 've* • Decodable Reader: "The Great Plains"

Shared Read Reread: Craft and Structure, T42–T43

Respond to Reading T44–T45

Study Skill/Research and Inquiry T48–T49

Grammar Action Verbs, T64

Word Work T84–T85, T88
• Phonemic Awareness: Categorization • Phonics: Review Long *a* • High-Frequency Words Review

Fluency Expression, T46–T47

Grammar Talk About It, T64

Spelling Words with Long *a*, T68

Expand Vocabulary T72

SMALL GROUP ⟩⟩ INSTRUCTION

APPROACHING

Leveled Reader
City Communities,
T132–T133
Literature Circles, T133

Genre Passage
"Helping Out in the Community,"
T134–T135

Vocabulary
Review Vocabulary Words, T136 ②
Identify Related Words, T137
Synonyms, T137

Fluency ②
Expression, T138

Comprehension
Key Details,
T138 ②
Review Author's
Purpose, T139

Word Work, T76–T103
Phonological/Phonemic Awareness
Phonics • Structural Analysis
High-Frequency Words
Decodable Reader

ON LEVEL

Leveled Reader
City Communities,
T140–T141
Literature Circles,
T141

Genre Passage
"Helping Out in
the Community,"
T142–T143

Vocabulary
Review Vocabulary
Words, T144

Synonyms, T144

Comprehension
Review Author's
Purpose, T145

Word Work
Phonics, T100

HOW TO DIFFERENTIATE ⟩

Use your Check for Success observations and Data Dashboard to determine each student's needs. Then select instructional support options throughout the week.

Customize your own lesson plans
my.mheducation.com

DAY 3

Word Work T90–T91, T95–T97
• Phonemic Awareness: Blending • Phonics: Introduce Long *a*: *eigh*, *ey* • High-Frequency Words • Decodable Reader: "Eight is Great!"

Read the Anchor Text
Biblioburro: A True Story from Colombia, T49A–T49K

Take Notes About Text T49A–T49K

Grammar/Mechanics Action Verbs, Book Titles, T65

Expand Vocabulary T64–T65

Word Work T92–T94
• Phonics: Blend, Build Words with Long *a* • Structural Analysis: Contractions with *'s, 're, 'll, 've*

Grammar Talk About It, T65

Spelling Words with Long *a,* T69

DAY 4

Word Work T99–T100
• Phonics: Blend, Build Words with Long *a*

Read the Anchor Text
Biblioburro: A True Story from Colombia, T49A–T49K

Take Notes About Text T49A–T49K

Respond to the Text T49L

Word Work T98–101
• Phonemic Awareness: Categorization • Structural Analysis Review • High-Frequency Words Review • Decodable Reader: "What a Day!"

Grammar Action Verbs, T65

Grammar Talk About It, T65

Spelling Words with Long *a,* T69

Expand Vocabulary T73

DAY 5

Word Work T102
• Phonics: Blend Words, Build Words

Reread the Anchor Text
Biblioburro: A True Story from Colombia, T49A–T49K

Writing Expert Model, T56–T57

Spelling Words with Long *a,* T69

Word Work T102–103
• Phonemic Awareness: Blending • Structural Analysis: Contractions with *'s, 're, 'll, 've* • High-Frequency Words

Grammar Action Verbs, T65

Grammar Talk About It, T65

Expand Vocabulary T73

BEYOND

Leveled Reader
City Communities, T146–T147
Literature Circles, T147
Synthesize, T147

Genre Passage
"Helping Out in the Community," T148–T149
Independent Study, T149

Vocabulary
Review Domain-Specific Words, T150
Synonyms, T150
Synthesize, T150

Comprehension
Review Author's Purpose, T151

ENGLISH LANGUAGE LEARNERS

Shared Read
"Lighting Lives," T152–T155
Interactive Question-Response Routine, T152
Text Reconstruction, T154
Grammar, T155

Anchor Text
Biblioburro: A True Story from Colombia, T156–T159
Reread, T156
Text Reconstruction, T158
Grammar in Context, T159

Leveled Reader
City Communities, T160–T161

Genre Passage
"Helping Out in the Community," T162–T163

Word Work T76–T103
Phonological/Phonemic Awareness • Phonics
Structural Analysis
High-Frequency Words
Decodable Reader

Suggested Lesson Plan

KEY

✏️ Writing activity

◀ Can be taught in small groups

DAY 6

CORE

Word Work T104–T111
• Phonemic Awareness: Isolation • Phonics: Introduce, Blend Long *i* • High-Frequency Words • Decodable Reader: "High in the Sky" • Handwriting

Reread the Anchor Text ◀
Biblioburro: A True Story from Colombia, T49A–T49K

Respond to Reading T50–T51 ✏️

Writing Plan, T58–T59 ✏️

Grammar Present-Tense Verbs, T66

Spelling Words with Long *i*, T70 ◀

OPTIONAL

Word Work T108
• Structural Analysis: Open Syllables

Grammar Talk About It, T66 ◀

Expand Vocabulary T72

DAY 7

Word Work T114–T116
• Phonics: Blend, Build Words with Long *i*
• Structural Analysis: Open Syllables

Read the Paired Selection
"Landing on Your Feet," T51A–T51D

Writing Plan, T60–T61 ✏️

Grammar Present-Tense Verbs, T66

Expand Vocabulary T72

Word Work T112-T113, T117 ◀
• Phonemic Awareness: Substitution • Phonics: Review Long *i* • High-Frequency Words Review • Decodable Reader: "High in the Sky"

Grammar Talk About It, T66 ◀

Spelling Words with Long *i*, T70 ◀

SMALL GROUP ⟩⟩ INSTRUCTION

APPROACHING

Genre Passage "Helping Out in the Community," T134-T135
Level Up, T135

Vocabulary
Cumulative Vocabulary Review, T136 ②
Identify Related Words, T137
Synonyms, T137

Fluency Rate and Phrasing, T138 ②

Comprehension
Key Details, T138 ②
Review Author's Purpose, T139
Self-Selected Reading, T139

Word Work T104–T131 ②
Phonemic Awareness
Phonics
Structural Analysis
High-Frequency Words
Decodable Reader

Leveled Reader Library Online
Children can choose additional titles for the same genre, topic, or skills.

ON LEVEL

Genre Passage "Helping Out in the Community," T142–T143
Level Up, T143

Vocabulary
Review Vocabulary Words, T144
Synonyms, T144

Comprehension
Review Author's Purpose, T145
Self-Selected Reading, T145

Word Work
Phonics, T113

Leveled Reader Library Online
Children can choose additional titles for the same genre, topic, or skills.

HOW TO DIFFERENTIATE ⟩

Use your Check for Success observations and Data Dashboard to determine each student's needs. Then select instructional support options throughout the week.

Digital Tools

Customize your own lesson plans
my.mheducation.com

Digital Tools

Customize your own lesson plans
my.mheducation.com

DAY 8

Word Work T118– T125
• Phonemic Awareness: Blending • Phonics: Contrast Vowel Sounds • High-Frequency Words • Decodable Reader: "A Bright Flight"

Reread the Paired Selection "Landing On Your Feet," T51A–T51D

Author's Craft Time Words, T52–T53

Writing Draft, T62–T63

Grammar/Mechanics Present-Tense Verbs, Commas in a Series, T67

Expand Vocabulary T73

Word Work T120-T122
• Phonics: Blend, Build Words with Long *i* • Structural Analysis: Open Syllables

Grammar Talk About It, T66

Spelling Words with Long *i*, T71

DAY 9

Word Work T127–T128
• Phonics: Blend, Build Words with Long *i*

Fluency Expression and Phrasing, T54–T55

Writing Draft, T62–T63

Integrate Make Connections, T74

Word Work T126, T129
• Phonemic Awareness: Categorization • Structural Analysis Review • High-Frequency Words Review • Decodable Reader: "A Bright Flight"

Grammar Present-Tense Verbs, T67

Grammar Talk About It, T66

Spelling Words with Long *i*, T71

Expand Vocabulary T73

DAY 10

Word Work T130
• Phonics: Blend, Build Words with Long *i*

Writing Draft, T62–T63

Spelling Words with Long *i*, T71

Research and Inquiry Present Your Work, T75

Progress Monitoring T164–T165

Word Work T130–T131
• Phonemic Awareness: Blending • Structural Analysis: Open Syllables • High-Frequency Words

Grammar Present-Tense Verbs, T67

Grammar Talk About It, T66

Expand Vocabulary T73

BEYOND

Genre Passage "Helping Out in the Community," T148–T149

Independent Study, T149

GIFTED and TALENTED

Vocabulary
Review Domain-Specific Words, T150
Synonyms, T150
Synthesize, T150

GIFTED and TALENTED

Comprehension
Review Author's Purpose, T151
Self-Selected Reading, T151
Independent Study, T151

GIFTED and TALENTED

Leveled Reader Library Online
Children can choose additional titles for the same genre, topic, or skills.

ENGLISH LANGUAGE LEARNERS

Anchor Text
Biblioburro: A True Story from Colombia, T156–T159
Reread, T156
Text Reconstruction, T158
Grammar in Context, T159

Leveled Reader
Self-Selected Reading, T161

Genre Passage
"Helping Out in the Community," T162–T163
Level Up, T163

Word Work T104–T131
Phonological/Phonemic Awareness
Phonics
Structural Analysis
High-Frequency Words
Decodable Reader

Leveled Reader Library Online
Children can choose additional titles for the same genre, topic, or skills.

Introduce the Concept

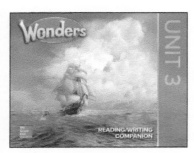

Reading/Writing Companion

OBJECTIVES

Follow agreed-upon rules for discussions (e.g., gaining the floor in respectful ways, listening to others with care, speaking one at a time about the topics and texts under discussion).

Build on others' talk in conversations by linking their comments to the remarks of others.

Ask and answer questions about what a speaker says in order to clarify comprehension, gather additional information, or deepen understanding of a topic or issue.

ACADEMIC LANGUAGE

• *idea, solution*
• Cognates: *idea, solución*

Digital Tools

Show the image during class discussion. Then play the video.

Discuss the Concept

Watch Video

Talk About It

 Essential Question

How can people help out their community?

Display the online **Student Learning Goals** for this genre study. Read the key concept: Ways People Help. Tell children that they will read narrative nonfiction texts that tell about how people help their communities.

Read the Essential Question on **Reading/Writing Companion** page vi. Point to the photograph. Ask children to tell what they think is happening.

Ask partners to use clues in the photograph to figure out how these children are helping out in their community.

• Explain that the garden in the photograph was once an empty lot filled with trash. This was a problem for the community. Then neighbors came up with an **idea**. They thought of a **solution** to the problem. They cleaned up the lot and planted a garden.

Ask: *What are some ways you could help out in the community?*

*Think of a community problem. What are some **ideas** you have for a **solution** to the problem?* Have children discuss in pairs or groups.

Model how to use the graphic organizer to generate words associated with helping out in the community. Have children add their ideas to complete the graphic organizer.

Have small groups develop ideas by discussing ways in which people can help out in the community. Ask groups to use as many words from the organizer as possible in their discussion.

 Collaborative Conversations

Add New Ideas As children engage in partner, small-group, and whole-group discussions, encourage them to

• stay on topic.

• build on the ideas of others.

• connect their personal experiences to the conversation.

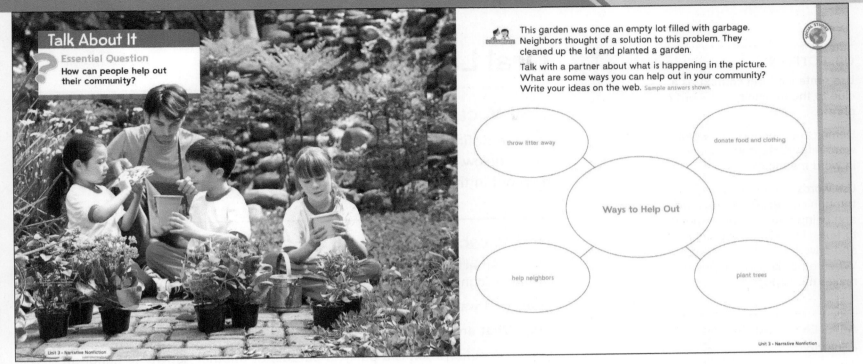

Talk About It

Essential Question
How can people help out their community?

This garden was once an empty lot filled with garbage. Neighbors thought of a solution to this problem. They cleaned up the lot and planted a garden.

Talk with a partner about what is happening in the picture. What are some ways you can help out in your community? Write your ideas on the web. Sample answers shown.

- throw litter away
- donate food and clothing
- Ways to Help Out
- help neighbors
- plant trees

Unit 3 • Narrative Nonfiction

Reading/Writing Companion, pp. vi–1

  Share the "Making Our Lives Better . . . Together" Blast assignment with children. Point out that you will discuss their responses in the Integrate Ideas lesson at the end of this two-week genre study.

English Language Learners SCAFFOLD

Use the scaffolds with **Ask** to help children develop vocabulary.

Beginning
Discuss the meaning of *community*. Help children describe places and people in their community. Describe the photograph and elicit that the kids are helping in a community garden. Ask: *What can you do to help your community?* Discuss to generate ideas. Then help partners describe what they can do using: We can <u>plant trees</u> to help our community.

Intermediate
Review the meaning of *community* by having children describe places and people in their community. Use the photograph to discuss how people help their community. Ask: *What can you do to help your community?* Have children generate ideas. Then have partners describe things they can do using: We can <u>plant trees</u> and <u>throw away trash</u> to help our community.

Advanced/Advanced High
Have children describe a *community,* including places and people and things that happen in their community. Use the photograph to generate ideas for how they can help their community. Then have partners describe things they can do.

 Vocabulary

community (*comunidad*) a group of people living in the same place

garden (*jardín*) an area where people grow plants and flowers

donate (*donar*) to give something to people who need it

help (*ayudar*) to give assistance

idea (*idea*) a thought about something

neighbor (*vecino*) someone who lives in the same community

problem (*problema*) something bad that needs to be fixed

solution (*solución*) a way to fix a problem

Newcomers

To help children develop oral language and build vocabulary, use **Newcomer Cards 5-9** and the accompanying materials in the **Newcomer Teacher's Guide**. For thematic connection, use Newcomer Cards 15 and 16 with the accompanying materials.

OBJECTIVES

Use sentence-level context as a clue to the meaning of a word or phrase.

Demonstrate understanding of word relationships and nuances in word meanings.

Use words and phrases acquired through conversations, reading and being read to, and responding to texts, including using adjectives and adverbs to describe (e.g., When other kids are happy that makes me happy).

ACADEMIC LANGUAGE

• *questions*

Digital Tools

Read or play the Interactive Read Aloud.

Interactive Read Aloud

SOCIAL EMOTIONAL LEARNING

Initiative Children who recognize initiative are better able to take initiative themselves. Before children listen, have them consider these questions:

• Name a problem in your local community that a group of people solved.
• Who initiated, or started, the project?
• How many other people worked on the project?
• What did all the people accomplish?

Oral Language

🕙 **10 Mins**

Oral Vocabulary Words

Use the Define/Example/Ask routine to introduce the Oral Vocabulary words below. Prompt children to use the words as they discuss ways people help out in their community.

Oral Vocabulary Routine

<u>Define:</u> An **artist** is someone who makes drawings, paintings, or things like statues. (Cognate: *artista*)

<u>Example:</u> I watched the artist painting a picture of an outdoor scene.

<u>Ask:</u> What are some things an artist might paint or draw?

<u>Define:</u> A **celebration** is a party, a parade, or another activity to honor an important or special day or event. (Cognate: *celebración*)

<u>Example:</u> Our town's celebration of the New Year began with a big parade.

<u>Ask:</u> What things would you need for a holiday celebration?

<u>Define:</u> **Commented** means explained something or gave an opinion about something. (Cognate: *comentar*)

<u>Example:</u> After the game, the coach commented on how well the team worked together.

<u>Ask:</u> What have you commented about at school?

<u>Define:</u> A **community** is a group of people who live together in the same place. (Cognate: *comunidad*)

<u>Example:</u> Our community voted to build a new library.

<u>Ask:</u> What are some places in your community?

<u>Define:</u> A **mural** is a large picture painted on a wall.

<u>Example:</u> The mural at school is a painting of a beautiful garden. (Cognate: *mural*)

<u>Ask:</u> What would you like to paint on a mural?

Introduce the Genre

10 Mins

Connect to Concept: Ways People Help

Tell children that you will read a selection about how people in Tucson, Arizona, helped their community by painting a mural.

Preview Narrative Nonfiction

Discuss the features:

- a story about a real person or people
- may have a beginning, a middle, and an end
- may include text features, such as photos and captions

Interactive Read-Aloud Cards

Anchor Chart Use the narrative nonfiction anchor chart and ask children to add characteristics of the genre.

Preview Text Structure

Explain that narrative nonfiction has a structure, which includes the order in which things happen in the real world. Sometimes the structure is based on a problem that needs to be solved. In "Color Your Community," the problem facing the Miracle Manor neighborhood is a loss of pride and spirit.

Read and Respond

Read the text aloud to children. Preview the comprehension strategy, Ask and Answer Questions, by using the Think Aloud below.

Display the online **Think Aloud Cloud: I figured out _____ because...** to reinforce how to use the strategy to understand content. Say: As I look at the photos, I wonder how the community decided on what to paint in the mural. As I read, I will listen to details to find the answer to this question.

Think Aloud As I read, I learned that people in the community shared stories about the neighborhood's history. This is what they painted.

Genre Features After reading, discuss the elements of the Interactive Read Aloud that let children know the text is narrative nonfiction. Ask them to think about other texts they read in class or independently that were narrative nonfiction.

Retell Have children use their own words to retell "Color Your Community" in logical order.

OBJECTIVES

Ask and answer such questions as *who, what, where, when, why,* and *how* to demonstrate understanding of key details in text.

Recount or describe key ideas or details from a text read aloud or information presented orally or through other media.

ACADEMIC LANGUAGE

- *narrative nonfiction, text features, questions*
- Cognate: *narrativa*

ELL Spotlight on Language

Card 1: Read aloud the first paragraph. Explain that *used to be* means "the way something was in the past." Say: *The wall is not blank now. The wall used to be blank. When was the wall blank?* The wall was blank <u>in the past</u>.

Card 2: Point out the words *older* and *younger.* Tell children that the words describe the ages of people in the community who shared stories for the mural. Help children use *older* and *younger* to describe residents in their community.

Card 3: Read aloud the second paragraph. Tell children that *took part* means "participated." Ask: *How many people took part in community paint day?* (over fifty people)

Card 4: Focus on the word *finally* in the second paragraph. Explain that *finally* means "after a long time" or "in the end." With a partner, ask and answer: *What did people do when they finally finished the mural?* (had a party)

"Lighting Lives"

Reading/Writing Companion

Text Complexity: 650
Lexile

420L   650   820L

OBJECTIVES

Ask and answer such questions as *who, what, where, when, why,* and *how* to demonstrate understanding of key details in a text.

Know and use various text features (e.g., captions, bold print, subheadings, glossaries, indexes, electronic menus, icons) to locate key facts or information in a text efficiently.

Participate in collaborative conversations with diverse partners about grade *2 topics and texts* with peers and adults in small and larger groups.

 Identify ways to actively practice good citizenship, including involvement in community service.

Close Reading Routine

Read   DOK 1–2

- Identify key ideas and details about how people can help out in their communities.
- Take notes and summarize.
- Use **ACT** prompts as needed.

Reread   DOK 2–3

- Analyze the text, craft, and structure.
- Use the **Reread minilessons** and **prompts**.

Integrate   DOK 4

- Integrate knowledge and ideas.
- Make text-to-text connections.
- Use the Integrate lesson.
- Inspire action.

SHARED READ

TAKE NOTES
Asking questions helps you figure out what information you want to learn.

Write your questions here to gain information.

_____

_____

_____

As you read, make note of:

Interesting Words: _____

_____

Key Details: _____

_____

_____

_____

_____

Lighting Lives

Essential Question

? **How can people help out their community?**

Read to learn how one person is helping people in her community.

2   Unit 3 · Narrative Nonfiction

Reading/Writing Companion, pp. 2–3

Take Notes Before children begin, have them think about the Essential Question and what they know about helping in a community, and then set a purpose for reading. As children read, they should use the left column of page 2 to note their questions, list interesting words they would like to learn, and identify key details from the text. Remind children to read accurately.

Focus on the Read prompts now. For additional support, there are extra prompts not included in the **Reading/Writing Companion.** Use the Reread prompts during the Craft and Structure lesson on pages T42–T43.

Preteach vocabulary words to children who need support.

DIFFERENTIATED READING

Approaching Level Talk with children about their note-taking techniques. Complete all Read prompts with the group.

On Level Have partners do the Read prompts before you meet.

Beyond Level Discuss partners' responses to the Read prompts.

 English Language Learners Preteach the vocabulary. Have Beginning/Early-Intermediate ELLs listen to the selection summary, available in multiple languages, and use the **Scaffolded Shared Read.** See also the Small Group pages.

When Debby Tewa was your age, her home had no electricity. She could not flip a light switch to read at night. She lit a candle. She could not cook on a stove or in a microwave oven. Her family cooked over a fire.

Debby lived in Arizona. When she was ten, she moved to a new home. Her new home had electricity! She could turn on a lamp and use a phone. She liked it!

Debby Tewa lived in a home that had small windows like this one. There was not a lot of light.

---

candle to read. Her family cooked over a fire. Then, when she moved, she had electricity and liked it. I think the author's purpose is going to be to explain something about Debby Tewa's relationship with electricity. **Ask:** *How is the title of the story another clue to the author's purpose?* (The title is "Lighting Lives," and electricity makes light. The author's purpose may be to tell us about how Debby helped people get electricity in their homes.)

Combine Information

Paragraph 2: Read the second paragraph. Ask: *How did Debby's life change when she was ten?* (Her new home had electricity.) Remind children that Debby had to light a candle at night to read in her old home. **Ask:** *How did having electricity change the way Debby read at night?* (Debby could turn on a lamp for light. She didn't have to light a candle anymore.)

Narrative Nonfiction

Paragraph 1: Read the title and look at the photograph on pages 2 and 3.

Think Aloud I know this is narrative nonfiction, and that helps me understand something about this photograph. Narrative nonfiction tells a story about real people and events. The woman I see in the photograph is a real person, and when I read I will find out about her. Who is she? What does she have to do with lighting lives? What is this interesting place in the photograph? Ask children to identify one other clue in the photograph to what the story is about. What question could they ask about it? (The woman is holding something that looks like a kind of tool. What is it?)

Skill: Author's Purpose

Paragraph 1: Read page 3. Model how to determine the author's purpose. Ask: *Which details tell about Debby's home when she was your age? How did Debby read at night, and how did her family cook?*

Think Aloud The author starts this story by telling us something about the woman in the photograph, Debby Tewa. When Debby was your age, her home didn't have any electricity. She lit a

---

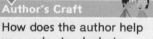 ## Spotlight on Language

Page 3, Paragraphs 1 and 2: Demonstrate the meaning of the phrase *flip a switch* using a light switch in the classroom. Flip the switch and explain that you are turning the lights on and off. Then, demonstrate the phrasal verb *turn on* from paragraph 2 and say: *I turn on the light.* Flip the light off and say: *I turn off the light.* Ask: *What could Debby turn on in her new home?* (a lamp) *What other things do we turn on?* Encourage children to give examples, such as a TV, computer, or radio.

Monitor Comprehension

Paragraph 1: Read paragraph 1. Ask questions to help children understand how solar power works. Ask: *What is solar power?* (electricity that comes from the sun) *What is a solar panel?* (a roof panel that turns sunlight into electricity) *What happens when sunlight hits the solar panel?* (It turns into electricity that can be used in a home.)

Skill: Author's Purpose

Paragraph 1: Read the first paragraph. Ask: *Which details tell about how people use solar panels?* (Solar panels are put on the roof of a building. The sunlight hits these panels and turns into electricity.) *What might be the purpose of this paragraph?* (The purpose of the paragraph is to explain to the reader how solar power works.) *Why might this be important?* (This is important because Debby realized she wanted to learn more about solar power as she grew up.)

Strategy: Ask and Answer Questions

Paragraph 2: Read the second paragraph. Ask: *What question could you ask about where Debby decided to work?* (Why did Debby go to work for a company that provided solar power to homes?) *Which details help to answer your question?* (She believed that solar power would be a good solution for people who had no electricity.) Have children work in pairs to ask and answer questions about the text.

SHARED READ

FIND TEXT EVIDENCE 🔍

Read

Paragraph 1
Author's Purpose
Underline details that explain the way people use solar panels.

Paragraph 2
Ask and Answer Questions
Ask a question about where Debby went to work. Write it below.

Why did she go to work for a company
that provided solar power to homes?

Circle text evidence that helps you to answer it.

Reread
Author's Craft

How does the author use punctuation to show when Debby was excited?

4   Unit 3 · Narrative Nonfiction

As she grew, Debby realized she wanted to learn more about solar power. Solar power is electricity that comes from the Sun. Solar panels are put on the roof of a building. The sunlight hits these panels and turns into electricity.

Debby thought a lot about solar power. Then she had an **idea**! She was excited. She went to work for a company that provided solar power to people's homes. She believed it would be a good **solution** for people who had no electricity. Debby likes solving problems!

Reading/Writing Companion, pp. 4–5

A C T   Access Complex Text

Connection of Ideas

Children may need help connecting to the idea that Debby is motivated to help her own community because of her own experience growing up.

- Make sure children understand that because Debby grew up without electricity, there were many things she could not do.

- Discuss how growing up without electricity would motivate Debby to help bring electricity to others in her community.

- Help children identify photos, captions, and other text evidence that illustrates how Debby lived as a child and how her work is changing the community in which she grew up.

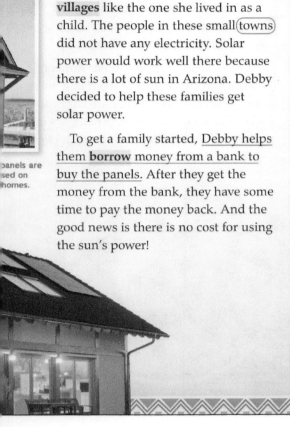

Debby also thought of people in **villages** like the one she lived in as a child. The people in these small (towns) did not have any electricity. Solar power would work well there because there is a lot of sun in Arizona. Debby decided to help these families get solar power.

To get a family started, Debby helps them **borrow** money from a bank to buy the panels. After they get the money from the bank, they have some time to pay the money back. And the good news is there is no cost for using the sun's power!

panels are
sed on
homes.

NARRATIVE NONFICTION

FIND TEXT EVIDENCE 🔍

Read
Paragraph 1
Synonyms
Circle a word with almost the same meaning as *villages*. What did Debby decide to do for families in places without electricity?

She decided to help them get solar

power.

Author's Purpose
Underline the sentence that explains how Debby helps a family buy panels.

Reread
Author's Craft
How does the author help you understand why solar energy is a good solution for people Debby helps?

Unit 3 · Narrative Nonfiction 5

Vocabulary: Synonyms

Paragraph 1: Read the first paragraph. Point out the word *villages* in the first sentence. Ask: *Which word in the paragraph has almost the same meaning as the word* villages*?* (*towns*) *What is something that people in the towns and villages had in common?* (They did not have any electricity.) *What did Debby decide to do for the people in these places?* (She decided to help the people get solar power for their homes.)

 ## Spotlight on Language

Page 5, Paragraph 2: Remind children that the word *after* is a connecting word that tells the order in which things happen. Help partners ask and answer: What happens first? First, Debby helps the family borrow money from a bank. What can the family do after they borrow money? After the family borrows money, they can buy solar panels.

Strategy: Ask and Answer Questions

Paragraph 1: Reread the last sentence of the first paragraph. Ask: *What question could you ask here to help you understand the story better?* (Why would solar power work well in the towns and villages?) *Reread the paragraph to find an answer to the question.* (Solar power would work well because there is a lot of sun in Arizona.) *What is one more question you can ask about the text?* (How does Debby help the families get solar power?) **Explain that reading the next paragraph will provide part of the answer.**

Skill: Author's Purpose

Paragraph 2: Read the second paragraph. Ask: *Which sentence explains how Debby helps a family buy panels?* (To get a family started, Debby helps them borrow money from a bank to buy the panels.) *What does Debby do at her job?* (She helps people borrow money from a bank.) *How does this help people get electricity in their homes?* (They use the money to pay for solar panels.) *What is the purpose of this paragraph?* (The purpose is to show how Debby helps people in her community get electricity for their homes.)

Monitor Comprehension

Paragraph 2: Ask: *How is borrowing money from a bank to buy panels helpful for people in the community?* (After borrowing money from the bank, the families Debby helps have some time to pay the money back. There is also no cost for using the sun's power.)

Photos and Captions

Paragraph 1: Read the first paragraph and the caption. Ask: *Which information tells about the photograph?* (The caption tells us that Debby helps many Hopi people.) *What does Debby do when she travels to the countryside?* (She helps Hopi and Navajo people get solar power.) *What do you see in the photograph?* (a young girl and an older woman) *Based on the information from the caption and the paragraph, who are these people?* (These are Hopi people. These must be some of the Hopi people that Debby helps.)

Strategy: Ask and Answer Questions

Paragraph 2: Read paragraph 2. Ask: *How does Debby help Hopi children?* (Debby travels to schools and summer camps. She teaches Hopi children there about solar energy.) Have children turn to a partner and ask and answer questions about the text.

SHARED READ

FIND TEXT EVIDENCE 🔍
Read

Paragraph 1
Photos and Captions
Draw a box around information that tells about the photograph.

What does Debby do when she travels to the countryside?

She helps Hopi and Navajo people

get solar power.

_____

Paragraph 2
Ask and Answer Questions
Underline text evidence that answers the question: How does Debby help Hopi children?

Debby travels **across** lands outside cities in Arizona and New Mexico. She travels to the **countryside**. She helps Hopi and Navajo people get solar power.

Debby believes deeply in her work and **insists** that families learn about how solar power can help them. They are happy to do what she demands. Debby also travels to schools and summer camps to teach Hopi children about solar energy.

Debby helps many Hopi people.

6   Unit 3 • Narrative Nonfiction

Reading/Writing Companion, pp. 6–7

Skill: Author's Purpose

Paragraph 2: Read the second paragraph and the caption. Ask: *What is the author's purpose in writing the second paragraph?* (to explain how Debby helps people) *What is one clue that supports this purpose?* (She insists that families learn about how solar power can help them, and they are happy to do what she demands.)

A C T **Access Complex Text**

Genre

Help children understand that when an author writes narrative nonfiction, the events in the selection are included because they support the author's purpose.

• Remind children that narrative nonfiction tells a story about a real person. Narrative nonfiction often tells events in sequence.

• Focus on events at the beginning of the selection. Say: *On page 3, the author tells about Debby's childhood.*

Does the author tell about Debby's school or how she played sports? (No.) *What is the main event that the author talks about?* (Debby's family had no electricity. They moved to a house with electricity.)

• *What does the information about Debby's childhood have to do with the rest of the selection?* (Debby helps families get electricity, just like her family.)

Debby drives her truck from place to ~~ce.~~ It is **lonely** with no one riding along. ~~...n~~ she thinks about how exciting it was ~~...se~~ electricity for the first time. Now ~~...ilies~~ can do the things you do without ~~...nking~~ about them. They can heat their ~~...mes~~ or turn on a light! Debby says she is ~~...hting~~ up people's lives."

Summarize

Use the most important details from "Lighting Lives" to orally summarize how Debby Tewa helps her community get electricity.

FIND TEXT EVIDENCE

Read

Author's Purpose
Circle the description of what it is like when Debby drives from place to place. **Underline** what Debby thinks about.

Fluency

With a partner, read aloud page 7. Use the author's ideas and end punctuation to guide your expression.

Reread
Author's Craft

What does Debby mean when she says she is "lighting up people's lives"? Why does the author include this quote?

Unit 3 · Narrative Nonfiction   7

Skill: Author's Purpose

Paragraph 1: Read the paragraph. Ask: *What is it like when Debby drives from place to place?* (The author says "It is lonely with no one riding along." But then the author says that when Debby is driving, she thinks about how exciting it was to use electricity for the first time.)

Ask: *What does the author explain about Debby's work?* (Her work brings solar power to people so that they can do more things with electricity.) Ask: *How do you think that makes Debby feel? Cite text evidence.* (She probably feels very happy. According to the author, she says she is "lighting up people's lives.")

 ## Spotlight on Language

Page 7: Point out that on page 6 the text says Debby travels "across lands outside cities in Arizona and New Mexico." Then, point out the phrase *from place to place* in the first sentence on page 7. Say: *"From place to place" means "to many places." Debby drives to many places to do her job. Name one place Debby drives.* (Arizona countryside) *Name another.* (New Mexico countryside) Have children complete the frame: Debby drives from the Arizona countryside to the New Mexico countryside.

Strategy: Ask and Answer Questions

Paragraph 1: Read the second sentence. Point out the word *lonely.* Ask: *What does it mean when it gets lonely with no one driving along?* (Debby is alone while driving.) *What might make the drive less lonely?* (Debby's thoughts about her work helping others.)

Summarize

 After their first read, have partners summarize the selection orally using their notes. Then have them write a summary in their writer's notebooks. Remind children to include important ideas and to use their own words. Children may decide to digitally record presentations of summaries.

Fluency

Have partners choral read the paragraph on page 7 for accuracy and expression. Circulate and provide corrective feedback. For a full lesson and additional fluency practice, see pages T46–T47.

Vocabulary

Reading/Writing Companion

OBJECTIVES

Determine or clarify the meaning of unknown and multiple-meaning words and phrases based on grade 2 reading and content, choosing flexibly from an array of strategies.

Use sentence-level context as a clue to the meaning of a word or phrase.

ACADEMIC LANGUAGE

- *synonym*
- Cognate: *sinónimo*

Digital Tools

Use the Visual Vocabulary Cards

Visual Vocabulary Cards

TEACH IN SMALL GROUP ≪

Synonyms

Approaching Level and ELL
Preteach the words before children begin the Shared Read.

On Level and Beyond Level
Have children look up each word in the online **Visual Glossary.**

Words in Context

Use the routines on the **Visual Vocabulary Cards** to introduce each word.

To go **across** something is to go from one side to the other.

If you **borrow** something, you take it and agree to return it later.

The **countryside** is land that is away from cities or large towns.

An **idea** is a thought or plan you have for something. **Cognate:** *idea*

If my mom **insists** on something, she says firmly that it must be done. **Cognate:** *insistir*

A **lonely** place is one that very few people visit.

A **solution** is a way to answer a problem. **Cognate:** *solución*

Villages are very small towns in the country.

Synonyms

1 Explain

Explain to children that synonyms are words that have almost the same meaning. Sometimes authors include synonyms in the same sentence or in a nearby sentence. Knowing the meaning of one word can help readers understand the unknown word. Replace the unknown word with the synonym to see if it makes sense in the context of the sentence.

2 Model

Model using the synonym *demands* to figure out the meaning of *insists* on page 6 of "Lighting Lives." *I'm not sure what* insists *means on page 6. I read that Debby "insists that families learn about how solar power can help them" and "They are happy to do what she demands." I know that* demands *means "asks for something in a strong way." When I replace* insists *with* demands, *it makes sense in the sentence.* Insists *and* demands *are synonyms.*

3 Guided Practice

Have partners identify synonyms for the words *home* (page 3) and *power* (page 4) in "Lighting Lives." As needed, work with children to brainstorm synonyms. Have them check their synonyms by replacing the story words with the synonyms to see if they make sense. Invite children to share their synonyms with the class.

Reading/Writing Companion, pp. 8–9

The page 8–9 content shown:

Vocabulary

Use the sentences to talk with a partner about each word. Then answer the questions. Sample answers shown.

across
We walked **across** the street.
What are other things you can walk across?

I can walk across a bridge or a field of grass.

borrow
I like to **borrow** books from the library.
What can you borrow from a friend?

I can borrow a book or a pencil from a friend.

Build Your Word List Choose a word that you noted while reading. Use a print or digital thesaurus to look up synonyms for the word. Use one pair of synonyms in your own sentences.

countryside
The **countryside** is full of grass and trees.
What else may be in the countryside?

There may be flowers and birds in the countryside.

idea
Kate has an **idea** for the class project.
Name an idea you have for a game to play.

My idea is to play tag.

insists
Mom **insists** we wear our seatbelts.
What is something your teacher insists that you and your classmates do?

Our teacher insists that we follow directions.

lonely
The boy was **lonely** when his friend moved away.
When have you felt lonely?

I felt lonely when I first went to a new school.

solution
Dylan found a **solution** for his problem.
What is a solution for spilled milk?

A solution is to clean it up with a sponge.

villages
Few people live in the small **villages** on the mountain.
What would it be like to visit a small village?

It would be quiet in a small village.

Synonyms

Synonyms are words that have almost the same meaning. *Big* and *large* are synonyms.

FIND TEXT EVIDENCE

I read that Debby "insists that families learn about how solar power can help them" and "They are happy to do what she demands." Insists and demands are synonyms. They both mean "asks for something in a strong way."

Debby believes deeply in her work and insists that families learn about how solar power can help them. They are happy to do what she demands.

Your Turn Think of a synonym for these words in "Lighting Lives."

home, page 3 house; apartment

power, page 4 energy; electricity

8 Unit 3 • Narrative Nonfiction   Unit 3 • Narrative Nonfiction 9

 English Language Learners SCAFFOLD

Use the following scaffolds with **Guided Practice**.

Beginning

Ask children to find and circle the word *home* on page 3, and then point to the home in the photo. Ask: *What is a home?* A home is a place where you <u>live</u>. *You live in a home. Do you live in an apartment building or a house?* (Children answer.) Have partners ask and answer: Where do you live? I live in <u>an apartment</u>. What two words are synonyms? The words home and <u>apartment</u> are synonyms. Then help mixed-proficiency pairs work together to find a synonym for *power* on page 4.

Intermediate

Have partners discuss their own homes: What is your home like? I live in <u>a house</u>. What about you? Then have them complete the frame: The words <u>home</u> and <u>house</u> are synonyms. Repeat the procedure for *power*. *Which phrase helps you find a synonym for power?* (*Solar power is electricity that comes from the sun.*) *Name the two synonyms.* The words <u>power</u> and <u>electricity</u> are synonyms.

Advanced/Advanced High

Have children find the word *home* on page 3. Have partners discuss the meaning of the word and list synonyms. Have them confirm that the words are synonyms by substituting the word in the original sentence and telling if it makes sense. Repeat for *power*.

 Build Your Word List

Children might choose *electricity* from page 4. Have partners use text clues and photographs to find the meaning.

✓ Check for Success

Rubric Use the online rubric to record student progress.

Are children able to identify synonyms for *home* and *power*?

Differentiate
SMALL GROUP INSTRUCTION

If No
Approaching Reteach p. T136
ELL Develop p. T162

If Yes
On Review p. T144
Beyond Extend p. T150

Comprehension Strategy

Reading/Writing Companion

OBJECTIVES

Ask and answer such questions as *who, what, where, when, why,* and *how* to demonstrate understanding of key details in a text.

Read with sufficient accuracy and fluency to support comprehension. Read on-level text with purpose and understanding.

ACADEMIC LANGUAGE

- *questions, key details, author's purpose*
- Cognate: *detalles*

Ask and Answer Questions

1 Explain

Remind children that when they read narrative nonfiction, such as "Lighting Lives," they may come across new information and detailed explanations. Children can ask themselves questions about the text before, during, and after they read. Their questions will help them understand the key details in the selection, deepen their understanding, and gain information. They can reread the part or all of the selection to find answers to their questions.

- Before reading, children can ask themselves questions about what they are about to read. For example: *What will this selection be about? Who are the people in the photo?* Asking questions also helps children set a purpose for reading.

- As children read, they can ask themselves questions to make sure they understand what they just read. For example: *What is the main point of that paragraph? Do I need to reread?*

- After children finish reading, they can ask themselves questions, such as: *Are there any details that I still don't understand? What was the author's purpose for writing this selection?*

Anchor Chart Have volunteers add information about asking and answering questions to the comprehension strategy chart and reread the chart.

2 Model

Model how asking and answering questions can help you understand what solar power is. Reread the first paragraph on page 4.

Think Aloud The text says that Debby became interested in solar power. I ask myself "What is solar power?" When I reread, I learn that solar power is electricity that comes from the sun. From this, I understand that solar panels use energy from the sun.

3 Guided Practice

Direct children to the first paragraph on page 5 of the **Reading/Writing Companion**. Reread the paragraph aloud as children follow along. Then have children work in pairs to write a question about how solar power can help people. Have pairs share their questions with the rest of the class.

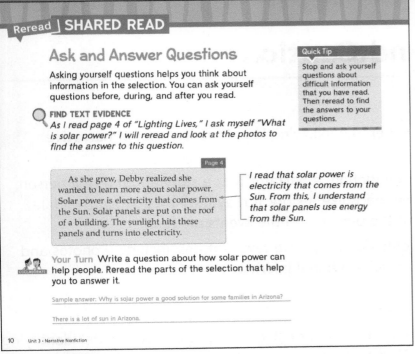

Reading/Writing Companion, p. 10

English Language Learners SCAFFOLD

Use the following scaffolds with **Guided Practice**.

Beginning

Ask sample questions about the first paragraph on page 4, such as: *What did Debby want to learn? What is solar power? Where do you put solar panels? How do solar panels work?* Have children repeat your questions. Help them find answers in the text. Then have mixed-proficiency pairs write a few questions about another chunk of text. Tell children to use one of those questions to complete **Your Turn**.

Intermediate

Review the 5-W question words with children. Then read aloud the first paragraph on page 4, and help children think of questions about the information. Remind them they can ask questions to clarify things they didn't understand, and to confirm their comprehension. Have partners write their questions and circle the answers in the text.

Advanced/Advanced High

Review the 5-W question words. Have children ask questions about different paragraphs. Challenge them to ask a few questions that are answered in a different paragraph. For example, "Why was Debby interested in solar panels?" can be asked on page 4, but the answer is on page 3. (Debby was probably interested in solar panels because she grew up without electricity.)

HABITS OF LEARNING

I can think critically about what I'm reading. When children think critically about what they are reading, they are better able to understand, appreciate, and apply what they've read. Have children ask and answer the following questions before, during, and after reading:

- **Before Reading:** What do I think this text will be about? What is my purpose for reading this text?
- **During reading:** Are there any details I do not understand in this text? What can I reread to help me understand the details?
- **After reading:** What was the author's purpose for writing this text? What does this text inspire me to do?

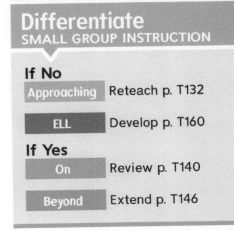

✔ Check for Success

Do children think of questions as they read? Do they reread to find the answers to their questions?

Differentiate
SMALL GROUP INSTRUCTION

If No

| Approaching | Reteach p. T132 |
| ELL | Develop p. T160 |

If Yes

| On | Review p. T140 |
| Beyond | Extend p. T146 |

Reading/Writing Companion

OBJECTIVES

Know and use various text features (e.g., captions, bold print, subheadings, glossaries, indexes, electronic menus, icons) to locate key facts or information in a text efficiently

Recognize the characteristics and text features of narrative nonfiction.

ACADEMIC LANGUAGE

• *narrative nonfiction, photos, captions, narrator*
• Cognates: *fotos, narrador*

Photos and Captions

1 Explain

Share with children the following key characteristics of **narrative nonfiction**.

• In narrative nonfiction, a narrator tells a story about a real person. The narrative reads like a story. It may have a beginning, middle, and end, but the person and the events are real.

• Narrative nonfiction may have text features, including photos and captions, to give additional information.

2 Model

Model identifying the genre of "Lighting Lives." Then model identifying and using the text features on page 6.

Photos Point out the photograph of the people. Explain that photographs help show who or what is described in the text.

Captions Read the caption aloud. Explain that it gives more information about the photograph and helps readers better understand the text.

3 Guided Practice

Have partners look at the photographs and caption on pages 4 and 5 of "Lighting Lives." Guide children to identify the information they gained from these text features. Ask: *Where are solar panels used?* (on many homes) *Where do the solar panels go?* (on the roof) Have partners continue to study the photos and caption in more detail. Ask them to share what they learned about solar panels with the class.

Independent Practice Have children read the online **Differentiated Genre Passage** "Helping Out in the Community."

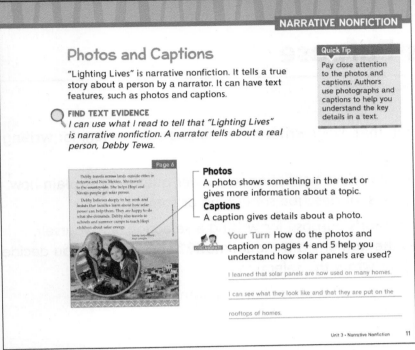

Reading/Writing Companion, p. 11

 # English Language Learners SCAFFOLD

Use the following scaffolds with **Guided Practice.**

Beginning

Have children look at the photo on page 5 as you read aloud the caption. Ask: *What does the photo show?* The photo shows solar panels. *Where do people use solar panels?* People use solar panels on roofs/houses.

Intermediate

Pair children to discuss the photos and caption on pages 4–5. Provide sentence frames to help children share information they learn from the photos and the caption: What do you learn from the caption? The caption tells me that solar panels are used on houses. What do you learn from the photos? This photo shows solar panels. This photo shows that solar panels go on the roof.

Advanced

Have partners use the photos and caption on pages 4 and 5 to explain how solar panels work in more detail. Ask questions to help them: *Where do solar panels go?* (on the roof of a house) *Why do they go on the roof?* (so that sunlight hits them) *How do solar panels use sunlight?* (They turn sunlight into electricity.)

✓ Check for Success

Rubric Use your online rubric to record student progress.

Can children explain what they learned about solar panels from photos and captions?

Differentiate
SMALL GROUP INSTRUCTION

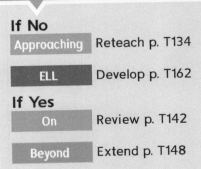

If No
Approaching Reteach p. T134
ELL Develop p. T162

If Yes
On Review p. T142
Beyond Extend p. T148

Reading/Writing Companion

OBJECTIVES

Identify the main purpose of a text, including what the author wants to answer, explain, or describe.

Describe how reasons support specific points the author makes in a text.

ACADEMIC LANGUAGE

- *author's purpose, reason*
- Cognate: *razón*

Digital Tools

To differentiate instruction for key skills, use the result of the activity.

 # Author's Purpose

1 Explain

Remind children that every writer has a purpose, or reason, for writing a selection.

- Writers write narrative nonfiction to answer questions, explain how something works, or describe something or someone.

- To find the author's purpose for writing a selection, ask yourself, "What does the author want me to know?" This will help you decide why the author wrote the selection.

Anchor Chart Begin an anchor chart on author's purpose.

2 Model

Tell children to think about what the author wants them to know. Then reread page 4 and model finding a clue to the author's purpose.

Think Aloud On page 4, the author tells how Debby Tewa got the idea to help others who do not have electricity in their homes. I think this is a clue to the author's purpose.

 ### 3 Guided Practice

Have children work in pairs to identify another clue to help them determine the author's purpose. Then have partners identify and record the author's purpose. Discuss each section as children complete the graphic organizer.

Write About Reading: Author's Purpose Have partners use their graphic organizers and text evidence to discuss the text's clues and the author's purpose for writing "Lighting Lives." Choose partners to share their writing.

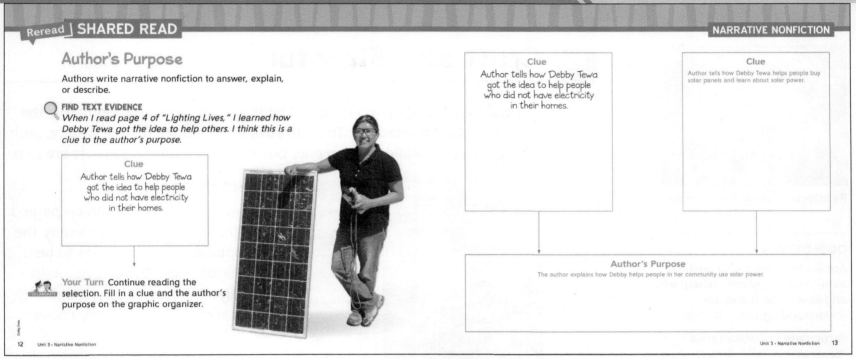

Reading/Writing Companion, pp. 12-13

English Language Learners SCAFFOLD

Use the following scaffolds with **Guided Practice**.

Beginning

Read aloud page 6 as children follow along. Then ask: *What does the author want me to know about Debby?* Debby helps Hopi and Navajo people get solar power. She travels to schools and summer camps to teach children about solar energy.

Intermediate

Have partners reread page 6 and identify clues to the author's purpose. Ask questions to help them: *Where does Debby travel? What does she help people get? What does she help them learn about?* Then have them complete the sentence starter to state the author's purpose: The author wants me to know that Debby helps people in her community use solar power.

Advanced/Advanced High

Have partners focus on page 6. Encourage them to identify clues from the page and add them to the graphic organizer. Help them to state the clue and the author's purpose as complete sentences. Ask them to explain how the clues helped them determine the author's purpose.

✔ Check for Success

Rubric Use your online rubric to record student progress.

Can children identify and use text clues to determine the author's purpose?

Differentiate
SMALL GROUP INSTRUCTION

If No

| Approaching | Reteach p. T138 |
| ELL | Develop p. T162 |

If Yes

| On | Review p. T145 |
| Beyond | Extend p. T151 |

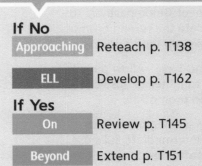

Reading/Writing Companion

OBJECTIVES

Ask and answer such questions as who, what, where, when, why, and how to demonstrate understanding of key details.

Participate in collaborative conversations with diverse partners about *grade 2 topics and texts* with peers and adults in small and larger groups.

Use knowledge of language and its conventions when writing, speaking, reading, or listening.

ACADEMIC LANGUAGE

- *narrative nonfiction, events*
- Cognate: *eventos*

TEACH IN SMALL GROUP ◀

Approaching Level Use the scaffolded questions to help children cite text evidence and answer the Reread prompts.

On Level Guide partners to complete the reread prompts and explain their answers.

Beyond Level Allow pairs to work together to answer the Reread prompts.

ELL Have Beginners and Early-Intermediate ELLs use the **Scaffolded Shared Read**.

 Craft and Structure

Tell children that they will reread "Lighting Lives" to learn about how the author wrote the selection. The narrative nonfiction reads like a story, with a beginning, a middle, and an end, but the person and the events are real.

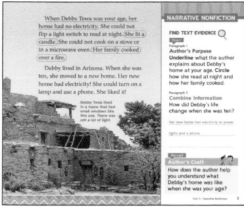

Reading/Writing Companion, p. 3

AUTHOR'S CRAFT

Reread the first paragraph on page 3 with children. Have them identify the descriptions the author uses to help them understand Debby's home at their age. (...home had no electricity; She lit a candle; Her family cooked over a fire.)

 Point out the use of past-tense verbs: *was, had, could not, lit, cooked. These signal the author is describing the past*

How does the author help you understand what Debby's home was like when she was your age? (The author describes what Debby's home was like without electricity.)

Reading/Writing Companion, p. 4

AUTHOR'S CRAFT

Reread the second paragraph on page 4 with children. Ask children to tell how you read the sentences that end with an exclamation point. (with excitement and strong belief)

 Show how punctuation can show emotion. Read aloud the quotes with exclamation points, first without and then with enthusiasm.

How does the author use punctuation to show when Debby was excited? (The author uses an exclamation point to show excitement and strong belief.)

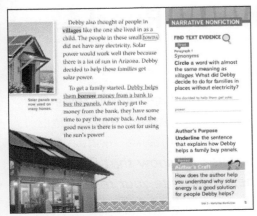

Reading/Writing Companion, p. 5

AUTHOR'S CRAFT

Reread page 5 with children. Have them tell why solar power would work well in the small towns of Arizona. (There is a lot of sun.) Ask: *What is the good news about the sun's power?* (There is no cost for using it.)

 Explain that *solar* means from the sun. Read aloud the first paragraph, and ask: *Why is solar power good for Arizona?* Solar power is good because there is a lot of <u>sun</u> in Arizona.

How does the author help you understand why solar energy is a good solution for people Debby helps? (There is a lot of sun in Arizona. There is no cost for using the sun's power.)

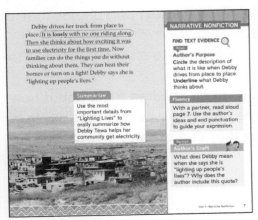

Reading/Writing Companion, p. 7

AUTHOR'S CRAFT

Reread page 7 with children. Have children tell how electricity changes people's lives. (They can heat their homes or turn on a light.) *Who helps people get the electricity that lets them heat their homes or turn on a light?* (Debby Tewa) *What does Debby say she is doing?* ("lighting up people's lives")

 Practice the two pronunciations of the words *lives* (as a noun and as a verb). *Is the author using the word as a noun or a verb?* (noun)

What does Debby mean when she says she is, "lighting up people's lives"? Why does the author include this quote? (Debby means she is bringing people electricity and also making their lives better.)

Evaluate Information

Explain that to evaluate information, you think about what you are reading and either agree or disagree with the information.

Think Aloud The author says that solar power would work well in small towns like the one where Debby grew up because there is a lot of sun in Arizona. On page 4, I read that solar power is electricity from the sun. Therefore, I agree with the author. If solar power is electricity from the sun, it should work well in a place where there is a lot of sun.

Respond to Reading

Reading/Writing Companion

OBJECTIVES

Know and use various text features (e.g., captions, bold print, subheadings, glossaries, indexes, electronic menus, icons) to locate key facts or information in a text efficiently.

Explain how specific images (e.g., a diagram showing how a machine works) contribute to and clarify a text.

Ask and answer such questions as *who, what, where, when, why,* and *how* to demonstrate understanding of key details in a text.

ACADEMIC LANGUAGE

• *text, photograph, detail*
• Cognate: *texto, fotografía, detalle*

TEACH IN SMALL GROUP

Respond to Reading

Approaching Level Model how to analyze the prompt and find text evidence.

On Level Have children work with a partner to analyze the prompt, find text evidence, and write their response.

Beyond Level Have children work independently to write their responses. Invite them to share their analysis of how the author presents ideas.

ELL Group children of mixed proficiency levels to discuss and respond to the prompt.

Write About the Shared Read

Analyze the Prompt

Read the prompt aloud: *How does the author show how Debby Tewa "is lighting up people's lives"?* Ask: *What is the prompt asking for?* (details from the text and photographs that show how Debby Tewa "lights up people's lives") Say: *Let's reread to find details that show that Debby Tewa lights up people's lives. Taking notes will help you write your response.*

Analyze Text Evidence

Remind children that the author uses the sequence text structure to show how Debby Tewa lights up people's lives. First, the author describes how electricity changed Debby's life when she was a child (page 3). Then the author explains what solar power is and what Debby wants to do—work for a company that provides solar power to homes (page 4). Finally, the author explains how Debby travels to small towns in Arizona and New Mexico helping people get electricity (page 6). In the **Reading/Writing Companion,** have children scan page 3 to find details about Debby's life before and after electricity. (before—read by candlelight, could not use a stove or microwave; after—could turn on a lamp and use a phone) Then have them scan the text on page 4 for details in the text and photos that tell what solar power is and how it works. (energy from the sun; sunlight hits solar panels and turns into electricity) Ask them to reread pages 5–7 to find details that show how Debby helps people. (helps people get money for solar panels; teaches about solar power) Have children think about how Debby's work with electricity helps change people's lives and how the text and photographs show this. Tell them that they can use this information to write their responses.

Respond

Direct children to the sentence starters on **Reading/Writing Companion** page 14. Have partners use the sentence starters to focus on how the author shows that Debby Tewa lights up people's lives.

Think Aloud I read that Debby grew up without electricity and it changed her life when she got it. She wanted to help other people get electricity, too. The author explains what solar power is and how Debby helps others use it. The photos show solar panels and the people whom Debby helps.

 Children should use the sentence starters to form their responses. The first sentence should state the main idea, such as "The author explains how Debby Tewa lights up people's lives with solar power." Children should then provide specific details about how the author shows that Debby helps people get electricity. Children may continue their responses on a separate sheet of paper.

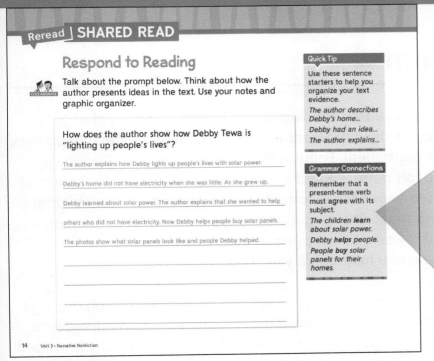

Reading/Writing Companion, p. 14

English Language Learners SCAFFOLD

Use the following scaffolds with **Respond**.

Beginning

Help children respond to the prompt. Read aloud the first paragraph on page 3, and ask: *Why couldn't Debby read at night?* Her home had no <u>electricity</u>. Have children look at page 4 and ask: *What idea did Debby have to help people?* Debby wanted people to have <u>solar power.</u>

Intermediate

Have partners reread pages 3 and 4 to complete the sentence starters. Provide questions to help them, ask: *Why couldn't Debby read or cook on a stove in her first home?* (She didn't have electricity.) *What idea did Debby have to help people?* (She decided to bring solar power to people.)

Advanced/Advanced High

Encourage partners to discuss how Debby helps light up people's lives. Provide guiding questions for discussion: *Describe Debby's childhood home.* (There was no electricity.) *What was it like living in a home without electricity?* (You couldn't turn on the lights or cook at a stove.) *How does Debby want to help people?* (She wants to help them get solar panels.)

Newcomers

Have children listen to the summaries of the **Shared Read** in their native language and then in English to help them access the text and develop listening comprehension. Help children ask and answer questions with a partner. Use these sentence frames: What is the text about? The text is about ___. Then continue the lessons in the **Newcomer Teacher's Guide**.

Reading/Writing Companion

OBJECTIVES

Read with sufficient accuracy and fluency to support comprehension.

Read on-level text with purpose and understanding.

Read on-level text orally with accuracy, appropriate rate, and expression on successive readings.

Use context to confirm or self-correct word recognition and understanding, rereading as necessary.

Rate: 74-94 WCPM

ACADEMIC LANGUAGE
• *expression, accurately, rate*
• Cognate: *expresión*

OPTION
10 Mins

Expression

Explain/Model Review that reading with expression means changing your tone of voice to show different emotions, such as sadness, happiness, fear, anger, and excitement. Point to the last paragraph on **Reading/Writing Companion** page 3. Read it aloud using your voice to show that Debby was excited about the electricity in her new home. Ask children what punctuation mark they noticed when you read with excitement. (an exclamation mark) Review that punctuation marks, such as an exclamation mark, can help guide your expression.

Ask children to follow the text as you read the second paragraph on page 4. Model reading with accuracy, good expression, and at an appropriate rate. Point out how you used your expression to show that Debby is excited about her idea and about solving problems.

Practice/Apply Invite children to echo read as you read aloud the first paragraph on **Reading/Writing Companion** page 5.

Divide the class into three groups. Have at least one slightly higher reader in each group. Ask children to follow along as you read the last paragraph on page 5. After reading the first sentence, have the first group echo read the sentence. Then read the second sentence, and have the second group echo read. Continue until all the groups have had a chance to read. Repeat for subsequent paragraphs.

Have groups work together to practice reading accurately and with good expression. Each group will choose a paragraph to read. Have half the group read the sentence and the other half of the group echo read. Then have children change roles within the group.

Listen in on the groups, providing corrective feedback as needed. Remind children to read with accuracy, or to say all the words correctly, and to read at an appropriate rate and with good expression.

Daily Fluency Practice

Children can practice fluency using **Differentiated Genre Passage,** "Helping Out in the Community."

English Language Learners SCAFFOLD

Before **Practice/Apply**, point out the potential pronunciation challenges in each section of text so children can practice the words in isolation beforehand. Refer to the **Language Transfers Handbook** to identify fluency challenges in different languages.

Use the following scaffolds with the collaborative activity in **Practice/Apply**.

Beginning

Before reading, have children listen to the audio recording of the **Shared Read** as a model for fluency. Allow them to listen and read along silently a few times. Then have them pause after each sentence to echo read. Invite them to record themselves and compare their readings with the original. Children may also record themselves reading one sentence several times, then select their favorite recording to play for you.

Intermediate

After groups select a paragraph to practice, have them listen to the audio recording of the Shared Read as a model for fluency. First have the group pause after each sentence to echo read. Then divide the group in half to take turns chorally reading a few sentences at a time with the audio. Invite them to record themselves and compare their readings with the original audio. Children may also record themselves reading a few sentences at a time, then select their favorite recording to play for you.

Advanced/Advanced High

Have these children join the rest of the class for group fluency practice. Encourage them to listen to the audio recording of the selection for additional practice as needed. Have children work with mixed proficiency groups to help them compare their own readings with the audio recordings.

Language Transfers Handbook

✔ Check for Success

Can children read at an appropriate rate and with expression?

Differentiate
SMALL GROUP INSTRUCTION

If No

| Approaching | Reteach pp. T82, T138 |
| ELL | Develop pp. T82, T160 |

If Yes

| On | Apply p. T140 |
| Beyond | Apply p. T146 |

Reading/Writing Companion

OBJECTIVES

Participate in shared research and writing projects (e.g., read a number of books on a single topic to produce a report; record science observations).

Recall information from experiences or gather information from provided sources to answer a question.

Participate in collaborative conversations with diverse partners about grade 2 topics and texts with peers and adults in small and larger groups.

ACADEMIC LANGUAGE

• *primary source, secondary source, topic*
• Cognates: *primero, secundario*

TEACH IN SMALL GROUP

You may wish to teach the Research and Inquiry lesson during Small Group time. Have groups of mixed abilities complete the page and work on the History Picture Book.

 # Primary and Secondary Sources

1 Explain

Explain that primary sources are original items that come from a person's life or experience. Letters, interviews, and photographs are primary sources. Secondary sources are created to give information about an event, person, or topic. They include textbooks and encyclopedias.

Work with children to identify the primary and secondary sources on **Reading/Writing Companion** page 15. Have them circle the primary sources and underline the secondary sources. Have them explain why "Lighting Lives" is a secondary source.

2 Model

Model how to identify and use reliable primary and secondary sources. Discuss with children which kinds of sources they might use to research a person or event that has shaped their town or state. Have children brainstorm questions they would want to answer in their research. Children might want to use a KWL chart to record the questions. They can divide up the questions with partners or group members.

3 Guided Practice

Review with children how to identify and record primary and secondary sources that they will use to gather information about their person or event. Have each pair or group make an Accordion Foldable® to record ideas and facts from sources. Model recording the names of the sources, and review children's entries with them.

Create a History Picture Book Have children work with their group or partner to create a history picture book. Explain that they will create a book with illustrations and captions to show and tell how a person or event shaped their town or state. Encourage them to use at least one primary source and one secondary source. Tell them that they will be working on the project over the next two weeks. Have partners or groups discuss their research plan.

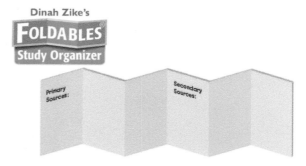

Accordion Book Foldable®

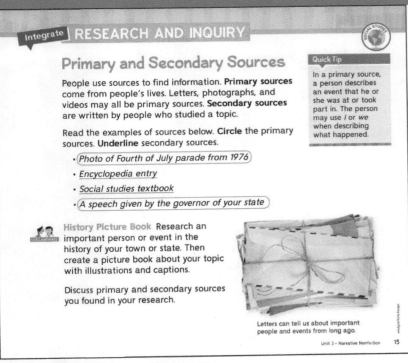

Reading/Writing Companion, p. 15

 ## English Language Learners SCAFFOLD

Before **Create a History Picture Book**, help children use prior knowledge about important historical figures to learn some new words and phrases they can use in their books. Invite them to name people they know about, including from other countries. Provide linguistic support so they can tell about who they are, what they did, and why they are important. Write words and phrases on the board for children to refer to as they complete the whole group assignment. Then use the following scaffolds with **Guided Practice**.

Beginning

If needed, suggest some important historical figures children can research. Have children work in mixed-proficiency pairs to complete the assignment. Help Beginning ELLs prepare labels and captions for the book.

Intermediate

Have partners use guiding questions to plan their research, such as *Who is the person? Where is he or she from? What did he or she do? Why is he or she important?* And, if the person is not living, *When did he or she live?*

Advanced/Advanced High

Challenge children to use longer phrases or complete sentences to create text and captions for their picture books. Encourage them to include interesting details about the person or event they chose.

 ## Digital Tools

RESOURCE TOOLKIT Children may watch the Take Notes: Print (Animated Tutorial) and Organize Notes (Animated Tutorial)

Research Process

Share the online **Research Roadmap** with children.

Step 1: Set Research Goals

- Reread the instructions for the History Picture Book and have children restate them. Then offer feedback as pairs brainstorm questions and make a research plan.

Step 2: Identify Sources

- Check that partners are following their research plan to find relevant sources on the topic they chose. Ask what primary sources they will use.

Step 3: Find and Record Information

- Review how to take notes and record source information.

Step 4: Organize

- Have partners check their understanding of the information they gathered.

Step 5: Synthesize and Present

- Make sure children decide on a clear main idea for the topic of their History Picture Book and agree on what role each partner will play during the presentation.

Genre • Narrative Nonfiction

BIBLIOBURRO
A True Story From Colombia
Jeanette Winter

Essential Question
How can people help out in their community?

Read about a man who travels to bring books to faraway villages that have none.

Go Digital!

212

Deep in the jungles of Colombia, there lives a man who loves books.

His name is Luis.

213

Wonders

Literature Anthology

Text Complexity Range
Lexile

420   700   820

Have children apply what they learned as they read.

 Identify other individuals who exemplify good citizenship.

Biblioburro

Close Reading Routine

Read DOK 1–2

• Identify key ideas and details about ways people help.
• Take notes and retell.
• Use **ACT** prompts as needed.

Reread DOK 2–3

• Analyze the text, craft, and structure.
• *Reading/Writing Companion,* 16–18.

Integrate DOK 4

• Integrate knowledge and ideas.
• Make text-to-text connections.
• Use the Integrate lesson.
• Inspire action.

Literature Anthology, pp. 212–213

Read

Tell children they will read about a man who brings books to people who do not have any. Ask children to predict how the story will help answer the **Essential Question.**

DIFFERENTIATED READING

Approaching Level Have children listen to the selection summary. Use the Reread prompts during Small-Group time.

On Level and **Beyond Level** Pair children or have them independently complete the Reread prompts on **Reading/Writing Companion** pages 16–18.

 ELL Before reading, have Beginning/Early-Intermediate ELLs listen to a selection summary, available in multiple languages. See the small group pages for more support.

As soon as he reads one book, he brings home another. Soon the house is filled with books.

His wife, Diana, grumbles.

What are we going to do, eat books with our rice?

214

Luis thinks long and hard.

At last an **idea** pops into his head.

"I can bring my books into the faraway hills to share with those who have none.

 One burro could carry books, and another burro could carry me—and more books!"

215

Literature Anthology, pp. 214–215

Note Taking: Use the Graphic Organizer

Guide children to fill in their Author's Purpose graphic organizer as they read. Have them record clues from the illustrations and text. Ask them to note questions they may have.

Reread

❶ Use Illustrations

Reading/Writing Companion, 16

How does the author help you to understand Luis's idea? (The author uses an illustration to show Luis riding over hills with burros carrying books. She uses text to tell how Luis would ride burros to bring books to people.)

Build Vocabulary pages 214–215

Throughout, have children add the Build Vocabulary words to their writer's notebooks.

grumbles: complains

faraway: a long distance away

ⒶⒸⓉ Access Complex Text

Purpose of the Text Because the nonfiction narrative reads as a story and has illustrations, children may assume the author's purpose is to entertain. As you read, remind children that the story tells a true story about a real man named Luis who helps people.

Specific Vocabulary Children may need help with specific vocabulary.

Organization Children may need help understanding the organization of sentences.

Luis buys two sturdy little burros.

He names them Alfa and Beto.

He builds crates to hang on their backs, and paints signs: BIBLIOBURRO— "The Burro Library."

Then Diana fills the crates with books.

Literature Anthology, pp. 216–217

Access Complex Text

Specific Vocabulary

Luis names his burros *Alfa* and *Beto* on page 216. Say the names aloud, *Alfa Beto*. Ask children what the names sound like. Explain that *alfabeto* is Spanish for *alphabet*. Luis lives in Colombia, and Spanish is spoken there. Ask children why Luis may name his burros *Alfa* and *Beto*. Then point out the word *biblioburro*. Explain that *biblioteca* is Spanish for *library*. Guide children to see why Luis chose the word *biblioburro*.

Build Vocabulary pages 216–217

sturdy: strong

crate: case

Read

2 Strategy: Ask and Answer Questions

Let's ask a question to make sure we understand what has happened. Why did Luis buy two burros? Ask another question about what you have read so far.

ELL Spotlight on Language

Page 217 Use pantomime to clarify the meaning of *build*s. Say: *To build means to make or create.* Ask: *What does Luis build?* (crates) *Why?* (to fill with books and hang on the backs of his burros)

Every week, Luis and Alfa and Beto set off **across** the **countryside** to faraway **villages** in the **lonely** hills. 3

This week they travel to El Tormento.

STOP AND CHECK
Ask and Answer Questions
Why are Luis, Alfa, and Beto going to El Tormento? Go back to the text to find the answer.

218   219

Literature Anthology, pp. 218–219

Build Vocabulary page 218

set off: leave

3 **Skill: Author's Purpose**

Let's think about what we have read so far. What does the author want us to know? Add this information to the first Clue box on our Author's Purpose graphic organizer.

Clues	Clues
Luis travels to faraway villages to bring books to people.	

Synthesize Information

Explain I can use specific words I read in the story to better understand where Luis travels with his books.

Model On page 215, the author uses the word *faraway* to describe the hills Luis will travel to. On page 216, Luis chooses *sturdy* burros.

Apply What specific words on page 218 describe where Luis travels every week? (across, faraway, lonely)

✓ STOP AND CHECK

Strategy: Ask and Answer Questions Why are Luis, Alfa, and Beto going to El Tormento? Use the text to find the answer. (Possible response: to bring books to people)

When the sun burns high in the sky,
Luis and the burros stop at a stream
to drink the cool water.

After they have their fill,
Beto balks.

220

Luis pulls and pulls on Beto's reins,
but Beto won't budge. 4

The children are waiting for us!

At last the burro gives in
and steps across the stream.

221

Literature Anthology, pp. 220–221

Read

4 Vocabulary

Teacher Think Aloud I'm not sure what *budge* means. I can use picture clues and reread the text to try to figure it out. The picture shows the burro refusing to move. The text says "Luis pulls and pulls on Beto's reins." So I think *budge* means *move*. I'll reread to check if it makes sense with the picture and the text.

 English Language Learners

Request Assistance Remind children of expressions they can use to request assistance from the teacher or a peer, such as *Can you show me a "stream" in the picture?*

Reread

Use Illustrations

Reading/Writing Companion, 17

How does the author help you understand what it was lik to travel to the villages? (The illustration shows the sun high in the sky, a stream, the burros Alfa and Beto carryi books, and Luis pulling on Beto's reins. Traveling to the villages was hot and difficult for the burros and Luis.)

<u>**Build Vocabulary** pages 220–221</u>

balks: resists

stream: small river

The Biblioburro continues on its way
over the hills, until at last,
Luis sees houses below.

The children of El Tormento run to meet him. **5**

Literature Anthology, pp. 222–223

Read

5 Strategy: Ask and Answer Questions

Teacher Think Aloud We read about how Luis and the Biblioburro travel to faraway villages each week. What question can you ask about their trip to El Tormento?

Student Think Aloud On pages 220 and 221, I read that Luis and the burros stop to drink some cool water and that after they are done drinking, Beto *balks*. I am not sure what *balks* means. Why does Beto do this? I will look for the answer in the text and illustrations as I read on. I see in the illustrations and read in the text that Luis is trying to get Beto to cross the stream, but he won't budge. This is the answer to my question.

Reread

Use Illustrations

Look at the illustrations on pages 222–223. How would you describe Luis's journey with the burros? Why do you think he continues? (The mountains look steep. It must be difficult to move around with books. I think Luis is determined to bring books to people who don't have any.)

Author's Craft: Word Choice

What do the words *at last* on page 223 help you understand about Luis's journey? (It tells me how long it has taken Luis to reach El Tormento. He traveled far to get the books to the children.)

Luis **insists** on reading a story before they choose books to **borrow**.

"Today I have a surprise for you," he says.

He reaches behind the books and pulls out a bundle of masks—little piglets!

"Put on a mask, and I'll read you a tale about pigs." **6** **7**

224

225

8

Literature Anthology, pp. 224–225

Read

6 Skill: Author's Purpose

As we read, we continue to think about why the author wrote the selection. She tells readers facts about Luis. We have already recorded that she tells how Luis travels a long way to bring books to people. What other information have we read that will help us determine the author's purpose? Add the information to the graphic organizer.

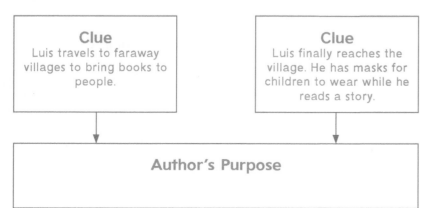

| **Clue** Luis travels to faraway villages to bring books to people. | **Clue** Luis finally reaches the village. He has masks for children to wear while he reads a story. |

Author's Purpose

7 Vocabulary: Synonyms

I'm not sure what the word *tale* means in the last sentence. I'm going to reread the page to see if there's a synonym that might help me. The first sentence says Luis wants to read a story. The last sentence says "I'll read you a tale." So I think *story* is a synonym for *tale* since the author uses both words to refer to what Luis is going to read.

 Spotlight on Language

Page 224 Focus on the phrasal verb *put on*. Explain that *put on* means "to start wearing something." Point to the illustration and ask: *What does Luis want the children to put on?* (masks) *What do you put on before you come to school?* (Possible answer: clothes)

When the story ends, it's time for everyone to choose a book.

The children hold their books close as they say good-bye and walk home. **9**

Literature Anthology, pp. 226–227

8 Reread for Understanding

Teacher Think Aloud After reading page 224, I will make sure I understand what I have read. Now that I have checked my understanding, I realize that I may have missed something. Why does Luis tell the children to put on piglet masks? I can reread page 224 and retell what I read in my own words, or paraphrase. Paraphrasing will help me understand the text better. Luis reads a story to the children and has a surprise for them. Luis's surprise is piglet masks for the children. He gives the children piglet masks because he is going to read a story about piglets.

9 Skill: Main Topic and Key Details

What key detail on pages 226 and 227 supports the main topic that Luis helps out his community? (Luis gives the children books to take home.)

Reread
Use Illustrations

Reading/Writing Companion, 18

What clues does the author use to show you how the children felt about the books? (The children are looking through books; this shows they are excited to discover new books. The children are smiling; this shows how happy they are to have their own books. The children are carrying the books home; this shows they are eager to read them.)

Build Vocabulary page 224

bundle: bunch

tale: story

Luis and Alfa and Beto head back, over and around the hills,

across the grasslands and streams, and into the sunset.

STOP AND CHECK

Reread Where are Luis, Alfa, and Beto going now? Reread to check your understanding.

228

229

Literature Anthology, pp. 228–229

Access Complex Text

Organization

Help children understand the structure of the sentence on pages 228–229.

- Point out that the text on pages 228–229 is just one sentence.
- Ask: *Why might the author have written one long sentence across the two pages?* (Possible response: to point out that Luis's journey was long)

Read

STOP AND CHECK

Reread Where are Luis, Alfa, and Beto going now? Reread to check your understanding. (Luis, Alfa, and Beto are going back home.)

Spotlight on Language

Page 228 Focus on the expression *head back*. Explain that *head back* means to go back, or return. *In the morning, you leave home. You come to school. After school, you head back home.* Ask: *Where are Luis and the burros heading back to?* (home)

Connect to Content

Ben Franklin

Like Luis Soriano, Benjamin Franklin wanted to share books with others. In 1731 few people had books and there were no public libraries. Franklin and some friends in Philadelphia decided to create a place where people could borrow books. The idea caught on. Now there are public libraries all across the United States. Franklin believed all citizens should help out in their communities.

At home, Luis feeds his hungry burros.

And Diana feeds her hungry husband.

But then, instead of sleeping,
Luis picks up *his* book,
and reads deep into the night.

And far away in the hills,
candles and lanterns burn
as the children read borrowed books
deep into *their* night, too.

Literature Anthology, pp. 230–231

Skill: Author's Purpose

What clues have we added to the Author's Purpose graphic organizer? Think about what the author of *Biblioburro* wants you to know. Why do you think she wrote the selection? Let's add the author's purpose to our graphic organizer.

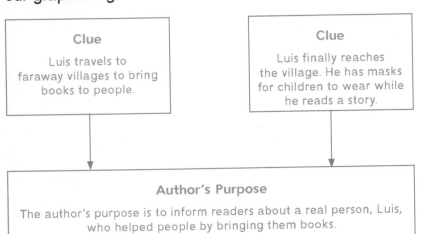

Clue	Clue
Luis travels to faraway villages to bring books to people.	Luis finally reaches the village. He has masks for children to wear while he reads a story.

Author's Purpose

The author's purpose is to inform readers about a real person, Luis, who helped people by bringing them books.

Reread

Author's Craft: Repetition

Reread pages 230–231. Why does the author repeat the phrase *deep into night*? (It shows the connection between Luis and the children. They are all enjoying their books at the same time.)

Return to Purposes

Review children's predictions. Ask them if their predictions were correct. Guide them to use evidence in the text to confirm whether their predictions turned out to be accurate. Discuss how Luis helped people. Did children learn what they wanted to by reading the selection?

Build Vocabulary page 231

lanterns: lamps

About the Author and Illustrator

Jeanette Winter loved to write stories and draw pictures as a child. She wanted to be an artist when she grew up. Jeanette studied painting, drawing, and sculpture. She taught herself about illustrating books. As an adult Jeanette has won many awards for her books.

Jeanette likes to write stories about real people. She often finds her ideas while she is reading the newspaper. *Biblioburro* tells the true story of Luis Soriano, a schoolteacher in Colombia. When Luis started sharing books with villages, he had 70 to share. Now he has over 4,800 books to loan!

Author's Purpose

Why do you think Jeanette tells Luis's story? What do you think her purpose is?

232

Respond to the Text

Summarize

Use important details to summarize what happens in the selection. Information from your Author's Purpose chart may help you.

Clue	Clue

Author's Purpose

Write

How does the author use illustrations to show the difficulty of Luis's journey? Use these sentence starters:

The author showed Luis thinking about his journey by . . .

There are images of the burros carrying . . .

Make Connections

How did Luis help out in his community? ESSENTIAL QUESTION

What is something you learned about reading or libraries from *Biblioburro*? TEXT TO WORLD

233

Literature Anthology, pp. 232–233

Read

Meet the Author

Jeanette Winter

Read aloud page 232 with children. Ask them why Jeanette Winter may have chosen to write Luis's story.

• How might Jeanette have gotten the idea for the book *Biblioburro*?

• What might she have done before she wrote the text?

• What question would you like to ask Jeanette about this story?

Author's Purpose

To Inform: Tell children that authors write narrative nonfiction to share information about real people, places, or events. Ask them why they think the author wrote about Luis's story. Have children record their answers. *The author's purpose is to _____.*

Summarize

Tell children they will use details from their Author's Purpose graphic organizer to summarize. As I read, I collected information from the selection by taking notes on the clues and the author's purpose. To summarize, I will paraphrase the most important details.

Analyze the Text

After children summarize the selection, have them reread to develop a deeper understanding of the text and answer the questions on pages 16–18 of the **Reading/Writing Companion**. For children who need support in citing text evidence, use the Reread prompts on pages T49B, T49F, T49H, and T49J.

Write About the Text

Review the writing prompt with children. Remind them to use their responses from the **Reading/Writing Companion** to cite text evidence and support their answers. For a full lesson on writing a response using text evidence, see pages T50–T51.

Make Connections

Essential Question <u>Answer</u>: Luis took books to children who live in a faraway place where there aren't many books. <u>Evidence</u>: The children are happy to have the books. They read *deep into their night*.

Text to World <u>Answer</u>: Books make people happy. <u>Evidence</u>: The children walk away smiling and holding their books close.

Reading/Writing Companion

OBJECTIVES

Ask and answer such questions as who, what, where, when, why, and how to demonstrate understanding of key details in a text.

Write informative/explanatory texts in which they introduce a topic, use facts and definitions to develop points, and provide a concluding statement or section.

ACADEMIC LANGUAGE

• *text, illustrations*
• Cognates: *texto, ilustraciones*

TEACH IN SMALL GROUP

You may wish to use the Respond to Reading lesson during Small Group time.

Approaching Level and **On Level** Have partners work together to plan and complete the response to the prompt.

Beyond Level Ask children to respond to the prompt independently and also to write a response to their self-selected reading selection.

ELL Group ELLs of mixed proficiency levels to discuss and respond to the prompt.

Write About the Anchor Text

Analyze the Prompt

Read the prompt aloud: *How does the author use illustrations to show the difficulty of Luis's journey?* Ask: *What is the prompt asking you to do?* (to explain how the author uses the text and illustrations to describe Luis's journey) Say: *Let's reread to see how the author uses words and illustrations to support the text and help us answer the prompt.*

Analyze Text Evidence

Remind children that narrative nonfiction text may require the reader to notice how the author uses both the key details in the text and the illustrations to tell the story. Have children look at the **Literature Anthology**, pages 212–213. *Look at the illustrations on these pages. What do the jungles of Colombia look like? Do you think it would be difficult to travel in a jungle? Explain why or why not.* (There are many trees, plants, and animals. It may be difficult to travel in a jungle because of this. There may not be many roads.) **Next, have children look at pages 218–219.** Say: *Look at the illustration. What do you think it would be like to travel up and down steep hills in the jungle carrying many books?* (It looks like it would be difficult. Books are heavy and would make it even more difficult for the burros to climb the hills.) **Then have children look at pages 226–227.** Say: *Look at the illustration on these pages. What are the children doing? Why are they excited?* (The children are choosing books and taking their books home with them. They are excited because they like getting the books.)

Respond

Review pages 16–18 of the **Reading/Writing Companion**. Have partners or small groups refer to and discuss their completed charts and writing responses from those pages. Then direct children's attention to the sentence starters on page 19. Have them take notes as necessary. Children should focus on details presented in the text and illustrations that tell how the author showed that Luis's journey was difficult. Their first sentence should state their main idea, such as "The author uses details in the text and illustrations to help readers understand how difficult Luis's journey is."

Analytical Writing Children should go through the text to find examples that show the challenges that Luis faces as he makes his journey. Remind children that they can use additional paper to complete their responses.

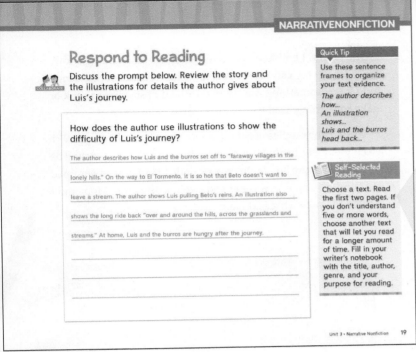

NARRATIVENONFICTION

Respond to Reading

Discuss the prompt below. Review the story and the illustrations for details the author gives about Luis's journey.

How does the author use illustrations to show the difficulty of Luis's journey?

The author describes how Luis and the burros set off to "faraway villages in the lonely hills." On the way to El Tormento, it is so hot that Beto doesn't want to leave a stream. The author shows Luis pulling Beto's reins. An illustration also shows the long ride back "over and around the hills, across the grasslands and streams." At home, Luis and the burros are hungry after the journey.

Quick Tip

Use these sentence frames to organize your text evidence.
The author describes how...
An illustration shows...
Luis and the burros head back...

Self-Selected Reading

Choose a text. Read the first two pages. If you don't understand five or more words, choose another text that will let you read for a longer amount of time. Fill in your writer's notebook with the title, author, genre, and your purpose for reading.

Unit 3 • Narrative Nonfiction   19

Reading/Writing Companion, p. 19

Self-Selected Reading

Allow children free time to read a book of their choosing. As they preview books, tell them that one way to check if a book is a good fit is to count the number of words they don't know on a page. If they get to five, they might want to choose another book. Before reading, have them set a purpose for reading and write it in their writer's notebook with the title, author, and genre of the book.

English Language Learners SCAFFOLD

Use the following scaffolds with **Respond.**

Beginning

Have children look at pages 218–219 of the **Literature Anthology.** Read aloud the text, and ask: *What word describes the hills?* (lonely) Have them look at the illustration, and ask: *Are there any people in the hills?* (no) *What are the hills like?* The hills are lonely. There are no people.

Intermediate

Guide children to show how the illustrations support the details in the text. Have them look at the text and illustration on pages 218–219 in the **Literature Anthology.** Ask: *How does the illustration show that Luis is going to "faraway" villages?* (The illustration shows Luis leaving home.) *How does the illustration show that the hills are lonely?* (There are no people in the hills.)

Advanced/Advanced High

Have partners reread the text and look at the illustrations on pages 218–219 in the **Literature Anthology.** Elicit how the illustration supports the details that the villages are far away and the hills are lonely. Have them use the information to complete the sentence starters. Provide support to help children elaborate and write complete sentences.

Newcomers

Have children listen to the summaries of the **Anchor Text** in their native language and then in English to help them access the text and develop listening comprehension. Help children ask and answer questions with a partner. Use these sentence frames: *What is the text about? The text is about ___.* Then have them complete the online **Newcomer Activities** individually or in pairs.

Genre · Personal Narrative

Compare Texts
Read about how a girl helped her dad, the gymnastics coach.

Landing on Your Feet

Before I wake up for school, Dad is already at work. He is an ironworker in the city. Ironworkers build tall buildings and repair giant bridges. They build with heavy metal beams made of iron. When Dad comes home, he likes to cook or do things for our house. He also teaches his favorite sport to kids. Dad is a gymnastics coach at a community center. He teaches girls like me at the same gym where he learned gymnastics as a boy.

Gymnastics is fun but hard to learn. Dad encourages us to practice to get better. He teaches older kids amazing skills like backflips and handstands. We all feel proud after we work hard and learn a cool new skill.

234

One Friday, I had free time after school. I was building a toy house for my toy cat. When Dad came home from work, Mom and I knew something was wrong. Instead of starting to cook or make something, Dad went to the couch to lie down.

"Ryan, can you please get me an ice pack from the freezer?" he asked me. I was having fun playing, but I got up right away. The ice pack froze my hands the few seconds I held it. Dad wrapped it around his ankle. It was big and swollen and blue. Mom and I wanted to know what had happened.

235

Literature Anthology, pp. 234–235

"Landing on Your Feet"

Literature Anthology

Text Complexity Range
Lexile

420   610   820

Have children apply what they learned as they read.

Compare Texts

Analytical Writing As children read and reread the selection, encourage them to think about the Essential Question: *How can people help out their community?* Ask children to think about how Luis in *Biblioburro* and Ryan and her dad in "Landing on Your Feet" helped people in their communities. Children should discuss how the texts are alike and different.

(A C T) Access Complex Text

Genre

Tell children that a personal narrative is a true story from a writer's life. It uses words, such as *I, me, my,* and *we*. It also uses time words to help readers understand when the events happened. Ask children to identify time order words that tell when different events take place in "Landing on Your Feet."

Read

1 Skill: Author's Purpose

Read the first paragraph on page 234. Ask: *What does the author tell you about her dad's favorite sport?* (His favorite sport is gymnastics.) *How does this detail help support the author's purpose?* (The author wants readers to know that her dad helps others by teaching his favorite sport at the community center.)

2 Strategy: Ask and Answer Questions

Read the first paragraph on page 235. Ask: *What question can you ask about what happened when Dad came home?* (Why did Dad go to the couch to lie down?) Read the second paragraph to find the answer. (Dad had hurt his ankle.)

3 Skill: Author's Purpose

Reread the first paragraph on page 234. Ask: *What else does the author's father do besides teach gymnastics?* (He is an ironworker, and he likes to cook and help around the house.) *Why might the author tell the reader all the different things that her dad does?* (It helps the reader to understand why the author is so happy to help her dad feel better. He does a lot for her, so she is happy to return the favor.)

Build Vocabulary pages 234, 236

beams: long support structures
sideways: on the edge
relax: rest

Reread

Author's Craft

What time words or phrases does the author use on page 235 to help you understand the order of the events? (She uses the time words *One Friday, after school, when,* and *right away* to tell when the events happened.)

"I was leading warm-ups at practice last night," he said. Dad teaches the oldest kids after I go home. "I jumped up high and came down hard on my ankle."

I had an **idea** of how Dad hurt himself. He probably landed on his foot sideways. Everyone at the gym must have gone, "Oooh!" Dad explained that a nurse was at the gym. The nurse told Dad how to take care of his ankle.

The ice pack seemed to help Dad relax on the couch. I got pillows so he could put his leg up. Dad said, "I hope my ankle gets better soon. I need to coach the kids on Monday." Now I was really worried. Dad is always there for the kids at the gym. *I have until Monday to help Dad feel better,* I thought.

236

Over the weekend, Mom and I stayed home with Dad. I got fresh ice packs for his ankle, and I made him lunch and snacks. We watched movies, and I got Dad books to read. Even our kitty, Toast, helped. He lay **across** Dad to keep him company.

Dad's ankle was still a little sore, or hurting, on Monday. It wasn't easy for him to walk. But Dad coached! After practice, I got more ice for his ankle. I am glad I made Dad feel better so he could keep teaching kids gymnastics. I think they're very lucky to have him as a coach. I know I'm lucky to have him as both a coach and my Dad.

> **Make Connections**
> How did the girl and her father help out their community? ESSENTIAL QUESTION
>
> Think about the other selections you've read. What are some other ways people helped in their communities? TEXT TO TEXT

237

Literature Anthology, pp. 236–237

(A)(C)(T) Access Complex Text

Genre

Help children understand that when an author writes a personal narrative, the events in the selection are included because they support the author's purpose. Because a personal narrative often reads like a story, children may need help understanding that the events described are actual events that the narrator wants readers to know about. As children read, remind them of the author's purpose--to share that her dad helps others--and that they are reading a true story about a girl who helps her dad.

On page 235, what detail supports the author's purpose of telling readers about a time when she helped her dad? (The author writes that when Dad asked Ryan for an ice pack, she got up right away to get it, even though she was playing.)

Read

❹ Ask and Answer Questions

Read the first paragraph on page 237. Ask: *What is a question you might ask after reading the paragraph?* (Did what the author and her mother do help her dad feel better?) *Where would you find the answer to that question?* (I would probably find it in the next paragraph.)

❺ Skill: Author's Purpose

Why is it important for the author to talk about the things that she did for her dad? (She wants to show that she appreciates the work that her father does. She also wants to show that she wants him to continue to do his work, and so she will help him feel better.)

Reread

Author's Craft

Point out the last sentence on page 236 and guide children to notice that it looks different. Say: *The author wants you to notice something about this sentence. It is written in italics, a different kind of print, to indicate that these are words that the author is thinking, but not saying to someone else.* Have children note the words *I thought.* Ask: *What do Ryan's thoughts tell you about her?* (They tell us that she cares about her dad and also the kids that he coaches.)

Read

Summarize

Guide children to use the key details to summarize the selection.

Reread

Analyze the Text

 After children summarize the selection, have them reread to develop a deeper understanding of the text by annotating and answering questions on pages 20–22 of the **Reading/Writing Companion.** For children who need support citing text evidence, use the reread prompts on pages T51B and T51D.

Integrate

Make Connections

Essential Question The author's dad helped his community by sharing his knowledge and skills of his favorite sport, gymnastics. Ryan helped by taking care of her dad so he could return to the gym and coach the kids.

Text to Text People helped their communities in different ways. Luis helped by taking books to people who lived far away and didn't have access to them.

Page 236, Paragraph 1 Focus on the phrase "warm-ups." Explain that warm-ups are exercises people do to prepare to play a sport or other physical activity. Invite a volunteer to demonstrate how a runner might stretch or do some other type of warm-up before a run. *What warm-up was Ryan's dad doing when he hurt his ankle?* (He was jumping high.) *When do you do warm-ups?* (Possible response: At the beginning of gym class.)

Author's Craft

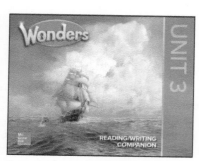

Reading/Writing Companion

OBJECTIVES

Ask and answer such questions as *who, what, where, when, why,* and *how* to demonstrate understanding of key details in a text.

Participate in collaborative conversations with diverse partners about *grade 2 topics and texts* with peers and adults in small and larger groups.

ACADEMIC LANGUAGE

- *time words, phrase, order, events, clause*
- Cognates: *frase, evento, cláusula*

Time Words

1 Explain

Have children turn to page 23 of the **Reading/Writing Companion.** Share with children the following key points about the use of time words in a personal narrative:

- Time words help readers understand the order of events in a personal narrative.

- Authors use special words or phrases, such as "now," "on Monday," and "over the weekend" to help readers keep track of when things happen.

- Readers can better understand a personal narrative when they know the correct order in which the events happen.

2 Model

Model time words by showing children how to tell when an event takes place. Point out the first paragraph on page 235 of "Landing on Your Feet." Say: *Let's look at the phrases that the narrator uses to tell about when things happen.* Guide children to identify the phrases "one Friday" and "after school." Then ask children to identify a clause that helps them understand when Mom and the author knew something was wrong. ("When Dad came home from work")

3 Guided Practice

Guide partners to work together to identify the words or phrases that tell when Dad hurt his ankle, what day he got hurt, and how they know. Have them begin by rereading the first paragraph on page 235 of "Landing on Your Feet." Allow children time to enter their responses on page 23 of the **Reading/Writing Companion.**

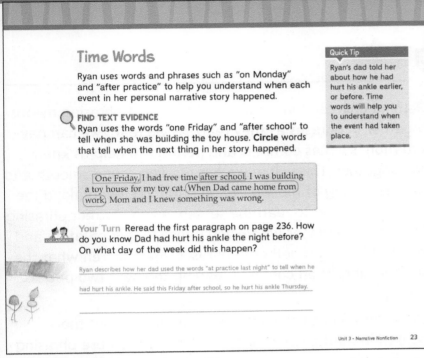

Time Words

Ryan uses words and phrases such as "on Monday" and "after practice" to help you understand when each event in her personal narrative story happened.

Quick Tip

Ryan's dad told her about how he had hurt his ankle earlier, or before. Time words will help you to understand when the event had taken place.

FIND TEXT EVIDENCE

Ryan uses the words "one Friday" and "after school" to tell when she was building the toy house. **Circle** words that tell when the next thing in her story happened.

One Friday, I had free time after school. I was building a toy house for my toy cat. When Dad came home from work, Mom and I knew something was wrong.

Your Turn Reread the first paragraph on page 236. How do you know Dad had hurt his ankle the night before? On what day of the week did this happen?

Ryan describes how her dad used the words "at practice last night" to tell when he

had hurt his ankle. He said this Friday after school, so he hurt his ankle Thursday.

Unit 3 • Narrative Nonfiction   23

Reading/Writing Companion, p. 23

English Language Learners SCAFFOLD

Use the following scaffolds with **Guided Practice**.

Beginning

Read the first paragraph on page 235. Ask: *Did Ryan build a toy house before or after school?* She built a toy house <u>after</u> school. *Which phrase tells when the story takes place?* ("One Friday") Now read the first paragraph on page 236. Ask: *Which phrase tells when Dad hurt his ankle?* ("last night") *So when did Dad hurt his ankle? What day?* Dad hurt his ankle on <u>Thursday</u>.

Intermediate

Have partners reread the first paragraph on page 235. Ask: *When did Ryan work on a toy house for her toy cat?* She worked on the toy house <u>after school</u>. Have partners reread the first paragraph on page 236. Say: *Ryan is talking about one day. What day is it?* (Friday) *When did Dad hurt his ankle?* He hurt his ankle <u>last night.</u> *What day of the week is that?* (Thursday)

Advanced/Advanced High

Have partners discuss the order of events on pages 235–236. Provide guiding questions: *Did Ryan work on a toy house or go to school first?* (She went to school first.) *How do you know?* (The text says Ryan worked on it "after school.") *When did Dad get hurt?* (Dad got hurt Thursday night.) *How do you know?* (The text says "last night.")

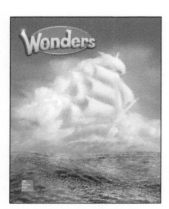

Literature Anthology

OBJECTIVES

Read with sufficient accuracy and fluency to support comprehension. Read on-level text orally with accuracy, appropriate rate, and expression on successive readings.

Rate: 74-94 WCPM

ACADEMIC LANGUAGE

• *phrase, phrasing, commas, punctuation*

• Cognates: *frase, comas, puntuación*

Phrasing

Explain/Model Remind children that reading with correct phrasing means grouping words together in phrases as they read. As we read, we can pay attention to punctuation, such as commas and periods, to help us know how to group words together. This will make our reading sound smooth and natural. Point to the beginning of *Biblioburro* on page 213. Read aloud the first sentence. Demonstrate how to read the sentence with correct phrasing and expression. Point out the places where you pause for punctuation and for groups of words that belong together in phrases. Ask children what they noticed about your phrasing. Then continue reading the next two pages, using correct phrasing.

Ask children to follow the text as you continue to read. Point out the commas and punctuation marks. Ask children to listen as you use phrasing to read smoothly and naturally.

Practice/Apply Invite children to echo read as you read aloud pages 216–217, pausing at the commas and end punctuation.

Divide the class into four groups. Have at least one slightly higher reader in each group. Ask children to follow along as you read the first paragraph on page 216. After reading the first sentence, have the first group echo read the sentence. Then read the second sentence and have the second group echo read. Continue until all groups have read a sentence. Repeat with subsequent paragraphs.

Have groups work together to practice reading with good phrasing. Each group will choose a paragraph to read. Have half the group read the sentence and the other half of the group echo read. Then have children change roles within the group.

Listen in on the groups, providing corrective feedback as needed. Remind children to read with accuracy, or to say all the words correctly, and to read at an appropriate rate.

Daily Fluency Practice

Children can practice fluency using **Differentiated Genre Passage,** "Helping Out in the Community."

English Language Learners SCAFFOLD

During the teacher-led portion of **Practice/Apply**, include English Language Learners in heterogeneous groups with the rest of the class. Before you begin the echo read routine, point out the potential pronunciation challenges in each section of text so children can practice the words in isolation beforehand. Refer to the **Language Transfers Handbook** to identify potential fluency challenges.

Beginning

After groups select a paragraph to practice, have them listen to the audio recording of the **Anchor Text** as a model for fluency. Allow them to listen and read along silently a few times. Then have them pause after each sentence to echo read. Children may record themselves reading one sentence several times, then select their favorite recording to play for you.

Intermediate

After groups select a paragraph to practice, have them listen to the audio recording of the Anchor Text as a model for fluency. First have the group pause after each sentence to echo read. Then have half the group choral read one sentence at a time with the audio and the other half echo read. Then have children switch roles. Children may also record themselves reading a few sentences several times, then select their favorite recording to play for you.

Advanced/Advanced High

Have these children join the rest of the class for group fluency practice. Encourage them to listen to the audio recording of the selection for additional practice as needed.

Language Transfers Handbook

✔ Check for Success

Can children read text accurately, at an appropriate rate, and with appropriate phrasing?

Differentiate
SMALL GROUP INSTRUCTION

If No

| Approaching | Reteach pp. T117, T132 |
| ELL | Develop pp. T117, T160 |

If Yes

| On | Review p. T140 |
| Beyond | Extend p. T146 |

Personal Narrative

Reading/Writing Companion

OBJECTIVES

Read on-level text with purpose and understanding.

Identify the main purpose of a text, including what the author wants to answer, describe, or explain.

ACADEMIC LANGUAGE

• *personal narrative, narrator, first person, event, details*

• Cognates: *narrador, detalles*

DIFFERENTIATED WRITING ≪

Approaching Level For Plan: Organization phase (T60), provide questions to guide children: *Beginning—Where did you help? Middle—What did you do? End—How did you feel?*

On Level Before children begin the Draft phase (T62), remind them to use sequence words *first, next, then,* and *finally.*

Beyond Level For the Draft phase (T62), have children choose words, such as *thankful, satisfying,* and *rewarding* to describe their feelings.

ELL Have pairs find an example of each feature listed on the Anchor Chart.

Expert Model

Features of Personal Narratives

Explain that after reading "Lighting Lives" and "Landing on Your Feet," children will begin writing a personal narrative about a time when they helped others. Invite children to recall other texts that tell a true story about a person who helped someone else.

Review the features of a personal narrative on **Reading/Writing Companion** page 26.

Anchor Chart Have a volunteer begin listing features of personal narratives on an anchor chart.

• It tells a true story about an event that happened to the narrator.

• It is usually written in the first person.

• It has a beginning, a middle, and an end.

• It uses words and phrases to tell about events in order.

• It explains how the narrator feels about the event.

Analyze an Expert Model

Remind children that the narrator of "Landing on Your Feet" in the **Literature Anthology** is telling about the time her dad hurt his ankle while coaching gymnastics.

Have children reread the first paragraph on page 235 of the **Literature Anthology**. Ask: *What detail does the narrator include to help readers know that something is wrong with her dad?* (When her dad came home from work, he went to the couch to lie down.) Have children reread the second paragraph on page 235. Ask: *What does the narrator's dad ask her?* ("Ryan, can you please get me an ice pack from the freezer?") *What does her dad do with the ice pack?* (He wraps it around his ankle.) *What describing words does Ryan use to describe her dad's ankle?* ("big and swollen and blue") Have children write the answers to the questions on page 26 of the **Reading/Writing Companion**.

Then review how the author includes other quotes and details in the personal narrative to help tell the story. For example, ask children to tell what Ryan's dad says on page 236 of the **Literature Anthology**. ("I was leading warm-ups at practice last night...." "I jumped up high and came down hard on my ankle.") *What does this help explain in the personal narrative?* (how Ryan's dad hurt his ankle) Have partners discuss other quotes and details that the author uses to help tell the story on pages 236 and 237.

WRITING

Expert Model

Features of a Personal Narrative

A personal narrative tells a story from the writer's life.
- It is usually written in the first person.
- It has a beginning, middle, and end.
- It uses words and phrases to tell events in order.

Literature Anthology: pages 234-237

Analyze an Expert Model Studying "Landing on Your Feet" will help you learn more about writing a personal narrative. Reread page 235. Answer the questions below.

How does Ryan use dialogue to tell an important detail?

She uses her dad's question to show he is hurt and needs her help.

How does Ryan use describing words?

She uses the words "big and swollen and blue" to describe her dad's hurt ankle.

26   Unit 3 · Narrative Nonfiction

Reading/Writing Companion, p. 26

English Language Learners SCAFFOLD

Use the following scaffolds with **Analyze an Expert Model**.

Beginning

Help children find the line of dialogue on page 235 and complete the sentence frame: Ryan uses dialogue to show that her dad is <u>hurt</u> and he needs her <u>help</u>. Ask: *Which phrase tells what Dad did with the ice pack?* ("wrapped it around his ankle") Make sure children know that "It" in the next sentence refers to "ankle," not "ice pack." *Which words does Ryan use to describe her Dad's ankle?* (*big, swollen, blue*)

Intermediate

Ask children to read the dialogue on page 235. *When do you use an ice pack?* You use an ice pack when <u>you are hurt</u>. *Why does Ryan use dialogue?* She uses dialogue to show that <u>her dad is hurt</u>. *Which sentence tells how Dad used the ice pack?* ("He wrapped it around his ankle.") *How does Ryan describe his ankle?* (*big, swollen, blue*).

Advanced/Advanced High

Have partners discuss the dialogue and describing words before they complete the activity on **Reading/Writing Companion** page 26. Encourage them to discuss the following questions: *How does the dialogue make the narrative stronger?* (Possible: It makes it more interesting to read.) *How do the describing words make the narrative stronger?* (Possible: They help me picture what his ankle looks like.)

Reading/Writing Companion

OBJECTIVES

Write narratives in which they recount a well-elaborated event or short sequence of events, include details to describe actions, thoughts, and feelings, use temporal words to signal event order, and provide a sense of closure.

Recall information from experiences or gather information from provided sources to answer a question.

Participate in collaborative conversations with diverse partners about *grade 2 topics and texts* with peers and adults in small and larger groups.

ACADEMIC LANGUAGE

- *audience, brainstorm, purpose*
- Cognate: *audiencia*

Digital Tools

Use these digital tools to enhance the lesson.

Model Graphic Organizer

Purpose of Narrative Writing Slide Show, Write for Your Audience video

Plan: Choose Your Topic

Brainstorm

Point out that a personal narrative is about a real event, but it should also be entertaining and help the reader make connections with the narrator. Children will need to think about developing their narratives with specific and relevant details that help readers picture the event and connect with the narrator's feelings about it.

Have children list or draw ideas for their narratives in the box on **Reading/Writing Companion** page 27. Encourage them to choose an experience that was important to them and that they felt strongly about. To get them started, ask: *What did you do? Whom did you help?*

Review the Quick Tip box. Help children to use specific words to express how they felt about their actions.

Writing Prompt

Children should use the events and feelings they brainstormed to write a personal narrative about a time when they helped others. Have children record a time they helped and their feelings about it on **Reading/Writing Companion** page 28.

Purpose and Audience

Tell children to look over their brainstorming pictures and notes and talk with a partner about the important experience they want to describe. Have them ask and answer questions about the experience. Remind children that they can add or change details based on their discussions.

Review the Quick Tip box, and explain that authors often write personal narratives to share their thoughts and feelings about an important event in their lives. Also explain that authors give specific details about the people, places, and events to help readers better understand the experience. Point out that the author of "Landing on Your Feet" explained how she felt about her dad and why it was important to help him.

Plan

Have partners explain why they chose the specific experience they will describe. Then challenge children to expand on their reasons for choosing their experiences. Ask: *What was important or special about this experience? What will your audience learn about you as they read your narrative?*

Have children preview the rubric on page 35 to help them understand what is expected of them for this assignment.

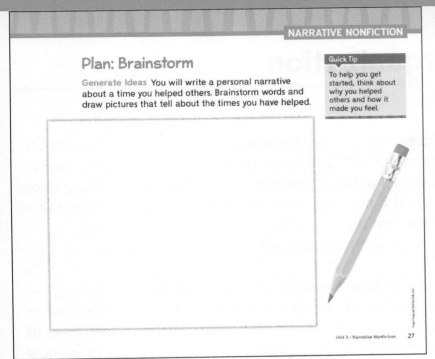

Reading/Writing Companion, p. 27

Reading/Writing Companion, p. 28

 English Language Learners SCAFFOLD

Use the following scaffolds with **Brainstorm**.

Beginning

Help children generate words and phrases to create labels and simple captions for their pictures. Help them share information by pointing to a picture and completing the sentence starters: I helped the garden club. I helped by cleaning up trash. I felt good.

Intermediate

After children draw pictures, ask guiding questions to help them share information about why and how they helped. For example, ask: *Who did you help? How did you help that person? What happened after you helped?* Encourage them to use their details from their responses in the captions for their drawings.

Advanced/Advanced High

Encourage children to brainstorm specific details about the events in their narratives and their feelings about them. Ask: *Which details tell what happened? Which details will entertain the reader? Can you explain why you helped?*

Reading/Writing Companion

OBJECTIVES

Write narratives in which they recount a well-elaborated event or short sequence of events, include details to describe actions, thoughts, and feelings, use temporal words to signal event order, and provide a sense of closure.

ACADEMIC LANGUAGE

• *details, sequence*
• Cognates: *detalles, secuencia*

Digital Tools

Use this digital tool to enhance the lesson.

 How to Create a Story Map video

Plan: Organization

Sequence

Review with children why sequence is important in a story. Ask volunteers to retell the main events in "Landing on Your Feet." Point out that events need to follow a logical order so that the story makes sense. Writing about events in sequence also makes it easier for readers to remember and retell a story. Tell children that they are going to organize their personal narrative in sequence—with a beginning, a middle, and an end.

Read aloud the sentences in the sequence chart on **Reading/Writing Companion** page 29. Ask volunteers to identify the words that show when things take place in the different parts of the story. Elicit what happens at the beginning, in the middle, and at the end of the narrative. Discuss how the clear organization and specific details work together to help readers understand what happens in the personal narrative.

Plan

Tell children that before they write their personal narratives, they will make a Sequence Chart to plan their ideas. Say: *Write details about your personal narrative in sequence. Tell what happens in the beginning, in the middle, and at the end of your narrative.* Then have children draw and fill in a sequence chart in their writer's notebooks.

Have children preview the rubric on page 35 of the **Reading/Writing Companion** to help them understand what is expected of them in this assignment.

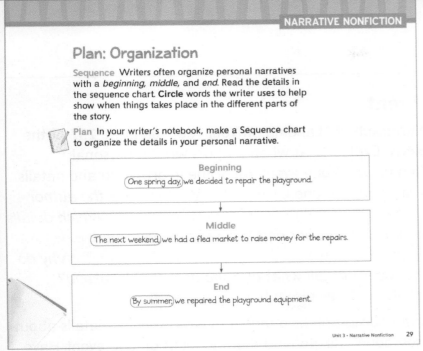

Plan: Organization

Sequence Writers often organize personal narratives with a *beginning, middle,* and *end.* Read the details in the sequence chart. **Circle** words the writer uses to help show when things takes place in the different parts of the story.

 Plan In your writer's notebook, make a Sequence chart to organize the details in your personal narrative.

> **Beginning**
> (One spring day,) we decided to repair the playground.

> **Middle**
> (The next weekend,) we had a flea market to raise money for the repairs.

> **End**
> (By summer,) we repaired the playground equipment.

Unit 3 · Narrative Nonfiction   29

Reading/Writing Companion, p. 29

English Language Learners   SCAFFOLD

Use the following scaffolds with **Plan.**

Beginning

Remind children that the words *first, next,* and *then* show the sequence, or order, of events. Help partners draw or write words and simple phrases in their sequence charts. Ask: *What do you do first? What happens next? Then what happens?* Provide support to help children respond orally and then in writing.

Intermediate

Encourage children to write their events in complete sentences. Guide them to organize the events in sequence. Ask: *What happened first? Then what happened? What happened in the end?* Have partners use the questions to discuss the sequence of events. As they discuss, guide them to add details to their story descriptions.

Advanced/Advanced High

Encourage children to write their story events in complete sentences with some specific details. Remind them to use words and phrases that show sequence, such as *first, next, then,* and *finally.* Then have children share their ideas with a partner. Encourage them to ask and answer questions about each other's narratives.

Personal Narrative

Reading/Writing Companion

OBJECTIVES

Write narratives in which they recount a well-elaborated event or short sequence of events, include details to describe actions, thoughts, and feelings, use temporal words to signal event order, and provide a sense of closure.

ACADEMIC LANGUAGE

- *event, details, focus, draft, time words*
- Cognates: *detalles, enfocar*

Draft

10 Mins

Focus on an Event

Reread the first paragraph of "Landing on Your Feet" on page 237 of the **Literature Anthology**. Explain that when authors write a personal narrative, they often focus on one event. All of the information and details they include tell just about the one event. Ask: *What event is the author focusing on?* (how she helps her dad after he hurts his ankle) *Which details tell about how the author helps her dad?* (stays home with Dad; gets fresh ice packs for his ankle; makes him lunch; gets Dad books to read) *Why do you think the author does not tell what else she does that weekend?* (because those details don't tell about helping her dad)

Have children use the paragraph as a model to write specific details about how they helped someone else. Remind them to focus on one event. Have them write their details in the space provided on **Reading/Writing Companion** page 30.

Write a Draft

Remind children that they will be writing a draft of a personal narrative about a time they helped someone. Point out that they should use details to describe their actions and feelings during the event.

Have children review the sequence charts they created during the Plan phase. They will use their sequence charts as they write their drafts. Remind children that their narratives should have a beginning, a middle, and an end. Help children organize their ideas into paragraphs with descriptive details and time words and phrases that show sequence.

Pair children to identify and discuss the details in each other's draft that tell about the narrator's actions and feelings during the event.

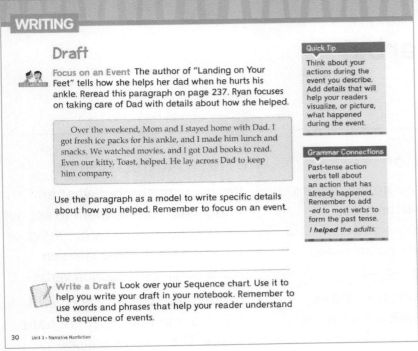

Reading/Writing Companion, p. 30

English Language Learners SCAFFOLD

Use the following scaffolds with **Write a Draft**.

Beginning

Help children expand the ideas and notes in their sequence charts. Model how to turn a word into a simple phrase, and a simple phrase into a sentence. Help children express their ideas orally, then support them in translating their spoken ideas into written language. Guide them to use appropriate first-person pronouns, such as *I, me,* and *my.*

Intermediate

Have children work in pairs to help each other add details describing the important events in their sequence charts. Model asking questions, such as: *Where were you? Why did you do that? What happened? How did you feel about that?*

Advanced/Advanced High

As children draft, help them incorporate signal words to show sequence. Write examples on the board for reference, such as *then, before, after, yesterday, later,* and *when.* Remind children that because they are writing about an event that already happened, they should use the past tense. Model forming the past tense with *-ed,* and provide assistance with irregular past tense verbs, such as *went* and *ran.*

Practice Book

OBJECTIVES

Demonstrate command of the conventions of standard English grammar and usage when writing or speaking.

Use knowledge of language and its conventions when writing, speaking, reading, or listening.

Participate in collaborative conversations with diverse partners about *grade 2 topics and texts* with peers and adults in small and larger groups.

DAILY LANGUAGE ACTIVITY

Use the online review for grammar, practice, and usage.

TEACH IN SMALL GROUP

You may wish to use the Talk About It activities during Small Group time.

Approaching Level, On Level and Beyond Level: Pair children of different proficiency levels.

ELL According to their language proficiency, children should contribute to discussions by using short phrases, asking questions, and adding relevant details.

Action Verbs

 DAY 1 Teach

Introduce Action Verbs

- Demonstrate some simple actions such as walking, sitting, or writing. Ask volunteers to demonstrate other actions, and write a list on the board.

- Explain that a word that shows action, such as *walk, sit,* or *write,* is an **action verb**.

- Tell children that they can identify the action verb in a sentence by asking: *What is the person or thing in the sentence doing?*

- Display the following sentences:

  Chad jumps rope.

  Sarah sings a song.

- Model identifying the action verb in the first sentence. Ask children to identify the action verb in the second sentence.

See **Practice Book** page 183 or online activity.

 DAY 2 Teach

Review Action Verbs

- Review with children what an **action verb** is. Ask them to act out some actions, such as *laughing,* or *clapping.* Have other children name some other action verbs.

- Explain that some action verbs tell about actions that are hard to see. These verbs include *wishes, loves, listens,* and *enjoys.*

- Display sentences using action verbs. Underline the action verbs and model how you identified them.

  1. Maureen <u>enjoys</u> this book about magnets. (enjoys)

  2. Ellen <u>wishes</u> for a telescope. (wishes)

  3. Jay <u>loves</u> his dog. (loves)

  4. Marcello <u>listens</u> to music in the morning. (listens)

See **Practice Book** page 184 or online activity.

 OPTION **Talk About It**

Play Charades

Have each child in a small group write an action, such as jump, on a slip of paper and place the paper in a pile. They take turns selecting and acting out the action, as the others guess what it is.

Sentence Making

Have children generate sentences with action verbs, making sure that the verb agrees with the subject of the sentence.

DAY 3 Mechanics and Usage

 OPTION DAY 4 Proofread and Write

 OPTION DAY 5 Assess and Reteach

Book Titles

- Explain to children that book titles follow special rules for capitalization.
- Demonstrate capitalizing the first word and each important word in the title, <u>The Story of a Horse</u>. Underline all the words in the title.
- Give children a list of articles, conjunctions, and prepositions that are not capitalized in book titles.
- Guide children to identify the book title in each sentence below. Point out capital letters, underlined words, and lowercase words in the titles.
  1. Wendy read a book called <u>At Home in Your Neighborhood.</u>
  2. <u>Thunder and Lightning</u> is a very good book.
  3. I think <u>Our Village</u> is a better book than <u>Water for Everyone</u>.

See **Practice Book** page 185 or online activity.

Proofread

Have children underline and properly capitalize the book titles in this blog entry.

This is my reading summer! The first book I will read is called Jenny finds a friend. it tells about a girl who finds a puppy in the park. The next book, the history of numbers, begins thousands of years ago. It's really interesting!

(This is my reading summer! The first book I will read is called <u>Jenny Finds a Friend</u>. It tells about a girl who finds a puppy in the park. The next book, <u>The History of Numbers</u>, begins thousands of years ago. It's really interesting!)

Write

Have children find a piece of their own writing in their writer's notebook and correct spelling and usage errors in book titles.

See **Practice Book** page 186 or online activity.

Assess

Use the Daily Language Activity and **Practice Book** page 187 for assessment.

Rubric Use your online rubric to record children's progress.

Reteach

Use the online Grammar Handbook page 481 and Practice Book pages 183-186 for additional reteaching. Remind children that every sentence needs to have a subject.

Check children's writing for use of the skill and listen for it in their speaking. Assign grammar revision assignments in their writer's notebooks as needed.

Talk About Titles

Have groups generate imaginary book titles. The books can be about anything, fiction or nonfiction. Have children capitalize the titles properly. Be sure that children are supplied with lists of words that are not capitalized in titles.

Real Titles

Have partners find books on the classroom shelves. A child reads the title of a book aloud to his or her partner, who writes it using correct underlining and capitalization. Then the partners switch tasks.

Action Sentences

Have partners take turns giving each other action verbs to use in orally generated sentences.

Grammar

Practice Book

TEACH IN SMALL GROUP ◀

You may wish to use the Talk About It activities during Small Group time.

Approaching Level, On Level and Beyond Level: Pair children of different proficiency levels.

ELL According to their language proficiency, children should contribute to discussions by using short phrases, asking questions, and adding relevant details.

Present-Tense Verbs

 DAY 6 Teach

Introduce Present-Tense Verbs

- Explain that **present-tense verbs** tell about actions that are happening right now.

- Display the following sentences:
  I see my lunch on the table.
  Do you hear the wind outside?

- Ask: *When do I see my lunch?* (right now) Say: *This action did not happen in the past, and the sentence does not tell about the future. It tells about what is happening right now. The verb see is in the present tense.* Model the second sentence.

- Guide children to identify which sentence is in the present-tense:

  The birds will fly away soon. (future)

  She feels the cold wind. (present)

  I saw her yesterday. (past)

  See **Practice Book** page 200 or online activity.

 DAY 7 Teach

Review Present-Tense Verbs

Have partners identify the sentences that are in the present tense. Ask: *When does the action in these sentences take place?*

1. Last week we worked in the park. (not present tense, the action happened last week)

2. I see a whale in the ocean. (present tense; see)

3. I will help with the mural tomorrow. (not present tense, the action will happen tomorrow)

4. She knows the answer. (present tense; she knows the answer now.)

Point out that the verb *know* ends in *s* in sentence 4. The verb *see* does not end in *s* in sentence 2. Explain that when the subject is in the third person (*he, she, it, Miguel, Meg*), the verb often ends in *s.*

See **Practice Book** page 201 or online activity.

  OPTION

Talk About It

About My Community

Ask partners to take turns telling about events and people they see, hear, and know about. Children should use present-tense verbs and identify them in their sentences, e.g., I feel hot! (feel). I see your book. (see)

Sentence Making

Have partners use present-tense verbs that agree with first- and third-person subjects in cloze sentences. Supply cards with sentences such as:

Jane _____see/sees the clouds. (sees)

I ___hear/hears the thunder. (hear)

DAY 8 Mechanics and Usage

 ## OPTION DAY 9 Proofread and Write

 ## OPTION DAY 10 Assess and Reteach

Commas in a Series

- Explain to children that writers use commas to separate the different items in a list of three or more things. Commas make lists in sentences easier to read.

- Display the following sentence: The boys picked up paper, cans, and bottles at the park.

- Guide children to identify the list of the three things the boys picked up in the park. Point out the comma after each item (except the last). Explain that the commas help readers see and understand each thing in the list.

- Have children punctuate the following sentences:

I brought paper, pencils, and books in my book bag.

She's baking cookies, cupcakes, and pies for the fair.

Kim has marbles, a doll, and a truck.

See **Practice Book** page 202 or online activity.

Proofread

Have children identify and correct errors in the passage below:

Matty work in the garden. He plant seeds for carrots beets lettuce and cucumbers. Steve Laura and Pat help Matty with the shovels and rakes. I helps with the water apples and cheese to keep us going.

(Matty works in the garden. He plants seeds for carrots, beets, lettuce, and cucumbers. Steve, Laura, and Pat help Matty with the shovels and rakes. I help with the water, apples, and cheese to keep us going.)

Write

Apply to Writing Have children find a piece of their own writing in their writer's notebook and correct errors in using commas in a series. Then have them correct errors they made using present-tense verbs.

See **Practice Book** page 203 or online activity.

Assess

Use the Daily Language Activity and **Practice Book** page 204 for assessment.

Rubric Use your online rubric to record children's progress.

Reteach

Use the online **Grammar Handbook** page 482 and Practice Book pages 200–203 for additional reteaching. Remind children to make sure their sentences have a subject and a verb when they speak and write.

Check children's writing for use of the skill and listen for it in their speaking. Assign grammar revision assignments in their writer's notebooks as needed.

List It!

Have partners write sentences that list three of their favorite things. Have them trade papers to check each other's use of commas in sentences with three or more things.

Words in Agreement

Have children work in groups. Each child gives the group a present-tense verb such as: *hear, see, listens, skates, run,* etc. The other children in the group write and share or orally generate sentences with correct subject-verb agreement.

Character Sketch

Ask partners to use present-tense verbs to talk about a character from a story they have read or a movie they have seen. As they talk, their partners should listen for present-tense verbs and identify them.

Practice Book

OBJECTIVES

Generalize learned spelling patterns when writing words (e.g., *cage → badge; boy → boil*).

Use sentence-level context as a clue to the meaning of a word or phrase.

Distinguish long and short vowels when reading regularly spelled one-syllable words.

DIFFERENTIATED SPELLING

Go online for Dictation Sentences for differentiated spelling lists.

On Level and ELL

nail	train	main
hay	stay	break
steak	weigh	sleigh
prey		

Review scrape, strange
High-Frequency good, often, two

Approaching Level

nail	rain	main
ray	day	break
steak	weigh	sleigh
they		

Review spring, shrug
High-Frequency good, often, two

Beyond Level

nails	train	mainland
haystack	staying	breaking
steaks	weighed	sleighs
preying		

Review throne, split
High-Frequency good, often, two

Long *a: a, ai, ay, ea, ei, eigh, ey*

 DAY 1 Assess Prior Knowledge

Read the spelling words aloud, drawing out the vowel sounds.

Point out the long *a* sound in *nail*. Draw a line under *ai* as you say the word. Explain that not all words with the long *a* sound are spelled in the same way.

Demonstrate sorting the spelling words under the key words *nail, hay, break, weigh, prey, scrape,* and *strange*.

Use the Dictation Sentences from Day 5 to give the pretest. Say the underlined word, read the sentence, and repeat the word. Have children write the words. Then have children check their papers.

See **Practice Book** page 179 for a pretest.

 OPTION **DAY 2** Spiral Review

Review 3-letter blends *scr, spr, str, thr, spl, shr.*

1. Don't <u>scratch</u> that itch!
2. We need to <u>scrape</u> the ice off the window.
3. The <u>spring</u> in this toy is broken.
4. I sat on the king's <u>throne</u>.
5. I like that blue <u>stripe</u> on your bike.
6. That's a <u>strange</u> thing to say!
7. I'll <u>shred</u> some cheese for the tacos.
8. Rover is hiding under that <u>shrub</u>.
9. Kids love to <u>splash</u> in the pool.
10. Ray <u>split</u> his sandwich with me.

Have children trade papers and check each other's work.

 Word Sorts

OPEN SORT

Have children cut apart the **Spelling Word Cards** available online and initial the back of each card. Have them read the words aloud with partners. Then have partners do an open sort. Have them record their sorts in their writer's notebook.

PATTERN SORT

Complete the pattern sort from Day 1 by using the boldfaced key words on the **Spelling Word Cards**. Point out the consonant blends. Partners should compare and check their sorts. See **Practice Book** pages 180, 180A, and 180B for differentiated practice.

 **Word Meanings**

Have children copy the three word groups below into their writer's notebooks. Say the words aloud. Then ask children to add a spelling word that fits with the group.

1. airplane, bus, boat (train)
2. burger, meatloaf, bacon (steak)
3. snap, crash, crack (break)
4. cut, grate, scratch (scrape)

Challenge children to create groups for their other spelling or review words. Have children post their word groups on the board.

 Proofread and Write

Write the sentences below on the board. Have children circle and correct each misspelled word. Have children use a print or a digital dictionary to check and correct their spellings.

1. Hey covered the floor of the barn. (hay)
2. The trane came into the station. (train)
3. Those rocks way a lot. (weigh)
4. A screw often works better than a nale. (nail)

Error Correction Point out that the words *hay* and *hey,* and *weigh* and *way* are homophones. Homophones have the same pronunciation but different spellings and meanings.

Apply to Writing Have children correct a piece of their own writing.

 Assess

Use the Dictation Sentences for the posttest. Have children list the misspelled words in their writer's notebook. Look for children's use of these words in their writing.

See **Practice Book** page 179 for a posttest. Use pages 180, 180A, and 180B for review.

Dictation Sentences

1. Hit the <u>nail</u> with the hammer.
2. He rode on the <u>train</u>.
3. This is the <u>main</u> branch of the library.
4. Horses like to eat <u>hay</u>.
5. Please <u>stay</u> in your seats until the bell rings.
6. Some toys <u>break</u> too easily.
7. My dad cooks <u>steak</u> on the grill.
8. How much do you <u>weigh</u>?
9. A horse pulled the <u>sleigh</u> through the snow.
10. Lions hunted their <u>prey</u> in the tall grass.
11. I did not <u>scrape</u> my knee when I fell.
12. Joe saw a <u>strange</u> animal at the zoo.
13. My dog is <u>good</u> and can sit and stay.
14. Deb's parents <u>often</u> read a book with her.
15. Jim has <u>two</u> black cats.

SPEED SORT

Have partners do a speed sort to see who is fastest. Then have them do a word hunt in this week's readings to find words with the long /ā/ sound. Have them record the words in their writer's notebook.

BLIND SORT

Have partners do a blind sort: one reads a **Spelling Word Card**; the other tells under which key word it belongs. Then have partners hunt for other words with the same spelling pattern and add them to their writer's notebook.

Long *i: i, y, igh, ie*

Practice Book

OBJECTIVES

Generalize learned spelling patterns when writing words (e.g., *cage* → *badge*; *boy* → *boil*).

Use sentence-level context as a clue to the meaning of a word or phrase.

Distinguish long and short vowels when reading regularly spelled one-syllable words.

DIFFERENTIATED SPELLING

Go online for Dictation Sentences for differentiated spelling lists.

On Level and ELL

light	sight	mind
cry	tie	high
wild	dry	try
lie		

Review hay, steak
High-Frequency begin, those, apart

Approaching Level

pie	right	mind
cry	tie	high
wild	dry	my
find		

Review main, weigh
High-Frequency begin, those, apart

Beyond Level

lightning	sight	minds
kindness	child	highway
skies	drying	trying
lie		

Review train, staying
High-Frequency begin, those, apart

 DAY 6 Assess Prior Knowledge

Read the spelling words aloud, drawing out the vowel sounds.

Point out the long *i* sound in *tie*. Draw a line under *ie* as you say the word. Explain that not all words with the long *i* sound are spelled in the same way.

Demonstrate sorting the spelling words under the key words *tie, light, mind,* and *cry*.

Use the Dictation Sentences from Day 5 to give the pretest. Say the underlined word, read the sentence, and repeat the word. Have children write the words. Then have children check their papers.

See **Practice Book** page 196 for a pretest.

 **OPTION DAY 7** Spiral Review

Review words with the long *a* sound. Read each sentence below, repeat the review word, and have children write the word.

1. He will <u>nail</u> the sign to the post.
2. The <u>train</u> goes very fast.
3. The <u>main</u> dish was spaghetti.
4. Do you have <u>hay</u> for the horse?
5. She cannot <u>stay</u> long.
6. Don't <u>break</u> that mirror!
7. We had <u>steak</u> for dinner.
8. I need to <u>weigh</u> that box.
9. We rode through the snow in a <u>sleigh</u>.
10. That hawk is looking for <u>prey</u>.

Have children trade papers and check each other's work.

 Word Sorts

OPEN SORT

Have children cut apart the **Spelling Word Cards** available online and initial the back of each card. Have them read the words aloud with partners. Then have partners do an open sort. Have them record their sorts in their writer's notebook.

PATTERN SORT

Complete the pattern sort from Day 6 by using the boldfaced key words on the **Spelling Word Cards**. Point out the short *a* and long *a* vowel sounds. Partners should compare and check their sorts. See **Practice Book** pages 197, 197A, and 197B for differentiated practice.

OPTION DAY 8 Word Meanings

Have children copy the four riddles below into their writer's notebooks. Read the riddles aloud. Then ask children to write a spelling word that answers the riddle.

1. When you are very happy, you laugh. When you are very sad, you do this. (cry)

2. You do this with a ribbon, a rope, or a shoelace. (tie)

3. An ocean is wet and a desert is this. (dry)

4. You sleep in the dark, but to read you need this. (light)

Challenge children to create riddles for their other spelling or review words. Have children post their riddles on the board.

OPTION DAY 9 Proofread and Write

Write the sentences below on the board. Have children circle and correct each misspelled word. Have children use a print or a digital dictionary to check and correct their spellings.

1. Please turn off the lite. (light)

2. Will you change your miend? (mind)

3. Has your brother learned to ty his shoes? (tie)

4. That shelf is very hie. (high)

Error Correction Point out that the word *light* is sometimes spelled *lite* in the names of products. That spelling is not correct in academic reading and writing.

Apply to Writing Have children correct a piece of their own writing.

DAY 10 Assess

Use the Dictation Sentences for the posttest. Have children list the misspelled words in their writer's notebook. Look for children's use of these words in their writing.

See **Practice Book** page 196 for a posttest. Use pages 197, 197A, and 197B for review.

Dictation Sentences

1. I turned on the <u>light</u> in my room.
2. You use your eyes for <u>sight</u>.
3. He has many good ideas in his <u>mind</u>.
4. Did you hear the baby <u>cry</u>?
5. Can you <u>tie</u> your shoes?
6. Pam jumped <u>high</u> in the air.
7. We saw <u>wild</u> animals at the zoo.
8. Please <u>dry</u> the dishes.
9. I will <u>try</u> to do my homework.
10. Janet never tells a <u>lie</u>.
11. A horse eats <u>hay</u>.
12. We had <u>steak</u> for dinner.
13. The game will <u>begin</u> now.
14. Where did you put <u>those</u> toys?
15. This book is falling <u>apart</u>.

SPEED SORT

Have partners do a speed sort to see who is fastest. Then have them do a word hunt in this week's readings to find words with the same vowel sounds as the spelling words. Have them record the words in their writer's notebook.

BLIND SORT

Have partners do a blind sort: one reads a **Spelling Word Card**; the other tells under which key word it belongs. Then have partners hunt for other words with the same spelling pattern and add them to their writer's notebook.

Expand Vocabulary

Practice Book

OBJECTIVES

Determine or clarify the meaning of unknown and multiple-meaning words and phrases based on grade 2 reading and content, choosing flexibly from an array of strategies.

Use sentence-level context as a clue to the meaning of a word or phrase.

Determine the meaning of the new word formed when a known prefix is added to a known word (e.g., *happy/unhappy, tell/retell*).

Use a known root word as a clue to the meaning of an unknown word with the same root (e.g., *addition, additional*).

Use glossaries and beginning dictionaries, both print and digital, to determine or clarify the meaning of words and phrases.

Digital Tools

For more practice, have children use the Vocabulary Activities.

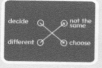

Vocabulary Activities

 English Language Learners

Pair children of different language proficiency levels to practice vocabulary.

 OPTION DAY 1 Connect to Words

Practice the target vocabulary.

1. What is **across** the street from your school?

2. What items can you **borrow** from a neighbor?

3. What kind of animals live in the **countryside**?

4. Describe an **idea** you have for a story, song, or dance.

5. What do your parents **insist** you do every day?

6. What can you do to help someone who feels **lonely**?

7. Tell about a time you found a **solution** to a problem.

8. What do you think it's like to live in a **village**?

 OPTION DAY 6 Build Vocabulary

Display *strong, bundle,* and s*team.*

- Define each word and discuss the meanings with children.

- Write *steamer* under *steam.* Have partners write other words with the same root and define them. Then have partners ask and answer questions using the words.

- Repeat with *strong* and *bundle.*

 OPTION DAY 2 Related Words

Help children create different forms of target words by adding, changing, or removing affixes.

- Write *lonely* in the first column of a T-chart. Then write *lone* and *lonesome* in the next two columns.

- Discuss each form of the word and its meaning. Then have children share aloud sentences using the words.

- Have children work in pairs to fill in charts for *across, borrow, countryside, ideas, insists, solution,* and *villages.*

- Have children copy the chart in their writer's notebook.

See **Practice Book** page 188 or online activity.

 DAY 7 Homophones

Help children make homophone pairs.

- Write the word *sun.* Say it aloud and talk about what it means. Then ask children to give you another word that sounds the same.

- Write the words *new, buy,* and *knight.* Have children write homophones for each of the words in their writer's notebook.

See **Practice Book** page 206 or online activity.

DAY 3 Spiral Review **Reinforce the Words**

Have children orally complete each cloze sentence to review words.

1. I'm sure I can find a _____ to that problem. (solution)

2. Elaine wants to _____ my table for just a minute. (borrow)

3. I have so many sisters I never feel _____. (lonely)

4. Ed's house is _____ the street. (across)

5. Helga _____ she's right. (insists)

6. Driving through the _____ is quiet and peaceful. (countryside)

Display previous genre study's vocabulary words: *behave, express, feathers, flapping*. Have pairs ask and answer questions for the words.

See **Practice Book** page 189 or online activity.

 OPTION **DAY 4** **Connect to Writing**

• Have children write sentences in their writer's notebook using the target vocabulary.

• Tell them to write sentences that provide context to show what the words mean.

• **ELL** Provide the Day 3 cloze sentences 1–6 for children needing extra support.

Write Using Vocabulary

Have children write something they learned from this week's target words in their writer's notebook. For example, they might write about different kinds of places to live.

 OPTION **DAY 5** **Word Squares**

Ask children to create Word Squares for each vocabulary word.

• In the first square, children write the word (e.g., *ideas*).

• In the second square, children write their own definition of the word and any related words, such as synonyms (e.g. *thoughts, plans*).

• In the third square, children draw an illustration that will help them remember the word (e.g., *a person's head*).

• In the fourth square, children write nonexamples, including antonyms for the word (e.g. *blank*).

Have partners discuss their squares.

 DAY 8 **Synonyms**

Remind children that synonyms are words that have the same or almost the same meaning.

• Show children these words from the On Level **Differentiated Genre Passage**, "Helping Out in the Community": *journey, route, touch, harmless*. Have children find a synonym for each word using a thesaurus.

• Have pairs find other words in the readings that have synonyms.

See **Practice Book** page 205 or online activity.

 OPTION **DAY 9** **Shades of Meaning**

Help children generate words related to the word *lonely*. Draw a T-chart with the labels "Synonyms and Antonyms."

• Have partners generate words to add to the T-chart. Ask children to use a thesaurus.

• Add words not given, such as synonyms (*alone, lonesome*) and antonyms (*unlonely, social*).

• Have children copy the words into their writer's notebook.

 OPTION **DAY 10** **Word Study**

Have children explore the suffix *–ity*.

• Have children begin with the word *electricity*. Ask them what part of the word turns the noun *electric* into an adjective. Guide them to point to the suffix *–ity*.

• Have partners use a dictionary or an online site to find other words that are nouns formed from adjectives by adding *-ity*. (*activity, similarity, oddity, modernity*, etc.)

Write Using Vocabulary

Have children use vocabulary words in their stories.

Make Connections

Reading/Writing Companion

OBJECTIVES

Ask and answer such questions as who, what, where, when, why, and how to demonstrate understanding of key details in a text.

Compare and contrast the most important points presented by two texts on the same topic.

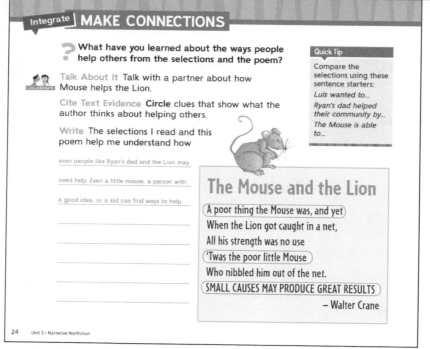

Integrate MAKE CONNECTIONS

? What have you learned about the ways people help others from the selections and the poem?

Talk About It Talk with a partner about how Mouse helps the Lion.

Cite Text Evidence Circle clues that show what the author thinks about helping others.

Write The selections I read and this poem help me understand how

even people like Ryan's dad and the Lion may

need help. Even a little mouse, a person with

a good idea, or a kid can find ways to help.

Quick Tip

Compare the selections using these sentence starters:
Luis wanted to...
Ryan's dad helped their community by...
The Mouse is able to...

The Mouse and the Lion

A poor thing the Mouse was, and yet
When the Lion got caught in a net,
All his strength was no use
'Twas the poor little Mouse
Who nibbled him out of the net.
SMALL CAUSES MAY PRODUCE GREAT RESULTS

– Walter Crane

24   Unit 3 • Narrative Nonfiction

Reading/Writing Companion, p. 24

Close Reading Routine

Read   DOK 1–2

- Identify key ideas and details about how people help others.
- Take notes and summarize.
- Use prompts as needed.

Reread   DOK 2–3

- Analyze the text, craft, and structure.
- Use the *Reading/Writing Companion*.

Integrate   DOK 4

- Integrate knowledge and ideas.
- Make text-to-text connections.
- Use the Integrate/Make Connections lesson.
- Use *Reading/Writing Companion*, page 24.
- Inspire action.

 Text Connections

Talk About It

Share and discuss children's responses to the "Making Our Lives Better... Together" Blast. Then write the Essential Question on the board or chart paper: *How can people help out their community?* Below that, draw a chart with headings for all the texts children have read. Have children read through their notes, annotations, and responses and add what they learned from each text to the chart. Then ask children to complete the Talk About It activity on **Reading/Writing Companion** page 24.

Cite Text Evidence

Guide children to use text evidence to make connections among the poem on page 24 of the **Reading/Writing Companion** and the selections they have read. Remind children to read the poem carefully and to use the Quick Tip.

Write

Children should refer to the notes on the chart as they respond to the writing prompt at the bottom of the page. When children have finished writing, have them share and discuss their responses.

Show What You Learned Have children write a final response synthesizing the knowledge they built about how people help out in their communities.

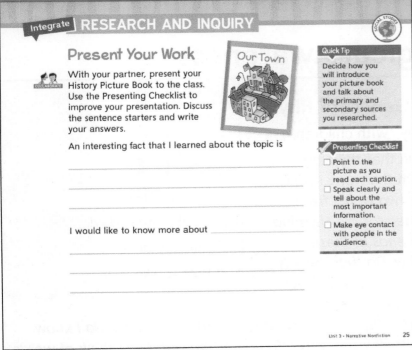

Reading/Writing Companion, p. 25

OBJECTIVES

With guidance and support from adults, use a variety of digital tools to produce and publish writing, including in collaboration with peers.

Recall information from experiences or gather information from provided sources to answer a question.

ACADEMIC LANGUAGE

- presentation, audience, role
- Cognate: presentación, audiencia

Present Your Work

Planning the Presentation

Remind children that careful preparation is necessary in order to successfully present their work. Discuss each item on the Presenting Checklist in the **Reading/Writing Companion** page 25. Allow partners time to rehearse.

Discuss options for a multimodal presentation, such as including audio or video of the person or event, which would give the audience additional information. Model ways to highlight the most important information.

Remind children that they will be part of the audience for other children's presentations, and that listeners play an important role. Review with and model for children the behaviors of an effective listener. You may want to show children the Listening Checklist from the Toolkit.

During the Presentation

Encourage children to be active listeners by having them write down any questions they have during the presentation. Guide a discussion of the presentation, asking some children to retell what they learned about the person or event. You may want to have children use the frames on the bottom of **Reading/Writing Companion** page 25 to focus the discussion. Allow time for children to ask the presenters the questions they recorded during the presentation.

Digital Tools

Use these digital tools to enhance the lesson.

How to Give a Presentation (Collaborative Conversations video), Record and Edit Audio (video)

TEACH IN SMALL GROUP

You may wish to teach the Research and Inquiry lesson during Small Group time and then have groups present their work to the class.

Daily Focus

Phonological Awareness
• Identify and Generate Rhyme

Phonics
• Introduce and Blend Words with Long *a*: *a, ai, ay, ea, ei*

Structural Analysis
• Contractions with *'s, 're, 'll, 've*

High-Frequency Words

Read
• Decodable Reader: Vol. 3: "Ray Saves the Play"

Handwriting
• Lowercase Cursive *h, k, g, q*

OBJECTIVES
• Identify and generate rhyme.

ACADEMIC LANGUAGE
• *identify, rhyme*
  Cognate: *identificar, rima*

Phonological Awareness: page 173

⏱ 5 Mins Phonological Awareness

Identify and Generate Rhyme

Read "A Great Day" with children.

1 **Model** Explain that rhyming words end with the same sounds. Say: *I will say two words from the poem. Listen for the rhyming sounds at the ends of these words.* Day, stay. *Do these words rhyme?* Day *and* stay *both end with the* /ā/ *sound. They rhyme.* Listen: /d/ /ā/, day; /s/ /t/ /ā/, stay. *What other words do I know that rhyme with* day *and* stay? *To figure that out, I will think of words that end with the same* /ā/ *sound.* Hay *ends in* /ā/, *so it rhymes with* day *and* stay. Repeat with *break, steak; sleigh, weigh; brain, train.*

> ## A Great Day
> Hey, hey, hooray!
> It's a really great day!
> Let's all stay outside
> And take a bike ride.

2 **Guided Practice/Practice** *Say: I will say two words. If the two words rhyme, say two more words that rhyme with them.* Guide children and offer corrective feedback until children can work independently.

spray, clay	they, prey	sand, gain	mail, tail
rain, rail	paint, faint	raise, praise	bat, bait
neigh, weigh	lay, line	paid, stayed	fail, file

Have children independently practice identifying and generating rhyme using **Practice Book** page 173.

English Language Learners

Model Choose rhyming words from the poem and focus on their ending sounds. Have children repeat the words *hooray* and *day*. Say: *When I say a word, I want you to tell me the ending sound:* Hooray (/ā/) Day (/ā/) *What sound do both words end in?* (/ā/) Repeat this routine with *outside* and *ride*. Then invite volunteers to complete this frame: When two words <u>rhyme</u> they end with the same sound. The words <u>hooray</u> and <u>day</u> rhyme. (<u>outside</u>/<u>ride</u>)

DIFFERENTIATED INSTRUCTION

TIER 2

Approaching Level If children need extra support to generate rhymes:

I Do Tell children they will be identifying and naming rhyming words. Say: *Listen as I say two words:* play, day. *The words* play *and* day *end with the same sounds:* /ā/. Play *and* day *rhyme.*

We Do *Listen as I say two more words:* train, tray. *Do the words rhyme? No,* train *and* tray *do not rhyme.* Train *ends with the sounds* /ān/. Tray *ends with the sound* /ā/. Train *and* rain *rhyme. They end with the same sounds.* Guide children with the following examples, giving corrective feedback as needed:

mail, nail	pain, pan	bank, thank	trail, train
stay, play	know, go	raise, gaze	wait, gate

You Do *Tell me if the words rhyme. If they do, say another word that rhymes with the two words.*

stain, stay	that, mat	great, steak	trust, rust
late, bait	mast, cast	most, boast	pain, hail

Repeat the rhyme routine with additional words with long *a: a, ai, ay, ea, ei.*

You may wish to review Phonological Awareness with **ELL** using this section.

ELL English Language Learners

See page 5 in the **Language Transfers Handbook** for guidance in identifying sounds that may or may not transfer for speakers of certain languages and for support in accommodating those children. See the chart on pages 6–9 for specific sound transfer issues for multiple languages.

Digital Tools

For more practice, have children use this activity.

Phonological Awareness

OBJECTIVES

- Know and apply grade-level phonics and word-analysis skills in decoding words.
- Know spelling-sound correspondences for additional common vowel teams.
- Identify words with inconsistent but common spelling-sound correspondences.

Phonics: page 175

---

5 Mins **Phonics**

Introduce Long *a: a, ai, ay, ea, ei*

Sound-Spelling Card

1 Model Display the *Train* **Sound-Spelling Card**. Teach /ā/ spelled *ai,* using *train.* Say: *This is the* Train *Sound-Spelling Card. The sound is /ā/. What sound do you hear? Yes, the sound is: /āāā/. This is the sound in the middle of the word* train. *Listen: /trrrāāānnn/,* train. *The letters* a *and* i *together can stand for /āāā/. I'll say /āāā/ as I write the letters* a, i *several times.*

Repeat for sound-spellings *a, ay, ea,* and *ei,* using the words *baby, spray, break,* and *veil.*

2 Guided Practice/Practice Have children practice connecting the letters *a, i* to the sound /ā/. Say: *This time, write the letters* a,i *five times as you say the /ā/ sound.* Repeat for the sound-spellings *a, ay, ea,* and *ei.*

Have children independently practice long *a: a, ai, ay, ea, ei* using **Practice Book** page 175.

DIFFERENTIATED INSTRUCTION ▶

TIER 2

Approaching Level **If children have difficulty with long *a: a, ay, ea, ei*:**

I Do Display the *Train* Sound-Spelling Card. Say: *This is the* Train *Sound-Spelling Card. The sound is /ā/. The /ā/ sound can be spelled with the letters* a, i. *Write the letters* a, i *while saying /ā/ five times. Repeat with* a, ay, ea, *and* ei.

We Do Say: *Now you do it with me.* Have children write *a, i* while saying /ā/. Say: *Write the letters* a, i *five times and say /ā/ together with me.* Repeat with *a, ay, ea,* and *ei.* Provide corrective feedback if necessary.

You Do Have children connect *ai* and *ay* to the sound /ā/ by writing lowercase letters *a, i* while saying /ā/. They should then write the letters *a, i* while saying /ā/ five to ten times. Repeat with *a, ay, ea,* and *ei.*

Repeat, connecting *ai, ay, a, ea, ea,* and *ei* to /ā/ through writing these long *a* sound-spellings throughout the week.

You may wish to review Phonics with **ELL** using this section.

Blend Words with Long *a: a, ai, ay, ea, ei*

1 **Model** Display **Word-Building Cards** r, a, i, n. Model how to blend the sounds. Say: *This is the letter* r. *It stands for /r/. Together the letters* a *and* i *stand for /ā/. This is the letter* n. *It stands for /n/. Listen as I blend these sounds together: /rrrāāānnn/. The word is* rain.

Continue with *stray, great, veil* for the *ay, ea, ei* sound-spellings.

2 **Guided Practice/Practice** Display the Day 1 Phonics/Fluency Practice chart. Read and blend each word in the first row; for example, say: */sssnnnāāālll/. The word is* snail. Have children blend each word with you. Prompt children to read the connected text, sounding out decodable words. Offer corrective feedback if needed.

snail	bay	trains	play	great	veil
break	vein	ways	gain	paid	sway
may	main	braid	raid	steak	stay
shame	shred	spray	thrive	graph	strain

The bride has a veil that trails.
Jay paid bills when the mail came.
At daybreak he got up and ate a steak.

Day 1 Phonics/Fluency Practice

DIFFERENTIATED INSTRUCTION ＞＞

TIER 2

Approaching Level If children are having difficulty blending words:

I Do Display Word-Building Cards r, a, i, n. Say: *This is* r. *It stands for /r/. These are letters* a, i. *Together they stand for /ā/. Let's say it: /āāā/. This is* n. *It stands for /n/. I'll blend the sounds: /rrrāāānnn/,* rain. Repeat with *pay, break,* and *vein.*

We Do Say: *Let's do some together.* Guide children to blend and read:

wait	way	day	steak	veil	nail
great	rein	gain	plain	clay	bacon

Offer corrective feedback until children can work on their own.

You Do Have children blend and read *nail, aim, train, basic, say, tray, stay, break,* and *rein.* Give corrective feedback if children need support.

Repeat, blending additional words with long *a: a, ai, ay, ea, ei.*

You may wish to review Phonics with **ELL** using this section.

Corrective Feedback

Sound Error Model the sounds that children missed, then have them repeat the sounds. Say: *My turn.* Tap under the letters and say: *Sound? /ā/. What's the sound?* Return to the beginning of the word. Say: *Let's start over.* Blend the word with children again.

English Language Learners

See page 5 in the **Language Transfers Handbook** for guidance in identifying phonics skills that may or may not transfer for speakers of certain languages and for support in accommodating those children. See the chart on pages 10–13 for specific phonics transfer issues for multiple languages.

Digital Tools

To differentiate instruction for key skills, use the results of this activity.

Phonics

OBJECTIVES

- Identify and read contractions with *'s, 're, 'll,* and *'ve.*

ACADEMIC LANGUAGE

- *contraction*
  Cognate: *contracción*

Digital Tools

For more practice, have children use this activity.

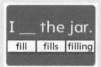

Structural Analysis

OPTION
5
Mins

Structural Analysis

Contractions with *'s, 're, 'll, 've*

1 **Model** Write and read aloud *that* and *that's*. Underline the *'s*. Say: *The word* that's *is a contraction that means "that is" or "that has." A contraction is a short way of writing two words. Contractions use an apostrophe to stand for one or more missing letters. I will use a contraction with* 's *meaning "*is*" in a sentence:* That's right! Then write and say *That is right* and *That's right*. Say: *Now I'll use a contraction with* 's *meaning "*has*" in a sentence:* He's gone home. Write and say *He has gone home* and *He's gone home.*

Repeat for contractions with *'re* meaning "are," contractions with *'ll* meaning "will," and contractions with *'ve* meaning "have."

2 **Guided Practice/Practice** Write the following words: *he, who, you, that, I,* and *they*. Have children write a contraction for each word and then use each word in a sentence. Give corrective feedback as necessary.

DIFFERENTIATED INSTRUCTION

TIER 2

Approaching Level If children are having difficulty with contractions:

I Do Write and read aloud *it is* and *it's*. Say: *The word* it's *is a contraction for* it is. *A contraction is a short way to write two words. An apostrophe replaces the missing letter* i *in* is: It is time for lunch. It's time for lunch.

We Do Write *they are*. Say: *Let's write a contraction for* they are. *The contraction is* they're. Write *they're*. Say: *The apostrophe replaces the missing letter* a *in* are. *Now let's use* they're *in a sentence:* They're at school today. Repeat with *I will (I'll)* and *you have (you've)*. Guide children and give additional support if needed.

You Do Have children work with partners. Give them several words and have them form contractions with *'s, 're, 'll,* and *'ve*. Circulate and give corrective feedback as necessary.

Repeat Have children use their contractions in sentences.

High-Frequency Words

about, around, good, great, idea, often, part, second, two, world

OBJECTIVES

- Know and apply grade-level phonics and word-analysis skills in decoding words.

- Recognize and read grade-appropriate irregularly spelled words.

1 **Model** Display the **High-Frequency Word Cards** and use the Read/Spell/Write routine to teach each word.

- **Read** Point to and say the word *about*. *This is the word* about. *Say it with me:* about. *That book is about jungle animals.*

- **Spell** *The word* about *is spelled* a-b-o-u-t. *Spell it with me.*

- **Write** *Let's write the word in the air as we say each letter:* a-b-o-u-t.

- Point out to children any irregularities in sound-spellings; for example, *good* has the letters *oo*, but it is pronounced /gŭd/ and does not rhyme with *food*.

- Have partners create sentences using each word.

2 **Guided Practice/Practice** Have children identify the high-frequency words in connected text and blend the decodable words.

1. Pam's family is **about** to move.
2. Ana rode **around** the block.
3. Len and May are **good** friends.
4. You did a **great** job with that!
5. Was it your **idea** to sing?
6. Mom **often** lets me wash the dog.
7. She ate a little **part** of her steak.
8. Ken is in **second** grade now.
9. Dad worked there for **two** years.
10. The **world** has land and water.

English Language Learners

Model Use visual cues, gestures, and examples to help children learn the meanings of the high-frequency words. Point out the Spanish cognates *Idea, parte,* and *segundo.* Point out and explain multiple-meaning words *about, around, good, great,* and *part.*

DIFFERENTIATED INSTRUCTION

TIER 2

Approaching Level If children need support with high-frequency words:

I Do Use the High-Frequency Word Cards. Follow this routine for each word: Display the word. Read the word. Spell the word.

We Do Ask children to state the word and spell the word with you. Model using the word in a sentence, and have children repeat.

You Do Display the words randomly for children to say and spell. Provide opportunities for children to use the words in conversation. Have children write each word in their writer's notebook.

Digital Tools

For more practice, have children use this activity.

High-Frequency Words

OBJECTIVES

- Know and apply grade-level phonics and word-analysis skills in decoding words.

- Recognize and read grade-appropriate irregularly spelled words.

- Read on-level text with purpose and understanding.

- Read with sufficient accuracy and fluency to support comprehension.

- Identify, trace, and write lowercase cursive letters *h, k, g,* and *q*

 **English Language Learners**

Check Comprehension Use frames, as needed, to help children answer questions:

p. 2 They were <u>putting on a play</u>. p. 3 Ray wanted to <u>have a part in the play</u>. p. 4 Max <u>broke the tree</u>. pp. 5–7 They used <u>a sheet and branches</u> to solve the problem. p. 8 Ray <u>was a tree</u> in the play.

 5 Mins

Decodable Reader: "Ray Saves the Play"

Focus on Foundational Skills

Review the words and letter-sounds that children will find in the **Decodable Reader**. Review the high-frequency words *about, around, good, great, idea, often, part, second, two,* and *world*. Remind children that *a, ai, ay, ea,* and *ei* can stand for the /ā/ sound.

Preview and Predict Help children sound out the words in the title of the story. Ask: *What do you see in the picture? What has Max the dog done?*

Read the Decodable Reader

Begin to read the story. On page 2, have children point to each word, sounding out decodable words and saying high-frequency words quickly. If children need support with decodable words, model blending. If they need support with high-frequency words, reread in isolation and then in context.

Check Comprehension

p. 2   *What were April and her pals doing?*
p. 3   *What did Ray want to do?*
p. 4   *What problem did April's dog Max make?*
pp. 5–7 *How did Ray and April's dad solve the problem?*
p. 8   *How was Ray able to be in the play?*

Retell Have partners use key ideas and details to retell "Ray Saves the Play."

 COLLABORATE ## Focus on Fluency

With partners, have children read "Ray Saves the Play" to focus on accuracy. Guide them to run their fingers under the text as they read. Children should note whether they are correctly reading the words on the page, monitor themselves, and provide feedback to their partners.

Listen in: If children are having difficulty reading accurately, have them start again at the beginning of the page. If children are reading too quickly, suggest that they should slow down and read as they speak.

 ## English Language Learners

Focus on Fluency Before reading "Ray Saves the Play," point out the potential pronunciation challenges in each section so children can practice the words in isolation beforehand. Have children first echo read each section after you, then choral read with you.

Handwriting: *h, k, g, q*

Model Say the handwriting cues as you write lowercase *h, k, g, q.*

Begin at the bottom line and curve up to the top line. Loop left to the bottom line, curve over, then slant down to the bottom line. Curve up to the middle line.

Begin at the bottom line and curve up to the top line. Loop left to the bottom line. Curve over, and close. Slant right and down; curve up to the middle line.

Begin at the middle line, curve down to the bottom line, and curve up to close at the starting point. Retrace down slanting through the bottom line to the top of the next row. Loop up left, cross over at the bottom line, and curve up to the middle line.

Begin at the middle line, curve down to the bottom line, and curve up to close at the starting point. Retrace down through the bottom line to the top of the next row. Loop right and join at the bottom line. Curve up to the middle line.

Guided Practice/Practice

- Observe children's pen grip and paper placement, and correct as needed. Have children say the name of each letter as they write it.
- Point out that the *q* must be closed at the starting point and the loop should meet the downstroke at the bottom line.

Daily Handwriting

During the week, use the models to review letter formation. Have children independently practice *h, k, g, q* using **Practice Book** pages 181–182.

Handwriting: pages 181–182

✓ Check for Success

Rubric Use the online rubric to record children's progress.

Can children decode words with long *a: a, ai, ay, ea, ei?*

Can children identify and read the high-frequency words?

Differentiate
SMALL GROUP INSTRUCTIONS

If No

| Approaching | pp. T78–T79, T81 |
| ELL | pp. T78–T79, T81 |

If Yes

| On | p. T140 |
| Beyond | p. T146 |

Daily Focus

Phonemic Awareness
• Phoneme Categorization

Phonics
• Blend and Build Words with Long a: *a, ai, ay, ea, ei*

Structural Analysis
• Contractions with *'s, 're, 'll, 've*

Read
• Decodable Reader, Vol. 3: "The Great Plains"

OBJECTIVES

• Categorize medial and final phonemes.

ACADEMIC LANGUAGE

• *category*
Cognate: *categoria*

OPTION 5 Mins

Phonemic Awareness

Phoneme Categorization

1 **Model** Show children how to listen for the medial and final /ā/ sound and identify the word that does not belong. Say: *Listen carefully as I say three words:* face, gave, keep. *Two have* /ā/ *in the middle, and one does not. The words* face *and* gave *have the* /ā/ *vowel sound. The word* keep *doesn't. It doesn't belong.* Repeat with *gray, me, may* to model listening for the final /ā/.

2 **Guided Practice/Practice** *Let's do some together. I will say three words. Listen to the vowel sounds in each word. Tell me which word does not belong and why. The words are* late, sleep, game. *That's right;* late *and* game *have* /ā/. *The word* sleep *does not belong. It has the vowel sound* /ē/. Repeat with *tray, flea, hay* and *braid, tail, kite*.

Continue guiding children as they categorize phonemes for medial and final /ā/. Provide corrective feedback as needed.

wait, read, tails	sleigh, weigh, croak	nice, nail, whale
meet, stay, play	great, goat, steak	tray, neigh, knee

DIFFERENTIATED INSTRUCTION

TIER 2

Approaching Level If children have difficulty with phoneme categorization:

I Do Explain to children that they will be categorizing phonemes today. Say: *Listen as I say three words:* cap, main, save. *When I say* main *and* save, *I can hear the* /ā/ *sound in the middle.* Cap *has the* /a/ *sound.* Cap *does not belong.*

We Do Say: *Listen as I say three words:* pay, they, hi. *Two have the sound* /ā/ *at the end:* pay *and* they. Hi *does not have* /ā/. Hi *does not belong.* Repeat this routine with the following word sets:

spray, tree, play	past, chain, wait	brain, tail, snap
weigh, prey, plow	plate, glass, bake	miss, main, made

You Do *Now it's your turn. Which words go together and which word does not belong?* Offer corrective feedback if needed.

may, day, see	track, rain, nail	sleigh, sigh, they
cake, fine, pail	tape, fail, white	gray, way, pie

Repeat the categorization routine with additional word sets.

You may wish to review Phonemic Awareness with **ELL** using this section.

Phonics

OPTION 5 Mins

Review Long a: a, ai, ay, ea, ei

1 **Model** Display the *Train* **Sound-Spelling Card**. Review the sound /ā/ spelled *ai, a, ay, ea, ei* using the words *train, baby, day, break, veil.*

2 **Guided Practice/Practice** Point to each spelling on the Sound-Spelling Card. *What are these letters? Together what sounds do they stand for?* Give corrective feedback as necessary.

DIFFERENTIATED INSTRUCTION

TIER 2

Approaching Level If children are having difficulty with long *a* spelled *a, ai, ay, ea, ei:*

I Do Display the *Train* Sound-Spelling Card. Say: *This is the* Train *Sound-Spelling Card. The sound is /ā/. The /ā/ sound can be spelled with the letters* a *and* i. Write the letters *ai* while saying /ā/ five times. Repeat with *a, ay, ea,* and *ei.*

We Do Say: *Now do it with me.* Have children write *ai* while saying /ā/. Write the letters *ai* five times and say /ā/ together. Repeat with *a, ay, ea,* and *ei.*

You Do Have children connect the letters *a* and *i* to the sound /ā/ by writing lowercase *ai* while saying /ā/. They should then write the letters *ai* while saying /ā/ five to ten times. Repeat with *a, ay, ea,* and *ei.*

Repeat, connecting the letters *ai, ay, a, ea,* and *ei* to the /ā/ sound through tracing and writing the letters throughout the week.

You may wish to review Phonics with **ELL** using this section.

OBJECTIVES

- Know and apply grade-level phonics and word-analysis skills in decoding words.

- Know spelling-sound correspondences for additional common vowel teams.

SOUND-SPELLING REVIEW

Build Fluency

Display the **Word-Building Cards** for *a, a_e, ai, ay, ea, ei, ch, tch, sh, th, ph, ng, scr, spr, str, thr, spl, shr.* Have children say each sound. Repeat, and vary the pace.

Digital Tools

For more practice, have children use this activity.

Phonemic Awareness

To differentiate instruction for key skills, use the results of this activity.

Phonics

OBJECTIVES

- Know and apply grade-level phonics and word-analysis skills in decoding words.
- Blend and build words with long *a* spelled *a, ai, ay, (ea, ei).*

ACADEMIC LANGUAGE

- *blend, build*

⏱ 5 Mins

Phonics

Blend Words with Long *a: a, ai, ay, ea, ei*

1 **Model** Display **Word-Building Cards** *p, a, i, d* to form the word *paid.* Model how to generate and blend the sounds to say the word. *This is the letter* p. *It stands for /p/. Together the letters* a *and* i *stand for /ā/. This is the letter* d. *It stands for /d/. Listen as I blend these sounds together: /pāāād/. The word is:* paid.

Continue by modeling the words *they, day, train, sail,* and *vein.*

2 **Guided Practice/Practice** Repeat the routine with children with the following words:

chain	break	day	hail	gray
way	rein	plain	clay	great

Guide practice until children can work independently. Provide corrective feedback as needed.

DIFFERENTIATED INSTRUCTION ›

Approaching Level If children are having difficulty blending words with long *a: a, ai, ay, ea, ei:*

I Do Display Word-Building Cards *c, l, a, i, m.* Say: *This is* c. *It stands for /k/. Listen as I say it: /c/. This is* l. *It stands for /l/. Listen as I say it: /l/. These are letters* a, i. *Together they stand for /ā/. Listen: /ā/. This is* m. *It stands for /m/. I'll blend the sounds together: /kllllāāāmmm/,* claim.

Repeat with *way, steak,* and *veil.*

We Do Guide children to blend sounds and read: *wait, sway, day, break,* and *rein.* Give corrective feedback if children need further support.

You Do Have children blend and read *nail, aim, train, say, tray, clay, stay, great,* and *vein.*

Repeat, blending additional words with long *a* spelled *a, ai, ay, ea, ei.*

You may wish to review Phonics with **ELL** using this section.

Build Words with Long *a: a, ai, ay, ea, ei*

Provide children with **Word-Building Cards** for the alphabet. Have children put the letters in order from *a* to *z*.

1 **Model** Display Word-Building Cards *m, a, i, n*. Blend /m/ /ā/ /n/, /mmmāāānnn/, *main*.

- Replace *m* with *ch* and repeat with *chain*.
- Change *ch* to *br* and repeat with *brain*.

2 **Guided Practice/Practice** Continue with *train, trail, rail, mail, jail, tail, sail, say, stay, gray, ray, hay, hail*. Guide children to build and blend each word.

Once children have built the words, dictate the words to children and have them write the words down. Children can work with a partner to check their spelling.

DIFFERENTIATED INSTRUCTION ▶

TIER 2

Approaching Level If children are having difficulty building words:

I Do Display Word-Building Cards *a, i, d*. These are letters *a, i, d*. *The letters* a *and* i *together stand for /ā/ The letter* d *stands for /d/. I will blend /ā/ and /d/: /āāād/,* aid. *The word is* aid.

We Do Say: *Let's do one together. Make* aid *using your Word-Building Cards. Place letter* m *in front of it. Let's blend the sounds in the new word: /mmmāāād/,* maid. *Now we'll change the letter* d *in* maid *to the letter* l. *Let's blend and read the new word: /m/ /ā/ /l/, /mmmāāālll/,* mail.

You Do Have children build *sail, stay, stain, steak, break, veil, vein*. Give corrective feedback if children need more support.

You may wish to review Phonics with **ELL** using this section.

Guided Practice During your word-building routine, say a sentence for each word to provide ELLs with some context. For example: *Train. I take a train to school. Train. Trail. We walk on a trail in the woods. Trail.* **Practice** Provide frames for partners to use when they check each other's spelling after the dictation: How did you spell <u>train</u>? I spelled it <u>t-r-a-i-n</u>. Which letters stand for the /ā/ sound in <u>train</u>? The letters <u>a-i</u> stand for the /ā/ sound in <u>train</u>.

Digital Tools

To differentiate instruction for key skills, use the results of this activity.

Phonics

OBJECTIVES

- Identify and read contractions with *'s, 're, 'll,* and *'ve.*
- Form contractions.

Digital Tools

For more practice, have children use this activity.

I __ the jar.
| fill | fills | filling |

Structural Analysis

Structural Analysis: page 177

⏱ **5 Mins**

Structural Analysis

Contractions with *'s, 're, 'll,* and *'ve*

1 **Model** Write and read aloud *you are* and *you're.* Underline the *'re.* Tell children the word *you're* is a contraction that means "you are." Say: *You know that a contraction is a short way of writing two words. Contractions use an apostrophe to stand for missing letters. I will use a contraction with 're meaning "are" in a sentence.* Write and say: *We are home!* and *We're home!* Say: *The apostrophe stands for the a in* are. Then use the contraction with *'s* meaning "has" in a sentence. Write and say: *He is at his desk* and *He's at his desk.* Repeat for contractions with *'ll* meaning "will" and with *'ve* meaning "have."

2 **Guided Practice/Practice** Write these words: *I, she, who, it, they, that, I, you.* Have children write contractions for each word and then use each contraction in a sentence.

Have children independently practice contractions with *'s, 're, 'll,* and *'ve* using **Practice Book** page 177.

DIFFERENTIATED INSTRUCTION ❯❯

TIER 2

Approaching Level If children are having difficulty with contractions with *'s, 're, 'll,* and *'ve:*

I Do Write *what is* and *what's.* Say: What's *is a contraction. A contraction is a short way to write two words. An apostrophe replaces the missing letters. The apostrophe in* what's *stands for the letter* i *in* is.

We Do Write *she will* and *she'll.* Say: She'll *is a contraction for* she will. *The apostrophe in* she'll *stands for the letters* w, i *in* will. *Let's use* she will *and* she'll *in sentences.* Repeat this routine with the following examples:

that is	we are	I will	we have
we will	I have	it is	you have

You Do Say: *Now it's your turn. Write the contraction for each word pair. Say each contraction and then use it in a sentence.* Offer corrective feedback if needed.

you will	that will	we are	I have
I will	we will	that has	you are

Repeat Have children form more *'s, 're, 'll, 've* contractions.

Decodable Reader: "The Great Plains"

Focus on Foundational Skills

Review that *a, ai, ay, ea,* and *ei* can stand for /ā/, as well as the high-frequency words *great* and *two,* that children will find in the **Decodable Reader**.

Preview and Predict Have children sound out each word in the title. Ask: *What is in the photograph? How would you describe the land in the Great Plains?* Elicit children's responses; then explain that *plains* means "an area of flat or almost flat land."

The Great Plains

The Great Plains is a nice place with big wide open spaces. It is inside of the United States.

9

Decodable Reader, Vol. 3

Read the Decodable Reader

Begin to read "The Great Plains." On page 11, have children point to each word, sounding out decodable words and saying high-frequency words quickly. If children need support reading decodable words, model blending. If children are having difficulty with high-frequency words, reread the word in isolation and then in context.

Check Comprehension

pp. 9 and 12   *What is the Great Plains? Where is it located?*
p. 10   *What are things you can see on the Great Plains?*
p. 11   *What can you do on the Great Plains?*
p. 12   *What might you see in the sky over the Great Plains?*

Retell Have partners use key ideas and details to retell "The Great Plains."

Focus on Fluency

With partners, have children read "The Great Plains" to focus on accuracy, as well as appropriate rate. Guide them to run their fingers under the text as they read. Children should note whether they are correctly reading the words on the page, monitor themselves, and give feedback to their partners.

English Language Learners

Check Comprehension Provide sentence frames, as needed, to help children answer the questions:
pp. 9 and 12 The Great Plains is <u>a place of big open spaces</u>. It is in <u>the United States</u>. p. 10 On the Great Plains you can see <u>big hay bales and waves of grain</u>. p. 11 On the Great Plains you can <u>hike</u> <u>on a trail</u>. p. 12 In the sky over the Great Plains, you might see <u>sun, rain, or a rainbow</u>.

OBJECTIVES

- Know and apply grade-level phonics and word-analysis skills in decoding words.
- Recognize and read grade-appropriate irregularly spelled words.
- Read on-level text with purpose and understanding.
- Read with sufficient accuracy and fluency to support comprehension.

✓ Check for Success

Rubric Use the online rubric to record children's progress.

Can children decode words with long *a: a, ai, ay, ea, ei?*

Can children identify and read the high-frequency words?

Differentiate
SMALL GROUP INSTRUCTIONS

If No
Approaching pp. T85–T88
ELL pp. T85–T88
If Yes
On p. T140
Beyond p. T146

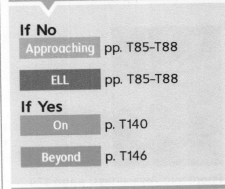

Daily Focus

Phonemic Awareness
• Phoneme Blending

Phonics
• Introduce Long *a*: *eigh*, *ey*

Structural Analysis
• Contractions with *'s, 're, 'll, 've*

High-Frequency Words

Read
• Decodable Reader, Vol. 3:
"Eight Is Great!"

OBJECTIVES
• Blend phonemes to form words.

Phonemic Awareness: page 174

⏱ 5 Mins Phonemic Awareness

Phoneme Blending

1 Model Place markers on the **Response Board** to represent sounds. Say: *I'll put one marker in each box as I say each sound. Then I'll blend the sounds to form a word.* Place a marker for each sound you say: /w/ /ā/ /t/. *This word has three sounds:* /w/ /ā/ /t/. *Listen as I blend the sounds to form a word:* /wwwāāāt/, wait. *The word is* wait.

2 Guided Practice/Practice Say: *Let's do some together. Using your own boards, place a marker for each sound you hear. I'll say one sound at a time. Then we will blend the sounds to say the word.* Do the first three with children. Offer corrective feedback as needed.

/r/ /ā/ /n/ (rain)	/s/ /p/ /i/ /n/ (spin)	/s/ /t/ /ā/ /k/ (steak)
/th/ /ā/ (they)	/s/ /w/ /ā/ (sway)	/m/ /a/ /d/ (mad)
/r/ /e/ /d/ (red)	/w/ /ā/ (weigh)	/v/ /ā/ /l/ (veil)

Have children independently practice blending phonemes using **Practice Book** page 174.

DIFFERENTIATED INSTRUCTION >>

TIER 2 | **Approaching Level** If children are having difficulty blending phonemes:

I Do Listen as I say two sounds: /rrr/ /āāā/. I'll blend the sounds together: /rrrāāā/, ray. The word is ray.

We Do Listen as I say three sounds: /t/ /āāā/ /lll/. Say the sounds with me: /t/ /āāā/ /lll/. Let's blend: /t/ /āāā/ /lll/, /tāāālll/, tail. We made the word tail. Repeat the routine with these words:

/t/ /r/ /ā/ /l/ (trail)	/p/ /r/ /ā/ (prey)	/m/ /ā/ (may)
/g/ /r/ /ā/ /n/ (grain)	/b/ /r/ /ā/ /k/ (break)	/v/ /ā/ /n/ (vein)
/g/ /r/ /ā/ /t/ (great)	/b/ /r/ /ā/ /d/ (braid)	/s/ /l/ /ā/ (sleigh)

You Do It's your turn now. I want you to blend the sounds I say together to form a word. Offer corrective feedback as necessary.

/p/ /ā/ /n/ /t/ (paint)	/t/ /r/ /ā/ (tray)	/s/ /ā/ /l/ (sail)
/s/ /t/ /ā/ /k/ (steak)	/m/ /ā/ /l/ (mail)	/ā/ /t/ (eight)
/t/ /r/ /ā/ /n/ (train)	/k/ /l/ /ā/ (clay)	/g/ /ā/ /n/ (gain)
/s/ /p/ /r/ /ā/ (spray)	/p/ /ā/ /l/ (pail)	/v/ /ā/ /l/ (veil)

Repeat the blending routine with additional long *a* words.

You may wish to review Phonemic Awareness with **ELL** using this section.

Phonics

5 Mins

Introduce Long *a: eigh, ey*

1 **Model** Display the *Train* **Sound-Spelling Card.** Teach /ā/ spelled *eigh*, using *weigh*. Say: *This is the* Train Sound-Spelling Card. The sound is /ā/. Say it with me: /āāā/. This is the sound in the middle of the word train. Listen: /trrrāāānnn/, train. You know that the letters a, i together and the letters e, a together can stand for /āāā/. The letters e, i, g, h together can also stand for /āāā/. The letters e, y together can stand for /āāā/ as well. I will write the letters e, i, g, h and the letters e, y several times. Review the sound-spellings a, ai, ay, ea, and ei, using basic, tail, tray, great, rein.

Sound-Spelling Card

2 **Guided Practice/Practice** Have children practice connecting the letters *e, i, g, h* and the letters *e, y* to the sound /ā/. Say: *This time, write the letters* e, i, g, h *and* e, y *five times as you say the /ā/ sound.* Repeat for the review sound-spellings *a, ay, ea,* and *ei.*

Have children independently practice long *a: a, ai, ay, ea, ei, eigh, ey* using **Practice Book** page 176.

DIFFERENTIATED INSTRUCTION

TIER 2

Approaching Level If children are having difficulty with long *a: eigh, ey*:

I Do Display the **Word-Building Cards** for *e, i, g,* and *h.* Say: *The letters* e, i, g, h *together stand for the /ā/ sound. Listen to this word:* weigh. *Add the Word-Building Card for* w. *Listen as I say the word again:* weigh. Repeat with /ā/ spelled *e, y* as in the word *prey.*

We Do Provide children with the Word-Building Cards for *e, i, g, h* and *e, y.* Help children trace each group of letters as they say the /ā/ sound. Circulate and give corrective feedback if necessary.

You Do Have children connect the letters *e, i, g, h* to /ā/ by tracing *e, i, g, h* with their fingers, while saying /ā/ three times. Then have them write the letters *e, i, g, h* while saying /ā/ five to ten times. Repeat for the *e, y* spelling of /ā/. Give extra support and feedback if necessary.

You may wish to review Phonics with **ELL** using this section.

OBJECTIVES

- Know and apply grade-level phonics and word-analysis skills in decoding words.

- Know spelling-sound correspondences for additional common vowel teams.

SOUND-SPELLING REVIEW

Build Fluency

Display Word-Building Cards: *a, ai, ay, ea, ei, eigh, ey, a_e, i, i_e, o, o_e, u, u_e, ch, sh, th, wh, tch, ph, ng, scr, spr, str, thr, spl, shr, dge, ge, lge, nge.* Have children say each sound.

Digital Tools

For more practice, have children use this activity.

Phonemic Awareness

To differentiate instruction for key skills, use the results of this activity.

Phonics

Phonics: page 176

OBJECTIVES

- Know and apply grade-level phonics and word-analysis skills in decoding words.

- Identify letter-sound correspondence /ā/ spelled *a, ai, ay, ea, ei, eigh, ey.*

- Blend and build words with long *a* spelled *a, ai, ay,* (*ea, ei, eigh, ey*).

- Decode words with long *a.*

 OPTION **5** Mins

Phonics

Blend Words with Long *a: a, ai, ay, ea, ei, eigh, ey*

1. **Model** Display **Word-Building Cards** *g, r, e, y.* Model how to blend the sounds. *This is the letter* g. *It stands for /g/. This is the letter* r. *It stands for /r/. Together, the letters* e *and* y *stand for /ā/. Listen as I blend the sounds: /grrrāāā/.* Continue modeling *stray, great, vein.*

2. **Guided Practice/Practice** Display the Day 3 Phonics/Fluency Practice chart. Blend and read each word in the first row; say: */āāāt/. The word is* eight. Have children blend each word with you. Prompt children to read the connected text, sounding out the decodable words. Guide practice and give feedback until children can work on their own.

eight	may	break	they	unveil	wail
great	stray	chain	basic	gain	prey
hey	hay	weigh	way	weights	waits
shade	fifth	phone	sprint	throne	whale

I weigh the grain and then pay for it.

Hey, watch it—or it may break!

Gail gained a lot of weight.

Day 3 Phonics/Fluency Practice

DIFFERENTIATED INSTRUCTION ▶

TIER 2

Approaching Level If children are having difficulty blending words:

I Do Display Word-Building Cards *t, h, e, y.* Say: *These are the letters* t, h. *Together, they stand for /th/. These are the letters* e, y. *Together, they stand for /ā/. Listen as I blend both sounds together: /thāāā/,* they. *The word is* they.

We Do *Now let's do some together.* Guide children to blend sounds and read these words with you: *play, rain, wait, break, veil, eight.* Give corrective feedback if necessary.

You Do Have children blend and read the following words. Provide corrective feedback if children need support.

main	hay	break	sleigh	prey
hey	weigh	faint	great	rein

You may wish to review Phonics with **ELL** using this section.

Build Words with Long *a*: *a, ai, ay, ea, ei, eigh, ey*

1 Display the **Word-Building Cards** *w, e, i, g, h, t.* Blend the sounds /w/ /ā/ /t/, /wwwāāāt/, *weight.*

- Delete *t* and repeat with *weigh.*
- Change *w* to *n* and repeat with *neigh.*

2 **Guided** Continue having children blend and build words with *sleigh, ray, way, sway, say, sail, wail, tail, trail, hail, hey, prey.* Guide children and provide corrective feedback as needed until they can work independently.

Once children have built the words, dictate the words to children and have them write the words down. Children can work with a partner to check their spelling.

Digital Tools

To differentiate instruction for key skills, use the results of this activity.

Phonics

DIFFERENTIATED INSTRUCTION 〉〉

TIER 2

Approaching Level If children need more support building words with /ā/:

I Do Display Word-Building Cards *a, i, d. The letters* a *and* i *together stand for /ā/. The letter* d *stands for /d/. I will blend /ā/ and /d/ together: /āāād/,* aid. *The word is* aid. *I will add the letter* p *at the beginning of the word* aid. *I made the new word* paid.

We Do *Now, let's do one together.* Make the word *aid* using Word-Building Cards. *Let's blend and say the word: /āāād/,* aid. *Now we'll change the word* aid. *Place the letter* r *in front of it. Let's blend the new word: /rrr/ /āāā/ /d/, /rrrāāād/,* raid. *Change the letter* d *in* raid *to the letter* l. *Say: Let's blend and read the new word: /rrr/ /āāā/ /lll/, /rrrāāālll/,* rail.

You Do Have children continue to build these words: *rain, main, gain, gay, hay, hey, they, prey, ray, way, weigh, weight, wait, bait.* Guide children and provide feedback as needed until they can work on their own.

You may wish to review Phonics with **ELL** using this section.

OBJECTIVES

- Identify and read contractions with *'s, 're, 'll,* and *'ve.*
- Form contractions.

Digital Tools

For more practice, have children use this activity.

Structural Analysis

English Language Learners

Guided Practice Provide frames for children to confirm their understanding of the spelling rules for contractions: The word <u>here's</u> is a contraction for <u>here is</u>. The apostrophe in <u>here's</u> stands for the letter(s) <u>i</u> in <u>is</u>. You spell the contraction <u>h-e-r-e-'-s</u>.

OPTION
5 Mins

Structural Analysis

Contractions with *'s, 're, 'll,* and *'ve*

1 **Model** Say the words *she* and *she's*. Ask children to listen closely to hear what is different. Point out the /z/ sound at the end of *she's*.

- Write the words *she is* and *she's*. Underline the *'s* at the end of *she's*. Say: *You know that a contraction is a short way to say two words.* Tell children that the word *she's* is the contraction for *she is*. Remind them that the apostrophe replaces missing letters in a contraction.

Repeat for the contractions *they're, he'll,* and *we've*.

2 **Guided Practice/Practice** Help children form contractions for *here is, that is, you are, we will, they will, you have,* and *I have*. Remind children to place the apostrophe to replace the missing letter or letters. Offer corrective feedback if more support is needed.

DIFFERENTIATED INSTRUCTION ➤

TIER 2

Approaching Level If children are having difficulty with contractions with *'s, 're, 'll,* and *'ve:*

I Do Write: *you have, you've*. Say: You've *is a contraction. A contraction is a short way to write two words. An apostrophe replaces the missing letters. The apostrophe in* you've *stands for the letters* h, a *in* have.

We Do Write *he will, he'll*. Say: He'll *is a contraction for* he will. *The apostrophe in* he'll *stands for the letters* w, i *in* will. *Let's use* he will *and* he'll *in sentences.*

Repeat this routine with the following examples:

| I have | you are | she will | that is |
| we will | I will | it will | we have |

You Do Say: *Now it's your turn. Write the contraction for each word pair. Say each contraction and then use it in a sentence.* Give corrective feedback as needed.

| we are | she is | it is | you will |
| I have | you are | we have | that will |

Repeat Have children work in pairs to form contractions with *'s, 're, 'll,* and *'ve*.

---

5 Mins

High-Frequency Words

about, around, good, great, idea, often, part, second, two, world

OBJECTIVES

- Know and apply grade-level phonics and word-analysis skills in decoding words.

- Recognize and read grade-appropriate irregularly spelled words.

1 **Model** Say each word and have children Read/Spell/Write it. Ask children to picture the word, and then write it the way they see it. Display the answers for children to self-correct.

2 **Guided Practice** Have children identify the high-frequency words in connected text and blend the decodable words.

1. We're **about** to run out of air!
2. The men ran **around** a track.
3. Oranges are a **good** food.
4. I hope you'll have a **great** day!
5. Tim's **idea** is the best one.

6. My family shops here **often.**
7. This **part** of the tape is funny.
8. He is the **second** one in line.
9. Can **two** children sit there?
10. The **world** is a very big place.

Point out any irregularities in sound-spellings; for example, the *t* in *often* is silent.

Have children independently practice the high-frequency words using **Practice Book** page 178.

COLLABORATE

Practice Add the high-frequency words to the cumulative word bank. Have children work in pairs to make up new sentences for each word.

Cumulative Review Review last week's words using the Read/Spell/ Write routine. Repeat; mix the words and have children say each one.

Digital Tools

For more practice, have children use this activity.

High-Frequency Words

DIFFERENTIATED INSTRUCTION

TIER 2

Approaching Level If children need support with high-frequency words:

I Do Use the **High-Frequency Word Cards**, one at a time. Follow this routine: Display the word. Read the word. Spell the word.

We Do Ask children to state the word and spell the word with you. Model using the word in a sentence, and have children repeat.

You Do Display each word for children to say and spell. Flip through the card set as children chorally read the words. Give opportunities for children to use the words in conversation. Have children write each word in their writer's notebook.

High-Frequency Words: page 178

Decodable Reader, Vol. 3

OBJECTIVES

- Know and apply grade-level phonics and word-analysis skills in decoding words.

- Recognize and read grade-appropriate irregularly spelled words.

- Read on-level text with purpose and understanding.

- Read with sufficient accuracy and fluency to support comprehension.

Decodable Reader: "Eight Is Great!"

5 Mins

Focus on Foundational Skills

Review the words and letter-sounds that children will find in the **Decodable Reader.**

- Review the high-frequency words *great, good, idea,* and *two.*

- Remind children that *a, ai, ay, ea, ei, eigh,* and *ey* can stand for the /ā/ sound.

Preview and Predict Point to the title of the selection and have children sound out each word with you as you run your finger under it. Ask: *What do you see in the photograph? How does the boy feel about being eight years old?*

Read the Decodable Reader

Begin guiding children to read the selection "Eight Is Great!" On page 18, have children point to each word, sounding out the decodable words and saying the high-frequency words quickly. If children need support reading decodable words, model blending for them. If children are having difficulty with high-frequency words, reread the high-frequency word in isolation and then reread the word in context.

Check Comprehension

p. 13 *What eight items are being counted?*

p. 14 *What are the girls in the photograph doing?*

p. 15 *What are two activities you can do when it's cold outside?*

p. 16 *What can you do to have fun in hot weather?*

p. 17 *In rainy weather, what can you do to have fun?*

p. 18 *What did the girl in the photograph do?*

Retell Have partners use key ideas and details to retell "Eight Is Great!"

Focus on Fluency

With partners, have children read "Eight Is Great!" to focus on accuracy. Guide them to run their fingers under the text as they read. Children should note whether they are correctly reading the words on the page. As children read, they can monitor themselves and provide feedback to their partners.

Listen in: If children are having difficulty reading accurately, have them start again at the beginning of the page. If children are reading too quickly, suggest to them that they should slow down and read as they speak.

English Language Learners

Check Comprehension Provide sentence frames, as needed, to help children answer the questions:

p. 13 The items are eight nice things to try on your birthday.

p. 14 The girls are taking a hike to a lake.

p. 15 When it's cold outside, you can ice skate and play in the snow.

p. 16 You can go to a beach and wade in the water.

p. 17 You can stay inside and play games with clay and paint.

p. 18 The girl baked a cake.

Focus on Fluency Before reading "Eight Is Great!" point out the potential pronunciation challenges in each section of the selection so children can practice the words in isolation beforehand. Have children first echo read each section after you, then choral read with you.

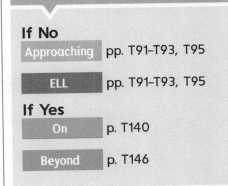

✔ Check for Success

Rubric Use the online rubric to record children's progress.

Can children decode words with long *a: a, ai, ay, ea, ei, eigh, ey*?

Can children identify and read the high-frequency words?

Differentiate
SMALL GROUP INSTRUCTIONS

If No

| Approaching | pp. T91–T93, T95 |
| ELL | pp. T91–T93, T95 |

If Yes

| On | p. T140 |
| Beyond | p. T146 |

Daily Focus

Phonemic Awareness
• Phoneme Categorization

Phonics
• Blend and Build Words with Long *a: a, ai, ay, ea, ei, eigh, ey*

Read
• Decodable Reader, Vol. 3: "What a Day!"

What a Day!

OBJECTIVES

• Categorize medial and final phonemes.

OPTION 5 Mins

Phonemic Awareness

Phoneme Categorization

1 Model Say: *Listen as I say three words:* crate, string, sprain. *Two of these words have the long* a *sound, /ā/, in the middle. One does not. The word* string *does not have the /ā/ sound. It does not belong.* Repeat for final /ā/ with *bee, stray, neigh.*

2 Guided Practice/Practice Have children practice categorizing medial and final vowel sounds. Do the first one together. Provide corrective feedback as children progress to work on their own.

sleigh/prey/key	stream/great/steak	spring/grain/train
they/weigh/thump	break/cube/weight	spray/sway/tree
bay/band/clay	trail/paint/sent	strike/neigh/tray

DIFFERENTIATED INSTRUCTION >>

TIER 2

Approaching Level If children are having difficulty with phoneme categorization:

I Do Explain to children that they will be categorizing phonemes today. Say: *Listen as I say three words /man/, /māl/, /gāv/. When I say* mail *and* gave, *I can hear the /ā/ sound in the middle.* Man *has the /a/ sound.* Man *does not belong.*

We Do Say: *Listen as I say three words:* tray, they, hot. *Two have the sound /ā/ at the end:* tray *and* they. *Which word does not belong? That's right,* hot *does not have /ā/.* Hot *does not belong.* Repeat the routine with children using these examples:

spray, tree, play	past, chain, wait	brain, tail, snap
trail, pain, fresh	save, sad, sail	flat, gain, braid

You Do *It's your turn. Which words go together and which word does not belong?* Give corrective feedback if needed.

may, day, see	track, rain, nail	sleigh, sigh, they
train, fail, mat	pot, play, hey	eight, late, badge

Repeat the categorization routine with additional long *a* words

You may wish to review Phonemic Awareness with **ELL** using this section.

Phonics

Blend Words with Long *a: a, ai, ay, ea, ei, eigh, ey*

1 **Model** Display **Word Building Cards** *p, l, a, i, n.* Say: *This is the letter* p. *It stands for /p/. This is the letter* l. *It stands for /l/. These are the letters* a *and* i. *The letters* a *and* i *together stand for /ā/. This is the letter* n. *It stands for /n/. Let's blend all four sounds: /plllāāānnn/. The word is* plain.

Continue by modeling the words *break, case, paint, weigh,* and *tray.*

2 **Guided Practice/Practice** Repeat the routine with *sway, great, neigh, blaze, stay, braid,* and *prey.*

DIFFERENTIATED INSTRUCTION

TIER 2

Approaching Level If children are having difficulty blending words:

I Do Display Word-Building Cards *c, l, a, y.* Say: *This is the letter* c. *It stands for /k/. This is the letter* l. *It stands for /l/. These are the letters* a, y. *Together, they stand for /ā/. Listen as I blend all the sounds together: /klllāāā/,* clay. *The word is* clay.

We Do *Now let's do some together.* Guide children to blend sounds and read these words with you: *wail, tray, break, veil, weigh, hey.* Give corrective feedback if needed.

You Do Display the following words:

gray	strain	hay	pail	great
they	weight	fail	steak	braid

Have children blend and read the words. Offer corrective feedback if children need more support.

You may wish to review Phonics with **ELL** using this section

---

OBJECTIVES

- Know and apply grade-level phonics and word-analysis skills in decoding words.

- Blend and build words with long *a* spelled *a, ai, ay, (ea, ei, eigh, ey).*

SOUND-SPELLING REVIEW

Build Fluency
Display Word-Building Cards: *a, ai, ay, ea, ei, eigh, ey, scr, spr, str, thr, spl, shr, dge, ge, lge, nge, ch, sh, th, wh, tch, ph, ng.* Have children say each sound. Repeat and vary the pace.

Digital Tools

For more practice, have children use this activity.

Phonemic Awareness

To differentiate instruction for key skills, use the results of this activity.

Phonics

OBJECTIVES

- Know and apply grade-level phonics and word-analysis skills in decoding words.

- Blend and build words with long *a* spelled *a, ai, ay, (ea, ei, eigh, ey)*.

- Decode words with long *a*.

STRUCTURAL ANALYSIS REVIEW

Remind children that a contraction is a short way to write two words. An apostrophe replaces one or more letters. Write *she's, we're, you'll, I've.* Have children work in pairs to identify the words that make up each contraction and which letters were replaced by an apostrophe. Have pairs write sentences for each contraction.

Digital Tools

To differentiate instruction for key skills, use the results of this activity.

Phonics

 Phonics 5 Mins

Build Words with Long *a: a, ai, ay, ea, ei, eigh, ey*

1 **Review** Display **Word-Building Cards** *r, a, i, n.* *The long a sound, /ā/, can be represented by the letters* a, ai, ay, ea, ei, eigh, *and* ey. *We'll use Word-Building Cards to build words with long* a. Point to the letters for *rain. Let's blend the sounds together and read the word: /rrrāāānnn/. Now, we'll change the* r *to* ch. Blend the sounds and read the word with children: *chain.* Continue building with *train, strain, stray, spray, way, weigh, weight.*

2 **Practice** Have children continue to build words with *wail, tail, sail, say, sleigh, slay, stay, steak, break, great, grey, they.*

Once children have built the words, dictate the words and have children write the words on a piece of paper. Children can work with a partner to check their words for spelling.

DIFFERENTIATED INSTRUCTION »

On Level For more practice building words:

I Do Display Word-Building Cards *t, r, a, i, n.* Say: *This is the letter* t. *It stands for /t/. This is the letter* r. *It stands for /r/. The letters* a *and* i *together stand for /ā/, and* n *stands for /n/. Listen as I blend all four sounds together: /trrrāāānnn/,* train.

We Do *Now, let's do one together.* Make the word *train* using Word-Building Cards.

Change the letter *t* to *b. Let's blend: /b/ /r/ /ā/ /n/, /brān/,* brain. *The new word is* brain. Change the letters *br* to *ch. I am going to change the letters* br *in* brain *to the letters* ch. *Let's blend and read the new word: /ch/ /āāā/ /nnn/, /chāāānnn/,* chain. *The new word is* chain.

You Do Have children build and blend the words: *way, sway, stay; steak, break; eight, eighth; hey, they.* Give corrective feedback if children need additional support.

Decodable Reader: "What a Day!"

OPTION 5 Mins

Focus on Foundational Skills

Review the words and letter-sounds that children will find in the **Decodable Reader**. Review the high-frequency words *great* and *two*. Remind children that *a, ai, ay, ea, ei, eigh,* and *ey* can stand for the /ā/ sound.

Preview and Predict Have children read each word in the title of the story with you. Ask: *What do you see in the picture? Where is the ape, and what is he doing?*

What a Day!

An ape ate seven grapes in space. What did he say? "They're great!" 19

Decodable Reader, Vol. 3

Read the Decodable Reader

Begin to read the story. On page 20, have children point to each word, sounding out decodable words and saying high-frequency words quickly. If children need support with decodable words, model blending. If they need support with high-frequency words, reread in isolation and then in context.

Check Comprehension

p. 19   *What did the ape do in space?*
p. 20   *What did Gail and Dale do on their play date?*
p. 21   *What things are described with which colors?*
p. 22   *What is May doing? What did Dad compare May's dream to?*

Retell Have partners use key ideas and details to retell "What a Day!"

Focus on Fluency

With partners, have children read "What a Day!" to focus on accuracy. Guide them to run their fingers under the text as they read. Children should note whether they are correctly reading the words on the page, monitor themselves, and provide feedback to their partners.

English Language Learners

Check Comprehension Provide sentence frames, as needed, to help children answer the questions:
p. 19 The ape ate seven grapes in space. p. 20 Gail and Dale played games. p. 21 Some things and their colors are a gray whale, its red and pink tail, and the white waves. p. 22 May is dreaming. Dad said a dream is like a play that takes place inside the brain.

OBJECTIVES

- Know and apply grade-level phonics and word-analysis skills in decoding words.
- Recognize and read grade-appropriate irregularly spelled words.
- Read on-level text with purpose and understanding.
- Read with sufficient accuracy and fluency to support comprehension.

HIGH-FREQUENCY WORDS REVIEW

about, around, good, great, idea, often, part, second, two, world
Have children Read/Spell/Write each word and use it in a sentence. Review last week's words using the same routine.

✓ Check for Success

Rubric Use the online rubric to record children's progress.

Can children decode words with long *a: a, ai, ay, ea, ei, eigh, ey?*

Can children read the high-frequency words?

Differentiate
SMALL GROUP INSTRUCTIONS

If No
Approaching pp. T99–T101
ELL pp. T99–T101
If Yes
On p. T140
Beyond p. T146

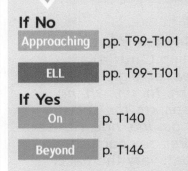

Daily Focus

Phonemic Awareness
• Phoneme Blending

Phonics
• Blend and Build Words with Long a: a, ai, ay, ea, ei, eigh, ey

Structural Analysis
• Contractions with 's, 're, 'll, 've

High-Frequency Words

OBJECTIVES

• Blend phonemes to form words.

• Know and apply grade-level phonics and word-analysis skills in decoding words.

• Know sound-spelliing correspondences for additional common vowel teams.

• Blend and build words with long a spelled a, ai, ay, (ea, ei, eigh, ey).

• Identify and read contractions with 's, 're, 'll, and 've.

• Recognize and read grade-appropriate irregularly spelled words.

SOUND-SPELLING REVIEW ▶

Build Fluency

Display the Word-Building Cards a, ai, ay, ea, ei, eigh, ey, ch, tch, sh, th, ph, wh, ng, scr, spr, str, thr, spl, shr, dge, ge, lge, nge. Have children say each sound. Repeat; vary the pace.

Phonemic Awareness

Phoneme Blending

Review Say: *Listen as I say a group of sounds. Blend them to form a word.*

/s/ /l/ /ā/ (sleigh)	/th/ /ā/ (they)	/k/ /l/ /ā/ /m/ (claim)
/t/ /r/ /ā/ (tray)	/n/ /ā/ /z/ (neighs)	/g/ /r/ /ā/ /n/ (grain)
/v/ /ā/ /l/ (veil)	/w/ /ā/ /t/ (weight)	/s/ /p/ /r/ /ā/ (spray)

Phonics

Blend and Build Words: Long a: a, ai, ay, ea, ei, eigh, ey

Review Write these words: *bacon, train, play, tame, weight, prey, break.* Have children read and say the words. If children have difficulty, remind them to segment the word and blend the sounds together. Then have children follow the word-building routine with **Word-Building Cards** to build *steak, stay, stray, tray, they, hey, hail, nail, neigh, weigh.* Once children have built the words, dictate the words to children and have them write the words. Children can work with a partner to check their spelling.

Word Automaticity Help children practice by displaying decodable words and pointing to each one as children chorally read it. Test how many words children can read in one minute. Model blending words children miss.

> ### DIFFERENTIATED INSTRUCTION ▶
>
> **TIER 2**
>
> **Approaching Level** If children need extra support blending and building words with long a: a, ai, ay, ea, ei, eigh, ey:
>
> **I Do** Display **Word-Building Cards** f, a, i, l, s. Say: *These letters stand for the sounds /fff/, /āāā/, /lll/, and /zzz/. Listen as I blend all four sounds: /fffāāālllzzz/, fails. The word is fails.*
>
> **We Do** Say: *Let's make the word break using Word-Building Cards. Let's blend: /b/ /rrr/ /āāā/ /k/, /brrrāāāk/, break. We'll change the letters br in break to st. Let's blend and read the new word: /sss/ /t/ /āāā/ /k/, /ssstāāāk/, steak.* Continue building with: *stay, grey, great, ray, rail, trail, train, rein.* Give corrective feedback until children can work independently.
>
> **You Do** Have children blend and build these words: *break, brake, bake, basic, bay, pay, play, prey, they, that, vat, veil, vein, vain, wail, way, weighs.* Review the meanings of the words.

You may wish to review Phonics with **ELL** using this section.

Structural Analysis

Contractions with 's, 're, 'll, 've

Review Have children decode and spell contractions. Have children explain that a contraction is a shortened form of two words joined together and that an apostrophe replaces the missing letters. Have children write the two words for such contractions as *I'll*, *she's*, *we've*, and *they're*.

High-Frequency Words

about, around, good, great, idea, often, part, second, two, world

Review Have children identify and read the high-frequency words. Display the **High-Frequency Word Cards** for each of the words. Have children Read/Spell/Write each word. Have pairs use the words in conversation. Then have children write a sentence for each word.

DIFFERENTIATED INSTRUCTION

TIER 2

Approaching Level If children need extra support with high-frequency words:

I Do Use the High-Frequency Word Cards. Display one word at a time, following the routine: Display the word. Read the word. Then spell the word.

We Do Ask children to state the word and spell the word with you. Model using the word in a sentence and have children repeat after you.

You Do Display the words in random order. Ask children to say the word and then spell it. When completed, quickly flip through the word card set as children chorally read the words. Provide opportunities for children to use the words in speaking and writing. For example, supply sentence starters, such as *One idea I have for helping around the house is ___* . Ask children to write each word in their writer's notebook.

Digital Tools

To differentiate instruction for key skills, use the results of this activity.

Phonics

For more practice, have children use this activity.

I __ the jar.
fill | fills | filling

Structural Analysis

✔ Check for Success

Rubric Use the online rubric to record children's progress.

Can children decode words with long *a: a, ai, ay, ea, ei*?

Can children identify and read the high-frequency words?

Differentiate
SMALL GROUP INSTRUCTIONS

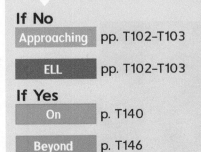

If No

| Approaching | pp. T102–T103 |
| ELL | pp. T102–T103 |

If Yes

| On | p. T140 |
| Beyond | p. T146 |

Daily Focus

Phonemic Awareness
• Phoneme Isolation

Phonics
• Introduce and Blend Words with Long *i*: *i, y, igh, ie*

Structural Analysis
• Open Syllables

High-Frequency Words

Read
• Decodable Reader, Vol. 3: "High in the Sky"

Handwriting
• Lowercase Cursive *j, p, r, s*

OBJECTIVES
• Isolate phonemes in words.

Phonemic Awareness: page 190

Phonemic Awareness

5 Mins

Phoneme Isolation

1 **Model** Introduce /ī/. Tell children you are going to say a word and that you want them to listen for the middle sound in that word. Say: *Listen: /sssīīīt/, sight. What sound do you hear in the middle of the word* sight*? Yes,* sight *has the /ī/ sound in the middle. Listen: /īīī/.*

Have children listen for the final, or ending, sound in the word *dry*.

2 **Guided Practice/Practice** Have children practice isolating medial and final vowel sounds. Say: *I will say some more words. Tell me what sound you hear in the middle of each word.*

bright	mind	chain	mule
wild	steak	light	broke

Then have children listen for the final vowel sound in these words.

shy	gray	me	tie
weigh	cry	why	tree

Have children independently practice isolating phonemes using **Practice Book** page 190.

English Language Learners

Guided Practice Reinforce the initial vocabulary needed to discuss phoneme isolation: *vowel sound, middle, end.* Use examples to clarify meaning, as needed. Provide sentence frames for partners to use while asking and answering questions about isolating medial and final vowel sounds. *What vowel sound do you hear in the middle of the word* bright*? I hear /ī/ in the middle of the word* bright*. What vowel sound do you hear at the end of the word* shy*? I hear /ī/ at the end of the word* shy*.* If children need additional support with phonemes, use the articulation support on the **Sound-Spelling Cards**.

English Language Learners

See page 5 in the **Language Transfers Handbook** for guidance in identifying sounds that may or may not transfer for speakers of certain languages and for support in accommodating those children. See the chart on pages 6–9 for specific sound transfer issues for multiple languages.

DIFFERENTIATED INSTRUCTION

TIER 2

Approaching Level If children are having difficulty isolating phonemes:

I Do Explain to children that you will say a word and you want them to listen to and identify the middle sound. Say: *Listen as I say this word: /n/ /ī/ /t/. When I say* night, *I hear the sound /ī/ in the middle*: Repeat for final /ī/ with *fly*.

We Do Say: *Listen as I say a word*: climb. *Say it with me*: climb. *What vowel sound is in the middle of* climb? /k/ /lll/ /īī/ /mmm/. *We can hear /ī/ in the middle of* climb. Repeat this routine with additional medial vowels in *fight, find, rain, might, home*.

Repeat for final vowels with *hay, hi, sky, play, cry, why*.

You Do Say: *It's your turn. What vowel sound do you hear in these words?*

mild	life	rose	might	leaf
sigh	tie	me	stay	try

Repeat the isolation routine with additional words with medial and final /ī/ spelled *i, y, igh, ie*.

You may wish to review Phonemic Awareness with **ELL** using this section.

Digital Tools

For more practice, have children use this activity.

Phonemic Awareness

OBJECTIVES

- Know and apply grade-level phonics and word analysis skills in decoding words.

- Distinguish long and short vowels when reading regularly spelled one-syllable words.

- Apply phonics when decoding words with long *i*.

(5 Mins) ## Phonics

Introduce Long *i*: *i, y, igh, ie*

1 **Model** Display the *Five* **Sound-Spelling Card.** Teach /ī/ spelled *i* as in *idea, y* as in *fly, igh* as in *high,* and *ie* as in *pie.* Model writing the letters *i, y, igh,* and *ie.* *This is the* Five *Sound-Spelling Card. The sound is /ī/. The /ī/ sound can be spelled i, y, ie, or igh. Say the sound with me: /īīī/. This is the middle sound in* five. *Listen: /fffīīīvvv/,* five. *I'll say /īīī/ as I write the letters of the sound-spellings several times.*

Sound-Spelling Card

2 **Guided Practice/Practice** Have children practice connecting the letters *i, y, igh,* and *ie* to the sound /ī/ by writing them. *Now do it with me. Say /ī/ as I write the letters* i, y, ie, *and* igh. *This time, write the letters three times as you say the /ī/ sound.*

Have children independently practice long *i*: *i, y, igh, ie* using **Practice Book** page 192.

DIFFERENTIATED INSTRUCTION ❱

TIER 2

Approaching Level If children are having difficulty with long *i*: *i, y, igh, ie*:

I Do Display the *Five* Sound-Spelling Card. Say: *This is the* Five *Sound-Spelling Card. The sound is /ī/. The /ī/ sound can be spelled with the letters* i, g, h. *Write the letters* i, g, h *while saying /ī/ five times. Repeat for the sound-spellings* y, ie, *and* i.

We Do *Now do it with me.* Have children write the letters *i, g, h* while saying /ī/. Write the letters *i, g, h* five times and say /ī/ with children. Repeat for *y, ie,* and *i*.

You Do Have children connect the letters *i, g, h* to the sound /ī/ by tracing lowercase *i, g, h* in the air while saying /ī/. They should then write the letters *i, g, h* while saying /ī/ five to ten times. Repeat with *y, ie,* and *i*.

Repeat, connecting the letters *i, y, igh,* and *ie* to the sound /ī/ through tracing and writing the letters throughout the week.

You may wish to review Phonics with **ELL** using this section.

Phonics: page 192

Blend Words with Long *i: i, y, igh, ie*

1 **Model** Display **Word-Building Cards** *t, i, e.* Say: *This is the letter* t. *It makes the /t/ sound. These are the letters* i *and* e. *Together,* i *and* e *can make the /ī/ sound. Listen as I blend: /tīīī/. The word is* tie.

Continue by modeling the words *mild, my, shy, night,* and *lie,* pointing out the *i, y, igh,* and *ie* sound-spellings.

2 **Guided Practice/Practice** Display the Phonics/Fluency Practice chart. Read each word in the first row, blending the sounds—for example, say: */ssskīīī/. The word is* sky. Have children blend each word with you. Prompt children to read the connected text, sounding out the decodable words.

sky	high	wild	rind	fry
grind	my	tie	try	pie
night	shy	spy	bright	mind
grain	spill	weigh	spray	will

Bright lights shine high in the night sky.

The girls shine their lights right at the tent.

What a nice sight it is in the daylight!

Phonics/Fluency Practice

DIFFERENTIATED INSTRUCTION

TIER 2

Approaching Level If children are having difficulty blending words:

I Do Display Word-Building Cards *f, i, n, d.* Say: *This is the letter* f. *It stands for /fff/. This is the letter* i. *It can stand for the sound /ī/. Listen: /īīī/. This is the letter* n. *It stands for /nnn/. This is the letter* d. *It stands for /d/. I'll blend all the sounds together: /fff īīīnnnd/,* find. *Repeat with* child, dry, right, sight, lie, tried.

We Do Guide children to blend the sounds and read these words: *my, cry, hi, kind, night, might, tie, pie.* Provide corrective feedback until children can work on their own.

You Do Have children blend and read: *try, shy, mind, wild, bright, fright, cried, die.* Offer corrective feedback if necessary.

Repeat, blending additional words with long *i* spelled *i, y, igh, ie.*

You may wish to review Phonics with **ELL** using this section.

Corrective Feedback

Sound Error Model the sound that children missed, and then have them repeat the sound. Say: *My turn.* Tap under the letter or letters and say: *Sound? /ī/. What's the sound?* Return to the beginning of the word. Say: *Let's start over.* Blend the word with children again.

 **English Language Learners**

See page 5 in the **Language Transfers Handbook** for guidance in identifying phonics skills that may or may not transfer for speakers of certain languages and for support in accommodating those children. See the chart on pages 10–13 for specific phonics transfer issues for multiple languages.

Digital Tools

To differentiate instruction for key skills, use the results of this activity.

Phonics

OBJECTIVES

- Read words with open syllables.
- Decode regularly spelled two-syllable words with long vowels.

ACADEMIC LANGUAGE

- *syllable*

English Language Learners

Model Confirm children understand the basic and academic vocabulary for the lesson: *syllable, long/short vowel sound, open syllable.*

Guided Practice Provide frames for children to use when they identify open syllables: The <u>first</u> syllable in <u>silent</u> is <u>/sī/</u>. The syllable <u>/sī/</u> is an open syllable. I know because <u>/sī/</u> has the <u>long i sound /ī/</u>.

Digital Tools

For more practice, have children use this activity.

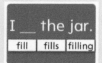

I __ the jar.
fill	fills	filling

Structural Analysis

Structural Analysis

OPTION **5** Mins

Open Syllables

1 **Model** Write the word *pilot* and read it aloud. Draw a line to divide the word into syllables. Explain to children that some words can be divided into syllables, or word parts. Explain that every syllable in a word has one vowel sound. Say: *Look at the word:* pilot. *I will clap the syllables as I say it:* pi *(clap)* lot *(clap). The word* pilot *has two syllables, or word parts:* pi-lot. *The first syllable is* /pī/. *The first syllable ends in one vowel. This is called an open syllable. Most open syllables have a long vowel sound. The first syllable in* pilot *has the long i sound,* /ī/: pi. Point out the second syllable in the word *pilot.* Guide children to understand that they may need to approximate sounds when reading multisyllabic words.

2 **Guided Practice/Practice** Write the following words: *silent, item, basic, bison.* Read each word with children. Next, have children clap out the syllables as they read each word again. Then have children identify the open syllables. (<u>si</u>/lent, <u>i</u>/tem, <u>ba</u>/sic, <u>bi</u>/son).

DIFFERENTIATED INSTRUCTION ››

TIER 2

Approaching Level If children are having difficulty with open syllables:

I Do Write *agent.* Read the word aloud and clap the syllables. *The word* agent *has two syllables, or word parts. The first syllable,* /ā/, *ends in a vowel sound,* /āāā/. *This is called an open syllable. An open syllable ends in a vowel sound, which is almost always a long vowel sound.*

We Do Write *item.* Say: *Let's read the word and clap the syllables:* /ī/ *(clap)* /təm/ *(clap). The word* item *has two syllables:* /ī/ *and* /təm/. *The first syllable,* /ī/, *ends with a vowel sound. It is an open syllable. The second syllable,* /təm/, *ends with the consonant* /m/ *sound. It is not an open syllable.*

You Do Have partners work together. Give them several one- or two-syllable words with long *i* and long *a.* Have them say the words and circle the open syllables.

Repeat Have children use their open syllable words in sentences.

High-Frequency Words

also, apart, begin, either, hundred, over, places, those, which, without

1 **Model** Display the **High-Frequency Word Cards** and use the Read/Spell/Write routine to teach each word.

- **Read** Point to and say the word *also*. *This is the word* also. *Say it with me:* also. *I like soccer, but I also like baseball.*

- **Spell** *The word* also *is spelled* a-l-s-o. *Spell it with me.*

- **Write** *Let's write the word in the air as we say each letter:* a-l-s-o.

- As children spell each word with you, point out any patterns in sound-spellings; for example, *which* has two consonant digraphs: *wh* and *ch*.

- Have partners create sentences using each word.

2 **Guided Practice/Practice** Have children identify the high-frequency words in connected text and blend the decodable words.

1. Bill and I will be there **also**.
2. She rips the tickets **apart**.
3. Do not **begin** until I am done.
4. You can pick **either** A, B, or C.
5. We won one **hundred** games!
6. I'll jump **over** those logs.
7. Are these good **places** to rest?
8. **Those** are Luke's green pants.
9. **Which** way should we go?
10. I go right home **without** a stop.

DIFFERENTIATED INSTRUCTION

TIER 2

Approaching Level If children need support with high-frequency words:

I Do Use the High-Frequency Word Cards. Follow this routine for each word: Display the word. Read the word. Spell the word.

We Do Ask children to state the word and spell the word with you. Model using the word in a sentence, and have children repeat.

You Do Display the words randomly for children to say and spell. Provide opportunities for children to use the words in conversation. Have children write each word in their Writer's Notebook.

OBJECTIVES

- Know and apply grade-level phonics and word-analysis skills in decoding words.

- Recognize and read grade-appropriate irregularly spelled words.

English Language Learners

Model Use visual cues, gestures, and examples to help children learn the meanings of the high-frequency words. Point out the Spanish cognate *aparte*. Point out and explain the multiple-meaning words *over* and *places*.

Digital Tools

For more practice, have children use this activity.

High-Frequency Words

Decodable Reader, Vol. 3

OBJECTIVES

- Know and apply grade-level phonics and word-analysis skills in decoding words.

- Recognize and read grade-appropriate irregularly spelled words.

- Read on-level text with purpose and understanding.

- Read with sufficient accuracy and fluency to support comprehension.

- Identify, trace, and write lowercase cursive letters *j, p, r,* and *s.*

 **English Language Learners**

Check Comprehension Use frames, as needed, to help children answer questions: p. 25 Stars shine because they are made of hot gases that let off light. p. 26 Stars are different sizes. p. 27 The sun is closest to Earth. p. 30 You can use a telescope to see stars.

Decodable Reader: "High in the Sky"

Focus on Foundational Skills

Review the words and letter-sounds that children will find in the **Decodable Reader.** Review the high-frequency words *also, apart, begin, either, hundred, over, places, those, which,* and *without.* Remind children that *i, y, igh,* and *ie* can stand for the /ī/ sound.

Preview and Predict Point to the title of the selection and have children sound out each word with you. Ask: *What do you see in the photograph?*

Read the Decodable Reader

Begin to read the selection "High in the Sky." On page 24, have children point to each word, sounding out decodable words and saying high-frequency words quickly. If children need support reading decodable words, model blending. If children are having difficulty with high-frequency words, reread the word in isolation and then in context.

Check Comprehension

p. 25 *Why do stars shine in the sky?*
p. 26 *Are all stars the same size?*
p. 27 *Which star is closest to Earth?*
p. 30 *How can you watch stars in the night sky?*
Retell Have partners use key ideas and details to retell "High in the Sky."

Focus on Fluency

 With partners, have children read "High in the Sky" to focus on accuracy. Guide them to run their fingers under the text as they read. Children should note whether they are correctly reading the words on the page. As children read, they can monitor themselves and provide feedback to their partners.

Listen in: If children are having difficulty reading accurately, have them start again at the beginning of the page. If children are reading too quickly, suggest to them that they should slow down and read as they speak.

 English Language Learners

Focus on Fluency Before reading "High in the Sky," point out the potential pronunciation challenges in each section so children can practice the words in isolation beforehand. Have children first echo read each section after you, then choral read with you.

5 Mins

Handwriting: *j, p, r, s*

Model Say the handwriting cues as you write lowercase *j, p, r, s.*

 *Begin at the bottom line and curve up to the middle line. Slant down through the bottom line. Loop left, cross over just below the bottom line and curve up to the middle line. Lift. Place a dot above the letter.*

 *Begin at the bottom line, curve up to the middle line, and slant down through the bottom line to the top line of the next row. Loop left and curve over at the middle line. Continue curving around to meet the bottom and slant lines. Curve up to the middle line.*

 *Begin at the bottom line and curve up to the middle line. Slant slightly to the right, then slant downward to the bottom line. Curve up to the middle line.*

 *Begin at the middle line. Curve up to the middle line. Curve over and back to touch the first stroke. Curve up to the middle line.*

Guided Practice/Practice

- Distribute **Response Boards**. Have children say the name of each letter as they write it. When finished, have children note the differences.
- Point out that both *j* and *p* should have a point at the top and that the bottom slant and loop should reach the top of the next row.
- Remind children to bring the *r* back down to the bottom line and end with a stroke that curves up before connecting to another letter.

Daily Handwriting

During the week, use models to review cursive letter formation. Have children independently practice *j, p, r, s* with **Practice Book** pp. 198–199.

Handwriting: pages 198–199

✔ Check for Success

Rubric Use the online rubric to record children's progress.

Can children decode words with long *i: i, y, igh, ie?*

Can children identify and read the high-frequency words?

Differentiate
SMALL GROUP INSTRUCTION

If No

| Approaching | pp. T106–T107, T109 |
| ELL | pp. T106–T107, T109 |

If Yes

| On | p. T140 |
| Beyond | p. T146 |

Daily Focus

Phonemic Awareness
• Phoneme Substitution

Phonics
• Blend and Build Words with Long *i: i, y, igh, ie*

Structural Analysis
• Open Syllables

Reread
• Decodable Reader, Vol. 3: "High in the Sky"

OBJECTIVES
• Substitute phonemes to form new words.

ACADEMIC LANGUAGE
• substitute
• Cognate: *substituto*

Phonemic Awareness: page 191

OPTION 5 Mins

Phonemic Awareness

Phoneme Substitution

1 Model Show children how substituting a new sound for the medial or final vowel sound in a word can form a new word. Say: *Listen for the sounds in the word* pie: /p/ /ī/. *Now listen as I substitute, or change, the vowel sound in* pie *from /ī/ to /ā/. The vowel sound in the new word is /ā/. The new word is /p//ā/,* pay. *I changed* pie *to* pay.

Continue by changing the medial or final vowel sound. Use these pairs:

sleigh/sly	tray/try	mend/mind	low/lie

2 Guided Practice/Practice *Listen for the vowel sound in each word. Then listen for the new sound. Substitute the new vowel sound and say the new word. The word is* shy, /sh/, /ī/. *The new sound is /ō/. Change the /ī/ to /ō/. What's the new word?* (show) Repeat by substituting /a/ for /ī/ in *hind;* /ō/ for /ī/ in *sigh.* (hand, so) Then have children substitute the vowel sound in the middle or at the end of each of the following words to create new words.

hay/high	my/me	shy/show
pine/pain	sigh/say	tie/toe

Have children independently practice phoneme substitution using **Practice Book** page 191.

DIFFERENTIATED INSTRUCTION >

TIER 2

Approaching Level If children have difficulty with phoneme substitution:

I Do Explain to children that they will be substituting sounds to form words. *When you substitute a sound, you trade it for a different sound. When I trade the /m/ sound in* mild *for /w/, I change the word from* mild *to* wild.

We Do *Listen as I say a word:* high. *Let's change /h/ in* high *to /s/: /sī/,* sigh. *The new word is* sigh. Repeat with these word pairs:

dried/fried	my/by	mind/kind	slight/flight

You Do *It's your turn. Substitute the first sound to form a new word.*

child/wild	sly/fly	thigh/high	wind/bind

Repeat the substitution routine with additional long *i* words.

You may wish to review Phonemic Awareness with **ELL** using this section.

Phonics

OPTION 5 Mins

Review Long *i: i, y, igh, ie*

1 **Model** Display the *Five* **Sound-Spelling Card**. Review the sound /ī/ spelled *i, y, igh,* and *ie* using the words *mind, by, tight,* and *pie.*

2 **Guided Practice/Practice** Have children practice connecting the letters to the long *i* sound. Point to the *i, y, igh,* and *ie* spellings on the Sound-Spelling Card. *What are the letters? What sound do these letters stand for?*

DIFFERENTIATED INSTRUCTION ›

TIER 2

Approaching Level If children are having difficulty with long *i: i, y, igh, ie:*

I Do Display the *Five* Sound-Spelling Card. Say: *This is the* Five *Sound-Spelling Card. The sound is /ī/. The /ī/ sound can be spelled with the letters* i *and* e. Write *ie* while saying /ī/ five times. Repeat with the *y, igh,* and *i* spellings.

We Do *Now do it with me.* Have children write *ie* while saying /ī/. Write *ie* five times and say /ī/ with children. Repeat with the long *i* spellngs *y, igh, i.*

You Do Have children connect the letters *i, e* to the sound /ī/ by tracing *i, e* in the air while saying /ī/. They should then write the letters *ie* while saying /ī/ five to ten times. Repeat with *y, igh, i.*

Repeat, connecting the letters *i, y, igh,* and *ie* to the sound /ī/ through tracing and writing the letters throughout the week.

You may wish to review Phonics with **ELL** using this section.

OBJECTIVES

- Know and apply grade-level phonics and word analysis skills in decoding words.
- Distinguish long and short vowels when reading regularly spelled one-syllable words.

SOUND-SPELLING REVIEW ›

Build Fluency

Display the **Word-Building Cards** for *i, igh, ie, y, a, ai, ay, ei, eigh, ey, scr, spr, str, thr, spl, shr.* Have children say each sound. Repeat, and vary the pace.

Digital Tools

For more practice, have children use this activity.

Phonemic Awareness

To differentiate instruction for key skills, use the results of this activity.

Phonics

OBJECTIVES

- Know and apply grade-level phonics and word analysis skills in decoding words.
- Blend and build words with long vowels.
- Apply phonics when decoding words with long *i*.

English Language Learners

Guided Practice/Practice
Use visuals, gestures, and examples to teach children the meanings of any example words that are unfamiliar. For example, ask children to point to a *light* or something that is *high*. Model actions. Say, "I will *try* a slice of *pie*." Have children repeat. Provide sentence starters for children to complete, such as: A bird can fly in the <u>sky</u>.

Phonics

(5 Mins)

Blend Words with Long *i*: *i, y, igh, ie*

1 **Model** Display **Word-Building Cards** *c, r, y* to form the word *cry*. Model how to generate and blend the sounds. *This is the letter* c. *It stands for* /k/. *This is the letter* r. *It stands for* /r/. *This is the letter* y. *It stands for* /ī/. *Listen as I blend these sounds together:* /krrrīī/. *The word I made is* cry.

Continue modeling by blending the words *my, tie, bright,* and *kind*.

2 **Guided Practice/Practice** Repeat the routine with children with *light, pie, try, high, fly, sky, sight, wild, mild,* and *fright*.

Guide practice until children can work independently. Provide corrective feedback as necessary.

DIFFERENTIATED INSTRUCTION ➤

TIER 2

Approaching Level If children are having difficulty blending words with long *i: i, y, igh, ie*:

I Do Display Word-Building Cards *m, i, n, d.* Say: *This is the letter* m. *It stands for* /m/. *Listen:* /m/. *This is the letter* i. *It can stand for the sound* /ī/. *Listen to the sound:* /īī/. *This is the letter* n. *It stands for* /n/. *This is the letter* d. *It stands for* /d/. *Listen:* /d/. *I'll blend all four sounds together:* /mmmīīnnnd/, mind. Repeat with *wild, fry, night, slight, lie, cried.*

We Do Guide children to blend the sounds and read: *by, why, hi, mild, sight, flight, tie.* Offer corrective feedback if children need further support.

You Do Have children blend and decode: *shy, spy, find, child, slight, fight, tried, died.*

Repeat, blending additional words with long *i* spelled *i, y, igh, ie.*

You may wish to review Phonics with **ELL** using this section.

Build Words with Long *i: i, y, igh, ie*

Provide children with **Word-Building Cards** for the alphabet. Have children put the letters in order from *a* to *z*.

1 **Model** Display the Word-Building Cards *l, i, g, h, t.* Blend /lll/ /ī/ /t/, /lllīīīt/, *light.*

- Replace *l* with *br* and repeat with *bright.*
- Replace *br* with *fl* and repeat with *flight.*

2 **Guided Practice/Practice** Continue with *tight, thigh, tie, try, dry, sty, sky, why, wild, wind, kind, find.* Guide children to build and blend each word.

Once children have built the words, dictate the words to children and have them write the words. Children can work with a partner to check their spelling.

Digital Tools

To differentiate instruction for key skills, use the results of this activity.

Phonics

DIFFERENTIATED INSTRUCTION

TIER 2

Approaching Level If children are having difficulty building words:

I Do Display Word-Building Cards *f, r, y. These are letters* f, r, y. *They stand for the sounds* /f/ /r/ /ī/. *I will blend* /fff/ /rrr/ /īī/ *together:* /fffrrrīī/, fry. *The word is* fry.

We Do Say: *Let's do one together.* Change the letter *f* to *t. Let's blend:* /t/ /rrr/ /īī/, /trrrīī/, try. Change the letter *t* to *c.* Say: *Let's blend and read the new word:* /k/ /rrr/ /īī/, /krrrīī/, cry.

You Do Have children continue to build with the words: *cried, tried, try, tie, lie, light, sight, sigh.* Offer corrective feedback if necessary.

You may wish to review Phonics with **ELL** using this section.

OBJECTIVES

- Read words with open syllables.
- Decode regularly spelled two-syllable words with long vowels.

Digital Tools

For more practice, have children use this activity.

Structural Analysis

Structural Analysis: page 194

(5 Mins) Structural Analysis

Open Syllables

1 Model Write the word *final* and read it aloud. Draw a line to divide the word into syllables. Explain to children that some words can be divided into syllables, or word parts. Explain that every syllable in a word has one vowel sound. Say: *Look at the word:* final. *I will clap the syllables as I say it:* fi *(clap)* nal *(clap). The word* final *has two syllables, or word parts. The first syllable is /fī/. The first syllable ends with one vowel. This is called an open syllable. Most open syllables have a long vowel sound. The first syllable in* final *has the long* i *sound. Listen:* fi-nal. Point out the second syllable in the word *final.* Explain to children that they may need to approximate sounds when reading multisyllabic words.

2 Guided Practice/Practice Write the following words: *minus, tiger, vacant, bison.* Read each word with children. Next, have children clap out the syllables as they read each word again. Then have children identify the open syllables. (mi/nus, ti/ger, va/cant, bi/son)

Have children independently practice words with open syllables using **Practice Book** page 194.

DIFFERENTIATED INSTRUCTION

TIER 2

Approaching Level If children are having difficulty with open syllables:

I Do Say: *Words are made of parts called syllables. A syllable contains a vowel sound.* Write *siren* and clap the syllables. Say: *The word* siren *has two syllables. The first syllable,* si-, *ends in a vowel sound. It is an open syllable.*

We Do Say: *Listen to this word:* pilot. *Let's clap the syllables. Listen for a long vowel sound. Say it with me:* pilot. *What sound do you hear at the end of the first syllable? We hear an /ī/ at the end of* pi. *The first syllable is an open syllable.*

Repeat this routine with the following examples: *halo, crisis, diver, iris.* Provide corrective feedback as necessary.

You Do Say: *Now it's your turn. Clap the syllables in each word. Tell which syllables are open syllables.*

vital   bison   rhino   climate   cider   silent

Repeat Have children identify open syllables in additional words with long *i: i, y, igh, ie.*

Decodable Reader:
Reread "High in the Sky"

OPTION 5 Mins

Focus on Foundational Skills

Review the words with long *i* spelled *i, y, igh, ie* as well as the high-frequency words *also, apart, begin, either, hundred, over, places, those, which,* and *without* that children will find in the **Decodable Reader**.

Decodable Reader, Vol. 3

Reread the Decodable Reader

Guide children in rereading "High in the Sky." Point out the high-frequency words and the words with long *i: i, y, igh, ie.*

Reread the Book On page 27, have children point to each word, sounding out the decodable words and saying the high-frequency words quickly.

Check Comprehension

Remind children that they can ask themselves questions to make sure they understood what they have read. Have children use both text and photographs to answer their questions.

Retell Have partners use key ideas and details to retell "High in the Sky."

Focus on Fluency

Review Remind children that part of reading with expression is using your voice to show feeling. When they read an exclamation, they can show surprise, shock, or excitement. When they read a question, their voice can go up at the end to show curiosity, interest, or confusion.

COLLABORATE

Practice Have children practice reading from the Decodable Reader to a partner. Have them concentrate on both accuracy and appropriate rate. Remind them to raise their voice at the end of a question and to read with appropriate emphasis and excitement. Offer corrective feedback as necessary.

OBJECTIVES

- Know and apply grade-level phonics and word-analysis skills in decoding words.
- Recognize and read grade-appropriate irregularly spelled words.
- Read on-level text with purpose and understanding.
- Read with sufficient accuracy and fluency to support comprehension.

✓ Check for Success

Rubric Use the online rubric to record children's progress.

Can children decode words with long *i: i, y, igh, ie?*

Can children identify and read the high-frequency words?

Differentiate
SMALL GROUP INSTRUCTION

If No

| Approaching | pp. T113–T116 |
| ELL | pp. T113–T116 |

If Yes

| On | p. T140 |
| Beyond | p. T146 |

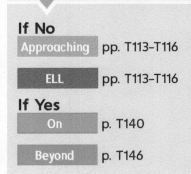

Daily Focus

Phonemic Awareness
• Phoneme Blending

Phonics
• Contrast Vowel Sounds; Blend and Build Words with Long *i: i, y, igh, ie*

Structural Analysis
• Open Syllables

High-Frequency Words

Read
• Decodable Reader, Vol. 3: "A Bright Flight"

A Bright Flight

OBJECTIVES

• Blend phonemes to form new words.

Phonemic Awareness

5 Mins

Phoneme Blending

1 **Model** Place markers on the **Response Board** to represent sounds. Show children how to orally blend phonemes. *I'll say three sounds. As I say each sound, I'm going to put one marker in each box. Then I'll blend the sounds to form a word.* Place a marker for each sound you say: /l/ /ī/ /t/. *This word has three sounds: /l/ /ī/ /t/. Listen as I blend the sounds to form a word: /lllīīīt/, light. The word is* light.

2 **Guided Practice/Practice** *Let's do some together. Using your own boards, place a marker for each sound you hear. I will say one sound at a time. Then we will blend the sounds to say the word.*

/t/ /r/ /ī/ (try)   /p/ /r/ /ī/ /z/ (prize)   /s/ /l/ /ī/ /t/ (slight)

/p/ /ā/ (pay)   /p/ /r/ /ī/ (pry)   /ch/ /ī/ /l/ /d/ (child)

/s/ /ī/ (sigh)   /m/ /ī/ /t/ (might)   /g/ /r/ /ī/ /n/ /d/ (grind)

/t/ /ī/ (tie)   /th/ /i/ /s/ (this)   /d/ /r/ /ī/ /d/ (dried)

> **DIFFERENTIATED INSTRUCTION**
>
> **TIER 2**
>
> **Approaching Level** If children have difficulty blending phonemes:
>
> **I Do** Explain to children that they will be blending sounds to form words. *Listen as I say two sounds: /h/ /ī/. Say the sounds with me: /h/ /īīī/. I'm going to blend the sounds together to say a word: /h/ /īīī/, /hīīī/. We blended the word* high.
>
> **We Do** *Listen as I say three sounds: /rrr/ /īīī/ /t/. Say the sounds with me: /rrr/ /īīī/ /t/. Let's blend the sounds: /rrr/ /īīī/ /t/, /rrrīīīt/,* right. *We made a word:* right. Repeat this routine with:
>
> find   child   cry   sight   by   wild   fly
>
> **You Do** Say: *It's your turn. I want you to blend the sounds I say to form a new word.* Give corrective feedback to children as needed.
>
> /sh/ /ī/ (shy)   /f/ /r/ /ī/ /t/ (fright)   /k/ /r/ /ī/ /d/ (cried)
>
> /h/ /ī/ (high)   /k/ /ī/ /n/ /d/ (kind)   /n/ /ī/ /t/ (night)
>
> /l/ /ī/ (lie)   /m/ /ī/ /l/ /d/ (mild)   /t/ /r/ /ī/ (try)
>
> **Repeat** the blending routine with additional words with long *i: i, y, igh, ie.*
>
> You may wish to review Phonemic Awareness with **ELL** using this section.

Phonics

5 Mins

Contrast Vowel Sounds

1 **Model** Say: *Let's listen to some words that have one sound that is different.* Display **Word-Building Cards** for long *i: i_e, i, y, igh, ie* and for long *a: a_e, ay, ai, ei, eigh.* As you say each vowel sound, point to the letter(s) for that sound. For example, say: *These are the letters* i,e. *They stand for the /ī/ sound.* Repeat for all the sound-spellings. Say: *I will say two words and point to the letters that stand for the vowel sound.* lie, lay. *When I say* lie, *I point to* ie. *The vowel sound in* lie *is /īīī/. When I say* lay, *I point to* ay. *The vowel sound in* lay *is /āāā/.* Repeat the routine with these word pairs: *high/hay, pile/pail.*

COLLABORATE

2 **Guided Practice/Practice** *Let's do some together. Listen as I say two words:* wild, wailed. *What vowel sounds can we hear in each word? Let's hold up Word-Building Cards for the vowel sounds.* Hold up *i* for *wild* and *ai* for *wailed.* Continue, having children work with a partner and take turns with their own set of Word-Building Cards. Say: *When I say a word, listen to the vowel sound. Then pick up the correct Word-Building Card that stands for that sound and hold it up.* Guide practice and give corrective feedback to partners as needed with these pairs:

tried/trade   sigh/say   bite/bait   spied/spade   why/weigh

DIFFERENTIATED INSTRUCTION

TIER 2

Approaching Level If children are having difficulty with contrasting vowel sounds, reteach:

I Do Display Word-Building Cards for long *i: i, y, igh, ie* and long *a: ay, ai, ei, eigh.* Say: *I will say the vowel sound as I point to the sound-spelling.* Review sound-spellings with example words.

We Do Provide children with the Word-Building Cards for long *i: i, y, igh, ie* and long *a: ay, ai, ei, eigh.* Have children trace the letters of each sound-spelling as they say the long vowel sound.

You Do Say: *Listen to each word and hold up the cards that stand for the vowel sound you hear.* Say one word at a time, emphasizing the vowel sound. Use the following words:

tie   stay   fly   mind   pail   vein   sleigh   sigh

Guide practice and provide corrective feedback as necessary until children are able to work on their own.

You may wish to review Phonics with **ELL** using this section.

OBJECTIVES

- Know and apply grade-level phonics and word analysis skills in decoding words.

- Distinguish long and short vowels when reading regularly spelled one-syllable words.

SOUND-SPELLING REVIEW

Build Fluency
Display the Word-Building Cards: *i, igh, ie, y, a, ai, ay, ei, eigh, ey, scr, spr, str, thr, spl, shr.* Have children say each sound. Repeat, and vary the pace.

Digital Tools

For more practice, have children use this activity.

Phonemic Awareness

To differentiate instruction for key skills, use the results of this activity.

Phonics

OBJECTIVES

- Know and apply grade-level phonics and word analysis skills in decoding words.

- Distinguish long and short vowels when reading regularly spelled one-syllable words.

- Identify letter-sound correspondences for long *i* spelled *i, y, igh, ie*.

- Apply phonics when decoding words with long *i*.

Phonics

OPTION 5 Mins

Blend Words with Long *i: i, y, igh, ie*

1 **Model** Display the **Word-Building Cards** *f, l, y*. Remind children that the letter *y* can stand for the long *i* sound. Model how to blend the sounds. Say: *Let's blend these letters to make a word. This is the letter f. It stands for /f/. This is the letter l. It stands for /l/. This is the letter y. It can stand for /ī/. Listen ; I will blend the three sounds together: /ffflllīī/. The word is* fly.

Continue by modeling the words *spy, tie, kind,* and *night*.

2 **Guided Practice/Practice** Repeat the blending routine with the words *sky, cry, might, pie, fried, lie, sigh, pint, rind,* and *by*.

Have children independently practice long *i: i, y, igh, ie* using **Practice Book** page 193.

DIFFERENTIATED INSTRUCTION ≫

TIER 2

Approaching Level If children are having difficulty blending words with long *i* spelled *i, y, igh, ie:*

I Do Display Word-Building Cards *w, i, n, d*. *This is the letter* w. *It stands for /w/. This is the letter* i. *It can stand for /ī/. This is the letter* n. *It stands for /n/. The letter* d *stands for /d/. Listen as I blend all four sounds together: /www/ /īī/ /nnn/ /d/,* wind. *The word is* wind.

We Do Say: *Let's do some together.* Blend and read the words *find, fly, sky, bright, sight, lie, tie*. Give corrective feedback if children need additional support.

You Do Display the words *right, try, mind, blind, high*. Have children blend and read the words.

You may wish to review Phonics with **ELL** using this section.

Phonics: page 193

Build Words with Long *i: i, y, igh, ie*

Provide children with **Word-Building Cards** *a* to *z*. Have children put the letters in alphabetical order as quickly as possible.

1 **Model** Display the Word-Building Cards *s, i, g, h*. Blend /s/ /ī/, /sssīī/, *sigh*.

- Add *t* and repeat with *sight*.
- Replace *s* with *sl* and repeat with *slight*.
- Replace *ight* with *y* and repeat with *sly*.

2 **Guided Practice/Practice** Continue with *cry, cried, dried, dry, why, wild, mild, mind, might, fight, flight, fly*. Guide children to build and blend each word. Children can work with a partner to check their spelling.

DIFFERENTIATED INSTRUCTION

TIER 2 | **Approaching Level** If children need more support building words:

I Do Display Word-Building Cards *c, r, y. These are letters* c, r, y. *They stand for the sounds* /k/ /r/ /ī/. *I will blend* /k/ /rrrr/ /īīī/ *together:* /krrrīī/, *cry. The word is* cry.

We Do Say: *Now, let's do one together.* Change the letter *c* to *t. Let's blend:* /t/ /rrr/ /īīī/, try. Change the letter *t* to *f.* Say: *Let's blend and read the new word:* /fff/ /rrr/ /īīī/, /fffrrrīī/, fry.

You Do Have children build the words: *dry, pry, pie, tie, lie, light, night, fright, right*. Children can work with a partner to check their spelling.

You may wish to review Phonics with **ELL** using this section.

DAY 8 >> Word Work

OBJECTIVES

- Read words with open syllables.
- Decode regularly spelled two-syllable words with long vowels.

Digital Tools

For more practice, have children use this activity.

Structural Analysis

OPTION 5 Mins

Structural Analysis

Open Syllables

1 **Model** Say and write the word *silent*. Say: *Remember that words are made of parts called syllables. Each syllable in a word has one vowel sound. Listen for the number of syllables in this word: /sī/ /lent/.* Clap as you say each syllable.

Say: *The word* silent *has two syllables. The first syllable in* silent *ends with one vowel. This is called an open syllable. The vowel sound in an open syllable is most often a long vowel sound. Listen for the long vowel sound in the first syllable: /sī/ /lent/.* Circle the *si.*

2 **Guided Practice/Practice** Display and have children say the words *bacon, Friday, icicle, vacant, siren, April,* and *item.* Lead children to clap out the syllables in each word. Have them identify the open syllable in each word and then identify the letters that make the long vowel sound at the end of each open syllable.

DIFFERENTIATED INSTRUCTION >>

TIER 2

Approaching Level If children are having difficulty with open syllables, reteach:

I Do Say: *Words are made of parts called syllables. A syllable contains a vowel sound.* Write *prefix* and clap the syllables. Say: Prefix *has two syllables. The first syllable,* pre-, *ends in a vowel sound. It is an open syllable.*

We Do Say: *Listen to this word:* minus, *Let's clap the syllables. Listen for a long vowel sound. Say it with me:* minus. *What sound do you hear at the end of the first syllable? We hear an /ī/ at the end of* mi. *The first syllable is an open syllable.*

Repeat this routine with the following examples: *bicycle, tiger, opening, rhino, iron, favor.*

You Do Say: *Now it's your turn. Clap the syllables in each word. Tell which syllables are open syllables.*

wider   agent   bison   climate   digest   basic

Repeat Have children identify open syllables in additional words with two and three syllables.

High-Frequency Words

OBJECTIVES
- Know and apply grade-level phonics and word-analysis skills in decoding words.
- Recognize and read grade-appropriate irregularly spelled words.

also, apart, begin, either, hundred, over, places, those, which, without

1 **Model** Say each word and have children Read/Spell/Write it. Ask children to picture the word, and write it the way they see it. Display the answers for children to self-correct.

2 **Guided Practice** Have children identify the high-frequency words in connected text and blend the decodable words. Encourage children to make up their own sentences for more practice.

1. Dan **also** wants another snack.
2. Move the beds far **apart**.
3. I will **begin** to learn math.
4. You can go **either** way.
5. Two **hundred** days is a lot.
6. That branch is **over** the house.
7. Here are some **places** to see.
8. Are **those** blue pens mine?
9. Tell me **which** one you chose.
10. I went home **without** my hat.

Have children independently practice the high-frequency words using **Practice Book** page 195.

Practice Add the high-frequency words to the cumulative word bank. Have children work in pairs to make up new sentences for each word.

Cumulative Review Review last week's words using the Read/Spell/Write routine. Repeat the above routine, mixing the words and having children say each one.

Digital Tools

For more practice, have children use this activity.

High-Frequency Words

DIFFERENTIATED INSTRUCTION

TIER 2

Approaching Level If children need support with high-frequency words:

I Do Use the **High-Frequency Word Cards**. Display one word at a time, following the routine: Display the word. Read the word. Then spell the word.

We Do Ask children to state the word and spell the word with you. Model using the word in a sentence and have children repeat after you.

You Do Display the word. Ask children to say the word then spell it. When completed, quickly flip through the word card set as children chorally read the words. Provide opportunities for children to use the words in speaking and writing. For example, provide sentence starters such as: *I like to ride a bike, and I also _____.* Ask children to write each word in their Writer's Notebook.

High-Frequency Words: page 195

Decodable Reader, Vol. 3

OBJECTIVES

- Know and apply grade-level phonics and word-analysis skills in decoding words.

- Recognize and read grade-appropriate irregularly spelled words.

- Read on-level text with purpose and understanding.

- Read with sufficient accuracy and fluency to support comprehension.

Decodable Reader: "A Bright Flight"

5 Mins

Focus on Foundational Skills

Review the words and letter-sounds that children will find in the **Decodable Reader**.

- Review the high-frequency words *over, places,* and *those.*
- Remind children that *i, y, igh, ie* can stand for the /ī/ sound.

Preview and Predict Point to the title of the story and have children sound out each word with you as you run your finger under it. Ask: *What do you see in the picture? Where are Sy and his Mom?*

Read the Decodable Reader

Begin to read the story "A Bright Flight." On page 33, have children point to each word, sounding out the decodable words and saying the high-frequency words quickly. If children need support reading decodable words, model blending for them. If children are having difficulty with high-frequency words, reread the word in isolation and then reread the high-frequency word in context.

Check Comprehension

p. 31 *When was Sy's last flight?*

p. 32 *What did Sy eat on his flight?*

p. 33 *Why did Sy lean over?*

p. 34 *What did Sy see out the window?*

Retell Have partners use key ideas and details to retell "A Bright Flight."

Focus on Fluency

With partners, have children read "A Bright Flight" to focus on accuracy. Guide them to run their fingers under the text as they read. Children should note whether they are correctly reading the words on the page. As children read, they can monitor themselves and provide feedback to their partners.

Listen in: If children are having difficulty reading accurately, have them start again at the beginning of the page. If children are reading too quickly, suggest that they should slow down and read as they speak.

English Language Learners

Check Comprehension Provide sentence frames, as needed, to help children answer the questions:

p. 31 Sy's last flight was on July Fourth.

p. 32 Sy ate rice and a slice of pie on his flight.

p. 33 Sy leaned over so he could see out the window.

p. 34 Sy saw a slight light and then bright fireworks out the window.

Focus on Fluency Before reading "A Bright Flight," point out the potential pronunciation challenges in each section of the story so children can practice the words in isolation beforehand. Have children first echo read each section after you, then choral read with you.

✔ Check for Success

Rubric Use the online rubric to record children's progress.

Can children decode words with long *i: i, y, igh, ie?*

Can children identify and read the high-frequency words?

Differentiate
SMALL GROUP INSTRUCTION

If No

| Approaching | pp. T119–T121, T123 |

| ELL | pp. T119–T121, T123 |

If Yes

| On | p. T140 |

| Beyond | p. T146 |

Daily Focus

Phonemic Awareness
• Phoneme Categorization

Phonics
• Blend and Build Words with Long *i: i, y, igh, ie*

Reread
• Decodable Reader, Vol. 3: "A Bright Flight"

OBJECTIVES
• Sort words by phonemes.

OPTION 5 Mins

Phonemic Awareness

Phoneme Categorization

1 **Model** Say: *Listen carefully as I say three words:* grind, sip, bright. *The words* grind *and* bright *have the /ī/ long vowel sound. The word* sip *does not. The word* sip *does not belong. Repeat with* play, dry, sky.

2 **Guided Practice/Practice** Have children practice with the following examples. Do the first one with them. *I will say three words. Tell me which word does not belong and why.*

fly, see, lie	way, my, shy	tin, mind, sight
map, might, bride	kind, gate, time	why, cry, lay
night, lit, light	sigh, hi, hay	sleep, slight, sly

Provide corrective feedback as children progress to work on their own.

DIFFERENTIATED INSTRUCTION ⟩⟩

TIER 2

Approaching Level If children are having difficulty with phoneme categorization:

I Do Explain to children that they will be categorizing phonemes today. Say: *Listen as I say three words /kīnd /, /brik/, /rīt/. When I say* kind *and* right, *I can hear the /ī/ sound in the middle.* Brick *has the /i/ sound.* Brick *does not belong.*

We Do Say: *Listen as I say three words:* my, high, see. *Which two words have the sound /ī/ at the end?* My *and* high. See *does not have /ī/. It does not belong. Repeat this routine with the following examples:*

paid, child, night	day, cry, way	light, cried, hint

You Do Say: *It's your turn. Which words go together and which word does not belong?*

cake, skate, fright	try, spray, pie	sight, mind, bat

Repeat the categorization routine with additional long *i* words.

You may wish to review Phonemic Awareness with **ELL** using this section.

Phonics

5 Mins

Blend Words with Long *i: i, y, igh, ie*

1 **Model** Display **Word-Building Cards** *s, p, y.* Remind children that the letter *y* can stand for the long *i* sound. Model how to blend the sounds. Say: *Let's blend these letters to make a word. This is the letter s. It stands for /s/. This is the letter p. It stands for /p/. This is the letter y. It can stand for /ī/. Let's blend the three sounds together: / ssspīī/. The word is* spy. Continue by modeling the words *fry, tie, rind,* and *sight.*

2 **Guided Practice/Practice** Repeat the routine with *sky, try, bright, pie, fried, high, pint, grind, highlight,* and *my.*

DIFFERENTIATED INSTRUCTION

TIER 2

Approaching Level If children are having difficulty with blending:

I Do Display Word-Building Cards *k, i, n, d. This is the letter* k. *It stands for /k/. This is the letter* i. *It can stand for /ī/. This is the letter* n. *It stands for /n/. The letter* d *stands for /d/. Listen as I blend all four sounds: /k/ /īī/ /nnn/ /d/, /kīīnnnd/,* kind. *The word is* kind.

We Do Say: *Let's do some together.* Blend and read the words *mind, fly, shy, might, sight, lie, tie.*

You Do Display the words *light, by, pie, bind, blind, sigh.* Have children blend and read the words. Give corrective feedback if children need more support.

You may wish to review Phonics with **ELL** using this section.

OBJECTIVES

- Know and apply grade-level phonics and word analysis skills in decoding words.
- Blend and build words with long vowels.
- Apply phonics when decoding words with long *i.*

SOUND-SPELLING REVIEW

Build Fluency
Display these Word-Building Cards: *i, igh, ie, y, a, ai, ay, ei, eigh, ey, scr, spr, str, thr, spl, shr.* Have children say each sound. Repeat, and vary the pace.

Digital Tools

For more practice, have children use this activity.

Phonemic Awareness

To differentiate instruction for key skills, use the results of this activity.

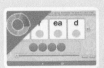

Phonics

OBJECTIVES

- Know and apply grade-level phonics and word analysis skills in decoding words.
- Blend and build words with long vowels.
- Apply phonics when decoding words with long *i*.

STRUCTURAL ANALYSIS REVIEW

Write *lilac* and have children read the word aloud. Remind children that an open syllable ends in one vowel, usually long. Repeat *lilac*, asking children which syllable is open. (li) Then write *siren, pilot, item, biceps,* and *raven* and read them with children. Have partners identify the number of syllables and which syllables are open syllables.

Digital Tools

To differentiate instruction for key skills, use the results of this activity.

Phonics

 ## Phonics

5 Mins

Build Words with Long *i: i, y, igh, ie*

1 **Review** Remind children that the long *i* sound, /ī/, can be spelled *i, y, igh,* and *ie.* Say: *We'll use* **Word-Building Cards** *to build words with long* i. Place the letters *n, i, g, h, t.* Say: *Let's blend the sounds together and read the word. Remember, the letters* igh *together stand for the* /ī/ *sound:* /nnnīīīt/. *Now change the* n *to* f. Blend the sounds and read the word with children: *fight.*

2 **Practice** Have children continue with *sight, slight, light, lie, lied, tied, tie, try, fry,* and *find.*

COLLABORATE

Once children have built the words, dictate the words and have children write the words on a piece of paper. Children can work with a partner to check their words for spelling.

DIFFERENTIATED INSTRUCTION

On Level For more practice building words:

I Do Display Word-Building Cards *w, i, l, d.* Say: *This is the letter* w. *It stands for* /w/. *This is the letter* i. *It can stand for* /ī/. *This is* l. *It stands for* /l/. *This is* d. *It stands for* /d/. *Now listen as I blend the four sounds together:* /wīīīlld/, *wild.*

We Do Say: *Now, let's do one together. let's make the word* wild *using Word-Building Cards. Now we'll change the letter* w *to the letter* m. *Let's blend:* /mmm/ /īī/ /lll/ /d/, /mmmīīīlld/, *mild. The new word is* mild. *Change the letter* m *to* ch. *I will change the letter* m *in* mild *to the letters* ch. *Now let's blend the sounds and read the new word:* /ch/ /īī/ /lll/ /d/, /chīīīlld/, *child. The new word is* child.

You Do Have children build and blend the words: *mild, mind, find, kind; sky, shy, spy, spied, cried, tried, try, tie, pie, lie, light, right, fright., fried, fry, fly, flight.*

Decodable Reader:
Reread "A Bright Flight"

Focus on Foundational Skills

Review with children the words with /ī/ spelled *i, y, igh, ie,* as well as the high-frequency words *over, places,* and *those* that they will find in the **Decodable Reader.**

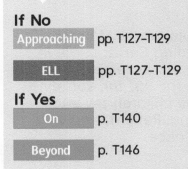

Decodable Reader, Vol. 3

Reread the Decodable Reader

Guide children in rereading "A Bright Flight." Point out the high-frequency words and the words with long *i: i, y, igh, ie.*

Reread the Book On page 34, have children point to each word, sounding out the decodable words and saying the high-frequency words quickly. If children struggle sounding out words, model blending for them.

Check Comprehension

Remind children that they can ask themselves questions to make sure they understand what they are reading. Have them use both text and illustrations to answer their questions.

Retell Have partners use key ideas and details to retell "A Bright Flight."

Focus on Fluency

Review Remind children that part of reading with expression is using your voice to show feeling. When they read an exclamation, they can show surprise, shock, or excitement. When they read a question, their voice can go up at the end to show curiosity, interest, or confusion.

Practice Have children practice reading to a partner with accuracy and at a suitable rate. Remind them to read with appropriate emphasis and excitement. Offer corrective feedback as necessary.

OBJECTIVES

- Know and apply grade-level phonics and word-analysis skills in decoding words.

- Recognize and read grade-appropriate irregularly spelled words.

- Read on-level text with purpose and understanding.

- Read with sufficient accuracy and fluency to support comprehension.

HIGH-FREQUENCY WORDS REVIEW

also, apart, begin, either, hundred, over, places, those, which, without

Have children Read/Spell/Write each word and use it in a sentence. Review last week's words using the same routine.

✓ Check for Success

Rubric Use the online rubric to record children's progress.

Can children decode words with long *i: i, y, igh, ie?*

Can children read the high-frequency words?

Differentiate
SMALL GROUP INSTRUCTION

If No

| Approaching | pp. T127–T129 |
| ELL | pp. T127–T129 |

If Yes

| On | p. T140 |
| Beyond | p. T146 |

Daily Focus

Phonemic Awareness
• Phoneme Blending

Phonics
• Blend and Build Words with Long *i: i, y, igh, ie*

Structural Analysis
• Open Syllables

High-Frequency Words

OBJECTIVES

• Blend phonemes to form words.

• Know and apply grade-level phonics and word-analysis skills in decoding words.

• Know spelling-sound correspondences for additional common vowel teams.

• Blend and build words with long vowels.

• Identify letter-sound correspondences for long *i*.

• Apply phonics when decoding words with long *i*.

• Read words with open syllables.

• Recognize and read grade-appropriate irregularly spelled words.

SOUND-SPELLING REVIEW ≫

Build Fluency
Display these Word-Building Cards: *i, igh, ie, y, a, ai, ay, ei, eigh, ey, scr, spr, str, thr, spl, shr.* Have children say each sound. Repeat, and vary the pace.

OPTION 5 Mins

Phonemic Awareness

Phoneme Blending

Review Guide children to blend phonemes to form words. *Listen as I say a group of sounds. Then blend those sounds to form a word.*

/n/ /ī/ /t/ (night)   /f/ /l/ /ī/ (fly)   /m/ /ī/ /n/ /d/ (mind)

/s/ /k/ /ī/ (sky)   /k/ /r/ /ī/ /d/ (cried)   /ch/ /ī/ /l/ /d/ (child)

5 Mins

Phonics

Blend and Build Words with Long *i: i, y, igh, ie*

Review Write *try, lie, light,* and *kind.* Have children read and say the words. If children have difficulty, remind them to segment the word and blend the sounds. Have children follow the word-building routine with **Word-Building Cards** to build *mild, mind, find, flight, might, my, by, pry, pie, tied.* Once children have built the words, dictate the words and have children write them. Children can work in pairs to check their spelling.

Word Automaticity Help children practice by displaying decodable words and pointing to each one as children chorally read it. Test how many words children can read in one minute. Model blending words that children miss.

DIFFERENTIATED INSTRUCTION ≫

TIER 2

Approaching Level If children need extra support blending and building words with long *i: i, y, igh, ie*

I Do Explain to children that they will be blending sounds to form words. *Listen as I say two sounds: /m/ /ī/. Say the sounds with me: /m/ /īīī/. I'm going to blend the sounds together to say a word: /m/ /īīī/, /mīīī/. We blended the word my.*

We Do *Listen as I say three sounds: /rrr/ /īīī/ /t/. Say the sounds with me: /rrr/ /īīī/ /t/. Let's blend the sounds: /rrr/ /īīī/ /t/, /rrrīīīt/,* right. *We made one word:* right.

Repeat this routine with the following words:

pie   child   sky   shy   night   by   kind   might

You Do Have children blend and build these words: *dry, fly, flies, cries, tries, tight, sight, slight, sly.* Review the meanings of the words.

Repeat, blending/building other words with long *i: i, y, igh, ie.*

You may wish to review Phonics with **ELL** using this section.

Structural Analysis

Open Syllables

Review Remind children that an open syllable ends with one vowel and usually has a long vowel sound. Have children listen to the following words: *virus, minus, finally, unit, opening, silent.* For each word, have children tell the number of syllables. Then have children identify and repeat the open syllables.

High-Frequency Words

also, apart, begin, either, hundred, over, places, those, which, without

Review Have children identify and read the high-frequency words. Display the **High-Frequency Word Cards** for each of the words. Have children Read/Spell/Write each word. Have pairs use the words in conversation. Then have children write a sentence for each word.

DIFFERENTIATED INSTRUCTION

TIER 2 **Approaching Level** If children need extra support with high-frequency words:

I Do Use the High-Frequency Word Cards. Display one word at a time, following the routine: Display the word. Read the word. Then spell the word.

We Do Ask children to state the word and spell the word with you. Model using the word in a sentence and have children repeat after you.

You Do Display the words in random order. Ask children to say the word and then spell it. When completed, quickly flip through the word card set as children chorally read the words. Provide opportunities for children to use the words in speaking and writing. For example, supply sentence starters, such as *Which foods do you like best? I like to eat ___ without ___ .* Ask children to write each word in their Writer's Notebook.

Digital Tools

To differentiate instruction for key skills, use the results of this activity.

Phonics

For more practice, have children use this activity.

Structural Analysis

✓ Check for Success

Rubric Use the online rubric to record children's progress.

Can children decode words with long *i: i, y, igh, ie?*

Can children identify and read the high-frequency words?

Differentiate
SMALL GROUP INSTRUCTIONS

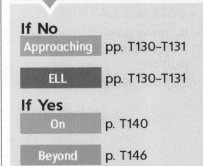

If No

Approaching pp. T130–T131

ELL pp. T130–T131

If Yes

On p. T140

Beyond p. T146

Lexile 290L

OBJECTIVES

Read with sufficient accuracy and fluency to support comprehension.

Ask and answer such questions as *who, what, where, when, why,* and *how* to demonstrate understanding of key details in a text.

Know and use various text features (e.g., captions, bold print, subheadings, glossaries, indexes, electronic menus, icons) to locate key facts or information in a text efficiently.

Explain how specific images (e.g., a diagram showing how a machine works) contribute to and clarify a text.

Identify the main purpose of a text, including what the author wants to answer, explain, or describe.

Participate in collaborative conversations with diverse partners about *grade 2 topics and texts* with peers and adults in small and larger groups.

ACADEMIC LANGUAGE

• *narrative nonfiction, narrator, text features, photographs, captions*

• Cognate: *fotografías*

Approaching Level

Leveled Reader *City Communities*

Preview and Predict

• Read the Essential Question: *How can people help out their community?*

• Have children preview the title, opening pages, headings, and photographs of *City Communities* to make a prediction about the selection. Then discuss the predictions.

Review Genre: Narrative Nonfiction

Have children recall that in narrative nonfiction, a narrator tells a story about a real person. It can have text features, such as headings, photos, and captions.

Close Reading

Note Taking: Ask children to use a copy of the online Author's Purpose **Graphic Organizer 07** as they read to record clues that help them determine the author's purpose.

Think Aloud As I read, I look for clues about the author's purpose. On pages 4 and 6, the author describes ways people help others in a city. Let's add these clues to the Author's Purpose chart.

Guide children to use the clues to determine the author's purpose.

Pages 2–3 *Turn to a partner and explain how neighbors helped the Sanchez family.* (Neighbors helped the family pack their car.) *What did their friends give them to help with the trip?* (a map)

Pages 4–7 *Turn to a partner and each take a turn asking the other a question about people who help in cities. Then answer each other's questions.* (Possible response: How does the neighbor help Mrs. Pavi? The neighbor shows her where to go to buy food and where the library is.) *Who helps children walk to school safely?* (crossing guards)

Pages 8–11 *How does the new friend help Billy Trent?* (The new friend takes Billy to the playground.) *What word on page 10 means almost the same as, or is a synonym for, exhibits?* (displays) *Add this word to your writer's notebook. What do neighbors do at block parties?* (They spend time together and raise money for the neighborhood.)

Pages 12–15 *What features on pages 12 and 13 tell you that this is narrative nonfiction?* (photos and captions) *Talk with a partner. Explain why you think the author wrote this selection.*

Retell Have children take turns retelling the selection using the Retelling cards. Help children make a personal connection by asking: *Do you live in a city or a smaller town? How do people help each other where you live?*

Respond to Reading Have children complete the Respond to Reading questions on page 16.

 Write About Reading In children's responses to question 4 on page 16, check that they are able to accurately determine the author's purpose.

Fluency: Accuracy and Expression

Model Fluency Read aloud pages 2 and 3, one sentence at a time, with accuracy and expression. Have children chorally repeat. Point out that the question mark indicates you should raise your voice at the end of the question and the exclamation mark indicates you should read that sentence with excitement.

Apply Have children practice reading with partners. Provide feedback.

Paired Read: "Magic Anansi"

 Make Connections: Write About It

Before reading, ask children to note that this text is a folktale. Then discuss the Essential Question. After reading, ask children to make connections between what they read in "Magic Anansi" and *City Communities*.

Leveled Reader

Focus On Social Studies

Children can extend their knowledge of ways people help in communities by completing the social studies activity on page 20.

Literature Circles

Lead children in conducting a literature circle using the Thinkmark questions to guide the discussion. You may wish to discuss what children have learned about ways people help in communities from both selections in the Leveled Reader.

LEVEL UP

IF children read the Approaching Level fluently and answered the questions

THEN pair them with children who have proficiently read the On Level and have approaching children

- echo-read the On Level main selection.

- use self-stick notes to mark a clue in each section that helps them determine the author's purpose.

A C T Access Complex Text

The On Level challenges children by including more specific vocabulary and complex sentence structures.

"Helping Out in the Community"
Lexile 420L

OBJECTIVES

Know and use various text features to locate key facts or information in a text efficiently.

Identify the main purpose of a text, including what the author wants to answer, explain, or describe.

Determine or clarify the meaning of unknown and multiple-meaning words and phrases based on grade 2 reading and content, choosing flexibly from an array of strategies.

Recall information from experiences or gather information from provided sources to answer a question.

ACADEMIC LANGUAGE

• *narrative nonfiction, narrator, text features, photographs, captions*

• Cognates: *narrador, texto, fotografías*

Approaching Level

Genre Passage "Helping Out in the Community"

Build Background

- Read aloud the Essential Question: *How can people help out their community?* Ask children to tell how different people help out their communities in the selections they read this week. Use these sentence starters to help focus discussion:

  In City Communities, *people help by* _____

  In "Lighting Lives," Debby Tewa helps by _____

  Helping people is important because _____

- Let children know that the online **Differentiated Genre Passage** "Helping Out in the Community" shows how one man uses bicycles to help out children in his community.

Review Genre: Narrative Nonfiction

Review with children that in narrative nonfiction, a narrator tells a story about a real person and events. The selection may have a beginning, a middle, and an end, like a fiction story, but the person and the events are real. The selection may have text features, such as photographs and captions, to give more information.

Close Reading

Note Taking As children read the passage the first time, ask them to annotate the text. Have them note key ideas and details, unfamiliar words, and questions they have. Then read again and use the following questions. Encourage children to cite text evidence from the selection.

> **Read**

Genre: Narrative Nonfiction *Read the three paragraphs on page A1. Who is telling the story?* (the narrator) *Who is the story about?* (Doug Long) *Is Doug Long a real person or a made-up character?* (He is a real person.) *Is the narrator telling about real events or about imaginary things that could not happen in real life?* (The narrator is telling a story about real events.) **Look at page A2. What text features can you identify?** (a photograph and a caption)

Synonyms Reread the second sentence in the first paragraph on page A1. *Which word in the fourth sentence in this paragraph means almost the same thing as solo?* (alone)

Author's Purpose Reread pages A1 and A2. *Who does the author want the reader to learn about?* (Doug Long) *What does the author want the reader to learn?* (that Doug Long helps children experience nature and helps children earn points to buy their own bikes)

Text Features Reread the caption on page A2. *What key detail does the photograph tell the readers about Doug Long?* (that Doug Long helps children learn about nature) *Turn to a partner and share other key details the author wants the readers to learn about Doug Long.*

Summarize Have children use their notes to summarize the ways that Doug Long helps out in his community.

Reread

Use the questions on page A3 to guide children's rereading of the passage.

Genre: Narrative Nonfiction *How do you know this passage is narrative nonfiction?* (A narrator is telling a true story about a real person. There is also a photograph with a caption to give more information about the text.)

Author's Purpose *Why did the author write this selection?* (to give information about how Doug Long helps in his community)

Text Features: Narrative Nonfiction *Why did the author include the photograph and caption on page A2?* (to show Doug on a ride with children; the caption tells about the photo)

Integrate

Make Connections Guide children to understand the connections between "Helping Out in the Community" and other selections they have read. Have partners find text evidence to answer this question: *How do authors help you understand how people help out in their communities?*

Compare Genres Draw or use **Graphic Organizer 119**, a Compare and Contrast chart. Help children show how different people help out in their communities. Record ways that the community helpers are alike, and ways that they are different. Use information from all of the selections in the genre study.

Differentiate and Collaborate

Be Inspired Have children think about selections they read. Ask: *"What do the texts inspire you to do?"* Use the following activities or have partners think of a way to respond to the texts.

Make a Community Service Poster Have children think about things that people do to help out their communities. Have partners make a poster with suggestions on ways to help out in your community.

Serve Your School Have partners think of a way to help your school. Have them write a proposal for their idea, and share it with the class. If you wish, you can have your class vote on their favorite school service idea, and then work together to organize the event.

Readers to Writers

Text Features: Photographs and Captions Remind children that authors of narrative nonfiction often include photographs of their subjects. The captions of the photographs may add information that is not in the text. Ask: *What photograph would you add to this passage? What would your caption say?*

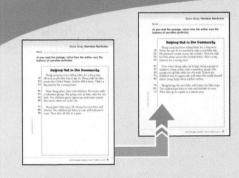

LEVEL UP

IF children read the Approaching Level fluently and answered the questions

THEN pair them with children who have proficiently read the On Level. Have them

- partner read the On Level passage.
- summarize a problem described in the text and identify its solution.

Approaching Level

Vocabulary

REVIEW VOCABULARY WORDS

TIER 2

OBJECTIVES
Determine or clarify the meaning of unknown and multiple-meaning words and phrases based on grade 2 reading and content, choosing flexibly from an array of strategies

I Do Display each **Visual Vocabulary Card** from this genre study and state the word. Explain how the photograph illustrates the word. State the example sentence and repeat the word.

We Do Point to the word on the card and read the word with children. Ask them to repeat the word. Engage children in structured partner talk about the image as prompted on the back of the vocabulary card.

You Do Display each visual in random order, hiding the word. Have children match the definitions and context sentences of the words to the visuals displayed.

CUMULATIVE VOCABULARY REVIEW

TIER 2

OBJECTIVES
Demonstrate understanding of word relationships and nuances in word meanings.

Determine or clarify the meaning of unknown and multiple-meaning words and phrases based on grade 2 reading and content, choosing flexibly from an array of strategies.

I Do Use **Visual Vocabulary Cards** from the previous genre study to review previously taught vocabulary. Display one card at a time. Read the definition and example sentence and repeat the word.

We Do Point to the word and read with children. Read the question on the back of the card or make up a new question. Ask children to answer the question using the vocabulary word. If a response is an incomplete sentence, restate using a complete sentence.

You Do Engage children in structured partner talk using a Partner Talk prompt from the back of the card.

IDENTIFY RELATED WORDS

OBJECTIVES

Demonstrate understanding of word relationships and nuances in word meanings.

Participate in collaborative conversations with diverse partners about grade 2 topics and texts with peers and adults in small and larger groups.

I Do Display the ideas **Visual Vocabulary Card** and say aloud the word set *ideas, pictures, thoughts*.

Point out that *ideas* means almost the same thing as *thoughts*.

We Do Display the vocabulary card for *solution*. Say aloud the word set *solution, test, answer*. With children, identify the word that has almost the same meaning as *solution* and discuss why.

You Do Have children work in pairs to choose the word that means almost the same as the first word in the group.

insists, claims, denies

lonely, friendly, alone

villages, towns, countries

Have children choose words from their writer's notebook and use an online thesaurus to find synonyms and a dictionary to check their pronunciation.

SYNONYMS

OBJECTIVES

Demonstrate understanding of word relationships and nuances in word meanings.

Participate in collaborative conversations with diverse partners about grade 2 topics and texts with peers and adults in small and larger groups.

I Do **Model:** Remind children that a synonym is a word that means almost the same thing as another word. Explain that finding a synonym can help them figure out the meaning of an unknown word. Ask children to listen for the synonym for *solo* as you read the first paragraph of "Helping Out in the Community" from the Approaching Level online **Differentiated Genre Passages**, page A1.

Think Aloud To find a synonym, I need to look for two words that mean almost the same thing. The first paragraph has the word *solo*. I'm not sure what it means, so I'll keep on reading. In the fourth sentence, I see the word *alone*. If Doug took a *solo* bike trip, then he was alone. Now I know that *solo* and *alone* are synonyms, because they mean about the same thing.

We Do Read the first paragraph on page A2 with children and point out the word *safe*. Work with them to find the synonym. (harmless)

You Do Ask children to work with a partner to find other words in the passage that have synonyms. Have them take turns naming the synonyms for the words they have selected. (big/huge, often/usually, community/neighborhood)

Approaching Level

Fluency/Comprehension

FLUENCY

TIER 2

OBJECTIVES

Read with sufficient accuracy and fluency to support comprehension.

Read on-level text with purpose and understanding.

I Do Read the first paragraph of page A1 of "Helping Out in the Community" in the Approaching Level online **Differentiated Genre Passages**. Model using appropriate expression.

We Do Read the next two paragraphs and have children repeat each sentence after you. Point out how you change your rate when you read with proper expression.

You Do Have children read the rest of the selection aloud. Remind them to read this narrative nonfiction with the proper expression.

KEY DETAILS

TIER 2

OBJECTIVES

Ask and answer questions such as *who, what, where, when, why,* and *how* to demonstrate understanding of key details in a text.

Identify the main topic of a multiparagraph text as well as the focus of specific paragraphs within the text.

I Do Remind children that details in a narrative nonfiction text tell about the main topic, which is what the selection is mostly about. *When I read narrative nonfiction, I look for details in the text and pictures. These details help me identify the main topic.*

We Do Read page A1 of "Helping Out in the Community" in the Approaching Level online **Differentiated Genre Passages** aloud. Pause to point out details that can help children figure out the main topic. *The title is "Helping Out in the Community." The first three paragraphs are all about Doug Long. They tell how he rides bikes with groups of children. I think the main topic is how Doug Long rides bikes and how he helps children by riding with them.*

You Do Guide children to read the rest of the **Differentiated Genre Passage**. After each paragraph, prompt them to identify key details that tell them about the main topic. Help children state the main topic.

REVIEW AUTHOR'S PURPOSE

OBJECTIVES

Identify the main purpose of a text, including what the author wants to answer, explain, or describe.

I Do Remind children that the author's purpose is the reason why the author wrote the selection. Authors write narrative nonfiction to answer questions, to explain, or to describe. *To find the author's purpose, I ask myself what the author wants me to know.*

We Do Read page A1 of "Helping Out in the Community" in the Approaching Level online **Differentiated Genre Passages** together. Pause to discuss clues about the author's purpose. *We read that Doug works with a volunteer group. He goes on rides with children. That's a clue to the author's purpose.* Record the clue on a copy of online Author's Purpose **Graphic Organizer 07**.

You Do Guide children as they read the rest of the selection, prompting them to identify clues. Record the clues on the graphic organizer. Then guide children to use the clues to determine the author's purpose.

SELF-SELECTED READING

OBJECTIVES

Read with sufficient accuracy and fluency to support comprehension.

Read on-level text with purpose and understanding.

Read Independently

Have children choose a narrative nonfiction selection for sustained silent reading and set a purpose for reading that selection. Children can check the online **Leveled Reader Database** for selections. Remind them that:

- they should determine the topic and read to understand information.
- the author's purpose is the reason the author wrote the text.
- they can ask themselves questions and then reread to find the answer.

Read Purposefully

As they read independently, have children record clues (key details) and the author's purpose on a copy of online Author's Purpose **Graphic Organizer 07**. After reading, guide children to participate in a book talk about the selection they read. Guide children to:

- share the information they recorded on their graphic organizer.
- tell what interesting facts they learned reading the selections.
- share what questions they asked and how they found the answers.

Offer assistance and guidance with self-selected assignments.

Lexile 500L

OBJECTIVES

Read with sufficient accuracy and fluency to support comprehension.

Ask and answer such questions as *who, what, where, when, why,* and *how* to demonstrate understanding of key details in a text.

Know and use various text features (e.g., captions, bold print, subheadings, glossaries, indexes, electronic menus, icons) to locate key facts or information in a text efficiently. Explain how specific images (e.g., a diagram showing how a machine works) contribute to and clarify a text.

Identify the main purpose of a text, including what the author wants to answer, explain, or describe.

Participate in collaborative conversations with diverse partners about *grade 2 topics and texts* with peers and adults in small and larger groups.

ACADEMIC LANGUAGE

• *narrative nonfiction, narrator, text features, photographs*

• Cognates: *narrador, texto, fotografías*

On Level

Leveled Reader *City Communities*

Preview and Predict

• Have children read the Essential Question: *How can people help out their community?*

• Next, have them preview the title, opening pages, text features, and photographs of *City Communities* to make a prediction about the selection. Have children discuss their predictions.

Review Genre: Narrative Nonfiction

Have children recall that in narrative nonfiction, a narrator tells a story about a real person and events. It may have a beginning, a middle, and an end, like a fiction story, but the person and the events are real. Have children identify features of narrative nonfiction in *City Communities.*

Close Reading

Note Taking: Ask children to use a copy of the online Author's Purpose **Graphic Organizer 07** as they read to record clues that help them determine the author's purpose.

Pages 2–3 *Turn to a partner and share questions you can ask as you read. Then answer your questions.* (Possible response: What is the Sanchez family doing? They are moving from the country to the city. What is a suburb? A town outside the city.) *What is the author's purpose for writing Chapter 1?* (The author wants to describe how a family begins the move from country to city.)

Pages 4–7 *What questions can you ask to help you understand how Mrs. Pavi gets help?* (Possible response: Who helps Mrs. Pavi? How does the neighbor help her?)

Pages 8–10 *What is the author's purpose for writing these pages?* (to describe indoor and outdoor fun in the city) *Which word is a synonym for* exhibits *on page 10,* museums *or* displays? (displays)

Pages 11–14 *What questions can you ask to better understand these pages?* (Possible response: What is a block party? How do people give back to their new city?)

Retell Have children take turns retelling the selection using the retelling cards. Help children make a personal connection by asking: *Have you ever had a new family move into your community? How can you make a new family feel welcome? What could you do to help them learn about your community?*

Respond to Reading Revisit the Essential Question and ask children to complete the Text Evidence questions on page 15.

 Write About Reading In children's responses to question 4 on page 15, check that they used details from the selection to determine that the author's purpose is to tell how people help each other in cities.

Fluency: Accuracy and Expression

Model Fluency Model reading page 3 with accuracy and expression. Have children chorally repeat. Point out how the exclamation mark indicates that you should read that sentence with excitement. Explain that your voice changes when you read about how the children feel about moving, showing their feelings of excitement.

Apply Have children practice reading with partners. Provide feedback as needed.

Paired Read: "Magic Anansi"

 Make Connections: Write About It

Before reading, ask children to note that this text is a folktale. Then discuss the Essential Question. After reading, ask children to make connections between what they read in *City Communities* and "Magic Anansi."

Leveled Reader

 Focus On Social Studies

Children can extend their knowledge of ways people help in communities by completing the social studies activity on page 20.

Literature Circles

Lead children in conducting a literature circle using the Thinkmark questions to guide the discussion. You may wish to discuss what children have learned about ways people help in communities from both selections in the leveled reader.

LEVEL UP

IF children read the On Level fluently and answered the questions

THEN pair them with children who have proficiently read the Beyond Level and have on-level children

- partner-read the Beyond Level main selection.

- Identify a part of the selection they would like to learn more about.

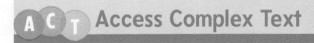 **Access Complex Text**

The Beyond Level challenges children by including more **specific vocabulary** and **complex sentence structures**.

"Helping Out in the Community"
Lexile 510L

OBJECTIVES

Know and use various text features to locate key facts or information in a text efficiently.

Identify the main purpose of a text, including what the author wants to answer, explain, or describe.

Determine or clarify the meaning of unknown and multiple-meaning words and phrases based on *grade 2 reading and content,* choosing flexibly from an array of strategies.

Recall information from experiences or gather information from provided sources to answer a question.

ACADEMIC LANGUAGE

• *narrative nonfiction, narrator, text features, photographs, captions*

• Cognates: *narrador, texto, fotografías*

On Level

Genre Passage "Helping Out in the Community"

Build Background

• Read aloud the Essential Question: *How can people help out their community?* Ask children to tell how different people they read about this week help out in their communities. Use these sentence frames to help focus discussion:

> *In the city, workers _____.*
>
> *In* Lighting Lives, *Debby Tewa _____.*
>
> *Helping people is important because _____.*

• Let children know that the online **Differentiated Genre Passage** "Helping Out in the Community" shows how one man uses bicycles to help children in his community and explains why his work is important.

Review Genre: Narrative Nonfiction

Review with children that in narrative nonfiction, a narrator tells a story about a real person and events. The selection may have a beginning, a middle, and an end, like a fiction story, but the person and the events are real. The selection may have text features, such as photographs and captions, to give more information.

Close Reading

Note Taking As children read the passage the first time, ask them to annotate the text. Have them note key ideas and details, unfamiliar words, and questions they have. Then read again and use the following questions. Encourage children to cite text evidence from the selection.

Read

Genre: Narrative Nonfiction *Read pages O1-O2. Who is the selection about?* (Doug Long.) *Is Doug Long a real person or a made-up character?* (He is a real person.) *What does the beginning of the selection describe?* (Doug's solo bike trip) *What does the middle of the selection describe?* (Doug's volunteer work with kids) *What does the end of the selection describe?* (It tells why his work is important.) *Are these events in the selection real events or imaginary events that the writer made up?* (The events really happened.) *What text feature do you notice?* (a photograph with a caption)

Synonyms *Which two words in the first paragraph on page O1 are synonyms?* (solo, alone) *In the second paragraph on page O1, which word is a synonym for kids?* (children)

Author's Purpose Reread the narrative nonfiction selection on pages O1 and O2. After reading, ask: *How can you figure out what the author wants the readers to learn from this selection?* (Possible response: The author includes details about what Doug Long does. I think the author wants to tell how Doug Long helps his community.)

Summarize Have children use their notes to summarize how Doug volunteers, why he does this, and how his work helps the community.

Reread

Use the questions on page O3 to guide children's rereading of the passage.

Genre: Narrative Nonfiction: *How do you know this passage is narrative nonfiction?* (A narrator is telling a true story about a real person. There is a photograph with a caption that gives more information about the text.)

Author's Purpose *Why did the author write this selection?* (The author wrote the selection to give information about how Doug Long helps in his community.)

Text Features *Why did the author include the photo and caption on page O2?* (The author included the photo to show Doug on a ride with children. The caption tells what the photo shows.)

Integrate

Make Connections Guide children to understand the connections between "Helping Out in the Community" and the other selections they have read. Tell them to work with a partner to find text evidence and respond to this question: *How do the authors help you understand how people help out in their communities?*

Compare Genres Have partners use **Graphic Organizer 119**, a Compare and Contrast chart, to show how different people help out in their communities. Children should record details about how the community helpers are alike, and how they are different. Use information from all of the selections in the genre study.

Differentiate and Collaborate

Be Inspired Have children think about "Helping Out in the Community" and other selections they read. Ask: *"What do the texts inspire you to do?"* Use the following activities or have partners think of a way to respond to the texts.

Create a Public Service Announcement Have partners choose one way that people can help out in the community. Then have partners record a public service announcement. They should tell why people should help, and what they can do.

Report on an Organization Have children report on an organization in your community that helps people. Have children research what they do, whom they help, and how their work makes a difference in the community. Children can share their reports with the class.

Readers to Writers

Vivid Verbs Remind children that authors of narrative nonfiction choose specific verbs to clearly explain what the subject of the selection says, does, or thinks. Read pages O1 and O2 aloud with children. Ask: *What are some of the verbs that clearly describe what Doug does?*

LEVEL UP

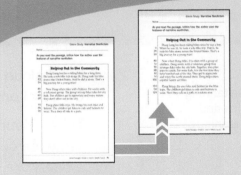

IF children read the On Level fluently and answered the questions

THEN pair them with children who have proficiently read the Beyond Level. Have them

- partner read the Beyond Level passage.
- identify the author's purpose in the selection and explain how they know it.

On Level

Vocabulary

REVIEW VOCABULARY WORDS

OBJECTIVES

Determine or clarify the meaning of unknown and multiple-meaning words and phrases based on grade 2 reading and content, choosing flexibly from an array of strategies.

Use sentence-level context as a clue to the meaning of a word or phrase.

I Do Use the **Visual Vocabulary Cards** to review the key selection words *across, borrow, countryside, idea, insists, lonely, solution,* and *villages.* Point to each word, read it aloud, and have children chorally repeat it.

We Do Ask these questions and help children record and explain their answers:

- What is **across** the street from your school?
- How many books can you **borrow** at one time from the school library?
- What might you see in the **countryside**?
- What is one **idea** that you have?

You Do Have children work in pairs to respond to these questions and explain their answers.

- What is something that your teacher **insists** that you do?
- What do you do when you feel **lonely**?
- How do you find the **solution** when you have a problem?
- How are cities different from **villages**?

Have children choose words from their writer's notebook and use an online thesaurus to find synonyms.

SYNONYMS

OBJECTIVES

Demonstrate understanding of word relationships and nuances in word meanings.

I Do Read aloud the first paragraph of "Helping Out in the Community" in the On Level online **Differentiated Genre Passages,** page O1.

Think Aloud I want to identify a synonym for the word *solo* in the second sentence of the first paragraph. In the fourth sentence, I see the word *alone.* I use context clues as I reread the paragraph. If Doug took a solo bike trip, then he was alone. Now I know that *solo* and *alone* are synonyms, because they mean almost the same thing.

We Do Have children read the second paragraph and find a synonym for the word *volunteer.* (helps)

You Do Have children work in pairs to identify the synonym for the word *safe* in the first paragraph on page O2. (harmless)

Comprehension

REVIEW AUTHOR'S PURPOSE

OBJECTIVES

Identify the main purpose of a text, including what the author wants to answer, explain, or describe.

I Do Remind children that authors write text for different reasons. Say: *An author usually writes narrative nonfiction to give or explain information about a topic. An author may write fiction to entertain readers. An author may want to convince readers to feel the same way about a topic that he or she does. We can look for clues in the text or text features to help us understand the author's purpose.*

We Do Read page O1 of "Helping Out in the Community" in the On Level online **Differentiated Genre Passages** aloud. Pause to point out information in the text and text features. Say: *We read that Doug Long works with a volunteer group. The group sets up bike rides for city kids.*

You Do Guide children to read the rest of the On Level online **Differentiated Genre Passage** on pages O1 and O2. Remind them to identify clues to the author's purpose as they read. Then have children use the clues to determine the author's purpose.

SELF-SELECTED READING

OBJECTIVES

Ask and answer such questions as *who, what, where, when, why,* and *how* to demonstrate understanding of key details in a text.

Identify the main purpose of a text, including what the author wants to answer, explain, or describe.

Read Independently

Have children choose a narrative nonfiction book for sustained silent reading. They can check the online **Leveled Reader Database** for selections.

- Before they read, have children use text and text features as clues to help them understand and identify the author's purpose.
- Remind children to ask themselves questions and then look for the answers in the text and images.

Read Purposefully

Have children record clues and the author's purpose on a copy of online Author's Purpose **Graphic Organizer O7**. After reading, guide partners to:

- share the information they recorded on their graphic organizers.
- tell what interesting facts they learned reading the selections.
- share what questions they asked themselves and how they found the answers.

 You may want to include **ELL** students in On Level vocabulary and comprehension lessons. Offer language support as needed.

Lexile 620L

OBJECTIVES

Read with sufficient accuracy and fluency to support comprehension.

Ask and answer such questions as *who, what, where, when, why,* and *how* to demonstrate understanding of key details in a text.

Know and use various text features (e.g., captions, bold print, subheadings, glossaries, indexes, electronic menus, icons) to locate key facts or information in a text efficiently.

Explain how specific images (e.g., a diagram showing how a machine works) contribute to and clarify a text.

Identify the main purpose of a text, including what the author wants to answer, explain, or describe.

Participate in collaborative conversations with diverse partners about *grade 2 topics and texts* with peers and adults in small and larger groups.

ACADEMIC LANGUAGE

- *narrative nonfiction, narrator, text features, photographs, captions*
- Cognates: *narrador, texto, fotografías*

Beyond Level

Leveled Reader *City Communities*

Preview and Predict

- Read the Essential Question: *How can people help out their community?*
- Read the title and author name. Have children preview the title page and the photos of *City Communities* to make a prediction. Then discuss their predictions.

Review Genre: Narrative Nonfiction

Have children recall that, in narrative nonfiction, a narrator tells about a real person, place, or thing. Prompt children to name key characteristics of narrative nonfiction. Then tell them to look for these characteristics as they read *City Communities*.

Close Reading

Note Taking Ask children to use a copy of the online Author's Purpose **Graphic Organizer 07** while they read to record clues that will help them determine the author's purpose.

Pages 2–3 *Turn to a partner and share questions you can ask as you read. Answer your questions.* (Possible response: How do the Sanchez kids feel about their move? They are sad to leave their home and friends but excited about moving to the city. What does the Sanchez family see in the city skyline? Tall buildings and a bridge.) *What is the author's purpose for writing Chapter 1?* (to describe how a family begins their move from country to city)

Pages 4–7 *What is a synonym for* arrives *on page 5?* (reaches; comes) *What questions can you ask to help you understand what happens when people move to the city? Answer your questions.* (Possible response: How do people know where to buy groceries? A neighbor can tell them. How do kids get to school? They might walk with their parents.)

Pages 8–10 *What is the author's purpose for including the information in the green box on page 9?* (to give readers an example of what might be listed in the park pamphlet discussed in the main text)

Pages 11–14 *What questions can you ask to better understand the text?* (Possible response: What is a block party? How do people give back to their new city?) *What is a synonym for* donates *on page 12?* (gives)

Retell Have children take turns retelling the selection. Help children make a personal connection by writing about how they are similar to and different from a character, setting, or event in the selection. Say: *Write about how you are similar to or different from the Sanchez family.*

Respond to Reading Revisit the Essential Question and ask children to complete the Text Evidence Questions on page 15.

 Write About Reading In children's response to question 4 on page 15, check that they used details from the selection to tell how people help each other in cities.

Fluency: Accuracy and Expression

Model Model reading page 2 with accuracy and expression. Point out how your voice changes based on the content of the sentences. Then read the next page and have children read along with you.

Apply Have children practice reading the passage with a partner.

Paired Read: "Magic Anansi"

 Make Connections: Write About It

Before reading "Magic Anansi," have children preview the title page and prompt them to identify the genre. Then discuss the Compare Texts statement. After reading, have children work with a partner to discuss what they read in "Magic Anansi" and *City Communities*. Ask children to make

Leveled Reader

connections by comparing and contrasting the communities described in each selection. Prompt children to discuss what they learned about how people help out their communities.

 Focus On Social Studies

Children can extend their knowledge of ways people help in communities by completing the social studies activity on page 20.

 Literature Circles

Lead children in conducting a literature circle using the Thinkmark questions to guide the discussion. You may wish to discuss what children have learned about how people help out their communities from both selections in the Leveled Reader.

 Gifted and Talented

Synthesize Challenge children to learn more about people who helps out in cities. Ask them to choose a person discussed in *City Communities,* such as an apartment superintendent. Children should write a job description for the person.

Extend Have children use facts they learned during the week and do additional research.

"Helping Out in the Community"
Lexile 610L

Beyond Level

Genre Passage "Helping Out in the Community"

Build Background

- Read the Essential Question: *How can people help out their community?* Ask partners to compare the ways the people they read about help out their communities. Use the following sentence frames to help focus discussion:

  Friends helped the Sanchez family by _____.

  In the city, _____ help out by _____.

  Helping people is important because _____.

- Let children know that the online **Differentiated Genre Passage** "Helping Out in the Community" shows how one man helps out in his community, and explains why his work is important.

Review Genre: Narrative Nonfiction

Review with children that in narrative nonfiction, a narrator tells a story about a real person and describes real events. The selection may have a beginning, a middle, and an end, like a fiction story, but the person and the events are real. It may include details about what the person says, does, and thinks. The selection may have text features, such as photographs and captions, to give information.

Close Reading

Note Taking As children read the passage the first time, ask them to annotate the text. Have them note key ideas and details, unfamiliar words, and questions they have. Then read again and use the following questions. Encourage children to cite text evidence from the selection.

> **Read**

Genre: Narrative Nonfiction *Read page B1. Who is this selection about?* (Doug Long) *Is Doug Long a real person, or a made-up character?* (He is a real person.) *Who is telling the story?* (a narrator) *Are the events real events or are the events made up by the writer?* (The events are real events.)

Author's Purpose *How does the author help you understand why Doug Long's work is important? Use evidence from the text in your answer.* (Possible response: The author gives details about how Doug helps the children. He shows them things about nature that they did not know. For example, they didn't know that a caterpillar was safe to pick up until Doug showed them.)

Text Features Reread the caption for the photograph on page B2. What key detail does the photograph tell the readers about Doug Long? (Doug Long helps children learn more about nature.) Have partners discuss other details that the author wants the reader to learn about Doug Long. Then have children discuss other photos and captions the author might have included to add more key details about this topic.

Summarize Have children use their notes to summarize how Doug helps out in his community, why he helps, and why his work is important.

Reread

Use the questions on page B3 to guide children's rereading of the passage.

Genre: Narrative Nonfiction: *How do you know this selection is narrative nonfiction?* (A narrator is telling a true story about a person. In addition, a photograph shows information from the text and a caption tells about the photo.)

Author's Purpose *What is the author's purpose for writing "Helping Out in the Community?"* (The author's purpose is to give information about how Doug Long helps in his community.)

Text Features *What is the purpose of the photo and caption on page B2?* (The photo shows something from the text. It shows Doug on a ride with children in the community. The caption gives more information about the photo.)

Integrate

Make Connections Guide children to make connections between "Helping Out in the Community" and the other two selections they have read. Tell them to work with a partner and find text evidence to respond to this question: *How do the authors help you understand how different people help out in their communities, and why their work is important?*

Compare Genres Ask children to use online **Graphic Organizer 119**, a Compare and Contrast chart. Help children show how different people help out in their communities. Have children identify ways the community helpers are alike, and ways they are different. Use information from all of the selections in the genre study.

Differentiate and Collaborate

Be Inspired Have children think about "Helping Out in the Community" and other selections they read. Ask: *What do the texts inspire you to do?* Use the following activities or have partners think of a way to respond to the texts.

Write a Newspaper Editorial Ask children to write an editorial for a newspaper. Children should take the position that people should help out in their communities, and explain why it is important.

Propose a Community Service Event Ask partners to think of one way to help out your community. Have partners write a letter to your mayor outlining their proposal for the community service idea. Have partners share their letters with the class.

Readers to Writers

Word Choice Remind children that authors of narrative nonfiction choose specific verbs, or action words, to clearly explain what the person they are writing about does. Read the second paragraph on page B1 aloud with children. Ask: *What are some vivid verbs that grabs your attention? Why are those verbs interesting to you? How do they help you picture what Doug and the children do?*

 Gifted and Talented

Independent Study Have children synthesize information from their notes and the selections they read to create a list of ways that they might help out in their communities. Have children trade their lists with a partner for evaluation.

Beyond Level

Vocabulary

REVIEW DOMAIN-SPECIFIC WORDS

OBJECTIVES
Determine or clarify the meaning of unknown and multiple-meaning words and phrases based on *grade 2 reading and content,* choosing flexibly from an array of strategies.

Use sentence-level context as a clue to the meaning of a word or phrase.

Model Use the **Visual Vocabulary Cards** to review the meaning of the words *idea* and *solution.* Write social studies-related sentences on the board using the words.

Write the words *volunteer* and *neighborhood* on the board and discuss the meanings with children. Then help children write sentences using these words. Discuss the meaning of *neighborhood* as a small area of a city where people live. Explain that people who live in a *neighborhood* sometimes live in the same building.

Apply Have children work in pairs to review the meanings of the words *across* and *cooperate.* Then have partners write sentences using the words.

SYNONYMS

OBJECTIVES
Determine or clarify the meaning of unknown and multiple-meaning words and phrases based on *grade 2 reading and content,* choosing flexibly from an array of strategies.

Use sentence-level context as a clue to the meaning of a word or phrase.

Model Read aloud the first two paragraphs of "Helping Out in the Community" in the Beyond online **Differentiated Genre Passages,** page B1.

Think Aloud When I read these paragraphs, I want to understand the word *solo.* I'll look for context clues to help me. It says that Doug rode his bike alone. So, I think a *solo* trip is a trip someone takes alone.

Help children figure out the meaning of *nature* in the second paragraph.

Apply Have pairs of children read the rest of the passage. Ask them to use synonyms to determine the meaning of the following words: *discovered, harmless, repair.*

Synthesize Have children work with a partner to review the Essential Question. Have them write sentences explaining how people help out in their communities. Then have them identify synonyms for some of the words used in their sentences.

Have children repeat the activity by finding words in their writer's notebook to use as synonyms for words in the passage.

Comprehension

REVIEW AUTHOR'S PURPOSE

OBJECTIVES
Identify the main purpose of a text, including what the author wants to answer, explain, or describe.

Model Remind children that the author's purpose is the reason the author writes a text. Authors write texts for different reasons. An author usually writes nonfiction narratives to give or explain information about a topic. Authors may also write to entertain readers or to convince readers to feel the same way about a topic that they do. Look for clues in the words and text features to help identify the author's purpose.

Have children read the first paragraph on page B1 of "Helping Out in the Community" in the Beyond Level online **Differentiated Genre Passages**. Ask open-ended questions to facilitate discussion, such as: *What is the author explaining in this paragraph? What does the author want us to know?* Children should support their responses with examples from the text.

Apply Have children identify clues on each page as they independently fill in a copy of online Author's Purpose **Graphic Organizer 07**. Then have partners vuse their work to determine the author's purpose.

SELF-SELECTED READING

OBJECTIVES
Ask and answer such questions as *who, what, where, when, why,* and *how* to demonstrate understanding of key details in a text.

Identify the main purpose of a text, including what the author wants to answer, explain, or describe.

Read Independently

Have children choose a narrative nonfiction book for sustained silent reading. They can check the online **Leveled Reader Database** for selections.

- As children read, have them fill in a copy of the online Author's Purpose **Graphic Organizer 07**.
- Remind them to ask questions about what they read and to look for the answers in the text and images.

Read Purposefully

Encourage children to keep a reading journal. Ask them to read different books in order to learn about a variety of subjects.

- Ask children to share their reactions to the books with classmates.

 Independent Study Challenge children to discuss how their books relate to the weekly theme of ways people help. Have children compare ways people help.

Reading/ Writing Companion

Scaffolded Shared Read

OBJECTIVES

Read with sufficient accuracy and fluency to support comprehension.

Read on-level text with purpose and understanding.

LANGUAGE OBJECTIVES

Children will show understanding of a nonfiction text by answering questions about key details and author's purpose.

ACADEMIC LANGUAGE

- *purpose, expression*
- Cognate: *expresión*

Digital Tools

Have children listen to the selection to develop comprehension and practice fluency and pronunciation.

English Language Learners

"Lighting Lives"

Plan Your ELL Small Group Instruction for the Shared Read		
Beginning	**Intermediate**	**Advanced/Advanced High**
Use the online **Scaffolded Shared Read** to focus on comprehension of a sheltered version of "Lighting Lives." Then have all ELL levels participate together in the activities on pages T154–T155.	Use pages T152-T153 to support student comprehension of the on-level text, reinforce skills and strategies, and develop oral language. Then have all ELL levels participate in the activities on pages T154-T155.	Use pages T152-T153 to support student comprehension of the on-level text, reinforce skills and strategies, and develop oral language. Then have all ELL levels participate in the activities on pages T154-T155.

Prepare to Read

Build Background Turn on the lights and then turn them off. Talk about how houses and buildings need electricity in order to have lighting. Have children brainstorm things that work with electricity and produce lighting.

Vocabulary Explain that the expression *light up one's life* means to make someone's life better. Invite children to suggest some examples, such as how children can light up their parents' lives or a beloved pet can light up a person's life. Use the **Visual Vocabulary Cards** to review the vocabulary: *across, borrow, countryside, ideas, insists, lonely, solution, villages*. Then use the online **Visual Vocabulary Cards** to teach ELL Vocabulary from the Shared Read: *company, demands, electricity, heat, provided, realized* (Cognates: *electricidad, realizar*)

Set Purpose Today we will read "Lighting Lives" and focus on understanding the language in the text. As we read, think about the Essential Question: *How can people help out their community?*

Interactive Question-Response Routine

After each paragraph, ask questions that help children understand the meaning of the text. Explain difficult or unfamiliar concepts and words. Provide sentence stems for **Intermediate** children. Have **Advanced/ Advanced High** children retell the information. Reinforce the meaning of new vocabulary. Ask children questions that require them to use the vocabulary. Reinforce weekly strategies and skills through modeling and questions. Use the images and captions to aid children's comprehension.

Page 3

When Debby was younger, did she have electricity at home? (no)
What did she use for light? (a candle)

Intermediate *Complete the frames using the verb "have":* Debby's old home <u>did not have</u> electricty. Her new home <u>had</u> electricity.

Advanced/Advanced High *Work with a partner. Ask and answer questions about Debby's home before and after she was ten.*

Page 4

Where does solar power come from? (the sun)
What does solar power turn sunlight into? (electricity)
How does Debby feel about solar power? (excited)
What does Debby like to do? (Debby likes to solve problems.)

 Intermediate *Turn to a partner and explain how solar panels work.* Use these sentence frames: Solar panels are put on the roof. They collect sunlight and turn it into electricity.

Advanced *How do you think solar panels work?* (Solar panels collect energy from the sun.) *Why are solar panels on the rooftops of houses?* (They are on the rooftops because that is where the sun shines directly.)

Advanced High *What was Debby's idea?* (to work for a solar panel company). *Why did her idea make her feel excited?* (Because Debby wanted to help people, especially people who had no electricity.) *What kind of person is Debby?* (Debby is kind/ a problem solver.)

Page 5

 Why is Arizona a good place to use solar power? Have children ask and answer the question with a partner: Arizona is a good place for solar power because there is a lot of sun.

Intermediate Have children point to the word *bank*. Explain that a bank is a place where people put their money to keep it safe. Then have them find the word *borrow*. Model what it means to *borrow* by borrowing a pencil from a child and then giving it back.

Advanced *Why does the author say it's good news that the sun's power is free?* Use this sentence frame: People save money when they don't have to pay for electricity.

 Advanced High *When you borrow something from someone, what do you have to do later?* (Pay it back.) *What does Debby help people borrow?* (money from banks)

Page 6

Where does Debby travel? (in Arizona and New Mexico, in the countryside) Point to Arizona and New Mexico on a map.

Intermediate Tell children that when you "believe deeply" in something, that thing is very important to you. *What is very important to Debby?* (her work) Have children circle the word *insist*. *If I insist on something, do I ask for something only once and give up, or do I keep asking?* (You keep asking.)

Page 7

How does Debby feel sometimes? (lonely) *When you feel lonely, are you happy or sad?* (sad) *But then, what does Debby think about?* (how exciting it is for people to have electricity) *How do you think this makes her feel?* (excited)

Intermediate *Point to the words that tell what families with electricity can do.* (heat their homes; turn on a light) Flip the classroom light switch and ask: *How am I using electricity now?* I am using electricity to turn on the light.

 Advanced/Advanced High *Tell your partner what Debby means when she says she is "lighting up people's lives."* Debby makes people's lives better by helping them get electricity and light.

*Now that we have finished the text, look back at page 3. Think about **Author's Purpose**. Why do you think the author described Debby's childhood home? Discuss with a partner.* (Possible: Debby grew up without electricity. She knows it's hard. That's why she wants to help people.)

Reading/Writing Companion

OBJECTIVES

Identify the main purpose of a text, including what the author wants to answer, explain, or describe.

Ask and answer such questions as who, what, where, when, why, and how to demonstrate understanding of key details in a text.

LANGUAGE OBJECTIVE

Children will take notes on a nonfiction text that is read aloud and analyze the author's purpose.

ACADEMIC VOCABULARY

• *author's purpose, details*
• Cognate: *detalles*

DIFFERENTIATED READING

ELL Have Beginning and Early-Intermediate children use the **Scaffolded Shared Read** Glossary Activities during Vocabulary Building.

English Language Learners

"Lighting Lives"

 Text Reconstruction

Focus on a single chunk of text to support comprehension and language development across the four domains.

1. Read aloud paragraph 1 on page 5 while children just listen.

2. Write the following on the board, providing definitions as needed: *thought, villages, small towns, solar power, because, decided, help.* Have children listen for these words as you read the paragraph a second time.

3. Read the paragraph a third time. Tell children to listen and take notes.

4. 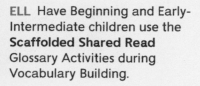 **COLLABORATE** Have children work in pairs to reconstruct the text from their notes. Help them write complete sentences as needed.

5. Have children look at the original text. Ask them to tell what the paragraph is mostly about. (Debby decided to help people in small towns get solar power.) Tell children they are going to discuss the author's purpose in this paragraph.

6. *What does Debby know about the people who live in small towns?* (They don't have electricity.) *Why does the author include the phrase "in villages like the one she lived in as a child?"* (To remind the reader that Debby has something in common with the people she wants to help; she knows their lives are hard.) *Why does the author include the sentence "Solar power would work well..." in this paragraph?* (To show a second reason Debby decided to help bring in solar power.)

7. Have children compare their text reconstructions to the original text and check if they understand the author's purpose for including details about the people in the villages and why solar power would work well.

Beginning Have children follow along in the **Reading/Writing Companion** as you read aloud, and have them circle the words from Step 2 as they hear them.

Make Connections

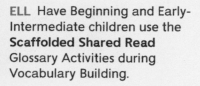 **COLLABORATE** **Mixed Levels** Combine children at different English proficiency levels to discuss how "Lighting Lives" relates to the Essential Question, *How can people help out their community?* and the Key Concept, *Ways People Help.* Beginning children will base their answers on the **Scaffolded Shared Read**. Intermediate and Advanced/Advanced High children will base theirs on the **Reading/Writing Companion**.

Grammar in Context

Notice the Form Display sentences from the text. Underline the action verbs.

> 1. The sunlight <u>hits</u> these panels and <u>turns</u> into electricity.
>
> 2. Debby <u>believes</u> deeply in her work and <u>insists</u> that families <u>learn</u> about how solar power can <u>help</u> them.
>
> 3. They can <u>heat</u> their homes or <u>turn</u> on a light.

What do the underlined words have in common? (They are all verbs.) **Help** children select the action verbs. In the first sentence, they describe the action of the sun on the panels. In the other sentences, they tell about Debby's mental or physical actions, or about the actions of families.

Apply and Extend Have children write about something they do to help at home. Make sure they use action verbs in their sentences. Use sentence frames to guide them in using action verbs: I help at home. I do chores. Every night I wash the dishes. In the mornings I make my bed. I also clean my room.

Independent Time

Vocabulary Building Have children build their glossaries.

Beginning/Early Intermediate Have children continue the Glossary Activities in the **Scaffolded Share Read,** then add words to a chart like the one below.

Intermediate/Advanced/Advanced High After children add vocabulary from **Reading/Writing Companion** pages 8-9 to the chart below, have them scan the text for self-selected words they would like to learn and add to the chart.

WORD/PHRASE	DEFINE	EXAMPLE	ASK
solar	from the sun	Solar energy can be turned into electricity.	When can we collect solar energy?

All Levels Combine children at different proficiency levels to teach one another new vocabulary. Beginning and Early-Intermediate ELLs will teach vocabulary from their Scaffolded Shared Read glossaries. Intermediate and Advanced/Advanced High children will teach their self-selected words.

Oral and Written Summaries Have partners work together to complete the online **Shared Read Writing Frame** for "Lighting Lives." First they will orally summarize the text, then they will write a summary in their notebooks. Have partners share their summaries.

OBJECTIVES

Demonstrate command of the conventions of standard English grammar and usage when writing or speaking.

LANGUAGE OBJECTIVE

Children will write sentences using action verbs.

ACADEMIC LANGUAGE

- *action verb, dialogue*
- Cognates: *verbo do acción, diálogo*

Language Transfers Handbook page 18 for Action Verbs

Literature Anthology

OBJECTIVES

Determine or clarify the meaning of unknown and multiple-meaning words and phrases based on grade 2 reading and content, choosing flexibly from an array of strategies.

Ask and answer such questions as *who, what, where, when, why,* and *how* to demonstrate understanding of key details in a text.

LANGUAGE OBJECTIVES

Children will work together to analyze how illustrations, word choice, and repetition, support the author's purpose.

ACADEMIC LANGUAGE

• *illustration, word choice, repetition*
• Cognates: *ilustración, repetición*

Digital Tools

🎧 Have children listen to the selection to develop comprehension and practice fluency and pronunciation.

English Language Learners

Biblioburro

Reread

Before focusing on Using Illustrations and Author's Craft in *Biblioburro,* support children's basic comprehension of the text.

• Provide context and background information: *Many of us have libraries near our homes or in our school. We can go to the library when we want to. But libraries are rare in some parts of the world, especially in the countryside, far from cities. This is a true story about a man who brings books to children who live far away from a library.*

• Use the **Visual Vocabulary Cards** to review vocabulary *(across, borrow, countryside, idea, insists, lonely, solution, villages).*

• Use the point-of-use Spotlight on Language tips on pages T49A–T49L to break down linguistic barriers to comprehension.

• Use the **Interactive Question-Response Routine** to help children access small chunks of text in the selection. (See page T152 for the complete routine).

• Have **Advanced/Advanced High** ELLs work with native speakers to fill in an Author's Purpose chart with clues about why the author wrote this story.

Pages 214–215, Use Illustrations

Explain that illustrations can give readers additional information in a story. Encourage children to run their finger along the pink cloud bubble outline of the illustration of page 215. Read aloud the sentence "At last an idea pops into his head." Explain that the illustration in the bubble shows the idea.

Beginning *Point to Luis's wife, Diana. Ask: Does Diana look happy or angry in this picture?* (angry) *Why is Diana angry at Luis?* Diana is angry at Luis because he brings home too many books. *Find the sentence that tells Luis's idea.* ("I can bring my books...") *Does the illustration match the text?* (yes)

Intermediate *Luis's problem is that he has too many books. Turn to a partner and tell how Luis decides to solve the problem of having too many books.* Provide sentence frames, such as: *Luis's problem is that he has too many books. Luis wants to solve his problem by taking his books to faraway hills to share with people who have no books.*

Advanced/Advanced High *Where do you think Luis is going?* (to a place with no books.) *Turn to a partner and read aloud the phrase on this page that supports your answer.* ("with those who have none") *Tell your partner what the words* those *and* none *refer to.* (children, books)

Pages 218–219, Use Illustrations

Now Luis isn't imagining, he is really carrying out his idea. Look at the picture on pages 218 and 219. Point to Luis's wife, Diana. Does she look big or small? (small) *That means she is far away. Are they going uphill or downhill?* (uphill) *What does the picture tell?* (Luis has traveled far from Diana. They are going uphill.)

Beginning *Where do Luis and the burros go?* They go to villages. *Are the places close by or far away?* The places are far away. *Does the journey, or trip, look easy or hard?* (hard)

Intermediate *How do the burros look?* (tired) *Why do you think the burros feel this way?* The burros look tired because they are going uphill. Luis and the burros are traveling far away.

Advanced/Advanced High *Talk to a partner about what you see in the illustration.* Use these sentence frames if needed: Luis and the burros are traveling to villages. The villages are far away. The burros look tired because they are going uphill. The hill looks steep.

Pages 222–223, Author's Craft: Word Choice

Reread the text on page 223. Emphasize the phrase "at last." Use the phrase to talk about something you did that took a long time. *The drive to my mother's house took 6 hours. That is a long time! At last, I arrived. I was tired and had to take a nap.*

Beginning Read the sentence with the words "at last." *Another word for "at last" is "finally." "At last" and "finally" are* **synonyms**. *Let's read the sentence again, using the word* finally. Have children repeat. Explain that "at last" and "finally" mean "after a long time."

Intermediate *Do you think Luis and the burros' journey was a long trip, or a short trip?* (a long trip) *Which phrase helps you understand that the trip took a long time?* ("at last")

Advanced *What do the children do when they see Luis?* (They run to him.) *Why do you think the author chose the word "run" instead of "go?" Discuss with a partner.* (Possible: to show they were excited)

Advanced High Cover the phrase "at last" and read the paragraph aloud again, without that phrase. Ask: *How does the meaning of the paragraph change without this phrase? Talk to your partner about this.* Have partners use the phrase in a sentence.

Pages 230–231, Author's Craft: Repetition

The author repeats two ideas on these pages. The first is about feeding. Luis feeds his hungry burros. They have worked hard for him. Diana feeds Luis, who has also worked hard and is also hungry. Luis cares for his burros. They all worked hard. Let's look for another repeated phrase on these pages.

Beginning *Which phrase tells when Luis reads?* (deep into the night) *If you read deep into the night, it means you read until it's very late. Which phrase tells when the children read?* (deep into their night) *Why do Luis and the children stay up late to read? Tell a partner.* Luis and the children both love to read books.

Intermediate *Do you think the phrase "Deep into the night" means for a short time or until it's very late?* (until it's very late) *Why does Luis read deep into the night? What about the children?* They all love reading. *Why do you think the author repeats this phrase? Discuss with a partner.* Use sentence frames: The phrase shows that Luis and the children have a connection. They all love to read. This is like the connection between Luis and his burros. They all worked hard.

Advanced/Advanced High *Why do you think the author repeats the same phrase about Luis and the children, "deep into the night"?* (Possible: to show a connection, that they have something in common)

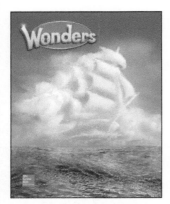

Literature Anthology

OBJECTIVES

Ask and answer such questions as *who, what, where, when, why,* and *how* to demonstrate understanding of key details in a text.

Identify the main purpose of a text, including what the author wants to answer, explain, or describe.

Demonstrate understanding of word relationships and nuances in word meanings.

LANGUAGE OBJECTIVES

Children will show listening comprehension by taking notes during multiple read-alouds.

ACADEMIC LANGUAGE

• *illustration, author's purpose*
• Cognate: *ilustración*

English Language Learners

Biblioburro

Text Reconstruction

Focus on a single chunk of text to support comprehension and language development across the four domains.

1. Read aloud page 224 of *Biblioburro*.

2. Write the following key words and phrases on the board, providing definitions as needed: *insists, choose, borrow, surprise, bundle, masks, piglets, tale.* Instruct children to listen for these words as you read the page a second time.

3. Read the page a third time while children listen and take notes.

4. Have children work with a partner to reconstruct the text from their notes. Help them write complete sentences as needed.

5. Have children look at the original text. Ask them to tell what the text is mostly about. (Luis gives the children masks and reads them a story about pigs.) Tell children they are going to think about how this page helps them understand the author's purpose for writing this story.

6. *Why does Luis insist on reading the children a story?* (because he loves to read) *Why does Luis give the children masks?* (to make the reading fun for the children) *Luis must be tired after the long journey. What does it tell you about Luis that he wants to read to the children?* (He loves reading, and he wants the children to love reading too.) *How does this help you understand the author's purpose in writing the story?* (The author wants the readers to understand how much Luis is helping children by bringing books to them.)

7. Have children compare their text reconstructions to the original text. Have them confirm they understood the author's purpose.

Beginning Allow children to follow along in their Literature Anthologies as you read the text aloud. Have them point to the words from Step 2 as they hear them.

Apply: Using Illustrations

Have children each select an illustration from *Biblioburro* and write a few sentences describing the picture. Guide them with questions: *What's happening? What do you see? What are the people doing? What details are in the picture but not in the text?* Then have children take turns reading their descriptions so the group can guess which illustration they are describing. Provide sentence frames for **Beginning** ELLs to use.

Grammar in Context: Text Deconstruction

Write this sentence from page 220 on the board: *When the sun burns high in the sky, Luis and the burros stop at a stream to drink the cool water.* Facilitate deconstructing this sentence for better comprehension:

- Underline *When the sun burns high in the sky.* Say, *The word "when" is a time signal word. When does the sun burn high in the sky? What time of day?* (midday) *Which word is an action word?* (*burns*) *Why does the author use the word "burn."* (The strong word helps us know it is hot.)

- Underline the second part of the sentence. *What are the two action words?* (*stop* and *drink*) *Who stops?* (Luis and the burros) *Where do they stop?* (at the stream) *What do they do there?* (drink) *What do they drink?* (cool water) *When do they stop?* (the middle of the day)

- *Rephrase the sentence in your own words. You can simplify it into two sentences.* (Possible: At midday they stop. Luis and the burros drink water from a stream.)

Independent Time

Vocabulary Building: Synonyms Remind children that synonyms are words that have the same or similar meaning. Have them work in small groups to complete a two-column chart with selection vocabulary. Children list words from the selection in one column and possible synonyms in the second column. Display the following chart with examples and ask groups to add to it.

Word	Synonym
idea	thought
little	small
tale	story

Beginning/Early Intermediate Have children work in mixed-proficiency pairs to use the **Visual Vocabulary Cards** or a dictionary to find synonyms.

Intermediate/Advanced/Advanced High Have children provide more than one synonym for some of the words.

Home-School Connections Help children connect the Essential Question to their own lives. Review how Debby and Luis helped people. Have partners brainstorm ways to help people in your community. Have them use the online **Oral Language Sentence Frames** for "Modifying to Add Details," available for all ELL levels, to elaborate on their ideas.

Beginning/Early Intermediate Help children write labels and simple phrases to express their ideas. If they are ready, provide a sentence stem to help them write a complete sentence as a caption: I can help clean the classroom.

Intermediate/Advanced/Advanced High Have children add another sentence with additional details to their captions.

OBJECTIVES

Demonstrate command of the conventions of standard English grammar and usage when writing or speaking.

Demonstrate understanding of word relationships and nuances in word meanings.

LANGUAGE OBJECTIVES

Children will identify synonyms from the text.

ACADEMIC LANGUAGE

- *action verb, synonym*
- Cognates: *verbo de acción, sinónimo*

Digital Tools

Use the additional grammar resources and the vocabulary activity related to this lesson.

Grammar Song

Vocabulary Activity

DIFFERENTIATED WRITING

ELL Have Beginning and Early-Intermediate ELLs use their **Scaffolded Shared Read** glossaries during Vocabulary Building.

Lexile 400L

OBJECTIVES

Ask and answer such questions as *who, what, where, when, why,* and *how* to demonstrate understanding of key details in a text.

LANGUAGE OBJECTIVES

Children will help each other read a leveled nonfiction text by asking and answering questions.

ACADEMIC LANGUAGE

- *narrative nonfiction, photograph, caption*
- Cognates: *narrativa, fotografía*

Digital Tools

Have children listen to the selections to develop comprehension and practice fluency and pronunciation.

English Language Learners

Leveled Reader: *City Communities*

Build Background

- Read the Essential Question: *How can people help out their communities?* Have children share their ideas about how people help out their communities.

- Choral read the title. Explain that this is a nonfiction text about real people and events, and it takes place in a city.

Vocabulary

Use the routine on the **Visual Vocabulary Cards** to pre-teach the ELL vocabulary: *community* and *exhibits.* Use the glossary definitions on page 19 of the selection to define additional vocabulary in context. Have children add these words to their glossaries.

Interactive Question-Response Routine

After each paragraph, use Interactive Question-Response prompts such as the following to provide language support and guide comprehension.

Chapter 1

Have children look at the photo and caption on page 2. *What clues in the text and in the photo tell you this is a narrative nonfiction story?* (The Sanchez family members are real people. They are moving from one place to another.)

Beginning *Where is the Sanchez family moving to?* (the city) *How do the children feel?* (sad but excited) *Let's read the sentences that support your answer.*

Intermediate *What places does the family pass and see as they drive?* First, they drive by <u>farms in the countryside</u>. They then drive by <u>houses and stores</u>. Later, they stop for <u>gas</u> in a <u>suburb</u>.

Chapter 2

*Take turns with your partner to **ask and answer questions** about living in the city. Ask questions about things you do not understand. Talk about where the people live, what they do, and how they get around town.* (Partners' questions will vary.)

Intermediate *Talk with your partner about the photograph on page 6. What do you see?* I see <u>two women</u> carrying a <u>basket</u>. The <u>basket</u> has <u>fresh vegetables</u>. *Look at the label. What do you think the women just did?* They just picked the <u>vegetables</u> from the <u>garden</u>.

Chapter 3

Advanced *Talk with your partner about what happens at a "block party."* (Answers should reflect the text)

Chapter 4

Beginning *What does Mrs. Lee do to help her community?* Mrs. Lee runs <u>races</u> for groups that help people. She asks people to pay for the miles she <u>runs</u>. She then <u>donates,</u> or gives money, to groups.

Intermediate *What does Mr. Lee do to help his community?* Mr. Lee <u>volunteers</u> in the park gardens. He helps to make the park <u>beautiful</u>. *What do the Lee children do to help the community?* They <u>read</u> to younger children at the <u>library</u>.

Fluency: Expression and Phrasing

Read pages 3–4 with appropriate expression and phrasing. Point out that the exclamation marks help you know to express excitement about being close to the city on page 3. Point out how to read the list of transportation options on page 4 with proper phrasing, based on the comma placement.

Respond to Reading Have partners **ask and answer questions** about the selection to check their understanding and clarify anything they are confused about. Then have partners discuss the questions on page 15 using the new vocabulary.

Paired Selection: "Magic Anansi"

Analytical Writing **Make Connections: Write About It**

Before children write, use sentence frames to discuss the question on page 18:

In *City Communities*, city workers help people by <u>giving them maps, helping them cross the street, showing them where to find things.</u> The neighbors have block parties to <u>raise money for their community.</u> In "Magic Anansi," Anansi helps the goats by <u>changing them to stones</u> and <u>throwing them across the river.</u>

Self-Selected Reading Have children select another nonfiction selection from the online **Leveled Reader Library**.

ELL Leveled Reader

Focus On Social Studies

Children can learn more about how people help in their communities by completing the activity on page 20.

Literature Circles

Ask children to conduct a literature circle using the Thinkmark questions to guide the discussion.

LEVEL UP

IF children read the ELL Level fluently and answered the questions

THEN pair them with children who have proficiently read the On Level and have children

- echo-read the On Level main selection with their partner.

- list difficult words and phrases and discuss them with their partners.

Access Complex Text

The On Level challenges children by including more **domain-specific words** and **complex sentence structures**.

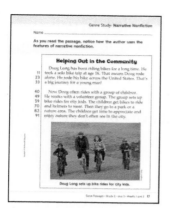

"Helping Out in the Community"
Lexile 480L

OBJECTIVES

Ask and answer such questions as *who, what, where, when, why,* and *how* to demonstrate understanding of key details in a text.

Demonstrate understanding of word relationships and nuances in word meanings.

LANGUAGE OBJECTIVES

Children will read a leveled nonfiction text with support, as needed.

ACADEMIC LANGUAGE

- *narrative nonfiction, purpose, photographs, captions, synonym*
- Cognates: *narrativa, fotografías, sinónimo*

Digital Tools

🎧 Have children listen to the selection to develop comprehension and practice fluency and pronunciation.

English Language Learners

Genre Passage: "Helping Out in the Community"

Build Background

- Remind children that they have been reading and talking about ways people in communities help each other. Tell children they will be reading a narrative nonfiction passage about a man who helps children in his community.

Vocabulary

Use the **Define, Example, Ask** routine to pre-teach difficult words or unfamiliar concepts, such as *journey, helmets, sets up, nature, caterpillar,* and *workshop*. Invite children to add new vocabulary to their glossaries.

Interactive Question-Response Routine

After each paragraph, use Interactive Question-Response prompts such as the following to provide language support and guide comprehension. As you read, remind children to ask for help if they do not understand something in the text.

Page E1

Look at the photograph on page E1. Point to the bikes. Point to the helmets. Where are the children riding? (in a park or nature area)

Paragraph 1

Review **synonyms**. Have children underline the second and third sentences in the first paragraph. *Which two words are synonyms?* (solo, alone) *Which phrase helps you find those **synonyms**?* ("That means")

Paragraph 2

Beginning *Does Doug often ride alone or with others?* (with others) *Who does he ride with?* (a group of children) *What does the volunteer group do for the children?* The volunteer group sets up <u>bike rides</u> for the children.

Intermediate *Does Doug get money for these bike trips?* (no) *How do you know?* (The text says it is a volunteer group. Volunteers do not get paid.) *What do the kids get from the group?* They get <u>bikes</u> and <u>helmets</u>. *Where do they ride?* They ride in a <u>park</u> or <u>nature area</u>.

Advanced Pair children to discuss why Doug's volunteer work is important. (Possible: It's important for children in the city to learn to appreciate nature.)

Page E2

Paragraph 1

Beginning *What did the children see on one trip?* They saw a <u>caterpillar</u>. *Do the kids touch it at first?* (no) *Why not?* The children think it can <u>hurt</u> them. *How do they learn that the caterpillar will not hurt them?* Doug <u>picked up</u> the caterpillar.

Intermediate *Does* harmless *mean that the caterpillar can hurt the children?* (No.) *What did the children do after they found out that the caterpillar was harmless?* They took turns <u>holding</u> it.

Paragraphs 2–3

Beginning *What do the children learn at a bike workshop?* They learn to <u>fix bikes</u>. *What do the children earn when they do this?* They earn <u>points</u>. *What can they use their points for?* They can use points to get their own <u>bikes</u>.

Advanced/Advanced High *The last sentence says, "He makes his community a better place." Tell your partner what that means.* (Possible response: Doug helps children learn new things about nature. He also helps them learn how to fix bikes.)

Dialogue Use this dialogue based on E2 Paragraph 1 to support comprehension while reinforcing listening and speaking skills.

Juan: Look at that! It looks scary. What is it?

Doug: That's a caterpillar. Don't worry it won't hurt you.

Olivia: I don't want to touch it. Are you sure it's harmless?

Doug: I promise. Do you want to hold it?

Olivia: Okay, I'll hold it. Juan, you can have a turn after me.

Doug: Here you go. Be gentle so you don't hurt it.

Respond to Reading

Use the following instruction to help children answer the questions on page E3.

1. *How do you know this selection is narrative nonfiction?* (A narrator is telling a true story about a real person. There is a photograph and caption.)

2. Author's Purpose *Why did the author write this selection?* (to give information about how Doug Long helps in his community)

3. *Why did the author include the* **photo and caption** *on page E1?* (The author included the photo to show Doug on a ride with children. The caption tells about the photo.)

Fluency Have partners take turns reading the passage.

Make Connections

COLLABORATE Have partners discuss ways they help their communities now, or ways they would like to help. Provide sentence frames for support. I help in my community when I (Answers will vary.) I would like to help in my community by (Answers will vary.) and by (Answers will vary.)

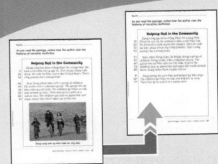

LEVEL UP

IF children read the ELL Level fluently and answered the questions,

THEN pair them with children who have proficiently read the On Level. Have them:

- partner-read the On Level passage.

- state a main idea about one part of the text and give supporting details from the text.

 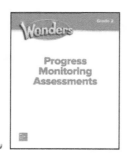  

GENRE STUDY: NARRATIVE NONFICTION
Skills assessed in Progress Monitoring Assessment

FORMALLY ASSESSED SKILLS	INSTRUCTIONAL FOCUS
Author's Purpose	Comprehension Skill
Synonyms	Vocabulary Strategy

Informal Assessment

INFORMALLY ASSESSED SKILLS	INSTRUCTIONAL FOCUS	HOW ASSESSED
Analytical Writing	• Comprehension Skill • Written Response • English Language Conventions	Reading/Writing Companion: Respond to Reading
Grammar, Mechanics, Usage	English Language Conventions	Practice Book, digital activities, writing activities
Spelling	English Language Conventions	Practice Book, word sorts, digital activities, writing activities
Phonics	Foundational Skills	Practice Book, digital activities
Listening/Collaborating/Research	• Listening • Speaking • Research	Checklists, rubrics
Oral Reading Fluency (ORF) Fluency Goal: 74–94 words correct per minute (WCPM) Accuracy Rate Goal: 95% or higher	• Reading Accuracy • Prosody	Fluency Assessment

 A* Assign practice pages online for auto-grading.

Making the Most of Assessment Results

Make data-based grouping decisions by using the following reports to verify assessment results. For additional support options for your students, refer to the reteaching and enrichment opportunities.

ONLINE ASSESSMENT CENTER

- *Item Analysis Report*
- *Standards Analysis Report*

DATA DASHBOARD

- *Recommendations Report*
- *Activity Report*
- *Skills Report*
- *Progress Report*

 RETEACHING OPPORTUNITIES with Intervention Online PDFs

IF CHILDREN SCORE . . .	THEN ASSIGN . . .
below 70% in **comprehension**	Lesson 82–84 on Author's Purpose in **Comprehension PDF**
below 70% in **vocabulary**	Lesson 115 on Synonyms in **Vocabulary PDF**
65–73 WCPM in **fluency**	lesson from Sections 1, 9 or 10 of **Fluency PDF**
0–64 WCPM in **fluency**	lesson from Sections 2–8 of **Fluency PDF**

Use the Phonemic Awareness *and* Phonics/Word Study PDFs *for additional reteaching lessons.*

ENRICHMENT OPPORTUNITIES for Gifted and Talented students

Beyond Level small group lessons include suggestions for additional activities in the following areas to extend learning opportunities for gifted and talented students:

- *Leveled Readers*
- *Genre Passages*
- *Vocabulary Strategy*
- *Comprehension*
- *Leveled Readers Library Online*
- *Workstation Activities*

Genre Study
Fiction

Key Features

- Has a text structure that includes sequence, and may be based on problem and solution

- Uses made-up characters, settings, and events to tell a story with a beginning, a middle, and an end

- Is sometimes told from the point of view of a narrator, instead of a character in the story

Teach It Your Way
Incorporate your own resources to customize your text set!

Make Learning Visible

Genre Study - Fiction

Students learn to think critically as they explore the fiction genre and apply new knowledge and skills encompassing the four domains of language.

Active Engagement in Learning

Students Know What They Are Learning

Students review the Learning Goals for the Fiction Genre Study. The Home/School Family Letter includes a list of the Learning Goals and activities related to student outcomes.

Students Document Their Learning

Anchor Chart

Students will create the following Anchor Charts:
- Fiction Genre Features
- Plot: Sequence
- Reread
- Compound Words
- Personal Narrative

Students Learn From Each Other

- Collaborative Conversations
- Talk About It digital message board
- Blasts

Model Anchor Chart

Genre: Fiction

- Has made up characters and events
- Stories have a beginning, a middle, and an end
  May include dialogue
- Dialogue is the words the characters say
- Writers use quotation marks to show dialogue

Student Outcomes

Comprehension/Genre/Author's Craft

- Cite relevant evidence from text
- ✓ Make inferences to support understanding
- ✓ Understand the author's use of sequence in the story's plot
- Reread to monitor comprehension
- Evaluate heads and subheads
- ✓ Identify and use literary elements

Writing

Writing Process
- Revise, edit, and publish a personal narrative

Analytical Writing
- ✓ Write responses that demonstrate understanding.

Speaking and Listening

- Engage in collaborative discussions
- Retell "The Hidden Sun"
- Present information about one phase of the moon

Language Development

Oral Language Acquisition

exactly	present	reports	telescopes	total

Vocabulary Acquisition
- Acquire and use academic vocabulary

adventure	delighted	dreamed	enjoyed
grumbled	moonlight	neighbor	nighttime

Vocabulary Strategy
- ✓ Recognize and understand compound words

Grammar
- ✓ Understand and use past- and future-tense verbs
- ✓ Understand and use subject-verb agreement

Foundational Skills

Word Work
- Phonological Awareness: Identify Syllables
- Phoneme Awareness: Deletion, Substitution, Addition, Blending, Categorization
- ✓ Phonics: Long *o: o, oa, ow, oe;* Long *e: e, ee, ea, ie, y, ey, e_e*
- Structural Analysis: Contractions, Plurals
- Use High-Frequency Words
- Handwriting: Cursive *y, z, v, x;* Letter/Word Spacing

Spelling Words

Week 3

told	most	float	coat	toast	grow	mow
show	Joe	toe	light	mind	only	our	who

Week 4

we	bee	need	queen	mean	leaf	thief
chief	pony	keys	grow	toe	after	every	special

- Differentiated Spelling Lists, pages T224 and T226

Fluency
- Read fluently with Intonation and Expression

Research and Inquiry

- Develop a research plan to locate information
- Research and write a short report about one phase of the Moon; draw and label a picture of this phase

Content Area Learning

- Research patterns of objects that can be observed in the sky

 Scaffolded supports for English Language Learners are embedded throughout the instruction.

Use the Data Dashboard to filter class, group, or individual student data to guide group placement decisions. It provides recommendations to enhance learning for gifted and talented children and offers extra support for children needing remediation.

Focus on Word Work

Support Foundational Skills

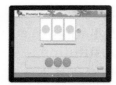

Phonological/Phonemic Awareness Activities

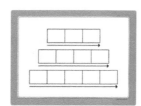

Response Board

Sound-Spelling Cards

Word-Building Cards online

Phonics Activities

Practice Book

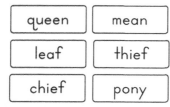

Spelling Word Cards online

High-Frequency Word Cards

High-Frequency Word Activities

Phonological/Phonemic Awareness
- Identify Syllables, Phoneme Deletion, Substitution, Addition, Blending, Categorization

Phonics: Words with Long *o*, Words with Long *e*
- Introduce and blend words
- Use manipulatives for sound-spelling review
- Structural Analysis: Contractions with *not*, Plurals with *-s, -es*

Spelling: Words with Long *o*, Words with Long *e*
- Differentiated spelling instruction
- Encode with sound-spellings
- Explore relationships with word sorts
- Apply spelling to writing

High-Frequency Words
- Read/Spell/Write routine

See Word Work pages, T232–T287

Apply Skills to Read
- Reads are designed to incorporate foundational skills

Decodable Readers

Decodable Passages

Short Vowels; Consonant Blends; Long Vowels › Soft c and g; Consonant Digraphs › 3-Letter Consonant Blends › Silent Letters › *r*-Controlled Vowels › Diphthongs › Varient Vowels › Vowel Digraphs › Syllables

Explicit Systematic Instruction

Word Work instruction expands foundational skills to enable students to become proficient readers.

Daily Review

Review prior sound-spellings to build fluency.

Explicit Minilessons

Use daily instruction in both whole and small groups to model, practice, and apply key foundational skills. Provide corrective feedback. ELL support is provided in all lessons.

Check for Success

Check that students are on track and ready to move forward. Follow up with:

Differentiated Instruction

To strengthen skills, provide targeted review and reteaching lessons to meet students' specific needs.

Approaching

- Includes Tier 2

On Level

Beyond

- Includes Gifted and Talented

ELL

Independent Practice

Students who have the key skills can work independently or with partners.

Workstation Activity Cards

Digital Activities

Word-Building Cards online

Decodable Readers

Practice Book

Foster a Love of Reading

Fiction Text Set

🔑 **Key Concept**
Look At the Sky

❓ **Essential Question**
What can we see in the sky?

Students read and write about different objects to see in the sky.

"The Hidden Sun"
Interactive Read Aloud Cards
Genre Fiction

"Starry Night"
Reading/Writing Companion pp. 38–43
Genre Fiction • Lexile 540L

Mr. Putter & Tabby See the Stars
Literature Anthology pp. 238–257
Genre Fiction • Lexile 580L

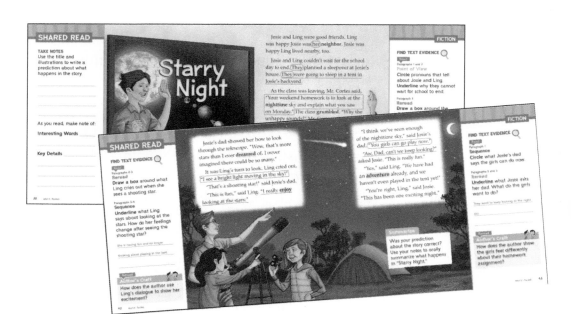

"Day to Night"
Literature Anthology pp. 258–261
Genre Expository Text • Lexile 550L

Scaffolded Shared Read

"Starry Night"
Available online

ELL Scaffolded Shared Read

Lexile 200L
GR G
Approaching

Lexile 390L
GR K
On Level

Lexile 590L
GR N
Beyond

Lexile 330L
GR J
ELL

Leveled Readers with Paired Reads

Approaching **Lexile** 350L
On Level **Lexile** 440L
Beyond **Lexile** 540L
ELL **Lexile** 390L

Genre Passages

Independent Reading Focus

Classroom Library

Henry and Mudge and the Starry Night
Lexile 440L
Lessons available online

More Leveled Readers to Explore

How Many Stars in the Sky?
Lexile 500L

Bonus Leveled Readers

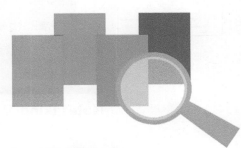

Leveled Reader Library Online

Bibliography

Have students self-select independent reading texts about friends helping friends. Share the online **Unit Bibliography.**

Reading Across Genres

Mezzanotte, Jim. *Hailstorms*. Gareth Stevens Publishing, 2010.
Expository **Lexile** 530L

Simon, Seymour. *The Moon (Revised Edition)*. Simon & Schuster Books for Young Readers, 2003.
Expository **Lexile** 730L

More Fiction

Prigger, Mary Skillings. *Aunt Minnie and the Twister*. Clarion Books, 2002. Fiction **Lexile** 380L

Rylant, Cynthia and Preston McDaniels. *The Lighthouse Family: The Storm*. Simon & Schuster 2003. Fiction **Lexile** 700L

Inspire Confident Writers

Analytical Writing: Fiction

> Develop student habits of writing while reading.

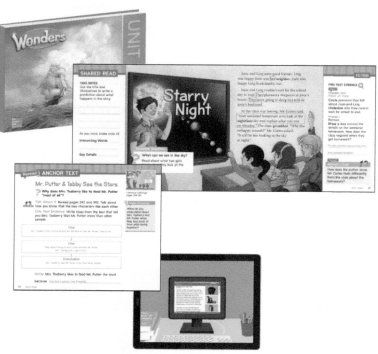

Notetaking Video

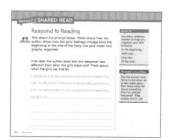
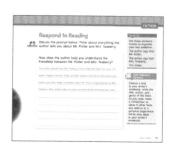

Take Notes to monitor comprehension

Shared Read - Model
"Starry Night"
Reading/Writing Companion pp. 38–43

Anchor Text - Practice and Apply
Mr. Putter & Tabby See the Stars
Literature Anthology pp. 238–255
Reading/Writing Companion pp. 52–54

Summarize using important details

Shared Read - Model
"Starry Night"
Reading/Writing Companion p. 43

Anchor Text - Practice and Apply
Mr. Putter & Tabby See the Stars
Literature Anthology p. 257

Respond using text evidence

Shared Read - Model
"Starry Night"
Reading/Writing Companion p. 50

Anchor Text - Practice and Apply
Mr. Putter & Tabby See the Stars
Literature Anthology p. 257
Reading/Writing Companion p. 55

Genre Writing:
Write Your Own Personal Narrative

WRITING PROCESS

Expert Model ▷ Plan ▷ Draft ▷ Revise ▷ Edit and Proofread ▷ Publish

WEEKS 1 AND 2   WEEKS 3 AND 4

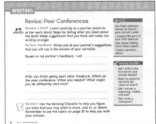

Revise and Peer Conference
Reading/Writing Companion pp. 31–32

- Revise the personal narrative checking for strong openings
- Revise the personal narrative based on partner feedback

Edit and Proofread
Reading/Writing Companion p. 33

- Edit the personal narrative checking for correct grammar
- Proofread the personal narrative checking for correct spelling

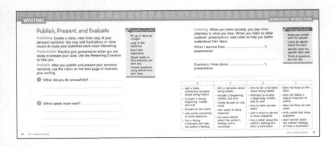

Publish, Present, and Evaluate
Reading/Writing Companion pp. 34–35

- Publish and present the personal narrative
- Self-evaluate using a rubric

Grammar, Spelling, and Handwriting Resources

Practice Book, pp. 213–221, 230–238

A⁺ Assign practice pages online for auto-grading.

Grammar Handbook

Digital Activities

Student Choice
OPTIONS FOR SMALL GROUP TIME

Develop self-directed, critical thinkers.

Independent Reading

Classroom Library

Henry and Mudge and the Starry Night
Genre Fiction
Lexile 440L

How Many Stars in the Sky?
Genre Fiction
Lexile 500L

Leveled Readers

Leveled Reader Library Online
Additional Leveled Readers allow for flexibility.

Bonus Leveled Readers
Students can read more fiction texts.

Reading Across Genres

Literature Anthology
Wild Weather p. 288
Genre Expository Text

"Can You Predict the Weather?" p. 300
Genre Expository Text

Differentiated Genre Passages
Six leveled sets of passages are available on diverse genres.

Self-Selected Reading

Share book room resources as well as the online **Unit Bibliography**. Students choose books for 30–40 minutes of daily independent reading and respond in their writer's notebooks.

Differentiated Workstation Activities

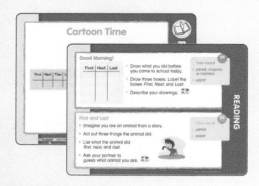

Reading 9

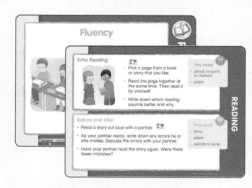

Reading 25

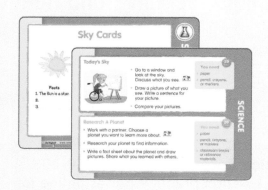

Science 12

Independent Writing

ONLINE Writer's Notebook

Self-Selected Writing

Have students revise and edit their stories or use these suggestions and choose the form they write in.

RESOURCE TOOLKIT

Resource Toolkit

Imagine two friends are looking at the sky. What do they see that surprises them?

Imagine a second-grader speaks to a grandparent and learns something surprising.

Think about a time you learned something new that surprised you. What did you learn?

Think about something a person looking through a telescope could be surprised to see.

What do Josie and Ling learn by looking at the night sky?

Research and Inquiry Project

Students conduct research about the night sky and choose how to present their work.

Digital Activities

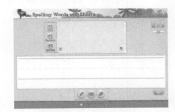

Grammar:
Past- and Future-Tense Verbs
Subject-Verb Agreement

Spelling:
Words with Long *o*
Words with Long *e*

Phonics/Word Study 12

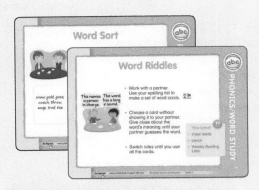

Phonics/Word Study 13, 14

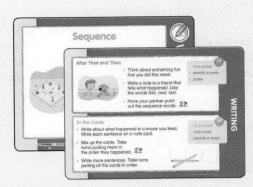

Writing 7

Suggested Lesson Plan

KEY

✎ Writing activity

◀ Can be taught in small groups

CORE

DAY 1	DAY 2
Introduce the Concept T180–T181	**Strategy** Reread, T192–T193
Oral Vocabulary/Listening Comprehension T182–T183	**Literary Elements** Point of View, T194–T195
Word Work T232–T239 • Phonemic Awareness: Deletion • Phonics: Introduce, Blend Long *o* • High-Frequency Words • Decodable Reader: "Three Goats and a Troll" • Handwriting ◀	**Skill** Plot: Sequence, T196–T197 ✎
	Word Work T242–T244 • Phonics: Blend, Build Words with Long *o* • Structural Analysis: Contractions with *not*
Read the Shared Read "Starry Night," T184–T189	**Shared Read** Reread: Craft and Structure, T198–T199
Summarize Quick Write, T189 ✎	**Respond to Reading** T200–T201 ◀
Vocabulary Words in Context, Compound Words, T190–T191	**Study Skill/Research and Inquiry** T204–T205 ◀
Grammar Past- and Future-Tense Verbs, T220	**Grammar** Past- and Future-Tense Verbs, T220
Spelling Words with Long *o: o, oa, ow, oe*, T224 ◀	

OPTIONAL

DAY 1	DAY 2
Word Work T236 • Structural Analysis: Contractions with *not* ◀	**Word Work** T240–T245 • Phonemic Awareness: Substitution • Phonics: Review Long *o* • Decodable Reader: "Three Goats and a Troll" • High-Frequency Words Review ◀
Preteach Vocabulary T190–T191	
Grammar Talk About It, T220 ◀	**Fluency** Intonation, T202–T203
Expand Vocabulary T228	**Grammar** Talk About It, T220 ◀
	Spelling Words with Long *o: o, oa, ow, oe*, T224 ◀
	Expand Vocabulary T228

SMALL GROUP ▶▶ INSTRUCTION

APPROACHING

Leveled Reader
A Special Sunset,
T288–T289
Literature Circles, T289

Genre Passage
"A Shooting Star,"
T290–T291

Vocabulary
Review Vocabulary Words,
T292 ②
Identify Related Words, T293
Compound Words, T293

Fluency
Intonation, T294 ②

Comprehension
Identify Plot,
T294 ②
Review Plot: Sequence,
T295

Word Work T232–T259 ②
Phonological/Phonemic Awareness
Phonics
Structural Analysis
High-Frequency Words
Decodable Reader

ON LEVEL

Leveled Reader
*A Different Set of
Stars,* T296–T297
Literature Circles,
T297

Genre Passage
"A Shooting Star,"
T298–T299

Vocabulary
Review Vocabulary
Words, T300
Compound Words,
T300

Comprehension
Review Plot:
Sequence, T301

Word Work
Phonics, T256

HOW TO DIFFERENTIATE ▶▶ Use your Check for Success observations and Data Dashboard to determine each student's needs. Then select instructional support options throughout the week.

Customize your own lesson plans
my.mheducation.com

DAY 3

Word Work T246–T253
• Phonemic Awareness: Addition • Phonics: Contrast Vowel Sounds • High-Frequency Words • Decodable Reader: "A Rose Grows"

Read the Anchor Text *Mr. Putter & Tabby See the Stars*, T205A–T205K

Take Notes About Text T205A–T205K

Grammar/Mechanics Past- and Future-Tense Verbs, Letter Punctuation, T221

Expand Vocabulary T229

Word Work T248–T250
• Phonics: Blend, Build Words with Long *o* • Structural Analysis: Contractions with *not*

Grammar Talk About It, T221

Spelling Long *o*: *o, oa, ow, oe*, T225

DAY 4

Word Work T255–T256
Phonics: Blend, Build Words with Long *o*

Read the Anchor Text *Mr. Putter & Tabby See the Stars*, T205A–T205K

Take Notes About Text T205A–T205K

Respond to the Text T205L

Word Work T254–T257
• Phoneme Blending • Structural Analysis Review • High-Frequency Words Review • Decodable Reader: "A Rose Grows"

Grammar Past -and Future-Tense Verbs, T221

Grammar Talk About It, T221

Spelling Words with Long *o*, T225

Expand Vocabulary T229

DAY 5

Word Work T258
• Phonics: Blend and Build Long *o*

Reread the Anchor Text *Mr. Putter & Tabby See the Stars*, T205A–T205K

Writing Revise, T212–T213

Spelling Words with Long *o*: *o, oa, ow, oe*, T225

Word Work T258–T259
• Phonemic Awareness: Substitution • Structural Analysis: Contractions with *not* • High-Frequency Words

Grammar Past- and Future-Tense Verbs, T221

Grammar Talk About It, T221

Expand Vocabulary T229

BEYOND

Leveled Reader
Shadows in the Sky, T302–T303
Literature Circles, T303
Synthesize, T303

GIFTED and TALENTED

Genre Passage
"A Shooting Star," T304–T305
Independent Study, T305
GIFTED and TALENTED

Vocabulary
Review Domain–Specific Words, T306
Compound Words, T306
Shades of Meaning, T306
GIFTED and TALENTED

Comprehension
Review Plot: Sequence, T307

ENGLISH LANGUAGE LEARNERS

Shared Read
"Starry Night," T308–T311
Interactive Question, T308–T309
Text Reconstruction, T310
Grammar in Context, T311

Anchor Text
Mr. Putter & Tabby See the Stars, T312–T315
Reread, T312–T313
Text Reconstruction, T314
Grammar in Context, T315

Leveled Reader
A Different Set of Stars, T316–T317

Genre Passage
"A Shooting Star," T318–T319

Word Work
T232–T259
Phonological/Phonemic Awareness
Phonics
Structural Analysis
High-Frequency Words
Decodable Reader

Suggested Lesson Plan

KEY

 Writing activity   ◀ Can be taught in small groups

CORE

DAY 6

Word Work T260–T267
• Phonological Awareness: Identify Syllables • Phonics: Introduce, Blend Long *e* • High-Frequency Words • Decodable Reader: "It Won't Be Easy" • Handwriting ◀

Reread the Anchor Text
Mr. Putter & Tabby See the Stars, T205A–T205K ◀

Respond to Reading T205L

Writing Revise, T212–T213

Grammar Subject-Verb Agreement, T222

Spelling Words with Long *e: e, ee, ea, ie, y, ey, e_e*, T226 ◀

DAY 7

Word Work T269–T272
• Phonics: Blend, Build Words with Long *e* • Structural Analysis: Plurals with -*s*, -*es* s ◀

Read the Paired Selection "Day to Night," T207A–T207B

Writing Peer Conferencing, T214–T215

Grammar Subject-Verb Agreement, T222

Expand Vocabulary T228

OPTIONAL

DAY 6

Word Work T264
• Structural Analysis: Plurals with -*s*, -*es* ◀

Grammar Talk About It, T222

Expand Vocabulary T228

DAY 7

Word Work T268–T273
Phonemic Awareness: Categorization • Phonics: Review Long *e* • Decodable Reader: "It Won't Be Easy"• High-Frequency Word Review

Grammar Talk About It, T222 ◀

Spelling Words with Long *e: e, ee, ea, ie, y, ey, e_e*, T226

 INSTRUCTION

SMALL GROUP

APPROACHING

Genre Passage
"A Shooting Star," T290–T291
Level Up, T291

Vocabulary
Cumulative Vocabulary Review, T292 ②
Identify Related Words, T293
Compound Words T293

Fluency Expression T294 ②

Comprehension
Identify the Plot, T294 ②
Review Plot: Sequence T295
Self-Selected Reading, T295

Word Work T260–T287 ②
Phonological/Phonemic
Awareness
Phonics
Structural Analysis
High–Frequency Words
Decodable Reader

**Leveled Reader
Library Online**
Students can choose additional titles for the same genre, topic, or skills.

ON LEVEL

Genre Passage
"A Shooting Star," T298
Level Up, T299

Vocabulary
Review Vocabulary Words, T300
Compound Words T300

Comprehension
Review Plot: Sequence T301
Self–Selected Reading, T301

Word Work
Phonics, T284

**Leveled Reader
Library Online**
Students can choose additional titles for the same genre, topic, or skills.

HOW TO DIFFERENTIATE

Use your Check for Success observations and Data Dashboard to determine each student's needs. Then select instructional support options throughout the week.

DAY 8

Word Work T274–T281
• Phonemic Awareness: Blending • Phonics: Contrast Vowel Sounds • High-Frequency Words • Decodable Reader: "The Beach Is a Treat"

Reread the Paired Selection "Day to Night," T207A–T207B

Author's Craft Heads, T208–T209

Writing Edit and Proofread, T216–T217

Grammar/Mechanics Abbreviations, T223

Expand Vocabulary T229

Word Work T276–T278
• Phonics: Blend, Build Words with Long *e* • Structural Analysis: Plurals with *-s, -es*

Grammar Talk About It, T223

Spelling Words with Long *e: e, ee, ea ie, y, ey, e_e,* T227

DAY 9

Word Work T283–T284
Phonics: Blend, Build Words with Long *e*

Fluency Reread Genre Passage, T285

Writing Edit and Proofread, T216–T217

Integrate Make Connections, T230

Word Work T282–T285
Identify Syllables • Structural Analysis Review • High-Frequency Words Review • Decodable Reader: "The Beach Is a Treat"

Grammar Subject-Verb Agreement, T223

Grammar Talk About It, T223

Spelling Words with Long *e,* T227

Expand Vocabulary T229

DAY 10

Word Work T286
Phonics: Blend and Build Words with Long *e*

Writing Publish, Present, and Evaluate, T218–T219

Spelling Words with Long *e: e, ee, ea, ie, y, ey, e_e,* T227

Research and Inquiry Present Your Work, T231

Progress Monitoring T320–T321

Word Work T286–T287
• Phonemic Awareness: Blending • Structural Analysis: Plurals with *-s, -es* • High-Frequency Words

Grammar Subject-Verb Agreement, T223

Grammar Talk About It, T223

Expand Vocabulary T229

BEYOND

Genre Passage "A Shooting Star," T304–T305
Independent Study, T305 *GIFTED and TALENTED*

Vocabulary
Review Domain-Specific Words, T306
Compound Words, T306
Shades of Meaning, T306 *GIFTED and TALENTED*

Comprehension
Review Plot: Sequence T307
Self-Selected Reading, T307
Independent Study, T307 *GIFTED and TALENTED*

Leveled Reader Library Online
Children can choose additional titles for the same genre, topic, or skills.

ENGLISH LANGUAGE LEARNERS

Anchor Text
Mr. Putter & Tabby See the Stars, T312–T315
Reread, T312–T313
Text Reconstruction, T314
Grammar in Context, T315

Leveled Reader
Self-Selected Reading, T316

Genre Passage
"A Shooting Star," T318
Level Up, T319

Word Work T260–T287
Phonological/Phonemic Awareness
Phonics
Structural Analysis
High-Frequency Words
Decodable Reader

Leveled Reader Library Online
Students can choose additional titles for the same genre, topic, or skills.

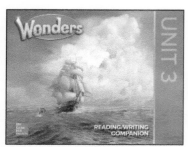

Reading/Writing Companion

OBJECTIVES

Ask and answer questions about what a speaker says in order to clarify comprehension, gather additional information, or deepen understanding of a topic or issue.

Participate in collaborative conversations with diverse partners about *grade 2 topics and texts* with peers and adults in small and larger groups.

(a) Follow agreed-upon rules for discussions (e.g., gaining the floor in respectful ways listening to others with care, speaking one at a time about the topics and texts under discussion).

(b) Build on others' talk in conversations by linking their comments to the remarks of others.

ACADEMIC LANGUAGE

• *moonlight, nighttime, daytime*

Digital Tools

Show the image during class discussion. Then play the video.

Discuss Concept

Watch Video

Talk About It

10 Mins

Essential Question

What can we see in the sky?

Display the online **Student Learning Goals** for this genre study. Read the key concept: Look at the Sky. Tell children that they will be reading fictional stories about people who are outside in the nighttime. The characters all notice that they see different things at night than during the daytime.

Read the Essential Question on **Reading/Writing Companion** page 36. Discuss the photograph with children. Point out that the photo shows a girl looking at the daytime sky. Explain that we can see things during the day because the Sun lights the sky. Ask children what they might see in the daytime sky.

Explain that during **nighttime**, it is dark outside. The Sun does not light the sky then, but sometimes there is light from the Moon. Have children describe the Moon. **Moonlight** is the light we see from the Moon at night.

Ask: *How is the sky different in the daytime and nighttime? What kinds of things can you see in the nighttime sky?* Have children discuss in pairs or groups.

Model using the graphic organizer. Ask children what they might see in the sky. Record one or two answers in the appropriate column on the graphic organizer. Then have children work in pairs to generate more things they might see in the sky and record them on the graphic organizer in the appropriate column.

Collaborative Conversations

Take Turns Talking As children engage in partner, small-group, and whole-group discussions, encourage them to follow discussion rules by taking turns speaking. Remind children to

• wait for a person to finish before they speak.

• quietly raise their hand when they want to speak.

• ask others to share their ideas and opinions.

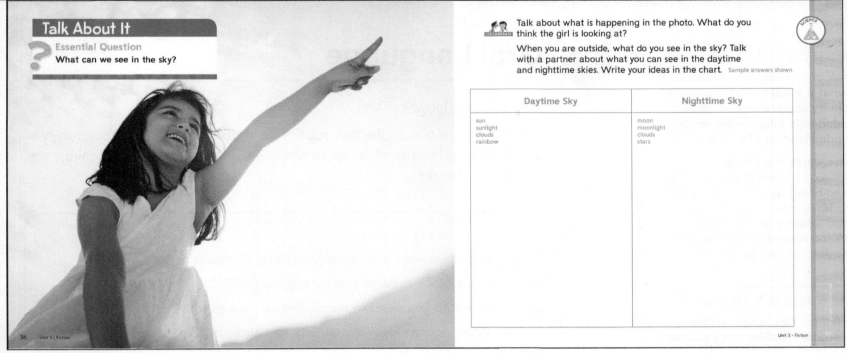

Talk About It

Essential Question
What can we see in the sky?

Talk about what is happening in the photo. What do you think the girl is looking at?

When you are outside, what do you see in the sky? Talk with a partner about what you can see in the daytime and nighttime skies. Write your ideas in the chart. Sample answers shown.

Daytime Sky	Nighttime Sky
sun sunlight clouds rainbow	moon moonlight clouds stars

Reading/Writing Companion, pp. 36–37

Share the "When the Night Sky Dances" Blast assignment with children. Point out that you will discuss their responses in the Integrate Ideas lesson at the end of this two-week genre study.

 English Language Learners SCAFFOLD

Use the following scaffolds during **Ask** to help children use their prior knowledge to talk about things they can see in the sky.

Beginning

Use the photo to prompt a discussion of things you can see in the sky. Point and say: *She is looking at the daytime sky. What do you see in the daytime sky?* Elicit responses: I see clouds in the daytime sky. *What do you see in the nighttime sky?* I see stars in the nighttime sky. Provide linguistic support, as needed, to help children share their prior knowledge. Help children use their responses to complete the graphic organizer on page 37.

Intermediate

Have partners ask and answer: What can you see in the daytime sky? I can see clouds in the daytime sky. Provide linguistic support, as needed, to help children share their prior knowledge.

Advanced/Advanced High

As you access prior knowledge with the group, invite children to record ideas on the board for the class to refer to. Then have partners ask and answer about the sky: *What can you see in the daytime/ nighttime sky? How is the sky different in the daytime and nighttime?*

 Vocabulary

clouds (*nubes*) tiny pieces of ice and water suspended in the air (use a visual for clarification)

daytime (*durante el día*) the time between sunrise and sunset

Moon (*Luna*) Earth's satellite body (use a visual for clarification)

outside (*afuera*) not in a building

star (*estrella*) bright celestial body visible at night (use a visual for clarification)

Sun (*Sol*) the star in the center of our solar system (use a visual for clarification)

Newcomers

To help children develop oral language and build vocabulary, use **Newcomer Cards 10–14** and the accompanying materials in the **Newcomer Teacher's Guide.**

OBJECTIVES

Ask and answer questions about what a speaker says in order to clarify comprehension, gather additional information, or deepen understanding of a topic or issue.

Use words and phrases acquired through conversations, reading and being read to, and responding to texts, including using adjectives and adverbs to describe (e.g., *When other kids are happy that makes me happy*).

ACADEMIC LANGUAGE

• *fiction, characters, settings, events, narrator, story structure*

Digital Tools

Read or play the Interactive Read Aloud.

Interactive Read Aloud

SOCIAL EMOTIONAL LEARNING

Curiosity Children who demonstrate curiosity are better able to generate questions to help them better understand content. As children listen, have them consider this question: *What things in the sky do you want to learn more about? Why?*

Oral Language

🕙 10 Mins

Oral Vocabulary Words

Use the **Define/Example/Ask** routine to introduce the Oral Vocabulary Words below. Prompt children to use the words as they discuss things we can see in the sky.

Oral Vocabulary Routine

<u>Define:</u> **Exactly** means without any mistake. (Cognate: *exactamente*)

<u>Example:</u> The clock showed exactly eight o'clock.

<u>Ask:</u> Why would you need to measure your feet exactly?

<u>Define:</u> When you **present** something, you show or tell about it before an audience. (Cognate: *presentar*)

<u>Example:</u> Lillian will present her report about dolphins to the class.

<u>Ask:</u> Show and tell how you would present a new friend to your class.

<u>Define:</u> When you give a **report**, you tell or write about something you've heard.

<u>Example:</u> The class enjoyed listening to Kara's report about dolphins.

<u>Ask:</u> What would you like to write a report about?

<u>Define:</u> **Telescopes** make things that are far away seem closer and larger. (Cognate: *telescopio*)

<u>Example:</u> Telescopes are useful for looking at the stars.

<u>Ask:</u> Describe what telescopes can help you see.

<u>Define:</u> **Total** means the whole or entire thing. (Cognate: *total*)

<u>Example:</u> Max spent the total amount of his money.

<u>Ask:</u> What is the total number of apples you will buy?

Introduce the Genre

Connect to Concept: Look at the Sky

Tell children that you are going to read a story about children who want to know about things in the sky. The story is fiction, but it tells facts about things in the sky, including something called a solar eclipse.

Interactive Read-Aloud Cards

Preview Fiction

Discuss the features of fiction:

- has made-up characters, settings, and events.

- has a beginning, a middle, and an end.

- is sometimes told by a narrator, instead of a character in the story.

Anchor Chart Begin an anchor chart for fiction and ask children to add characteristics of the genre.

Preview Story Structure

Explain that fictional stories have a structure, which includes the order in which events happen. Sometimes the structure is based on a problem that needs to be solved. In "The Hidden Sun," the problem facing Hollie and Mike is *How can we learn about solar eclipses?*

Read and Respond

Read the text aloud to children. Preview the comprehension strategy. Reread, using the Think Alouds below.

Display the online **Think Aloud Cloud:** When I read . . . , I had to reread . . . to reinforce how to use the strategy to understand content. Say: I read about a *partial eclipse,* but now I'm not sure what it is. I'll reread to find out.

Think Aloud As I read, I learned that when the Moon hides part of the Sun, it's called a partial eclipse.

Genre Features With children, discuss the elements of the Interactive Read Aloud that let them know the text is fiction. Ask them to think about other texts they read in class or independently that were fiction.

Retell Have children use their own words to retell "The Hidden Sun" in logical order. Explain that they do not have to include every fact, but they should tell the important events in the story.

OBJECTIVES

Ask and answer questions about what a speaker says in order to clarify comprehension, gather additional information, or deepen understanding of a topic or issue.

Use information gained from the illustrations and words in a print or digital text to demonstrate understanding of its characters, setting, or plot.

ACADEMIC LANGUAGE

- *fiction, story structure*

 Spotlight on Language

Card 1: Reinforce the basic vocabulary listed on Card 1: *far, near, big, little, bright, dark, fast, slow.* Use visuals, gestures, and examples to clarify meaning. *Now turn to a partner and use some of these words to talk about things you see in the sky.* I can see the Moon. It is far.

Card 2: Point out the phrase *even when* (the Sun is hidden by the moon). Clarify meaning as needed.

Card 3: Use visuals to reinforce *total* and *partial* eclipses. The words *total* and *partial* have cognates in Spanish (*total, parcial*), French (*total, partiel*), Italian (*totale, parziale*).

Card 4: Help children use the pictures on the cards to retell the story. Provide additional frames to help them use new vocabulary, for example: (Card 1) Ms. Moore tells the class to write a report. (Card 2) Then Hollie and Mike decide to write about a solar eclipse. (Card 3) Then Hollie's mother helps them find a website to learn about solar eclipses. (Card 4) In the end, they visit an observatory. They wear special glasses to watch the eclipse. They look through a telescope.

"Starry Night"

Reading/Writing Companion

Text Complexity Range
Lexile

420   540   820

OBJECTIVES

Read with sufficient accuracy and fluency to support comprehension.

Read on-level text with purpose and understanding.

Read with sufficient accuracy and fluency to support comprehension.

Ask and answer such questions as *who, what, where, when, why,* and *how* to demonstrate understanding of key details in a text.

Close Reading Routine

Read   DOK 1–2

• Identify key ideas and details about what we can look at in the sky.
• Take notes and summarize.
• Use **A C T** prompts as needed.

Reread   DOK 2–3

• Analyze the text, craft, and structure.
• Use the Reread Minilessons and prompts.

Integrate   DOK 4

• Integrate knowledge and ideas.
• Make text-to-text connections.
• Use the Integrate lesson.
• Inspire action.

SHARED READ

TAKE NOTES
Use the title and illustrations to write a prediction about what happens in the story.

_____
_____
_____
_____

As you read, make note of:

Interesting Words _____

_____

Key Details _____

_____
_____
_____

38   Unit 3 · Fiction

Essential Question

What can we see in the sky?
Read about what two girls learn when they look at the nighttime sky.

Reading/Writing Companion pp. 38–39

Take Notes Before they begin, have children think about the Essential Question and what they know about looking at the sky. Then have them look at the title and illustrations and make a prediction about what will happen in the story. Have them write their prediction on page 38. As children read, remind them to use the left column of page 38 to note any interesting words they read, and to record key details from the text. Remind children to read accurately.

Focus on the Read prompts now. For additional support, there are extra prompts not included in the **Reading/Writing Companion.** Use the Reread prompts on pages T198-T199.

DIFFERENTIATED READING

Approaching Level Ask children to volunteer words they listed in their notes. Talk with students about the words' meanings.

On Level Have pairs of children work together to determine the meanings of interesting words they listed in their notes.

Beyond Level As a class, discuss key details students noted. Also discuss examples of the use of the third-person point of view.

  English Language Learners Preteach the vocabulary. Have Beginning/Early-Intermediate ELLs listen to the summary, available in many languages, and use the **Scaffolded Shared Read.** See the small group pages for additional support.

osie and Ling were good friends. Ling
s happy Josie was her neighbor. Josie was
ppy Ling lived nearby, too.

osie and Ling couldn't wait for the school
r to end. They planned a sleepover at Josie's
use. They were going to sleep in a tent in
ie's backyard.

As the class was leaving, Mr. Cortes said,
ur weekend homework is to look at the
httime sky and explain what you saw
Monday." The class grumbled. "Why the
happy sounds?" Mr. Cortes asked.
will be fun looking at the sky
ight."

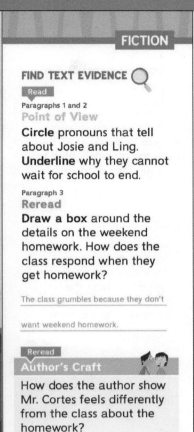

FIND TEXT EVIDENCE 🔍

Read

Paragraphs 1 and 2
Point of View

Circle pronouns that tell
about Josie and Ling.
Underline why they cannot
wait for school to end.

Paragraph 3
Reread

Draw a box around the
details on the weekend
homework. How does the
class respond when they
get homework?

The class grumbles because they don't

want weekend homework.

Reread
Author's Craft

How does the author show
Mr. Cortes feels differently
from the class about the
homework?

Unit 3 · Fiction   **39**

Point of View

Paragraphs 1-2: Read the first two paragraphs. Ask: *Who are the characters?* (Josie and Ling) *Who is telling the story?* (not one of the characters; someone not in the story) Explain that this story is told by someone outside the story called the narrator. Say: *The narrator gives information about the characters.* Encourage children to listen for other information about Josie, Ling, and other characters. Have children circle the pronouns that tell about Jose and Ling and underline why they cannot wait for school to end. (her; They; They; They are going to sleep in a tent in Josie's backyard.)

Vocabulary: Compound Words

Paragraph 3: Read the third paragraph. Remind children that a compound word is made up of two smaller words.

Think Aloud I see the word *weekend* in the paragraph. I can see two smaller words in this word: *week* and *end*. The weekend is the *end* of the *week*. When two words are put together to make a new word, it's called a compound word. Ask children to find two other compound words in the paragraph. Discuss how the two smaller words in each form the meaning of the compound word. (*homework* and *nighttime*; Homework is school work that you do at home. Nighttime is the time that happens at night.)

Strategy: Reread

Paragraph 3: Read the third paragraph. Model rereading for information.

Think Aloud There are a lot of details in this paragraph. I think I need to read the paragraph again to help me remember what the weekend homework is and how the class feels about it. Reread the paragraph and point out what the weekend homework is and how the class responds to it. Ask children to tell why they think the class responds that way. Encourage them to cite text evidence. (The class probably wants to have fun over the weekend. For example, Josie and Ling planned a sleepover at Josie's house. They are going to sleep in a tent in Josie's backyard.)

Ⓔ Spotlight on Language

Page 39, Paragraph 2: Focus on the use of the pronoun *they*. Explain that pronouns are words that replace nouns, including the names of characters. Read the sentence: *They planned a sleepover at Josie's house. I want to figure out who planned a sleepover. I need to find out what names are replaced by* They. *I'm going to look for the names that appear before* They. Read the sentence: *Josie and Ling couldn't wait for the school day to end. This tells me that* They *refers to Josie and Ling.*

Vocabulary: Compound Words

Paragraph 1: Read the first paragraph.

Think Aloud When I see a compound word I don't know, I look at the two smaller words. Sometimes I have to do a little thinking. If I didn't know the word *outdoors*, I would ask myself where I am when I go *out* through the *doors* of a house or other building. **Ask children to look for another compound word in the first paragraph. (flashlights) Discuss how two smaller words work together to make the meaning of** *flashlight*. (A flashlight flashes, or shines, a light brightly.) **Then ask why the girls are delighted to be sleeping outdoors. Have them cite text evidence.** (They are happy to play games in the tent, using the flashlights they brought with them.)

 English Language Learners

Request Assistance Remind children of expressions they can use to request assistance from the teacher or their partners, such as *Can you show me in the picture, please?*

SHARED READ

FIND TEXT EVIDENCE 🔍

Read
Paragraph 1
Compound Words
Circle the two smaller words in *outdoors*. Why are the girls delighted to be sleeping outdoors?

They are happy to play games in the

tent.

Paragraph 2
Sequence
Underline text evidence that shows how the girls feel about doing homework at the time.

Reread
Author's Craft
Why is the setting in Josie's backyard at night important to the story?

40   Unit 3 · Fiction

The girls arrived at Josie's house and were **delighted** to be sleeping outdoors. Josie said, "I'm happy that we get to sleep in the tent. It will be lo of fun." Then Ling said, "I'll get the sleeping bags and flashlights. I brought flashlights so we can pl games in the tent."

Josie's dad poked his head inside the tent. "Gir it is a good time to do your homework now becau it is getting dark," he said. "Awww," they both complained. "Dad," said Josie, "do we have to, no

"Yes, I already set up the telescope."

Reading/Writing Companion pp. 40–41

Skill: Sequence

Paragraph 2: Read the second paragraph. Ask: *What new event happens?* (Josie's father tells them to do their homework.) Ask: *What word in the second sentence tells you when he wants them to do their homework?* (now) Ask: *How do the girls feel about this? How do you know?* (They both complain. They say, "Awww.")

Strategy: Reread

Paragraph 3: Reread paragraph 3 with children to find out why Josie's father wants Josie and Ling to do their homework now. (It is getting dark outside, and he already set up the telescope.)

 **Access Complex Text**

Purpose

Remind children that sometimes an author has more than one purpose in writing a text. Point out that "Starry Night" is a fictional story with made-up characters and a plot. However, there are clues that the story will also give important factual information.

• Ask: *What does the illustration on the board on page 38 show?* (the Sun and planets) *What homework assignment does the teacher give?* (He tells the class to look at the nighttime sky.) *What do you think you might learn about as you read this story?* (The story will probably tell about what you can see in the nighttime sky.) *What clue in the illustration on page 41 lets you know that you might get more information about the sky?* (Josie's father is pointing a telescope at the sky.)

FIND TEXT EVIDENCE 🔍

[Read]
Paragraph 1
Reread

Why does Josie say, "It's funny that it's called moonlight"? **Circle** details that support your answer.

She knows that moonlight is light that
_____

comes from the Sun.
_____
_____
_____

Fluency

With a partner, practice reading with intonation. Try to raise the tone of your voice when asking a question.

...ing said, "I hope this won't take too long." Josie ...ked up and spotted a crescent moon. "Did you ...ow the moon's light comes from the sun?" said Josie. ...s funny that it's called **moonlight**." "Yes," said Ling, ...o was still thinking about playing in the tent.

...osie's dad smiled at the girls and said, ...ee the stars in the sky? Those points ...oright light can form shapes."

..."You can see the Big Dipper," he ...d. "It's a group of stars that look like a ...nt spoon in the sky."

The Big Dipper

Unit 3 · Fiction   41

Vocabulary: Compound Words

Paragraph 1: Read the first paragraph. Draw children's attention to the word *moonlight.* Ask them how they can figure out what the word means. (There are two smaller words in the word—*moon* and *light*—so it must mean light from the moon.)

Strategy: Reread

Paragraph 1: Ask children to reread paragraph 1 to find out why Josie says, "It's funny that it's called moonlight." Ask: What question does Josie ask that tells you where the moon's light comes from? (She asks, "Did you know the moon's light comes from the sun?")

Strategy: Reread

Paragraphs 1–3: Ask how Ling feels about leaving the tent to look at the telescope.

Think Aloud If I don't remember how Ling is feeling, I can reread. I go back to page 40 and find that she wants to play games in the tent. Then I can look at page 41 and discover more text evidence. Ask children to reread to find evidence in the first paragraph of page 41 about how Ling is feeling about leaving the tent to look at the stars. (She says, "I hope this won't take too long" and is still thinking about playing with flashlights in the tent.)

Fluency

Have partners choral read paragraphs 1 and 2 on page 41. Circulate and provide corrective feedback. For a full lesson and additional fluency practice, see pages T202–T203.

 Spotlight on Language

Page 41, Paragraph 1: Read aloud the sentence, *I hope this won't take too long. The word* hope *tells what the speaker wants. The word* this *is a pronoun that refers to looking at the sky through the telescope. The word* won't *is a contraction of the words* will not, *which are used to talk about the future. The word* take *has many meanings. In this sentence, it refers to time. The phrase* too long *means more time than you want. Invite children to restate the sentence in their own words.* (Possible: I want this to end soon.) *Turn to a partner and discuss: Why does Ling hope this won't take too long?* (Possible: The girls are having fun and don't want to be interrupted.)

Skill: Sequence

Paragraph 1: Read the first paragraph. Ask: *What does Josie's dad show her how to do?* (look through the telescope) What happens next? (She sees more stars than she ever dreamed of.) Discuss why this is an important event in the story. Explain that Josie is now excited about looking at the nighttime sky.

Author's Craft

Paragraph 1: Point out the word *Wow* in the second line. Remind children that this is an interjection, a word at the beginning of a sentence that shows emotion. *Why do you think the author used an interjection here?* (To show how amazed Josie is by the stars.) Ask children to find and discuss another interjection in the story. (*Aw* on pages 40 and 43)

Strategy: Reread

Paragraphs 2-3: Read the second and third paragraphs.

Think Aloud I've heard of shooting stars, but I've never actually seen one. I'm going to reread to understand what it is. I see. It looks like a bright light moving in the sky. After Ling says that she sees "a bright light moving in the sky," Josie's dad explains that what she sees is a shooting star. **Have children point to the shooting star in the illustration on pages 42-43.**

SHARED READ

FIND TEXT EVIDENCE 🔍

Read

Paragraphs 2-3

Reread

Draw a box around what Ling cries out when she sees a shooting star.

Paragraphs 3-4

Sequence

Underline what Ling says about looking at the stars. How do her feelings change after seeing the shooting star?

She is having fun and no longer

thinking about playing in the tent.

Reread

Author's Craft

How does the author use Ling's dialogue to show her excitement?

42   Unit 3 · Fiction

Josie's dad showed her how to look through the telescope. "Wow, that's more stars than I ever **dreamed** of. I never imagined there could be so many."

It was Ling's turn to look. Ling cried ou "I see a bright light moving in the sky!"

"That's a shooting star!" said Josie's dad

"This is fun," said Ling. "I really **enjoy** looking at the stars."

Reading/Writing Companion pp. 42–43

Skill: Sequence

Paragraphs 3-4: Read the third and fourth paragraphs. Say: *So far in the story, Ling hasn't been very excited about looking at the nighttime sky. How do her feelings change?* (She really enjoys it.) How do you know? (Ling says that she enjoys looking at the stars.) Discuss why this is an important event in the story. Explain that in most stories the characters change in some way.

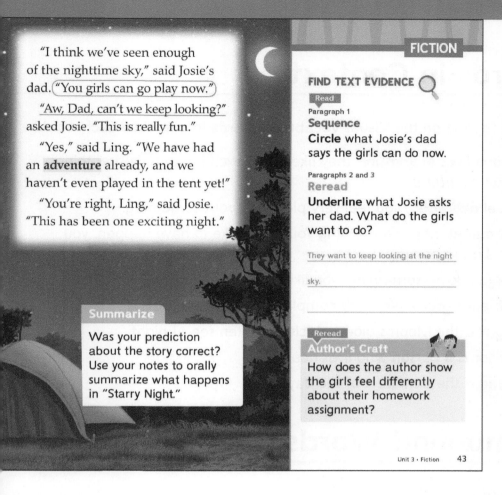

"I think we've seen enough of the nighttime sky," said Josie's dad. ("You girls can go play now.")

"Aw, Dad, can't we keep looking?" asked Josie. "This is really fun."

"Yes," said Ling. "We have had an **adventure** already, and we haven't even played in the tent yet!"

"You're right, Ling," said Josie. "This has been one exciting night."

Summarize

Was your prediction about the story correct? Use your notes to orally summarize what happens in "Starry Night."

FIND TEXT EVIDENCE 🔍

Read

Paragraph 1
Sequence
Circle what Josie's dad says the girls can do now.

Paragraphs 2 and 3
Reread
Underline what Josie asks her dad. What do the girls want to do?

They want to keep looking at the night sky.

Reread
Author's Craft
How does the author show the girls feel differently about their homework assignment?

Unit 3 · Fiction   43

Skill: Sequence

Paragraph 1: Read paragraph 1. Point out that writers often lead readers to expect a certain event to be next in a sequence. Sometimes, writers surprise their readers with a different event. Say: *When I read the first paragraph, I expect Josie and Ling to go back to the tent to play. That's because Josie's dad says, "You girls can go play now." But the girls surprise me. What do they want to do instead?* (keep looking at the sky) Ask children what they think will happen next.

Strategy: Reread

Paragraphs 2-3: Reread paragraphs 2-3. Ask: *After Josies's dad tells the girls that they can play, what does Josie ask her dad?* (She asks him if she and Ling can keep looking at the sky.) Ask: *Why does she ask him that?* (It has been fun.) Ask children what they think will happen next in the story.

Vocabulary: Context Clues

Paragraphs 3-4: Read paragraphs 3 and 4. Draw children's attention to the word *adventure*. Tell children they can use information in sentences before and after a word to help understand what it means. Ask children what clues the authors gives to help us understand the word *adventure*. (The girls look at the stars and see a shooting star. They say they are having fun and that it's been an exciting night.) Explain that when people do something new and exciting, it can be an adventure.

Summarize

Analytical Writing Have partners summarize the selection orally using the notes they have taken during their first read. Then have individual children write summaries in their writer's notebooks. Remind them to include only important events, not small details, and to use their own words. They may decide to digitally record presentations of their summaries.

ELL Spotlight on Language

Page 43, Paragraph 2 *When Josie asks "Can't we keep looking?" she is asking her father to allow the girls to spend more time looking at the night sky. If you keep doing something, you continue doing it. Why does Josie want to keep looking?* (The girls are having fun.)

Vocabulary

Reading/Writing Companion

OBJECTIVES

Recognize and read grade-appropriate irregularly spelled words.

Create audio recordings of stories or poems; add drawings or other visual displays to stories or recounts of experiences when appropriate to clarify ideas, thoughts, and feelings.

ACADEMIC LANGUAGE

• compound, figure out

Digital Tools

Visual Vocabulary Cards

TEACH IN SMALL GROUP

Compound Words

Approaching Level and ELL Preteach the words before children begin the Shared Read.

On Level and Beyond Level Have children look up each word in the online **Visual Glossary**.

 ## Words in Context

Use the routine on the **Visual Vocabulary Cards** to introduce each word.

If someone likes **adventure**, they like doing exciting and unusual things. (Cognate: *aventura*)

If you feel **delighted**, you feel very pleased about something.

If you **dreamed** about something you would like to have happen, you imagined it happening.

If you **enjoy** doing something, you like doing it.

If your friends **grumbled**, they complained about something.

Moonlight is the Moon's glow, which you often see at night.

A **neighbor** is a person who lives near you.

Nighttime is the dark part of the day.

 ## Compound Words

1 Explain

A compound word is made up of two smaller words. The meanings of the two smaller words can be used to figure out the meaning of the compound word.

2 Model

Model how to figure out the meaning of the compound word *sleepover* on page 39. Say: *First, I find the two smaller words in* sleepover. *The compound word contains the words* sleep *and* over. *The word* sleep *means "to close your eyes and rest." The word* over *can mean "at another place." I put those meanings together to figure out that the compound word* sleepover *means "resting at another place."*

3 Guided Practice

Have partners use the meaning of the smaller words in the compound words on page 39 to figure out the meanings of the compound words: *backyard* (the grassy area in back of a house) and *homework* (schoolwork to be done at home). Ask children to share their answers with the class to confirm everyone understands the words. Have children add these words to their vocabulary strategy anchor chart.

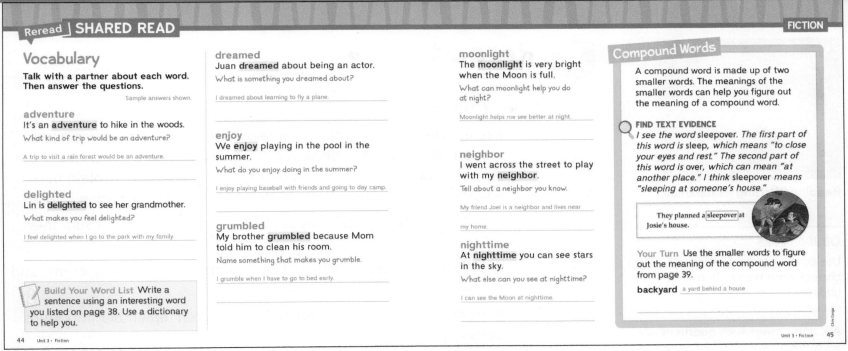

Reading/Writing Companion, pp. 44–45

 English Language Learners SCAFFOLD

Use the following scaffolds with **Guided Practice** to help children use accessible language to learn compound words.

Beginning

Have children point to *backyard* and *homework* on page 39. Write the words on the board and divide them to show *back, yard, home,* and *work*. Elicit meanings of these smaller words, using gestures or visuals for support. Then provide sentence frames to help children define each compound word: A backyard is the <u>yard</u> in the <u>back</u> of a house. Homework is <u>work</u> you do at <u>home</u>.

Intermediate

Write *backyard* and *homework* on the board. *What two words do you know in* backyard? (back and yard) *What two words do you know in* homework? (home and work) Have children work in pairs to complete sentence frames to define each word: A <u>backyard</u> is the <u>yard</u> in the <u>back</u> of a house. Your <u>homework</u> is <u>work</u> you do at <u>home</u>.

Advanced/Advanced High

Have partners circle the compound words on page 39. (sleepover, backyard, weekend, homework, nighttime) Have partners ask and answer for each word: *What two words do you know in ___? What do you think ___ means?*

 Build Your Word List

Children might choose *unhappy* from page 39. Have partners use context clues and word parts to figure out the meaning.

✔ Check for Success

Rubric Use the online rubric to record children's progress.

Can children figure out the meanings of *backyard* and *homework*?

Differentiate
SMALL GROUP INSTRUCTION

If No

| Approaching | Reteach p. T292 |
| ELL | Develop p. T318 |

If Yes

| On | Review p. T300 |
| Beyond | Extend p. T306 |

Reading/Writing Companion

OBJECTIVES

Use context to confirm or self-correct word recognition and understanding, rereading as necessary.

Ask and answer such questions as *who, what, where, when, why,* and *how* to demonstrate understanding of key details in a text.

ACADEMIC LANGUAGE

• *reread*

 Reread

1 Explain

Remind children that when they read fiction, they may come across sections they do not understand. They may also be unclear about the sequence of events or miss an event in that sequence. Explain that rereading text can help them better understand information.

- Children should reread any sections of text they are not sure they understood.

- Children can reread to build their understanding of story events and how those events fit together.

Point out that rereading will also help children remember important parts of a story.

Anchor Chart Have volunteers add information about rereading to the comprehension strategy chart and reread the chart.

2 Model

Model how rereading can help you understand what the Big Dipper is. Reread the last two paragraphs on page 41 of "Starry Night."

Think Aloud Rereading the text helps me understand that the Big Dipper is a group of stars that looks like a giant spoon in the sky. I also notice an illustration next to the text that shows a group of stars that looks like a spoon. Now I can picture and understand what the Big Dipper is.

3 Guided Practice

Have children work in pairs to explain what a telescope helps you do. Direct children to page 42. Have partners reread the first two paragraphs and discuss what each girl sees as she looks through the telescope. Then have partners discuss other parts of the story that they might want to reread. Circulate and listen in as children discuss, offering feedback and guidance as necessary.

Reread | SHARED READ

Reread

As you read, you can stop and reread the parts you do not understand or may have missed. This will help you understand what you read.

Quick Tip
Pay attention to words that tell about actions and words that describe sensory details, such as how something looks or sounds.

FIND TEXT EVIDENCE
On page 41 of "Starry Night," I am not sure what the Big Dipper is. I will reread this part of the story to see if I missed anything.

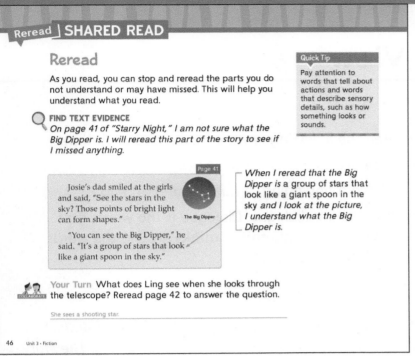

Page 41

Josie's dad smiled at the girls and said, "See the stars in the sky? Those points of bright light can form shapes."

"You can see the Big Dipper," he said. "It's a group of stars that look like a giant spoon in the sky."

The Big Dipper

When I reread that the Big Dipper is a group of stars that look like a giant spoon in the sky and I look at the picture, I understand what the Big Dipper is.

Your Turn What does Ling see when she looks through the telescope? Reread page 42 to answer the question.

She sees a shooting star.

46   Unit 3 · Fiction

Reading/Writing Companion, p. 46

ELL English Language Learners SCAFFOLD

Use the following scaffolds with **Guided Practice**.

Beginning

Choral read the first paragraph on page 42. Repeat the word *telescope* and have children point to the telescope in the illustration. Then choral read the second paragraph and ask: *What did Ling do?* (look through the telescope) Use gestures to convey the meaning of *look* and allow children to point to the word on the page. Choral read the rest of page 42. *What can you do with a telescope?* Help children complete this frame: You can look at the stars through a telescope.

Intermediate

Help children reread page 42. Then have partners work together to complete these frames: Josie used the telescope to look at the stars in the sky. Ling saw a moving light through the telescope. Josie's dad said the moving light in the sky was a shooting star. Then ask: *What does a telescope help you do?* Have partners complete this sentence starter: A telescope helps you look at stars and other things in the sky.

Advanced/Advanced High

Ask partners: *What did the girls use to look at the sky?* (a telescope) *What did Josie see through the telescope? What did Ling see through the telescope?* Have them find the answers on page 42. (the stars; a moving light in the sky; a shooting star) *What does a telescope help you do?* Have partners discuss possible answers.

HABITS OF LEARNING

I believe I can succeed. Rereading sections of text helps children develop this key habit of believing that they can succeed. Remind children to reread sections of text to better understand the content. Have them ask themselves the following questions to determine whether they need to reread sections of text:

- Do I understand this section?
- Do I understand the story events?
- Do I understand how the story events fit together?
- Do I understand the most important parts of this story?

✓ Check for Success

Can children reread to find important information in the text?

Differentiate
SMALL GROUP INSTRUCTION

If No
| Approaching | Reteach p. T288 |
| ELL | Develop p. T316 |

If Yes
| On | Review p. T296 |
| Beyond | Extend p. T302 |

Reading/Writing Companion

OBJECTIVES

Acknowledge differences in the points of view of characters, including by speaking in a different voice for each character when reading dialogue aloud.

ACADEMIC LANGUAGE

- *fiction, characters, point of view*
- Cognate: *ficción*

Point of View

1 Explain

Share with children the following key characteristics of **fiction**.

- Fiction has made-up characters and events.
- Fiction stories have a beginning, a middle, and an end.
- Fiction may also include dialogue. Dialogue is the words that characters say. Writers use quotation marks around the words characters say to show dialogue.

2 Model

Model identifying the genre of "Starry Night." Say: *I can tell that "Starry Night" is fiction. It tells about made-up characters. The story also tells about made-up events. It has a clear beginning, middle, and end. I notice that the characters also talk to each other, so there is dialogue.*

Point of View Tell children that "point of view" refers to who is telling the story. If a character is telling a story, then we say the story is in the first person. When the story is told by someone outside the story, then we say the story is in the third person. Explain that when a story is told in the third person, we call the person telling the story the narrator. The narrator is not a character in the story. Point out that the main characters in "Starry Night" are Josie, Ling, and Josie's dad. However, none of those characters is telling the story.

A story told in the third person uses pronouns, such as *he, his, she, her, they,* and *their* to tell what happens. Have children look for pronouns on page 39 that show this story is told in the third person. (her, they)

Anchor Chart Have children add information to the fiction anchor chart.

3 Guided Practice

Have partners work together to identify pronouns that show that this story is written in the third person. Guide children to identify an example. Say: *Turn to page 40. Point to two pronouns in the second paragraph that let you know this story is told in the third person.* (his, he) *What does the narrator explain about Josie's dad?* (The narrator explains what Josie's dad is doing and what he is saying.) Have partners discuss how the third-person point of view helps them understand all the characters in the story. Have them share their ideas with the class to make sure everyone has a clear understanding of third-person point of view.

Independent Practice Have children read the online **Differentiated Genre Passage**, "A Shooting Star."

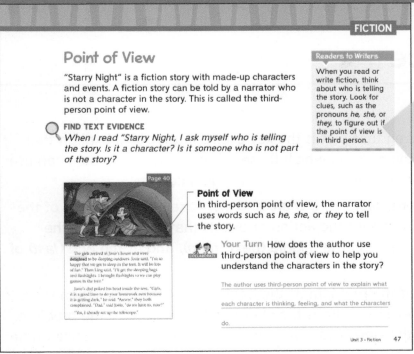

Reading/Writing Companion, p. 47

English Language Learners SCAFFOLD

Use the following scaffolds with **Guided Practice**.

Beginning

Write the words *he, his, she, her,* and *they* on the board. Review pronoun referents: *On page 40, it says* Josie's dad poked his head inside the tent. *Finish the sentence*: The word *his* refers to Josie's dad. *So is Josie's dad telling the story?* (no) *Repeat with the other characters. Then elicit* The story uses the third-person point of view.

Intermediate

Help children complete these sentence frames: The narrator tells the story. A third-person narrator is not one of the characters. A third-person narrator uses pronouns to talk about the characters. *Is "Starry Night" told from a third-person point of view?* (yes) *How do you know?* (The narrator uses words like *he, his,* and *they* to talk about characters.) Have partners circle the pronouns in the second paragraph on page 40. Review which noun each pronoun refers to.

Advanced/Advanced High

After partners identify the pronouns (*he* and *his*) and their referents, ask them to discuss: *I see the word* we *in the second paragraph. What does the word* we *usually tell you about point of view?* (Usually the word *we* means a story is in the first person.) *Why is this use of* we *different?* (The word "we" is used in a quote, not in narration.)

✓ Check for Success

Can children identify the pronouns in the story that let the reader know the story is written in the third person?

Differentiate
SMALL GROUP INSTRUCTION

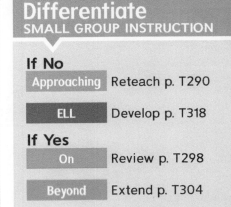

If No
Approaching Reteach p. T290
ELL Develop p. T318
If Yes
On Review p. T298
Beyond Extend p. T304

Comprehension Skill

Reading/Writing Companion

OBJECTIVES

Recount stories, including fables and folktales from diverse cultures, and determine their central message, lesson, or moral.

Describe how characters in a story respond to major events and challenges.

Use information gained from the illustrations and words in a print or digital text to demonstrate understanding of its characters, setting, or plot.

ACADEMIC LANGUAGE

• *sequence, events, order*
• Cognates: *secuencia*

Digital Tools

To differentiate instruction for key skills, use the results of the activity.

Sequence

1 Explain

Remind children that plot is the key events in the story. Explain that sequence is the order in which those events happen. Children can use these steps to help them think about sequence.

• Use the words *first, next, then,* and *last* to tell the sequence of the events. Think about the action or events that take place at the beginning (*first*), in the middle (*next, then*), and at the end (*last*) of the story.

• Think about the problem at the beginning of the story. Then think about the events or steps the characters take to solve the problem. How does the story end? This will help you find the sequence in the story.

Anchor Chart Begin an anchor chart on Sequence.

2 Model

Model using the graphic organizer to record what happens first in the sequence of the story.

Write About Reading: Sentences Model for children how to complete sentences about the story using notes from the graphic organizer. For example, *First, Josie and Ling plan a sleepover. Next, the girls meet in Josie's backyard. They want to play, but they have homework.* Continue with sentences for *Then* and *Last.*

3 Guided Practice

Have children work in pairs to complete the graphic organizer for "Starry Night," returning to the text to find events. Remind them to include the events that happened *next, then,* and *last* in the story. Lead children in a discussion of each event as they complete the graphic organizer.

Write About Reading: Summary Have pairs work together to write a brief summary of "Starry Night." Remind them to include information about the events at the beginning, in the middle, and at the end of the story and use sequence words to help show the order. Select pairs of children to share their summaries with the class.

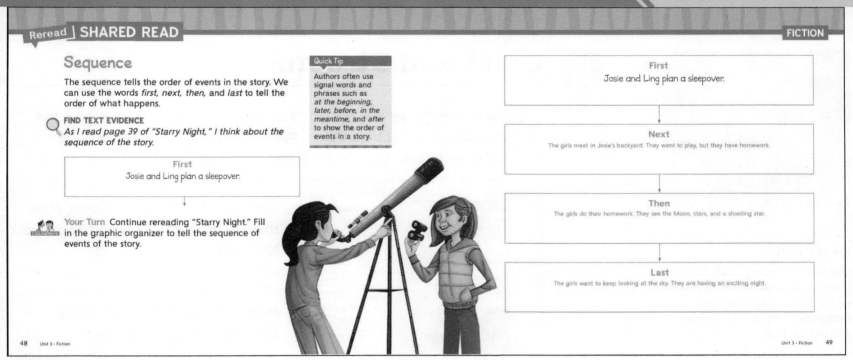

FICTION

Sequence

The sequence tells the order of events in the story. We can use the words *first, next, then,* and *last* to tell the order of what happens.

FIND TEXT EVIDENCE

As I read page 39 of "Starry Night," I think about the sequence of the story.

> **First**
> Josie and Ling plan a sleepover.

Your Turn Continue rereading "Starry Night." Fill in the graphic organizer to tell the sequence of events of the story.

Quick Tip

Authors often use signal words and phrases such as *at the beginning, later, before, in the meantime,* and *after* to show the order of events in a story.

> **First**
> Josie and Ling plan a sleepover.
>
> **Next**
> The girls meet in Josie's backyard. They want to play, but they have homework.
>
> **Then**
> The girls do their homework. They see the Moon, stars, and a shooting star.
>
> **Last**
> The girls want to keep looking at the sky. They are having an exciting night.

48   Unit 3 · Fiction   Unit 3 · Fiction   49

Reading/Writing Companion, pp. 48–49

 ## English Language Learners SCAFFOLD

Use the following scaffolds with **Guided Practice.**

Beginning

Write the main events in random order and help partners put them in order using the illustrations and the text. (Josie and Ling plan a sleepover. Josie and Ling meet in the backyard. Josie and Ling do their homework. They see the moon and stars. Josie and Ling want to keep looking through the telescope.) Help children read the sentences using signal words *first, next, then,* and *last.* Then have partners complete the graphic organizer to prepare for writing summaries.

Intermediate

Model the first sentence starter: First, Josie and Ling plan a sleepover. Have pairs complete these starters: Next, Josie and Ling meet in the backyard. Then, they do their homework and see the Moon and stars. Last, they want to keep looking through the telescope. Have children use the graphic organizer to list specific events details in order and then write their summaries.

Advanced/Advanced High

Display the graphic organizer. *What did Josie and Ling do first? What happened next? Then what happened? What happened last?* As children answer, have them record their answers in the graphic organizer. Have partners orally narrate the main events of the story using signal words in preparation for writing summaries.

✔ Check for Success

Rubric Use your online rubric to record children's progress.

Can children identify the order of events in the story?

Differentiate
SMALL GROUP INSTRUCTION

If No

| Approaching | Reteach p. T294 |
| ELL | Develop pp. T308, T316 |

If Yes

| On | Review p. T301 |
| Beyond | Extend p. T307 |

Comprehension

Craft and Structure

10 Mins

Tell children that they will reread "Starry Night" to learn about how the author wrote the selection. When authors write fiction, they include characters with feelings, a setting, and events in order.

Reading/Writing Companion

OBJECTIVES

Use information gained from the illustrations and words in a print or digital text to demonstrate understanding of its characters, setting, or plot.

ACADEMIC LANGUAGE

- *fiction, character, setting, dialogue, narrator*
- Cognates: *ficción, carácter, diálogo, narrador*

TEACH IN SMALL GROUP

Approaching Level Use the scaffolded questions to help children cite text evidence and answer the Reread prompts.

On Level Guide partners to complete the reread prompts.

Beyond Level Allow pairs to answer the prompts together.

ELL Have Beginning and Early Intermediate ELLs use the **Scaffolded Shared Read.**

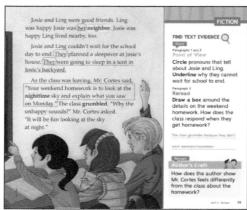

Reading/Writing Companion p. 39

AUTHOR'S CRAFT

Reread page 39 with children. Have them identify the weekend homework Mr. Cortes assigns. (The class is to look at the nighttime sky and be prepared to explain what they saw.) *How does the class react to the homework?* (They grumble.)

 What does Mr. Cortes ask that means: "Why are you grumbling and making sad noises?" ("Why...sounds?")

How does the author show that Mr. Cortes feels differently from the class about the homework? (The author uses dialogue. Mr. Cortes says, "Why the unhappy sounds?" and "It will be fun looking at the sky at night.")

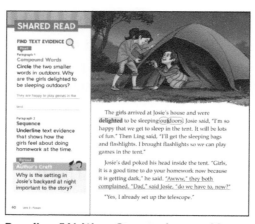

Reading/Writing Companion p. 40

AUTHOR'S CRAFT

Reread page 40 with children. Have them identify the sentence that tells where the girls went after school. ("The girls arrived at Josie's house and were delighted to be sleeping outdoors.") Have children describe what they see in the illustration. (Josie and Ling are outside by a tent after dark.)

 The setting tells where and when something happens. What is the setting for the story? (Josie's backyard/outside; nighttime)

Why is the setting in Josie's backyard at night important in this story? (The girls have to be outside in the dark to look at the nighttime sky for their homework.)

Reading/Writing Companion p. 42

AUTHOR'S CRAFT

Reread page 42 with children. *What does Ling cry out when she looks through the telescope?* (She cries out, "I see a bright light moving in the sky!") *What is the bright light?* (a shooting star) *What does Ling say about looking at the stars?* (She says it is fun. She really enjoys looking at the stars.)

ELL *The author writes that Ling cried out. In this case, does* cried out *mean sobbed in sadness (demonstrate) or spoke loudly in excitement (demonstrate)?* (spoke loudly in excitement)

How does the author use Ling's dialogue to show her excitement? (The author uses an exclamation point to show Ling's excitement. Ling cries out that she sees a bright light moving in the sky. Ling says she really enjoys looking at the stars.

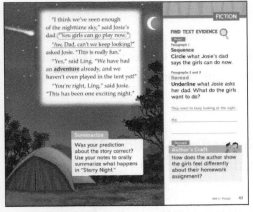

Reading/Writing Companion p. 43

AUTHOR'S CRAFT

Reread page 43 with children. *In the beginning, what did the class do when Mr. Cortes gave their homework assignment?* (They grumbled.) **Have children tell what Josie said on page 43.** ("...can't we keep looking? This is really fun." ... "You're right, Ling. This has been one exciting night.") **Have them tell what Ling said.** ("We have had an adventure already, and we haven't even played in the tent yet!")

 ELL Help children restate lines of dialogue in the story. For example, *"Can't we keep looking?" means "we want to continue looking."*

How does the author show that the girls feel differently about their homework assignment? (The author uses dialogue. Josie says that it's a lot of fun. Ling says that this is an adventure already, and they haven't even played yet.)

Respond to Reading

Reading/Writing Companion

OBJECTIVES

Ask and answer such questions as *who, what, where, when, why,* and *how* to demonstrate understanding of key details in a text.

Recount stories, including fables and folktales from diverse cultures, and determine their central message, lesson, or moral.

ACADEMIC LANGUAGE

• *prompt, analyze, respond*
• Cognates: *analizar, responder*

TEACH IN SMALL GROUP ≪

Respond to Reading

Approaching Level Have partners work together to plan and complete the response to the prompt.

On Level Discuss how the girls felt at the beginning and then at the end. Have children write their responses independently and then discuss them.

Beyond Level Have children brainstorm words to describe the girls' feelings at different points in the story. Encourage them to use the words in their responses.

ELL Group children of mixed proficiency levels to discuss and respond to the prompt.

Write About the Shared Read

Analyze the Prompt

Read the prompt aloud: *How does the author show that the sleepover was different from what the girls expected? Think about what the girls say and do.* Ask: *What is the prompt asking you to do?* (Tell what the girls expected and then how the sleepover turned out differently.) *Let's reread to find details in the text about what the girls first expected from the sleepover. Then let's find details that tell what happened. Taking notes on the details will help you write your response.*

Analyze Text Evidence

Remind children that the author tells the story events in order. At the beginning, the characters tell what they are looking forward to (page 40). Then the author tells about the characters using the telescope and how they feel about it (pages 42–43). Have partners scan page 40 in the **Reading/Writing Companion** to locate details and dialogue that tell how the girls feel. (Possible answers: "delighted to be sleeping outdoors," sleeping in a tent will be lots of fun, play games in the tent) Then have partners scan pages 42–43 to locate dialogue that tells how the girls feel about using the telescope. (Possible answers: "This is fun. I really enjoy looking at the stars." Josie doesn't want to stop. Ling says that it is an adventure. "This has been one exciting night.") Have children think about how the sleepover was different from what the girls expected. Tell children that they can use this information to write their responses.

Respond

Direct children to the sentence starters on **Reading/Writing Companion** page 50. Have partners use the sentence starters in their responses to focus on how the girls' expectations changed.

Think Aloud I read in the beginning that the girls are excited to sleep in a tent and look forward to playing games with flashlights. When Josie's dad tells them it's time to do their homework, they don't want to; they would rather play. Ling says she hopes looking at the nighttime sky doesn't take long. Then I read how the girls feel as they use the telescope. Josie says she wants to keep looking. Ling says she enjoys looking at the stars. The girls thought they would have fun at the sleepover by playing games in the tent, but instead they had fun looking at the stars through the telescope.

Analytical Writing Children should use the sentence starters to form their responses. The first sentence should tell how the girls feel about the sleepover at the beginning. The next sentences should tell about the girls' feelings in order. The last sentences should tell how the girls feel at the end. Children may continue their responses on a separate piece of paper.

Reread | **SHARED READ**

Respond to Reading

Talk about the prompt below. Think about how the author shows how the girls' feelings change from the beginning to the end of the story. Use your notes and graphic organizer.

How does the author show that the sleepover was different from what the girls expected? Think about what the girls say and do.

In the beginning of the story, the girls don't want to do their homework. Then

Josie's dad helps them look at the sky. At the end, the author uses pictures to

show Ling enjoying looking at the stars. Josie says she wants to keep looking.

They say it is fun.

Quick Tip

Use these sentence starters to help you organize your text evidence.

In the beginning....
Josie says....
Ling says....
At the end....

Grammar Connections

Use the correct verb tense to tell when an action takes place. Past tense verbs tell about something that has already happened. They usually end in *-ed*.

50 Unit 3 · Fiction

Reading/Writing Companion, p. 50

Grammar Connections

Children can use the online **Grammar Handbook** page 482 to review and practice using past-tense verbs.

English Language Learners SCAFFOLD

Use the following scaffolds with **Respond**.

Beginning

Make a two-column chart with the heads *Beginning* and *End*. Reread page 39. *Are the children happy?* (no) *Which words tell us how they feel?* (grumbled, unhappy) Write *grumbled, unhappy* under *Beginning*. Then reread page 43. *Which words show the girls are having a good time?* (really fun, adventure, exciting) Write *fun, adventure, and exciting* under *End*.

Intermediate

Chorally read the last paragraph on page 39. *Are they happy or unhappy about their homework?* (unhappy) *How do we know?* (They make unhappy sounds, they grumble.) Help them read page 43. *How do Josie and Ling describe the night they had?* (fun, exciting) Have children complete these frames: At first, Josie and Ling felt <u>unhappy</u> about their homework. In the end, they had a <u>fun</u> and <u>exciting</u> night.

Advanced/Advanced High

Have partners use the text to respond. *How did the girls feel about their homework?* (They were unhappy) *What did Josie say about looking through the telescope?* ("Wow!") *How did Ling feel about looking through the telescope?* (She enjoyed it.) Then, have partners work together to complete the sentence starters on page 50.

Newcomer

Have children listen to the summaries of the **Shared Read** in their native language and then in English to help them access the text and develop listening comprehension. Help children ask and answer questions with a partner. Use these sentence frames: What is the text about? The text is about ___. Then have children continue the lessons in the **Newcomer Teacher's Guide**.

Reading/Writing Companion

OBJECTIVES

Read on-level text orally with accuracy, appropriate rate, and expression on successive readings.

Rate: 74-94 WCPM

ACADEMIC LANGUAGE

• *tone, dialogue*
• Cognates: *tono, diálogo*

Intonation

Explain/Model Remind children that reading with intonation means changing your tone of voice when you read. As we read and understand a text, we can use our tone of voice to show what a character feels. Point to the first paragraph of "Starry Night" on **Reading/Writing Companion** page 41. Read aloud the third sentence in the first paragraph, raising your voice at the end of Josie's question. Ask children what they noticed about your tone of voice. Point out that Josie's dialogue ends with a question mark. Then point to the second paragraph on page 42. Read aloud the second sentence in this paragraph. Ask children what they noticed about your tone of voice. Point out that Ling's dialogue ends with an exclamation mark to show her excitement.

Ask children to follow the text as you read the second paragraph on page 43. Model reading with accuracy, good intonation, and at an appropriate rate. Point out how you pause briefly at commas in the first sentence. Also point out the question mark in the first sentence, which causes you to raise your voice at the end of the sentence.

Practice/Apply Invite children to echo read as you read aloud the second paragraph on page 41, raising your voice at the end of the question. Then have children echo read the second paragraph on page 42, reading Ling's dialogue in an excited tone.

Divide the class into two groups. Ask children to follow along as you read the second paragraph on page 43. Have the first group echo read the paragraph. Then read the third paragraph. Have the second group echo read the paragraph.

Have pairs work together to practice reading page 43 with good intonation. Remind children that quotation marks show that a character is talking. They should make the dialogue sound like speech.

Listen in on pairs, providing corrective feedback as needed. Remind children to read with accuracy, saying all the words correctly, and to read at an appropriate rate.

Daily Fluency Practice

Children can practice fluency using **Differentiated Genre Passage,** "A Shooting Star."

English Language Learners SCAFFOLD

Before you begin the echo read routine, point out the potential pronunciation challenges in each section of text so children can practice the words in isolation beforehand. Refer to the **Language Transfers Handbook** to identify potential fluency challenges. During the teacher-led portion of **Practice/Apply,** include English Language Learners in heterogeneous groups with the rest of the class.

Use the following scaffolds to support children during the paired fluency practice in **Practice/Apply.**

Beginning

Have partners listen to the audio recording of the Shared Read as a model for fluency. Allow them to listen and read along silently a few times. Then have them pause after each sentence to echo read. Children may record themselves reading one sentence several times. Then they may select their favorite recording to play for you.

Intermediate

Have partners listen to the audio recording of the Shared Read as a model for fluency, paying special attention to intonation patterns for questions. Have them echo read after the audio recording. Have children record themselves reading one sentence several times. Then have them compare their recordings to the original and adjust their intonation and pronunciation accordingly.

Advanced/Advanced High

Have partners listen to the audio recording of the selection for additional practice as needed. Then have children suggest ways their partners can improve their intonation, for example: *Your voice should go up at the end of the question.*

Language Transfers Handbook

✔ Check for Success

Can children read questions and exclamatory sentences with appropriate intonation?

Differentiate
SMALL GROUP INSTRUCTIONS

If No

| Approaching | Reteach pp. T245, T294 |
| ELL | Develop pp. T245, T316 |

If Yes

| On | Review p. T297 |
| Beyond | Extend p. T303 |

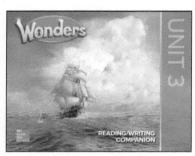

Reading/Writing Companion

OBJECTIVES

Participate in shared research and writing projects (e.g., read a number of books on a single topic to produce a report; record science observations).

Recall information from experiences or gather information from provided sources to answer a question.

ACADEMIC LANGUAGE

- *data, record, organize, sources, label*
- Cognates: *datos, organizar*

TEACH IN SMALL GROUP

You may wish to teach the Study Skill lesson during Small Group time. Have groups of mixed abilities complete the page and work on the short report.

 10 Mins

Develop a Research Plan

1 Explain

Tell children that when they research a topic, it is helpful to follow a research plan, or steps to take to find information. These steps may include:

1. Ask questions about the topic.
2. Find relevant, reliable sources.
3. Take notes.
4. Put information in a logical order.

2 Model

Ask children to identify the most prominent feature in the night sky—the Moon. Point out that the Moon looks a little different every night. Provide Internet and nonfiction book sources that show the different phases of the Moon.

Tell children that they will do research to learn more about phases of the Moon. Then, they will collect data about one phase and share the information in a short report. They will also draw a picture of the phase and label it for the report.

Model how to ask a question about phases of the Moon. Then demonstrate how to select a source that can answer the question. Show children how you take notes from the source, and let them know that this is an example of following a research plan.

3 Guided Practice

Have children ask questions about Moon phases, and help them identify sources they can use for their research. Review with children how to cite and record the sources they use to gather information for their short report. Have each pair or group use an online Layered Foldable™ to record their source information.

Write a Moon Phase Report Have partners choose sources and write a short report explaining one phase of the Moon. Have them also draw the phase and label it. Review their entries with children.

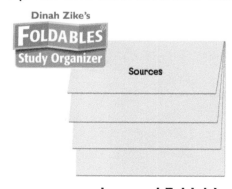

Layered Foldable

Integrate RESEARCH AND INQUIRY

Research Plan

A **research plan** explains how you will find sources and use information. Having a plan is helpful for staying focused on your topic and organized.

If you wanted to look at the nighttime sky and report on what you saw, how could you organize your plan?

I can make a chart.

 Moon Phase Report With a partner, make a drawing and write a short report explaining one phase of the Moon. Share your drawing and report with the class.

What source can you use to learn about Moon phases?

How will you remember what the Moon phase looks like and what it is called?

Remember to follow your research plan. Use your notes about sources and the information you get from them.

The Night Sky

Ling and Josie did research about the night sky. This picture shows how they recorded and organized their data. How do you think the drawings and words help them?

The drawings and words

helped make the information

more clear.

Unit 3 • Fiction   51

Reading/Writing Companion, p. 51

ELL English Language Learners SCAFFOLD

Use the following scaffolds with **Guided Practice**.

Beginning

Elicit children's knowledge of common meanings of *full*, *quarter*, and *new* by helping them complete these sentence frames: The word full can mean the same as the word *whole*. Four quarters make one whole dollar. Every January 1 we celebrate the beginning of a new year. Then as you show images of the phases of the Moon, have partners ask and answer: Which Moon is this? This is the full Moon.

Intermediate

As you show images of the phases of the Moon, provide sentence frames for partners to ask and answer about what they see: What does a full Moon look like? A full Moon looks like a round ball/ full circle. What does the Moon look like in the quarter Moon phase? It looks like a half circle. When is it hardest to see the Moon? It's hardest to see the Moon in the new Moon phase. If the Moon is waxing/waning, how does it change? It gets bigger/smaller.

Advanced/Advanced High

Challenge children to orally describe how the Moon changes through the eight phases. Have them compare the different Moons to something from their own lives, for example: *The full Moon looks like a ball. A crescent Moon looks like a letter* C.

Digital Tools

RESOURCE TOOLKIT   Children may watch Take Notes: Print.

Research Process

Provide the online Research Roadmap to guide children.

Step 1: Set Research Goals

- Direct children to develop and follow a research plan.
- Offer feedback as they generate inquiry questions.

Step 2: Identify Sources

- Help children identify relevant sources.
- Discuss how to choose reliable sources.

Step 3: Find and Record Information

- Review how to take notes.
- Discuss how to keep track of source information.

Step 4: Organize

- Have children analyze all gathered information.
- Encourage children to organize their notes.

Step 5: Synthesize and Present

- Make sure children decide on their final message.
- Guide children to choose appropriate delivery modes for their presentations.

Genre · Fiction

Essential Question
What can we see in the sky?
Read about what Mr. Putter and Tabby see in the **nighttime** sky.

Go Digital!

Mr. Putter & Tabby
See the Stars

by Cynthia Rylant
illustrated by Arthur Howard

Chapter ① **Logs**
Chapter ② **Grumble**
Chapter ③ **Stars**

Literature Anthology, pp. 238–239

Wonders

Literature Anthology

Text Complexity Range
Lexile

420 ▲580 820

Have children apply what they learned as they read.

Mr. Putter & Tabby
See the Stars

Close Reading Routine

Read DOK 1–2

- Identify key ideas and details about the sky.
- Take notes and retell.
- Use **ACT** prompts as needed.

Reread DOK 2–3

- Analyze the text, craft, and structure.
- *Reading/Writing Companion*, pp. 52–54.

Integrate DOK 4

- Integrate knowledge and ideas.
- Make text-to-text connections.
- Use the Integrate lesson.
- Inspire action.

Read

Tell children they will read a story about a man and his cat and what they see in the nighttime sky. Ask children to predict how the story will help answer the **Essential Question.**

DIFFERENTIATED READING ◀◀

Approaching Level Have children listen to the selection summary. Use the Reread prompts during Small-Group time.

On Level and **Beyond Level** Pair children or have them independently complete the Reread prompts on **Reading/Writing Companion** pages 52–54.

 English Language Learners Beforehand, have Beginning and Early-Intermediate ELLs listen to a text summary, available in many languages. See small group pages for additional support.

Chapter **1**

Logs

Mr. Putter and his fine cat, Tabby, loved
to sleep.
They could sleep anywhere.
They slept in chairs, in swings, in cars, in
tubs, and sometimes in the laundry room.

240

Mr. Putter and Tabby also slept in
a bed. Of course, most of the time,
sleeping in a bed was just fine.
Mr. Putter plumped his pillow. Tabby
squished hers. And then they slept like logs.

But one night, one of the logs could not sleep. **1** **2**

241

Literature Anthology, pp. 240–241

1 Strategy: Reread

Teacher Think Aloud I'm confused by the last sentence on page 241. It says one of the logs could not sleep. I know that a log is part of a dead tree. It's not something that sleeps! There must be a different meaning for *log* here. I'm going to reread this page to make sure I understand what the author means.

2 Skill: Sequence

Remember, sequence is the order of events in a story. The very beginning of the story tells us about Mr. Putter and Tabby. What is the first event that happens after we learn about Mr. Putter and Tabby?

Note Taking: Use the Graphic Organizer

Guide children to fill in the Sequence graphic organizer as they read. Have them record events of the story. Ask them to note any unfamiliar words or questions they have.

Build Vocabulary page 241

Throughout, have children add the Build Vocabulary words to their writer's notebooks.

plumped: made bigger

squished: made smaller

A C T Access Complex Text

What Makes This Text Complex?

Organization Children may be confused by how the story is organized. Events are not strictly chronological in some cases, and background information about characters and ongoing events might be confusing to children.

Connections of Ideas Children may need help in making connections between events in the plot.

Chapter **2**

Grumble

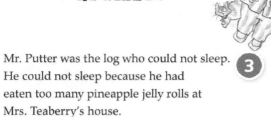

Mr. Putter was the log who could not sleep. **3**
He could not sleep because he had
eaten too many pineapple jelly rolls at
Mrs. Teaberry's house.

Mrs. Teaberry was Mr. Putter's good friend
and **neighbor**, and she liked to feed him.
She liked to feed everybody.
But most of all, she liked
to feed Mr. Putter.

242

She was always sending her good dog, Zeke,
over to Mr. Putter's house with a note.
The note always said, "Are you hungry?"
And Mr. Putter always said, "Yes." **4**
So he and Tabby went next door a lot.

But tonight Mr. Putter had been having
such a good time that he lost track and ate
twenty-one jelly rolls.
He forgot to count them as he popped them
one at a time into his mouth.

Before he knew it, twenty-one jelly rolls
were gone, and it was time to go home.

243

Literature Anthology, pp. 242–243

Access Complex Text

Read

Specific Vocabulary

Organization Help children understand the
organization of events at the beginning of the story.

- Explain that pages 242–243 go back in time to when
  Mr. Putter ate too many jelly rolls. This is why Mr.
  Putter's stomach is upset and why he can't sleep.
  Because he can't sleep, he gets the idea to take a
  walk with Tabby.

- Be sure children understand the sequence: first Mr.
  Putter ate too much, then he couldn't sleep, then he
  has the idea for a walk.

3 Skill: Problem and Solution

The main character in a story often encounters a
problem at the beginning. The middle and end of the
story describe how the problem is solved. On page
242, what is Mr. Putter's problem? (He ate too many
pineapple jelly rolls at Mrs. Teaberry's house, and now he
is unable to sleep.)

4 Dialogue

Fiction may include dialogue. Dialogue is the words
that characters say. Work with a partner to find the
dialogue on page 243. Identify who is speaking and the
character's words.

Build Vocabulary page 243

lost track: stopped paying attention

popped: ate

Mrs. Teaberry was happy that Mr. Putter **enjoyed** her jelly rolls so much. But Mr. Putter's stomach was not. It **grumbled** and grumbled and grumbled.

Mr. Putter looked at his nice soft bed when he got home. *G-R-U-M-B-L-E* grumbled his stomach. Mr. Putter knew he would not be able to sleep with all that grumbling. What to do? Mr. Putter looked at Tabby. Then he got an idea.

244

Chapter **3**

Stars

"Let's go for a walk," Mr. Putter said. He put his coat back on. He put his hat back on.

He picked up Tabby. And out the door they went.

6

245

Literature Anthology, pp. 244–245

5 **Strategy: Reread**

Teacher Think Aloud I read Mr. Putter loved to sleep. On page 244 it says he knew he would not be able to sleep. To understand this, I will reread this page and retell what I read. Mr. Putter's stomach is upset from the jelly rolls he ate. His stomach is grumbling, so he can't sleep.

6 **Skill: Sequence**

Turn to a partner and discuss the sequence of events. What happens after Mr. Putter gets an upset stomach? Why do you think he does this?

ELL Spotlight on Language

Page 245 Use pantomime to clarify *put on a hat.* If you *put your hat* back *on,* it means you were wearing your hat, you took it off, and then you put it on again. Play Simon Says to practice *put on, take off,* and *put back on.*

Reread

Make Inferences

Reread pages 243–244. Why does Mrs. Teaberry like to feed Mr. Putter "most of all"? (He loves her food.)

Reading/Writing Companion, 52

 Make Inferences

Explain: Thinking about your own friendships can help you understand the characters in a text better.

Model One day a good friend and I were so involved in writing a play together that we forgot to eat lunch! This helps me understand how Mr. Potter lost track of time.

Apply: Think of a time when you lost track of time.

What can you infer about Mr. Putter and Mrs. Teaberry's friendship from your experience?

It was a beautiful night.

The moon was full, and **moonlight** was everywhere.

Tabby looked. She listened.
She twitched her ears.
She twitched her tail.
She loved the night.
Mr. Putter loved it, too, even
with a grumbling stomach.

STOP AND CHECK

Reread Why is Mr. Putter's stomach grumbling? Reread to check your understanding.

Literature Anthology, pp. 246–247

Connect to Content

Seeing Stars

A star is a large ball of burning hydrogen gas in outer space. The burning gas creates the star's light. Our Sun is also a star. During the day, our Earth turns toward the Sun. The sunlight makes our sky too bright to see other stars. At night, Earth turns away from the Sun. The sky becomes dark. Then we can see the stars. We can also see the Moon and planets in our solar system. They appear bright because the Sun's light reflects off of them. Have children draw a line down the middle of a sheet of art paper. Ask them to draw a picture of the sky during the day on one side, and a picture of the sky at night on the other side.

Read

 STOP AND CHECK

Reread Why is Mr. Putter's stomach grumbling? Reread to check your understanding. (His stomach is growling because he ate twenty-one jelly rolls.)

❼ Strategy: Reread

Teacher Think Aloud I don't know the words *Big Dipper* and *Milky Way*, so I will reread page 248. After I reread, I understand that Mr. Putter is showing Tabby things in the night sky. What does Mr. Putter tell Tabby? Why do you think Mr. Putter does this? Reread to understand this part.

Student Think Aloud When I reread, I understood that Mr. Putter tells Tabby the Big Dipper is full of milk from the Milky Way. It's not really filled with milk. He tells her that because she loves milk.

Mr. Putter looked up at the sky.
He showed Tabby the stars, and he
told her all about them.
He told her that the Big Dipper was
full of milk from the Milky Way.
Tabby purred. She loved milk.

⑦

248

He told her about looking
at stars when he was a boy.
And how he had always wanted
to ride in a rocket ship.
He told her how he had always
dreamed of **adventure**.

Tabby purred some more.
Mr. Putter and Tabby made
a nice big circle around
the neighborhood.

⑧

249

Literature Anthology, pp. 248–249

⑧ Skill: Sequence

Turn to a partner and discuss what happened first in the story and what happened next. Add these events from the plot to the first two boxes of your graphic organizer.

> **First**
> Mr. Putter eats a lot of jelly rolls. His stomach grumbles and he can't sleep.

↓

> **Next**
> Mr. Putter and Tabby go outside for a walk. Mr. Putter tells Tabby about the sky.

Reread

Author's Craft: Repetition

How does the repetition of the word *she* on page 247 help you understand how Tabby feels about the night? (The text says she loves the night. Repetition of the word *she* makes me notice that part of the text. It helps me understand how much Tabby loves the night.)

Build Vocabulary page 249

rocket ship: space ship

 ## Spotlight on Language

Page 249, Paragraph 1 *Mr. Putter says he had* always wanted *to ride in a rocket ship. Ask and answer with a partner: What have you* always wanted *to do?*

They looked at the sky.
They looked at the yellow lights of the houses.

They looked at cats sitting in windows,
looking back at them.

250

And when at last they circled back home,
they stopped in front of Mrs. Teaberry's house.
Mrs. Teaberry and Zeke were on the front lawn!
"Mrs. Teaberry, what are you doing up?"
asked Mr. Putter.

STOP AND CHECK

Reread Mr. Putter asks why
Mrs. Teaberry is up. Why is
Mr. Putter up, too? Reread to
check your understanding.

251

Literature Anthology, pp. 250–251

Reread Mr. Putter asks why Mrs. Teaberry is up. Why is
Mr. Putter up, too? Reread to check your understanding.
(He is taking a walk to help his stomach feel better.)

9 Problem and Solution

Remember, the plot of a story often tells about a
problem and its solution. In this story, the problem is
that Mr. Putter can't sleep. Turn to a partner and discuss
what Mr. Putter does to solve the problem.

10 Compound Words

We can figure out the meaning of the compound word
moonlight by thinking about the meanings of the two
smaller words that are within it. What do the two
smaller words tell you about the meaning of *moonlight*?

11 Skill: Sequence

Discuss with a partner what happens after
Mr. Putter and Tabby finish their walk. Add
these events to your Graphic Organizer.

 Spotlight on Language

Page 250 Paragraphs 1-2 Point to *They* and *them. These
pronouns refer to Mr. Putter and Tabby.*

12 Summarize

Teacher Think Aloud To make sure I understand what
is happening in the story on pages 252 and 253, I can
summarize what I read.

"Zeke has a grumbling stomach," said
Mrs. Teaberry.
"He ate too many jelly rolls and we can't sleep."

Mr. Putter and Tabby were **delighted**.
They sat on the lawn with Mrs. Teaberry and Zeke.

252

Mr. Putter's stomach and Zeke's stomach
talked to each other while Mr. Putter
and Mrs. Teaberry talked to each other.

They told stories in the moonlight.
They told secrets.
They made each other laugh.

253

Literature Anthology, pp. 252–253

First
Mr. Putter eats a lot of jelly rolls. His stomach grumbles and he can't sleep.

↓

Next
Mr. Putter and Tabby go outside for a walk. Mr. Putter tells Tabby about the sky.

↓

Then
Mr. Putter and Tabby finish their walk and find Mrs. Teaberry and Zeke outside. They tell stories.

↓

Last

Reread

Author's Purpose

Reading/Writing Companion, 53

How do you know that Mrs. Teaberry and Mr. Putter are
becoming better friends? (They are telling stories and
secrets, and making each other laugh.)

 Combine Information

Explain: Think about how Mrs. Teaberry and Mr.
Putter's friendship is changing throughout the story.

Model: First, Mrs. Teaberry liked to feed Mr. Putter.
They talk and tell stories. That's what friends do.

Apply: What other details does the author give to
show they are becoming better friends?

Then when the stomachs on the front lawn stopped grumbling, everyone said good night, went to bed, and slept like logs.

254

In the morning, Mr. Putter heard a scratching at the door.
He opened it.

It was Zeke with a note.
The note said, "Are you hungry?"

Mr. Putter smiled.
He picked up Tabby and together they walked next door.

255

Literature Anthology, pp. 254–255

Reread

Skill: Sequence

Have children identify the events that happen at the end of the story for the Graphic Organizer.

Reread

Author's Craft: Text Structure

Reading/Writing Companion, 54

Why does the author end the story with a new note on a new day? (It shows how their good friendship has stayed the same and how it might be different.)

Return to Purposes

Ask children to use text evidence to show if their predictions about the selection were correct.

First
Mr. Putter eats a lot of jelly rolls. His stomach grumbles and he can't sleep.

Next
Mr. Putter and Tabby go outside for a walk.
Mr. Putter tells Tabby about the sky.

Then
Mr. Putter and Tabby finish their walk and find Mrs. Teaberry and Zeke outside. They tell stories.

Last
Mr. Putter finally goes to sleep. The next day he and Tabby return to Mrs. Teaberry's house.

About the Author and Illustrator

Cynthia Rylant was a teacher and a librarian before she became a writer. She began reading children's books while working at a library. That's when she decided she wanted to make her own. When she gets an idea, she says, "I sit down with pen and paper, and soon I've got a story going!"

Arthur Howard used to be an actor in plays and on television. Now he writes and illustrates books for children. When he started the Mr. Putter & Tabby series, Arthur drew Mr. Putter to look like his own father. Tabby is based on his mother's cat, Red.

Author's Purpose

Cynthia divides *Mr. Putter & Tabby See the Stars* into chapters. Why do you think she uses the chapter names "Logs," "Grumbles," and "Stars"?

256

Literature Anthology, p. 256

 Spotlight on Language

Page 254 Point out the phrase *slept like logs.* The verb *slept* *is the past-tense form of* sleep. *A* log *is a part of a tree trunk that has been cut off the tree. Imagine a log lying on the ground, not moving. If you sleep like a log, it means you sleep very deeply, nothing can wake you up, you don't move. Why did the characters sleep like logs?* (Possible: They were very tired.)

 Read

Meet the Author

Cynthia Rylant

Read aloud page 256 with children. Ask them what Cynthia Rylant did before she was a writer.

• How do you think being a librarian helped her be a writer?

• When Cynthia Rylant gets an idea for a story, what does she do?

• What do you do when you get a good idea for something?

Author's Purpose

To Entertain: Tell children that sometimes authors write stories for people to enjoy them.

Ask children to explain why the author uses the chapter names "Logs," "Grumbles," and "Stars." Have children record their answers in their Writer's Notebook. *The chapter name "Logs," / "Grumbles," / "Stars" tells about _____.*

Respond to the Text

Summarize

Use important details to summarize what happens in the story. Information from your Sequence chart may help you.

First
↓
Next
↓
Then
↓
Last

Write

How does the author show the connection between Mr. Putter and Mrs. Teaberry? Use these sentence frames:

The author says that Mr. Putter...
This shows a connection to Mrs. Teaberry because...

Make Connections

What do Mr. Putter and Tabby see in the sky?
ESSENTIAL QUESTION

Tell about something that you can see or have learned about the nighttime sky. TEXT TO WORLD

257

Literature Anthology, p. 257

 Spotlight on Language

Page 256, Paragraph 2 Focus on the sentence "Tabby is based on his mother's cat, Red." Explain that *based on* means that something is modeled after something else. *In the story, the illustrator drew Tabby to look like his mother's cat.* Ask children if they know of anything that is *based on* something else. (movies, books)

Newcomers

Use the **Newcomer Online Visuals** and their accompanying prompts to help children expand vocabulary and language about My Family and Me (10–14). Use the Conversation Starters, Speech Balloons, and the Games in the **Newcomer Teacher's Guide** to continue building vocabulary and developing oral and written language.

Read

Summarize

Tell children they will use details from their Sequence graphic organizer to retell the story. As I read Mr. Putter & Tabby See the Stars, I gathered information from the text by taking notes about what Mr. Putter and Tabby did first, next, then, and last. I will paraphrase the most important details.

Reread

Analyze the Text

 After children summarize the selection, have them reread to develop a deeper understanding of the text and answer the questions on pages 52–54 of the **Reading/Writing Companion**. For children who need support in citing text evidence, use the Reread prompts on pages T205D–T205I.

Write About the Text

Review the writing prompt with children. Remind them to use their **COLLABORATE** responses from the **Reading/Writing Companion** to cite text evidence and to support their answers. For a full lesson on writing a response using text evidence, see pages T206–T207.

Integrate

Make Connections

Essential Question <u>Answer</u>: Mr. Putter and Tabby see the Moon and stars. <u>Evidence</u> On p. 247, the text states that the Moon was full and moonlight was everywhere. I read on page 248 that Mr. Putter showed Tabby the stars.

Text to World <u>Answer</u> Possible response: I can see stars and the Moon at night. I learned that we can see the Moon at night because the sun reflects off it.

Reading/Writing Companion

OBJECTIVES

Ask and answer such questions as *who, what, where, when, why,* and *how* to demonstrate understanding of key details in a text.

Write narratives in which they recount a well-elaborated event or short sequence of events, include details to describe actions, thoughts, and feelings, use temporal words to signal event order, and provide a sense of closure.

ACADEMIC LANGUAGE

• fiction, text structure, sequence, text evidence

• Cognates: *ficcion, texto, sequencia, evidencia*

TEACH IN SMALL GROUP

You may wish to teach the Respond to Reading lesson during Small Group time.

Approaching Level and **On Level** Have partners work together to plan and complete the response to the prompt.

Beyond Level Ask students to respond to the prompt independently and also to write a response to their self-selected reading selection.

ELL Group ELLs of mixed proficiency levels to discuss and respond to the prompt.

Write About the Anchor Text

Analyze the Prompt

Read the prompt aloud: *How does the author help you understand the friendship between Mr. Putter and Mrs. Teaberry?* Ask: *What is the prompt asking you to do?* (explain what the author does to tell the reader about Mr. Putter and Mrs. Teaberry's friendship) Say: *Let's reread to see how the words, illustrations, and the text structure help us answer the prompt.*

Analyze Text Evidence

Remind children that sequence is the order of the events in a story, but sometimes the events that happen aren't told in order. Have children look at **Literature Anthology** *Mr. Putter and Tabby See the Stars, page 241. What problem does Mr. Putter have?* (Mr. Putter cannot sleep.) Next, have children look at pages 242–243. Ask: *What do we learn about why Mr. Putter has this problem?* (Mr. Putter cannot sleep because his stomach is grumbling from having eaten too many jelly rolls earlier in the day.) *Why did he eat too many jelly rolls?* (Because he was having such a good time with Mrs. Teaberry.) *What does this tell you about their friendship?* (They like to spend time together.) *What else do we learn about their friendship on these pages?* (Mrs. Teaberry often sends Mr. Putter a note asking if he's hungry and then feeds him.) Then have children look at page 253. Ask: *Why are Mrs. Teaberry and Zeke still awake?* (Mrs. Teaberry and Zeke are still awake because Zeke also has a grumbling stomach and cannot sleep.) *So what do Mrs. Teaberry and Mr. Putter do?* (They talk and tell stories.) Last, have children look at page 255. Ask: *Why does Mr. Putter smile when he gets the note from Mrs. Teaberry?* (He smiles because he's happy that his friend has invited him over again.)

Respond

COLLABORATE

Review pages 52–54 of the **Reading/Writing Companion**. Have partners or small groups refer to and discuss their completed charts and writing responses. Then direct children's attention to the sentence starters on page 55. Children should focus on details, including dialogue and illustrations, that the author uses to show that Mr. Putter and Mrs. Teaberry are friends. Their first sentence should state their main idea, such as: *The author uses details in the text, dialogue, and illustrations to help readers understand the friendship between Mr. Putter and Mrs. Teaberry.*

Analytical Writing Children should continue to go through the text to find examples that show the connection between Mr. Putter and Mrs. Teaberry. Remind children that they can use additional paper to complete their responses.

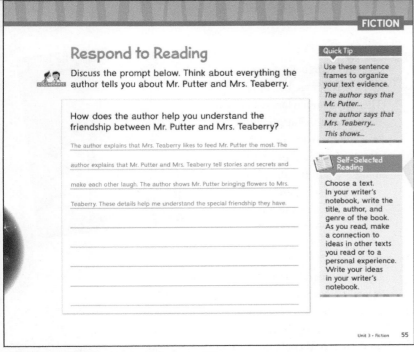

Reading/Writing Companion, p. 55

English Language Learners SCAFFOLD

Use these scaffolds during **Respond** to reinforce some vocabulary used in the prompts on **Reading/Writing Companion** pages 52-54.

Beginning

Write these words on the board: *cite, text evidence, clue, conclusion.* Next to each word, write a definition based on these explanations: *The word* cite *means to give proof of something* (cognate: *citar*). The *text* is the story or selection you're reading. *Evidence* is an example you use to prove your answer (Spanish: *prueba*). A *clue* is information that helps you figure something out (Spanish: *indicio*). A *conclusion* is a decision you make based on information. Review each term and use examples for clarification.

Intermediate

After discussing the terms above, have partners practice matching words and phrases with their definitions. Then ask them to paraphrase what it means to cite text evidence using this frame: When I cite text evidence, I give <u>examples</u> from the <u>story/selection</u> to <u>prove</u> my answer.

Advanced/Advanced High

Have children explain the tasks on pages 52-54 in their own words. for example, *On page 52, you have to prove Mrs. Teaberry likes Mr. Putter. You have to write examples from the story.*

Newcomers

Have children listen to the summaries of the **Anchor Text** in their native language and then in English to help them access the text and develop listening comprehension. Help children ask and answer questions with a partner. Use these sentence frames: What is the text about? The text is about ___. Then have them complete the online **Newcomer Activities** individually or in pairs.

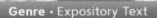

Genre · Expository Text

Compare Texts
Read about the daytime and nighttime skies.

Day to Night

Your alarm clock rings. *Beep! Beep! Beep!* You turn it off, stretch, and get out of bed. You look out the window and see the daytime sky.

The Daytime Sky

The sky is light today. It is blue with white clouds and the bright Sun. The Sun is the brightest object in the sky. It looks small, but that is because it is far from Earth.

Sometimes the daytime sky has clouds.

258

The Sun

The Sun is actually a star. Like all stars, it is a huge ball of hot gases. The Sun is much larger than the Earth. It is the Earth's closest star, but there are many stars in the sky. In fact, there are too many stars in the sky to count! We cannot see them during the day because the Sun's light makes our sky too bright.

Hello, Sun . . . Goodbye, Sun

If you watched the Sun all day, it would look like it moves across the sky. But the Sun does not move. Even though you cannot feel it, Earth is turning. It makes one full turn in 24 hours, or one day. For about half of those hours, the place where you live faces the Sun. It is daytime. The rest of the time, your home is not facing the Sun. Then it is dark.

When the Sun is shining on your home, it is daytime. Then the Earth turns. When your home faces away from the Sun, it is nighttime.

259

Literature Anthology, pp. 258–259

Wonders

Literature Anthology

"Day to Night"

Text Complexity Range
Lexile

420   550   820

Have children apply what they learned as they read.

🧪 Observe, describe, and record patterns of objects in the sky, including the appearance of the Moon.

Compare Texts

 Analytical Writing As children read and reread "Day to Night," encourage them to take notes and think about the Essential Question: *What can we see in the sky?* Tell children to think about how the information in "Day to Night" can explain what Mr. Putter sees in the nighttime sky. Children should discuss how the texts are alike and different.

Ⓐ Ⓒ Ⓣ Access Complex Text

Sentence Structures

Expository text often contains complicated sentences with multiple ideas. Point to the last sentence in the first paragraph on page 259. Explain the two ideas. *We cannot see stars in the day. When the sun is up the sky is too bright.* Say that *because* connects the first part of the sentence to the reason why we can't see the stars in the day.

Read

1 Skill: Key Details

Reread page 259. Does the Sun or the Earth make a full turn in one day? (The Earth does.) When the place you live in faces the Sun, is it daytime or nighttime? (It is daytime.) And when the place you live in faces away from the Sun? (It is nighttime.)

Reread

Author's Purpose

Reread the first paragraph on page 258. Ask: *How does the author begin the selection?* (with an alarm clock ringing, "Beep!" "Beep!" "Beep!") Point out the title of the selection. Ask: *Why do you think the author begins the selection this way?* (to show that it's the start of the day; also to interest readers)

Build Vocabulary page 258

stretch: move your body

 Spotlight on Language

Page 259, Paragraph 2 As you focus on the key details in the section about the movement of the Earth around the Sun, write these two sentences on the board: *You cannot feel it, but Earth is always turning. It makes one full turn in one day.* Check understanding of *turning* and *full turn,* using gestures or demonstrations with a classroom object to convey meaning. Then, underline *Earth* and *It.* Point to the second sentence and ask: *What does the word* it *stand for in this sentence?* (Earth) Guide children to rewrite the sentence using *Earth.* (*Earth makes one full turn in one day.*)

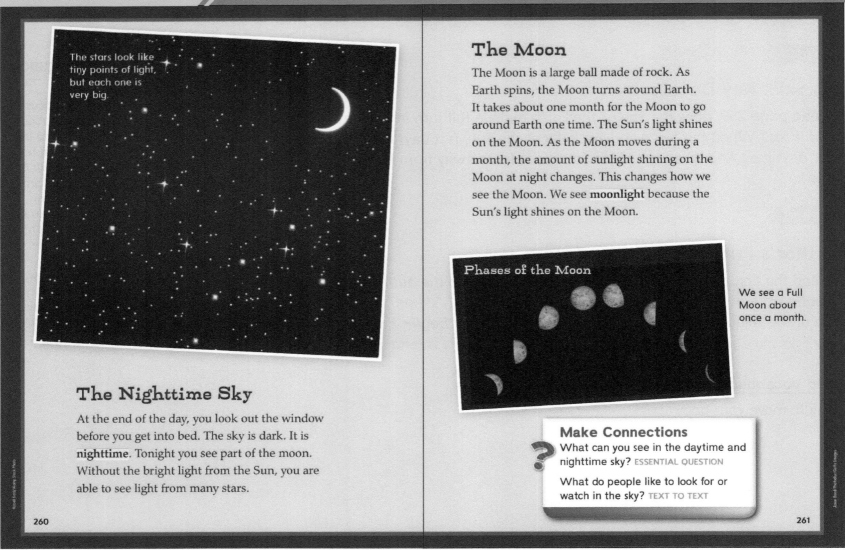

The stars look like tiny points of light, but each one is very big.

The Nighttime Sky

At the end of the day, you look out the window before you get into bed. The sky is dark. It is **nighttime**. Tonight you see part of the moon. Without the bright light from the Sun, you are able to see light from many stars.

260

The Moon

The Moon is a large ball made of rock. As Earth spins, the Moon turns around Earth. It takes about one month for the Moon to go around Earth one time. The Sun's light shines on the Moon. As the Moon moves during a month, the amount of sunlight shining on the Moon at night changes. This changes how we see the Moon. We see **moonlight** because the Sun's light shines on the Moon.

Phases of the Moon

We see a Full Moon about once a month.

Make Connections

What can you see in the daytime and nighttime sky? ESSENTIAL QUESTION

What do people like to look for or watch in the sky? TEXT TO TEXT

261

Literature Anthology, pp. 260–261

Read

② Strategy: Reread

Reread page 260 to understand why you can see stars in the sky at night. (You can see the stars against the dark sky at night because the Sun's bright light is not shining in the sky then.)

③ Text Features: Diagrams

What information can you learn from the diagram "Phases of the Moon"? (The diagram shows the different Moon shapes that we can see.)

Reread

Author's Craft: Text Structure

How do the headings help organize the information in a way that's easy to understand? (The orange headings cover information about the rise and setting of the Sun. The dark blue headings cover information about the nighttime sky and the Moon.)

Build Vocabulary pages 260–261

spins: stays in place but turns round

month: about 30 days

phases: stages, views

Read

Summarize

Guide students to use the key details to summarize the selection.

Reread

Analyze the Text

After children summarize the selection, have them reread to develop a deeper understanding of the text by annotating and answering questions on pages 56–58 of the **Reading/Writing Companion**. For children who need help citing text evidence, use the Reread prompts on pages T207B–T207C.

Integrate

Make Connections

Essential Question What can we see in the daytime and nighttime sky? <u>Answer:</u> We can see different things in the daytime and nighttime sky. <u>Evidence:</u> We can see the Sun in the daytime sky and the Moon and stars in the nighttime sky.

Text to Text Answers may vary, but encourage children to use evidence from both selections.

ELL Spotlight on Language

Page 260, Paragraph 1 *The word* without *is a compound word. Which two smaller words do you see?* (*with* and *out*) Provide additional clarification: *The word* without *means you do not have something.* If you wear glasses, take them off and pretend to squint like you cannot see. *I am without my glasses.* If you have an absent student, say, *Tom is not here today. We are without Tom today.* Reread the sentence from the text: *Without the bright light from the Sun, you are able to see light from many stars.* Provide a sentence stem to help children rephrase the sentence: You can see light from the stars when <u>the sun's light is not there</u>.

Reading/Writing Companion

Heads

1 Explain

Have children turn to page 59 of the **Reading/Writing Companion.** Explain that authors often use print features, such as headings to organize their work. Share with children the following key points about heads in expository texts.

• Heads are usually printed in big, bold type.

• Heads and subheads separate the text into sections, or parts.

• Authors use heads and subheads to tell readers what the different sections are about.

2 Model

Model showing children how to find the heads. Point out the first head on **Literature Anthology** page 258 of "Day to Night." Ask: *How does the head look different from the text around it?* (It's a bigger size and a different color.) *What does the head tell you about this section of text?* (This section is about things we can see in the sky during the day.) Discuss why the author used heads. *What is the purpose of the heads?* (Possible Answers: To organize the text, to help readers find information, to make the text easier to read)

3 Guided Practice

Guide partners to work together to identify each of the remaining heads. Ask them to discuss why the author included the heads. Then have children take turns telling what each section of text is about, based on the heads. Allow children time to enter their responses on page 59 of the **Reading/Writing Companion.** Circulate and offer assistance, as needed.

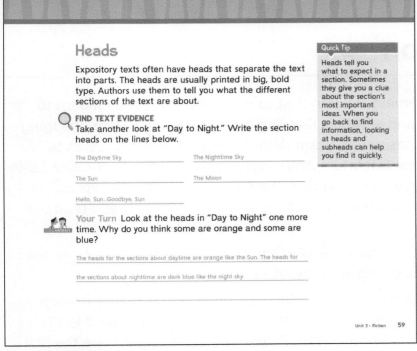

Reading/Writing Companion, p. 59

 English Language Learners SCAFFOLD

Use the following scaffold with **Guided Practice**.

Beginning

Review the meaning of *head.* Say: *A "head" tells you what a section of text is about.* Model identifying the heads in "Day to Night" in the **Literature Anthology.** Then have partners scan the text and ask and answer: What is the second head? The second head is The Sun. What do you think the section will be about? I think the section will be about the Sun. Have children look at each photograph or diagram. Ask: *Does the picture match the head?* (Yes.) Then, have children complete: I think this part will be about the Sun.

Intermediate

Direct children's attention to the third head in "Day to Night" in the Literature Anthology. Ask: *What is the third head?* (Hello, Sun... Goodbye, Sun) *What do you see in the photograph?* (the Sun shining on half the Earth) Have children complete: I think this part will be about how we can see the Sun in the daytime, but it is dark in the nighttime.

Advanced/Advanced High

Guide partners to identify the heads in "Day to Night." Help them record their answers on page 59. Then have them take turns explaining why each head matches the context of its section, using the photographs on the page as well as the heads to support their ideas.

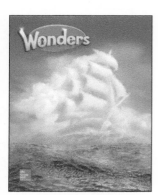

Literature Anthology

OBJECTIVES

Read on-level text orally with accuracy, appropriate rate, and expression on successive readings.

Rate: 74–94 WCPM

ACADEMIC LANGUAGE

fluency, expression

• Cognate: *expresión*

Expression

Explain/Model Remind children that to read with expression means to read with feeling and emotion. Reading with expression means changing your voice to emphasize important details in the story. Ask children to follow the text in the Literature Anthology, page 243, *Mr. Putter and Tabby See the Stars,* as you model reading the first paragraph with expression. Ask children to notice how you read the questions and how you read the statements.

Practice/Apply Read the same passage sentence by sentence. Have the class echo read, modeling your use of expression.

Divide the class into three groups. Have a slightly higher reader in each group. Ask children to follow along as you model reading page 244 of *Mr. Putter and Tabby See the Stars*. Read the first sentence. Have the first group echo read the sentence. Read the second sentence. Have the next group echo read. Continue until all groups have echo read.

Have groups work together to practice reading accurately and with appropriate expression. Have each group choose a paragraph to read. Have some children read the sentence and the others in the group echo read. Then have children change roles within the group.

Listen in on the groups, providing corrective feedback as needed. Remind children to read with accuracy and to read at an appropriate rate.

Daily Fluency Practice

Children can practice fluency using **Differentiated Genre Passage,** "A Shooting Star."

English Language Learners SCAFFOLD

During the teacher-led portion of **Practice/Apply**, include English Language Learners in heterogeneous groups with the rest of the class. Before you begin the echo read routine, point out the potential pronunciation challenges in each section of text so children can practice the words in isolation. Refer to the **Language Transfers Handbook** to identify fluency challenges in different languages.

Use the following scaffolds during **Practice/Apply** to help children apply self-corrective techniques to their own fluency practice.

Beginning

Before reading, have children listen to the audio recording of the selection as a model for fluency. Allow them to listen and read along silently a few times. Then have them pause after each sentence to echo read. Have them record themselves and listen to make sure they read with expression that shows emotion.

Intermediate

After groups select a paragraph to practice, have them listen to the audio recording of the selection as a model for fluency. First, have the group pause after each sentence to echo read. Then have half the group choral read one sentence at a time with the audio and the other half echo read. Have partners provide feedback by asking questions, such as: *How do you think the character is feeling? How can your voice show that feeling?*

Advanced/Advanced High

Have these children join the rest of the class for group fluency practice. Encourage them to listen to the audio recording for additional, independent practice. Praise children when they read with expression with specific comments, such as: I liked when you read ____ because your voice showed how happy Mr. Putter was.

Language Transfers Handbook

✔ Check for Success

Can children read text accurately and with expression?

Differentiate
SMALL GROUP INSTRUCTIONS

If No

| Approaching | Reteach pp. T273, T289 |
| ELL | Develop pp. T273, T316 |

If Yes

| On | Review p. T297 |
| Beyond | Extend p. T303 |

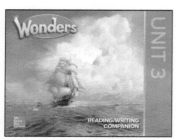

Reading/Writing Companion

OBJECTIVES

Write narratives in which they recount a well-elaborated event or short sequence of events, and provide a sense of closure.

With guidance and support from adults and peers, focus on a topic and strengthen writing as needed by revising and editing.

ACADEMIC LANGUAGE

- *revise, conclusion*
- Cognates: *revisar, conclusión*

DIFFERENTIATED WRITING

Revising personal narratives can be challenging. Check children's progress during Small Group time.

Approaching Level Review children's drafts for a clear beginning, middle, and end.

On Level Partners can review each other's drafts, focusing on a clear beginning, middle, and end.

Beyond Level Children can focus on adding effective signal words to show sequence.

ELL Provide sequence words, such as *before, after, when, then,* and *later,* for children to add as they revise.

Revise

Conclusion

Explain that writers end their personal narratives with a conclusion that wraps up the story and leaves an impression on the reader. A strong conclusion may share thoughts and feelings about the experience or what the narrator learned. Read aloud page 237 of "Landing on Your Feet" in the **Literature Anthology**. Point out how the narrator shares her feelings about her experience.

Have partners talk about how Ryan, the narrator, shows how she felt after helping. Ask them to underline specific words and phrases she uses to express her feelings. Then have them write their ideas on **Reading/Writing Companion** page 31.

Have volunteers share the details they recorded. Discuss how these details effectively wrapped up Ryan's writing. Ask: *What does Ryan want the reader to know after reading her personal narrative?* (She's happy that she was able to help him and that he went back to coach the kids. She thinks she is lucky, and she thinks the kids at the community center are lucky, too.)

Revision

Allow time for children to review their drafts, focusing on their conclusions. Remind children that their conclusion should share their thoughts and feelings about the experience and leave readers with something to think about.

NARRATIVE NONFICTION

Revise

Conclusion The conclusion of a personal narrative often shares how an author feels about an event. Think about what you want your readers to take away from your writing.

Reread the last paragraph of the selection on page 237. Think about how the author, Ryan, shares how she felt at the end of her story.

Explain how Ryan shows how she felt after helping.

Ryan uses an exclamation point to show she was happy her dad could coach. She

says she is glad she made him feel better. Ryan's final thought is that the kids at the

community center are lucky. She tells readers she feels lucky, too.

_____

_____

 Revise It's time to revise your draft. Make sure you write a conclusion that tells how you feel about what you did.

> **Grammar Connections**
>
> Remember, action verbs in the present tense tell about an action happening now.
>
> *Jen **looks** up and **watches** the birds.*

Unit 3 • Narrative Nonfiction   31

Reading/Writing Companion, p. 31

Grammar Connections

Remind children to use the past tense to tell about something they did yesterday or long ago. When they tell about something they are doing now, they should use the present tense. Point out that in the first paragraph on page 237 of "Landing on Your Feet" in the **Literature Anthology,** the author uses past-tense verbs, such as *made* and *watched* because she is telling about what she did over the weekend. In the last paragraph, she uses the present tense for the verbs *think* and *feel* because she is telling about what she thinks and feels at that moment.

English Language Learners   SCAFFOLD

Use the following scaffolds with **Conclusion**.

Beginning

Reread the last paragraph on page 237 and discuss the conclusion of the story. Have children circle the punctuation mark at the end of "But Dad coached!" Ask: *What mark is at the end?* (an exclamation mark) *This mark shows how Ryan feels. How does she feel?* She feels <u>excited</u>. *Ryan's dad feels better. How does Ryan feel about this?* She is <u>glad</u>. *How does Ryan feel to have her dad as her coach?* She feels <u>lucky</u>.

Intermediate

Have partners reread the last paragraph on page 237 and analyze the conclusion of the story. As needed, provide these questions to guide their discussion: *What punctuation mark does Ryan use to show that she is happy her dad can coach?* (an exclamation mark) *What are some words that tell how Ryan feels?* (glad, lucky)

Advanced/Advanced High

Have partners find and share words that tell Ryan's feelings about her experience. Ask children to include similar details about their feelings in their conclusions. Encourage them to use precise words to tell how they felt about their experience.

Digital Tools

Use these digital tools to enhance the lessons.

Revised Student Model

RESOURCE TOOLKIT   Revise Checklist

Newcomers

To help children review and develop their writing, display the online **Weekly Opener Image** and have them identify what they see with a partner. Provide sentence frames: What do you see? I see a/an ___. Have children point to the image as they ask and answer. Then have them write the sentences in their notebooks. Use the Progress Monitoring materials in the **Newcomer Teacher's Guide** to evaluate, assess, and plan instruction for your newcomers.

Reading/Writing Companion

OBJECTIVES

Ask for clarification and further explanation as needed about the topics and texts under discussion.

Ask and answer questions about what a speaker says in order to clarify.

ACADEMIC LANGUAGE

• feedback, revise, reflect

• Cognates: *revisar, reflejar*

Digital Tools

Use these digital tools to enhance the lesson.

 Peer Conferencing Checklist

 Peer Conferencing (Collaborative Conversation video)

---

 10 Mins

Peer Conferencing

Review a Draft

Review with children the routine for peer review of writing.

- Step 1: Listen carefully as the writer reads his or her work aloud.
- Step 2: Begin by telling what you liked about the writing.
- Step 3: Ask a question that will help the writer think more deeply about the writing.
- Step 4: Make a suggestion that will make the writing stronger.

Model using the sentence starters on **Reading/Writing Companion** page 32. Say: *I enjoyed your conclusion because....* Discuss the steps of the routine for peer conferencing. Ask: *Why does Step 1 tell you to listen carefully?* (So you hear all the important details.) *How can asking questions about a text be helpful?* (It helps the writer recognize parts of the text that might not be clear.)

Partner Feedback

Circulate and observe as partners review and give feedback on each other's drafts. Ensure that partners are following the routine and the agreed-upon rules. Have children reflect on partner feedback and write on **Reading/Writing Companion** page 32 about how they intend to use the feedback.

Revision

Review the revising checklist on **Reading/Writing Companion** page 32. Allow children time to implement suggestions. Remind children that the rubric on page 35 can also help with revision. After children have completed their revisions, allow them time to share how their partners' feedback helped improve their personal narratives.

WRITING

Revise: Peer Conferences

Review a Draft Listen carefully as a partner reads his or her work aloud. Begin by telling what you liked about the draft. Make suggestions that you think will make the writing stronger.

Partner Feedback Write one of your partner's suggestions that you will use in the revision of your narrative.

Based on my partner's feedback, I will _____

_____

After you finish giving each other feedback, reflect on the peer conference. What was helpful? What might you do differently next time?

_____

Revision Use the Revising Checklist to help you figure out what text you may need to move, add to, or delete. Remember to use the rubric on page 35 to help you with your revision.

Quick Tip

Use these sentence starters to discuss your partner's work.
I enjoyed this part of your draft because...
How about adding more details about...
I have a question about...

Revising Checklist

☐ Did I write in the first person and include details?
☐ Does my personal narrative tell about an event?
☐ Did I include a beginning, middle, and end?
☐ Did I write a conclusion?

32   Unit 3 • Narrative Nonfiction

Reading/Writing Companion, p. 32

English Language Learners SCAFFOLD

Use the following scaffolds with **Partner Feedback** to help children collaborate with peers.

Beginning

Pair children with more proficient speakers for peer conferencing. Supply simple sentence starters to help them ask questions and provide feedback: *Can you repeat ____? Can you read more slowly? I like ____ because ____. I learned about ____.* Model how to follow the routine for peer review.

Intermediate

Pair children with more proficient speakers for peer conferencing. Provide questions for children to use to help each other reflect on their narratives: *Why did this happen? What happened next? How did you feel? Does the word ____ show how you felt?*

Advanced/Advanced High

Encourage children to comment on their partner's conclusion and decide if the narrative needs more specific details. Have partners fill in their Partner Feedback on **Reading/Writing Companion** page 32 and then read each other's responses to check if their partner understood them correctly.

Teacher Conferences

As students revise, hold teacher conferences with individual students.

Step 1: Talk About Strengths

Point out strengths in the personal narrative. For example, say: *Your personal narrative has a beginning, a middle, and an end.*

Step 2: Focus on Skills

Give feedback on how the student could improve on features of the personal narrative. For example, say: *Certain phrases, such as* last night, *help readers understand when things take place in a story. Try adding these kinds of phrases.*

Step 3: Make Concrete Suggestions

Point out a section that needs to be revised. Have students use a specific strategy. For example, ask students to rewrite the conclusion to share how the author feels about the event.

CLASSROOM CULTURE

We promote ownership of learning.
To create a classroom where children take responsibility for their own learning, it is important for children to understand the importance of the routine for peer review of writing. After peer conferences, ask children: *How did Step 1 (Step 2/ Step 3/ Step 4) help you be responsible for your own learning?*

Reading/Writing Companion

OBJECTIVES

Demonstrate command of the conventions of standard English capitalization, punctuation, and spelling when writing.

Consult reference materials, including beginning dictionaries, as needed to check and correct spellings

With guidance and support from adults and peers, focus on a topic and strengthen writing as needed by revising and editing.

ACADEMIC LANGUAGE

• correct, error, verb, noun, capital letter

• Cognates: *correcto, error, verbo*

Edit and Proofread

Explain

Tell children that after they have revised their drafts, they must go back and edit and proofread. Explain that when we edit we correct our grammar, usage, capitalization, end punctuation, and spelling. We make sure all of our sentences start with a capital letter and end with correct punctuation.

Correct Mistakes

Review the editing checklist on **Reading/Writing Companion** page 33. Ask: *What should you check in sentences besides capital letters, end punctuation, and spelling?* (Did I use the word *have* correctly? Did I capitalize proper nouns?) **Write these sentences on the board:**

I *have* a sandwich and an apple for lunch today.

Anita *has* a sandwich and an apple, too.

Proofread and edit as a class. Ask volunteers to share mistakes they found when using the editing checklist for their own work. Identify each mistake, and write the corrected sentences on the board.

Using the Editing Checklist

Pair children to edit and proofread each other's drafts using the editing checklist as a guide. First, they should read their drafts aloud. Then have them mark each other's paper to show errors that need to be corrected. Help them look for grammar, usage, end punctuation and spelling errors, sentence by sentence. Remind children to be helpful and polite. When they are finished, have them write a reflection on how collaborating helped their writing.

NARRATIVE NONFICTION

Edit and Proofread

When you **edit** and **proofread,** you look for and correct mistakes in your writing. Rereading a revised draft several times will help you catch any errors. Use the checklist below to edit your sentences.

✓ Editing Checklist

- ☐ Do all sentences begin with a capital letter and end with a punctuation mark?
- ☐ Are present-tense and past-tense forms of action verbs used correctly?
- ☐ Are all the words spelled correctly?
- ☐ Are proper nouns capitalized?

List two mistakes you found as you proofread your narrative.

1 _____

2 _____

Grammar Connections

When you write your personal narrative, make sure you use capital letters for proper nouns. Check for nouns that name specific people, places, or things.

Unit 3 • Narrative Nonfiction   33

Reading/Writing Companion, p. 33

Grammar Connections

Have children proof their personal narratives for the use of capital letters with proper nouns. Review that a proper noun names a specific person, place, or thing. Examples include <u>Alice</u>, <u>the Pacific Ocean</u>, and the <u>Hubble Space Telescope</u>.

English Language Learners SCAFFOLD

Use the following scaffolds with **Using the Editing Checklist.**

Beginning

Model routine language and sentence frames children can use to communicate ideas. *Is there a capital letter at the beginning of this sentence/word? Yes, this is a capital <u>H</u>. Which punctuation mark is at the end of this sentence? It's <u>a period</u>. I'm not sure if ___ is spelled correctly. Let's check a dictionary.* Finally, have mixed proficiency pairs work together to confirm verb tenses are used correctly.

Intermediate

Have partners ask and answer about their drafts using routine language: Is there a capital letter at the beginning of this sentence/word? Yes, the letter <u>H</u> is capitalized/ No, the letter <u>H</u> should be capitalized. What punctuation mark did you use at the end of this sentence? I used <u>a question mark</u> because <u>this is a question</u>.

Advanced/Advanced High

After children check for capitalization and punctuation, have pairs check that verb tenses are used correctly. Provide some models for routine language they can use: *The word "yesterday" tells me you are talking about the past. You should change the verb to the past tense. In this sentence, you are talking about something that happens all the time. You should use the present tense.*

Reading/Writing Companion

OBJECTIVES

With guidance and support from adults, use a variety of digital tools to produce and publish writing, including in collaboration with peers.

Ask for clarification and further explanation as needed about the topics and texts under discussion.

ACADEMIC LANGUAGE

• *present, visual, publish, rubric*
• Cognates: *presentar, visual, publicar, rúbrica*

Digital Tools

Use these digital tools to enhance the lesson.

 Anchor Papers

 How to Give a Presentation video

 # Publish, Present, and Evaluate

Publishing

Once their drafts are final, children can prepare for publishing and presenting their work. Published work should be error-free with illustrations in place.

Presentation

For the final presentation of their personal narratives, have children choose a format for publishing: print or digital. Allow time for children to record an audio/video presentation of their writing. Review the points on the **Presenting Checklist.** Emphasize that a successful presentation depends on these skills. Have children consult the checklist as they practice their presentations before they present for the class.

Evaluate

Explain that rubrics show what is expected from the assignment and how it will be evaluated. Ideally, children should look at rubrics before they begin writing in order to fulfill all the requirements. When they finish, they should evaluate their work. Direct them to the rubric in the **Reading/ Writing Companion** page 35 to check their work.

• Have they written a lively, interesting narrative about being helpful?
• Is there a clear beginning, middle, and end?
• Is there a conclusion that expresses the author's feelings?
• Does the narrative focus on one event?
• Does the narrative use sequence words accurately?

If children answer "no" to any of these points, they should revisit their work. Make sure they note what they did successfully and what needs more work. After children have evaluated their personal narratives using the rubric, have them exchange texts with a partner. Have them go through each point and give the partner a score. Remind them to be respectful and helpful. When they are finished, have children reflect on the effectiveness of the collaboration and on their progress as writers. Have them note where they need improvement, and help them set writing goals.

WRITING

Publish, Present, and Evaluate

Publishing Create a clean, neat final copy of your personal narrative. You may add illustrations or other visuals to make your published work more interesting.

Presentation Practice your presentation when you are ready to present your work. Use the Presenting Checklist to help you.

Evaluate After you publish and present your personal narrative, use the rubric on the next page to evaluate your writing.

1 What did you do successfully? _____

_____

_____

2 What needs more work? _____

_____

_____

Presenting Checklist
- ☐ Sit up or stand up straight.
- ☐ Look at the audience.
- ☐ Read with expression.
- ☐ Speak loudly so that everyone can hear you.
- ☐ Answer questions using details from your story.

34   Unit 3 · Narrative Nonfiction

Listening When you listen actively, you pay close attention to what you hear. When you listen to other students' presentations, take notes to help you better understand their ideas.

What I learned from ....'s presentation:

_____

Questions I have about ....'s presentation:

Listening Checklist
- ☐ Make eye contact with the speaker.
- ☐ Listen for details about the topic.
- ☐ Identify what the speaker does well.
- ☐ Think of questions you can ask.

4	3	2	1
• tells a lively, interesting narrative about being helpful	• tells a narrative about being helpful	• tries to tell a narrative about being helpful	• does not focus on the topic
• includes a strong beginning, middle, and end	• includes a beginning, middle, and end	• attempts to include a beginning, middle, and an end	• does not follow a logical sequence of events
• focuses on one event	• mostly focuses on one event	• tries to focus on one event	• does not focus on one event
• uses words accurately to show sequence	• uses words to show sequence	• uses a word or phrase to show sequence	• lacks words that show sequence
• has a strong conclusion and tells the author's feelings	• has some details about the author's feelings and a conclusion	• has a detail about the author's feelings but lacks a conclusion	• does not tell about the author's feelings or have a conclusion

Unit 3 · Narrative Nonfiction   35

Reading/Writing Companion, pp. 34–35

English Language Learners SCAFFOLD

Use the following scaffolds with **Presentation** to help children share their personal narratives.

Beginning

Help children record their presentations so they can review their own performance against the checklist. Invite them to share their recorded presentations with you and tell you what pronunciation or fluency issues they feel they need help with. After providing support, then have children practice presenting in small groups.

Intermediate

Have partners take turns practicing their presentations and giving feedback to each other. Provide support for their pronunciation and phrasing, and provide sentence frames as needed. For additional support, videotape children's presentations. Then have them watch the videos. Using the checklist, discuss what went well and what needs more practice.

Advanced/Advanced High

Have partners take turns practicing their presentations and giving feedback to each other. Provide support for their pronunciation and phrasing. Using the checklist, have children identify what they did well and what they want to improve upon before presenting to the whole group.

Practice Book

OBJECTIVES

Demonstrate command of the conventions of standard English grammar and usage when writing or speaking. Form and use the past tense of frequently occurring irregular verbs (e.g., *sat, hid, told*).

Demonstrate command of the conventions of standard English capitalization, punctuation, and spelling when writing. (b) Use commas in greetings and closings of letters.

DAILY LANGUAGE ACTIVITY

Use the online review for grammar, practice, and usage.

TEACH IN SMALL GROUP

You may wish to use the Talk About It activities during Small Group time.

Approaching Level, On Level, and Beyond Level Pair children of different proficiency levels.

ELL According to their language proficiency, children should contribute to discussions by using short phrases, asking questions, and adding relevant details.

Past- and Future-Tense Verbs

 DAY 1 Teach

Past- and Future-Tense Verbs

- Remind children that most verbs are action words. Ask: *Do you use the same word to talk about an action that happened in the past and an action that happens in the present?* (No.)

- Explain that verbs telling about an action that happened in the past are called past-tense verbs: *I played ball yesterday*.

- Some verbs tell about an action that will happen in the future. These verbs are called future-tense verbs. The word *will* goes before the verb to make it future tense: *I will play ball tomorrow*.

- Display the following sentences: I walked in the park yesterday. I will run in a race tomorrow. Model identifying the past-tense verb and future-tense verb.

See **Practice Book** page 217 or online activity.

 DAY 2 Teach

Review Past- and Future-Tense Verbs

- Remind children that verbs can tell about an action that happened in the past or will happen in the future.

- The past tense of a verb is often formed by adding *-ed* to the present tense of the verb. Display the following sentences:

I count the birds in our tree. Yesterday, I counted the birds in our tree.

- Read the sentences aloud and point out the present-tense verb and the past-tense verb.

- Display the sentence below and ask children to rewrite it using a past-tense and a future-tense verb.
  He mows grass. (He mowed the grass. He will mow the grass.)

See **Practice Book** page 218 or online activity.

  OPTION

Talk About It

Yesterday and Tomorrow

Have partners talk with each other about what they did yesterday and what they will do tomorrow. Have each partner listen for past-tense and future-tense verbs.

Pick Two

Write these action verbs on cards: *walk, dream, help, paint, enjoy*. Write *tomorrow, later, yesterday, last week,* and *next week* on another set of cards. Have children generate sentences using the cards.

Mechanics and Usage — DAY 3

Letter Punctuation

- Letters have special punctuation. The greeting (the beginning of a letter) and the closing (the end of a letter) both begin with a capital letter.

- A comma is used after the greeting and closing.

- Write the brief letter below on the board. Read it aloud. Guide children to tell where to use capital letters and commas.

dear Tomás (Dear Tomás,)

I liked the selection "Lighting Lives." I think you would like it, too.

your friend (Your friend,)

sienna (Sienna)

See **Practice Book** page 219 or online activity.

 Proofread and Write — OPTION DAY 4

Proofread

Have children identify and correct errors in the letter below:

dear joan (Dear Joan,)

do (Do) you like your new school? we (We) miss you here. Last week, Patty and I join (joined) a new club. It's about science. we (We) wish you were in it, too. Next weekend, I invite (will invite) you to my birthday party.

your friend (Your friend,)

will (Will)

Write

Have children find a section of their own writing in their writer's notebook and correct errors they made using past- and future-tense verbs. Then have them correct spelling and capitalization errors.

See **Practice Book** page 220 or online activity.

 Assess and Reteach — OPTION DAY 5

Assess

Use the Daily Language Activity and **Practice Book** page 221 for assessment.

Rubric Use your online rubric to record student progress.

Reteach

Use the online **Grammar Handbook** pages 482-483 and Practice Book pages 217–220 for additional reteaching. Remind children to use past-tense verbs and future-tense verbs correctly as they speak and write.

Check children's writing for use of the skill and listen for it in their speaking. Assign grammar revision assignments in their writer's notebook as needed.

Pen Pal

Have groups talk about someone they would like to write a letter to. Have each group write a two-sentence letter, punctuating it correctly.

Fix It Up

Have groups trade the letters they wrote on Day 3. Ask each group to check the letter they receive for correct capitalization and punctuation.

Tell a Story

Ask partners to use action verbs to retell a story they have read or seen. As they talk, their partners should listen for and identify action verbs.

Subject-Verb Agreement

Practice Book

TEACH IN SMALL GROUP

You may wish to use the Talk About It activities during Small Group time.

Approaching Level, On Level and Beyond Level Pair children of different proficiency levels.

ELL According to their language proficiency, children should contribute to discussions by using short phrases, asking questions, and adding relevant details.

 DAY 6 Teach

Subject-Verb Agreement

- Explain that the **verb** in a sentence must agree with its **subject**. Tell children to identify the subject of a sentence and ask: "Is the subject one or more people or things?" Add *-s* or *-es* only if the subject tells about one person or thing in the present tense. Model finding the verb.

The boy (walk) up the stairs. (walks)

Display the sentence below:

Jamal and Robin is/are in the park.

- Underline *Jamal and Robin.* Explain that the word *and* connects *Jamal and Robin.* They make a plural subject. Use the third person plural verb *are.*

Ask children to pick the correct verb for the sentence below:

The book and pencil is/are on the table. (are)

See **Practice Book** page 234 or online activity.

 DAY 7 Teach

Review Subject-Verb Agreement

- Remind children that there must be subject-verb agreement in every sentence.

- Display the following sentences and guide children to underline the subject and choose the correct the verb.

The pencil are/is in the house. (is)

Ronan (cook) delicious food. (cooks)

- Remind children that sometimes a subject is a **collective noun,** such as the words *class* and *team.* These subjects represent more than one person. Say: *You must still ask, "How many?"* Display the sentence and ask: *Is there one—or more than one—team on the field? Choose the verb.*

The team is/are on the field. (one team/subject is on the field, is)

See **Practice Book** page 235 or online activity.

  ^OPTION ## Talk About It

Singular or Plural?

Have partners write *is, are, and, -s, -es,* and two names of people for a total of seven cards. Partners take turns drawing one or two "subject" cards and combining it/them with *is, are, and* or verbs with *-es, -s,* to create orally generated sentences.

How Many?

Partners add the singular and plural names of things (e.g., *book, books*) and collective nouns, such as *group* to their subjects' pile from the day before. Have children write sentences. Invite volunteers to share with the class.

DAY 8 Mechanics and Usage

 OPTION DAY 9 Proofread and Write

 OPTION DAY 10 Assess and Teach

Abbreviations

- Remind children that an abbreviation is a short way of writing a word.
- Abbreviations start with a capital letter and end with a period.
- Abbreviations can be used in street addresses and in titles before names. Explain to children that a title can describe someone's job. A good example is the word *doctor*. Display the word and abbreviation. Underline the capital D and circle the period.
- Doctor/ Dr.
- Explain that if you wanted to write to a doctor you would use the abbreviation for the title and abbreviations for road (Rd.), Street, (St.), Avenue, (Ave.), and Apartment (Apt.).

See **Practice Book** page 236 or online activity.

Proofread

Give children the list of abbreviations from the previous day and ask them to make corrections in the following email.

dear (Dear) Doctor (Dr.) Clifton,

My sister and I likes (like) you as our doctor. Please tell me what your address is so that i (I) can send something to your office. Is it 49 Plaza Road, (Rd.) 49 Plaza Street, (St.) or 49 Plaza Drive? (Dr.)

Best regards,

Milo Landers

Write

Apply to Writing Have children find a piece of their own writing in their writer's notebook and correct errors they made in subject-verb agreement. Then have them correct abbreviation errors.

See **Practice Book** page 237 or online activity.

Assess

Use the Daily Language Activity and **Practice Book** page 238 for assessment.

Rubric Use your online rubric to record student progress

Reteach

Use the online **Grammar Handbook** page 483 and Practice Book pages 234–237 for additional reteaching. Remind children to use present-tense and past-tense verbs correctly as they speak and write.

Check children's writing for use of the skill and listen for it in their speaking. Assign grammar revision assignments in their writer's notebooks as needed.

Proper Address

Have partners address letters. They should choose abbreviations from the following list: Doctor (Dr.), Captain (Capt.), Professor (Prof.), Road (Rd.), Drive (Dr.), Street (St.).

Places to Go

Partners write one sentence using the past-tense verb *visited*. Then they write about someplace they would like to visit. They must use the word *will* before the verb. Partners exchange sentences.

Charades

Write these verbs on slips of paper: *walk, jump, laugh, cough, sleep, drop, march, sneeze, snore.* Have children take turns drawing a slip of paper and acting out the verb. Others can guess, calling out the past-tense and the future-tense of the word.

Practice Book

OBJECTIVES

Demonstrate command of the conventions of standard English capitalization, punctuation, and spelling when writing. Generalize learned spelling patterns when writing words (e.g., cage → badge; boy → boil).

DIFFERENTIATED SPELLING

Go online for Dictation Sentences for differentiated spelling lists.

On Level and ELL

told	most	float
coat	toast	grow
mow	show	Joe
toe		

Review light, mind
High-Frequency only, our, who

Approaching Level

told	most	road
coat	toast	grow
crow	show	Joe
toe		

Review right, mind
High-Frequency only, our, who

Beyond Level

know	mostly	floating
cloak	toast	woe
bowl	showed	Joe
stows		

Review sight, kindness
High-Frequency only, our, who

Long *o: o, oa, ow, oe*

 DAY 1 Assess Prior Knowledge

Read the spelling words aloud, drawing out the vowel sounds.

Point out the long *o* sound in *told*. Write the word and draw a line under *o* as you say the word. Explain that not all words with the long *o* sound are spelled in the same way.

Write these words and underline the letter patterns that spell the long *o* sound: *told*, *float*, *grow*, and *toe*. Demonstrate sorting the spelling words under these key words.

Use the Dictation Sentences from Day 5 to give the pretest. Say the underlined word, read the sentence, and repeat the word. Have children write the words. Then have children check their paper.

See **Practice Book** page 213 for a pretest.

 OPTION **DAY 2** Spiral Review

Review the long *i* sound in *mind*, *cry*, *light*, and *lie*. Read each sentence below, repeat the review word, and have children write the word.

1. Dad turned on the <u>light</u>.
2. Owls have wonderful <u>sight</u>.
3. Keep your <u>mind</u> on the job.
4. We heard the baby <u>cry</u>.
5. We'll <u>tie</u> the boat to the dock.
6. The book is <u>high</u> on the shelf.
7. We ate <u>wild</u> berries.
8. My socks are <u>dry</u>.
9. I'll <u>try</u> to fix the lock.
10. My dog will <u>lie</u> on the couch.

Have children trade papers and check their partner's spelling.

  Word Sorts

OPEN SORT

Have children cut apart the **Spelling Word Cards** available online and initial the back of each card. Have them read the words aloud with partners. Then have partners do an open sort. Have them record their sorts in their writer's notebook.

PATTERN SORT

Have children complete the pattern sort you modeled on Day 1 by using the boldfaced key words on the **Spelling Word Cards**. Point out the long *o* vowel sounds. Partners should compare and check their sorts. See **Practice Book** pages 214, 214A, and 214B for differentiated practice.

Word Meanings

Have children copy the riddles below into their writer's notebooks. Read the riddles aloud. Then ask them to write a spelling word that answers the riddle.

1. You might put jam on this. (toast)
2. This is what you do on top of the water. (float)
3. This is how you cut down grass. (mow)
4. This is what you wear when you are cold. (coat)

Challenge children to create riddles for their other spelling or review words. Have them post their riddles on the board.

Proofread and Write

Write these sentences on the board. Have children circle and correct each misspelled word. Have them use a print or digital dictionary to check and correct their spellings.

1. I hurt my to. (toe)
2. The plant will groe tall. (grow)
3. Can you shoo me how to fix my bike? (show)
4. I have a new cote for winter. (coat)

Error Correction Point out that *toe* and *tow* are homonyms. They sound the same but have different meanings and are spelled differently.

Apply to Writing Have children correct a piece of their own writing.

Assess

Use the Dictation Sentences for the posttest. Have children list the misspelled words in their writer's notebook. Look for children's use of these words in their writing.

See **Practice Book** page 213 for a posttest. Use pages 214, 214A, and 214B for review.

Dictation Sentences

1. I <u>told</u> Mom about the party.
2. I ate <u>most</u> of my dinner.
3. I can <u>float</u> on my back.
4. My new <u>coat</u> is red.
5. I like <u>toast</u> with butter.
6. Apples <u>grow</u> on trees.
7. I like to <u>mow</u> the lawn.
8. Sam will <u>show</u> me how to play the game.
9. <u>Joe</u> is on our team.
10. I hurt my <u>toe</u> when I fell.
11. We needed <u>light</u> in the tent.
12. I like to see pictures in my <u>mind</u>.
13. I <u>only</u> read part of the book.
14. Did you like <u>our</u> idea?
15. <u>Who</u> can come to the party?

SPEED SORT

Have partners do a speed sort to see who is the fastest. Then have them do a word hunt in this week's readings to find words with the same vowel sounds as the spelling words. Have them record the words in their writer's notebook.

BLIND SORT

Have partners do a blind sort: one reads a **Spelling Word Card**; the other tells under which key word it belongs. Then have partners hunt for other words with the same spelling pattern and add them to their writer's notebooks.

Practice Book

OBJECTIVES

Demonstrate command of the conventions of standard English capitalization, punctuation, and spelling when writing. Generalize learned spelling patterns when writing words (e.g., cage → badge; boy → boil).

DIFFERENTIATED SPELLING

Go online for Dictation Sentences for differentiated spelling lists.

On Level and ELL

we	bee	need
queen	mean	leaf
thief	chief	pony
keys		

Review grow, toe
High-Frequency after, every, special

Approaching Level

we	bee	need
green	bean	seat
thief	chief	pony
key		

Review grow, toe
High-Frequency after, every, special

Beyond Level

we've	she's	needed
queen	meaning	leaves
grief	chiefs	fifty
keys		

Review bowl, toast
High-Frequency after, every, special

Long *e: e, ee, ea, ie, y, ey*

 DAY 6 Assess Prior Knowledge

- Read the spelling words aloud, drawing out the vowel sounds. Point out the long *e* sound in *we*. Draw a line under *e* as you say the word. Remind children that not all words with the long *e* sound are spelled in the same way and that two letters can stand for one vowel sound. The two letters act as a team and the vowel team stays together in the same syllable.

Write these words and underline the letter patterns that spell /ē/: *we, bee, mean, thief, pony,* and *keys*. Demonstrate sorting the spelling words under these key words.

- Use the Dictation Sentences from Day 10 to give the pretest. Say the underlined word, read the sentence, and repeat the word. Have children write the words. Have partners check their work.

See **Practice Book** page 230 for a pretest.

 Word Sorts

OPEN SORT

Have children cut apart the **Spelling Word Cards** available online and initial the back of each card. Have them read the words aloud with partners. Then have partners do an open sort. Have them record their sorts in their writer's notebook.

 OPTION **DAY 7** Spiral Review

Review the long *o* sound in *told, coat,* and *grow*. Read each sentence below, repeat the review word, and have children write the word.

1. Jack **told** me the answer.
2. Will you **show** me the book?
3. **Most** of us like pizza.
4. Flowers **grow** in the garden.
5. Tim will **mow** the grass in the yard.
6. Leaves **float** in the puddle.
7. Did you **scrape** the paint?
8. My favorite questions **begin** with *why?*
9. Do **those** books belong to you?
10. My sister and I don't spend much time **apart**.

Have children trade papers and check their partner's spelling.

PATTERN SORT

Have children complete the pattern sort you modeled on Day 6 by using the boldfaced key words on the **Spelling Word Cards**. Point out the long *e* vowel sounds. Partners should compare and check their sorts. See **Practice Book** pages 231, 231A, and 231B for differentiated practice.

Word Meanings

Have children copy the four words below into their writer's notebooks. Say the words aloud. Then ask them to write the spelling word that means the opposite of each word.

1. mean (kind)
2. after (before)
3. need (want)
4. special (common)

Challenge children to come up with antonyms for their other spelling or review words. Have them post their word groups on the board.

 Proofread and Write

Write these sentences on the board. Have children circle and correct each misspelled word. Remind children that the long e sound can be spelled with the vowel teams ee, ea, ie, ey and the letters e, y.

1. We nead the book. (need)
2. The quen wore a crown. (queen)
3. The theif stole the money. (thief)
4. I lost my kes. (keys)

Error Correction Point out that the words *bee* and *be* can be confused. Remind children to check their spelling of these words as they write.

Apply to Writing Have children use their knowledge of spelling rules and patterns to correct misspelled words in a piece of their own writing.

 Assess

Use the Dictation Sentences for the posttest. Have children list the misspelled words in their writer's notebook. Look for children's use of these words in their writing. See **Practice Book** page 230 for a posttest. Use pages 231, 231A, and 231B for review.

Dictation Sentences

1. Do <u>we</u> want to ride the bus?
2. The <u>bee</u> flew out the window.
3. Do you <u>need</u> a ticket?
4. The <u>queen</u> came to the window.
5. Do not be <u>mean</u> to others.
6. The <u>leaf</u> was green and yellow.
7. The <u>thief</u> ran away.
8. The <u>chief</u> told a story about nature.
9. The <u>pony</u> ran down the hill.
10. Put the <u>keys</u> on the table.
11. I <u>grow</u> taller each year.
12. I hurt my <u>toe</u> on the rock.
13. We'll read <u>after</u> lunch.
14. <u>Every</u> person got an award.
15. My birthday is a <u>special</u> day.

SPEED SORT

Have partners do a speed sort to see who is the fastest. Then have them do a word hunt in this week's readings to find words with the same vowel sounds as the spelling words. Have them record the words in their writer's notebook.

BLIND SORT

Have partners do a blind sort: one reads a **Spelling Word Card**; the other tells under which key word it belongs. Then have partners hunt for other words with the same spelling pattern and add them to their writer's notebooks.

Expand Vocabulary

Practice Book

OBJECTIVES

Use sentence-level context as a clue to the meaning of a word or phrase.

Determine the meaning of the new word formed when a known prefix is added to a known word (e.g., *happy/unhappy, tell/retell*).

Use a known root word as a clue to the meaning of an unknown word with the same root (e.g., *addition, additional*).

Digital Tools

For more practice, have children use the Vocabulary Activities.

 Vocabulary Activities

 English Language Learners

Pair children of different language proficiency levels to practice vocabulary.

OPTION
 DAY 1 Connect to Words

Practice the target vocabulary.

1. Where would you expect to have an **adventure**?
2. What would you be **delighted** to get as a present?
3. What have you **dreamed** of doing when you grow up?
4. What books have you **enjoyed** reading?
5. What have you **grumbled** about lately?
6. How is **moonlight** different from sunlight?
7. Who is your favorite **neighbor**?
8. What can you see in the **nighttime** sky?

OPTION
DAY 6 Build Vocabulary

Display *plumped, squished, lost track,* and *rocket ship*.

- Define each word or phrase and discuss the meanings with children.
- Write *squishing* under *squish*.

Have partners write other words with the same root and define them. Then have partners ask and answer questions using the words.

- Repeat with *plump*.

OPTION
 DAY 2 Related Words

Help children create different forms of target words by adding, changing, or removing affixes.

- Write *adventure* in the first column of a T-chart. Then write *adventuring* and *adventurous* in the next two columns.
- Discuss each form of the word and its meaning. Then have children share aloud sentences using the words.
- Have children work in pairs to fill in charts for *delighted, dreamed, enjoyed, grumbled, moonlight, neighbor,* and *nighttime*.
- Have children copy the chart into their writer's notebook.

DAY 7 Multiple-Meaning Words

Explain to children that some words have more than one meaning. Have them discuss the use of the word *play* in these three sentences.

We like to <u>play</u> on the swings.
I acted in a <u>play</u> at school.
Would you <u>play</u> that song again?

- Then discuss these three words: *light, point, ring*.
- Have partners discuss at least two meanings of each word and write the meanings of the words in their writer's notebook.

See **Practice Book** page 239 or online activity.

OPTION
DAY 3 · Spiral Review
Reinforce the Words

Have children orally complete each cloze sentence to review words.

1. A new _____ moved in next door. (neighbor)

2. I was _____ to see my friend. (delighted)

3. Our trip to the mountains was a great _____ . (adventure)

4. I like the soft glow of _____ . (moonlight)

5. My grumpy brother _____ during dinner. (grumbled)

6. There were many stars in the _____ sky. (nighttime)

7. It was a great party and everyone _____ it. (enjoyed)

Display previous vocabulary words: *across, borrow, countryside, ideas, insists, lonely, solution, villages.* Have pairs ask and answer questions for the words.

OPTION
DAY 4 · **Connect to Writing**

Have children write sentences in their writer's notebook using the target vocabulary from Day 1.

- Tell them to write sentences that provide context to show what the words mean.
- **ELL** Provide the Day 3 cloze sentences 1–6 for children needing extra support.

Write Using Vocabulary

- Have children write something they learned from this week's target words in their writer's notebook. For example, they might write about different kinds of light.

OPTION
DAY 5 · **Word Squares**

Ask children to create Word Squares for each vocabulary word.

- In the first square, children write the word (e.g., *delighted*).
- In the second square, children write their own definition of the word and any related words, such as synonyms (e.g. *happy, glad, thrilled*).
- In the third square, children draw an illustration that will help them remember the word (e.g., children smiling).
- In the fourth square, children write nonexamples, including antonyms for the word (e.g. *sad, unhappy*).

Have partners discuss their squares.

OPTION
DAY 8 · **Compound Words**

Remind children that some English words are made up of two smaller words. They are called **compound words**.

- Show children these words from the **Differentiated Genre Passage**, "A Shooting Star": *afternoon, campsite, overhead, nightfall,* and *daylight.* Explain that they can figure out the meaning of a compound word by thinking about the meaning of the two smaller words.
- Have pairs create a concept map for another compound word.

OPTION
DAY 9 · **Shades of Meaning**

Help children create a concept map for the word *adventure.*

- In the middle circle, write *adventure.* In circles on the left, write words that tell what an adventure should be (*fun, interesting, exciting*). On the right, write words that tell what an adventure should not be (*dull, uninteresting, boring*).
- Ask children to copy the words in their writer's notebook.

OPTION
DAY 10 · **Compound Word Chain**

Have children make a compound word chain beginning with the word *homework.* Provide these five words: *homework, lighthouse, daylight, workday,* and *houseboat* and have children order them so the second word of each compound becomes the first word of the next one.

- Have children find other compound words and see how long a chain they can make.

Write Using Vocabulary

Have children use vocabulary words in their stories.

VOCABULARY **T229**

Make Connections

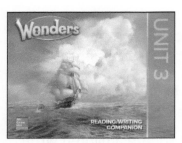

Reading/Writing Companion

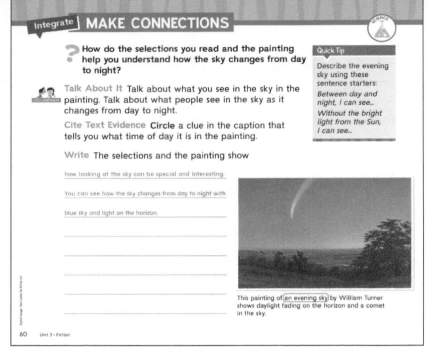

Reading/Writing Companion, p. 60

OBJECTIVES

Compare and contrast the most important points presented by two texts on the same topic.

Recall information from experiences or gather information from provided sources to answer a question.

Close Reading Routine

Read DOK 1–2

- Identify key ideas and details about objects that can be seen in the sky.
- Take notes and summarize.
- Use **A C T** prompts as needed.

Reread DOK 2–3

- Analyze the text, craft, and structure.
- Use the *Reading/Writing Companion*.

Integrate DOK 4

- Integrate knowledge and ideas.
- Make text-to-text connections.
- Use the Integrate/Make Connections lesson.
- Inspire action.

Text Connections

Talk About It

Share and discuss children's responses to the "When The Night Sky Dances" Blast. Then write the Essential Question on the board or chart paper: *What can we see in the sky?* Below that, draw a chart with headings for all the texts children have read. Have children read through their notes, annotations, and responses and add what they learned from each text to the chart. Then ask children to complete the Talk About It activity on **Reading/Writing Companion** page 60.

Cite Text Evidence

Guide children to use text evidence to make connections between the image on page 60 of the **Reading/Writing Companion** and the selections they have read. Remind children to read the caption below the image and to use the Quick Tip.

Write

Children should refer to the notes on the chart as they respond to the writing prompt at the bottom of the page. When children have finished writing, have them share and discuss their responses.

Show What You Learned Have children write a final response synthesizing the knowledge they built about what we can see in the sky.

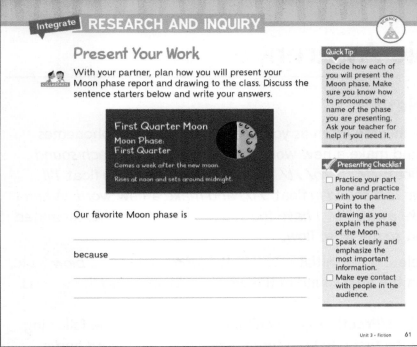

Reading/Writing Companion, p. 61

Recall information from experiences or gather information from provided sources to answer a question.

ACADEMIC LANGUAGE
- *report, presentation*
- Cognate: *presentación*

Digital Tools

Use this digital tool to enhance the lesson.

 RESOURCE TOOLKIT How to Give a Presentation (Collaborative Conversations video)

Present Your Work

10 Mins

Planning the Presentation

COLLABORATE

Tell children that they will need to prepare in order to best present their work. Discuss each item on the Presenting Strategies checklist in the **Reading/Writing Companion** page 61. Allow partners and small groups time to rehearse.

Discuss options for ways children can present their short reports. Model how to highlight the most important information. Suggest children complete the sentence starters on **Reading/Writing Companion** page 61, and use the sentences in their presentations.

Remind children that they will be part of the audience for other children's presentations, and that listeners play an important role. Review with and model for children the behaviors of an effective listener. You may wish to show children the Listening Checklist from the Toolkit.

During the Presentation

Tell children to write down any questions they have as speakers share information. Explain that doing so will help them remember their questions when a speaker is finished. Guide a discussion of the presentations, asking children to review the Moon phases in time order.

TEACH IN SMALL GROUP

You may wish to teach the Research and Inquiry lesson during Small Group time and then have groups present their work to the class.

Daily Focus

Phonemic Awareness
• Phoneme Deletion

Phonics
• Introduce and Blend Words with /ō/o, oa, ow, oe

Structural Analysis
• Contractions with *not*

High-Frequency Words

Read
• Decodable Reader, Vol. 3: "Three Goats and a Troll"

Handwriting
• lowercase cursive *y, z, v, x*

OBJECTIVES

• Delete phonemes in a word.

• Apply phonics when decoding words with long *o*.

Phonemic Awareness: page 207

Phonemic Awareness

5 Mins

Phoneme Deletion

1 **Model** Have children listen as you say a word with four phonemes, delete one, and make a new word. Say: *Listen as I say each sound in the word* float: */f/ /l/ /ō/ /t/. There are four sounds in* float. *I'll take away the last sound in* float, */t/, and make a new word. When I delete, or take away, /t/, I have the sounds /f/ /l/ /ō/ left. I changed the word* float *to the word* flow.

Repeat by deleting the initial sound in the words *scold* and *blow* (cold, low) and then the final sound in the words *gold* and *road* (goal, row).

2 **Guided Practice/Practice** Have children practice with the following examples. Do the first one with them. *Say: I will say a word and a sound to take away. Tell me the new word. We'll do the first one together.*

note (take away /t/)	bold (take away /b/)	soak (take away /s/)
groan (take away /n/)	boat (take away /b/)	spoke (take away /s/)
bread (take away /b/)	wait (take away /t/)	pail (take away /l/)

Provide corrective feedback to children as necessary.

Have children independently practice deleting phonemes using **Practice Book** page 207.

English Language Learners

Model Focus on articulation. Say /ō/ and note your mouth position. Have children repeat. Use the articulation photos on the **Sound-Spelling Cards**. Repeat for /o/. Have children say both sounds, noting the slight differences in mouth position. Continue with these word pairs: *road/rod; cloak/clock; goat/got; soak/sock.*

DIFFERENTIATED INSTRUCTION 》

TIER 2

Approaching Level If children need extra support with phoneme deletion:

I Do Explain to children that they will be deleting the first or the last phoneme to make new words. Say: *When you delete, you subtract, or take away. When you delete a phoneme, you are taking a sound away.*

Say: Listen as I say a word: gold, */gōōōllld/. I want to take away /g/ from gold. That leaves /ōōō/, /lll/, and /d/.* Gold *without /g/ is* old.

We Do Say: *Listen as I say another word:* boats. *Say the word with me, /bōōōtsss/. Let's take away /b/ from* boats. *That leaves /ōōō/ /t/ /sss/. Let's blend the sounds: /ōōōtsss/,* oats. Boats *without /b/ is* oats. Repeat the deletion routine with these word pairs:

stow/tow	hold/old	soak/oak	fork/for
shelf/elf	sold/sole	shrug/rug	clock/lock

You Do Say: *It's your turn. Take away a sound from one word to form a new word.* Provide corrective feedback if children need support.

stone/tone	train/rain	flow/low	throat/throw
scream/cream	grow/row	trap/rap	plane/lane

You may wish to review Phonemic Awareness with **ELL** using this section.

See page 5 in the **Language Transfers Handbook** for guidance in identifying sounds that may or may not transfer for speakers of certain languages and for support in accommodating those children. See the chart on pages 6–9 for specific sound transfer issues for multiple languages.

Digital Tools

For more practice, have children use this activity.

Phonemic Awareness

OBJECTIVES
- Know and apply grade-level phonics and word analysis skills in decoding words.

Build Fluency

Display the Word-Building Cards *i, igh, ie, y, scr, spr, str, thr, spl, shr, a, ai, ay, ea, ei, eigh, ey.* Have children say each sound.

⏱ 5 Mins **Phonics**

Introduce Long *o: o, oa, ow, oe*

1 **Model** Display the *Boat* **Sound-Spelling Card.** Teach /ō/ spelled *o, oa, ow, oe.* Say: *This is the* Boat *Sound-Spelling Card. The sound is /ō/. You learned that the /ō/ sound can be spelled with the letters* o_e. *The /ō/ sound can also be spelled with the letters* o, oa, ow, *and* oe. *Listen as I say it: /ōōō/. This is the sound in the middle of the word* boat. *Listen: /bōōōt/,* boat. *I'll say /ōōō/ as I write the letters* oa.

Sound Spelling Card

2 **Guided Practice/Practice** Have children practice connecting the letters *o, oa, ow, oe* to the /ō/ sound. Display the *Boat* Sound Spelling Card and write *oa. Now do it with me. Say /ōōō/ as I write the letters* oa. *This time, write the letters* oa *five times as you say the /ō/ sound.*

Repeat the routine with the letters *o* in *go, ow* in *own,* and *oe* in *toe.*

Have children independently practice long *o: o, oa, ow, oe* using **Practice Book** page 209.

TIER 2

Approaching Level If children have difficulty with long *o: o, oa, ow, oe:*

I Do Display the *Boat* Sound-Spelling Card. Say: *This is the* Boat *Sound-Spelling Card. The sound is /ō/. The /ō/ sound can be spelled with the letters* o, oa, ow, *and* oe. Display the **Word-Building Cards** *oa.* Trace the letters *oa* while saying /ō/ five times. Repeat with *o, ow,* and *oe.*

We Do Say: *Now do it with me.* Have children trace lowercase *oa* on the Word-Building Cards with their finger while saying /ō/. Trace the letters *oa* five times and say /ō/ with children. Repeat with the sound-spellings *o, ow,* and *oe.*

You Do Have children connect the letters *oa, o, ow,* and *oe* to the sound /ō/ by tracing lowercase *oa, o, ow,* and *oe* with their finger while saying /ō/. Once children have traced the letters on paper five to ten times, they should then write the letters *oa, o, ow,* and *oe* while saying /ō/ five to ten times.

Repeat, connecting the letters *oa, o, ow,* and *oe* to the sound /ō/ through tracing and writing the letters throughout the week.

You may wish to review Phonics with **ELL** using this section.

Phonics: page 209

Blend Words with Long *o*: *o, oa, ow, oe*

1 **Model** Display **Word-Building Cards** *s, o, a, p.* Model how to blend the sounds: *This is the letter* s. *It stands for /s/. These are the letters* oa. *Together they stand for /ō/. This is the letter* p. *It stands for /p/. Listen as I blend these sounds together: /sssōōōp/. The word is* soap.

Continue modeling blending with the words *cold, low,* and *doe.*

2 **Guided Practice/Practice** Display the Phonics/Fluency Practice chart. Read each word in the first row, blending the sounds—for example, say: */nnnōōō/. The word is* no. Have children blend each word with you. Prompt children to read the connected text, sounding out the decodable words.

no	toe	bold	float	row	Joe
coat	loan	so	mow	fold	slow
foe	go	woe	most	roast	pro
light	pay	switch	night	scrub	sway

Moe ate toast and oats.

The coach told Joan she made a goal!

Joe put on his coat to go out in the cold snow.

Phonics/Fluency Practice

DIFFERENTIATED INSTRUCTION »

TIER 2

Approaching Level If children are having difficulty blending words:

I Do Display Word-Building Cards *c, o, a, t. This is the letter* c. *It stands for /k/. Listen as I say it: /k/. These are the letters* oa. *Together they can stand for the sound /ō/. Listen: /ō/. This is the letter* t. *It stands for /t/. I will blend all the sounds together: /kōōōt/,* coat. Repeat with *most, low, toe.*

We Do Guide children to blend the sounds and read the following words: *coach, road, old, so, mow, grow, doe.* Offer corrective feedback to any children needing additional support.

You Do Have children blend and decode: *goat, toast, no, sold, own, throw,* and *foe.*

Repeat, blending additional long *o* words with *o, oa, ow, oe.*

You may wish to review Phonics with **ELL** using this section.

Corrective Feedback

Sound Error: Model the sound children missed, then have them repeat the sound. Say: *My turn.* Tap under the letters and say: *Sound? /ō/ What's the sound?* Return to the beginning of the word. Say: *Let's start over.* Blend the word with children again.

English Language Learners

See page 5 in the **Language Transfers Handbook** for guidance in identifying phonics skills that may or may not transfer for speakers of certain languages and for support in accommodating those children. See the chart on pages 10–13 for specific phonics transfer issues for multiple languages.

Digital Tools

To differentiate instruction for key skills, use the results of this activity.

Phonics

OBJECTIVES

• Form contractions with *not.*

• Know and apply grade-level phonics and word analysis skills in decoding words.

ACADEMIC LANGUAGE

• *contraction, apostrophe*

• Cognates: *contracción, apóstrofe*

Digital Tools

For more practice, have children use this activity.

I __ the jar.
| fill | fills | filling |

Structural Analysis

OPTION
5
Mins

Structural Analysis

Contractions with *not*

1 **Model** Remind children that a contraction is formed when two words are put together to make one shorter word. An apostrophe takes the place of one or more letters that are removed to make the contraction. Write *is* and *not.* Beneath them write *isn't* and underline the letters *n't.* Say: *When I make the words* is *and* not *into a contraction, I leave out the letter* o *in* not. *I use an apostrophe to show that there is a letter missing.* Read *isn't.*

COLLABORATE

2 **Guided Practice/Practice** Display the following words, read them with children, and then have children form the contractions. Discuss which letters were removed or changed to form each contraction. Do the first three with children. Provide corrective feedback as necessary.

do not (don't)	did not (didn't)	would not (wouldn't)
can not (can't)	is not (isn't)	were not (weren't)
was not (wasn't)	will not (won't)	could not (couldn't)
are not (aren't)	does not (doesn't)	should not (shouldn't)

DIFFERENTIATED INSTRUCTION ➤➤

TIER
2

Approaching Level If children need additional support with contractions with *not:*

I Do Write and read *is not* and *isn't.* Say: *The word* isn't *is a contraction for the words* is not. *A contraction is a short way to write two words. The apostrophe replaces the letter* o *in* isn't. *My artwork is not finished. My artwork isn't finished.*

We Do Write *have not.* Let's write a contraction for *have not. The contraction is* haven't. *The apostrophe replaces the missing letter* o *in* not. *Let's use* haven't *in a sentence.* Repeat with *can not, do not,* and *did not.*

You Do Have children work in pairs. Give each pair the words *was, would,* and *had* and have them form contractions with *not.*

Repeat Have children use their contractions in sentences.

High-Frequency Words

better, group, long, more, only, our, started, three, who, won't

1 **Model** Display the **High-Frequency Word Cards** and use the Read/Spell/Write routine for each word.

- **Read** Point to and say the word *better*. *This is the word* better. *Say it with me:* better.

- **Spell** *The word* better *is spelled* b-e-t-t-e-r. *Spell it with me.*

- **Write** *Let's write the word in the air as we say each letter:* b-e-t-t-e-r.

- Point out to children any irregularities in sound-spellings, such as the /ü/ sound spelled *o* in the word *who*.

- Have partners create sentences using each word.

2 **Guided Practice/Practice** Have children identify the high-frequency words in connected text and blend the decodable words.

1. Joe is much **better** today.
2. A **group** of kids played tag.
3. Ken has a **long** bus ride.
4. May I have **more** grapes?
5. **Only** one fish is in the bowl.
6. It is **our** time to play ball.
7. The race has just **started**.
8. Joan has **three** gifts for us.
9. **Who** is on the phone?
10. I **won't** go without you.

DIFFERENTIATED INSTRUCTION

TIER 2

Approaching Level If children need additional support with high-frequency words:

I Do Use the High-Frequency Word Cards. Follow this routine for each word: Display the word. Read the word. Spell the word.

We Do Ask children to state the word and spell the word with you. Model using the word in a sentence, and have children repeat.

You Do Display the words randomly for children to say and spell. Provide opportunities for children to use the words in speaking and writing. For example, provide sentence starters, such as *I think ____ is better than ____*. Have children write each word in their Writer's Notebook.

OBJECTIVES

- Know and apply grade-level phonics and word analysis skills in decoding words.

- Recognize and read grade-appropriate irregularly spelled words.

English Language Learners

Model Use visual cues, gestures, and examples to help children learn the meanings of the high-frequency words. Point out the Spanish cognate *grupo*. Use words in sentences to help clarify meaning.

Digital Tools

For more practice, have children use this activity.

High-Frequency Words

Decodable Reader: "Three Goats and a Troll"

5 Mins

Decodable Reader, Vol. 3

OBJECTIVES

- Know and apply grade-level phonics and word-analysis skills in decoding words.
- Recognize and read grade-appropriate irregularly spelled words.
- Read on-level text with purpose and understanding.
- Read with sufficient accuracy and fluency to support comprehension.
- Identify, trace, and write lowercase cursive letters *y, z, v,* and *x*.

English Language Learners

Check Comprehension
Provide sentence frames, as needed, to help children answer the questions:

p. 36 The three goats want to <u>eat the grass on the hill</u>.

p. 38 Moe tells Troll to <u>wait for Joe</u>.

p. 39 I know because Troll says Joe will be <u>better than a fresh pie</u>.

p. 40 Joe <u>throws</u> Troll in the <u>lake</u>.

Focus on Foundational Skills

Review the words and letter-sounds that children will find in the **Decodable Reader**.

- Review the high-frequency words *better, group, long, more, only, our, started, three, who,* and *won't.*
- Review that the letters *o, oa, ow, oe* can stand for the long *o* sound.

Preview and Predict Point to the title of the story and have children sound out each word with you. Ask: *What do you see in the illustration?*

Read the Decodable Reader

Begin to read the story "Three Goats and a Troll." On page 37, have children point to each word, sounding out the decodable words and saying the high-frequency words quickly. If children need support reading decodable words, model blending. If children are having difficulty with high-frequency words, reread the word in isolation and then in context.

Check Comprehension

p. 36 *Why do the three goats want to cross Troll's low bridge?*
p. 38 *What does Moe say to Troll to save himself from being eaten?*
p. 39 *How do you know that Troll wants to eat Joe?*
p. 40 *What does Joe do to Troll?*
Retell Have partners use key ideas and details to retell the story.

Focus on Fluency

COLLABORATE

With partners, have children read "Three Goats and a Troll" to focus on accuracy. Guide them to run their fingers under the text as they read. Children should note whether they are correctly reading the words on the page, monitor themselves, and provide feedback to their partners.

Listen in: If children are having difficulty reading accurately, have them start again at the beginning of the page. If children are reading too quickly, suggest that they should slow down and read as they speak.

 English Language Learners

Focus on Fluency Before reading "Three Goats and a Troll," point out the potential pronunciation challenges in each section so children can practice the words in isolation. Have children first echo read each section after you, then choral read with you.

Handwriting: *y, z, v, x*

Model Say the handwriting cues as you write lowercase *y, z, v, x*.

 *Begin at the bottom line; curve over at the middle line and down to the bottom line.* Curve up to the middle line, then slant left and down to the top of the next row. Loop left, closing the loop at the bottom line. Continue curving up to the middle line.

 *Begin at the bottom line; curve over at the middle line and down to the bottom line. Curve over a little and down to the top of the next row. Loop left, closing the loop at the bottom line. Continue curving up to the middle line.*

 *Begin at the bottom line. Curve over at the middle line and down to the bottom line.* Curve up to the middle line. Swing right.

 *Begin at the bottom line. Curve over at the middle line and down to the bottom line.* Curve up. Lift. Touch the middle line to the right of the starting point. Slant left and cross the first line by moving down to the bottom line.

Guided Practice/Practice
- Correct children's pen grip and paper placement, if needed.
- Have children identify each finished letter and note the differences.

Daily Handwriting
Throughout the week, use the models to teach how to form and join the cursive lowercase letters. Have children independently practice *y, z, v, x* using **Practice Book** pages 215–216.

Handwriting: pages 215–216

✔ Check for Success

Rubric Use the online rubric to record children's progress.

Can children decode words with long *o: o, oa, ow, oe*?

Can children identify and read the high-frequency words?

Differentiate
SMALL GROUP INSTRUCTIONS

If No
Approaching pp. T234–T235, T237
ELL pp. T234–T235, T237

If Yes
On p. T296
Beyond p. T302

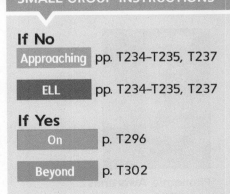

Daily Focus

Phonemic Awareness
• Phoneme Substitution

Phonics
• Review, Blend, and Build Words with /ō/o, oa, ow, oe

Structural Analysis
• Contractions with *not*

Reread
• Decodable Reader, Vol. 3: "Three Goats and a Troll"

OBJECTIVES

• Substitute phonemes to form new words.

• Blend and build words with long *o*.

ACADEMIC LANGUAGE

• *substitute*
• Cognate: *sustituir*

Phonemic Awareness: page 208

OPTION 5 Mins

Phonemic Awareness

Phoneme Substitution

1 **Model** Show children that substituting, or changing, the first sound in a word can form a new word. Say: *I'll say a word:* bold, */b/ /ō/ /l/ /d/. I will change the /b/ to /k/. The new word is* cold, */k/ /ō/ /l/ /d/.*

Now I'll substitute, or change, the last sound in a word. Listen again: cold, */k/ /ō/ /l/ /d/. I will change the /d/ to /t/ and make a new word. The new word is* colt, */k/ /ō/ /l/ /t/.*

Continue modeling phoneme substitution with the following words.

coal/coat   toe/Joe   soak/joke   stove/stone   vote/goat   blow/slow

2 **Guided Practice/Practice** Say: *Listen for the sounds in each word. Change the first sound and say a new word. Let's do the first one together. The word is* boat. *The sounds in* boat *are /b/ /ō/ /t/. We'll change the first sound, /b/, to /n/. Let's say the new word together:* note. Have children continue to substitute phonemes by changing the first or the last sound. Give corrective feedback if needed.

go/so	told/gold	road/code	tow/mow
soap/soak	doe/Moe	fold/hold	boat/bowl

Have children independently practice phoneme substitution using **Practice Book** page 208.

⟫ **DIFFERENTIATED INSTRUCTION** ⟫

TIER 2

Approaching Level If children need support for phoneme substitution:

I Do Explain to children that they will be substituting sounds in words. *When you substitute a sound, you trade it for a different sound. When I trade the /h/ sound in* hold *for /b/, I change the word from* hold *to* bold.

We Do *Listen as I say a word:* coast. *Say the word with me, /k/ /ōōō/ /sss/ /t/,* coast. *Let's change /k/ in* coast *to /t/: /tōōōssssst/,* toast. *The new word is* toast. Repeat with these word pairs:

boat/goat	toe/doe	coal/goal
coach/coat	crow/grow	loaf/load

You Do Say: *It's your turn. Substitute the first or last sound to form a new word. Use these words: gold/sold, road/roam, load/toad, mow/bow, no/go, flow/blow, low/show, Joe/hoe, soak/soap.*

You may wish to review Phonemic Awareness with **ELL** using this section.

Phonics

OPTION 5 Mins

Review Long *o: o, oa, ow, oe*

1 Model Display the *Boat* **Sound-Spelling Card**. Review the sound /ō/ spelled *o, oa, ow,* and *oe*.. Say: *The sound is /ō/ spelled* o. *Listen as I say the sounds in the word* fold: */f/ /ō/ /l/ /d/, /fffōōōllld/.* Repeat with /ō/ spelled *oa, ow, oe* using *boat, own,* and *toe*.

2 Guided Practice/Practice Have children practice connecting the letters and the sound. Point to each spelling for /ō/ on the Sound-Spelling Card and say: *What are these letters? What sound can they stand for when they are together?* Give corrective feedback if children need more support.

DIFFERENTIATED INSTRUCTION

TIER 2

Approaching Level If children are having difficulty with long *o* spelled *o, oa, ow, oe*:

I Do Display the *Boat* Sound-Spelling Card. Say: *This is the* Boat *Sound-Spelling Card. The sound is /ō/. The /ō/ sound can be spelled with the letters* o, oa, ow, *and* oe. Display the Word-Building Cards *oe.* Trace the letters *oe* while saying /ō/ five times. Repeat with *o, oa,* and *ow.*

We Do Say: *Now do it with me.* Have children trace lowercase *oe* on the Word-Building Cards with their finger while saying /ō/. Trace the letters *oe* five times and say /ō/ with children. Repeat with *o, oa,* and *ow.*

You Do Have children connect the letters *oa, o, ow,* and *oe* to the sound /ō/ by tracing lowercase letters with their finger while saying /ō/. Once children have traced the letters on paper five to ten times, they should then write the letters *oa, o, ow,* and *oe* while saying /ō/ five to ten times.

Repeat, connecting the letters *oa, o, ow,* and *oe* to the sound /ō/ through tracing and writing the letters during the week.

You may wish to review Phonics with **ELL** using this section.

OBJECTIVES

• Know and apply grade-level phonics and word analysis skills in decoding words.

SOUND-SPELLING REVIEW

Build Fluency
Display the Word-Building Cards *o, oa, ow, oe, i, igh, ie, y, scr, spr, thr, spl, shr, a, ai, ay, ea, e, eigh.* Have children say each sound. Repeat, and vary the pace.

Digital Tools

For more practice, have children use this activity.

Phonemic Awareness

To differentiate instruction for key skills, use the results of this activity.

Phonics

OBJECTIVES
• Know and apply grade-level phonics and word analysis skills in decoding words.

English Language Learners

Guided Practice/Practice
Review the meanings of example words. For example: Point out something gold and have children identify it as gold. Show a picture of a soccer goal and say, *The player scored a goal!* Pantomime shivering and say, *I feel cold*. In each case have children copy your gestures and repeat the words.

Phonics
5 Mins

Blend Words with Long *o*: *o, oa, ow, oe*

1 Model Display **Word-Building Cards** *g, o, a, t*. Model how to generate and blend the sounds to say the word. *This is the letter* g. *It stands for /g/. The letters* o *and* a *together stand for /ō/. This is the letter* t. *It stands for /t/. Listen as I blend all these sounds together: /gōōōt/. The word is* goat.

Continue by modeling how to blend words with long *o* spelled *o, oa, ow, oe* by using the words *sold, load, crow,* and *woe*.

2 Guided Practice/Practice Repeat the routine with children with the following words:

gold	both	toe	throw	goal
coach	blow	cold	snow	foe

Guide practice and give corrective feedback until children can work on their own.

DIFFERENTIATED INSTRUCTION >>

TIER 2

Approaching Level If children are having difficulty blending words with long *o*: *o, oa, ow, oe*:

I Do Display Word-Building Cards *c, o, a, l*. *This is the letter* c. *It stands for /k/. These are the letters* o *and* a. *Together they can stand for the sound /ō/. This is the letter* l. *It stands for /l/. I'll blend the sounds together: /kōōōlll/,* coal. Repeat the blending routine with *toe, slow, boast*.

We Do Guide children to blend the sounds and read: *loan, roam, told, sow, go,* and *Moe*.

You Do Have children blend and decode: *moat, pro, Joe, grow, goat, stow*. Offer corrective feedback if needed.

Repeat, blending additional long *o* words spelled *o, oa, ow,* and *oe*.

You may wish to review Phonics with **ELL** using this section.

Build Words with Long *o: o, oa, ow, oe*

Provide children with **Word-Building Cards** for the alphabet. Have children put the letters in order from *a* to *z*.

1 **Model** Display the Word-Building Cards *g, o, l, d.* Blend: /g/ /ō/ /l/ /d/, /gōōōllld/, *gold.*

- Remove *l* and *d* from *gold* and repeat with *go.*
- Add *a* and *l* to *go* and repeat with *goal.*
- Replace *g* with *s* and replace *a* and *l* with *l* and *d* and repeat with *sold.*

2 **Guided Practice/Practice** Continue to change letters to make *so, soap, sow, snow, mow, most, moat, coat, boat, bow, bowl.* Guide children to build and blend each word.

Once children have built the words, dictate the words to children and have them write the words down. Children can work with a partner to check their spelling.

DIFFERENTIATED INSTRUCTION

TIER 2

Approaching Level If children are having difficulty building words:

I Do Display Word-Building Cards *o, a, t.* Say: *These are letters* o, a, t. *Together* o *and* a *stand for the sound /ō/. The letter* t *stands for /t/. I will blend /ōōō/ and /t/ together: /ōōōt/,* oat. *The word is* oat.

We Do Make the word *oat.* *Let's place the letter* c *in front of* oat. *Let's blend: /k/ /ōōōt/, /kōōōt/,* coat.

You Do Have children build these sets of words: *oak, soak, cloak, croak; old, sold, fold, hold; bow, low, flow, show; toe, woe, doe, Joe.* Offer corrective feedback if children need additional support.

You may wish to review Phonics with **ELL** using this section.

OBJECTIVES

- Know and apply grade-level phonics and word analysis skills in decoding words.
- Form contractions with *not.*

HIGH-FREQUENCY WORDS REVIEW

better, group, long, more, only, our, started, three, who, won't

Say the words and have children Read/Spell/Write them. List the words so children can self-correct.

- Point out that *won't* is a contraction for *will not.*

Cumulative Review
Review last week's words using the same routine.

Digital Tools

For more practice, have children use this activity.

I __ the jar.
| fill | fills | filling |

Structural Analysis

Structural Analysis: page 211

⏱ 5 Mins Structural Analysis

Contractions with *not*

1 **Model** Remind children that a contraction is formed when two words are joined to make one shorter word. An apostrophe takes the place of one or more letters that are removed to make the contraction. Write *could* and *not.* Beneath them write *couldn't;* underline *n't.* Say: *When I make* could *and* not *into a contraction, I leave out the letter* o *in* not. *I use an apostrophe to show there is a letter missing.* Read *couldn't.*

2 **Guided Practice/Practice** Write the following words, read them with children, and then have children form the contractions. Discuss which letters were removed to form the contraction. Do the first two with children. Provide corrective feedback if needed.

does not (doesn't)	were not (weren't)	could not (couldn't)
is not (isn't)	are not (aren't)	can not (can't)
did not (didn't)	should not (shouldn't)	do not (don't)
was not (wasn't)	would not (wouldn't)	will not (won't)

Have children independently practice contractions with *not* using **Practice Book** page 211.

DIFFERENTIATED INSTRUCTION ➤

TIER 2 **Approaching Level** If children are having difficulty with contractions with *not:*

I Do Write *are not* and *aren't.* Say: *What is a contraction? I know that a contraction is a short way to write two words. An apostrophe replaces the missing letters. The apostrophe in* aren't *stands for the letter* o *in* not.

We Do Say: *Let's write* do not. *Now let's form the contraction* don't. Demonstrate joining the words and replacing the letter *o* with an apostrophe to form *don't.* Say: Don't *is a contraction. The apostrophe replaces the letter* o *in* not.

Repeat this routine with: *did not, has not, had not.*

You Do Say: *Now it's your turn. I will give you two words. Form the contraction for each word pair. Remember to replace the missing letters with an apostrophe.*

should not   does not   would not   have not

Repeat Have children form additional contractions with *not.*

OPTION 5 Mins

Decodable Reader: Reread "Three Goats and a Troll"

Decodable Reader, Vol. 3

Focus on Foundational Skills

Review with children the words with long *o: o, oa, ow, oe,* as well as the high-frequency words that they will find in the **Decodable Reader.**

Reread the Decodable Reader

Guide children in rereading "Three Goats and a Troll." Point out the high-frequency words and the words with long *o* spelled *o, oa, ow, oe.*

Reread the Book On page 38, have children point to each word, sounding out the decodable words and saying the high-frequency words quickly.

Check Comprehension

Remind children that they can ask themselves questions to make sure they understood what they have read. Have children use both text and illustrations to answer their questions.

Retell Have partners use key ideas and details to retell "Three Goats and a Troll."

Focus on Fluency

Review Remind children that part of reading with expression is using your voice to show feeling. When they read an exclamation, they can show surprise, shock, or excitement. When they read a question, their voice can go up at the end to show curiosity, interest, or confusion.

COLLABORATE

Practice Have children practice reading from the Decodable Reader to a partner. Have them concentrate on both accuracy and appropriate rate. Remind them to raise their voice at the end of a question and to read with appropriate emphasis and excitement. Offer corrective feedback as necessary.

OBJECTIVES

- Know and apply grade-level phonics and word-analysis skills in decoding words.
- Recognize and read grade-appropriate irregularly spelled words
- Read on-level text with purpose and understanding.
- Read with sufficient accuracy and fluency to support comprehension.

✔ Check for Success

Rubric Use the online rubric to record children's progress.

Can children decode words with long *o: o, oa, ow, oe?*

Can children identify and read the high-frequency words?

Differentiate
SMALL GROUP INSTRUCTIONS

If No

| Approaching | pp. T241–T244 |

| ELL | pp. T241–T244 |

If Yes

| On | p. T296 |

| Beyond | p. T302 |

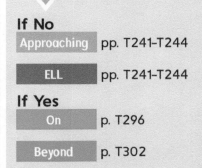

 Phonemic Awareness

Phoneme Addition

1 Model Show children how to add phonemes to words. *I'm going to say a word:* old. *I will add /s/ to the beginning of* old: */s/, /ssss/ /ōōōllld/,* sold. *The new word is* sold. *Repeat by adding /th/ to the word* row. *Say: /th/, /th/ /rrrōōō/. The new word is* throw.

2 Guided Practice/Practice *Let's do some together. I'll say a word. Then I'll say a sound. Add the sound I say to the beginning of the word. Tell me the new word. Let's do the first one together.* Offer corrective feedback if children need support.

/b/ oat   /f/ low   /g/ row   /s/ oak   /s/ cold

DIFFERENTIATED INSTRUCTION

TIER 2

Approaching Level If children are having difficulty adding phonemes:

I Do Explain to children that they will be adding phonemes. *When you add a phoneme, you are adding a sound. Listen as I say a word:* old. *I will add /k/ to the beginning of* old: */k/ /ōld/,* cold. Old *with /k/ added is* cold.

We Do Say: *Listen as I say a word:* oak. *Say the word with me, /ōk/. Let's add /s/ to the beginning of* oak: */sss/, oak,* soak. *The new word is* soak. Repeat this routine with the following word sets:

/b/ oat   /g/ low   /s/ tow   /t/ roll

You Do Say: *It's your turn. Add the sound to the beginning of the words to form a new word.*

/k/ row   /f/ low   /m/ oat   /sh/ own

Repeat the phoneme addition routine with additional long *o* words.

Daily Focus

Phonemic Awareness
• Phoneme Addition

Phonics
• Contrast Vowel Sounds; Blend and Build Words with /ō/o, oa, ow, oe

Structural Analysis
• Contractions with *not*

High-Frequency Words

Read
• Decodable Reader, Vol. 3: "A Rose Grows"

A Rose Grows

OBJECTIVES

• Add phonemes to make a new word.

Phonics

5 Mins

Contrast Vowel Sounds

1 **Model** Display **Word-Building Cards** for *o, oa, ow, oe*. Review that the letters can stand for long *o*. Display Word-Building Cards for long *a* spelled *ai, ay* and for long *i* spelled *y, igh*. As you say each vowel sound, point to the letters that represent that sound. Say: *Let's listen to two words that have one sound that is different. For each word, I'll point to the letters that stand for the vowel sound.* flow, fly. *When I say* flow, *I point to the letters* ow. *The vowel sound in* flow *is* /ōō/. *When I say* fly, *I point to the letter* y. *The vowel sound in* fly *is* /īī/. Repeat the routine with the word pairs *so/sigh, boat/bait, doe/day.*

2 **Guided Practice/Practice** *Let's do some together. Listen as I say two words:* grow, gray. *What sounds can we hear in each word? Let's hold up Word-Building Cards for the vowel sound in each word.* Hold up the *ow* cards for *grow* and the *ay* cards for *gray.* Continue, having children take turns with a partner. Give each pair of children Word-Building Cards for *o, oa, ow, oe, ai, ay, y, igh.* Say: *Hold up the correct Word-Building Cards that stand for the vowel sound you hear.* Use these word pairs and provide corrective feedback to partners as necessary.

woe/way	show/shy	road/raid	go/gay	moat/might
roll/rail	row/ray	hoe/high	crow/cry	groan/grain

DIFFERENTIATED INSTRUCTION

TIER 2

Approaching Level If children are having difficulty with contrasting vowel sounds, reteach:

I Do Display Word-Building Cards for *o, oa, ow, oe, ai, ay, y, igh.* Say: *I will say each vowel sound as I point to the sound-spelling.* Review each of the vowel sound-spellings, with example words.

We Do Provide children with Word-Building Cards for *o, oa, ow, oe, ai, ay, y, igh.* Have children trace the letters as they say each vowel sound.

You Do Say: *Listen to each word and hold up the cards that stand for the vowel sound you hear in the word.* Say one word at a time, emphasizing the long-vowel sound. Use the following words:

slow	brain	play	coal	dry
grown	night	no	bowl	hoe

Give corrective feedback as needed for extra support.

OBJECTIVES
- Know and apply grade-level phonics and word analysis skills in decoding words.

SOUND-SPELLING REVIEW

Build Fluency

Display the **Word-Building Cards** *o, oa, ow, oe, i, igh, ie, y, scr, spr, str, thr, spl, shr, a, ai, ay, ea, e, eigh.* Have children say each sound. Repeat, and vary the pace.

Digital Tools

For more practice, have children use this activity.

Phonemic Awareness

To differentiate instruction for key skills, use the results of this activity.

Phonics

OBJECTIVES

- Know and apply grade-level phonics and word analysis skills in decoding words.

OPTION 5 Mins

Phonics

Blend Words with Long *o: o, oa, ow, oe*

1 **Model** Display **Word-Building Cards** *t, o, l, d.* Model how to blend the sounds. Say: *This is the letter* t. *It stands for the sound /t/. This is the letter* o. *It stands for the sound /ō/. This is the letter* l. *It stands for the sound /l/. This is the letter* d. *It stands for the sound /d/. Let's blend the four sounds together: /tōōōllld/. The word is* told.

Continue by modeling the words *coast, bowl,* and *foe.*

2 **Guided Practice/Practice** Repeat the routine with *so, no, loan, soak, flown, glow,* and *doe.* Guide practice until children can work independently. Give corrective feedback as necessary.

Have children independently practice blending words with long *o: o, oa, ow, oe* using **Practice Book** page 210.

DIFFERENTIATED INSTRUCTION ➤

TIER 2 **Approaching Level** If children are having difficulty blending words with long *o: o, oa, ow, oe:*

I Do Display Word-Building Cards *l, o, w.* Say: *This is the letter* l. *It stands for /l/. These are the letters* ow. *Together they can stand for /ō/. Listen as I blend the sounds: /lll/, /ōōō/, /lllōōō/,* low. *The word is* low.

We Do Say: *Let's do some together.* Blend and read the words *hold, troll, goes, grows, showing, toes.* Provide children with corrective feedback if needed.

You Do Display the following words: *slow, croak, soaked, so, go.* Have children blend and read the words.

You may wish to review Phonics with **ELL** using this section.

Phonics: page 210

Build Words with Long *o: o, oa, ow, oe*

Provide children with **Word-Building Cards** for the alphabet. Have children put the letters in order from *a* to *z*.

1 **Model** Display the Word-Building Cards *f, l, o, a, t*. Blend the sounds and say the word: /fff/ /lll/ /ōōō/ /t/, /ffflllōōōt/, *float*.

- Change *f* in *float* to *g* and repeat with *gloat*.
- Delete *l* in *gloat* and repeat with *goat*.

2 **Guided Practice/Practice** Continue with *go, no, so, sow, stow, mow, Moe, toe, towing, blow, flow, glow, grow, grown, shown, own*. Guide children to build and blend each word, providing corrective feedback as necessary.

Once children have built the words, dictate the words to children and have them write the words down. Children can work with a partner to check their spelling.

Digital Tools

To differentiate instruction for key skills, use the results of this activity.

Phonics

DIFFERENTIATED INSTRUCTION ⟩

TIER 2

Approaching Level If children need more support with building words:

I Do Display Word-Building Cards *c, o, a, t*. Say: *This is the letter* c. *It stands for /k/. These are the letters* oa. *Together,* o *and* a *stand for the sound /ō/. This is the letter* t. *The letter* t *stands for /t/. I will blend /k/, /ōōō/, and /t/ together: /kōōōt/,* coat. *The word is* coat.

We Do Say: *Now, let's do one together. Let's make the word* oat *using the Word-Building Cards. Now we'll place the letter* b *in front of* oat. *Let's blend: /b/ /ōōōt/, /bōōōt/,* boat. *Now there is a new word,* boat.

You Do Say: *Now it's your turn.* Have children build the words: *boast, toast, roast, coast, coal, foal, foe, woe, hoe, toe, told, folding, scolded, cold, colt, jolt, bolt.* Offer any corrective feedback that is needed.

You may wish to review Phonics with **ELL** using this section.

OBJECTIVES

- Know and apply grade-level phonics and word analysis skills in decoding words.
- Form contractions with *not*.

Digital Tools

For more practice, have children use this activity.

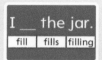

Structural Analysis

OPTION
5 Mins

Structural Analysis

Contractions with *not*

1 **Model** Say the words *do* and *not*. Then say *don't*. Ask children to listen closely to hear what is different. Point out *do* and *not* are two words. *Don't* is one word. Remind them that a contraction is a shortened form of a word. An apostrophe takes the place of the letters that are left out.

2 **Guided Practice/Practice** Write the words *do* and *not*. Say: *Let's change the words* do *and* not *into a contraction. Remember, we use an apostrophe to take the place of the letter or letters that are left out.* Have children direct you as you write *don't*. Point out the long *o* spelled *o* in *don't*.

Help children write the correct form of the contractions with *not* for these words: *can not, is not, do not, has not, did not.*

DIFFERENTIATED INSTRUCTION >>

TIER **2**

Approaching Level If children are having difficulty forming contractions with *not,* reteach:

I Do Write: *do not, don't.* Say: *What is a contraction? A contraction is a short way to write two words. An apostrophe replaces the missing letters. The apostrophe in* don't *stands for the letter* o *in* not.

We Do Write: *were not.* Say: *Let's form the contraction* weren't. Demonstrate joining the words and replacing the letter *o* with an apostrophe to form *weren't.* Say: Weren't *is a contraction. It is used in place of the words* were not. *The apostrophe replaces the letter* o *in* not.

Repeat this routine with the following examples: *had not, was not, would not.* Offer corrective feedback if needed.

You Do Have children form contractions for each word pair. Say: *Now it's your turn. Form contractions for each word pair. Remember to replace the missing letters with an apostrophe.*

did not does not could not have not is not

Repeat Have children form additional contractions with *not.* Give corrective feedback if children need more support..

High-Frequency Words

better, group, long, more, only, our, started, three, who, won't

1 **Model** Say each word and have children Read/Spell/Write it. Ask children to picture the words, and write them the way they see them. Display words so children can self-correct.

2 **Guided Practice** Have children identify the high-frequency words in connected text and blend the decodable words.

1. I ran the race **better** last May.
2. My new friend is in our **group**.
3. It's a **long** way to get home!
4. Do I have **more** time to find it?
5. I drank **only** one glass of milk.
6. **Our** bus is here right now!
7. We **started** the game early.
8. Which **three** teeth came out?
9. **Who** is ready for some fun?
10. He **won't** begin to walk yet.

Point out any irregularities in sound-spellings, such as the /ô/ in *long*.

Have children independently practice the high-frequency words using **Practice Book** page 212.

Practice Add the high-frequency words to the cumulative word bank. Have partners create more sentences using the words.

Cumulative Review Review last week's words using the Read/Spell/ Write routine. Repeat the above routine, mixing the words and having children say each one.

DIFFERENTIATED INSTRUCTION

Approaching Level If children are having difficulty with high-frequency words:

I Do Use the **High-Frequency Word Cards**. Display one word at a time, following the routine: Display the word. Read the word. Then spell the word.

We Do Ask children to state the word and spell the word with you. Model using the word in a sentence, and have children repeat after you.

You Do Display the word. Ask children to say the word then spell it. When completed, quickly flip through the word card set as children chorally read the words. Provide opportunities for children to use the words in conversation. Ask children to write each word in their writer's notebook.

OBJECTIVES
- Know and apply grade-level phonics and word analysis skills in decoding words.
- Recognize and read grade-appropriate irregularly spelled words.

Digital Tools

For more practice, have children use this activity.

High-Frequency Words

High-Frequency Words: page 212

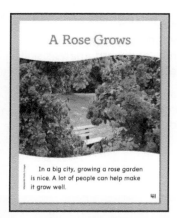

Decodable Reader, Vol. 3

OBJECTIVES

- Know and apply grade-level phonics and word analysis skills in decoding words.

- Recognize and read grade-appropriate irregularly spelled words.

- Read on-level text with purpose and understanding.

- Read with sufficient accuracy and fluency to support comprehension.

Decodable Reader: "A Rose Grows"

Focus on Foundational Skills

Review the words and letter-sounds that children will find in the **Decodable Reader**.

- Review the high-frequency word *group*.

- Review with children that the letters *o, oa, ow, oe* can stand for the long *o* sound.

Preview and Predict Point to the title of the selection and have children sound out each word with you as you run your finger under it. Ask: *What do you see in the picture? What plants are growing in this garden?*

Read the Decodable Reader

Begin guiding children to read the selection "A Rose Grows." On page 43, have children point to each word, sounding out the decodable words and saying the high-frequency words quickly. If children need support reading decodable words, model blending for them. If children are having difficulty with high-frequency words, reread the word in isolation and then reread the high-frequency word in context.

Check Comprehension

p. 41 *Why is growing a rose garden nice in a big city?*

p. 42 *What are two reasons that kids go to help a rose garden grow?*

p. 43 *How do kids learn about growing roses?*

p. 44 *What colors are some of the roses?*

Retell Have partners use key ideas and details to retell "A Rose Grows."

Focus on Fluency

With partners, have children read "A Rose Grows" to focus on accuracy. As children read, guide them to run their fingers under the text as they read. Children should note whether they are correctly reading the words on the page. As children read, they can monitor themselves and provide feedback to their partners.

Listen in: If children are having difficulty reading accurately, have them start again at the beginning of the page. If children are reading too quickly, suggest to them that they should slow down and read as they speak.

English Language Learners

Check Comprehension Provide sentence frames, as needed, to help children answer the questions.

p. 41 Growing a rose garden is nice because a lot of people can help.

p. 42 Kids help a rose garden grow because they hope to make the city a nice place and they know that roses will be a nice home for birds.

p. 43 Kids learn about growing roses from pros.

p. 44 Some of the roses are yellow, red, and pink.

Focus on Fluency Before reading "A Rose Grows," point out the potential pronunciation challenges in each section of the selection so children can practice the words in isolation. Have children first echo read each section after you, then choral read with you.

As you read, remember to model self-corrective techniques. For example, pretend to mispronounce a word and then self-correct. Encourage children to do the same as they read.

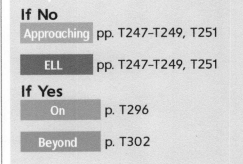

✓ Check for Success

Rubric Use the online rubric to record children's progress.

Can children decode words with long *o: o, oa, ow, oe?*

Can children identify and read the high-frequency words?

Differentiate
SMALL GROUP INSTRUCTIONS

If No

Approaching pp. T247–T249, T251

ELL pp. T247–T249, T251

If Yes

On p. T296

Beyond p. T302

Daily Focus

Phonemic Awareness
• Phoneme Blending

Phonics
• Blend and Build Words with
/ō/o, oa, ow, oe

Reread
• Decodable Reader, Vol. 3:
"A Rose Grows"

OBJECTIVES
• Blend phonemes to form words.

 OPTION 5 Mins

Phonemic Awareness

Phoneme Blending

1 **Model** Place markers on the **Response Board** to represent sounds. *I'm going to put one marker in each box as I say each sound. Then I will blend the sounds to form a word.* Place a marker for each sound: /t/ /ō/ /s/ /t/. Say: *This word has four sounds: /t/ /ōōō/ /sss/ /t/. Listen as I blend these sounds to form a word: /tōōōsst/. The word is* toast.

2 **Guided Practice/Practice** Guide children to place a marker on their own Response Boards for each sound they hear. Say one sound at a time. Then blend the sounds to say the word. Guide practice and provide corrective feedback as children progress to work on their own.

/r/ /ō/ /s/ /t/, roast	/s/ /ō/, so	/b/ /ō/ /l/, bowl
/b/ /ō/ /t/, boat	/t/ /ō/, toe	/r/ /ō/ /d/, road
/g/ /ō/ /l/, goal	/l/ /ō/, low	/f/ /ō/ /l/ /d/, fold

> **DIFFERENTIATED INSTRUCTION** ▶▶

 TIER 2

Approaching Level If children are having difficulty with phoneme blending:

I Do Explain to children that you will be blending sounds to form words. *Listen as I say three sounds: /sss/ /ōōō/ /p/. I'm going to blend the sounds together to say a word: /sssōōōp/,* soap.

We Do Say: *Listen as I say two sounds: /ōōō/ /nnn/. Say the sounds with me: /ōōō/ /nnn/. Let's blend the sounds: /ōōō/ /nnn/, /ōōōnnn/,* own. *We made one word:* own. Repeat this routine with the following words:

no   show   oat   toe   loaf   toast   cold   grow

Provide corrective feedback until children can work independently.

You Do Say: *It's your turn. I want you to blend the sounds I say together to form a new word.*

coat   glow   old   throw   both   own   float   doe

Repeat the blending routine with additional long *o* words spelled *o, oa, ow, oe.*

You may wish to review Phonemic Awareness with **ELL** using this section.

Phonics

Blend Words with Long *o: o, oa, ow, oe*

1 **Model** Display **Word-Building Cards** *b, o, l, t.* Model how to blend the sounds. Say: *This is the letter* b. *It stands for the sound /b/. This is the letter* o. *It stands for the sound /ō/. This is the letter* l. *It stands for /l/. This is the letter* t. *It stands for /t/. Let's blend the sounds together: /bōōōlllt/. The word is* bolt.

Continue by modeling the words *roast, shown,* and *Moe.*

2 **Guided Practice/Practice** Repeat the routine with *doe, toe, rolling, loan, flow, grown, soak,* and *going.* Guide practice until children can work independently. Give corrective feedback as necessary.

DIFFERENTIATED INSTRUCTION

TIER 2

Approaching Level If children are having difficulty blending words with long *o: o, oa, ow, oe:*

I Do Display Word-Building Cards *b, l, o, w.* Say: *This is the letter* b. *It stands for /b/. This is the letter* l. *It stands for /l/. These are the letters* ow. *Together they can stand for /ō/. Listen as I blend the three sounds: /b/, /lll/, /ōōō/, /blllōōō/,* blow. *The word is* blow.

We Do Say: *Let's do some together.* Blend and read the words *sold, troll, goes, glowing, show, hoed.* Give corrective feedback if necessary.

You Do Display the following words: *go, glowing, croak, flowed, toe.* Have children blend and read the words.

You may wish to review Phonics with **ELL** using this section.

OBJECTIVES

• Know and apply grade-level phonics and word analysis skills in decoding words.

SOUND-SPELLING REVIEW

Build Fluency

Display the **Word-Building Cards** *o, oa, ow, oe, i, igh, ie, y, scr, spr, thr, spl, shr, a, ai, ay, ea, e, eigh.* Have children say each sound. Repeat, and vary the pace.

Digital Tools

For more practice, have children use this activity

Phonemic Awareness

To differentiate instruction for key skills, use the results of this activity.

Phonics

OBJECTIVES

- Know and apply grade-level phonics and word analysis skills in decoding words.
- Build words.

Remind children that a contraction is a short form of two words, with an apostrophe replacing any letters left out. Write *can* and *not*. Model forming the contraction *can't*. Then write *will* and *not*. Say: *The contraction that means "will not" is* won't. Point out that the contraction *won't* has the long *o* sound, /o/: *won't*. Write these incorrect contractions: *do'nt, did'nt, arent', does'nt, werent*. Have pairs work to write each contraction correctly.

Digital Tools

To differentiate instruction for key skills, use the results of this activity.

Phonics

 Phonics (5 Mins)

Build Words with Long *o*: *o, oa, ow, oe*

Provide children with **Word-Building Cards** for the alphabet. Have children put the letters in order from *a* to *z*.

1 **Review** The letters *o, oa, ow,* and *oe* can stand for the long *o* sound /ō/. Use Word-Building Cards to build words with long *o* spelled *o, oa, ow,* and *oe*. Place the letters for *moan*. Say: *Let's blend the sounds and read the word: /mmmōōōnnn/.* Now change the *m* to *l*. *Let's blend the sounds and read the word: /lllōōōnnn/. The word is* loan.

2 **Practice** Continue with *load, road, roam, roast, boast., boat, float.*

Once children have built the words, dictate the words and have children write the words on a piece of paper. Children can work with a partner to check their words for spelling.

DIFFERENTIATED INSTRUCTION ⟩⟩

On Level For more practice building words:

I Do Display Word-Building Cards *t, o, a, d.* Say: *This is the letter* t. *It stands for /t/. These are the letters* o *and* a. *Together they stand for /ō/. This is the letter* d. *It stands for /d/. I will blend /t/, /ōōō/, and /d/ together: /tōōōod/,* toad. *The word is* toad.

We Do Say: *Now, let's do one together. Make the word* toast *using Word-Building Cards. Change the letter* t *to* r. *Let's blend: /rrr/ /ōōō/ /sss/ /t/, /rrrōōōsst/,* roast. *The new word is* roast. *Change the first letter* r *to* c. *Say: I am going to change the letter* r *in* roast *to the letter* c. *Let's blend and read the new word: /k/ ōōō/ /sss/ /t/, /kōōōsst/,* coast. *The new word is* coast.

You Do Have children build and blend these words: *no, go, so, sold, told, toad, road, load, loan.* Give corrective feedback if children need more support.

Decodable Reader:
Reread "A Rose Grows"

Focus on Foundational Skills

Review with children the words with long *o: o, oa, ow, oe* as well as the high-frequency word *group* that they will find in the **Decodable Reader**.

Decodable Reader, Vol. 3

Reread the Decodable Reader

Guide children in rereading "A Rose Grows." Point out the high-frequency words and the words with long *o: o, oa, ow, oe*.

Reread the Book On page 44, have children point to each word, sounding out the decodable words. If children struggle sounding out words, model blending for them.

Check Comprehension

Remind children that they can ask themselves questions to make sure they understood what they are reading. Have them use both text and photographs to answer their questions.

Retell Have partners use key ideas and details to retell "A Rose Grows."

Focus on Fluency

Review Remind children that part of reading with expression is using your voice to show feeling. When they read an exclamation, they can show surprise, shock, or excitement. When they read a question, their voice can go up at the end to show curiosity, interest, or confusion.

COLLABORATE

Practice Have children practice reading to a partner with accuracy and at a suitable rate. Remind them to read with appropriate emphasis and excitement. Offer corrective feedback as necessary. Remind them that they can ask themselves questions to make sure they understood what they are reading. Have them use both text and photographs to answer their questions.

OBJECTIVES

- Know and apply grade-level phonics and word analysis skills in decoding words.
- Recognize and read grade-appropriate irregularly spelled words
- Read on-level text with purpose and understanding.
- Read with sufficient accuracy and fluency to support comprehension.

HIGH-FREQUENCY WORDS REVIEW

better, group, long, more, only, our, started, three, who, won't
Have children Read/Spell/Write the words and use them in sentences. Review last week's words using the same routine.

✔ Check for Success

Rubric Use the online rubric to record children's progress.

Can children decode words with /ō/ *o, oa, ow, oe*?
Can children read the high-frequency words?

Differentiate
SMALL GROUP INSTRUCTIONS

If No
| Approaching | pp. T255–T257 |
| ELL | pp. T255–T257 |

If Yes
| On | p. T296 |
| Beyond | p. T302 |

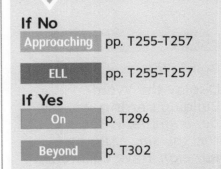

Daily Focus

Phonemic Awareness
• Phoneme Substitution

Phonics
• Blend and Build Words with /ō/o, oa, ow, oe

Structural Analysis
• Contractions with *not*

High-Frequency Words

OBJECTIVES
• Substitute phonemes in words.
• Decode words with long o.
• Form contractions with *not*.
• Know and apply grade-level phonics and word analysis skills in decoding words.
• Recognize and read grade-appropriate irregularly spelled words.

SOUND-SPELLING REVIEW >

Build Fluency
Display the Word-Building Cards *o, oa, ow, oe, i, igh, ie, y, scr, spr, thr, spl, shr, a, ai, ay, ea, eigh.* Have children say each sound. Repeat.

 OPTION **5** Mins

Phonemic Awareness

Phoneme Substitution

Review Guide children to substitute phonemes in words. *I will say a word. Then I'll say a new sound. Change the first or last sound in the word to make a new word.* Use the following word pairs:

row/show	load/loan	post/most	coax/coat
soak/soap	mold/bold	bow/low	tone/zone

 5 Mins

Phonics

Blend and Build Words with Long *o: o, oa, ow, oe*

Review Write the following words: *pro, boat, own,* and *woe.* Have children read and say the words. If children are having difficulty, remind them to segment the word and then blend the sounds together. Then have children follow the word-building routine with **Word-Building Cards** to build *so, sow, sold, hold, hoe, hoax, coax, coat,* and *boat.* Once children have built the words, dictate the words to children and have them write the words. Children can work with a partner to check their spelling.

Word Automaticity Display decodable words and point to each word as children chorally read it. Test how many words children can read in one minute. Model blending any words that children miss.

DIFFERENTIATED INSTRUCTION >>

 TIER 2

Approaching Level If children need extra support blending and building words with long *o: o, oa, ow, oe:*

I Do Display Word-Building Cards *r, o, a, m. These letters stand for the sounds /rrr/, /ōōō/, and /mmm/. Listen as I blend all three sounds: /rrrōōōmmm/, roam. The word is* roam.

We Do *Now let's do some together. Let's make the word* host *using Word-Building Cards. Let's blend: /h/ /ōōō/ /sss/ /t/, /hōōōssst/, host. We'll change the letter* h *in* host *to the letter p. Let's blend and read the new word: /p/ /ōōō/ /sss/ /t/, /pōōōssst/, post.* Continue to help children change letters and build: *most, mow, show, row, rowing, throwing, thrown, grown, own, flown, float.* Give corrective feedback as needed.

You Do *Now it's your turn.* Have children blend and build these words: *woe, toe, toad, road, row, low, slow, glow, grow, pro, go, no, so, soap, sold.*

You may wish to review Phonics with **ELL** using this section.

Structural Analysis

Contractions with *not*

Review Have children explain how to form a contraction with *not*. Then have children practice writing contractions for the following words: *do not, can not, did not, is not, are not, could not, were not, have not.*

High-Frequency Words

better, group, long, more, only, our, started, three, who, won't

Review Have children identify and read the high-frequency words. Display the **High-Frequency Word Cards** and have partners use the words in conversation. Then have children write a sentence with each word.

DIFFERENTIATED INSTRUCTION

TIER 2

Approaching Level If children need extra support with high-frequency words:

I Do Use the High-Frequency Word Cards. Display one word at a time, following the routine: Display the word. Read the word. Then spell the word.

We Do Ask children to state the word and spell the word with you. Model using the word in a sentence, and have children repeat after you. Have them make up more sentences for the words.

You Do Display the word. Ask children to say the word and then spell it. When completed, quickly flip through the word card set as children chorally read the words. Provide opportunities for children to use the words in speaking and writing. For example, provide sentence starters, such as *It won't be a long time for our _____ to _____* . Ask children to write each word in their writer's notebook.

Digital Tools

To differentiate instruction for key skills, use the results of this activity.

Phonics

For more practice, have children use this activity.

Structural Analysis

✔ Check for Success

Rubric Use the online rubric to record children's progress.

Can children decode words with long *o: o, oa, ow, oe*? Can children read the high-frequency words?

Differentiate
SMALL GROUP INSTRUCTIONS

If No
Approaching pp. T258–T259
ELL pp. T258–T259

If Yes
On p. T296
Beyond p. T302

Daily Focus

Phonological Awareness
• Identify Syllables

Phonics
• Introduce and Blend Words with /ē/e, ee, ea, ie, y, ey, e_e

Structural Analysis
• Plurals with –s, -es

High-Frequency Words

Read
• Decodable Reader, Vol. 3: "It Won't Be Easy!"

Handwriting
• Letter and Word Spacing

OBJECTIVES
• Identify syllables in words.

ACADEMIC LANGUAGE
• *syllable*
• Cognate: *sílaba*

Phonological Awareness: page 224

(5 Mins) Phonological Awareness

Identify Syllables

Read the poem "A Meal Complete" with children.

> **A Meal Complete**
>
> Meat and green beans I will eat,
> But my meal won't be complete
> Without (we really must agree)
> Some berries as a sweet treat!

1 **Model** *I am going to say two words from the poem:* Have children listen as you say the word *complete.* Tell them you will divide the word into syllables, or word parts, and clap for each syllable. Explain that each syllable has only one vowel sound. Say: *Listen carefully as I say* complete. *I will clap the syllables that I hear:* com *(clap)* plete *(clap). The word* complete *has two syllables.* Repeat with the words *money* (2), *teacher* (2), *week* (1), *bumblebee* (3).

2 **Guided Practice/Practice** Have children practice identifying syllables with the following examples from the poem. Do the first one together. *Say the word* agree *and clap the syllables. Count how many syllables you hear.*

agreeing (3)	must (1)	meal (1)	won't (1)
green (1)	berries (2)	treating (2)	be (1)
beans (1)	really (2)	without (2)	sweet (1)

Let's try some more words. Tell me how many syllables you hear.

teenager (3)	year (1)	uneasy (3)	chief (1)
sticky (2)	keys (1)	tiny (2)	disbelief (3)

Provide corrective feedback to children as necessary.

Have children independently practice identifying syllables using **Practice Book** page 224.

DIFFERENTIATED INSTRUCTION

TIER 2

Approaching Level If children need extra support with identifying syllables:

I Do Explain to children that they will be identifying syllables in words. Say: *A syllable is a word part that has a vowel sound. Listen as I say a word:* even. *I'll clap for each syllable:* e *(clap)* ven *(clap). The word* even *has two syllables.*

We Do *Listen as I say* zebra. *Say the word with me:* zebra. *Let's clap the syllables:* ze *(clap)* bra *(clap).* Zebra *has two syllables. Each syllable has a vowel sound.*

Repeat this routine with the following words:

valley (2) needless (2) insect (2) keyhole (2)
chief (1) employee (3) reasoning (3) family (3)

Provide corrective feedback until children can work independently.

You Do Say: *It's your turn. I'll say a word. Repeat the word. Then clap the syllables.*

sunset (2) alone (2) tadpole (2) reopen (3)
seventy (3) teapot (2) free (1) turkey (2)

You may wish to review Phonological Awareness with **ELL** using this section.

English Language Learners

See page 5 in the **Language Transfers Handbook** for guidance in identifying sounds that may or may not transfer for speakers of certain languages and for support in accommodating those children. See the chart on pages 6–9 for specific sound transfer issues for multiple languages.

Digital Tools

For more practice, have children use this activity.

Phonological Awareness

OBJECTIVES

• Know and apply grade-level phonics and word analysis skills in decoding words.

Introduce Long *e: e, ee, ea, ie, y, ey, e_e*

1 **Model** Display the *Tree* **Sound-Spelling Card.**
Teach /ē/ spelled *ee* using *tree.* Say: *This is the* Tree *Sound-Spelling Card. The sound is /ē/. One way to spell the /ē/ sound is with the letters* ee. *Listen: /ēēē/. This is the sound at the end of the word* tree. *Listen: /t/ /rrr/ /ēēē/,* tree. *I'll say /ē/ as I write the letters* ee *several times.* Explain that /ē/ can be spelled different ways. Repeat with the sound-spellings *e, ea, ie, y, ey, e_e* using *me, team, chief, funny, key, these.*

Sound Spelling Card

2 **Guided Practice/Practice** Have children practice connecting the long vowel sound /ē/ to the letters *ee. Say /ē/ as I write the letters* ee. *This time, write the letters* ee *five times as you say the /ē/ sound.* Repeat with *e, ea, ie, y, ey, e_e.*

Have children independently practice long *e: e, ee, ea, ie, y, ey, e_e* using **Practice Book** page 226.

SOUND-SPELLING REVIEW ➤➤

Build Fluency

Display the Word-Building Cards *o, oa, ow, oe, i, igh, ie, y, scr, spr, thr, spl, shr, a, ai, ay, ea, e, eigh.* Have children say each sound.

DIFFERENTIATED INSTRUCTION ➤➤

TIER 2

Approaching Level If children are having difficulty with long *e:*

I Do Display the *Tree* Sound-Spelling Card. *This is the* Tree *Sound-Spelling Card. The sound is /ē/. The /ē/ sound can be spelled with the letters* ee, ea, e, y, ie, ey, *and* e_e. Display **Word-Building Cards** for *ee.* Trace the letters *ee* while saying /ē/ five times. Repeat with *ea, e, y, ie, ey,* and *e_e.*

We Do *Now do it with me.* Guide children to trace lowercase *ee* on the Word-Building Cards with their finger while saying /ē/. Trace the letters *ee* five times and say /ē/ with children. Repeat the routine with *ea, e, ea, y, ie, ey,* and *e_e.*

You Do Have children connect the letters *e, ee, ea, ie, y, ey,* and *e_e* to the sound /ē/ by tracing lowercase *e, ee, ea, ie, y, ey,* and *e_e* with their finger while saying /ē/. Once children have traced on paper five to ten times, they should then write the letters *e, ee, ea, ie, y, ey,* and *e_e* while saying /ē/ five to ten times.

Repeat, connecting the letters *e, ee, ea, ie, y, ey,* and *e_e* to the sound /ē/ through tracing and writing the letters throughout the week.

You may wish to review Phonics with **ELL** using this section.

Phonics: page 226

Blend Words with Long *e: e, ee, ea, ie, y, ey, e_e*

1 Model Display **Word-Building Cards** *m, e, e, t.* Model how to blend the sounds. Say: *This is the letter* m. *It stands for /mmm/. These are the letters* ee. *Together, they stand for /ēēē/. This is the letter* t. *It stands for /t/. Listen as I blend these sounds together: /mmmēēēt/. The word is* meet.

Continue by modeling the words *me, peach, field, tiny, valley,* and *eve.*

2 Guided Practice/Practice Display the Phonics/Fluency Practice chart. Read each word in the first row, blending the sounds—for example, say: */bēēēk/. The word is* beak. Have children blend each word with you. Prompt children to read the connected text, sounding out the decodable words.

beak	key	deep	fancy	these	eve
we	brief	silly	heat	peach	feed
piece	teeth	be	mean	sunny	peek
boat	show	toe	no	snow	roam

She can sleep at the beach.

I read a lot each week.

Will you be on this field team with me?

Phonics/Fluency Practice

DIFFERENTIATED INSTRUCTION

TIER 2

Approaching Level If children are having difficulty blending words:

I Do Display Word-Building Cards *f, e, e, t. This is the letter* f. *It stands for /fff/. These are the letters* e *and* e. *Together they can stand for the sound /ē/. Listen as I say it: /ēēē/. This is the letter* t. *It stands for /t/. I'll blend all the sounds together: /fffēēēt/,* feet. *Repeat with* he, bead, field, any, key, *and* Steve.

We Do *Let's do some together.* Guide children to blend the sounds and read: *eel, teeth, teach, dream, me, the, chief, copy, valley, these.* Offer corrective feedback to any children needing extra support.

You Do *It's your turn. Blend the sounds and read the words.*

feed	free	leap	clean	be	we
piece	brief	messy	daddy	volley	eve

Repeat, blending other words with these long *e* spellings.

You may wish to review Phonics with **ELL** using this section.

English Language Learners

See page 5 in the **Language Transfers Handbook** for guidance in identifying phonics skills that may or may not transfer for speakers of certain languages and for support in accommodating those children. See the chart on pages 10–13 for specific phonics transfer issues for multiple languages.

Digital Tools

To differentiate instruction for key skills, use the results of this activity.

Phonics

OBJECTIVES

- Know and apply grade-level phonics and word analysis skills in decoding words.

ACADEMIC LANGUAGE

- *plural*
- Cognate: *plural*

English Language Learners

See page 15 in the **Language Transfers Handbook** for guidance in identifying grammatical forms that may not transfer for speakers of certain languages and for support in accommodating those children. See the chart on pages 16–19 for specific transfer errors for multiple languages.

Digital Tools

For more practice, have children use this activity.

I __ the jar.		
fill	fills	filling

Structural Analysis

OPTION 5 Mins

Structural Analysis

Plurals with -s, -es

1 **Model** Write the word *bean*. Explain that the word means "one bean." *To make the word* bean *mean "more than one," I add* -s. Write *beans* and read the new word. Repeat with the word *pony. The word* pony *ends with* y, *so I need to change the* y *to* i *before I add* -es *to make the word plural.* Write *ponies* and read the new word.

2 **Guided Practice/Practice** Write the following words: *puppy, ring, key, penny, kitten, baby.* Have children write the plural form of each word. Display models so children can check their spelling.

DIFFERENTIATED INSTRUCTION ▶▶

TIER 2

Approaching Level If children need more support with plurals *-s, -es*.

I Do Write the words *bead* and *beads.* Explain that *-s* was added to *bead* to make it plural. Write the word *pony* and change it to *ponies* as you say: *When a word ends with a consonant and* y, *change the* y *to* i *and then add* -es *to form the plural.*

We Do Write *baby* and *babies.* Say: *Let's read these words:* baby, babies. Remind children that when a noun ends with a consonant and *y,* you usually change the *y* to *i* and then add *-es* to form its plural. Say: *Let's use* baby *and* babies *in sentences.*

You Do Have children work with partners. Have them form plurals for the following nouns: *puppy, bunny, kitty, lily, penny.* Give corrective feedback as needed.

Repeat Have children create sentences using plural nouns with *–s* and *-es*.

High-Frequency Words

5 Mins

after, before, every, few, first, hear, hurt, old, special, would

1 **Model** Display the **High-Frequency Word Cards** and use the Read/ Spell/Write routine for each word.

- **Read** Point to and say the word *before*. *This is the word* before. *Say it with me:* before. *I wash my hands before I eat lunch.*

- **Spell** *The word* before *is spelled* b-e-f-o-r-e. *Spell it with me.*

- **Write** *Let's write the word in the air as we say each letter:* b-e-f-o-r-e.

- Point out to children any irregularities in sound/spellings, such as the /sh/ sound spelled *ci* in the word *special*.

- Have partners create sentences using each word.

2 **Guided Practice/Practice** Have children identify the high-frequency words in connected text and blend the decodable words.

1. Let's walk **after** the rain stops.
2. We can play **before** school.
3. Nan read **every** page!
4. I see a **few** birds in the tree.
5. My friend Sally is in **first** grade.
6. They can **hear** the bell ring.
7. Dad **hurt** his left hand.
8. How **old** are you now?
9. This picture is **special** to me.
10. **Would** you help clean it up?

> **DIFFERENTIATED INSTRUCTION**

TIER 2

Approaching Level If children need support with high-frequency words:

I Do Use the High-Frequency Word Cards. Follow this routine for each word: Display the word. Read the word. Spell the word.

We Do Ask children to state the word and spell the word with you. Model using the word in a sentence, and have children repeat.

You Do Display the words randomly for children to say and spell. Provide opportunities for children to use the words in speaking and writing. For example, provide sentence starters, such as *What special thing do you like to do after ___?* Have children write each word in their writer's notebook.

OBJECTIVES

- Know and apply grade-level phonics and word analysis skills in decoding words.

- Recognize and read grade-appropriate irregularly spelled words.

 English Language Learners

Model Use visual cues, gestures, and examples to help children learn the meanings of the high-frequency words. Point out the Spanish cognate *especial*. Ask questions and give examples to reinforce meaning.

Digital Tools

For more practice, have children use this activity.

they · together · how · eat

High-Frequency Words

Decodable Reader, Vol. 3

OBJECTIVES

- Know and apply grade-level phonics and word-analysis skills in decoding words.

- Recognize and read grade-appropriate irregularly spelled words.

- Read on-level text with purpose and understanding.

- Read with sufficient accuracy and fluency to support comprehension.

- Review spacing between cursive letters and spacing between words.

Decodable Reader: "It Won't Be Easy!"

🕐 5 Mins

Focus on Foundational Skills

Review the words and letter-sounds that children will find in the **Decodable Reader.**

- Review with children the high-frequency words *after, before, every, few, first, hear, hurt, old, special,* and *would.*

- Review that *e, ee, ea, ie, y, ey, e_e* can stand for the /ē/ sound.

Preview and Predict Point to the title of the story and have children sound out each word with you as you run your finger under it. Ask: *What do you see in the picture? How do the mice feel about the cat?*

Read the Decodable Reader

Begin to read the story "It Won't Be Easy!" on page 47, have children point to each word, sounding out the decodable words and saying the high-frequency words quickly. If children need support reading decodable words, model blending for them. If children are having difficulty with high-frequency words, reread the word in isolation and then in context.

Check Comprehension

p. 46 *Why did Sneaky Mouse have a meeting?*
p. 46 *Who was at the meeting?*
p. 47 *What was Pete's idea for being safe from Beast?*
p. 48 *What was Sneaky plan for being safe from Beast?*
p. 49 *What did Stanley ask that showed that Sneaky's plan would not be easy?*

Retell Have partners use key ideas and details to retell "It Won't Be Easy!"

 English Language Learners

Check Comprehension Provide sentence frames, as needed, to help children answer the questions:

p. 46 Sneaky Mouse had a meeting because she was <u>tired of fleeing</u> from <u>Beast</u>.

p. 46 <u>Joe, Moe, Pete</u>, and <u>Stanley</u> were at the meeting.

p. 47 Pete wants to <u>hide in the big field</u>.

p. 48 Sneaky's plan was to <u>tie a bell</u> on Beast.

p. 49 Stanley asked how they would <u>get a bell on Beast</u>.

Focus on Fluency

With partners, have children read "It Won't Be Easy!" to focus on accuracy. Guide them to run their fingers under the text as they read. Children should note whether they are correctly reading the words on the page, monitor themselves, and provide feedback to their partners.

Listen in: If children are having difficulty reading accurately, have them start again at the beginning of the page. If children are reading too quickly, suggest to them that they slow down and read as they speak.

English Language Learners

Focus on Fluency Before reading "It Won't Be Easy!" point out the potential pronunciation challenges in each section of the story so children can practice the words in isolation. Have children first echo read each section after you, then choral read with you.

Handwriting: Letter and Word Spacing

Model Review with children that both their manuscript and their cursive writing should have good letter and word spacing to make it easier for readers to read their writing. Tell children that in cursive writing, there should be space for a small *o* between words. Then demonstrate with several examples in which letters and words are too crowded or are too widely spaced.

Guided Practice/Practice

- Invite volunteers to point out the letter and word spacing errors in your demonstration examples.

- Distribute **Response Boards**. Observe children's pen grip and paper placement, and correct as needed. Check that children are writing the lowercase cursive letters correctly on the guidelines.

Daily Handwriting

Throughout the week, use the models to review good letter and word spacing in cursive writing. Have children independently practice spacing using **Practice Book** pages 232–233.

Handwriting: pages 232–233

✔ Check for Success

Rubric Use the online rubric to record children's progress.

Can children decode words with long *e*?

Can children identify and read the high-frequency words?

Differentiate
SMALL GROUP INSTRUCTIONS

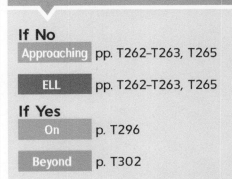

If No

| Approaching | pp. T262–T263, T265 |

| ELL | pp. T262–T263, T265 |

If Yes

| On | p. T296 |

| Beyond | p. T302 |

Daily Focus

Phonemic Awareness
• Phoneme Categorization

Phonics
• Review, Blend, and Build Words with /ē/e, ee, ea, ie, y, ey, e_e

Structural Analysis
• Plurals with –s, -es

Reread
• Decodable Reader, Vol. 3: "It Won't Be Easy!"

OBJECTIVES
• Categorize words by phoneme.

OPTION 5 Mins

Phonemic Awareness

Phoneme Categorization

1 **Model** Review /ē/. Have children listen for the medial sound in words. Say: *Listen closely as I say three words:* bean, joke, seat. *Two words have /ē/ in the middle, and one does not. I hear that the words* bean and seat *have the /ē/ vowel sound. The word* joke *does not.* Joke *doesn't belong.* Repeat with *feed, loaf, heat.*

2 **Guided Practice/Practice** Have children practice with the following word sets. Say: *I will say three words. Tell me which word does not belong and why.* Give corrective feedback if necessary.

deep, rose, meat	seed, beam, coal	bone, feet, keep
wheel, road, team	need, home, teach	vote, heap, read

English Language Learners

Guided Practice/Practice Provide sentence frames for children to use to respond; for example: I heard you say <u>deep, rose, and meat</u>. The word <u>rose</u> does not belong because it does not have the <u>/ē/</u> sound.

DIFFERENTIATED INSTRUCTION ▶

TIER 2 **Approaching Level** If children are having difficulty with phoneme categorization:

I Do Explain to children that you will be grouping phonemes. Say: *Listen as I say three words /nēd/, /red/, /lēf/. When I say* need and leaf, *I can hear the /ē/ sound in the middle.* Red *has the /e/ sound.* Red *does not belong.*

We Do *Do it with me. Listen as I say three words:* kite, green, theme. *Two have /ē/ in the middle:* green and theme. Kite *does not have /ē/. It does not belong.* Repeat with these word sets:

teeth, week, mail   coat, queen, soap   step, lake, dress

You Do Say: *It's your turn. Which words go together, and which word does not belong?* Provide corrective feedback if necessary.

soap, clean, bead   time, night, sneak   jeans, brain, team

Repeat the categorization routine with more long *e* words.

You may wish to review Phonemic Awareness with **ELL** using this section.

Phonics

OPTION 5 Mins

Review Long *e: e, ee, ea, ie, y, ey, e_e*

1 **Model** Display the *Tree* **Sound-Spelling Card.** Review the sound /ē/ using the word *free.* Say: *The sound is /ē/. Listen as I say the sounds in the word: /fff/ /rrr/ /ēēē/,* free. Repeat with the words *me, beet, meal, yield, funny, donkey,* and *theme.*

2 **Guided Practice/Practice** Point to each spelling pattern on the Sound-Spelling Card. Have children connect the letter(s) and the sound. Ask: *What are these letters? Together, what sound do they make? What is this letter? What sound does it stand for?* Offer corrective feedback as necessary.

DIFFERENTIATED INSTRUCTION

TIER 2

Approaching Level If children are having difficulty with long *e: e, ee, ea, ie, y, ey, e_e:*

I Do Display the *Tree* Sound-Spelling Card. *This is the* Tree *Sound-Spelling Card. The sound is /ē/. The /ē/ sound can be spelled with the letters* ee, ea, e, y, ie, ey, *and* e_e. Display the **Word-Building Cards** *ie.* Trace the letters *ie* while saying /ē/ five times. Repeat with *e, ee, ea, y, ey, e_e.*

We Do *Now do it with me.* Have children trace lowercase *ie* on the Word-Building Cards with their finger while saying /ē/. Trace the letters *ie* five times and say /ē/ with children. Repeat with *e, ee, ea, y, ey, e_e.*

You Do Have children connect the letters *e, ee, ea, ie, y, ey,* and *e_e* to the sound /ē/ by tracing each set of lowercase letters with their finger while saying /ē/. Once children have traced on paper five to ten times, they should then write the letters *e, ee, ea, ie, y, ey,* and *e_e* while saying /ē/ five to ten times.

Repeat, connecting the letters *e, ee, ea, ie, y, ey,* and *e_e* to the sound /ē/ through tracing and writing the letters throughout the week.

You may wish to review Phonics with **ELL** using this section.

OBJECTIVES
• Know and apply grade-level phonics and word analysis skills in decoding words.

SOUND-SPELLING REVIEW »

Build Fluency

Display the Word-Building Cards *e, e_e, ee, ea, y, ey, ie, o, oa, ow, oe, a, ai, ay, ea, ei, eigh, ey.* Have children say each sound. Repeat, and vary the pace.

Digital Tools

For more practice, have children use this activity.

Phonemic Awareness

To differentiate instruction for key skills, use the results of this activity.

Phonics

OBJECTIVES

• Know and apply grade-level phonics and word-analysis skills in decoding words.

• Recognize and read grade-appropriate irregularly spelled words.

• Read on-level text with purpose and understanding.

• Read with sufficient accuracy and fluency to support comprehension.

 English Language Learners

Guided Practice/Practice
Before practicing blending, review the meanings of example words. For example, close your eyes, pretending to nap, and say, "I will *sleep*." Show a picture of a peach and say, "I can eat a *peach*." Smile and say, "I am *happy*." Have children repeat the actions and sentences.

 Phonics

5 Mins

Blend Words with Long *e: e, ee, ea, ie, y, ey, e_e*

1 **Model** Display **Word-Building Cards** *w, e, a, k*. Model how to generate and blend the sounds to say the word. *This is the letter* w. *It stands for /www/. This is the letter* e. *This is the letter* a. *Together, they stand for /ēēē/. This is the letter* k. *It stands for /k/. Listen as I blend these sounds together: /wwwēēēk/. The word is:* weak.

Continue by modeling the words *me, meet, chief, lucky, key, these*.

2 **Guided Practice/Practice** Repeat the blending routine with children with the words *me, sleep, eat, peach, brief, happy, valley,* and *eve*. Provide corrective feedback until children can work on their own.

 DIFFERENTIATED INSTRUCTION >>

TIER 2

Approaching Level If children are having difficulty blending words with /ē/ spelled *e, ee, ea, ie, y, ey, e_e*:

I Do Display Word-Building Cards *t, e, e, t, h. Say: This is the letter* t. *It stands for /t/. These are the letters* ee. *Together they stand for the sound /ēēē/. These are the letters* t *and* h. *Together they stand for /th/. I'll blend all the sounds together: /tēēēth/,* teeth. Repeat with *be, seal, yield, tidy, volley,* and *Pete*.

We Do Guide children to blend the sounds and read: eel, beet, teach, dream, she, field, copy, key, and compete.

You Do Have children blend and decode: *deep, free, clean, speak, be, we, belief, penny, valley, eve*.

You may wish to review Phonics with **ELL** using this section.

Build Words with Long *e: e, ee, ea, ie, y, ey, e_e*

Provide children with **Word-Building Cards** for the alphabet. Have children put the letters in order from *a* to *z*.

1 **Model** Display Word-Building Cards *m, e.* Blend: /m/ /ē/, /mmmēēē/. The word is *me.*

- Replace *m* with *w* and repeat with *we.*
- Change *w* to *sh* and repeat with *she.*

2 **Guided Practice/Practice** Continue with the following word sets. Guide children to build and blend each word. Give corrective feedback until children can work on their own.

sheet, sheep, sleep, deep, peep, peel
field, yield, shield, shriek

chief, thief, grief, brief, belief, relief
Steve, eve, these, theme

sunny, funny, bunny, buggy, bumpy, lumpy
leaf, leak, peak, peach, beach, reach

Once children have built the words, dictate the words to children and have them write the words down. Children can work with a partner to check their spelling.

DIFFERENTIATED INSTRUCTION

TIER 2

Approaching Level If children are having difficulty building words with long *e: e, ee, ea, ie, y, ey, e_e:*

I Do Display Word-Building Cards *s, e, e.* Say: *These are letters* s, e, e. *They stand for the sounds* /sss/ *and* /ēēē/. *I will blend the two sounds together:* /sssēēē/, see.

We Do *Now let's do one together. We'll make the word* seed. *Place the letter* d *at the end of* see. *Let's blend:* /sssēēē/ /d/, /sssēēēd/, seed. *Now we will change the letter* s *to the letter* f. *Let's blend the new word:* /fff/ /ēēē/ /d/, /fffēēēd/, feed.

You Do *Now you do it.* Have children build and blend these words: *bee, beep, peep, seep, sea, seat, heat, he, she, shield, yield, field.*

You may wish to review Phonics with **ELL** using this section.

Digital Tools

To differentiate instruction for key skills, use the results of this activity.

Phonics

DAY 7 ›› **Word Work**

OBJECTIVES

- Know and apply grade-level phonics and word analysis skills in decoding words.

ACADEMIC LANGUAGE

- *plural*
- Cognate: *plural*

Digital Tools

For more practice, have children use this activity.

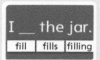

Structural Analysis

 Structural Analysis

Plurals with *-s, -es*

1 **Model** Write the word *field*. Explain that the word means "one field." *To make the word* field *mean "more than one," I add* -s. Write *fields* and read the new word. Repeat with the word *body*. *The word* body *ends with a consonant and* y, *so I need to change the* y *to* i *before I add* -es *to make the word plural.* Write *bodies* and read the new word.

2 **Guided Practice/Practice** Write the following words *daddy, thing, key, ferry, niece, lady*. Have children write the plural form of each word. Have children work with a partner to check their spelling.

Have children independently practice plurals with *-s* and *-es* using **Practice Book** page 228.

DIFFERENTIATED INSTRUCTION ››

TIER 2

Approaching Level If children are having difficulty with plurals *-s, -es:*

I Do Write the word *lady*. Read the word aloud. Say: *I know that when a noun ends with a consonant and* y, *I change the* y *to* i *and then add* -es. *The noun* lady *becomes* ladies. *The word* ladies *is plural. Two ladies met for lunch.*

We Do Write *penny*. Penny *is a noun. The word ends in a consonant and* y. *Let's change the* y *to* i *and then add* -es *to form* pennies. Pennies *is plural. I have many pennies.* Repeat this routine with the following examples: *guppy, sock, moon, pony*. Give corrective feedback to children needing extra support.

You Do *Now it's your turn. Write the plural form of each word and use each plural in a sentence.*

jelly   bean   daisy   mommy   cheek   cherry

Repeat Have children form plurals with long *e* nouns.

Decodable Reader: Reread "It Won't Be Easy!"

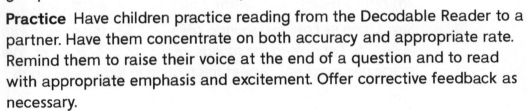

Focus on Foundational Skills

Review with children the words with long *e* as well as the high-frequency words that they will find in the **Decodable Reader**.

Decodable Reader, Vol. 3

Reread the Decodable Reader

Guide children in rereading "It Won't Be Easy!" Point out the high-frequency words and the words with long *e* spelled *e, ee, ea, ie, y, ey,* and *e_e*.

Reread the Book On page 48, have children point to each word, sounding out the decodable words and saying the high-frequency words quickly.

Check Comprehension

Remind children that they can ask themselves questions to make sure they understood what they have read. Have children use both text and illustrations to answer their questions.

Retell Have partners use key ideas and details to retell "It Won't Be Easy!"

Focus on Fluency

COLLABORATE

Review Remind children that part of reading with expression is using your voice to show feeling. When they read an exclamation, they can show surprise, shock, or excitement. When they read a question, their voice can go up at the end to show curiosity, interest, or confusion.

Practice Have children practice reading from the Decodable Reader to a partner. Have them concentrate on both accuracy and appropriate rate. Remind them to raise their voice at the end of a question and to read with appropriate emphasis and excitement. Offer corrective feedback as necessary.

OBJECTIVES

- Know and apply grade-level phonics and word-analysis skills in decoding words.
- Recognize and read grade-appropriate irregularly spelled words.
- Read on-level text with purpose and understanding.
- Read with sufficient accuracy and fluency to support comprehension.

HIGH-FREQUENCY WORDS REVIEW

after, before, every, few, first, hear, hurt, old, special, would

Say the words and have children Read/Spell/Write them. List the words so children can self-correct. Review last week's words using the same routine.

✔ Check for Success

Rubric Use the online rubric to record children's progress.

Can children decode words with long *e*?

Can children read the high-frequency words?

Differentiate
SMALL GROUP INSTRUCTIONS

If No

| Approaching | pp. T269–T273 |
| ELL | pp. T269–T273 |

If Yes

| On | p. T296 |
| Beyond | p. T302 |

Daily Focus

Phonemic Awareness
• Phoneme Blending

Phonics
• Contrast Vowel Sounds;
Blend and Build Words with
/ē/e, ee, ea, ie, y, ey, e_e

Structural Analysis
• Plurals with –s, -es

High-Frequency Words

Read
• Decodable Reader, Vol. 3:
"The Beach Is a Treat"

Phonemic Awareness: page 225

OBJECTIVES
• Blend phonemes to form new words.

---

5 Mins Phonemic Awareness

Phoneme Blending

1 Model Demonstrate how to say a word sound by sound and then blend the sounds to say the word as a whole. *Listen as I say the three sounds in a word: The beginning sound is /d/. The middle sound is /ē/. The ending sound is /p/. Now I'll blend the sounds together to say the word, /dēēēp/, deep. The word is* deep.

2 Guided Practice/Practice Say: *Let's do some blending together. I will say one sound at a time. Then we will blend the sounds to say the word. Do it with me.* Do the first one together. Offer corrective feedback if needed until children can work on their own.

/sss/ /ēēē/ /d/ (seed)   /sss/ /t/ /ēēē/ /mmm/ (steam)
/ch/ /ēēē/ /k/ (cheek)   /g/ /rrr/ /ēēē/ /nnn/ (green)
/sh/ /ēēē/ (she)   /fff/ /ēēē/ /lll/ /d/ (field)
/ch/ /ēēē/ /fff/ (chief)   /th/ /ēēē/ /mmm/ (theme)

Have children independently practice blending phonemes using **Practice Book** page 225.

DIFFERENTIATED INSTRUCTION ⟩

TIER 2

Approaching Level If children are having difficulty blending phonemes:

I Do Explain to children that you will be blending sounds to form words. Say: *Listen as I say three sounds: /t/ /ēēē/ /mmm/. I'm going to blend the sounds together to say a word: /t/ /ēēē/ /mmm/, /tēēemmm/, team. I blended the word* team

We Do Say: *Listen as I say two sounds: /ēēē/ /t/. Say the sounds with me: /ēēē/ /t/. Let's blend the sounds: /ēēē/ /t/, /ēēēt/ /, eat. We made one word:* eat. Repeat this routine to form these words:

teeth   key   leaf   east
keep   speak   chief   teach

You Do Say: *It's your turn. I want you to blend the sounds I say together to form a word.* Provide corrective feedback as necessary.

deep   she   icy   yield   delete
we   leap   feed   beach   valley

Repeat the blending routine with additional long *e* words.

You may wish to review Phonemic Awareness with **ELL** using this section.

Phonics

5 Mins

Contrast Vowel Sounds

1 **Model** Say: *Let's listen to some word pairs that have one sound that is different.* Display the **Word-Building Cards** for long *a, e, i, o.* As you say each long vowel sound, point to the letter combinations that represent that sound. Say: *These are the letters* ay. *They stand for /ā/.* Repeat for all sound-spellings. Say: *I will say two words. For each word, I will point to the letter or letters that stand for the vowel sound.* tray, tree. *When I say* tray, *I point to the letters* ay. *The vowel sound in* tray *is /āāā/. When I say* tree, *I point to the letters* ee. *The vowel sound in* tree *is /ēēē/. Listen:* tray, tree. *Repeat with these word pairs:* feed/fade, steal/stale; green/groan, weak/woke; free/fry, niece/nice.

2 **Guided Practice/Practice** *Let's do some together. Listen as I say two words:* niece, nice. *What sounds can we hear in the middle of each word? Let's hold up Word-Building Cards for the sound we hear in the middle.* Display the *ie* cards for *niece* and the *i_e* cards for *nice.* Continue the routine, having children take turns with a partner. Pairs should have Word-Building Cards for the long-vowel spellings. Guide practice with these word pairs. Give corrective feedback if needed:

sleep/slope	meet/might	wee/weigh	seam/same	she/shy
greed/grade	cheese/chose	wheel/while	breed/braid	tease/toes

DIFFERENTIATED INSTRUCTION

TIER 2

Approaching Level If children need support contrasting vowel sounds:

I Do Display Word-Building Cards for the long *a, e, i,* and *o* spellings. Say: *I will say each vowel sound as I point to the sound-spelling.* Review each of the vowel sound-spellings, with example words.

We Do Provide children with the Word-Building Cards for the long *a, e, i,* and *o* spellings. Have children trace the letters for each sound-spelling as they say the long-vowel sound.

You Do *Listen to each word. Hold up the cards that stand for the vowel sound you hear in the middle. of the word.* Say one word at a time, emphasizing the long-vowel sound. Use these words:

these	daze	might	weight	those
meal	while	beach	phone	break

Guide practice and give corrective feedback as needed.

You may wish to review Phonics with **ELL** using this section.

OBJECTIVES

- Know and apply grade-level phonics and word analysis skills in decoding words.

SOUND-SPELLING REVIEW

Build Fluency

Display the Word-Building Cards *e, e_e, ee, ea, y, ey, ie, o, oa, ow, oe, a, ai, ay, ea, ei, eigh, ey.* Have children say each sound.

Digital Tools

For more practice, have children use this activity.

Phonemic Awareness

To differentiate instruction for key skills, use the results of this activity.

Phonics

OBJECTIVES

• Know and apply grade-level phonics and word analysis skills in decoding words.

OPTION 5 Mins

Phonics

Blend Words with Long *e: e, ee, ea, ie, y, ey, e_e*

1 **Model** Display **Word-Building Cards** *h, e, a, t.* Model how to blend the sounds. *This is the letter* h. *It stands for /h/. This is the letter* e *and this is the letter* a. *Together, the letters* e, a *can stand for /ē/. This is the letter* t. *It stands for /t/. Let's blend all three sounds: /hēēēt/. The word is* heat.

Continue by modeling the words *teeth, key, study, be,* and *Steve.*

2 **Guided Practice/Practice** Repeat the routine with *pea, tiny, feed, we, seat, brief, meet, these, alley.* Guide practice until children can work independently. Give corrective feedback as necessary.

Have children independently practice blending words with long *e* using **Practice Book** page 227.

DIFFERENTIATED INSTRUCTION ➤➤

TIER 2

Approaching Level If children are having difficulty blending words:

I Do Display Word-Building Cards *s, l, e, e, p.* Say: *This is the letter* s. *It stands for /sss/. This is the letter* l. *It stands for /lll/. These are the letters* ee. *Together they stand for /ēēē/. This is the letter* p. *It stands for /p/. Listen as I blend all four sounds: /sss/ /lll/ /ēēē/ /p/, /ssslllēēēp/,* sleep. *The word is* sleep.

We Do Say: *Let's do some together.* Blend and read the words *green, read, speak, me, she, thief, penny, key, theme.* Offer corrective feedback if children need more support.

You Do Display the words *be, secret, beast, easy, meeting, seemed, key.* Have children blend and read the words.

You may wish to review Phonics with **ELL** using this section.

Phonics: page 227

Build Words with Long *e: e, ee, ea, ie, y, ey, e_e*

Provide children with **Word-Building Cards** *a* to *z*. Have children put the letters in alphabetical order.

1 **Model** Display Word-Building Cards *w, e, e*. Blend: /w/ /ē/ /wwwēēē/, *wee*.

- Replace *w* with *b* and repeat with *bee*.
- Add *t* to *bee* and repeat with *beet*.

2 **Guided Practice/Practice** Continue with *sheet, sheep, sleep, sleet, meet, me, mean, bean, clean, lean, leaf, leak, peak, peach, peachy*. Extend the building routine with these additional /ē/ words: *chief, thief, grief, grieve, eve, Steve*.

Guide children and provide feedback as needed until they can work independently. Once children have built the words, dictate the words and have children write each word.

Children can work with a partner to check their spelling.

Digital Tools

To differentiate instruction for key skills, use the results of this activity.

Phonics

DIFFERENTIATED INSTRUCTION ⟩

TIER 2

Approaching Level If children need more support building words:

I Do Display Word-Building Cards *c, h, e, a, p*. Say: *These are letters* c, h, e, a, p. *They stand for the sounds* /ch/, /ēēē/, *and* /p/. I *will blend* /ch/, /ēēē/, *and* /p/ *together:* /chēēēp/, *cheap*.

We Do Say: *Now let's do one together. Let's make the word* cheek. *Change the letter* p *at the end of* cheap *to the letter* k. *The spelling of* /ē/ *changes from* ea *to* ee. *Let's blend the new word:* /chēēēk/, *cheek*.

You Do Have children continue changing letters to build and blend these words: *cheese, ease, eat, heat, cheat, treat, tree, be, he, she, shield, field, feel, feet*. Give corrective feedback until children can work independently.

You may wish to review Phonics with **ELL** using this section.

OBJECTIVES

- Form plurals with -e and -es.

- Know and apply grade-level phonics and word analysis skills in decoding words.

Digital Tools

For more practice, have children use this activity.

Structural Analysis

OPTION 5 Mins

Structural Analysis

Plurals -s, -es

1 **Model** Write the words *seed* and *seeds*. Point out the -s that was added to make *seed* plural. Then write *penny* and *pennies*. Point out that you changed the *y* to *i* and then added -es to make *penny* plural.

2 **Guided Practice/Practice** Help children blend the words *teams, weeds, bunnies, fields, cities, keys,* and *babies*. Ask them to identify the ending that makes each word plural.

DIFFERENTIATED INSTRUCTION >>

TIER 2

Approaching Level If children are having difficulty with forming plurals with -s or -es:

I Do Write the word *jelly*. Read the word aloud. Say: *I know that when a noun ends with a consonant and y, I change the* y *to* i *and then add* -es. *The noun* jelly *becomes* jellies. *The word* jellies *is plural. There were two different jellies on the sandwich.*

We Do Write *penny*. Penny *is a noun. The word ends in consonant* y. *Let's change the* y *to* i *and then add* -es *to form* pennies. Pennies *is plural. I have many pennies.* Repeat this routine with the following examples: *pony, bungee, leak, guppy.*

You Do *Now it's your turn. Write plural form of each word and use each plural in a sentence.*

meal   family   cheese   daisy   feast   chimney   creek

Repeat Have children form plurals with long *e* nouns.

High-Frequency Words

after, before, every, few, first, hear, hurt, old, special, would

1 **Model** Say each word and have children Read/Spell/Write it. Ask children to picture the words, and write them the way they see them. Display words so children can self-correct.

2 **Guided Practice** Have children identify the high-frequency words in connected text and blend the decodable words.

1. Drink some water **after** you eat.
2. I played **before** Mom woke up.
3. I like **every** flower in the field.
4. I was sick for a **few** days.
5. Camp started on the **first** of May.
6. I **hear** people singing a tune.
7. Do not **hurt** the small puppy.
8. That **old** dress is very little.
9. Did you go to the **special** sale?
10. I **would** like to stay there.

Point out the long *e* sound-spelling *e* in *before*.

Have children independently practice the high-frequency words using **Practice Book** page 229.

Practice Add the high-frequency words to the cumulative word bank. Have partners create more sentences using the words.

Cumulative Review Review last week's words using the Read/Spell/Write routine. Repeat the above routine, mixing the words and having children say each one.

DIFFERENTIATED INSTRUCTION

TIER 2

Approaching Level If children are having difficulty with high-frequency words:

I Do Use the High-Frequency Word Cards. Display one word at a time, following the routine: Display the word. Read the word. Then spell the word.

We Do Ask children to state the word and spell the word with you. Model using the word in a sentence, and have children repeat after you.

You Do Display the word. Ask children to say the word then spell it. When completed, quickly flip through the word card set as children chorally read the words. Provide opportunities for children to use the words in conversation. Ask children to write each word in their Writer's Notebook.

OBJECTIVES

- Know and apply grade-level phonics and word analysis skills in decoding words.

- Recognize and read grade-appropriate irregularly spelled words.

Digital Tools

For more practice, have children use this activity.

| they | together |
| how | eat |

High-Frequency Words

High-Frequency Words: page 229

The Beach Is a Treat

It's the weekend! You are lucky if you can go to the beach and sit by the sea.

51

Decodable Reader, Vol. 3

OBJECTIVES

- Know and apply grade-level phonics and word-analysis skills in decoding words.

- Recognize and read grade-appropriate irregularly spelled words.

- Read on-level text with purpose and understanding.

- Read with sufficient accuracy and fluency to support comprehension.

Decodable Reader: "The Beach Is a Treat"

Focus on Foundational Skills

Review the words and letter-sounds that children will find in the **Decodable Reader.**

- Review the high-frequency words *few, hurt,* and *would.*

- Review with children that the letters *e, ee, ea, ie, y, ey,* and *e_e* can stand for the /ē/ sound.

Preview and Predict Point to the title of the selection and have children sound out each word with you as you run your finger under it. Ask: *What do you see in the photograph? Where is the family?*

Read the Decodable Reader

Begin guiding children to read the selection "The Beach Is a Treat." On page 52, have children point to each word, sounding out the decodable words and saying the high-frequency words quickly. If children need support reading decodable words, model blending for them. If children are having difficulty with high-frequency words, reread the word in isolation and then reread the high-frequency word in context.

Check Comprehension

p. 51 *When does this family go to the beach?*

p. 52 *What are some things you might see at the beach?*

p. 53 *What are some things you can do to stay safe at the beach?*

p. 54 *How can you clean your hands at the beach?*

Retell Have partners use key ideas and details to retell "The Beach Is a Treat."

Focus on Fluency

With partners, have children read "The Beach Is a Treat" to focus on accuracy. As children read, guide them to run their fingers under the text as they read. Children should note whether they are correctly reading the words on the page. As children read, they can monitor themselves and provide feedback to their partners.

Listen in: If children are having difficulty reading accurately, have them start again at the beginning of the page. If children are reading too quickly, suggest that they should slow down and read as they speak.

English Language Learners

Check Comprehension Provide sentence frames, as needed, to help children answer the questions:

p. 51 The family goes to the beach <u>on the weekend</u>.

p. 52 At the beach you might see <u>heaps of sand, many tiny shells, happy familes, sandy babies, seals swimming</u>.

p. 53 At the beach you can stay safe if you <u>do not go in deep water</u>, if you <u>put on sunscreen</u>, and if you <u>try not to get sand in your eyes</u>.

p. 54 To clean your hands at the beach, you can <u>put them in the sea</u>.

Focus on Fluency Before reading "The Beach Is a Treat," point out the potential pronunciation challenges in each section of the selection so children can practice the words in isolation beforehand. Have children first echo read each section after you, then choral read with you.

Remember to model self-corrective techniques on a regular basis as you read aloud. For example, pretend to mispronounce a word, then self-correct. Encourage children to follow your example as they read.

✓ Check for Success

Rubric Use the online rubric to record children's progress.

Can children decode words with long *e?*

Can children identify and read the high-frequency words?

Differentiate
SMALL GROUP INSTRUCTIONS

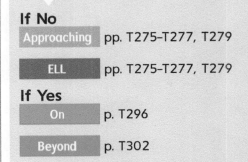

If No

| Approaching | pp. T275–T277, T279 |
| ELL | pp. T275–T277, T279 |

If Yes

| On | p. T296 |
| Beyond | p. T302 |

Daily Focus

Phonological Awareness
• Identify Syllables

Phonics
• Blend and Build Words with /ē/e, ee, ea, ie, y, ey, e_e

Reread
• Decodable Reader, Vol. 3: "The Beach Is a Treat"

The Beach Is a Treat

OBJECTIVES
• Identify syllables in words.

OPTION 5 Mins

Phonological Awareness

Identify Syllables

1 **Model** Say: *I will count the syllables in a word. Listen as I say this word:* weekend. *I hear two vowel sounds. Now I will clap the syllables:* week *(clap)* end *(clap). The word* weekend *has two syllables.*

2 **Guided Practice/Practice** Have children practice counting the syllables in the following words. Do the first one together.

teeth (1)   committee (3)   silly (2)   briefing (2)

leader (2)   feelings (2)   keys (1)   repeating (3)

Guide practice and provide corrective feedback as children progress to work on their own.

DIFFERENTIATED INSTRUCTION ⟩

TIER 2

Approaching Level If children are having difficulty with identifying syllables:

I Do Explain to children that they will be identifying syllables in words. Say: *A syllable is a word part that has a vowel sound. Listen as I say a word:* even. *I'll clap for each syllable:* e *(clap)* ven *(clap). The word* even *has two syllables.*

We Do *Listen as I say* zebra. *Say the word with me:* zebra. *Let's clap the syllables:* ze *(clap)* bra *(clap).* Zebra *has two syllables. Each syllable has a vowel sound.*

Repeat this routine with the following words:

valley (2)   bumblebee (3)   keyhole (2)   shield (1)
field (1)   seashell (2)   disagree (3)   needless (2)

Provide corrective feedback until children are able to work on their own.

You Do Say: *Now it's your turn. I'll say a word. Repeat the word. Then clap and count the syllables.*

sneaky (2)   employee (3)   disagreement (4)   reread (2)
maybe (2)   three (1)   streaming (2)   tadpole (2)

You may wish to review Phonological Awareness with **ELL** using this section.

Phonics

5 Mins

Blend Words with Long *e: e, ee, ea, ie, y, ey, e_e*

1 Model Display **Word-Building Cards** *t, e, a, c, h.* Model how to blend the sounds. *This is the letter* t. *It stands for /t/. This is the letter* e *and this is the letter* a. *Together, the letters* ea *can stand for /ē/. This is the letter* c *and this is the letter* h. *Together, the letters* ch *stand for /ch/. I will blend all three sounds: /tēēēch/. The word is* teach.

Continue by modeling the words *speed, key, study, we,* and *Pete.*

2 Guided Practice/Practice Repeat the routine with *clean, baby, sheet, me, team, brief, wheel, these, medley.*

Guide practice until children can work independently. Give corrective feedback as necessary.

DIFFERENTIATED INSTRUCTION

TIER 2

Approaching Level If children are having difficulty blending words:

I Do Display Word-Building Cards *g, r, e, e, n.* Say: *This is the letter* g. *It stands for /g/. This is the letter* r. *It stands for /rrr/. These are the letters* ee. *Together they stand for /ēēē/. This is the letter* n. *It stands for /nnn/. Listen as I blend all four sounds: /g/ /rrr/ /ēēē/ /nnn/, /grrrēēēnnn/,* green. *The word is* green.

We Do Say: *Let's do some together.* Blend and read the words *steep, deal, speak, be, she, grief, penny, key, theme.* Give corrective feedback until children can work on their own.

You Do Display the words *he, secret, least, easy, greeting, peeled, alley.* Have children blend and read the words.

You may wish to review Phonics with **ELL** using this section.

SOUND-SPELLING REVIEW

Build Fluency

Display the Word-Building Cards *e, e_e, ee, ea, y, ey, ie, o, oa, ow, oe, a, ai, ay, ea, ei, eigh, ey.* Have children say each sound. Repeat, and vary the pace.

Digital Tools

For more practice, have children use this activity.

Phonological Awareness

To differentiate instruction for key skills, use the results of this activity.

Phonics

OBJECTIVES

- Know and apply grade-level phonics and word analysis skills in decoding words.

Phonics

5 Mins

Build Words with Long *e: e, ee, ea, ie, y, ey, e_e*

1 **Review** Say: *Remember, the long* e *sound /ēēē/ can be represented by different letters:* e, e_e, ee, ea, ie, y, *and* ey. Display the **Word-Building Cards** *r, e, a, c, h.* Say: *Let's blend the sounds together and read the word: /rrrēēēch/,* reach. *Now let's change the* r *to* b. *We made the word* beach. *Read the word* beach *with me.*

2 **Practice** Continue building with these word sets: *be, me, she, sheep, keep, peep; buggy, bunny, sunny; brief, grief, grieve; these, theme.*

Once children have built the words, dictate the words and have children write the words on a piece of paper. Children can work with a partner to check their words for spelling.

DIFFERENTIATED INSTRUCTION

On-Level For more practice building words:

I Do Display Word-Building Cards *e, e, l.* Say: *This is the letter* e. *The letters* ee *together stand for /ē/. This is the letter* l. *It stands for /l/. Listen as I blend the two sounds together: /ēēēlll/,* eel. *The word is* eel.

We Do *Now, let's do one together. Make the word* eel *using Word-Building Cards. Add the letters* wh *to the beginning of the word. Let's blend: /hw/ /ēēē/, /lll/, /hwēēēlll/,* wheel. *Now there is a new word,* wheel. *Change the letters* wh *to* f. *Let's blend and read the new word: /fffēēēlll/,* feel. *The new word is* feel. Provide corrective feedback if children need additional support.

You Do Have children build and blend the words: *she, he, we, see, sea, tea, teak, beak, beam, seam, seem, seen, queen; brief, grief, chief; guppy, puppy, peppy; alley, valley; theme, these*

Digital Tools

To differentiate instruction for key skills, use the results of this activity.

Phonics

OPTION
5 Mins

Decodable Reader:
Reread "The Beach Is a Treat"

Focus on Foundational Skills

Review with children the words with long *e* sound spelled as well as the high-frequency words *few, hurt,* and *would* that they will find in the **Decodable Reader.**

Decodable Reader, Vol. 3

Reread the Decodable Reader

Guide children in rereading "The Beach Is a Treat." Point out the high-frequency words and the words with /ē/ spelled *e, ee, ea, ie, y, ey, e_e.*

Reread the Book On page 53, have children point to each word, sounding out the decodable words and saying the high-frequency words quickly. If children struggle sounding out words, model blending for them.

Check Comprehension

Remind children that they can ask themselves questions to make sure they understood what they are reading. Have them use both text and photographs to answer their questions.

Retell Have partners use key ideas and details to retell "The Beach Is a Treat."

Focus on Fluency

Review Remind children that part of reading with expression is using your voice to show feeling. When they read an exclamation, they can show surprise, shock, or excitement. When they read a question, their voice can go up at the end to show curiosity, interest, or confusion.

COLLABORATE

Practice Have children practice reading to a partner with accuracy and at a suitable rate. Remind them to read with appropriate emphasis and excitement. Offer corrective feedback as necessary. Remind them that they can ask themselves questions to make sure they understood what they read. Have them use both text and photographs to answer their questions.

OBJECTIVES

- Know and apply grade-level phonics and word analysis skills in decoding words.

- Recognize and read grade-appropriate irregularly spelled words.

- Read on-level text with purpose and understanding.

- Read with sufficient accuracy and fluency to support comprehension.

HIGH-FREQUENCY WORDS REVIEW

after, before, every, few, first, hear, hurt, old, special, would Have children Read/ Spell/Write each word and use it in a sentence. Repeat with last week's words.

✓ **Check for Success**

Rubric Use the online rubric to record children's progress.

Can children decode words with long *e*?

Can children read the high-frequency words?

Differentiate
SMALL GROUP INSTRUCTIONS

If No

Approaching	pp. T283–T285
ELL	pp. T283–T285

If Yes

On	p. T296
Beyond	p. T302

Word Work

 Phonemic Awareness

Phoneme Blending

Review Guide children to blend phonemes to form words. *Listen as I say a group of sounds. Then blend those sounds to form a word.*

/f/ /r/ /ē/ (free)	/k/ /l/ /ē/ /n/ (clean)	/t/ /ē/ /m/ (team)
/p/ /ē/ /z/ (peas)	/r/ /ē/ /l/ (real or reel)	/sh/ /ē/ (she)
/ch/ /ē/ /f/ (chief)	/b/ /l/ /ē/ /d/ (bleed)	/p/ /ē/ /t/ (Pete)

 # Phonics

Blend and Build Words: Long *e: e, ee, ea, ie, y, ey, e_e*

Review Write these words: *key, field, speak, we, fancy, these, see.* Ask children to read and say the words. If children are having difficulty, remind them to segment the word and then blend the sounds together. Then have children follow the word-building routine with **Word-Building Cards** to build *she, sheet; treat, tree; money, honey; dusty, rusty; chief, brief, thief.*

Word Automaticity Help children practice word automaticity. Display decodable words. Have children chorally read each word. Test how many words children can read in one minute. Model blending any missed words.

> **DIFFERENTIATED INSTRUCTION**
>
> **TIER 2**
>
> **Approaching Level** If children need support blending and building:
>
> **I Do** Display Word-Building Cards *r, e, a, c, h. These letters stand for the sounds /rrr/, /ēēē/, and /ch/. Listen as I blend all three sounds: /rrrēēēch/, reach. The word is* reach.
>
> **We Do** *Now let's do some together. Let's make the word* keep *using Word-Building Cards. Let's blend: /k/ /ēēē/ /p/, /kēēēp/, keep. Now we'll change the letter* k *in* keep *to the letter* w. *Let's blend and read the new word: /www/ /ēēē/ /p/, /wēēēp/, weep.* Continue to help children change letters and build with these words: *wheel, wheat, heat, heal, real, meal, me, fee,* and *free.* Provide corrective feedback as needed.
>
> **You Do** *Now it's your turn.* Have children blend and build these words: *fleet, feet, seat, beat, be, bee, see, seem, seam, team, steam, Steve, Eve.* Review the meanings of the words.
>
> **Repeat,** blending and building additional words with long *e*.

You may wish to review Phonics with **ELL** using this section.

Daily Focus

Phonemic Awareness
• Phoneme Blending

Phonics
• Blend and Build Words with /ē/e, ee, ea, ie, y, ey, e_e

Structural Analysis
• Plurals with –s, -es

High-Frequency Words

OBJECTIVES
• Blend phonemes to form words.
• Decode words with long *e*.
• Know and apply grade-level phonics and word analysis skills in decoding words.
• Form plurals with –s and -es.
• Recognize and read grade-appropriate irregularly spelled words.

SOUND-SPELLING REVIEW

Build Fluency
Display the Word-Building Cards *e, e_e, ee, ea, y, ey, ie, o, oa, ow, oe, a, ai, ay, ea, ei, eigh, ey.* Have children say each sound. Repeat, and vary the pace.

Structural Analysis

Plurals with –s, –es

Review With children, review the rules for forming plurals: adding –s or changing the final y to i before adding –es. Then have children practice writing the plural forms of these words: *baby, seat, weed, pony.* Have them write a sentence for each of the plural forms.

High-Frequency Words

after, before, every, few, first, hear, hurt, old, special, would

Review Have children identify and read the high-frequency words. Display **High-Frequency Word Cards** for each word. Have pairs use the words in conversation. Then have children write a sentence for each word.

DIFFERENTIATED INSTRUCTION

Approaching Level If children need extra support with high-frequency words:

I Do Use the High-Frequency Word Cards. Display one word at a time, following the routine: Display the word. Read the word. Then spell the word.

We Do Ask children to state the word and spell the word with you. Model using the word in a sentence, and have children repeat after you.

You Do Display the word. Ask children to say the word and then spell it. When completed, quickly flip through the word card set as children chorally read the words. Provide opportunities for children to use the words in speaking and writing. For example, provide sentence starters, such as *Before and after every _____, my family and I like to _____.* Ask children to write each word in their Writer's Notebook.

OBJECTIVES

- Decode words with common prefixes and suffixes.
- Recognize and read grade-appropriate irregularly spelled words.

✔ Check for Success

Rubric Use the online rubric to record children's progress.

Can children decode words with long *e?*

Can children identify and read the high-frequency words?

Differentiate
SMALL GROUP INSTRUCTIONS

If No

| Approaching | pp. T286–T287 |
| ELL | pp. T286–T287 |

If Yes

| On | p. T296 |
| Beyond | p. T302 |

Lexile 200L

OBJECTIVES

Recount stories, including fables and folktales from diverse cultures, and determine their central message, lesson, or moral.

Recount or describe key ideas or details from a text read aloud or information presented orally or through other media.

ACADEMIC LANGUAGE

• *expository text, problem, solution, context clues*

• Cognates: *texto expositivo, problema, solución*

Approaching Level

Leveled Reader *A Special Sunset*

Preview and Predict

• Read the Essential Question: *What can we see in the sky?*

• Have children preview the title, opening pages, and illustrations of *A Special Sunset* to make a prediction about the selection. Then discuss the predictions.

Review Genre: Fiction

Have children recall that fiction is a made-up story with characters, a setting, and plot. A fiction story has a beginning, a middle, and an end, which is the story's sequence. It can have dialogue, or words that characters say.

Close Reading

Note Taking: Ask children to use the online Sequence **Graphic Organizer 2** as they read to record events that will help them summarize the story.

Pages 2–3 *What happens in this part of the story?* (Maria and her father go to the airport to catch a plane.)

Think Aloud Let's add this event to the First box in our Sequence graphic organizer. As we read, we'll continue adding events to keep track of what happens.

Pages 4-5 *How do you know this story is written in the third person?* (The narrator is not a character.) *What pronoun on page 4 helps you know this?* (*She*)

Page 6 *What happens after Maria sits down?* (She looks out the window. The plane takes off.) *What clue word on page 6 helps you understand sequence?* (*soon*)

Pages 7-10 *What compound word can you find on page 10?* (*sunset*) *What two smaller words make up the word sunset?* (*sun* and *set*) Have children add this word to their writer's notebook.

Pages 12–13 *Turn to a partner and talk about details you did not understand the first time you read these pages. Which part can you reread to help you?* (Possible response: I didn't understand what Maria's dad said. I can reread page 12 to understand what her dad said.)

Pages 14–15 *How is the Moon similar to the Sun?* (The Moon makes the clouds glow; it is far away so it looks as though it follows the plane.)

Retell Have children take turns retelling the selection using the retelling cards. Help children make a personal connection by asking: *When have you noticed the Sun or Moon in the sky? What questions do you have about them?*

Analytical Writing **Respond to Reading** Have children complete the Respond to Reading questions on page 16.

Write About Reading In children's responses to question 4 on page 16, check that they wrote about what might happen next to Maria.

Fluency: Intonation

Model Fluency Read the sentences on pages 10–11 one at a time. Have children chorally repeat. Point out how your voice shows excitement when you see an exclamation mark and how it goes up at the end of a question.

Apply Have children practice reading pages 10–11 with partners.

Paired Read: "Shadows and Sundials"

 Analytical Writing **Make Connections: Write About It**

Before reading, ask children to note that the genre of this text is expository text. Then discuss the Essential Question. After reading, ask children to make connections between the information they learned from "Shadows and Sundials" and *A Special Sunset.*

Leveled Reader

Focus On Literary Elements

Children can learn more about plot and sequence by completing the activity on page 20.

 Literature Circles

Lead children in conducting a literature circle using the Thinkmark questions to guide the discussion. You may wish to discuss what children have learned about what they can see in the sky from both selections in the Leveled Reader.

LEVEL UP

IF children read the Approaching Level fluently and answered the questions

THEN pair them with children who have proficiently read the On Level and have children

- echo-read the On Level main selection.
- identify the sequence of events with their partners.

A C T Access Complex Text

The On Level challenges children by including more **specific vocabulary** and **complex sentence structures**.

"A Shooting Star"
Lexile 350L

OBJECTIVES

Ask and answer such questions as *who, what, where, when, why,* and *how* to demonstrate understanding of key details in a text.

Recount stories, including fables and folktales from diverse cultures, and determine their central message, lesson, or moral.

Recount or describe key ideas or details from a text read aloud or information presented orally or through other media.

Read with sufficient accuracy and fluency to support comprehension.

Read on-level text orally with accuracy, appropriate rate, and expression on successive readings.

ACADEMIC LANGUAGE

• *problem, solution, timelines, compare*

• Cognates: *problema, solución*

Approaching Level

Genre Passage "A Shooting Star"

Build Background

• Read aloud the Essential Question: *What can we see in the sky?* Have children share their experiences of looking at the sky. Use the following sentence starters to help focus discussion.

> *In the daytime sky, I can see...*
> *In the nighttime sky, I can see...*

• Let children know that the online **Differentiated Genre Passage** "A Shooting Star" tells a story about a family who sees a shooting star on a camping trip.

Review Genre: Fiction

Review with children that a fiction story has made-up characters and events. A fiction story has a beginning, a middle, and an end, which is the story's sequence. Sometimes the narrator is *not* a character in the story, so the story is told in the third person. Fiction may also have dialogue, or words that the characters say.

Close Reading

Note Taking As children read the passage the first time, ask them to annotate the text. Have them note key ideas and details, unfamiliar words, and questions they have. Then have them read the passage again and use the following questions. Encourage children to cite text evidence from the selection.

Read

Genre: Fiction Read paragraphs 1-4 on page A1. *What details from the text tell you that this is fiction?* (There are made-up characters and a setting. There is also dialogue.) *Who are the characters?* (Carla, Rosa, and their parents)

Point of View *Is the narrator one of the characters?* (No.) *How do you know?* (The narrator uses the characters' names and pronouns such as "they" to talk about them.) *What is this point of view called?* (third person)

Compound Words Read paragraph 1 on page A1. *What compound words can you find?* (afternoon; anywhere) *What two smaller words make up the word afternoon?* (after and noon) *How do these words help you understand what the word afternoon means?* (*After* means "later than" and *noon* means "12:00 in the day," so *afternoon* means "after, or later than, 12:00 in the day.")

Sequence *What happens in the beginning of the story?* (Carla's family arrives at a campsite.) *In the middle?* (The family sees a shooting star. Carla and Rosa make wishes.) *At the end?* (Mama explains what a shooting star really is.) **Read the first paragraph of A2.** *What word helps you understand the sequence, or order, of events?* (Then)

Dialogue Read the fifth paragraph of A2. *What does Mama say to Rosa and Carla?* ("That's not really a star. It's just dust flying close to Earth. The dust glows so it looks like a star.")

 Summarize Have children use their notes to summarize what happens in the beginning, middle, and end of the story.

Reread

Use the questions on page A3 to guide children's rereading of the passage.

Genre: Fiction How do you know "A Shooting Star" is fiction? (The story's characters and events are made up.)

Point of View Reread the first three paragraphs on page A2. How do you know this story is written in the third person? (The narrator uses the words *Carla's family, Carla and her sister Rosa, They,* and *Mama* to tell the story.)

Dialogue Reread the fifth paragraph on page A2. What is the purpose of Mama's dialogue? (Mama tells Rosa and Carla what a shooting star really is.)

Integrate

 Make Connections Guide children to understand the connections between "A Shooting Star" and other selections they have read. Tell them to work with a partner to find text evidence and respond to this question: *What do the authors help you learn about the sky?*

Compare Genres Draw or use a Compare and Contrast chart. Help children show what they learned about the daytime and nighttime sky. Have them use information from the selections in the genre study.

Differentiate and Collaborate

Be Inspired Have children think about "A Shooting Star" and other selections they read. Ask: *"What do the texts inspire you to do?"* Use the following activities or have partners think of a way to respond to the texts.

Draw a Picture Have children draw a picture showing what they see in the day sky on one side and in the night sky on the other side. Have them write a sentence about their drawings.

Write a Journal Entry Have children observe the night sky and draw and write about what they see in a journal entry.

Readers to Writers

Dialogue Explain that authors can use dialogue in fiction stories to help readers understand more about the characters. Reread paragraph 5 on page A2. *Why does the author include this dialogue? What does the author want to show about Mama?*

 **LEVEL UP**

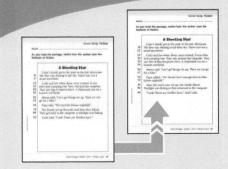

IF students read the Approaching Level fluently and answered the questions,

THEN pair them with students who have proficiently read the On Level. Have them

- partner-read the On Level passage.
- summarize what happens in the beginning, middle, and end of the story.

Approaching Level

Vocabulary

REVIEW VOCABULARY WORDS

TIER 2

OBJECTIVES
Determine or clarify the meaning of unknown and multiple-meaning words and phrases based on *grade 2 reading and content*, choosing <u>flexibly</u> from an array of strategies.

Use sentence-level context as a clue to the meaning of a word or phrase.

I Do Display each **Visual Vocabulary Card** from this genre study and state the word. Explain how the photograph illustrates the word. State the example sentence and repeat the word.

We Do Point to the word on the card and read the word with children. Ask them to repeat the word. Engage children in structured partner talk about the image as prompted on the back of the vocabulary card.

You Do Display each visual in random order, hiding the word. Have children match the definitions and context sentences of the word to the visuals displayed.

CUMULATIVE VOCABULARY REVIEW

TIER 2

OBJECTIVES
Determine or clarify the meaning of unknown and multiple-meaning words and phrases based on *grade 2 reading and content*, choosing <u>flexibly</u> from an array of strategies.

Use sentence-level context as a clue to the meaning of a word or phrase.

I Do Use the **Visual Vocabulary Cards** from the previous genre study to review previously taught vocabulary. Display one card at a time. Read the definition and example sentence and repeat the word.

We Do Point to the word and read with children. Read the question on the back of the card or make up a new question. Ask children to answer the question using the vocabulary word. If a response is an incomplete sentence, restate using a complete sentence.

You Do Engage children in structured partner talk using a Partner Talk prompt from the back of the card.

IDENTIFY RELATED WORDS

OBJECTIVES

Determine or clarify the meaning of unknown and multiple-meaning words and phrases based on *grade 2 reading and content,* choosing flexibly from an array of strategies.

Use sentence-level context as a clue to the meaning of a word or phrase.

I Do Display the *grumbled* **Visual Vocabulary Card** and say aloud the word set *grumbled, shouted,* and *complained.*

Point out that *complained* means almost the same thing as *grumbled.*

We Do Display the vocabulary card for *dreamed.* Say aloud the word set *dreamed, slept, imagined.* With students, identify the word that has almost the same meaning as *dreamed* and discuss why.

You Do Have students work in pairs to choose the word that means almost the same as the first word in the group.

delighted, happy, angry
enjoyed, loved, watched
adventure, lesson, trip

Have children choose words from their writer's notebook and use an online thesaurus to find synonyms and a dictionary to check their pronunciation.

COMPOUND WORDS

OBJECTIVES

Determine or clarify the meaning of unknown and multiple-meaning words and phrases based on *grade 2 reading and content,* choosing <u>flexibly</u> from an array of strategies.

Use sentence-level context as a clue to the meaning of a word or phrase.

I Do **Model** Remind children that a compound word is made up of two smaller words. Ask children to listen for a compound word as you read aloud the first paragraph of "A Shooting Star" in the Approaching Level online **Differentiated Genre Passage,** page A1.

Think Aloud I see the word *afternoon.* I can break this word into two smaller words: *after* and *noon.* This lets me know that the word is a compound word.

We Do Have children read the second paragraph and identify the compound words. Children should name the smaller words that make up each compound word. (camp/site; ever/green; over/head)

You Do Have children work in pairs to identify other compound words on page A1 and name the smaller words that make up each compound word. (paragraph 4: night/fall; paragraph 5: camp/site, day/light; paragraph 6: fire/flies)

Approaching Level

Fluency/Comprehension

FLUENCY

OBJECTIVES

Read with sufficient accuracy and fluency to support comprehension.

Read on-level text orally with accuracy, appropriate rate, and expression on successive readings.

I Do Read page A1 of "A Shooting Star" in the Approaching Level online **Differentiated Genre Passage**. Model reading with appropriate intonation. Point out how you change your voice to show excitement when you see an exclamation mark.

We Do Read the first three paragraphs on page A2 and have children repeat each sentence after you. Point out how you change your voice when you see a question mark.

You Do Have children read the rest of the selection aloud. Remind them to read with appropriate intonation.

IDENTIFY PLOT: SEQUENCE

OBJECTIVES

Recount stories, including fables and folktales from diverse cultures, and determine their central message, lesson, or moral.

Describe how characters in a story respond to major events and challenges.

Use information gained from the illustrations and words in a print or digital text to demonstrate understanding of its characters, setting, or plot.

I Do Remind children that fiction stories have a plot. Say: *The plot is the key events that happen in the beginning, the middle, and end of the story. Identifying the key events can help you better understand the story.*

We Do Read page A1 of "A Shooting Star" in the Approaching Level online **Differentiated Genre Passage**. Pause to help children identify important events. *Carla's family gets to the park in the late afternoon and sets up the tents. The family goes on a hike and returns as daylight is ending.*

You Do Guide children to read the rest of the selection. Prompt them to identify the important events that happen in the middle and at the end of the story.

REVIEW PLOT: SEQUENCE

OBJECTIVES

Describe how characters in a story respond to major events and challenges.

Use information gained from the illustrations and words in a print or digital text to demonstrate understanding of its characters, setting, or plot.

I Do Remind children that fiction stories have a plot, which is the events in the story. Say: *The events happen in a certain order, called the sequence. You can use signal words such as* first, next, then, *and* last *to describe the order in which events happen.*

We Do Read page A1 of "A Shooting Star" together in the Approaching Level online **Differentiated Genre Passage**. Pause to discuss the sequence of events. Say: *At the beginnning of the story, Carla's family gets to the park and sets things up. Then the family goes on a hike and returns to the campsite.* Have children record what happens first and next on a copy of online Sequence **Graphic Organizer 2**.

You Do Read paragraphs 1–4 on page A2. Ask: *Then what happens?* (They see a shooting star and make a wish.) Have children record the events on the graphic organizer. Then guide children to identify the last event. record it. (Mama explains what a shooting star really is.)

SELF-SELECTED READING

OBJECTIVES

Read with sufficient accuracy and fluency to support comprehension.

Read on-level text with purpose and understanding.

Read Independently

Have children choose a fiction book for sustained silent reading and set a purpose for reading that book. Children can check the online **Leveled Reader Database** for selections. Remind them that:

- they should identify the characters, the setting, and the events.
- the sequence is what happens in the beginning, middle, and end.
- they can reread to understand details about characters and events that didn't make sense the first time.

Read Purposefully

As they read independently, have children record the sequence of events described in their books on a copy of online Sequence **Graphic Organizer 2**. After they finish reading, they can conduct a Book Talk about what they read.

- Children should share the information they recorded on their graphic organizer.
- They should also tell what they enjoyed most about the selection.
- They should share what they reread and how it helped them understand the story.

Offer assistance and guidance with self-selected assignments.

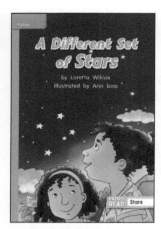

Lexile 390L

OBJECTIVES

Recount stories, including fables and folktales from diverse cultures, and determine their central message, lesson, or moral.

Recount or describe key ideas or details from a text read aloud or information presented orally or through other media.

ACADEMIC LANGUAGE

• *fiction, characters, setting, plot, sequence*

• Cognates: *secuencia, ficción*

On Level

Leveled Reader *A Different Set of Stars*

Preview and Predict

• Have children read the Essential Question: *What can we see in the sky?*

• Next, have them preview the title, table of contents, and illustrations for *A Different Set of Stars* to make a prediction about the selection. Have children discuss their predictions.

Review Genre: Fiction

Have children recall that fiction has made-up characters and events. A fiction story has a beginning, a middle, and an end, which is the story's sequence. Fiction may have dialogue, or words that the characters say.

Close Reading

Note Taking: Ask students to use a copy of the online Sequence **Graphic Organizer 2** as they read to record the main events of the story. Point out the labels in the graphic organizer: First, **Next**, **Then**, **Last**.

Pages 2–5 *Turn to a partner and discuss details you did not understand the first time you read these pages. Which part can you reread to help you?* (Possible response: I didn't understand what I learned about Anita and Isabel. I can reread on page 3 that the girls are twins, but Isabel is three minutes older than Anita and enjoys bossing her around.) *What compound word is on page 2?* (suitcase) Have children write the word in their writer's notebook.

Pages 6–8 *What is the sequence of events in Chapter 2?* (The family arrives at the jungle lodge. Then Mom looks for birds to photograph. Next, the family joins guests on the porch to watch the sunset and drink smoothies. Then Anita falls asleep and dreams of Muffin. Finally, the family goes to their room to get ready for dinner.)

Pages 9–10 *When does Chapter 3 take place?* (at night, after dinner) *What problem does Anita grumble about at the end of the chapter?* (She can't find the Big Dipper.)

Pages 11–15 *What can you reread if you want to know why Anita can't find the Big Dipper?* (I can reread pages 11, 12, and 13.) *Why does the mother compare the Earth to an orange?* (to help the girls understand why they see a different set of stars in Brazil.) *Why does Anita feel happy and excited at the end of the story?* (because she is learning new things)

Retell Have children take turns retelling the selection using the retelling cards. Help children make a personal connection by asking: *What do you see in the night sky? How is it different from what Anita sees?*

Respond to Reading Revisit the Essential Question and ask children to complete the Text Evidence questions on page 16.

 Write About Reading In children's responses to question 4 on page 16, check that they wrote about what they think will happen next on the family's trip.

Fluency: Intonation

Model Model reading page 3 with appropriate intonation. Point out how you raise your voice at the end of a question. Read the page aloud again and have children read along with you.

Apply Have children practice reading the page with a partner.

Paired Read: "Stars"

Leveled Reader

Analytical Writing **Make Connections: Write About It**

Before reading, ask children to note that the genre of this text is expository text. Then discuss the Essential Question. After reading, ask children to make connections between what they read in "Stars" and *A Different Set of Stars*.

Focus On Literary Elements

Children can learn more about the sequence of events in a story by completing page 20.

Literature Circles

Lead children in conducting a literature circle using the Thinkmark questions to guide the discussion. You may wish to discuss what children have learned about what they can see in the sky from both selections in the Leveled Reader.

LEVEL UP

IF children read the On Level fluently and answered the questions

THEN pair them with children who have proficiently read the Beyond Level and have children

- partner-read the Beyond Level main selection.
- list the sequence of events and discuss the plot with their partners.

Access Complex Text

The Beyond Level challenges children by including more **specific vocabulary** and **complex sentence structures**.

"A Shooting Star"
Lexile 440L

OBJECTIVES

Ask and answer such questions as *who, what, where, when, why,* and *how* to demonstrate understanding of key details in a text.

Recount stories, including fables and folktales from diverse cultures, and determine their central message, lesson, or moral.

Recount or describe key ideas or details from a text read aloud or information presented orally or through other media.

Read with sufficient accuracy and fluency to support comprehension.

Read on-level text orally with accuracy, appropriate rate, and expression on successive readings.

ACADEMIC LANGUAGE

• *dialogue, fiction, third person*
• Cognates: *diálogo, ficción*

On Level

Genre Passage *"A Shooting Star"*

Build Background

- Read the Essential Question: *What can we see in the sky?* Have children share their experiences of looking at the sky. Use the following sentence starters to help focus discussion.

  In the daytime sky, I can see...

  In the nighttime sky, I can see...

- Let children know that the online **Differentiated Genre Passage** "A Shooting Star" tells a story about a family who sees a shooting star on a camping trip.

Review Genre: Fiction

Review with children that a fiction story has made-up characters and events. A fiction story has a beginning, a middle, and an end, which is the story's sequence. Sometimes the narrator is *not* a character in the story, so the story is told in the third person. Fiction may also have dialogue, or words that the characters say.

Close Reading

Note Taking As children read the passage for the first time, ask them to annotate the text. Have them note key ideas and details, unfamiliar words, and questions they have. Then have children read the passage again and use the following questions. Encourage children to cite text evidence from the selection.

> **Read**

Genre: Fiction Read paragraphs 1-4 on page O1. *What details from the text tell you that this is fiction?* (There are made-up characters and a setting. There is also dialogue.) *Who are the characters?* (members of a family) *Where are they and what are they doing?* (They are setting up at a campsite.)

Point of View *Is the narrator a character in the story?* (No.) *How do you know?* (The narrator uses characters' names and pronouns such as "they" to talk about them.) *What is this point of view called?* (third person)

Compound Words Look at the first two paragraphs on page O1. *What compound words can you find? What two smaller words make up each word?* (after/noon; any/where; camp/site; ever/green; over/head) *How do the words* ever *and* green *help you understand the meaning of evergreen?* (Ever means "always." Ever and green help me understand that evergreen means "always green." The trees are always green.)

Dialogue *What does Mama tell Carla and Rosa on page O2?* (Mama tells Carla and Rosa that what they see in the sky is not really a shooting star.)

Sequence *What happens in the beginning, middle, and end of the story?* (The family arrives at a campsite and gets set up; they go hiking and return; they see a shooting star and make wishes; Mama explains what a shooting star really is.) *What sequence words do you notice?* (then, after, just then)

 Summarize Have children use their notes to summarize what happens in the beginning, middle, and end of the story.

Reread

Use the questions on page O3 to guide children's rereading of the passage.

Genre: Fiction How do you know "A Shooting Star" is fiction? (The story has characters and events that are made-up. The characters talk to each other.)

Point of View Reread the first three paragraphs on page O1. How do you know this story is written in the third person? (The narrator uses the words *Carla's family, Carla and her sister Rosa, They,* and *Mama* to tell the story.)

Dialogue Reread the fifth paragraph on page O2. What is the purpose of Mama's dialogue? (Mama explains what a shooting star really is. She tells Carla and Rosa.)

Integrate

 Make Connections Guide children to understand the connections between "A Shooting Star" and the other selections they read. Tell them to work with a partner to find text evidence and respond to this question: *What do the authors help you learn about the sky?*

Compare Genres Draw or use a Compare and Contrast chart. Help children show what they learned about the daytime and nighttime sky. Have them use information from each selection in the genre study.

Differentiate and Collaborate

Be Inspired Have children think about "A Shooting Star" and other selections they read. Ask: *"What do the texts inspire you to do?"* Use the following activities or have partners think of a way to respond to the texts.

Create a Diorama Have children create a diorama about what they see in the sky. They can split the diorama in two so that one side shows the daytime sky and one side shows the nighttime sky.

Create a Collage Have children create a collage showing either the daytime or nighttime sky. Children can use colored paper, magazine pictures, stickers, or other materials to show elements such as the Sun, clouds, the Moon, stars, and so on.

Readers to Writers

Dialogue Explain that authors can use dialogue in fiction stories to help readers understand more about the characters. Reread paragraph 5 on page O2. *Why does the author include this dialogue? What does the author want to show about Mama?*

LEVEL UP

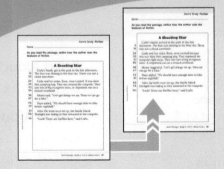

IF students read the On Level fluently and answered the questions,

THEN pair them with students who have proficiently read the Beyond Level. Have them

- partner-read the Beyond Level passage.

- summarize what happens in the beginning, middle, and end of the story.

On Level

Vocabulary

REVIEW VOCABULARY WORDS

OBJECTIVES
Determine or clarify the meaning of unknown and multiple-meaning words and phrases based on *grade 2 reading and content,* choosing <u>flexibly</u> from an array of strategies.

Use sentence-level context as a clue to the meaning of a word or phrase.

I Do Use the **Visual Vocabulary Cards** to review the key selection words *adventure, delighted, dreamed, enjoyed, grumbled, moonlight, neighbor,* and *nighttime.* Point to each word, read it aloud, and have children chorally repeat it.

We Do Ask these questions and help children record and explain their answers.
- What is one funny thing you have *dreamed* about at night?
- When can you see *moonlight*?
- What is something that makes you *grumble*?
- What is one event that you have *enjoyed*?

You Do Have children work in pairs to respond to these questions and explain their answers.
- What can you see in the *nighttime* sky?
- Where do your *neighbors* live?
- Where would you like to go to have an *adventure*?
- When was a time you felt *delighted*?

Have children choose words from their writer's notebook and use an online thesaurus to find synonyms.

COMPOUND WORDS

OBJECTIVES
Determine or clarify the meaning of unknown and multiple-meaning words and phrases based on *grade 2 reading and content,* choosing <u>flexibly</u> from an array of strategies.

Use sentence-level context as a clue to the meaning of a word or phrase.

Read aloud the first paragraph of "A Shooting Star" in the On Level online **Differentiated Genre Passage,** page O1.

Think Aloud *I want to identify a compound word in the first paragraph. To identify a compound word, I am going to look for a word that is made up of two smaller words. I see the word* afternoon. *I can break this word into two smaller words,* after *and* noon. *This shows me that the word is a compound word.*

We Do Have children read the second paragraph and identify the compound words. Children should name the smaller words that make up each compound word. (camp/site; ever/green; over/head)

You Do Have children work in pairs to identify other compound words on page O1 and name the smaller words that make up each word. (paragraph 4: night/fall; paragraph 5: camp/site; paragraph 6: fire/flies)

Comprehension

REVIEW PLOT: SEQUENCE

OBJECTIVES

Describe how characters in a story respond to major events and challenges.

Use information gained from the illustrations and words in a print or digital text to demonstrate understanding of its characters, setting, or plot.

I Do Remind children that fiction has characters, setting, and a plot. The plot is the sequence of events. *When we read fiction, we pay attention to what happens at the beginning, in the middle, and at the end. We identify the sequence, or order, of events.*

We Do Read aloud the first four paragraphs of "A Shooting Star" in the On Level online **Differentiated Genre Passages**, page O1. Help children identify the characters, setting, and what happens at the beginning of the story.

You Do Guide children to read the rest of the story. Remind them to identify what happens at the beginning, in the middle, and at the end of the story. Have children record the events on a copy of online Sequence **Graphic Organizer 2**.

SELF-SELECTED READING

OBJECTIVES

Read with sufficient accuracy and fluency to support comprehension.

Read on-level text with purpose and understanding.

Read Independently

Have children choose a fiction book for sustained silent reading. They can check the online **Leveled Reader Database** for selections. Before they read, they should consider their purpose for reading.

- Have children identify what characters do at the beginning, in the middle, and at the end of the story.
- Remind children to reread to understand difficult sections.

Read Purposefully

Encourage children to read different books to learn about a variety of characters, settings, and events.

As children read, have them record events on a copy of online Sequence **Graphic Organizer 2**.

- Have children share the information they recorded.
- Encourage them to tell what event they enjoyed reading the most.
- Have children share what they reread and how it helped them.

 You may want to include **ELL** students in On Level vocabulary and comprehension lessons. Offer language support as needed.

Lexile 540

OBJECTIVES

Recount stories, including fables and folktales from diverse cultures, and determine their central message, lesson, or moral.

Recount or describe key ideas or details from a text read aloud or information presented orally or through other media.

ACADEMIC LANGUAGE

- *compound word, fiction, intonation, prediction, sequence*
- Cognates: *entonación, ficción, predicción*

Beyond Level

Leveled Reader *Shadows in the Sky*

Preview and Predict

- Have children read the Essential Question: *What can we see in the sky?*
- Then have them read the title and preview the pages and the illustrations in order to make a prediction about *Shadows in the Sky*.

Review Genre: Fiction

Have children recall that fiction has characters and events that are made up. It also has a beginning, a middle, and an end. Fiction can also have dialogue, or the words characters say. Tell children to look for these things as they read *Shadows in the Sky*.

Close Reading

Note Taking: Ask students to use a copy of the online Sequence **Graphic Organizer 2** as they read to record details that will help them summarize the story.

Pages 2–6 *Turn to a partner and discuss Jamal and Malik's friendship. Reread Chapter 1 to help you remember specific details.* (Possible response: Jamal and Malik are neighbors, best friends, and classmates. Malik doesn't like waiting for Jamal because he likes to be first. Their teacher doesn't want them to have too much fun on this trip because they got into trouble on a class trip to the zoo.) *What compound word is on page 5?* (zookeeper) *What two smaller words make up this larger word?* (*zoo* and *keeper*)

Pages 7–11 *What are some clue words and phrases that tell you about the sequence of events in Chapter 2?* (finally, soon, then, began, once in a while, continued, during, can lead to)

Pages 12–13 *What words on page 12 tell you that this story is written in a third-person point of view?* (he, they) *What compound word is on page 12?* (outside) *What two smaller words make up the compound word?* (out and side) *What happens after Malik wakes up?* (The boys follow Mr. Washington outside to sit on benches and eat lunch.)

Pages 14–15 *What can you reread if you want to remember what happens during an eclipse?* (I can reread pages 9 through 11.) *Why does the picture on page 14 show the shadow of Malik's hand?* (It illustrates what he says to Jamal about eclipsing the leaf.)

Retell Have children take turns retelling the selection. Help children make a personal connection by writing about something interesting they have seen in the sky. Say: *Write about a time when you saw something interesting in the sky. What was it? How did you learn more about it?*

Respond to Reading Revisit the Essential Question and ask children to complete the Text Evidence questions on page 16.

 Write About Reading In children's responses to question 4 on page 16, check that they have written about what happened to the boys and have made logical predictions about what might happen next in the story.

Fluency: Intonation

Model Model reading pages 3-4 with appropriate intonation. Point out how you raise your voice at the end of a question. Read the page aloud again and have children read along with you.

Apply Have children practice reading the pages with a partner.

Paired Read: "Eclipses"

 Make Connections: Write About It

Before reading "Eclipses," have children preview the title page and prompt them to identify the genre. Then discuss the Compare Texts statement. After reading, discuss the Essential Question. Have partners discuss the information they learned from "Eclipses" and *Shadows in the Sky*. Ask children to make connections by  comparing and contrasting the eclipses described in each selection. Prompt children to discuss what they learned about eclipses.

Leveled Reader

Focus On Literary Elements

Children can learn more about plot and the sequence of events in a story by completing the activities on page 20.

A Shooting Star
Lexile 540L

OBJECTIVES

Ask and answer such questions as *who, what, where, when, why,* and *how* to demonstrate understanding of key details in a text.

Recount stories, including fables and folktales from diverse cultures, and determine their central message, lesson, or moral.

Recount or describe key ideas or details from a text read aloud or information presented orally or through other media.

Read with sufficient accuracy and fluency to support comprehension.

Read on-level text orally with accuracy, appropriate rate, and expression on successive readings.

ACADEMIC LANGUAGE

• *dialogue, fiction, third person*
• Cognates: *diálogo, ficción*

Beyond Level

Genre Passage "A Shooting Star"

Build Background

• Read the Essential Question: *What can we see in the sky?* Ask partners to share their experiences looking at the sky. Use the following sentence starters to help focus discussion.

> *One thing I can see in the daytime sky is...*
>
> *One thing I can see in the nighttime sky is...*

• Let children know that the online **Differentiated Genre Passage** "A Shooting Star" tells a story about a family who sees a shooting star on a camping trip.

Review Genre: Fiction

Review with children that a fiction story has made-up characters and events. A fiction story has a beginning, a middle, and an end, which is the story's sequence. Sometimes the narrator is *not* a character in the story, so the story is told in the third person. Fiction may also have dialogue, or words that the characters say.

Close Reading

Note Taking As children read the passage the first time, ask them to annotate the text. Have them note key ideas and details, unfamiliar words, and questions they have. Then have children read again and use the following questions. Encourage children to cite text evidence from the selection.

> **Read**

Genre: Fiction Reread paragraphs 1–4 on page B1. *What details from the text tell you that this is fiction?* (There are made-up characters and a setting. There is also dialogue.) *Who are the characters?* (members of a family) *What details tell you where the story takes place?* (park; campsite; evergreen trees)

Point of View *Is the narrator a character in the story?* (No.) *Which pronoun helps you know that this story is told in the third person?* (they)

Compound Words *Look at the first four paragraphs on page B1. What compound words can you find?* (afternoon; anywhere; campsite; evergreen; overhead; nightfall) *How do the two smaller words in each compound word help you understand the meaning of these words?* (If I know the meaning of each separate word, I can use that to understand the meaning of the compound word.)

Dialogue *What does Mama tell Carla and Rosa on page B2?* (Mama tells Carla and Rosa that what they see in the sky is not really a shooting star.)

Sequence *What happens in the beginning, middle, and end of the story?* (The family arrives at a campsite and gets set up; they go hiking and return; they see a shooting star and make wishes; Mama explains what a shooting star really is.) *What sequence words do you notice?* (then, after, just then)

 Summarize Have children use their notes to summarize what happens in the beginning, middle, and end of the story.

Reread

Use the questions on page B3 to guide children's rereading of the passage.

Genre: Fiction How do you know "A Shooting Star" is fiction? (The story has made-up characters and events. The characters talk to each other.)

Point of View Reread the first three paragraphs on page B1. How do you know this story is written in the third-person point of view? (The narrator tells the story using the words *Carla's family, Carla and her sister Rosa, they,* and *Mama.*)

Dialogue Reread the fifth paragraph on page B2. What is the purpose of Mama's dialogue? (Mama explains what a shooting star really is. She tells Carla and Rosa.)

Integrate

 Make Connections Guide children to understand the connections between "A Shooting Star" and the other selections they read. Tell them to work with a partner to find text evidence and respond to this question: *What do the authors help you learn about the sky?*

Compare Genres Draw or use a Compare and Contrast chart. Have children show what they learned about the daytime and nighttime sky. Have them use information from each selection in the genre study.

Differentiate and Collaborate

 Be Inspired Have children think about "A Shooting Star" and other selections they read. Ask: *What do the texts inspire you to do?* Use the following activities or have partners think of a way to respond to the texts.

Record a Podcast Have children summarize what they've learned about the night sky from the readings and then record the information in a podcast for others to learn from. They can conduct additional research if they choose.

Write a Poem Have children write and illustrate a poem about what they see in the day or night sky.

Readers to Writers

Dialogue Explain that authors can use dialogue in fiction stories to help readers understand more about the characters. Reread paragraph 5 on page B2. *Why does the author include this dialogue? What does the author want to show about Mama?*

Gifted and Talented

Independent Study Have children write the story "A Shooting Star" in a different genre. Have them report about the events in an informational text, such as a newspaper article. Or have them create a comic book version of the story with illustrations and speech bubbles. Allow students to choose the format they prefer.

Beyond Level

Vocabulary

REVIEW DOMAIN-SPECIFIC WORDS

OBJECTIVES

Demonstrate understanding of word relationships and nuances in word meanings.

Use words and phrases acquired through conversations, reading and being read to, and responding to texts.

Model Use the **Visual Vocabulary Cards** to review the meaning of the words *nighttime* and *moonlight.* Write science-related sentences on the board using the words.

Write the words *adventure, delighted,* and *grumbled* on the board and discuss the meanings with children. Have children write a sentence with each word and share with the group.

Apply Have children work in pairs to review the meanings of the following words from this week's selections: *starry, telescope,* and *shooting star.* Then have partners write sentences using the words.

COMPOUND WORDS

OBJECTIVES

Determine or clarify the meaning of unknown and multiple-meaning words and phrases based on *grade 2 reading and content,* choosing <u>flexibly</u> from an array of strategies.

Use sentence-level context as a clue to the meaning of a word or phrase.

Model Read aloud the first paragraph of "A Shooting Star" in the Beyond Level online **Differentiated Genre Passages**, page B1.

Think Aloud When I read this paragraph, I don't know the meaning of the compound word *afternoon.* I'll think about the meanings of the smaller words *after* and *noon.* Now I understand. *Afternoon* means "the time of day after noon."

With children, read the second, third, and fourth paragraphs. Help them figure out the meaning of *campsite, overhead,* and *nightfall.*

Apply Have pairs of children read the rest of the passage. Ask them to break down compound words to determine the meaning of the following words: *daylight; fireflies; everyone.*

Shades of Meaning Using their understanding of compound words, have partners write an explanation of *evergreen.* Encourage them to use artwork to depict the compound word.

Have children repeat the activity by finding compound words in their writer's notebook. Have them write an explanation of the words and illustrate them.

Comprehension

REVIEW PLOT: SEQUENCE

OBJECTIVES

Describe how characters in a story respond to major events and challenges.

Use information gained from the illustrations and words in a print or digital text to demonstrate understanding of its characters, setting, or plot.

Model Remind children that stories have characters, settings, and plots. Explain that the characters are who or what the story is about. The setting is where and when the story takes place. The plot is the action or the events in a story. Point out that the plot follows a sequence, which includes a beginning, a middle, and an end. The beginning introduces the events or problem of the story, while the end concludes the events or problem.

Have children read the first paragraph of "A Shooting Star" in the Beyond Level online **Differentiated Genre Passages,** page B1. Ask open-ended questions to facilitate discussion, such as: *What happens first in the story? What event happens next?* Children should support their responses with details from the text.

Apply Have children identify important events as they complete a copy of the online Sequence **Graphic Organizer 2.** Then have partners use their work to retell the selection.

SELF-SELECTED READING

OBJECTIVES

Read with sufficient accuracy and fluency to support comprehension.

Read on-level text with purpose and understanding.

Read Independently

Have children choose a fiction book for sustained silent reading. Children can check the online **Leveled Reader Database** for selections. As they choose, they should consider their purpose for reading.

- Have children record the sequence of events in their books on a copy of the online Sequence **Graphic Organizer 2.**
- Remind children to reread difficult sections of the text.

Read Purposefully

Encourage children to keep a reading journal. Ask them to read different books in order to learn about a variety of characters, settings, and plots.

- Ask children to share their reactions to the books with classmates.

 Independent Study Challenge children to discuss how their books relate to the weekly theme of what we can see in the sky. Have children compare the different objects in the daytime and nighttime sky.

Reading/ Writing Companion

Scaffolded Shared Read

OBJECTIVES

Determine or clarify the meaning of unknown and multiple-meaning words and phrases based on *grade 2 reading and content,* choosing <u>flexibly</u> from an array of strategies.

Use sentence-level context as a clue to the meaning of a word or phrase.

Read with sufficient accuracy and fluency to support comprehension.

Read on-level text with purpose and understanding.

Use context to confirm or self-correct word recognition and understanding, rereading as necessary.

Ask and answer such questions as *who, what, where, when, why,* and *how* to demonstrate understanding of key details in a text.

LANGUAGE OBJECTIVES

Children will use visual and contextual supports to read text and show comprehension through basic reading skills.

ACADEMIC LANGUAGE

• *define, predict*
• Cognates: *definir*

Digital Tools

🎧 Have children listen to the selection to develop comprehension and practice fluency and pronunciation.

English Language Learners

"Starry Night"

Plan Your ELL Small Group Instruction for the Shared Read		
Beginning	**Intermediate**	**Advanced/Advanced High**
Use the online **Scaffolded Shared Read** to focus on comprehension of a sheltered version of "Starry Night." Then have all ELL levels participate together in the activities on pages T310–T311.	Use pages T308–T309 to support student comprehension of the on-level text, reinforce skills and strategies, and develop oral language. Then have all ELL levels participate in the activities on pages T310–T311.	Use pages T308–T309 to support student comprehension of the on-level text, reinforce skills and strategies, and develop oral language. Then have all ELL levels participate in the activities on pages T310–T311.

Prepare to Read

Build Background Use pictures of the sun and moon to reinforce the concepts of day and night. Invite children to name things they see in the sky during the day and during the night. Provide translation and other linguistic support, as needed.

Vocabulary Use the **Visual Vocabulary Cards** to review the vocabulary: *adventure, delighted, dreamed, enjoy, grumbled, moonlight, neighbor, nighttime.* Use the online **Visual Vocabulary Cards** to teach ELL Vocabulary from the Shared Read: *complained, crescent, form, hope, poked, spotted.*

Set Purpose *As we read "Starry Night," think about the Essential Question: What can we see in the sky?*

Interactive Question-Response Routine

After each paragraph, ask questions that help children understand the meaning of the text. Explain difficult or unfamiliar concepts and words. Provide sentence starters for **Intermediate** ELLs. Have **Advanced/Advanced High** ELLs retell the information. Reinforce the meaning of new vocabulary. Ask children questions that require them to use the vocabulary. Reinforce weekly skills and strategies through modeling and questions. Use the images to aid children's comprehension.

Page 38

What is the title? ("Starry Night") *What does the word* starry *describe?* (the night sky) *What is a "starry night"?* (a night when there are many stars in the sky)

Page 39

Paragraphs 1–3 *What does Mr. Cortes ask the class to do for homework?* (Look at the nighttime sky, tell what they see.) *What does the word* nighttime *mean?* (during the night, after dark)

Intermediate *How do the children show how they feel about their homework?* The children grumble because they are unhappy. *What words in the story describe Josie and Ling?* Josie and Ling are friends and neighbors. *What words on the page help you understand what* neighbors *means?* (*lived nearby*)

Advanced *Which phrase tells when Mr. Cortes gives the class their homework.* ("As the class was leaving")

Advanced High *When the author writes "They were going to sleep in a tent....", she is using the "future in the past" verb tense.* With a partner, discuss why the author used the future in the past to discuss their plans for the evening. (The story is written in the past, but the sentence tells about what is going to happen at a point in the future.)

Page 40

Paragraph 1 *What two words make up the word* outdoors? (*out* and *doors*) *What does the word* outdoors *mean?* (a place that is not inside) *How do the girls feel about sleeping outdoors?* (They are delighted.) *What word helps you define* delighted? (*happy*)

Intermediate Encourage children to find a new **compound word** on the page. (*flashlights*) *How do we use flashlights?* Flashlights help us see in the dark.

Advanced/Advanced High *With a partner, names some other times people might use a flashlight.* (Answers will vary.)

Paragraph 2 *What happens first in this paragraph?* (Josie's dad poked his head into the tent) *What word tells what the girls do when it's time for homework?* (*complained*)

Intermediate *Why do the girls complain?* The girls complain because they don't want to do homework.

Page 41

Paragraphs 1–3 *What happened when Josie looked at the sky?* (She spotted a crescent moon.) *Look at the picture. What does the word* crescent *describe about the moon?* (its shape)

Intermediate *Which word is made up of two words that describe the moon's light?* The compound word moonlight is made up of the words moon and light.

Page 42

Paragraph 1 *How does Josie feel when she looks at the stars?* (Possible: excited; happy) *Which word helps you define the word* dreamed? (*imagined*)

Intermediate *Reread the paragraph. What does the telescope do?* The telescope lets people see things that are very far away.

Paragraphs 2–4 *What happens next in the story?* (Ling sees a shooting star.) *What does a shooting star look like?* (a bright light moving in the sky)

Intermediate *How do Ling's thoughts change?* At first, Ling complained about looking at the sky. Then, Ling enjoyed looking at the stars.

Advanced/Advanced High *What do you predict will happen next?* (The girls will like looking at the nighttime sky.)

Page 43

Paragraphs 1–4 What do Josie and Ling want to do next? (keep looking at the nighttime sky)

Intermediate *Which words show how Josie and Ling feel about their sleepover?* (*fun, adventure, exciting*)

Advanced/Advanced High How have the girls' plans for their sleepover changed since the beginning of the story? (At first, Josie and Ling wanted to play games in the tent. Now the girls want to spend more time looking at the nighttime sky.)

Have partners collaborate to practice **sequence**. Help them talk about important events using connecting words. For example, Dad set up the telescope before he poked his head in the tent. The girls wanted to keep looking after they saw a shooting star. Help partners use pictures in the text to help them recall events, if needed.

Reading/Writing Companion

OBJECTIVES

Ask and answer such questions as *who, what, where, when, why,* and *how* to demonstrate understanding of key details in a text.

Recount stories, including fables and folktales from diverse cultures, and determine their central message, lesson, or moral.

LANGUAGE OBJECTIVE

Children will retell text that is read aloud and analyze how an author uses sequence in a fiction story.

ACADEMIC LANGUAGE

• *sequence, summarize*
• Cognate: *secuencia*

DIFFERENTIATED READING

ELL Have Beginning and Early-Intermediate students use the **Scaffolded Shared Read** Glossary Activities during Vocabulary Building.

English Language Learners

"Starry Night"

 Text Reconstruction

Focus on a single chunk of text to support comprehension and language development across the four domains.

1. Read aloud paragraphs 2 and 3 on page 41 while children just listen.

2. Write the following on the board, providing definitions as needed: *points, bright, light, shapes, group, giant,* and *spoon.* Instruct children to listen for these words as you read the paragraph a second time.

3. Read the paragraphs a third time. Tell children to listen and take notes.

4. Have children work in pairs to reconstruct the text from their **COLLABORATE** notes. Help them write complete sentences as needed.

5. Have children look at the original text. Ask them to tell what the paragraphs are mostly about. (This part of the story is about Josie's dad teaching the girls how to see star shapes in the night sky.) Tell children they are going to look at how the author uses sequence to help readers understand the events in the story.

6. *What does Josie's dad teach the girls first?* (Josie's dad teaches the girls that points of bright light can form shapes in the night sky.) *What does Josie's dad show the girls next?* (Next, Josie's dad shows the girls the Big Dipper in the sky.) *What is the Big Dipper?* (The Big Dipper is a group of stars in the sky.) *What does Josie's dad tell the girls about the shape of the Big Dipper?* (It looks like a giant spoon.)

7. Have children compare their text reconstructions to the original text. Have them check if they included sequence words that tell the order of events in the paragraphs.

Beginning Have children follow along in the **Reading/Writing Companion** as you read the text aloud. Have them circle the words from Step 2 as they hear them.

Make Connections

Mixed Levels Combine children at different English proficiency levels to **COLLABORATE** discuss how "Starry Night" relates to the Essential Question, *What can we see in the sky?* and the Key Concept, *Look at the sky.* Beginning ELLs will base their answers on the **Scaffolded Shared Read.** Intermediate and Advanced/Advanced High students will base theirs on the **Reading/Writing Companion.**

Grammar in Context

Notice the Form Display sentences from the text. Underline the verbs.

> 1. The class <u>grumbled</u>.
> 2. Josie's dad <u>poked</u> his head inside the tent.
> 3. Josie <u>looked</u> up and <u>spotted</u> a crescent moon.

What do the underlined words have in common? (They are all past-tense verbs.)
Add them to a word wall. Include the past and future forms of each verb:
grumbled/ will grumble, poked/ will poke, looked/ will look.

Apply and Extend Have children write a paragraph about a time they looked at
the sky using past-tense verbs. Have partners trade papers and edit each other's
work to confirm verb tenses.

Independent Time

Vocabulary Building Have children build their glossaries by adding
words to a chart like the one below.

Beginning/Early Intermediate Have children also continue the Glossary Activities
in the **Scaffolded Share Read**.

Intermediate/Advanced/Advanced High After children add the vocabulary
from the **Reading/Writing Companion** pages 44–45 to the chart below, have
them scan the text for self-selected words they would like to learn and add to
the chart.

WORD/PHRASE	DEFINE	EXAMPLE	ASK
flashlight	tool to see in the dark	Josie uses a flashlight to see at night.	When do you use a flashlight?

Mixed Levels Combine children at different proficiency levels to teach each other
new vocabulary. Beginning and Early-Intermediate students will teach vocabulary
from their Scaffolded Shared Read glossaries. Intermediate and Advanced/
Advanced High students will teach their self-selected words.

Summarize the Story Have partners use the online **Shared Read Writing Frames**
to orally summarize "Starry Night" with a partner. Then have them use the writing
frame to write a summary of the story on a separate piece of paper.

OBJECTIVES

Demonstrate command of the
conventions of standard English
grammar and usage when writing
or speaking.

ACADEMIC LANGUAGE

- *abstract, concrete, noun*
- cognates: *abstracto, concreto*

Language Transfers Handbook
page 18 for Present and Future
Tense Verbs

Digital Tools

Use the additional grammar
resources and the vocabulary
activity.

Grammar Video

Grammar Song

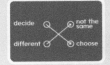
Vocabulary Activity

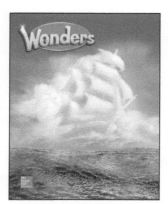

Literature Anthology

OBJECTIVES

Read with sufficient accuracy and fluency to support comprehension.

Use context to confirm or self-correct word recognition and understanding, rereading as necessary.

Use information gained from the illustrations and words in a print or digital text to demonstrate understanding of its characters, setting, or plot.

Recount stories, including fables and folktales from diverse cultures, and determine their central message, lesson, or moral.

LANGUAGE OBJECTIVE

Children will discuss author's craft and show comprehension through basic reading and inferential skills.

ACADEMIC LANGUAGE

• *inference, repetition, structure, summarize*
• Cognates: *estructura, repetición*

Digital Tools

🎧 Have children listen to the selection to develop comprehension and practice fluency and pronunciation.

English Language Learners

Mr. Putter & Tabby See the Stars

Reread

Before focusing on Making Inferences, Author's Craft, and Author's Purpose in *Mr. Putter & Tabby See the Stars*, support children's basic comprehension of the text.

• Provide a simple summary: Mr. Putter has a cat named Tabby. Mr. Putter and Tabby sleep in the same bed. But one night, Mr. Putter can't sleep. So, he and Tabby go for a walk and look at the nighttime sky.

• Use the **Visual Vocabulary Cards** to review vocabulary (*adventure, delighted, dreamed, enjoy, grumbled, moonlight, neighbor, nighttime*).

• Use the point-of-use Spotlight on Language tips on pages T205A–T205L to break down linguistic barriers to comprehension.

• Use the **Interactive Question-Response Routine** to help children access small chunks of text in the selection. (See page T308 for the complete routine.)

• Have **Advanced/Advanced High** ELLs work with native speakers to fill in a Sequence Graphic Organizer about the events of the story.

Pages 243–244, Make Inferences

Sometimes an author doesn't tell you everything about a character. Authors often include certain details to help you understand why a character says or does certain things. When you read fiction, you can make inferences about characters. An inference is an idea you get from reading details in the text.

Beginning *If you* lose track of time, *it means you forget what time it is. Sometimes you lose track of time when you're having fun. Why does Mr. Putter lose track of time while eating Mrs. Teaberry's jelly rolls?* He loses track of time because he is having <u>fun/a good time</u>.

Intermediate *Why does Mr. Putter eat so many of Mrs. Teaberry's jelly roles?* Mr. Putter thinks Mrs. Teaberry's jelly rolls taste <u>good/delicious</u>. *Does it make Mrs. Teaberry happy that Mr. Putter eats her jelly rolls?* (yes) *How do you know? Which sentence tells how Mrs. Teaberry feels about Mr. Putter eating the jelly rolls?* (Mrs. Teaberry was happy that Mr. Putter enjoyed her jelly rolls so much.)

Advanced/Advanced High *Talk with a partner about why Mrs. Teaberry likes to feed Mr. Putter.* (Mr. Putter likes the food Mrs. Teaberry cooks. This makes her happy.)

Pages 246–247, Author's Craft: Repetition

Authors often repeat a word or phrase to communicate an idea to readers. Repetition helps to teach us about a character, place, or event in a story.

 Beginning *With a partner, look for the word that appears several times on the page. Say the word aloud with your partner.* (she) *Who does this word refer to?* (Tabby)

Intermediate *Why does the author repeat the word she on this page?* The author repeats the word *she* to help me <u>notice</u> this part of the text.

Advanced/Advanced High *How does the author use the word she on this page to tell us about how Tabby feels about the night?* (The author repeats the word *she* to show Tabby's actions. She is happy. She loves the night.)

Pages 252–253, Author's Purpose

Authors explain what characters say and do to teach us more about those characters. Authors may use details to show how characters feel about one another, or to explain their relationships with others.

 Beginning *Find the word that is repeated on page 253.* (they) *Who does they refer to?* (Mr. Putter and Mrs. Teaberry) *With a partner, ask and answer:* What did they do? They <u>told stories in the moonlight</u>. *Do you tell stories with someone you like or someone you don't like?* (like) *Do you tell secrets to someone you like or someone you don't like?* (like) *Who makes you laugh? Someone you like, or someone you don't like?* (like)

 Intermediate *What do Mr. Putter and Mrs. Teaberry do together?* (sit on the lawn, talk to each other, tell stories, tell secrets, make each other laugh) *How does the author show that they are friends?* The author shows they are friends by <u>describing</u> what they do <u>together</u>.

 Advanced *Tell a partner how the author shows that Mr. Putter and Mrs. Teaberry are friends.* (The author shows they are friends by describing what they do together.)

 Advanced High *With a partner, write a conversation that Mr. Putter and Mrs. Teaberry might have on page 253.* (Answers will vary, but children should create short dialogues where the characters tell stories, tell secrets, or make each other laugh.)

Pages 254–255, Author's Craft: Text Structure

A good author ends a story in a way that makes sense to readers. The author of Mr. Putter & Tabby See the Stars *ends the story with a scene that is already familiar to readers.*

Beginning *Look at page 255. Which phrase tells you when this part of the story takes place?* (In the morning) *What does Mr. Putter hear?* (scratching at the door) *What made the scratching noise?* (Zeke) *What does Zeke's note say?* (Are you hungry?) *I think I've seen this note before. What do you notice about this note?* (It's the same as the other notes in the story.)

Intermediate *Look at the ending on page 255. Why does the author end the story on a new day?* The author ends the story on a new day to show that Mr. Putter and Mrs. Teaberry are <u>good friends</u>. They will continue to <u>visit each other</u>.

 Advanced *Talk to a partner about the end of the story on page 255. Talk about why the author chose to end the story this way.* (At the end of the story, Mr. Putter and Tabby return to Mrs. Teaberry's house to eat. The author ends the story on a new day to show that Mr. Putter and Mrs. Teaberry will continue to be friends.)

 Advanced High *With a partner, discuss what might happen next in the story. Can you predict what will happen the next evening?* (Answers will vary, but should reflect understanding that the story repeats, and it is likely Mr. Putter and Mrs. Teaberry will eat together and perhaps bump into each other that evening when they can't sleep.)

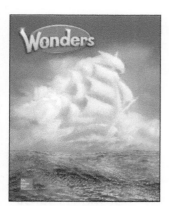

Literature Anthology

OBJECTIVES

Read with sufficient accuracy and fluency to support comprehension.

Read on-level text orally with accuracy, appropriate rate, and expression on successive readings.

Describe how words and phrases (e.g., regular beats, alliteration, rhymes, repeated lines) supply rhythm and meaning in a story, poem, or song.

LANGUAGE OBJECTIVE

Children will demonstrate listening comprehension by retelling text that is read aloud.

ACADEMIC LANGUAGE

• repetition, sequence
• Cognates: repetición, sequencia

English Language Learners

Mr. Putter & Tabby See the Stars

Text Reconstruction

Focus on a single chunk of text to support comprehension and language development across the four domains.

1. Read aloud page 248 of *Mr. Putter & Tabby See the Stars*.

2. Write the following key words and phrases on the board, providing definitions as needed: *sky, stars, Big Dipper, Milky Way, purred*. Instruct children to listen for these words as you read the page a second time.

3. Read the page a third time while children listen and take notes.

4. Have children work with a partner to reconstruct the text from their notes. Help them write complete sentences as needed.

5. Have children look at the original text. Ask what this section of text is mostly about. (Mr. Putter shows Tabby the Milky Way.) Tell children they are going to discuss how the author organizes the text into a logical sequence.

6. *What happens first on the page?* (Mr. Putter looks up at the sky.) *What happens next?* (Mr. Putter shows Tabby the stars and tells her all about them.) *Why does Mr. Putter tell Tabby about the Big Dipper and the Milky Way?* (They are things in the night sky.) *What happens last on the page?* (Tabby purrs because she loves milk.) *Why does the author write that Tabby purrs at the end of the section?* (Possible: The cat purrs after she hears the name "Milky Way" because it reminds her of milk.)

7. Have children compare their text reconstructions to the original text. Have them check if they told events of the story in the correct order.

Beginning Allow children to follow along in their **Literature Anthologies** as you read the text aloud. Have them point to words from Step 2 as they hear them.

Apply Author's Craft: Repetition

Have children write sentences about something they have seen in the night sky. Tell them they will use repetition to tell about their experience. Model the exercise first: *I saw the moon in the night sky. I saw bright stars. I saw stars that formed shapes.* As children work, provide vocabulary support. Allow **Beginning** ELLs to first say their sentences aloud, then help them write their sentences. Reconvene and have children share their sentences.

Grammar in Context: Text Deconstruction

Write this sentence from page 254 on the board: *Then when the stomachs on the front lawn stopped grumbling, everyone said good night, went to bed, and slept like logs.* Facilitate deconstructing this sentence for better comprehension:

- Circle *stopped. What is the subject? What stopped?* (the stomachs on the lawn) *What did they stop doing?* (grumbling) *Whose stomachs were grumbling?* (Mr. Putter's and Zeke's) *Why were they grumbling?* (They ate too much.) *How do you think Mr. Putter and Zeke felt after their stomachs stopped grumbling?* (They felt better.)

- *What are the other actions?* (said, went, slept) *Who said goodnight? Who went to bed? Who slept like logs?* (everyone) *Who does the word* everyone *refer to?* (Mr. Putter, Tabby, Mrs. Teaberry, and Zeke)

- The author tells us that everyone "slept like logs." What does this mean? (They slept without moving. They slept well.)

- *Say the sentence in your own words.* (Possible: Everyone felt better. Then they said good night and went to bed. They all slept well.)

Independent Time

Verb Tenses Have children copy the chart in their notebooks and add additional verbs from the texts. Have partners work together to write sentences based on this frame: Every day I _____. Yesterday/ Last week I _____. Tomorrow I will _____. Have partners trade papers to edit for appropriate verb tenses.

PRESENT TENSE	PAST-TENSE	FUTURE-TENSE	SENTENCES
look	looked	will look	Every day I look at the stars.
arrive	arrived	will arrive	
stop	stopped	will stop	Yesterday I ~~look~~ looked at the stars.
say	said	will say	
go	went	will go	Tomorrow I ~~look~~ will look at the stars.
sleep	slept	will sleep	

Advanced/Advanced High After children add several verbs to the chart, challenge them to use the examples to determine spelling rules for regular past-tense verbs (+ *-ed*, double the final consonant + *-ed*, change *y* to *i* + *-ed*).

Make Connections Help children connect the Essential Question to their own lives. Ask children to draw a picture of their own night sky, including as many details as they can. Then have partners share and describe their drawings. Use the online **Oral Language Sentence Frames** for "Use Nouns/ Noun Phrases," available for all ELL levels, to support oral language development.

OBJECTIVES

Demonstrate command of the conventions of standard English grammar and usage when writing or speaking.

Demonstrate understanding of word relationships and nuances in word meanings.

LANGUAGE OBJECTIVE

Children will study verb forms and practice using key vocabulary from the text.

ACADEMIC LANGUAGE

- *plural, noun*
- cognate: *plural*

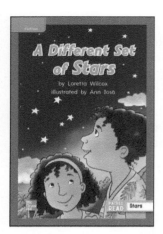

Lexile 390

OBJECTIVES

Ask and answer such questions as *who, what, where, when, why,* and *how* to demonstrate understanding of key details in a text.

LANGUAGE OBJECTIVE

Students will identify the elements of a fiction story and learn acccessible language using visual support.

ACADEMIC LANGUAGE

- *compare, fiction, label, plot, sequence*
- Cognates: *comparar, ficción*

Digital Tools

🎧 Have children listen to the selections to develop comprehension and practice fluency and pronunciation.

English Language Learners

Leveled Reader *A Different Set of Stars*

Build Background

- Read the Essential Question: *What can we see in the sky?* Have children discuss looking at the sky. *What can you see in the sky?* Brainstorm words for a word bank to help children answer: I can see <u>stars</u> in the sky.

- Choral read the title. Explain that a *set* is a group of things that go together. Show pictures of objects in a set, such as a set of cards, toys, or tools. Explain that there are many different groups, or sets, of stars in the sky.

Vocabulary

Use the routine on the **ELL Visual Vocabulary Cards** to pre-teach the ELL vocabulary: *equator* and *twin* (cognate: *ecuador*). Use the images and any labels to identify and model the use of key vocabulary in context.

Interactive Question-Response Routine

After each paragraph, use **Interactive Question-Response** prompts such as the following to provide language support and guide comprehension.

Chapter 1

Choral read the first paragraph on page 3. What new words did you learn? (twin, bossy) **Review the definition of** *twin.* Anita and Isabel are <u>twin sisters</u>.

Beginning *Let's read the label on page 3:* suitcase. *What two words make the word* suitcase? (*suit; case*) *When you pack a suitcase, you put clothing in it to go on a trip. Why do you think Mom asked "Are you all packed?"* (They're going on a trip.)

Intermediate *Reread paragraph 3 on page 3. Which words describe Isabel?* (neater, bossy) *Look at the picture. What does it show you about Anita's suitcase?* Anita's suitcase is <u>a mess.</u>

 Advanced/Advanced High *Isabel is bossy. How do bossy people behave? Discuss with a partner.* (They tell others what to do.)

Chapter 2

Have partners narrate the **sequence** of events in Chapter 2 using signal words like *first, then, next,* and *finally.*

Intermediate *A fruit smoothie is a drink. What do you think* sip *means?* (Possible: *drink*)

 Advanced/Advanced High *How does Anita feel about her drink?* (She thinks it is delicious.) *What other words are similar to the word* delicious? *Tell a partner.* (Possible: *tasty, yummy*)

Chapter 3

Beginning *Reread page 9. What can the girls see in the sky? Say the words aloud as you point to the pictures.* (stars, moon, clouds)

 Advanced/Advanced High *Isabel likes* correcting *Anita. What does this mean? Tell a partner.* (Isabel likes telling Anita that she is wrong.)

Chapter 4

 Focus on the picture of the Southern Cross on page 14, then read page 15 together. *Isabel has never seen the Southern Cross before. Why not? With a partner,* **reread** *to find key details to answer the question.* Provide sentence frames for children to answer: Earth is round like an <u>orange</u>. The <u>equator</u> is an imaginary line through the middle. Each <u>half</u> of the Earth sees a different sky. Isabel is looking at the <u>sky</u> from a different <u>half</u>.

Fluency: Intonation and Expression

Read page 3 to model proper intonation and expression. Have children echo read.

 Respond to Reading Have partners list the main events in **sequence** using the graphic organizer on page 16. Then have them discuss the questions.

Paired Selection: "Stars"

Analytical Writing **Make Connections: Write About It**

Before children write, use sentence frames to discuss the questions on page 19: We can see <u>stars</u> in the night sky. The texts are alike because they both tell about <u>stars</u>. They are different because one text <u>is a story</u>, but the other text <u>gives facts</u>.

ELL Leveled Reader

Self-Selected Reading Have children select another realistic fiction selection from the online **Leveled Reader Library.**

Focus On Literary Elements

Children can learn more about literary elements such as plot by completing the activity on page 20.

 Literature Circles

Ask children to conduct a literature circle using the Thinkmark questions to guide the discussion. You may wish to use the Leveled Reader selections to discuss what you learn about stars in both texts.

LEVEL UP

IF children read the ELL Level fluently and answered the questions

THEN pair them with children who have proficiently read the On Level and have children

- echo-read the On Level main selection with their partner.
- list difficult words and phrases and discuss them with their partners.

A C T **Access Complex Text**

The On Level challenges children by including more **domain-specific words** and **complex sentence structures.**

Lexile 390L

OBJECTIVES

Ask and answer such questions as *who, what, where, when, why,* and *how* to demonstrate understanding of key details in a text.

LANGUAGE OBJECTIVE

Students will identify the elements of and point of view for a fiction story.

ACADEMIC LANGUAGE

• *dialogue, fiction, third person*
• Cognates: *diálogo, ficción*

English Language Learners

Genre Passage "A Shooting Star"

Build Background

• Ask children what they can see in the sky at night. Elicit vocabulary, such as *moon* and *stars*. Ask children if they have ever seen a *shooting star*. Point to the illustration on page E2 of the story "A Shooting Star." Explain that a shooting star looks like it is moving across the sky. Tell children that they will be reading a story about a family that goes camping and sees a shooting star.

Vocabulary

Use the **Define, Example, Ask** routine to pre-teach difficult words or unfamiliar concepts, such as *campsite, set up, fireflies, shooting star, come true, dust, glows,* and *no matter.* Invite students to add new vocabulary to their glossaries.

Interactive Question-Response Routine

After each paragraph, use the Interactive Question-Response prompts such as the following to provide language support and guide comprehension.

Page E1

Paragraph 1 Review **compound words.** Have children underline the compound words in the first paragraph. (*afternoon, campsite, evergreen, overhead*) Then have children identify the two words that make up each compound word. Draw a line between the two words.

Intermediate *How do the two smaller words help you understand each compound word?* (Possible: The word *ever* means "always." I know the meaning of *green.* This helps me understand that *evergreen* means "always green." The trees are always green.)

Advanced/Advanced High *Which sentences tell what the family did when they got to the park?* (The family set up the tents. Then they hiked.) *Would you like to go camping and do these things? Why or why not? Talk to a partner.* (Answers will vary.)

Paragraph 4

Intermediate *When did the family come back to their campsite?* (in the evening) *Look at the phrase "daylight was almost gone." What does this mean?* (It was almost dark.)

Paragraphs 1–5

Have partners work together to write the events on page E1 in order. To reinforce the **sequence** of events, remind them to use connecting words like *first, then, next, after that,* and *finally.* Afterwards, guide the class in acting out the events while they narrate.

Beginning Have children underline the following: *got to the park, ran around the campsite, family set up the tents, they hiked, they returned.* Help children expand each underlined phrase into a complete sentence.

Intermediate Have children underline the main events on the page. Then have partners compare their notes by asking and answering: *What happened first? Then what happened? What happened after that?* Finally have them retell the section of the story by writing the events in order using connecting words.

Advanced/Advanced High Have children read the page aloud while a partner takes notes on the main events. Challenge them to write the main events in sequence using their notes.

Page E2

Paragraph 1

Beginning *What does the family see in the sky?* (fireflies; a shooting star) *Which phrase describes what the shooting star does?* ("cross the night sky")

Paragraph 3 Point out the text *you can wish on a shooting star.* Explain that to wish on a shooting star means that when you see a shooting star, you make a wish. *Why do you make a wish?* (Possible: to make something good happen) *What would you wish if you saw a shooting star? Tell a partner.* (Answers will vary.)

Paragraph 5 *Read paragraph 5. Underline the words that tell about shooting stars.* (dust; flying; glows)

Intermediate *What is a shooting star?* (glowing dust flying toward Earth) *Underline text evidence.* ("It's just dust flying toward Earth. The dust glows.")

Advanced/Advanced High *Why is Mama's dialogue important?* (because she explains what a shooting star really is)

Respond to Reading

Use the following prompts to help children answer the questions on page E3.

1. Review the features of the genre, fiction. (The story's characters and events are made up.)

2. Reread the first three paragraphs on page E1. Have children underline each instance of *they* and *their.* Then have them underline each instance of a name (*Carla, Rosa, Mama, Papa*). Remind children these signal the third-person **point of view.**

3. Reread the fifth paragraph on page E2. What did you learn from Mama's dialogue? I learned that shooting stars are just dust flying toward Earth.

Fluency Have children take turns reading the selection.

Make Connections

After reading this story, discuss with a partner all the things you can see in the sky.

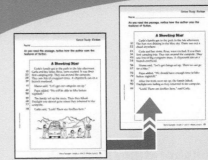

IF students read the **ELL Level** fluently and answered the questions,

THEN pair them with students who have proficiently read the **On Level.** Have them:

- partner-read the On Level passage.
- summarize what happens in the beginning, middle, and end of the story

GENRE STUDY: FICTION

Skills assessed in Progress Monitoring Assessment

FORMALLY ASSESSED SKILLS	INSTRUCTIONAL FOCUS
Plot: Sequence	Comprehension Skill
Compound Words	Vocabulary Strategy

Informal Assessment

INFORMALLY ASSESSED SKILLS	INSTRUCTIONAL FOCUS	HOW ASSESSED
Analytical Writing	• Comprehension Skill • Written Response • English Language Conventions	Reading/Writing Companion: Respond to Reading
Grammar, Mechanics, Usage	English Language Conventions	Practice Book, digital activities, writing activities
Spelling	English Language Conventions	Practice Book, word sorts, digital activities, writing activities
Phonics	Foundational Skills	Practice Book, digital activities
Listening/Collaborating/Research	• Listening • Speaking • Research	Checklists, rubrics
Oral Reading Fluency (ORF) Fluency Goal: 74–94 words correct per minute (WCPM) Accuracy Rate Goal: 95% or higher	• Reading Accuracy • Prosody	Fluency Assessment

 Assign practice pages online for auto-grading.

Making the Most of Assessment Results

Make data-based grouping decisions by using the following reports to verify assessment results. For additional support options for your students, refer to the reteaching and enrichment opportunities.

ONLINE ASSESSMENT CENTER

- *Item Analysis Report*
- *Standards Analysis Report*

DATA DASHBOARD

- *Recommendations Report*
- *Activity Report*
- *Skills Report*
- *Progress Report*

 RETEACHING OPPORTUNITIES with Intervention Online PDFs

IF CHILDREN SCORE . . .	THEN ASSIGN . . .
below 70% in **comprehension**	lessons 37–39 on Sequence in **Comprehension PDF**
below 70% in **vocabulary**	lesson 98 on Plurals with -s, -es in **Vocabulary PDF**
below 2 on **constructed-response items**	lessons 37–39 and/or Write About Reading lessons from Section 4 in **Comprehension PDF**
65–73 WCPM in **fluency**	lesson from Sections 1, 9 or 10 of **Fluency PDF**
0–64 WCPM in **fluency**	lesson from Sections 2–8 of **Fluency PDF**

Use the **Phonemic Awareness** *and* **Phonics/Word Study PDFs** *for additional reteaching lessons.*

 ENRICHMENT OPPORTUNITIES for Gifted and Talented Students

Beyond Level small group lessons include suggestions for additional activities in the following areas to extend learning opportunities for gifted and talented students:

- *Leveled Readers*
- *Genre Passages*
- *Vocabulary Strategy*
- *Comprehension*
- *Leveled Readers Library Online*
- *Workstation Activities*

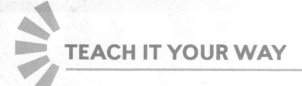

Genre Study

Expository INFORMATIONAL TEXT

Key Features

- Uses text structures to organize information, such as description

- Gives facts, examples, and explanations about a topic

- Provides details to support a main idea

- May include text features, such as photos, captions, and graphics

Teach It Your Way

Incorporate your own resources to customize your text set!

Make Learning Visible

Genre Study - Expository INFORMATIONAL TEXT

Children learn to think critically as they explore the expository text genre and apply new knowledge and skills encompassing the four domains of language.

Active Engagement in Learning

Students Know What They Are Learning

Children review the Learning Goals for the Expository Text Genre Study. The Home/School Family Letter includes a list of the Learning Goals and activities related to student outcomes.

Students Document Their Learning

Children will create the following Anchor Charts:

Anchor Chart

- Expository Text Genre Features
- Main Idea and Key Details
- Ask and Answer Questions
- Prefixes
- Expository Essay

Students Learn From Each Other

- Collaborative conversations
- Talk About It digital message board
- Blasts

Model Anchor Chart

Genre: Expository Text

- Gives facts, examples, and explanation about a topic, unlike fiction in which details are not real
- Presents information in a logical order
- Uses certain text structures to organize information
- May include text features, such as photos and captions

Student Outcomes

Comprehension/Genre/Author's Craft

- Cite relevant evidence from text
- ✓ Make inferences to support understanding
- ✓ Identify the main idea and key details
- Ask and answer questions
- Evaluate the use of graphic features
- ✓ Identify and use text features

Writing

Writing Process
- Plan and draft an expository essay

Analytical Writing
- Write responses that demonstrate understanding.

Speaking and Listening

- Engage in collaborative discussions
- Retell "Why People Drum"
- Present information about a patriotic song

Language Development

Oral Vocabulary Acquisition

carved   glide   sphere   suddenly   surface

Vocabulary Acquisition
- Acquire and use academic vocabulary

cheered   concert   instrument   movements
music   rhythm   sounds   understand

Vocabulary Strategy
- ✓ Recognize and understand prefixes

Grammar
- ✓ Understand and use the verb *have*

Foundational Skills

Word Work
- Phonological Awareness: Identify and Generate Alliteration
- Phonemic Awareness: Addition, Deletion, Blending
- ✓ Phonics: Long *u, u_e, ue, u, ew*
- Structural Analysis: Comparative Endings *-er, -est*
- Use High-Frequency Words
- Handwriting: Review Lower Case Letters

Spelling Words

Week 5

huge	cube	fumes	music	unit
menu	few	pew	fuel	cues
pony	queen	began	come	give

- Differentiated Spelling Lists, page T372

Fluency
- Intonation

Research and Inquiry

- Research Relevant Information
- Create a collage about a patriotic song

🌐 Content Area Learning

- Research and identify patriotic songs

ELL Scaffolded supports for English Language Learners are embedded throughout the instruction.

 Use the Data Dashboard to filter class, group, or individual student data to guide group placement decisions. It provides recommendations to enhance learning for gifted and talented children and offers extra support for children needing remediation.

Focus on Word Work

Support Foundational Skills

Phonological/Phonemic Awareness Activities

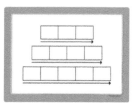

Response Board

Sound-Spelling Cards

Word-Building Cards online

Phonics Activities

Practice Book

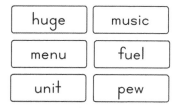

Spelling Word Cards online

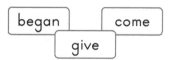

High-Frequency Word Cards

High-Frequency Word Activities

Phonological/Phonemic Awareness

- Phoneme Addition and Deletion, Identify and Generate Alliteration, Phoneme Blending

Phonics: Long *u*

- Introduce and blend words
- Use manipulatives for sound-spelling review
- Structural Analysis: Comparative Endings

Spelling: Long *u*

- Differentiated spelling instruction
- Encode with sound-spellings
- Explore relationships with word sorts
- Apply spelling to writing

High-Frequency Words

- Read/Spell/Write routine

  See Word Work, pages T378–T405

Apply Skills to Read

- Reads are designed to incorporate foundational skills

Decodable Readers

Decodable Passages

Short Vowels; Consonant Blends; Long Vowels〉 Soft c and g; Consonant Digraphs〉 3-Letter Consonant Blends〉 Silent Letters〉 r-Controlled Vowels〉 Diphthongs〉 Varient Vowels〉 Vowel Digraphs〉 Syllables

Explicit Systematic Instruction

Word Work instruction expands foundational skills to enable students to become proficient readers.

Daily Review

Review prior sound-spellings to build fluency.

Explicit Minilessons

Use daily instruction in both whole and small groups to model, practice, and apply key foundational skills. Provide corrective feedback. ELL support is provided in all lessons.

Check for Success

Check that children are on track and ready to move forward. Follow up with:

Differentiated Instruction

To strengthen skills, provide targeted review and reteaching lessons to meet students' specific needs.

Approaching

- Includes Tier 2

On Level

Beyond

- Includes Gifted and Talented

ELL

Independent Practice

Students who have the key skills can work independently or with partners.

Workstation Activity Cards

Digital Activities

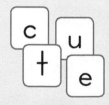

Word-Building Cards online

Decodable Readers

Practice Book

Expository Text Set

Key Concept
Express Yourself

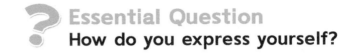

Essential Question
How do you express yourself?

Students read and write about different ways that people express their thoughts and feelings.

"Why People Drum"
Interactive Read Aloud Cards
Genre Expository Text

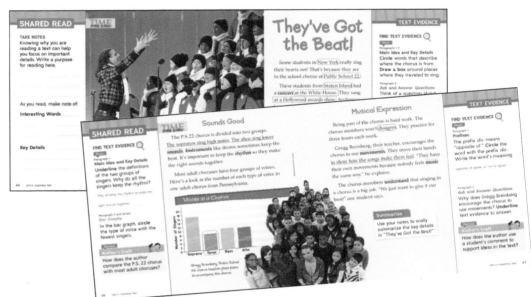

"They've Got the Beat!"
Reading/Writing Companion pp. 64–67
Genre Expository Text • **Lexile** 620L

Many Way to Enjoy Music
Literature Anthology pp. 262–265
Genre Expository Text • **Lexile** 680L

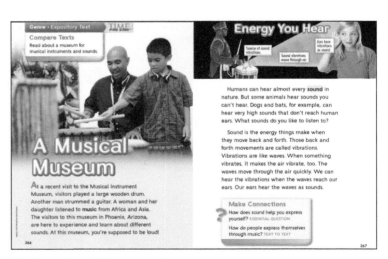

"A Musical Museum"
Literature Anthology pp. 266–267
Genre Expository Text • **Lexile** 640L

Scaffolded Shared Read

"Many Ways to Enjoy Music"

Available online

ELL Scaffolded Shared Read

Lexile 410L
GR G
Approaching

Lexile 530L
GR L
On Level

Lexile 590L
GR O
Beyond

Lexile 380L
GR J
ELL

Leveled Readers with Paired Reads

Approaching **Lexile** 480L
On Level **Lexile** 590L
Beyond **Lexile** 690L
ELL **Lexile** 550L

Genre Passages

Independent Reading Focus

Classroom Library

Fire Fighter!
Lexile 500L

One Plastic Bag
Lexile 480L

Lessons available online

More Leveled Readers to Explore

Bonus Leveled Readers

Leveled Reader Library Online

Bibliography

Have students self-select independent reading texts about different ways people express themselves. Share the online **Unit Bibliography.**

Reading Across Genres

Tello, Jerry. *Let's Read About César Chávez.* Scholastic, 2004. Biography **Lexile** 450L

Rylant, Cynthia. *Mr. Putter & Tabby Write the Book.* Houghton Mifflin Harcourt, 2004. Fiction **Lexile** 570L

More Expository Texts

Taylor-Butler, Christine. *Experiments with Magnets.* Cherry Lake Publishing, 2011. Expository Text **Lexile** 480L

Rendon, Marci. *Farmer's Market.* Carolrhoda Books, 2001. Expository Text

Inspire Confident Writers

Analytical Writing: Expository Text

Develop children's habits of writing while reading.

Notetaking Video

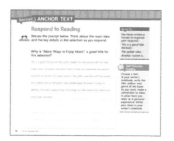

Take Notes to monitor comprehension

Shared Read - Model
"They've Got the Beat!"
Reading/Writing Companion pp. 64–67

Anchor Text - Practice and Apply
Many Ways to Enjoy Music
Literature Anthology pp. 262–264
Reading/Writing Companion pp. 76–77

Summarize using important details

Shared Read - Model
"They've Got the Beat!"
Reading/Writing Companion p. 67

Anchor Text - Practice and Apply
Many Ways to Enjoy Music
Literature Anthology p. 265

Respond using text evidence

Shared Read - Model
"They've Got the Beat!"
Reading/Writing Companion p. 74

Anchor Text - Practice and Apply
Many Ways to Enjoy Music
Literature Anthology p. 265
Reading/Writing Companion p. 78

Genre Writing:
Write Your Own Expository Essay

ONLINE Writer's Notebook

WRITING PROCESS

Expert Model ⟩ Plan ⟩ Draft ⟩ Revise ⟩ Edit and Proofread ⟩ Publish

WEEK 5 　　　　　　　　　　　　　　　　WEEK 6

Study the Expert Model
Reading/Writing Companion p. 84

- Discuss features of expository essay
- Discuss the mentor text (**Literature Anthology, pp. 262–265**)

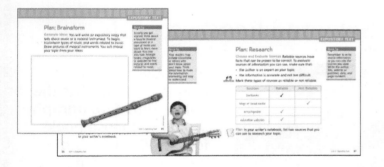

Plan the Essay
Reading/Writing Companion pp. 85–87

- Choose the topic
- Discuss purpose and audience
- Choose and evaluate sources
- Take notes

Write a Draft
Reading/Writing Companion p. 88

- Discuss sentence and coherence: Paragraph
- Write the draft

Grammar, Spelling, and Handwriting Resources

Practice Book, pp. 247–255

 Assign practice pages online for auto-grading.

Grammar Handbook

Digital Activities

Student Choice
OPTIONS FOR SMALL GROUP TIME

Develop self-directed, critical thinkers.

Independent Reading

Classroom Library

Fire Fighter!
Genre Narrative Nonfiction
Lexile 500L

One Plastic Bag
Genre Narrative Nonfiction
Lexile 480L

Reading Across Genres

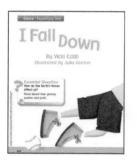

Literature Anthology
I Fall Down p. 268
Genre Expository Text

"Move It!" p. 286
Genre Expository Text

Differentiated Genre Passages
Six leveled sets of passages are available on diverse genres.

Leveled Readers

Leveled Reader Library Online
Additional Leveled Readers allow for flexibility.

Bonus Leveled Readers
Students can read more nonfiction titles.

Self-Selected Reading

Share book room resources as well as the online **Unit Bibliography**. Students choose books for 30-40 minutes of daily independent reading and respond in their writer's notebooks.

Blend/Image Source; FIRE FIGHTER. Copyright © 1998 by Angela Royston. Used by permission of DK Publishing; "One Plastic Bag; Isatou Ceesay and the Recycling Women of Gambia" by Miranda Paul, illustrated by Elizabeth Zunon. Text copyright © 2015 by Miranda Paul. Illustration copyright © 2015 by Elizabeth Zunon. Reprinted with the permission of Lerner Publications

Differentiated Workstation Activities

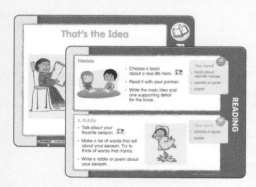

Reading 10

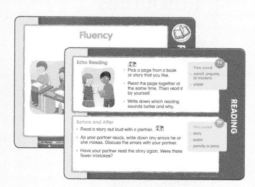

Reading 25

Science 15

Independent Writing

Self-Selected Writing

Have students plan and draft their essay or use these suggestions and choose the form they write in.

Resource Toolkit

> Think about different hobbies. How can people express themselves through hobbies?

> When was the last time you used writing to express yourself?

> Which instrument would you choose to express yourself? Why?

> Have you ever used technology to express yourself? Explain.

> How can people express themselves when they write and perform music?

Research and Inquiry Project

Students conduct research about patriotic songs and choose how to present their work.

Digital Activities

Grammar:
The Verb *have*

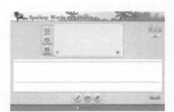

Spelling:
Long *u*

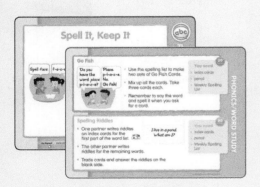

Phonics/Word Study 27

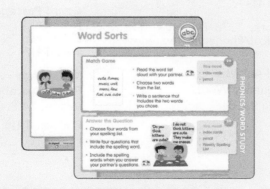

Phonics/Word Study 15

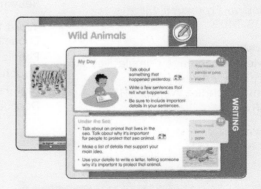

Writing 3

Suggested Lesson Plan

KEY

 Writing activity   ◀ Can be taught in Small Groups

DAY 1

Introduce the Concept T334–T335

Oral Vocabulary/Listening Comprehension T336–T337

Word Work T378–T385
• Phonemic Awareness: Addition and Deletion • Phonics: Introduce, Blend Words with Long *u* • High-Frequency Words • Decodable Reader: "Luke's Tune" • Handwriting ◀

Read the Shared Read "They've Got the Beat!" T338–T341

Summarize Quick Write, T341 ✏

Vocabulary Words in Context, Prefixes, T342–T343

Grammar The Verb *have*, T370 ◀

Spelling Words with Long *u* T372

Word Work T382
• Structural Analysis: Comparative Endings ◀

Preteach Vocabulary T342–T343

Grammar Talk About It, T370 ◀

Expand Vocabulary T374

DAY 2

Strategy Ask and Answer Questions T344–T345

Text Structure Bar Graphs, T346–T347

Skill Main Idea and Key Details, T348–349 ✏

Word Work T388–T390
• Phonics: Blend, Build Words with Long *u* • Structural Analysis: Comparative Endings ◀

Shared Read Reread: Craft and Structure, T350–T351 ◀

Respond to Reading T352–T353 ✏◀

Study Skill/Research and Inquiry T356–T357 ◀

Grammar The Verb *have*, T370

Fluency Intonation, T354–T355

Word Work T386–T387, T390–T391
Phonological Awareness: Identify and Generate Alliteration • Phonics: Review Long *u* • Decodable Reader: "Mules" • High-Frequency Words Review ◀

Grammar Talk About It, T370 ◀

Spelling Words with Long *u*, T372 ◀

Expand Vocabulary T374

CORE

OPTIONAL

SMALL GROUP ≫ INSTRUCTION

APPROACHING

Leveled Reader
The Sounds of Trash, T406–T407
Literature Circles, T407

Genre Passage
"Musical Expression," T408–T409

Vocabulary
Review Vocabulary, Cumulative Vocabulary Review, T410 ②
Identify Related Words, T411
Prefixes, T411

Fluency ②
Intonation, T412

Comprehension
Key Details, T412 ②
Review Main Idea and Key Details, T413
Self-Selected Reading T413

Word Work, T378–T405 ②
Phonological/Phonemic Awareness
Phonics
Structural Analysis
High-Frequency Words
Decodable Reader

ON LEVEL

Leveled Reader
The Sound of Trash, T414–T415
Literature Circles, T415

Genre Passage
"Musical Expression," T416–T417

Vocabulary
Review Vocabulary Words, T418
Prefixes, T418

Comprehension
Review Main Idea and Key Details, T419
Self-Selected Reading, T419

Self-Selected Reading, T419

Word Work
Phonics, T402

HOW TO DIFFERENTIATE ≫

Use your Check for Success observations and Data Dashboard to determine each student's needs. Then select instructional support options throughout the week.

Customize your own lesson plans
my.mheducation.com

DAY 3

Word Work T392–T399
• Phonemic Awareness: Blending • Phonics: Introduce Long *u,* • High-Frequency Words • Decodable Reader: "Growing Stew"

Read and Reread the Anchor Text
Many Ways to Enjoy Music, T357A–T357C

Take Notes About Text T357A–T357C

Respond to Reading T358-T359

Writing Analyze Expert Model, T362–T363

Grammar/Mechanics The Verb *have,* Sentence Punctuation, T371

Expand Vocabulary T375

Word Work T394–T396
• Phonics: Blend, Build Words with Long *u* • Structural Analysis: Comparative Endings

Grammar Talk About It, T371

Spelling Words with Long *u,* T373

DAY 4

Word Work T401–T402
Phonics: Blend, Build Words with Long *u*

Read and Reread the Paired Selection
"A Musical Museum," T359A–T359B

Author's Craft Text Features: Diagrams, T360-T361

Writing Plan, T364–T367

Word Work T400–T403
Phonemic Awareness: Addition and Deletion • Structural Analysis Review • High-Frequency Word Review• Decodable Reader "Dan and Jen Made Music"

Grammar The Verb *have,* T371

Grammar Talk About It, T371

Spelling Words with Long *u,* T373

Expand Vocabulary T375

DAY 5

Word Work T404
Phonics: Blend and Build Words with Long *u*

Writing Draft, T368–T369

Spelling Words with Long *u,* T373

Integrate Make Connections, T376

Word Work T404–T405
• Phonemic Awareness: Blending • Structural Analysis: Comparative Endings • High-Frequency Words

Grammar The Verb *have,* T371

Grammar Talk About It, T371

Expand Vocabulary T375

Fluency Intonation, T377

BEYOND

Leveled Reader
The Sounds of Trash, T420–T421
Literature Circles, T421
Synthesize, T421

GIFTED and TALENTED

Genre Passage
"Musical Expression," T422–T423
Synthesize, T423

GIFTED and TALENTED

Vocabulary
Review Domain-Specific Words, T424
Prefixes, T424
Synthesize, T424

GIFTED and TALENTED

Comprehension
Review Main Idea and Key Details, T425
Self-Selected Reading, T425
Independent Study T425

GIFTED and TALENTED

ENGLISH LANGUAGE LEARNERS

Shared Read
"They've Got the Beat," T426–T429
Interactive Question-Response Routine, T426–T427
Text Reconstruction, T428
Grammar in Context, T429

Anchor Text
Many Ways to Enjoy Music
Reread, T430–T433
Text Reconstruction, T432
Grammar in Context, T433

Leveled Reader
The Sounds of Trash, T434–T435

Genre Passage
"Musical Expression," T436–T437

Word Work,
T378–T405
Phonological/Phonemic Awareness
Phonics
Structural Analysis
High-Frequency Words
Decodable Reader

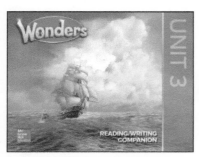

Reading/Writing Companion

OBJECTIVES

Ask and answer questions about what a speaker says in order to clarify comprehension, gather additional information, or deepen understanding of a topic or issue.

Follow agreed-upon rules for discussions (e.g., gaining the floor in respectful ways, listening to others with care, speaking one at a time about the topics and texts under discussion).

ACADEMIC LANGUAGE

• *music, sounds, instrument*
• Cognates: *música, instrumento*

Digital Tools

Show the image during class discussion. Then play the video.

Discuss Concept

Watch Video

 10 Mins

Talk About It

 Essential Question

How do you express yourself?

Display the online **Student Learning Goals** for this genre study. Read the key concept: Express Yourself. Tell children that they will read an expository text about how they can express themselves through music.

Read the Essential Question on the **Reading/Writing Companion** page 62. Point to the photograph. Explain that music is one way to express yourself. There are many different ways to make music just as there are many different ways of expressing yourself.

• You can play an **instrument**, such as a guitar, to make music and express yourself. You can sing, or make **sounds** with your voice, to make music and express yourself, too.

• Making music is just one of many ways to express yourself. Writing, drawing, and painting are some other ways.

Ask: *How would you express yourself through **music**—by making **sounds** with an **instrument** or with your voice? How do you like to express yourself?* Have children discuss in pairs or groups.

• Model how to use the graphic organizer to generate words that can describe some of the ways people express themselves.

• Have small groups develop ideas by discussing art forms they have been involved in or are interested in trying. Ask groups to use as many words from the organizer as possible in their discussion.

 Collaborative Conversations

Take Turns Talking As children engage in partner, small-group, and whole-group discussions, encourage them to

• wait for a person to finish before they speak.

• quietly raise their hand when they want to speak.

• ask others to share their ideas and opinions.

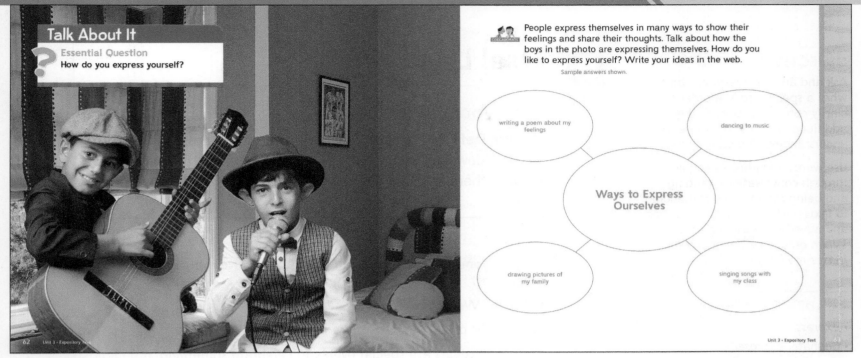

Reading/Writing Companion, pp. 62–63

 Share the "Show Yourself Through Your Art" Blast assignment with children. Point out that you will discuss their responses in the Integrate Ideas lesson at the end of this two-week genre study.

 # English Language Learners SCAFFOLD

Use the following scaffolds with **Ask**.

Beginning

Look at the boys. How are they expressing themselves? Ask and answer with a partner. Provide sentence frames and a word bank. What's the boy doing? The boy is making music with his <u>voice</u>. He is <u>singing</u>. (Word Bank: *guitar, voice, singing, playing an instrument*)

Intermediate

As children share ways they express themselves, encourage them to pantomime or use other strategies to share ideas they don't know in English. Provide linguistic support, as needed. Write ideas on the board for partners to refer to when completing the graphic organizer, such as *writing, painting, drawing, dancing, singing.* Use sentence frames to help partners share ideas. I express myself by <u>painting.</u>

Advanced/Advanced High

Help partners use more complex forms during conversations. Provide models for linguistic support, for example: *I express myself with my voice when I am singing. I express myself with my hands when I am painting. I express myself by dancing with my friends.*

 ## Vocabulary

express (*expresar*) to say or show

feelings (*sentimientos*) emotions; a tender part of a person's nature

guitar (*guitarra*) one type of musical instrument with strings

voice (*voz*) sound made with your mouth

play an instrument (*tocar un instrumento*) make music using a guitar, piano, or other music device

sing (*cantar*) make music with your voice, chant

thoughts (*pensamientos*) ideas or opinions

Newcomers

To reinforce children's development of oral language and vocabulary, review **Newcomer Cards 5-14** and the accompanying materials in the **Newcomer Teacher's Guide.**

Oral Language

10 Mins

OBJECTIVES

Ask and answer questions about what a speaker says in order to clarify comprehension, gather additional information, or deepen understanding of a topic or issue.

Use words and phrases acquired through conversations, reading and being read to, and responding to texts, including using adjectives and adverbs to describe (e.g., *When other kids are happy that makes me happy*).

ACADEMIC LANGUAGE

- *express*
- Cognate: *expresar*

Digital Tools

Read or play the Interactive Read Aloud.

Interactive Read Aloud

SOCIAL EMOTIONAL LEARNING

· · · · · · · · · · · · · · · ·

Creativity When children use their creativity to express themselves, they are better able to participate in class activities. Before children listen, have them think about their creativity by considering these questions:

- How do I like to express myself?
- Do I like to sing? Dance? Draw? Paint? Write? Act?
- How do I feel when I use my creativity to express myself?

Oral Vocabulary Words

Use the **Define/Example/Ask** routine to introduce the Oral Vocabulary words below. Prompt children to use the words as they discuss how people express themselves.

Oral Vocabulary Routine

<u>Define:</u> **Communicate** means to send and receive messages. (Cognate: *comunicar*)

<u>Example:</u> We communicate by sending e-mail every day.

<u>Ask:</u> What other ways are there to communicate?

<u>Define:</u> **Festivals** are special events to celebrate something. (Cognate: *festival*)

<u>Example:</u> We go on hayrides and have fun picking apples at the fall festivals in our town.

<u>Ask:</u> What would you like to do at a festival?

<u>Define:</u> **Respect** means high regard or honor. (Cognate: *respecto*)

<u>Example:</u> I treat my parents and grandparents with respect.

<u>Ask:</u> Whom do you treat with respect?

<u>Define:</u> **Squeezing** means pushing hard on the sides of something.

<u>Example:</u> Dad is squeezing the toothpaste to make it come out of the tube.

<u>Ask:</u> Why would someone squeeze a lemon?

<u>Define:</u> A **tradition** is a custom or belief that is passed down. (Cognate: *tradición*)

<u>Example:</u> Our family has a tradition of eating a turkey dinner together for Thanksgiving.

<u>Ask:</u> What is one tradition your family has?

Introduce the Genre

10 Mins

Connect to Concept: Express Yourself

Tell children that you will be reading an expository text about drums and how different cultures use drums as a way to express themselves.

Preview Informational Text: Expository Text

Discuss features of expository text:

- gives facts, examples, and explanations about a topic

- uses certain text structures to organize information

Interactive Read-Aloud Cards

- may include text features, such as photos and captions

Anchor Chart Use the expository text anchor chart and ask children to add characteristics of the genre.

Preview Text Structure

Point out that understanding text structure helps readers comprehend expository texts. Explain that expository texts give information about a topic. Point out that "Why People Drum" uses a description text structure. It includes descriptive details about drumming in different countries. It has a central idea and gives text evidence to support the central idea. It includes text features and graphics.

Read and Respond

Read the text aloud to children. Preview the comprehension strategy, Ask and Answer Questions, by using the Think Alouds below.

Display the online **Think Aloud Cloud: I figured out _____ because...** to reinforce how to use the strategy to understand content. Say: As I look at the photos, I wonder why one person is using hands to play drums while the other person is using sticks. As I read, I listen to details to find the answer to this question.

Think Aloud As I read, I learned that people can play a drum in many different ways because there are many different kinds of drums.

Genre Features After reading, discuss the elements of the Interactive Read Aloud that let children know the text is an expository text. Ask them to think about other texts they have read in class or independently that were expository texts.

Retell Have children use their own words to retell "Why People Drum" in logical order.

OBJECTIVES

Ask and answer questions about what a speaker says in order to clarify comprehension, gather additional information, or deepen understanding of a topic or issue.

Ask and answer such questions as *who, what, where, when, why,* and *how* to demonstrate understanding of key details in text.

ACADEMIC LANGUAGE

- *expository text, informational text*

ELL Spotlight on Language

Use these supports during **Read and Respond** to support children's listening comprehension.

Card 1: Repeat the sentence: *There are many kinds of drums.* Say: *The phrase "many kinds" means that there are different types, not all drums are the same.* As you read aloud the remaining cards, stop periodically to ask: *What kind of drum are we learning about now?* We are learning about talking drums.

Card 2: Before reading, write the words *talking drum, squeezing, louder,* and *softer* on the board. Demonstrate each word and have children mimic your gestures as they repeat the words. Explain that these words are used to describe how to play a *talking drum.* As you read the card aloud, ask children to raise their hands when they hear the words. Confirm children understood what they heard: *How does a drummer make the drum louder or softer?* A drummer makes the drum louder/softer by hitting it harder/more softly.

Card 3: Explain that a *soldier* (*soldado*) is a fighter in a war or *battle* (*batalla*). *How did drums help soldiers long ago?* Drums told soldiers where to go and what to do.

Card 4: Review *talking drum, taiko,* and *powwows.* Then have children take turns pretending to use one kind of drum and saying, I'm using a taiko drum. Ask: *Why are you drumming?* I'm drumming because I want to tell people that a storm is coming.

"They've Got the Beat!"

Reading/Writing Companion

Text Complexity Range

Lexile

420   620   820

OBJECTIVES

Ask and answer such questions as *who, what, where, when, why,* and *how* to demonstrate understanding of key details in text.

Identify the main topic of a multiparagraph text as well as the focus of specific paragraphs within the text.

Explain how specific images (e.g., a diagram showing how a machine works) contribute to and clarify a text.

Close Reading Routine

Read   DOK 1–2

- Identify key ideas and details about expressing ourselves.
- Take notes and summarize.
- Use **ACT** prompts as needed.

Reread   DOK 2–3

- Analyze the text, craft, and structure.
- Use the **Reread minilessons** and **prompts**.

Integrate   DOK 4

- Integrate knowledge and ideas.
- Make text-to-text connections.
- Use the Integrate lesson.
- Inspire action.

SHARED READ   TIME FOR KIDS

TAKE NOTES
Knowing why you are reading a text can help you focus on important details. Write a purpose for reading here.

_____

_____

_____

As you read, make note of:

Interesting Words _____

_____

_____

Key Details _____

_____

_____

Essential Question

How do you express yourself?

Read about how children in a school chorus express themselves.

64   Unit 3 • Expository Text

Reading/Writing Companion pp. 64–65

Take Notes Before children begin, have them think about the Essential Question and what they know about what a chorus does. Then have them set a purpose for reading. As children read, they should use the left column of page 64 to note their questions, list interesting words they would like to learn, and identify key details from the text.

Focus on the Read prompts now. For additional support, there are extra prompts not included in the **Reading/Writing Companion**. Use the Reread prompts during the Craft and Structure lesson on pages T350–T351. Consider preteaching vocabulary to some children.

DIFFERENTIATED READING

Approaching Level Elicit note-taking techniques and interesting words. Complete Read prompts with the group.

On Level Have partners do the Read prompts before you meet.

Beyond Level Discuss how partners responded to the Read prompts. Discuss how the bar graph supports the text.

English Language Learners Preteach the vocabulary. Have Beginning/Early-Intermediate ELLs listen to a selection summary, available in multiple languages, and use the **Scaffolded Shared Read**. Also see the small group pages.

They've Got the Beat!

Some students in New York really sing their hearts out! That's because they are in the school chorus at Public School 22.

These students from Staten Island had a **concert** at the White House. They sang at a Hollywood awards show. Audiences have clapped and **cheered** them on. These kids are always asked to return.

How does it feel to sing on stage? "I get nervous singing for a big audience," Brianna Crispino recalls. "But when I see the joy on their faces, I get excited."

Brianna Crispino, Public School 22 Chorus Member

TEXT EVIDENCE

FIND TEXT EVIDENCE

Read

Paragraphs 1-2
Main Idea and Key Details
Circle words that describe where the chorus is from.
Draw a box around places where they traveled to sing.

Paragraph 3
Ask and Answer Questions
Think of a question about the feelings Brianna describes. Write it here.

Sample answer: Why does she get

nervous?

Underline clues that help answer your question.

Reread

Author's Craft
How does the author grab your attention in the opening paragraph?

Unit 3 · Expository Text   65

Vocabulary: Context Clues

Paragraph 1: Read the first paragraph. Point out the word *chorus* in the second sentence. Ask: *What word in the first sentence helps us to understand the meaning of the word* chorus*?* (*sing*) *What is a chorus?* (a group of people who sing together for an audience)

Skill: Main Idea and Key Details

Paragraphs 1 and 2: Read the first two paragraphs. Ask: *Where is the chorus from?* Model using text evidence.

Think Aloud I can read to find out the details of where this chorus is from. I see that this chorus is from New York City. I also read that they are from Staten Island. I know that is in New York City. Last, I read that the members of this chorus attend Public School 22. Because real places are listed, I know that this story is nonfiction. **Ask:** *Where has the chorus traveled to sing?* (to the White House and a Hollywood awards show)

Strategy: Ask and Answer Questions

Paragraph 3: Read the third paragraph. Model using text evidence.

Think Aloud As I read, I can ask questions to help me better understand the text. As I read paragraph 3, I can ask, "Why does Brianna get nervous?" Where can I find the answer to my question? I read that Brianna gets nervous singing for a big audience. But I also read that she gets excited. I can ask another question: "When does Brianna get excited?" (when she sees the joy on the faces of the audience) Encourage partners to ask each other questions about details in the text as they read.

ELL   Spotlight on Idioms

Page 65, Paragraph 1 Focus on the phrase *sing their hearts out*. Help children understand the meaning of the phrase. Explain that to *sing one's heart out* means that you are *singing with passion or great enthusiasm*. Ask children to look at the photo and talk about how the chorus is singing: *How does the photo help you understand what "sing their hearts out" means?* (The children are singing. They look excited and happy.)

Skill: Main Idea and Key Details

Paragraph 1: Remind children that identifying the key details of a selection will help them to determine the main idea. Read the first paragraph. Ask: *What group sings high notes? What group sings low notes?* (Sopranos sing high notes and altos sing the lower notes.) *Why do all the singers need to keep the rhythm?* (They all keep the rhythm to make the right sounds together.)

Text Features: Bar Graph

Have children look at the bar graph at the bottom of page 66. Model how to read the bar graph.

Think Aloud This bar graph shows the four types of voices that might be found in a chorus. I can use the labels on the side and the bottom to understand the information in the bar graph. I see that the red bar that is labeled "Tenor" is the shortest one. This bar shows that there are fewer singers in this group than in any other group in this chorus. Ask: *Which group in this chorus has the most singers?* (soprano)

Vocabulary: Content Area Words

Paragraph 1 and Graph: Read the first sentence. Remind children that the chorus is divided into two groups: soprano and alto. Point out the other two groups listed in the

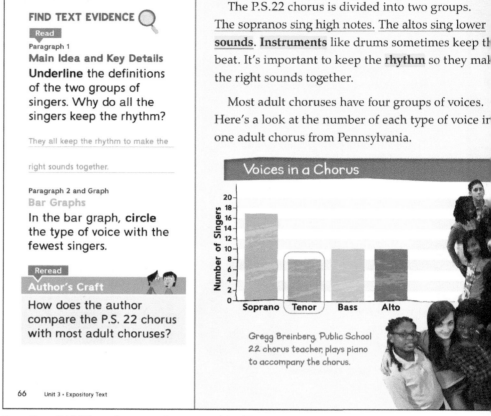

Reading/Writing Companion, pp. 66–67

graph: tenor and bass. Say: *Soprano, tenor, bass, and alto are different types of voices in a chorus. The singers in these groups sing different notes.* Ask: *Which two types of voices have the same number of singers?* (Bass and Alto)

Access Complex Text

Sentence Structure

Children may need additional support to help them understand complicated phrases and sentences in the selection. Direct children to page 67.

- Reread the second sentence on the page. Lead children to interpret the double negative, *won't disagree*.

- Read the first sentence in the second paragraph. Ask: *Who is Gregg Breinberg? What does he encourage the chorus to do?*

- Reread the last sentence in the second paragraph. Have children restate the sentence in their own words.

Musical Expression

Being part of the chorus is hard work. The chorus members won't (disagree). They practice for three hours each week.

Gregg Breinberg, their teacher, encourages the chorus to use **movements**. They move their hands to show how the songs make them feel. "They have their own movements because nobody feels **music** the same way," he explains.

The chorus members **understand** that singing in a chorus is a big job. "We just want to give it our best!" one student says.

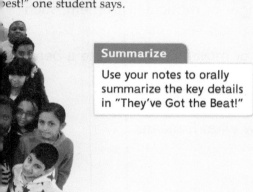

Summarize

Use your notes to orally summarize the key details in "They've Got the Beat!"

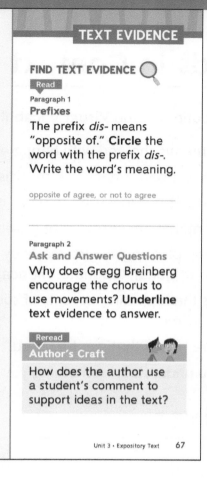

TEXT EVIDENCE

FIND TEXT EVIDENCE 🔍
Read

Paragraph 1
Prefixes
The prefix *dis-* means "opposite of." **Circle** the word with the prefix *dis-*. Write the word's meaning.

opposite of agree, or not to agree

Paragraph 2
Ask and Answer Questions
Why does Gregg Breinberg encourage the chorus to use movements? **Underline** text evidence to answer.

Reread
Author's Craft

How does the author use a student's comment to support ideas in the text?

Unit 3 · Expository Text   67

Vocabulary: Prefixes

Paragraph 1: Read the first paragraph. Remind children that a prefix is a group of letters added to the beginning of a word to change the word's meaning. *The prefix -dis can mean "opposite of." If I dislike something, then I don't like it. Which word in the paragraph has the prefix -dis?* (disagree) *What does* disagree *mean?* (not to agree) *What idea won't the members of the chorus disagree about?* (Being a part of the chorus is hard.)

Skill: Main Idea and Key Details

Paragraph 1: Read the first paragraph. Read the first sentence: "Being part of the chorus is hard work." Ask: *What is one detail that supports this idea?* (The chorus practices for three hours each week.)

Strategy: Ask and Answer Questions

Paragraph 2: Read the second paragraph. Remind children to ask questions about the text. Ask: *Why does Gregg Breinberg encourage the chorus to use movements?* (They can use movements to show how the songs make them feel.)

Summarize

Analytical Writing After their first read, have partners summarize the selection orally using their notes. Then have them write a summary in their writer's notebooks. Remind children to include important events and to use their own words. Children may decide to digitally record presentations of summaries.

Fluency

Have partners choral read the last paragraph on page 67 for intonation. Circulate and provide corrective feedback. For a full lesson and additional fluency practice, see pages T354–T355.

ELL Spotlight on Language

Page 67, Paragraph 2 Talk about the word *movement.* Say: *When I move, I make a movement. Watch me move my hands. Now, you move your hands. Turn to your partner. Are your movements different from your partner's?* Turn on some music. Encourage children to move to the music, either with their hands or with their whole bodies. Say: *Look around. Is everyone making the same movements?* (no) *Which phrase in paragraph 2 helps explain why everyone has their own movements?* ("because nobody feels music the same way") *How else can you say that?* (Possible: because everyone feels music differently)

Vocabulary

Reading/Writing Companion

OBJECTIVES

Determine the meaning of the new word formed when a known prefix is added to a known word (e.g., *happy/unhappy, tell/retell*).

ACADEMIC LANGUAGE

- *root word, prefix*
- Cognate: *prefijo*

Digital Tools

Visual Vocabulary Cards

TEACH IN SMALL GROUP ≪

Words in Context

Approaching Level and ELL Preteach the words before children begin the Shared Read.

On Level and Beyond Level Have children look up each word in the online **Visual Glossary**.

Words in Context

Use the routine on the **Visual Vocabulary Cards** to introduce each word.

Cheered means shouted with happiness or praise.

A **concert** is a performance by musicians or singers. (Cognate: *concierto*)

An **instrument** is a tool used to do or make something.

Our **movements** are our ways of moving.

Music is the pleasing sounds made by a singer or musical instrument, such as a piano or guitar. (Cognate: *música*)

Rhythm is the repeating accents of sounds or movements to create a beat. (Cognate: *ritmo*)

Sounds are noises that can be heard.

When you **understand** something you know what it means.

Prefixes

1 Explain

Tell children that a prefix is a word part added to the beginning of a root word to make a new word. They can separate the root word from a prefix to figure out the meaning of the word.

- The prefix *re-* means "again." If we *rebuild* something, we build it again.
- The prefix *dis-* means "opposite of" or "not." If you *disconnect* something, that means the opposite of connecting it.

Have children add information about prefixes to the vocabulary anchor chart.

2 Model

Model how to use the prefix *re-* to figure out the meaning of *return* on page 65. *I'm not sure what* return *means. I know that the word* turn *means "to move around in a circle." The prefix* re- *means "again." The word* return *means "to come around again."*

3 Guided Practice

Have children work with a partner to identify the meaning of the word *recalls* from page 65. Remind them to use the meaning of the prefix and the root word to determine the meaning. Have them write the definition, and then generate sentences using the word. Next, have pairs brainstorm other words with the prefix *re-*. Guide them to discuss the meaning of each and generate sentences using the words.

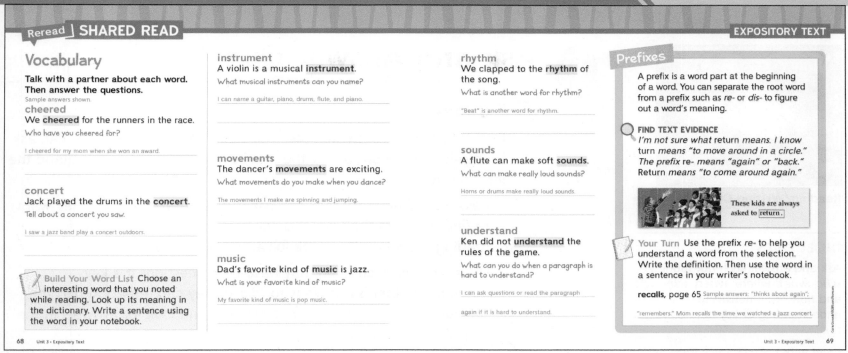

Reading/Writing Companion, pp. 68–69

 English Language Learners SCAFFOLD

Use the following scaffolds with **Guided Practice**.

Beginning

What prefix do you see in the word recall? (re-) *What does the prefix* re- *mean?* The prefix re- means again. *The word* call *has many meanings. What meanings of* call *do you know?* (Possible: give someone a name; cry out; contact using a telephone) Say: *In this case, the word* call *means to think about something.* Have partners ask and answer: *What does the word* recalls *mean?* The word *recalls* means thinks about again.

Intermediate

Help children understand how to use the prefix *re-* and root word *calls* to figure out that *recalls* means *thinks about again*. Provide a few more examples for practice, such as *retell*. Have partners ask and answer: What do you think retell means? The prefix re- means again. The root word tell means give information or say something. I think retell means say something again.

Advanced/Advanced High

Have children demonstrate that they can use what they know about the prefix *re-* to figure out the meaning of the word *recalls*. Ask: *What do you think recalls means? How do you know?* (I know re- means again and *calls* means thinks about, so I think *recalls* means thinks about something again, or remembers something.)

 Build Your Word List

Children might choose *recalls* from page 65. Have them create a word web with synonyms and antonyms. Have them write the word web in their writer's notebook.

✔ **Check for Success**

Rubric Use the online rubric to record children's progress.

Can children use the root word and prefix to figure out the meaning of the word *recalls?*

Differentiate
SMALL GROUP INSTRUCTION

If No

| Approaching | Reteach p. T410 |

| ELL | Develop p. T436 |

If Yes

| On | Review p. T418 |

| Beyond | Extend p. T424 |

Comprehension Strategy

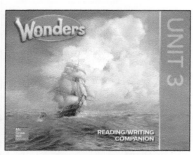

Reading/Writing Companion

OBJECTIVES

Ask and answer such questions as *who, what, where, when, why,* and *how* to demonstrate understanding of key details in a text.

Read with sufficient accuracy and fluency to support comprehension.

Read on-level text with purpose and understanding.

ACADEMIC LANGUAGE

• *bar graph, expository text*

Ask and Answer Questions

1 **Explain**

Remind children that when they read an expository text, they can ask themselves questions about the text to make sure they understand the information.

- Before children read, they can ask questions about what they want to find out from the text. This will help them set a purpose for reading. They can then look for answers as they read.

- During reading, children may have new questions if a key detail in the text is not clear to them. They can reread to find the answer. They can also continue reading and look for answers in the rest of the selection.

- If children still have questions about key details after reading, they can go back and reread parts of the text to find the answers.

Anchor Chart Have volunteers add information about asking and answering questions to the ask-and-answer strategy chart and reread the chart.

2 **Model**

Model how asking and answering questions can help children understand the text better. Point out the last paragraph on page 67 of "They've Got the Beat!" to answer the question, "What is it like for students to sing on stage?"

Think Aloud I can reread the last paragraph on page 67 to answer my question, "What is it like for students to sing on stage?" I learn that all the chorus members think that singing on stage is hard work. I also learn that they just want to give it their best. Therefore, they don't mind all the hard work.

3 **Guided Practice**

Have partners think of a question they have about the selection. Guide them to reread the part of the selection that will help them answer their question. Ask partners to share their questions and answers with the class.

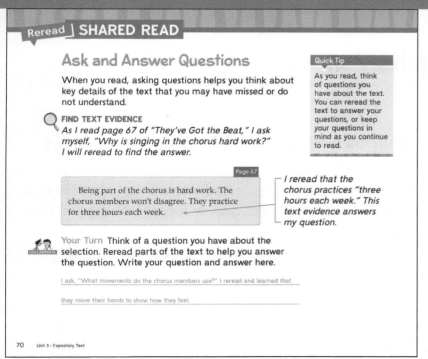

Reading/Writing Companion, p. 70

 English Language Learners SCAFFOLD

Use the following scaffolds with **Guided Practice**.

Beginning

Write the question words on the board: *who, what, where, why, when,* and *how.* Display the photograph on page 64 and ask questions, such as *Who is singing? What is this girl doing? Where are the children? Why is she smiling? When do they perform? How do they feel?* For each question, help children locate an answer in the photo or in the text. Then have children scan the text and find a fact they want to ask a partner about. Help them formulate a question so they can ask and answer with a partner.

Intermediate

Display the 5W + How question words. Using the photographs and text, model asking and answering questions about the passage. Then have pairs work together to ask and answer a question about the passage. Provide examples as needed, such as *Where did the chorus sing?* The chorus sang <u>at the White House</u>.

Advanced/Advanced High

Review the 5W + How question words. Have pairs take turns asking and answering questions about the passage. Provide support so they can use complete sentences.

 HABITS OF LEARNING

I ask questions. When children ask questions about an expository text, they are better able to understand the text. Have children consider the following questions:

- **Before reading:** What do I think this text will be about? What is my purpose for reading this text?
- **During reading:** Are there any details I do not understand? What can I reread to help me understand the details?
- **After reading:** What was the author's purpose for writing this text?

✓ Check for Success

Do children ask and answer questions about expository text?

Differentiate
SMALL GROUP INSTRUCTION

If No

| Approaching | Reteach p. T406 |
| ELL | Develop p. T434 |

If Yes

| On | Review p. T414 |
| Beyond | Extend p. T420 |

Reading/Writing Companion

OBJECTIVES

Ask and answer such questions as *who, what, where, when, why,* and *how* to demonstrate understanding of key details in a text.

Know and use various text features (e.g., captions, bold print, subheadings, glossaries, indexes, electronic menus, icons) to locate key facts or information in a text efficiently.

Explain how specific images (e.g., diagram showing how a machine works) contribute to and clarify a text.

Recognize the characteristics and text features of expository text.

ACADEMIC LANGUAGE
• *bar graph, expository text*
• Cognate: *gráfico*

Bar Graphs

1 Explain

Share with children the following key characteristics of **expository text**.

• Expository text gives important facts and information about a topic. This kind of text can tell about a person or a place or explain how something works.

• Expository text may include text features such as subheadings, photographs and captions, and graphs.

2 Model

Model identifying and using the text features in "They've Got the Beat!" Tell children that previewing text features can help them make predictions about what they will read.

Bar Graph Remind children that a bar graph uses bars. The bars help readers compare numbers or amounts. Authors use bar graphs to compare information between groups. Point out the bar graph and read the title and labels. Have children repeat after you. Ask: *What is the topic of this bar graph?* (the different kinds of voices in a chorus)

Anchor Chart Have a volunteer add this text feature and information about it to the expository text anchor chart.

3 Guided Practice

Have partners work together to learn what the bar graph compares. Guide children by asking the following questions: *What are the four different groups in an adult chorus?* (soprano, tenor, bass, and alto) *Which group has the fewest singers?* (tenor) *Which group has the most singers?* (soprano) *How many singers does the bass group have?* (10) Have children share the information they learned with the class. Have them discuss how the graph helps them compare amounts easily.

Independent Practice Have children read the online **Differentiated Genre Passage**, "Musical Expression."

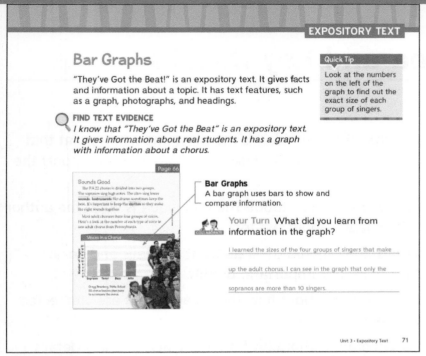

Reading/Writing Companion, p. 71

 English Language Learners **SCAFFOLD**

Use the following scaffolds with **Guided Practice** to help children give information based on the bar graph.

Beginning

Read aloud the words on the graph and have children repeat after you. Make sure children know the number words by pointing to the numbers and having children chorally count with you. Provide sentence frames to help partners give information about the graph: How many sopranos are there? There are 16 sopranos.

Intermediate

After partners ask and answer basic questions about the bar graph, help children use words to compare: *more, most, fewer, fewest.* Model as needed, then have partners ask and answer: Which group has the most/fewest singers? The sopranos have the most singers. The tenors have the fewest singers. Are there more tenors or altos? There are more altos. Are there fewer tenors or altos? There are fewer tenors.

Advanced/Advanced High

Have pairs take turns asking each other and answering questions about the bar graph, for example: *How many tenors are there? Are there more sopranos or altos? Are there fewer basses than tenors? Which two groups have the same number?*

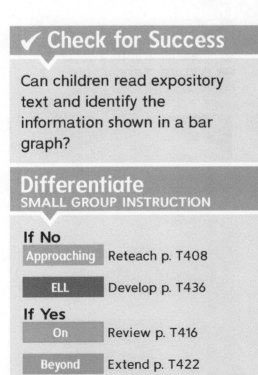

✔ **Check for Success**

Can children read expository text and identify the information shown in a bar graph?

Differentiate
SMALL GROUP INSTRUCTION

If No
Approaching Reteach p. T408

ELL Develop p. T436

If Yes
On Review p. T416

Beyond Extend p. T422

Comprehension Skill

Reading/Writing Companion

OBJECTIVES

Ask and answer such questions as *who, what, where, when, why,* and *how* to demonstrate understanding of key details in a text.

Identify the main topic of a multiparagraph text as well as the focus of specific paragraphs within the text.

ACADEMIC LANGUAGE

• *key detail, main idea*
• Cognate: *detalle*

Digital Tools

To differentiate instruction for key skills, use the results of the activity.

Main Idea and Key Details

1 Explain

Remind children that the main idea is the most important point that an author makes about a topic. Key details tell about and support the main idea.

- The topic is what the text is about. The main idea is what the author wants readers to learn about the topic.

- As children read, they should think about the details and decide which details are key, or important, details.

- Children can then think about how these key details are connected to determine the main idea.

Anchor Chart Begin an anchor chart on main idea and key details and encourage children to add information to it.

2 Model

Model identifying a key detail on page 65 of the **Reading/Writing Companion** and recording it in the graphic organizer. Point out that the key details will be connected and support the main idea.

Model for children how you chose the first key detail to include in the graphic organizer. *I see from the photo, title, and first paragraph that the text is about a school chorus; that's the topic. The second paragraph tells about the chorus singing at the White House at an awards show. The fact that the chorus sings at important events is a key detail about the chorus. It tells me they must be very good! Let's continue reading for more details so we can put them together to figure out the main idea, or what the author wants us to learn about the chorus.*

3 Guided Practice

Have children work in pairs to complete the graphic organizer. Guide them to identify a key detail from each section of the text. When they have collected their details, have partners discuss them and think about what the author wants readers to understand about the chorus by providing those details. Help children understand that the details all need to support the main idea the author is writing about.

Write About Reading: Key Details Have partners work together to write a paragraph about how they chose the key details and how they used those details to determine the main idea. Choose partners to share their writing.

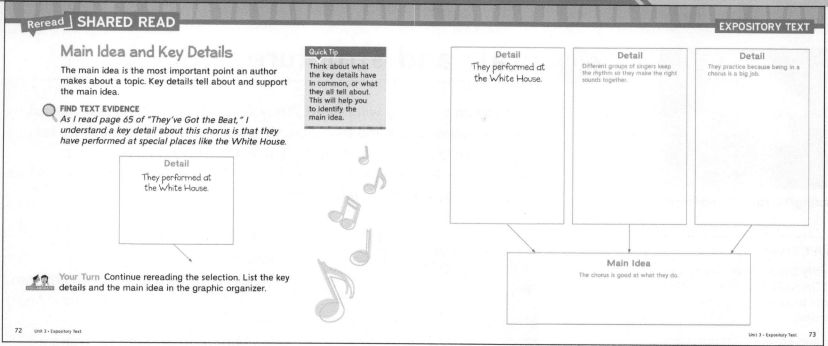

Reading/Writing Companion, pp. 72–73

English Language Learners SCAFFOLD

Use the following scaffolds with **Guided Practice**.

Beginning

Help children complete the graphic organizer. Point to the photos for support. Provide a word bank of action words, then provide sentence frames to state key details: They <u>performed</u> at the White House. They <u>sang</u> at a Hollywood awards show. The audience <u>clapped</u> and <u>cheered</u>. They <u>keep</u> the rhythm. The chorus <u>practices</u> for three hours a week.

Intermediate

Have partners work together to find key details to complete the graphic organizer. As needed, prompt them with questions and by pointing to details in the photos: *Where did the chorus perform?* (the White House) *Where else did they sing?* (a Hollywood awards show) *What did the audience do?* (clapped and cheered) *What does the chorus do every week?* (practice three times)

Advanced/Advanced High

Have partners work together to complete the graphic organizer. To help them focus, suggest partners scan one paragraph at a time, and ask: *What important detail did we read in this paragraph?* Remind them to look at the photos for additional details. Ask them to try to write complete sentences. Then have partners discuss how the details are connected to determine the main idea.

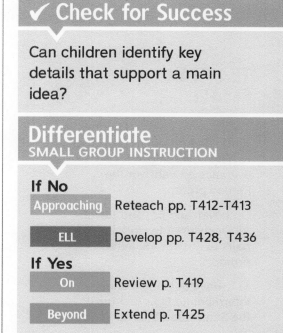

✓ Check for Success

Can children identify key details that support a main idea?

Differentiate
SMALL GROUP INSTRUCTION

If No

| Approaching | Reteach pp. T412-T413 |
| ELL | Develop pp. T428, T436 |

If Yes

| On | Review p. T419 |
| Beyond | Extend p. T425 |

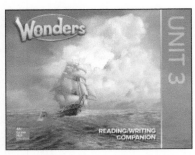

Reading/Writing Companion

OBJECTIVES

Identify the main purpose of a text, including what the author wants to answer, explain, or describe.

Ask and answer such questions as *who, what, where, when, why,* and *how* to demonstrate understanding of key details in a text.

ACADEMIC LANGUAGE

- *phrase, compare*
- Cognates: *frase, comparer*

 ## Craft and Structure

Tell children that they will reread "They've Got the Beat!" to learn about how the author wrote the selection. When authors write expository text, they give facts and information. They may use text features, such as headings, photographs with captions, and graphs. They often use a definite structure to present their information.

Reading/Writing Companion p. 65

AUTHOR'S CRAFT

Reread the first paragraph of "They've Got the Beat!" with children. *What does it mean to sing your heart out?* (It means to sing with feeling.) Explain that the author is using a colorful phrase to tell how the students feel about singing. *If you are singing your heart out, how are you singing?* (with great feeling, singing your best)

ELL Explain that when something is done "with heart," it is done with feeling. Demonstrate singing a familiar song in a monotone voice and then with feeling. Reread the first sentence of "They've Got the Beat!" with children. Lead children in singing a familiar song with great feeling. Explain that they just "sang their hearts out."

Why does the author use the phrase "sing their hearts out" to begin the selection? (The author wants readers to know that the students really love to sing and do their best. The author wants the reader to be interested in the singers.)

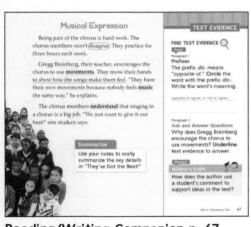

Reading/Writing Companion p. 66

AUTHOR'S CRAFT

Reread the first paragraph of page 66 with children. *How is the P.S. 22 chorus divided?* (It is divided into two groups: sopranos and altos.) Read the second paragraph with children. *How are most adult choruses divided?* (They are divided into four groups of voices.)

 Reread "Sounds Good" on page 66. *How many groups are in the P.S. 22 chorus?* (two) *How many groups are in most adult choruses?* (four) *How are adult choruses and the P.S. 22 chorus alike?* (They divide the singers into groups.) *How are they different?* (The P.S. 22 chorus has two groups and most adult choruses have four groups.)

How does the author compare the P.S. 22 chorus with most adult choruses? (Both the P.S. 22 chorus and adult choruses divide the singers into groups. The P.S. 22 chorus is divided into two groups while most adult choruses are divided into four groups.)

Reading/Writing Companion p. 67

AUTHOR'S CRAFT

Reread the first paragraph on page 67 with children. *What do the chorus members do each week?* (They practice three hours.) *Why?* (Being part of the chorus is hard work.) Reread the last paragraph on page 67 with children. *The author includes a quote from a student. What does the student say?* ("We just want to give it our best!") *How do you think this student feels about being in the chorus?* (The student feels that being in the chorus is important.)

 Use gestures and context to help children understand the phrases *hard work, big job,* and *give it our best.*

How does the author use a student's comment to support ideas in the text? (The students practice a lot and work hard. The author quotes a student, "We just want to give it our best!" Even though they work hard, they want to do their best because the chorus is important to them.)

Make Inferences

Remind children that to make inferences, they use text evidence and what they already know. They connect details to make inferences.

Think Aloud On page 67, I read that the chorus members practice three hours each week. This tells me they are willing to dedicate a lot of their time and work very hard to be in the chorus. I can infer that being in the chorus is important to the students. In the last paragraph, when a student says, "We just want to give it our best," I can infer that the student is proud to be in the chorus. I can infer that the chorus is important to this student.

Respond to Reading

Reading/Writing Companion

OBJECTIVES

Ask and answer such questions as *who, what, where, when, why,* and *how* to demonstrate understanding of key details in a text.

ACADEMIC LANGUAGE

• *detail, quote*
• Cognate: *detalle*

TEACH IN SMALL GROUP

Approaching Level Have partners work together to complete sentence frames with key details from the passage.

On Level Have partners work together to find text evidence and complete the response to the prompt.

Beyond Level Have children work independently to identify key details, and then work as partners to write their response.

ELL Group ELLs of mixed proficiency levels to discuss and respond to the prompt.

Write About the Shared Read

Analyze the Prompt

Read the prompt aloud: *How does the author help you understand what being in the chorus is like for the students?* Ask: *What is the prompt asking?* (for details to show what being in the chorus is like for the students) Say: *Let's reread to find details in the text that show what being in the chorus is like for the students. Taking notes will help you write your response.*

Analyze Text Evidence

Remind children that the author provides examples of different things the chorus members do in the passage. The author also provides quotes from students that let you know how they feel about being in the chorus. In the **Reading/Writing Companion,** have children scan the second paragraph on page 65 to find places the chorus performed. (They went to the White House and a Hollywood awards show.) Then have them read the quote at the bottom of page 65 to learn how a student feels. (Brianna gets excited when she sees joy on the faces of audience members.) Next, have them find details on page 67 that tell what the chorus members do. (They work hard. They practice three hours each week. They use movements to show how they feel. They give it their best.) Tell children that they can use these details to write their responses.

Respond

Direct children to the sentence starters on **Reading/Writing Companion** page 74. Have partners use text evidence they found to complete the sentence starters. They can use the sentence starters in their responses to tell what being in the chorus is like for the students.

Think Aloud When I read that Brianna is nervous to sing in front of a big audience but also excited when she sees the joy on the faces of the audience, I understood what being in the chorus is like for the students. I thought about how the chorus members make other people happy.

 Children should use the sentence starters in their responses. The first sentence should state the main idea, or what the response is about, such as "The author explains that the students practice a lot because they have a big job." Then children should use specific details from the passage to support the main idea. If needed, children may continue their responses on a separate sheet of paper.

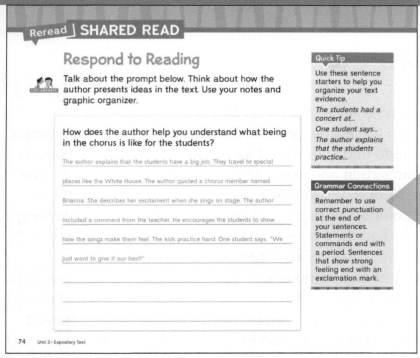

Reading/Writing Companion, p. 74

 English Language Learners SCAFFOLD

Use the following scaffolds with **Analyze Text Evidence**.

Beginning

Clarify the meaning of the words *joy* and *excited*. Reread the last sentence on page 65. *Which word describes how the audience feels when the chorus sings?* (joy) *How do the singers feel when they see joy on the faces of the audience?* (excited) Lead children in writing a sentence using a sentence frame: The singers feel <u>excited</u> when they see <u>joy</u> in the audience.

Intermediate

Reread page 65. *Which text clues help you guess how the audience reacted when the students performed at the White House and the awards show?* (clapped, cheered; always asked to return) *How do you think that made the singers feel?* (happy, proud) *Which text clues confirm your guess?* The singers feel <u>excited</u> when <u>they see joy in the audience</u>.

Advanced/Advanced High

Have partners focus on how the interview with Brianna helps them understand what being in a chorus is like. Provide guiding questions to ask each other: *Which words describe how Brianna feels?* (She feels nervous and excited.) *What makes her change from nervous to excited?* (She gets excited when she sees joy on their faces.)

Newcomers

Have children listen to the summaries of the **Shared Read** in their native language and then in English to help them access the text and develop listening comprehension. Help children ask and answer questions with a partner. Use these sentence frames: What is the text about? The text is about _____. Then have children continue the lessons in the **Newcomer Teacher's Guide**.

Reading/Writing Companion

OBJECTIVES

Read with sufficient accuracy and fluency to support comprehension. Read on-level text orally with accuracy, appropriate rate, and expression on successive readings.

Rate: 74-94 WCPM

ACADEMIC LANGUAGE

• *intonation, punctuation, exclamation*

• Cognates: *entonación, puntuación, exclamación*

Intonation

Explain/Model Remind children that reading with intonation means changing your tone of voice when you read to express meaning to listeners. Explain that as we read and understand a text, we can adjust our voice in response to the punctuation and in response to the importance of certain words and phrases. Point to the beginning of "They've Got the Beat!" on **Reading/Writing Companion** page 65. Read the first paragraph, showing excitement when reading the exclamatory sentence and stress when reading the words "the school chorus." Model reading with accuracy, good intonation, and at an appropriate rate. Remind children that an appropriate rate is not as fast as they can read. They should think about what is comfortable for someone to listen to and be able to comprehend the message. Point out how you read at an appropriate rate when you read aloud. Ask children what they noticed about your tone of voice. Point out the exclamation mark at the end of the first sentence, which is read with an excited tone. Point out the important words "the school chorus," which is read at a slower rate.

Practice/Apply Invite children to echo read the last paragraph on page 67, reading the quotation in an excited tone.

Divide the class into two groups. Have at least one slightly higher reader in each group. Ask children to follow along as you reread the last paragraph on page 67 of the **Reading/Writing Companion.** Have the first group echo read the first sentence and the second group echo read the second sentence. Repeat, so that each group reads each sentence.

Have groups work together to practice reading with good intonation and at an appropriate rate. Each group should choose either page 65 or page 67 to read. Remind children to read with accuracy, or to say all the words correctly, and to read with good intonation, adjusting their voices in response to the punctuation and to the importance of certain words and phrases. Ask children to give each other feedback on the rate at which they read.

Listen to the groups, providing corrective feedback as needed.

Daily Fluency Practice

Children can practice fluency using **Differentiated Genre Passage** "Musical Expression."

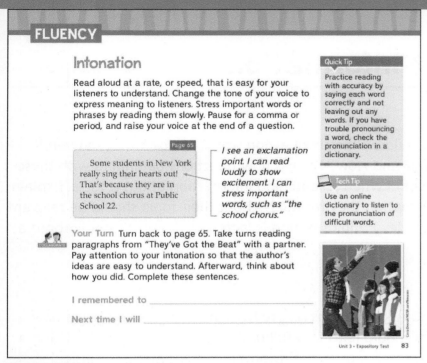

FLUENCY

Intonation

Read aloud at a rate, or speed, that is easy for your listeners to understand. Change the tone of your voice to express meaning to listeners. Stress important words or phrases by reading them slowly. Pause for a comma or period, and raise your voice at the end of a question.

Quick Tip

Practice reading with accuracy by saying each word correctly and not leaving out any words. If you have trouble pronouncing a word, check the pronunciation in a dictionary.

Page 65

Some students in New York really sing their hearts out! That's because they are in the school chorus at Public School 22.

I see an exclamation point. I can read loudly to show excitement. I can stress important words, such as "the school chorus."

Tech Tip

Use an online dictionary to listen to the pronunciation of difficult words.

Your Turn Turn back to page 65. Take turns reading paragraphs from "They've Got the Beat" with a partner. Pay attention to your intonation so that the author's ideas are easy to understand. Afterward, think about how you did. Complete these sentences.

I remembered to _____

Next time I will _____

Unit 3 · Expository Text   83

Reading/Writing Companion, p. 83

 # English Language Learners SCAFFOLD

Before fluency practice, point out the potential pronunciation challenges in each section of text so children can practice the words in isolation. Refer to the **Language Transfers Handbook** for sounds that may or may not transfer in English.

Use the following scaffolds during the group activity in **Practice/Apply**.

Beginning

Before reading, have students listen to the audio recording of the Shared Read as a model for fluency. Allow them to listen and read along silently a few times. Then have them pause after each sentence to echo read. Children may record themselves reading one sentence several times, then select their favorite recording to play for you.

Intermediate

After groups pick a page to practice, have them listen to the audio of the Shared Read as a model for fluency. Have the group pause after each sentence to echo read. Encourage children to record themselves reading one page several times and compare their reading to the audio recording so they can self-correct, as needed.

Advanced/Advanced High

Have children join the rest of the class for group fluency practice. Encourage them to listen to the audio recording of the selection for additional practice as needed.

Language Transfers Handbook

 ✓ **Check for Success**

Can children read text accurately, with good intonation, and at an appropriate rate?

Differentiate
SMALL GROUP INSTRUCTION

If No

| Approaching | Reteach pp. T384, T406 |
| ELL | Develop pp. T385, T434 |

If Yes

| On | Apply p. T414 |
| Beyond | Apply p. T420 |

Reading/Writing Companion

OBJECTIVES

Participate in shared research and writing projects (e.g., read a number of books on a single topic to produce a report; record science observations).

Ask and answer such questions as *who, what, where, when, why,* and *how* to demonstrate understanding of key details in a text.

ACADEMIC LANGUAGE

• *relevant, paraphrase, patriotic, collage*

• Cognate: *patriótico*

Relevant Information

1 Explain

Review with children the six question words *Who? What? When? Where? Why?* and *How?* Discuss how questions beginning with these words are helpful when researching information about a topic. Explain that the information they research about their topic should be relevant information. Relevant information is facts and details that tell about a topic.

2 Model

Model how to ask questions before beginning research. Discuss how the questions should lead to a full understanding of the topic. Using a few of the question words, brainstorm questions about a musical instrument, such as an electric guitar.

Discuss using research materials to locate relevant information, or details and facts, that answer their questions. If needed, show an example of how to research the answer to one of the questions. Remind children to paraphrase relevant information by taking notes in their own words.

3 Guided Practice

Group children by their chosen song and have them brainstorm a list of four questions about it. Children can work as a group or in pairs to use the questions to guide their research. Guide children in using their questions as they research their song.

Patriotic Song Collage After children have answered their questions, guide them in finding pictures that show the important ideas. Have children use the pictures to create a collage. Tell them to write the title of the song at the top of the collage and to write sentences about the song using their notes.

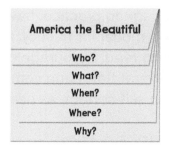

Layered-Look Book

TEACH IN SMALL GROUP

You may wish to teach the Study Skill lesson during Small Group time. Have groups of mixed abilities complete the page and work on the collage.

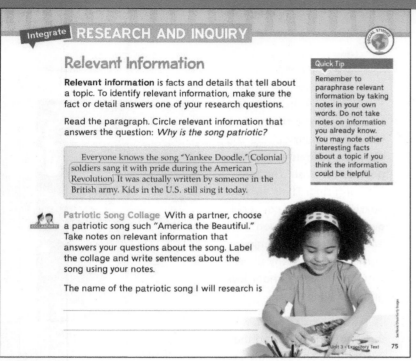

Digital Tools

Use this digital tool to enhance the lesson. Evaluate Video Sources for Relevance (Video)

Research Process

Provide the online **Research Roadmap** to guide children.

Step 1: Set Research Goals

- Direct children to develop and follow a research plan.
- Offer feedback as they generate research questions.

Step 2: Identify Sources

- Help children identify relevant and reliable sources.

Step 3: Find and Record Information

- Help children find relevant information and take notes.
- Discuss how to keep track of source information.

Step 4: Organize

- Have children analyze gathered information.
- Encourage children to organize their notes.

Step 5: Synthesize and Present

- Make sure children create a collage about a patriotic song.
- Guide children to choose appropriate delivery modes.

 # English Language Learners SCAFFOLD

Use the following scaffolds with **Patriotic Song Collage**.

Beginning

Pair children with native speakers who can suggest patriotic songs and help explain the language in each one. Provide sentence frames for discussion: Which song are you going to research? We are going to research "America the Beautiful." Help children contribute ideas to the planning process by providing frames to discuss the imagery and descriptions in the song. For example: In "America the Beautiful," I hear the phrase "sea to shining sea." Let's add a picture of a sea.

Intermediate

Pair children with native speakers who can suggest patriotic songs and help explain the language in each one. As partners assemble their collages, provide sentence frames for children to use to discuss their collages. For example, The song "America the Beautiful" is about our beautiful country. I hear the phrase "sea to shining sea." Let's add a picture of a sparkling, shining sea.

Advanced/Advanced High

Pair children with native speakers who can help explain the language in a few patriotic songs. After partners assemble their collages, ask pairs to work together to write captions and labels for them. Encourage them to write captions in complete sentences.

Genre · Expository Text TIME FOR KIDS

Many Ways to Enjoy Music

? Essential Question
How do you express yourself?
Read about how people express
themselves through music.

▶ Go Digital!

262

How do music lovers who are deaf enjoy concerts?

At a **concert**, loud **music** booms from the stage. The band rocks their guitars and other **instruments**. Drums pound and clash. The fans clap and sing. Their ears are buzzing when the concert is over. However, you don't need to listen up to enjoy a music concert. Many people who are unable to hear love going to concerts.

At this rock concert, a fan who is deaf sensed the excitement. She saw the band take the stage. She **cheered** by shaking her fist in the air. Her big smile showed that she really loved the concert! **1**

A fan who is deaf and her son enjoy a concert. They sat in seats close to an interpreter.

2

STOP AND CHECK

Ask and Answer Questions What things will happen at a concert? Go back to the text to find the answer.

263

Literature Anthology, pp. 262–263

Literature Anthology

Text Complexity Range
Lexile

420   ▲680   820

Have children apply what they learned as they read.

"Many Ways to Enjoy Music"
Close Reading Routine

▼ **Read**   DOK 1–2

- Identify key ideas and details about expressing ourselves.
- Take notes and retell.
- Use A C T prompts as needed.

▼ **Reread**   DOK 2–3

- Analyze the text, craft, and structure.
- *Reading/Writing Companion*, pp. 76–77.

▼ **Integrate**   DOK 4

- Integrate knowledge and ideas.
- Make text-to-text connections.
- Use the Integrate lesson.
- Inspire action.

T357A UNIT 3 WEEK 5

Read

Tell children they will read about how deaf music lovers enjoy concerts. Ask children to predict how the text might answer the **Essential Question.**

DIFFERENTIATED READING

Approaching Level Have children listen to the selection summary. Use the Reread prompts during Small-Group time.

On Level and **Beyond Level** Pair children or have them independently complete the Reread prompts on **Reading/Writing Companion** pages 76–77.

 English Language Learners Beforehand, have Beginning/Early-Intermediate ELLs listen to a text summary, available in many languages. See small group pages for additional support.

Note Taking

Use the Graphic Organizer

Guide children to take notes as they read. Distribute copies of the Main Idea and Key Details **Graphic Organizer**. Ask them to note words they do not understand or questions they may have.

① Skill: Main Idea and Key Details

Ask: *What is a key detail we learn on page 263 about how music lovers who are deaf enjoy music at concerts?* (We learn that fans who are deaf sense the excitement at the concert.) *We'll add this information to the first detail box on our Main Idea and Key Details Chart.*

② Text Features: Photos and Captions

Say: *Look at the photograph and caption on page 263. What additional information does the caption give you?* (A fan who is deaf and her son are enjoying a concert. They are sitting in seats close to an interpreter.)

✓ STOP AND CHECK

Ask and Answer Questions What things will happen at a concert? Go back to the text to find the answer. (Loud music will boom from the stage. The band will play their instruments. The fans will clap and sing.)

Reread

Author's Craft

Reading/Writing Companion, 76

Reread page 263. Ask: *What words and phrases does the author use to help you sense the excitement of a concert?* (loud music booms; band rocks their guitars; drums pound and clash; fans clap and sing)

Make Inferences

Explain I can use text evidence to help me figure out why the author wants me to sense the excitement of the concert.

Model In the first paragraph, the author describes the music and the fans' responses. In the second paragraph, the author describes how a fan who is deaf senses the excitement and responds.

Apply By sensing the excitement of the concert myself, I can understand what the music fans are sensing, too.

Purpose The purpose of the text is to give children information about the ways in which people who are deaf enjoy music. Discuss both the ways fans who are deaf perceive the music and the ways they respond to it. Explain that, as the title suggests, there are many ways for people to enjoy music.

 Spotlight on Language

Page 263, Paragraph 1 Point out the words *booms, pound, clash, clap,* and *buzzing.* Work with children to describe the noises named by these words. Help them "hear" how the definition of *boom* is the same as the sound it names. Repeat the activity for *buzzing, pound, clash,* and *clap,* which also sound similar to the sounds that they name. Have partners work together to practice the words. One partner says a word and the other makes a sound to demonstrate it.

Making Music

At some concerts, rock bands perform. At others, orchestras play. An orchestra is a group of musicians playing instruments together. Most orchestras have four sections.

③

Here is a look at the number of instruments in each section.

Orchestra Instruments

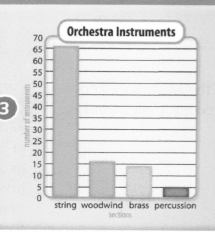

(bar graph: vertical axis labeled "number of instruments" from 0 to 70; horizontal axis "sections" with bars for string, woodwind, brass, percussion)

Watching the Signs

One way people who are deaf enjoy a concert is by watching an interpreter. Interpreters use body **movements**, like swaying or jumping, to communicate what is happening on stage. By watching interpreters move, fans can **understand** what the band is singing.

An interpreter is a person who uses sign language to show the words of the song.

264

TIME FOR KIDS

The movements help users feel what the music expresses. These chairs really rock!

Rock and Relax

④ Another way for people who are deaf to enjoy a concert is with technology. A special chair moves with the music's **rhythm**. A loud, pounding sound makes the chair beat hard. Fans who are deaf feel the rhythm on their backs. Low, quiet **sounds** makes the chair beat softer. The fans can feel the rhythm on the lower parts of their bodies.

⑤ Interpreters and technology are just some of the many ways people who are deaf can enjoy a concert.

Respond to the Text

Use details from the selection to summarize. SUMMARIZE

Is "Many Ways to Enjoy Music" a good title for this selection? Why or why not? WRITE

? How can people express themselves through music? TEXT TO WORLD

265

Literature Anthology, pp. 264–265

Read

③ Text Features: Bar Graph

Review with children the bar graph on page 264.
Ask: *What does the bar graph help explain?* (how many instruments are in each section of an orchestra) Ask: *How many instruments are in the percussion section?* (5)

④ Strategy: Ask and Answer Questions

We've learned about different ways a person who is deaf can enjoy music. With a partner, ask a question about that topic. Reread to see if you can find an answer.

⑤ Skill: Main Idea and Key Details

What important details have we read about how fans who are deaf enjoy concerts and music? Let's add these to our chart. Now think about what these details tell us about the main idea. Talk with a partner, and then write the main idea on your chart.

Main Idea	Key Details
Fans who are deaf can enjoy music in many ways.	Fans who are deaf sense the excitement.
	Fans who are deaf can enjoy a concert by watching a sign language interpreter.
	Fans who are deaf can use a special chair to feel the music.

Reread

Author's Purpose

Reading/Writing Companion, 77

Ask: *Why does the author describe watching an interpreter and using technology? Cite evidence from the text in your answer.* (The author wants readers to understand how people who are deaf can enjoy the words of songs, understand what is happening on stage, and feel the rhythm of music.)

Return to Purposes

Review children's predictions. Guide them to use text evidence to confirm or revise predictions. Discuss what they learned about how music lovers who are deaf enjoy concerts.

Read

Summarize

Guide children in retelling the selection. Remind them that as they read, they noted key details and answered questions about the text. Have them use this and the information they recorded on their Main Idea and Key Details Chart to help retell the selection.

Reread

Analyze the Text

After children retell the selection, have them reread and answer the questions on **Reading/Writing Companion** pages 76–77. For children who need more support, use the Reread prompts on pages T357B and T357C.

Write About the Text

Review the writing prompt with children. Remind them to use their responses from the **Reading/Writing Companion** to support their answers. For a full lesson on writing a response using text evidence, see pages T358-T359.

Integrate

Make Connections

Text to World Answer: Technology helps people who are deaf feel the rhythm of music. Evidence: There is a special chair that moves along with the rhythm of the music. The person in the chair can feel the beats.

Connect to Content

Sound is a type of energy that is made when molecules in the air move rapidly back and forth in waves. Clap your hands. The sound travels in waves to your ears and your brain.

English Language Learners

Monitor Oral Production Help children summarize by asking a prompt about each page, such as *How are people expressing themselves here? How does a person who is deaf enjoy the music?* Provide sentence starters to help children retell the selection, such as: *This person is enjoying the music by ____.*

Remember to model self-corrective techniques as you speak to children. For example, pretend to answer one of your guiding questions above, but use the wrong verb form, then self-correct.

Newcomers

Review the **Newcomer Online Visuals** and their accompanying prompts to help children reinforce and expand vocabulary and language about Life at School (5-9) and My Family and Me (10-14). Use the Conversation Starters, Speech Balloons, and the Games in the **Newcomer Teacher's Guide** to continue building vocabulary and developing oral and written language.

Respond to Reading

Reading/Writing Companion

OBJECTIVES

Write opinion pieces in which they introduce the topic or book they are writing about, state an opinion, supply reasons that support the opinion, use linking words (e.g., because, and, also) to connect opinion and reasons, and provide a concluding statement or section.

ACADEMIC LANGUAGE
• *title, prompt*
• Cognate: *título*

TEACH IN SMALL GROUP ◀◀

You may wish to use the Respond to Reading activities during Small Group time.

Approaching Level, **On Level** and **Beyond Level** Pair children of different proficiency levels.

ELL According to their language proficiency, children should contribute to discussions by using short phrases, asking questions, and adding relevant details.

Write About the Anchor Text

Analyze the Prompt

Read the prompt aloud: *Why is "Many Ways to Enjoy Music" a good title for this selection?* Ask: *What is the prompt asking you to do?* (to explain why the title of the article is a good title for the text) Say: *Let's reread to see how the title of this text sums up the most important ideas of the text.*

Analyze Text Evidence

Explain that a title usually sums up the most important ideas of a text. Have children look at **Literature Anthology** "Many Ways to Enjoy Music," page 263. Ask: *How does the author help you sense the excitement of a concert?* (The author uses word choice.) Next, have children look at pages 264–265. Ask: *What are the most important ideas on these pages that tell how music lovers who are deaf enjoy music?* (They enjoy music by watching an interpreter. They also enjoy music by using a special chair that moves with the music's rhythm.)

Respond

Review pages 76–77 of the **Reading/Writing Companion**. Have partners or small groups refer to and discuss their completed charts and writing responses from those pages. Then direct children's attention to the sentence starters on page 78 of the **Reading/Writing Companion**. Children should focus on how the author uses word choice, text details, and text features to explain that there are many ways to enjoy music. Their first sentence should state their main idea, such as "This is a good title because the author taught me many ways people who are deaf enjoy music."

Analytical Writing Children should continue to go through the text to find specific elements that support their explanation of why "Many Ways to Enjoy Music" is a good title for the selection. Remind children that they can use additional paper to complete their responses.

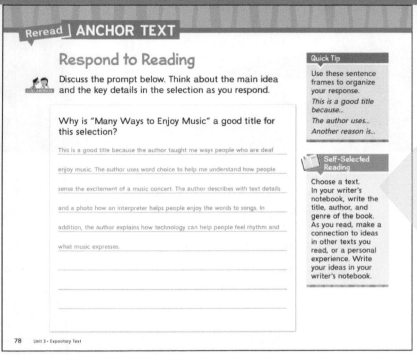

Reading/Writing Companion, p. 78

English Language Learners SCAFFOLD

Use the following scaffold during **Respond**.

Beginning

Read the title together. *Look at your answers on page 76. Which words describe the concert?* (Children read aloud their graphic organizer responses.) *Why does the author include these details?* The author includes these details to show how <u>exciting</u> a concert is. *Look at your answers on page 77. Why does the author include these details?* The author includes these details to show how people who are <u>deaf</u> can enjoy <u>music</u>.

Intermediate

Teach children the phrases *even if* and *even though*. Then provide sentence frames to help them craft their responses. The author describes the excitement of a concert using words like <u>booms</u> and <u>rocks.</u> The author explains how <u>interpreters</u> can help people who are deaf enjoy the words to songs even though <u>they can't hear</u>. The author also explains how <u>technology</u> can help people feel the rhythm of the music even if <u>they can't hear</u>.

Advanced/Advanced High

Have partners find text evidence to support their answers. Have them discuss their answers before writing them. Encourage them to use phrases like *even though* and *even if* in their responses.

Newcomers

Have children listen to a summary of the **Anchor Text** in their native language and then in English to help them access the text and develop listening comprehension. Help children ask and answer questions with a partner. Use these sentence frames: What is the text about? The text is about ___. Then have them complete the online **Newcomer Activities** individually or in pairs.

Compare Texts

Read about a museum for musical instruments and sounds.

A Musical Museum

1 **A**t a recent visit to the Musical Instrument Museum, visitors played a large wooden drum. Another man strummed a guitar. A woman and her daughter listened to **music** from Africa and Asia. The visitors to this museum in Phoenix, Arizona, are here to experience and learn about different sounds. At this museum, you're supposed to be loud!

266

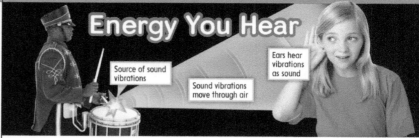

Energy You Hear

Source of sound vibrations

Sound vibrations move through air

Ears hear vibrations as sound

Humans can hear almost every **sound** in nature. But some animals hear sounds you can't hear. Dogs and bats, for example, can hear very high sounds that don't reach human ears. What sounds do you like to listen to?

2 Sound is the energy things make when they move back and forth. Those back and forth movements are called vibrations. Vibrations are like waves. When something vibrates, it makes the air vibrate, too. The waves move through the air quickly. We can hear the vibrations when the waves reach our ears. Our ears hear the waves as sounds.

Make Connections

How does sound help you express yourself? ESSENTIAL QUESTION

How do people express themselves through music? TEXT TO TEXT

267

Literature Anthology, pp. 266–267

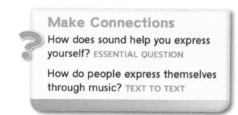

"A Musical Museum"

Literature Anthology

Text Complexity Range
Lexile

420   640   820

Identify governmental services such as museums and explain their value to the community.

Compare Texts

Analytical Writing

As children read and reread "A Musical Museum," encourage them to think about the Essential Question: *How do people express themselves?* Have children compare the ways the people in "A Musical Museum" and the people in "Many Ways to Enjoy Music" experience and enjoy music. Children should discuss how these texts are similar and different.

ACT Access Complex Text

Specific Vocabulary

Point out the words *energy, vibrations,* and *waves.* Tell children that they will need to be familiar with these words before they read the selection. Discuss definitions. Refer children to the diagram in their student book. The diagram will help clarify the concepts.

Read

1 Skill: Main Idea and Details

Read the paragraph on page 266. Ask: *Why do people go to the musical museum in Phoenix, Arizona?* (They go there to experience and learn about different sounds.)

2 Skill: Key Details

Read the second paragraph on page 267. *What is sound?* (It is the energy things make when they move back and forth.) *How does sound travel from one place to another?* (Sound waves move through the air.)

Summarize

Guide children to use the key details to summarize the selection.

Reread

Analyze the Text

After children summarize, have them reread to develop a deeper understanding of the text by annotating and answering questions on pages 79–80 of the **Reading/Writing Companion**. For children who need support citing text evidence, use the Reread questions on this page.

Author's Craft: Diagrams

Reread page 267. Ask: *How does the diagram help you understand sound?* (The diagram shows the drum as a source of sound vibrations, the sound vibrations moving through the air, and the ears hearing the vibrations as sounds.)

Author's Craft: Text Structure

Reread pages 266–267. Ask: *Why is the selection organized with "Musical Museum" first and "Energy You Hear" next?* ("Musical Museum" talks about a place where people experience and learn about sound. "Energy You Hear" talks about how people hear sound and what sound is.)

Integrate

Make Connections

Essential Question <u>Answer:</u> I can make sounds that show how I am feeling.

Text to Text Answers may vary, but have children cite text evidence from *Many Ways to Enjoy Music* and "A Musical Museum."

Spotlight on ELL Language

Page 267, Paragraph 1 Point out the phrase *almost every. If you can hear "every" sound, it means you can hear all of the sounds. But if you hear "almost every" sound, it means you can hear most, but not all, of them. What is one example of a sound humans cannot hear?* (very high sounds) *Work with a partner to use "almost every" in a sentence. For example: I like almost every kind of ice cream. The only kind I don't like is strawberry.*

Author's Craft

Reading/Writing Companion

Text Features: Diagrams

1 Explain

Have children turn to page 81 of the **Reading/Writing Companion**. Share with children these key points about diagrams.

• Diagrams use both words and images to explain important concepts.

• Diagrams can include photos, charts, arrows, drawings, and a variety of other elements.

• Diagrams, just like regular text, are usually read from left to right and from top to bottom.

2 Model

Model showing children how to read the diagram on **Literature Anthology** page 267. Point out the design elements of the diagram. Say: *The girl has her hand cupped around her ear.* Ask: *Why is she making that gesture?* (to help her hear the drumbeat) *How does the diagram indicate that she's listening for sounds from the drum?* (with the yellow cone-shaped image of the sound waves coming off the stick hitting the drum) **Point out that the author only includes the most important information in the diagram. Model identifying the first step in the diagram.** (Source of sound vibrations) **As a group, identify steps two and three.** (Sound vibrations move through air. Ears hear vibrations as sound.)

3 Guided Practice

Guide partners to work together to read the diagram. Ask: *What is an example of a detail the author did not include in the diagram?* Then have partners discuss information in the paragraph that the diagram shows.

Allow children time to discuss and write responses to the question on **Reading/Writing Companion** page 81.

Diagrams

A diagram is a graphic feature used in expository texts. Authors use diagrams to show the special parts of something or to explain how something works.

FIND TEXT EVIDENCE
Look back at the diagram on page 267. What three steps are shown in the diagram?

1. Source of sound vibrations

2. Sound vibrations move through air

3. Ears hear vibrations as sound

Your Turn Reread the second paragraph. Discuss the information from the text shown in the diagram. What is an example of a text detail the author did not include in the diagram?

The author does not include that the vibrations are like waves.

Readers to Writers
Label each step in a diagram with a simple sentence or a phrase. Include only the most important information. You may number each step to show sequence, or the correct order of the information.

Unit 3 - Expository Text   81

Reading/Writing Companion, p. 81

Readers to Writers

Ask children to explain how a listener hears a sound when someone strikes a drum. Ask what would be included in a diagram explaining this process. Have children partner to design diagrams explaining how we hear sounds. Encourage them to use simple sentences or phrases and to number the steps in order.

English Language Learners SCAFFOLD

Use the following scaffolds with **Guided Practice.**

Beginning

Draw a drum with drum sticks. Pretend to drum on a table and say, *This is the source.* Write the word *source* under your drum. Then draw sound waves emanating from the drum. *These are sound vibrations.* Write a label: *vibrations.* Then draw a face with ears. Write and say, *Ears hear the vibrations as sounds.* Draw a line from the words to the ear. Then have volunteers narrate the steps using your drawing and labels for guidance.

Intermediate

Have children narrate the steps shown in the diagram before they complete page 81. Provide sentence frames for support: First, there is a <u>source</u> of sound vibrations. Next, the <u>sound vibrations</u> travel through the air. Finally, our ears <u>hear</u> the vibrations as sound. Then help partners notice that the author does not use the word "waves" in the diagram.

Advanced/Advanced High

Have children narrate the steps shown in the diagram before they complete page 81. Have partners scan the text to find additional information not shown in the diagram.

Reading/Writing Companion

OBJECTIVES

Identify the main purpose of a text, including what the author wants to answer, describe, or explain.

Explain how specific images (e.g., a diagram showing how a machine works) contribute to and clarify a text.

ACADEMIC LANGUAGE

• *expository essay, inform, introduction, conclusion, word choice*

DIFFERENTIATED WRITING

Approaching and **On Level** For Plan: Research phase (T366), show children a helpful way to take notes using index cards. Explain that one idea is written on each card (in their own words) with the source information on the back. When it is time to begin drafting, children can put the cards in the order in which they will present the ideas.

Beyond Level For Plan: Research phase (T366), challenge children to find some direct quotes from an expert that they can include in their essays.

ELL Have partners find an example of each feature listed on the Anchor Chart.

Expert Model

Features of an Expository Essay

Explain that after reading the expository texts "They've Got the Beat!" and *Many Ways to Enjoy Music,* children will write a short expository essay. Invite children to recall other texts they have read that gave facts about a topic they found interesting.

Review that an expository essay is a type of expository text. Since it uses facts, details, and information to inform readers about a topic, children will need to do research to write their essay.

Anchor Chart Have a volunteer add these features of an expository essay to the anchor chart.

• It provides information on a topic.

• It has a strong introduction, or opening.

• It presents facts, details, and information in a logical order.

• It can include text features, such as graphs and photos with captions.

• It has a strong conclusion, or ending.

Analyze an Expert Model

Explain to children that analyzing expository texts closely will help them learn how to write expository essays. *Many Ways to Enjoy Music* is about the ways people who are deaf can enjoy music. Point out that the text is one way the author gives information. Text features also help readers understand the important ideas. Have children look at the photograph and caption on page 264. Ask: *What does this photograph help you understand?* (Possible responses: It shows what sign language looks like. It shows that the interpreter is right next to the musician.) *Why is the caption helpful?* (It tells what is happening in the picture.)

Point out other text features on the page, including the bar graph and the heading. Ask: *Why is the bar graph in a section that is a different color?* (The bar graph gives information that is not in the text.) Explain that the information is about another type of music that people enjoy.

Have children work with a partner to look at the photograph on page 265 and read the caption together. Have them discuss why the photo and caption are helpful. Then have children write their answers to the questions on page 84 of the **Reading/Writing Companion**.

WRITING

Expert Model

Features of Expository Essay

Authors write expository essays to give information about a topic.

- Expository essays give facts and information.
- It can have text features such as photos and captions.
- It has a strong opening and a conclusion.

Analyze an Expert Model Studying "Many Ways to Enjoy Music" will help you learn to write an expository essay. Reread page 265. Answer the questions below.

 How does the author use language to help you understand how the special chair works?

The author uses words like "loud, pounding sound" and "beat hard" to help me

understand how the fans feel rhythm in the chair.

What is the author's concluding statement?

The concluding statement is that interpreters and technology are ways people who

are deaf can enjoy a concert.

84   Unit 3 · Expository Text

Literature Anthology: pages 262-265

Word Wise

The author uses phrases, such as *one way* and *another way* to help you understand that there are different ways to enjoy music.

Reading/Writing Companion, p. 84

Word Wise

Explain that signal words or phrases point out that a certain type of information is being shared. In *Many Ways to Enjoy Music,* the phrases "One way" and "Another way" signal that the writer is giving first one way and then another way that deaf people's experiences at concerts are made more enjoyable. If the author had wanted to include another way, the author could have used the signal phrase "A third way."

 ## English Language Learners SCAFFOLD

Use the following scaffolds with **Analyze an Expert Model.**

Beginning

Find the phrase "another way" on page 265. Read the first two sentences in this paragraph with me. (Choral read.) *Look at the next sentence. Which two words describe a kind of sound?* (loud, pounding) *What happens when there is a loud, pounding sound?* (the chair beats hard) Provide a sentence frame to help children respond to the prompt: The author uses words like <u>loud, pounding sound</u> and <u>beat hard</u> to help me understand how the chair works.

Intermediate

Read the first paragraph in "Rock and Relax." With a partner, find the phrases that help you understand how the chair works. (loud, pounding; beat hard; low, quiet; beat softer; feel the rhythm) Provide a sentence frame to help children respond to the prompt: The author uses words like <u>loud, pounding and beat hard</u> to help me understand how fans feel <u>the rhythm</u> of the music.

Advanced/Advanced High

Have partners examine the "Rock and Relax" section and discuss the prompts. Children may identify the last sentence as the concluding statement, but challenge them to paraphrase it in their own words.

Newcomers

To help children review and develop their writing, display the online **Weekly Opener Image** and have them identify what they see with a partner. Provide sentence frames: What do you see? I see a/an ___. Have children point to the image as they ask and answer. Then have them write the sentences in their notebooks. Use the Progress Monitoring materials in the **Newcomer Teacher's Guide** to evaluate, assess, and plan instruction for your newcomers.

Reading/Writing Companion

OBJECTIVES

With guidance and support from adults and peers, focus on a topic.

Recall information from experiences or gather information from provided sources to answer a question.

ACADEMIC LANGUAGE
• *describe, explain, purpose*
• Cognates: *describir, propósito*

Digital Tools

Use these digital tools to enhance the lesson.

 Model Graphic Organizer

 Purpose of Informative Writing (slide show), Create a Research Plan (video), Organize Notes (animated tutorial)

🕙 10 Mins — Plan: Choose Your Topic

Brainstorm

Remind children that an expository essay includes factual information, but it should be presented in a way that will interest readers. Point out how the author of *Many Ways to Enjoy Music* engages readers at the beginning by using a story line about a mother and her son. Explain that many expository essay writers especially enjoy writing about topics that they find interesting or exciting.

Children will choose a favorite kind of music or instrument to write about. Encourage them to think about what type of music or instrument interests them as they brainstorm. Have them draw and write these ideas on **Reading/Writing Companion** page 85.

Review the Quick Tip box. Reinforce that ideas for writing can come from all types of sources: visual, audio, and personal experiences. Tell children that some of the words they brainstorm might describe the ways they feel when they listen to music. Details and descriptions of feelings will help readers understand more about the music.

Writing Prompt

Point out that children are to focus on one topic: one instrument or one type of music. Choosing one topic will help them to be thorough in providing information about the topic. Tell children to look over their brainstorming pictures and lists and talk with a partner about which idea is their favorite. Part of the discussion should include why they are interested in the particular instrument or type of music. Have children record their topic and why they are interested in the topic on **Reading/Writing Companion** page 86.

Purpose and Audience

Have children think about their audience, or their readers. Their audience might be their classmates, teacher, friends, or others. Have children consider what questions about their topic they would like to answer for their readers. Then have them explain their purpose for writing in their writer's notebook.

Review the Quick Tip box. Remind children that as they plan their essay, they need to think about their readers. How can they make the information interesting and clear for their readers? Text features can make the information clearer for readers. Signal words are also helpful, as they help readers understand why the information is being presented in a certain way.

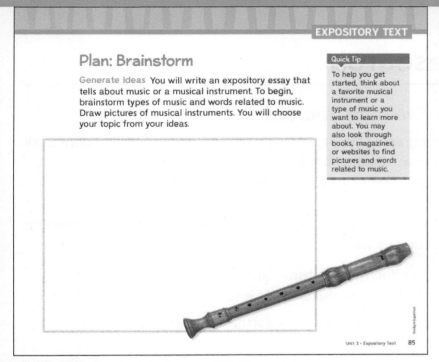

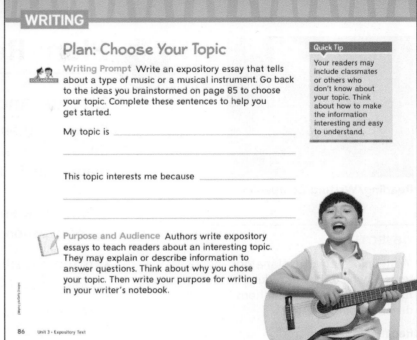

Reading/Writing Companion, pp. 85–86

English Language Learners SCAFFOLD

Use the following scaffolds with **Brainstorm**.

Beginning

Pair children with more proficient partners for the brainstorming session. Invite the class to listen to different types of music. Then they can focus their planning on the types of music they enjoy. Remind children they can always draw pictures and use pantomime to express themselves when they don't have words in English, then their peers or the teacher can provide linguistic support, as needed.

Intermediate

Children can get ideas from each other during the discussion. Model an example, such as: *My favorite instrument is a drum. My partner saw a drummer use his feet! I'm going to find out more about drummers who use their feet.* Remind children to use a variety of speaking strategies to express themselves during the discussion.

Advanced/Advanced High

As partners collaborate and brainstorm, encourage them to ask questions to clarify their ideas and request assistance, as needed. For example: *My partner said he wanted to write about the cello. I don't know what a cello is. Can you show me a picture of a cello? My partner said she wanted to write about technology that helps blind people play music. Where can she find information about that?*

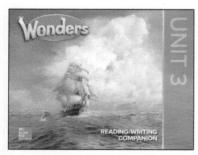

Reading/Writing Companion

OBJECTIVES

Write informative/explanatory texts in which they introduce a topic, use facts and definitions to develop points.

Recall information from experiences or gather information from provided sources to answer a question.

ACADEMIC LANGUAGE

• *evaluate, sources, reliable, accurate*

• Cognate: *evaluar*

Digital Tools

Use this digital tool to enhance the lesson.

 Evaluate Sources for Reliability (video)

Plan: Research

Choose and Evaluate Sources

Explain that finding accurate information about a topic is dependent upon using reliable sources, such as books, encyclopedias, websites, and magazines. Reliable sources can be trusted as factual.

Discuss different ways that children can identify reliable sources. Provide a list of questions, such as the following one:

• Is the website an education website, an organization website, or a government website? Does the website end in .edu, .org, or .gov?

• Does the website or book have the information you need about your topic?

• Is the website or book up to date? When was it created?

• Was the information created by someone who is an expert?

• Can the facts be checked in other sources?

Have children focus on the chart on page 87 of the **Reading/Writing Companion** as you discuss each source. Have them identify the sources as reliable or not reliable and discuss why.

Cite Sources

Remind children to credit all sources used for their research. Review that they should include the name of the website or publisher, the title of the source, the name of the author, the date of publication, and the page numbers.

Plan

In their writer's notebook, have children list two reliable sources that they can use to research their topic.

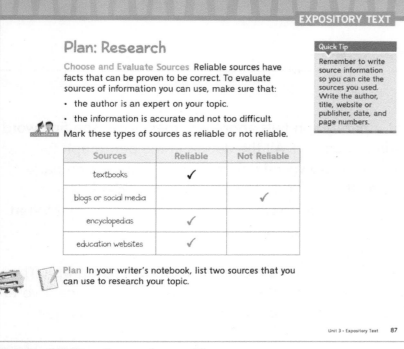

Plan: Research

Choose and Evaluate Sources Reliable sources have facts that can be proven to be correct. To evaluate sources of information you can use, make sure that:

- the author is an expert on your topic.
- the information is accurate and not too difficult.

Mark these types of sources as reliable or not reliable.

Quick Tip

Remember to write source information so you can cite the sources you used. Write the author, title, website or publisher, date, and page numbers.

Sources	Reliable	Not Reliable
textbooks	✓	
blogs or social media		✓
encyclopedias	✓	
education websites	✓	

Plan In your writer's notebook, list two sources that you can use to research your topic.

Unit 3 · Expository Text   **87**

Reading/Writing Companion, p. 87

English Language Learners SCAFFOLD

Use the following scaffolds with **Choose and Evaluate Sources**.

Beginning

Use yes/no questions to help children think about specific sources. Use classroom resources and ask questions such as: *Will this book tell you about guitars? Can our music teacher tell you about guitars?* Help children make a list of sources that will be helpful and share their ideas: I think the city orchestra website is a good source of information.

Intermediate

Ask children how they might decide if a person is an expert source. What questions might they ask? Provide two examples, such as: How long have you played the harp? How did you learn about traditional Korean music? Then have partners continue thinking of specific questions.

Advanced/Advanced High

Challenge children to come up with a list of specific questions they can ask about an Internet source when determining if it is reliable. Start the list: *Is there information provided about the writer that proves he or she knows the topic? Does the URL end with .edu, .gov, or .org? What is the purpose of the website?*

CLASSROOM CULTURE

We build knowledge. Children build their knowledge as they investigate what they want to know more about. As children research their topics for an expository essay, have them consider these questions:

- Which kinds of sources are reliable? Books? Encyclopedias? Websites?
- Which education websites (ending in .edu), organization websites (ending in .org), and government websites (ending in .gov) have been helpful?
- What information do I use to credit a source?

Reading/Writing Companion

OBJECTIVES

Compose informational texts using genre characteristics and craft.

Plan a first draft by selecting a genre for a particular topic, purpose, and audience using a range of strategies such as brainstorming, free writing, and mapping.

Write using newly acquired basic vocabulary and content-based grade-level vocabulary.

ACADEMIC LANGUAGE

• *draft, paragraph, main idea, supporting details*
• Cognate: *detalle*

Digital Tools

Use this digital tool to enhance the lesson.

RESOURCE TOOLKIT Outline to Draft (Animated Tutorial)

Draft

Paragraphs

Remind children that a paragraph tells about one main idea. The first word of a paragraph is usually indented. All the details in the paragraph tell about that one main idea. Have volunteers read the paragraph on page 264 of the **Literature Anthology**. Ask: *What is the main idea?* (One way people who are deaf enjoy a concert is by watching an interpreter.) What details tell about this? (the details in sentences 2 and 3).

Have children use the paragraph as a model for their own paragraph. The paragraph they write should have a main idea as the first sentence. Two to three other sentences in the paragraph should provide details that tell about the main idea.

Write a Draft

Have children take notes as they study the reliable sources they have chosen. Remind them that as they take notes, they should write in their own words. They should also write information identifying the source from which they get each piece of information.

Encourage children to carefully focus on their topic. If they are writing about drums, for example, they do not need to look at information about keyboard instruments.

 Pair children after they have done their research and taken notes. They can work together to figure out the best way to organize the information into paragraphs. Have children focus on making sure that each paragraph is about one idea. Point out that often the main idea of the paragraph is in the first sentence. Explain that usually there are at least three sentences in one paragraph. Each paragraph should have a main idea and supporting details.

Suggest that children list their main ideas and decide what order to present them in before they begin drafting. As they start to draft, remind them to use the model on page 264 of the **Literature Anthology** as an example of a model paragraph.

WRITING

Draft

Paragraphs A paragraph is a group of sentences that tell about one idea. The first word of a paragraph is usually indented. Reread page 264 of "Many Ways to Enjoy Music" in the **Literature Anthology**.

What idea do the details in the paragraph tell about?

People who are deaf can enjoy concerts by watching an interpreter.

Now use the paragraph as a model to write a paragraph of your essay. Make sure the details tell about one idea.

_____

_____

_____

 Write a Draft Use the information you gathered from your sources to write a draft in your writer's notebook.

Digital Tools
To learn more about creating an outline, watch "Outline to Draft." Go to **my.mheducation.com**.

> **Quick Tip**
> Outline paragraphs for your essay. Write a sentence that tells what a paragraph will be about. Under the sentence, list details from your notes that tell about the idea.

88   Unit 3 • Expository Text

Reading/Writing Companion, p. 88

English Language Learners   SCAFFOLD

Use the following scaffolds with **Write a Draft**.

Beginning

Guide children to understand that "one idea" refers to one topic, or piece of information. Draw a simple main idea and details graphic organizer on the board. Invite volunteers to name ideas and details from their own essays. Use the graphic organizer to help them identify which of their details properly fit under a main idea.

Intermediate

Encourage partners to use simple main idea and detail graphic organizers to organize their ideas into logical paragraphs.

Advanced/Advanced High

Point out that although their text is about one topic, each paragraph also has one idea that connects to the main topic of the text. Model by saying: _I am going to write about drums. My first paragraph will tell what drums look like. The next paragraph will tell what drums sound like. My third paragraph will tell why I like drums._ Help partners analyze their writing by having them ask and answer: What is the main topic of your (first) paragraph? My (first) paragraph is about (what drums look like).

Practice Book

OBJECTIVES

Demonstrate command of the conventions of standard English grammar and usage when writing or speaking.

Produce, expand, and rearrange complete simple and compound sentences

Form and use the past tense of frequently occurring irregular verbs

Demonstrate command of the conventions of standard English capitalization, punctuation, and spelling when writing.

TEACH IN SMALL GROUP ◂◂

You may wish to use the Talk About It activities during Small Group time.

Approaching Level, On Level and Beyond Level Pair children of different proficiency levels.

ELL Children should contribute to discussions by using short phrases, asking questions, and adding relevant details.

The Verb *have*

 Teach

Introduce the Verb *have* (subject-verb agreement)

- Explain that the verb **have** has two forms in the present tense: *has* and *have*. Say and display:

- Use *has* when the subject is singular.

  She <u>has</u> a trumpet.

- Use *have* when the subject is plural or *I* or *you*.

  They <u>have</u> brass instruments.

  I <u>have</u> a flute.

  You <u>have</u> a piano.

Say: *Ask yourself "Is the subject singular or plural? Is the subject I? Is the subject you?"*

  She ___ a flute. (has, singular)

  I ___ a new drum. (have, *I*)

  We ___ a band. (have, plural)

  You ___ a guitar. (have, You)

See **Practice Book** page 251 or online activity.

 Teach

Review the Verb *have* (subject-verb agreement)

Have partners orally generate sentences using singular and plural forms of the verb *have*.

Introduce the Past Tense of the Verb *have (had)*

- Explain that the past tense of the verb *have* has just one form—*had*. We use *had* with any subject-- singular or plural.

- Model identifying the use of *had*.

  I <u>had</u> a trumpet, but I gave it to my sister.

  They <u>had</u> a set of drums.

- Ask children to use the past and present tense of the verb *have*.

1. You ___ new drum sticks. (have/ had)

2. Hannah ___ a big book of music. (has/had)

See **Practice Book** page 252 or online activity.

Talk About It

Sentences and Verbs

Have children work with a partner. Have them write five sentences using the verb form *has*. Ask them to read their sentences aloud and identify the subject and verb. Repeat the process by having partners write five sentences using the verb form *have*.

Complete the Sentences

Partners should imagine they are watching a marching band during a parade. Have them create sentences using the present-tense and the past-tense form of the verb *have*.

He ___.   I ___.   You ___.

They ___.   She ___.   We ___.

DAY 3 Mechanics and Usage

Sentence Punctuation

- All sentences begin with a capital letter and end with an end mark.

- A "telling sentence" is called a **statement** and ends with a period. An "asking sentence" is a **question** and ends with a question mark. Display the following sentences. Ask partners to correct and punctuate them.

  will you play with me (Will/?)

  we played in the park (We/.)

- A **command** is a sentence that tells someone to do something and ends with a period. An **exclamation** is a sentence that expresses excitement and ends with an exclamation point.

- Guide children to tell where to put the capital letter and which end punctuation is needed.

  what time does it start (What/?)

  that is my favorite song (That/.)

  wow, that was awesome (Wow/!)

See **Practice Book** page 253 or online activity.

 OPTION DAY 4 Proofread and Write

Proofread

Have children identify and correct errors in the sentences, and supply the correct end punctuation mark.

he have a good story to tell you

(He has a good story to tell you.)

what did you has for lunch today

(What did you have for lunch today?)

what a great time we has

(What a great time we had!)

Write

Have children find a piece of their own writing in their writer's notebook and correct errors in subject-verb agreement with the verb *have*, capitalization, and end punctuation.

See **Practice Book** page 254 or online activity.

 OPTION DAY 5 Assess and Reteach

Assess

Use the Daily Language Activity and **Practice Book** page 255 for assessment.

Rubric Use your online rubric to record children's progress.

Reteach

Use the online **Grammar Handbook** page 484 and **Practice Book** pages 251–255 for additional reteaching. Remind children to use the verb *have* correctly as they speak and write.

Check children's writing for use of the skill and listen for it in their speaking. Assign grammar revision assignments in their writer's notebooks as needed.

Simon Says

Have partners write five simple, polite commands in a game of "Simon Says." Then have them write five simple exclamations in a game of "Simon Exclaims!" Last, have them write five questions in a game of "Simon Questions."

I, You, He, She, We, They

Place index cards with the following pronouns face down: *I, You, He, She, We, They.* Ask each partner to choose a card and say a sentence using the correct present-tense form of the verb *have.* Have partners take turns until all cards are drawn.

Sentence Types

Have partners orally generate sentences using a present-tense or past-tense form of the verb *have.* Partners should challenge each other to use different sentence types: statement, command, question, exclamation.

Practice Book

DIFFERENTIATED SPELLING

Go online for Dictation Sentences for differentiated spelling lists online.

On Level and ELL

cute	cube	fumes
music	unit	menu
few	pew	fuel
cues		

Review: pony, queen
High-Frequency: began, come, give

Approaching Level

cute	cube	fumes
music	unit	menu
few	pew	fuel
cue		

Review: green, seat
High-Frequency: began, come, give

Beyond Level

cute	using	cues
humid	units	menus
few	pews	rescue
continue		

Review: queen, meaning
High-Frequency: began, come, give

Words with Long *u: u_e, ew, ue, u*

 DAY 1 Assess Prior Knowledge

 OPTION **DAY 2** Spiral Review

Display the spelling words and read them aloud, focusing on the long *u* sound. Point out the /ū/ sound spelled *u_e* as in *cute*. Draw a line under *u* as you say the word. Then point out the /ū/ sound spelled *u* as in *music*. Draw a line under *u* as you say the word. Explain that the sound /ū/ can be spelled different ways. Give some examples, such as *mule, mew, cue,* and *unit*.

Demonstrate sorting the spelling words under the key words *cute, few, cue,* and *music*. Sort a few words. Point out the long *u* sound in each word.

Use the Dictation Sentences from Day 5 to give a pretest. Say the underlined word, read the sentence, and repeat the word. Have children write the words. Then have children trade their papers with a partner and check their papers.

See **Practice Book** page 247 for a pretest.

 Word Sorts

Review words with long *e*. Read each sentence below, repeat the review word, and have children write the word.

1. Can <u>we</u> go with you?
2. A <u>bee</u> sting can hurt!
3. I <u>need</u> a good book to read.
4. The <u>queen</u> wears a crown.
5. What does this word <u>mean</u>?
6. There is one red <u>leaf</u> on the branch.
7. A <u>thief</u> took the money from the bank.
8. The police <u>chief</u> spoke at our school.
9. There were <u>pony</u> rides at the fair.
10. I need the <u>keys</u> to lock the door.

Have children trade papers with a partner to check their spelling.

OPEN SORT

Have children cut apart the **Spelling Word Cards** available online and initial the back of each card. Have them read the words aloud with partners. Then have partners do an open sort by sorting long *u* sounds into four catagories: *u_e, ew, ue,* and *u*. Have them record their sorts in their writer's notebook.

PATTERN SORT

Complete the pattern sort from Day 1 by using the boldfaced key words on the Spelling Word Cards. Point out the long *u* sounds. Partners should compare and check their sorts. See **Practice Book** pages 248, 248A, and 248B for differentiated practice.

Word Meanings

Have children copy the three riddles below into their writer's notebooks. Read each riddle aloud. Then ask children to answer each riddle with a spelling word.

1. *I am the same shape as the dice you use in a game. I have six equal, square sides. What am I?* (cube)

2. *I am a pleasing combination of sounds. People listen to me. People dance to me. What am I? _____.* (music)

3. *I am not very many. And I rhyme with "you." What am I? _____.* (few)

Challenge children to create riddles for their other spelling or review words. Have children write their riddles in their notebooks. Then allow time for children to read their riddles to the class.

See online activity for additional practice.

Proofread and Write

Write these sentences on the board. Have children circle and correct each misspelled word. Have children use a print or digital dictionary to check and correct their spellings.

1. We listened to muzik while sitting in a pue. (music/pew)

2. I saw a cewt baby deer. (cute)

3. I could smell fewms for a fue minutes. (fumes/few)

4. I ordered a salad from the menue. (menu)

Error Correction Point out that although the words *menu* and *cue* both contain the long *u* sound, *cue* ends with a silent *e* and *menu* does not.

Apply to Writing Have children correct a piece of their own writing.

See online activity for additional practice.

Assess

Use the Dictation Sentences for the posttest. Have children list the misspelled words in their writer's notebook. Look for children's use of these words in their writing.

See **Practice Book** page 247 for a posttest.

Dictation Sentences

1. The baby panda is very <u>cute</u>!
2. Joan put an ice <u>cube</u> in her drink.
3. Can you smell the <u>fumes</u> from the fire?
4. We listen to <u>music</u> on the radio.
5. The class is studying a <u>unit</u> on energy.
6. Martin will order lunch from the <u>menu</u>.
7. There are a <u>few</u> birds in the tree.
8. The family sits in the <u>pew</u>.
9. How much <u>fuel</u> does the car need?
10. The actor uses <u>cues</u> to learn his lines.
11. Can I ride the <u>pony</u>?
12. The <u>queen</u> sits on her throne.
13. We <u>began</u> dance lessons last week.
14. Will you <u>come</u> to my party?
15. They <u>give</u> presents to their friends.

SPEED SORT

Have partners do a speed sort to see who sorted the words correctly and the fastest. Then have them do a word hunt in this week's readings to find words with the same vowel sounds as the spelling words. Have them record the words in their writer's notebook.

BLIND SORT

Have partners do a **blind sort**: one reads a Spelling Word Card; the other tells under which key word it belongs. Have children explain how they sorted the words. Then have partners use their word cards to play Go Fish, using this week's spelling patterns as the "fish."

Expand Vocabulary

Practice Book

OBJECTIVES

Determine or clarify the meaning of unknown and multiple-meaning words and phrases.

Determine the meaning of the new word formed when known affixes are added.

Use a known root word as a clue to the meaning of an unknown word with the same root

Use sentence-level context as a clue to the meaning of a word or phrase.

Digital Tools

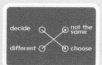

Vocabulary Activities

English Language Learners

Pair children of different language proficiency levels to practice vocabulary.

OPTION

DAY 1 Connect to Words

Practice the target vocabulary.

1. What is an event that you have **cheered** at?

2. What kinds of **concerts** do you like best?

3. What is your favorite musical **instrument**?

4. What **movements** do you like to do?

5. How would you describe your favorite **music**?

6. Would you keep the **rhythm** with your hands or with your feet?

7. How many different **sounds** can you make?

8. What would you like your friends to **understand** about you?

Build Vocabulary

- Display *cheer, movements,* and *understanding*.

- Define each word and discuss the meanings with children.

- Write *cheers* under *cheered*. Have pairs write other words with the same root and define them, such as *cheering, cheery,* and *cheerful*. Then have pairs ask and answer questions using the words.

- Repeat with *movements* and *understanding*. *(moves, moving, moved; understand, understands, understood)*

OPTION

DAY 2 Related Words

Help children create different forms of target words by adding, changing, or removing affixes.

- Write *cheered* in the first column of a T-chart. Then write *cheer* and *cheering* in the next two columns.

- Discuss each form of the word and its meaning. Then have children share aloud sentences using the words.

- Have children work in pairs to fill in charts for *concert, instrument, movements, music, rhythm, sounds,* and *understand*.

- Have children copy the chart into their writer's notebook.

Spiral Review

- Display previous vocabulary words: *delighted, flapping, idea, lonely, neighbor*. Have children orally complete each sentence stem with one of the words.

1. My ____ lives next door to me. (neighbor)

2. Sometimes I feel sad and ____ . (lonely)

3. Maria has a great ____. (idea)

4. I was ____ when I opened the present. (delighted)

5. The bird was ____ its wings. (flapping)

See Practice Book page 257.

DAY 3 Prefixes

OPTION **DAY 4** Connect to Writing

OPTION **DAY 5** Word Squares

- Display On Level **Differentiated Genre Passage** "Musical Expression." Read the third paragraph. Discuss the meaning of *unhappy*. (not happy) Tell children that the prefix *-un* means *not*.

- Have children think of other words with the prefix *un-*. Ask: *What word means "not (true, finished, safe, able)"?*

- Have pairs use the words in sentences.

See **Practice Book** page 256.

Reinforce the Words

Have children orally complete each sentence stem to review words.

1. Some ____ you might hear outside are loud. (sounds)

2. I ____ for my team when they played. (cheered)

3. I would like to play an ____ because my uncle is in a band. (instrument)

4. My favorite kind of ____ is pop. (music)

5. The dancer made graceful ____ with her body. (movements)

6. I can better ____ something when I do it. (understand)

Display previous vocabulary words: *adventure, delighted, dreamed, enjoyed, grumbled, moonlight, neighbor,* and *nighttime*. Have pairs ask and answer questions about the words.

- Have children write sentences in their writer's notebook using the target vocabulary.

- Tell them to write sentences that provide context to show what the words mean.

- **ELL** Provide the Day 3 sentence stems 1–6 for children needing extra support.

Write Using Vocabulary

Have children write something they learned from this week's target words in their writer's notebook. For example, they might write about how they use *movements, music,* or *instruments* to express themselves.

Shades of Meaning

- Have children refer to "Many Ways to Enjoy Music" on pages 262-265 in the **Literature Anthology**.

- Draw a T-chart with the heads "Loud" and "Quiet."

- Have pairs find synonyms for *loud* and *quiet* in the text. Children should add the words to the T-chart. (*loud: boom, pound(ing); quiet: low, soft*)

- Pairs can use a thesaurus to generate more words.

- Ask children to copy the T-chart into their writer's notebook.

Ask children to create Word Squares for each vocabulary word.

- In the first square, children write the word (e.g. *rhythm*).

- In the second square, children write their own definition of the word and any related words, such as synonyms (e.g. a pattern of beats or sounds; *pattern, tempo, movement*).

- In the third square, children draw an illustration that will help them remember the word (e.g. a person dancing to music).

- In the fourth square, children write nonexamples, including antonyms for the word (e.g. *nonrepeating; off beat*).

Have partners discuss their squares.

Word Study

- In the center circle of a web, write *music*. In three outer circles, write: *people, places, things*. Add more circles that branch out.

- Have children find words in "Many Ways to Enjoy Music" on pages 262–265 in the **Literature Anthology** to add to the outer circles. (people: *band, fans, singer, musicians;* places: *concert, stage;* things: *instruments, guitars, drums*)

- Have children copy the web into their writer's notebook.

Write Using Vocabulary

Have children use vocabulary words in their expository essays.

Make Connections

Reading/Writing Companion

OBJECTIVES

Participate in collaborative conversations with diverse partners about grade 2 topics and texts with peers and adults in small and larger groups.

Follow agreed-upon rules for discussions (e.g., gaining the floor in respectful ways listening to others with care, speaking one at a time about the topics and texts under discussion).

Close Reading Routine

 Read DOK 1-2

- Identify main ideas and key details about expressing ourselves.
- Take notes and summarize.
- Use prompts as needed.

Reread DOK 2-3

- Analyze the text, craft, and structure.
- Use the *Reading/Writing Companion*.

Integrate DOK 4

- Integrate knowledge and ideas.
- Make text-to-text connections.
- Use the Integrate/Make Connections lesson.
- Use the **Reading/Writing Companion**, p. 82.
- Inspire action.

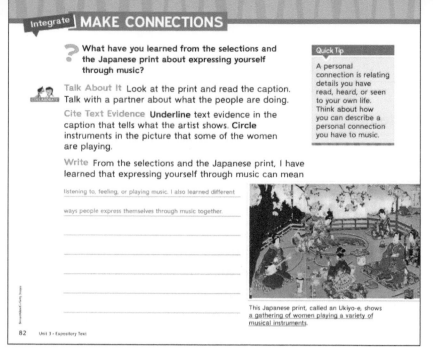

Integrate | MAKE CONNECTIONS

What have you learned from the selections and the Japanese print about expressing yourself through music?

Talk About It Look at the print and read the caption. Talk with a partner about what the people are doing.

Cite Text Evidence **Underline** text evidence in the caption that tells what the artist shows. **Circle** instruments in the picture that some of the women are playing.

Write From the selections and the Japanese print, I have learned that expressing yourself through music can mean

listening to, feeling, or playing music. I also learned different

ways people express themselves through music together.

Quick Tip

A personal connection is relating details you have read, heard, or seen to your own life. Think about how you can describe a personal connection you have to music.

This Japanese print, called an Ukiyo-e, shows a gathering of women playing a variety of musical instruments.

82 Unit 3 - Expository Text

Reading/Writing Companion, p. 82

(10 Mins) Text Connections

Talk About It

Share and discuss children's responses to the "Show Yourself Through Your Art" Blast. Then write the Essential Question on the board or chart paper: *How do you express yourself?* Below that, draw a chart with headings for all the texts children have read. Have children read through their notes, annotations, and responses and add what they learned from each text to the chart. Then ask children to complete the Talk About It activity on **Reading/Writing Companion** page 82.

Cite Text Evidence

Guide children to use text evidence to make connections between the Ukiyo-e print on page 82 of the **Reading/Writing Companion** and the selections they have read. Remind children to read the caption below the Ukiyo-e print and to use the Quick Tip.

Write

Children should refer to the notes on the chart as they respond to the writing prompt at the bottom of **Reading/Writing Companion** page 82. When children have finished writing, have them share and discuss their responses.

Show What You Learned Have children write a final response synthesizing the knowledge they built about how people express themselves.

Intonation

Explain/Model Remind children that reading with intonation means changing the tone of your voice as you read to express meaning to listeners. While children follow along, read aloud the first two paragraphs of "Many Ways to Enjoy Music" on page 263. Use appropriate intonation, for example, lowering your tone at the end of the statements and emphasizing the "sound effects" such as *booms, rocks, pound, clash, clap,* and *sing.*

Practice/Apply Invite children to echo-read as you read aloud page 263 a second time. Make sure to model reading with accuracy, with good intonation, and at an appropriate rate.

Divide the class into groups, with at least one slightly higher-level reader in each group. Ask children to follow along as you read the first paragraph on page 265 with good intonation and at an appropriate rate. Have the groups of children echo-read until each group has read a sentence.

Next, have each group work to read page 265 aloud with accuracy, with good intonation, and at an appropriate rate. Children can take turns reading, or echo-read, until everyone has had a chance to read. Circulate while the groups are working, providing feedback as needed.

Daily Fluency Practice

Children can practice fluency using **Differentiated Genre Passage,** "Musical Expression."

English Language Learners SCAFFOLD

Use the following scaffolds with **Practice/Apply.**

Beginning
Have children listen to the audio recording as a model for pronunciation, fluency, and intonation. Have them pause after each sentence to echo read. Invite children to record themselves reading and help them compare their own readings to the audio.

Intermediate
Have children listen to the audio recording as a model for pronunciation, fluency, and intonation. Have them choral read with the recording. Invite children to record themselves a few times, then help them select their best recording.

Advanced/Advanced High
Have children join the rest of the class for fluency practice. Allow them to listen to the audio recording, as needed, for additional practice.

OBJECTIVES

Read with sufficient accuracy and fluency to support comprehension.

Read on-level text orally with accuracy, appropriate rate, and expression on successive readings.

Rate: 74-94 WCPM

ACADEMIC LANGUAGE
- *intonation, tone*

Digital Tools

Assign children "A Musical Museum." Ask them to record themselves reading it aloud, and then play it back.

Audio Recorder

✔ Check for Success

Can children read text accurately, with good intonation, and at an appropriate rate?

Differentiate
SMALL GROUP INSTRUCTION

If No

| Approaching | Reteach pp. T391, T406 |
| ELL | Develop pp. T391, T434 |

If Yes

| On | Apply p. T414 |
| Beyond | Apply p. T420 |

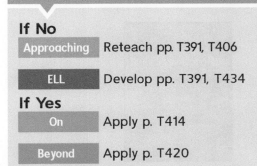

Daily Focus

Phonemic Awareness
• Phoneme Addition and Deletion

Phonics
• Introduce and Blend Words with Long *u: u_e, ue*

Structural Analysis
• Comparative Endings *-er, -est*

High-Frequency Words

Read
• Decodable Reader, Vol. 3: "Luke's Tune"

Handwriting
• Review Lowercase Letters

OBJECTIVES
• Add or delete sounds to make new words.

Phonemic Awareness: page 241

⏱ Phonemic Awareness
5 Mins

Phoneme Addition and Deletion

1 **Model** Tell children you will add a sound to the beginning of a word to make a new word. Say: *Listen carefully to this word:* use. *I will add /f/ to the beginning of* use: /f/ /ūz/, /fffūūūzzz/, fuse. *The new word is* fuse. Repeat with /k/ *oat,* /t/ *aim,* /n/ *eel,* /r/ *ice.* Then tell children you will take away a sound in a word to make a new word. Say: *The word is* goat, /g/ /ō/ /t/. *When I take away the first sound, /g/, I have the sounds /ō/ /t/ left. I changed the word* goat *to* oat. Repeat by taking away /r/ from *raid* (aid), taking away /s/ from *speech* (peach), taking away /m/ from *muse* (use).

2 **Guided Practice/Practice** Have children practice adding sounds to words. Do the first one together.

/g/ old (gold)   /n/ eat (neat)
/t/ ape (tape)   /f/ low (flow)

Then have children practice deleting sounds from words. Do the first one together.

Take away the /s/: *smile.* (mile)   Take away the /l/: *wild.* (wide)

Take away the /p/: *plate.* (late)   Take away the /s/: *grace* (gray)

Provide corrective feedback for both addition and deletion of phonemes until children can work on their own.

Have children independently practice adding and deleting phonemes using **Practice Book** page 241.

English Language Learners

Guided Practice Remind children of the initial vocabulary needed to discuss phoneme addition and deletion: *add, take away, sound.* Use examples to clarify meaning, as needed. Provide frames for children to talk about adding and deleting phonemes: The word is old. When I add /g/ the new word is gold. The word is smile. When I take away /s/ the new word is mile. If children need additional support with phonemes, use the articulation support on the **Sound-Spelling Cards.**

DIFFERENTIATED INSTRUCTION

TIER 2

Approaching Level If children are having difficulty adding and deleting phonemes:

I Do Explain to children that they will be adding and deleting phonemes to make new words. *Listen as I say a word:* use. *I will add /f/ to the beginning of* use: /f/, /ūz/, /fffūūūzzz/, fuse. *The new word is:* fuse.

Now listen for the first sound in flute: /f/. *Listen as I take away the first sound in* flute: lute. *When I took away the first sound in* flute, *I got a new word,* lute.

We Do *Listen as I say a word:* rude. *Say the word with me,* /rüd/. *Let's add /k/ to the beginning of* rude: /k/, /rüd/, crude. *Say it with me:* crude. Rude *with /k/ added is* crude. *Repeat with adding /s/ to* cream (scream), */f/ to* light (flight), */s/ to* mile (smile), *and /t/ to* rain (train).

Now let's practice deleting sounds. Take away the first sound of a word I say, and say the new word. Give corrective feedback as necessary.

speak (peak)	**trace** (race)
fluke (Luke)	**space** (pace)

You Do *It's your turn now. Add the sound to the beginning of the words to form new words. Add /k/ to* row (crow), */g/ to* round (ground), */k/ to* oat (coat), *and /n/ to* ice (nice).

Now take away the first sound, and say the new word. Take away /g/ from gold (old), */s/ from* stone (tone), *and /p/ from* preach (reach).

You may wish to review Phonemic Awareness with **ELL** using this section.

English Language Learners

See page 5 in the **Language Transfers Handbook** for guidance in identifying sounds that may or may not transfer for speakers of certain languages and for support in accommodating those children. See the chart on pages 6–9 for specific sound transfer issues for multiple languages.

Digital Tools

For more practice, have children use this activity.

Phonemic Awareness

OBJECTIVES

- Know and apply grade-level phonics and word analysis skills in decoding words.

- Apply phonics when decoding words with long *u*.

Phonics: page 243

 Phonics

Introduce Long *u*: *u_e, ue*

1 **Model** Display the *Cube* **Sound-Spelling Card**. Teach /ū/ spelled *u_e* and *ue*. Say: *This is the* Cube *Sound-Spelling Card. The vowel sound is /ū/. The long u sound can be spelled u_e. I'll say /ū/ as I write the letters u_e several times.* Repeat with *ue*.

Sound-Spelling Card

2 **Guided Practice/Practice** Have children practice connecting the letters *u_e* and *ue* to the sound /ū/ by writing them. *Say: Say /ū/ as I write the letters u_e. Now write the letters five times as you say the /ū/ sound.* Repeat with *ue*.

Have children independently practice long *u*: *u_e, ue* using **Practice Book** page 243.

DIFFERENTIATED INSTRUCTION ➤

TIER 2

Approaching Level If children are having difficulty with long *u* spelled *u_e, ue*:

I Do Display the **Word-Building Cards** *u* and *e*. *This is lowercase u and lowercase e. The letters ue can stand for the /ū/ sound. I am going to trace the letters ue while I say /ū/, the sound that the letters ue can stand for.* Trace the letters *ue* while saying /ū/ five times.

We Do Say: *Now do it with me.* Have children trace lowercase *ue* on the Word-Building Cards with their finger while saying /ū/. Trace the letters *ue* five times and say /ū/ with children. Repeat the process with long *u* spelled *u_e*.

You Do Have children connect the letters *ue* to the sound /ū/ by tracing lowercase *ue* with their finger, while saying /ū/ five to ten times. Then have them write the letters *ue* while saying /ū/ five to ten times. Repeat the process with *u_e*.

Repeat, connecting the letters *u_e* and *ue* to /ū/ through tracing and writing the letters throughout the week.

You may wish to review Phonics with **ELL** using this section.

Blend Words with Long *u: u_e, ue*

1 **Model** Display **Word-Building Cards** *h, u, g, e*. Model blending the sounds. Say: *This is the letter* h. *It stands for /h/. This is the letter* u. *When you see* e *at the end of the word,* u *can stand for the /ū/ sound. This is the letter* g. *It can stand for /j/. This is the letter* e. *In this word, the* e *is silent. Listen as I blend the sounds: /hūūūj/. The word is* huge.

Continue by modeling the words *fume, cue,* and *cube.*

2 **Guided Practice/Practice** Display the Day 1 Phonics/Fluency Practice chart. Read each word in the first row, blending the sounds; for example, say: *Listen: /mmmyūūūt/. The word is* mute. Have children blend each word with you. Prompt children to read the connected text, sounding out the decodable words.

mute	use	fuse	fume	using
cute	fuel	mule	huge	refuse
cube	cues	hue	amuse	useful
team	she	piece	wheel	keys

That mule refuses to go.

The huge plane uses a lot of fuel.

Sue is amused by her cute kitten.

Day 1 Phonics/Fluency Practice

DIFFERENTIATED INSTRUCTION

TIER 2

Approaching Level If children are having difficulty blending words with /ū/ spelled *u_e, ue:*

I Do Display Word-Building Cards *m, u, l, e. This is the letter* m. *It stands for /m/. This is the letter* u. *It stands for /ū/ in this word. This is the letter* l. *It stands for /l/. The letter* e *is silent. Listen as I blend these sounds: /mmmūūūlll/,* mule.

We Do Guide children to blend the sounds and read: *use, fuel, muse, cube.* Offer corrective feedback to children if needed.

You Do Have children blend and decode: *huge, mute, cues, hue, unit.*

You may wish to review Phonics with **ELL** using this section.

Corrective Feedback

Sound Error: Model the sound that children missed, then have them repeat the sound. Say: *My turn.* Tap under the letters and say: *Sound? /ū/. What's the sound?* Return to the beginning of the word. Say: *Let's start over.* Blend the word with children again.

English Language Learners

See page 5 in the **Language Transfers Handbook** for guidance in identifying phonics skills that may or may not transfer for speakers of certain languages and for support in accommodating those children. See the chart on pages 10–13 for specific phonics transfer issues for multiple languages.

Digital Tools

To differentiate instruction for key skills, use the results of this activity.

Phonics

OBJECTIVES

- Identify and read words with comparative endings *-er* and *-est*.
- Know and apply grade-level phonics and word analysis skills in decoding words.

ACADEMIC LANGUAGE

- *compare*
- Cognate: *comparar*

English Language Learners

See page 15 in the **Language Transfers Handbook** for guidance in identifying grammatical forms that may or may not transfer for speakers of certain languages and for support in accommodating those children. See page 19 for transfer issues related to *-er* and *-est* endings.

Digital Tools

For more practice, have children use this activity.

Structural Analysis

OPTION 5 Mins

Structural Analysis

Comparative Endings *-er*, *-est*

1 **Model** Write the words *higher* and *highest*. Underline the endings *-er* and *-est*. Tell children that they can use adjectives to compare nouns. Explain that you can add the ending *-er* to an adjective to compare two nouns. You can add the ending *-est* to an adjective to compare more than two nouns. Write these sentences: *Your kite is higher than my kite. Jan's kite is the highest one of all.* Read each sentence with children. Point out that the word *higher* compares two kites and the word highest compares more than two kites.

2 **Guided Practice/Practice** Write the following words: *fresh, sweet, slow.* Have children add *-er* and *-est* to each word and then use each new word in a sentence. Provide corrective feedback as necessary.

DIFFERENTIATED INSTRUCTION ➤➤

TIER 2

Approaching Level If children are having difficulty with comparative endings *-er* and *-est*:

I Do Write *faster* and *fastest*. Remind children that you can use adjectives to compare nouns. Say: *Add* -er *to compare two nouns. Add* -est *to compare more than two nouns. Jen had a faster time in the race than Pat did. Lily had the fastest time in the whole class.*

We Do Write *light, clean,* and *soft*. With children, read each word. Guide them to add the endings *-er* and *-est* to each word and to read the new words. Guide them to use each one in a sentence. Give corrective feedback if needed.

You Do Have partners work together to add the endings *-er* and *-est* to each of the following words and to use the new words in sentences: *weak, cold, rich.*

Repeat Have children create sentences using words with the endings *-er* and *-est*.

High-Frequency Words

America, beautiful, began, climbed, come, country, didn't, give, live, turned

1 **Model** Display the **High-Frequency Word Cards** and use the Read/Spell/Write routine to teach each word.

- **Read** Point to and say the word *America. This is the word* America. *Say it with me*: America. *We live in America.*

- **Spell** *The word* America *is spelled* A-m-e-r-i-c-a. *Spell it with me.*

- **Write** *Let's write the word in the air as we say each letter:* A-m-e-r-i-c-a.

- Point out to children any irregularities in sound-spellings; for example, the short *u* sound is spelled *o_e* in the word *come* and is spelled *ou* in the word *country*.

- Have partners create sentences using each word.

2 **Guided Practice** Have children identify the high-frequency words in connected text and blend the decodable words.

1. When did he live in **America**?
2. That sunset is **beautiful**!
3. Sid **began** to sing a new tune.
4. They **climbed** over the fence.
5. He will **come** up to your home.
6. What **country** is on that map?
7. Lee **didn't** eat lunch yet.
8. Dad will **give** Gran a ride.
9. Where do you **live** now?
10. Ben **turned** the pages for me.

DIFFERENTIATED INSTRUCTION

TIER 2

Approaching Level If children need support with high-frequency words:

I Do Use the High-Frequency Word Cards. Follow this routine for each word: Display the word. Read the word. Spell the word.

We Do Ask children to state the word and spell the word with you. Model using the word in a sentence, and have children repeat.

You Do Display the words randomly for children to say and spell. Provide opportunities for children to use the words in speaking and writing; for example, provide sentence starters such as *One beautiful place in America I have seen is _____*. Have children write each word in their writer's notebook.

OBJECTIVES

- Know and apply grade-level phonics and word analysis skills in decoding words.

- Recognize and read grade-appropriate irregularly spelled words.

 English Language Learners

Model Use visual cues, gestures, and examples to help children learn the meanings of the high-frequency words. Point out the Spanish cognate *América* and explain the multiple-meaning word *country*.

Digital Tools

For more practice, have children use this activity.

 High-Frequency Words

Decodable Reader, Vol. 3

OBJECTIVES

- Know and apply grade-level phonics and word-analysis skills in decoding words.

- Recognize and read grade-appropriate irregularly spelled words.

- Read on-level text with purpose and understanding.

- Read with sufficient accuracy and fluency to support comprehension.

- Review all lowercase cursive letter forms.

Decodable Reader: "Luke's Tune"

Focus on Foundational Skills

Review the words and letter-sounds that children will find in the **Decodable Reader**.

- Review the high-frequency words *America, beautiful, began, climbed, come, country, didn't, give, live,* and *turned*.

- Review with children that *u_e* and *ue* can stand for the long *u* sound.

Preview and Predict Point to the title of the story and have children sound out each word with you as you run your finger under it. Ask: *What do you see in the picture? What do you think Luke is doing?*

Read the Decodable Reader

Begin to read the story "Luke's Tune." On page 58, have children point to each word, sounding out the decodable words and saying the high-frequency words quickly. If children need support reading decodable words, model blending for them. If children are having difficulty with high-frequency words, reread the word in isolation and then in context.

Check Comprehension

p. 56 *What idea does Luke have for the field near his new house?*
p. 57 *What two things does Luke do because he knows what all plants need?*
p. 58 *Why does Luke think about his home country, India?*
p. 59 *Why does Luke hum a tune?*
p. 60 *Why was Luke so happy?*

Retell Have partners use key ideas and details to retell "Luke's Tune."

Focus on Fluency

COLLABORATE

With partners, have children read "Luke's Tune" to focus on accuracy. Guide them to run their fingers under the text as they read. Children should note whether they are correctly reading the words on the page. They can monitor themselves and provide feedback to their partners.

Listen in: If children are having difficulty reading accurately, have them start again at the beginning of the page. If children are reading too quickly, suggest that they should slow down and read as they speak.

English Language Learners

Check Comprehension Provide sentence frames, as needed, to help children answer the questions:

p. 56 Luke wants to <u>grow green plants</u> in the <u>field</u> near his new house.

p. 57 Luke chooses <u>a sunny spot</u> and gives his plants <u>a drink of water</u>.

p. 58 Luke asks why his new plants won't <u>grow</u>. Luke thinks about how <u>plants</u> in India <u>grow big and beautiful</u>.

p. 59 Luke likes to <u>hum</u> while he is <u>making a plan</u>.

p. 60 Luke was happy because <u>his plants grew</u>.

Focus on Fluency Before reading "Luke's Tune," point out the potential pronunciation challenges in each section of the story so children can practice the words in isolation beforehand. Have children first echo read each section after you, then choral read with you.

Handwriting: Review Lowercase Letters

Review Call on volunteers to take turns writing the lowercase letters *u, w, b, f, h, k, g, q, j, p, r, s, y, z, v,* and *x*. Review the stroke directions with children as each letter is written.

After all the letters are written, ask volunteers to circle each letter that starts with a stroke that curves up. (u, w, b, f, h, k) Then have them draw a box around each letter that has a loop that reaches below the bottom line. (f, g, q, j, p, y, z) Next, have children draw a line under each letter that starts with a stroke that curves over. (y, z, v, x)

Ask questions as you continue to call attention to possible problem areas in the letters, such as: *Which letters have a closed oval?* (q, g)

Guided Practice/Practice
- Have children take turns describing how to form each letter. Have the rest of the class use their **Response Boards** to write the letters.
- Correct children's pen grip and paper placement as needed.

Daily Handwriting
Throughout the week, use the models to review the formation of the lowercase cursive letters. Have children independently practice lowercase letters using **Practice Book** pages 249–250.

Handwriting: pages 249–250

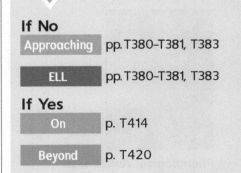

✔ Check for Success

Rubric Use the online rubric to record children's progress.

Can children decode words with long *u* spelled *u_e, ue*?

Can children identify and read the high-frequency words?

Differentiate
SMALL GROUP INSTRUCTIONS

If No
| Approaching | pp. T380–T381, T383 |
| ELL | pp. T380–T381, T383 |

If Yes
| On | p. T414 |
| Beyond | p. T420 |

DAY 2 ›› Word Work

OBJECTIVES

• Identify and generate alliteration.

Phonological Awareness: page 242

⏱ 5 Mins — Phonological Awareness

Identify and Generate Alliteration

1 **Model** Show children how to identify alliteration. Ask children to listen to the beginning sound in each word. *Listen:* Hal has horses. Hal, has, *and* horses *all begin with /h/. I can change the name* Hal *to another name that begins with /h/,* Heather. *Listen:* Heather has horses.

2 **Guided Practice/Practice** Have children identify the sound that forms the alliteration and change each name to another name that begins with the same sound. Do the first one together. Say: *Listen:* Sam sells soup. *What is the beginning sound in each word? Yes, /sss/. I'll replace* Sam *with another name that begins with /sss/:* Sue sells soup.

Sam sells soup.	Rita runs races.
Felix feels fine.	Dave dislikes dancing.
Lucy likes lemons.	Bob buys buttons.

Have children independently practice identifying and generating alliteration using **Practice Book** page 242.

DIFFERENTIATED INSTRUCTION ››

TIER 2

Approaching Level If children are having difficulty with alliteration:

I Do Explain to children that they will listen to and say words with the same beginning sound. Say: *Listen to the beginning sound of each word in this sentence:* Seth sings silly songs. *Each word begins with /s/. I'll change* Seth *to another name with /s/:* Sarah sings silly songs.

We Do Say: *Listen to the first sound in each word:* Lily likes lemonade. *Each word begins with /l/. Let's change* Lily *to another name with /l/:* Luke likes lemonade. Continue with these sentences:

Tony takes toys to town.	Rick races rockets.
Judy juggles giant jars.	Nancy needs notebooks.

You Do *It's your turn. Listen to the first sound in each word. Change the name to another name with the same sound.*

Ben bought big books.   Pat plays piano.   Hank hears hail.

Repeat the alliteration routine with additional initial consonant sounds.

You may wish to review Phonological Awareness with **ELL** using this section.

Phonics

Review Long *u: u_e, ue*

1 **Model** Display the *Cube* **Sound-Spelling Card**. Review the long *u* sound /ū/ spelled *u_e*, and *ue*. Use the words *cute* and *cues*. Say: *The long* u *sound can be spelled* u_e. *It can also be spelled* ue.

2 **Guided Practice/Practice** Have children practice connecting the letters and sounds. Point to the *u_e* and *ue* spellings on the Sound-Spelling Card. Ask: *What are these letters? What is the sound?*

DIFFERENTIATED INSTRUCTION

Approaching Level If children are having difficulty with long *u* spelled *u_e, ue:*

I Do Display the **Word-Building Cards** *u_e. This is lowercase* u *and lowercase* e, *with a consonant in between. The letters* u_e *can stand for the /ū/ sound. I am going to trace the letters* u_e *while I say /ū/, the sound that these letters can stand for.* Trace the letters *u_e* while saying /ū/, five times.

We Do Say: *Now do it with me.* Have children trace lowercase *u_e* on the Word-Building Cards with their finger while saying /ū/. Repeat the process with long *u* spelled *ue*.

You Do Have children connect the letters *u_e* to the sound /ū/ by tracing lowercase *u_e* with their finger while saying /ū/ five to ten times. Say: *Write the letters* u_e *five times as you say /ū/.* Repeat the process with *ue*.

Repeat, connecting the letters *u_e* and *ue* to /ū/ through tracing and writing the letters throughout the week.

You may wish to review Phonics with **ELL** using this section.

OBJECTIVES

• Know and apply grade-level phonics and word-analysis skills in decoding words.

SOUND-SPELLING REVIEW

Build Fluency
Display the **Word-Building Cards** *u, u_e, ew, ue, o, oa, ow, oe, i, igh, ie, y, e, ee, ea, y, ey, ie, a, ai, ay, ea, ei, eigh*. Have children say each sound.

Digital Tools

For more practice, have children use this activity.

Phonological Awareness

To differentiate instruction for key skills, use the results of this activity.

Phonics

OBJECTIVES
- Know and apply grade-level phonics and word-analysis skills in decoding words.
- Blend and build words with long *u*.

English Language Learners

Model Build vocabulary by reviewing the meanings of example words. Ask children to *use* a pencil to write their name. Have them point to or draw something that is *huge*. Explain that a *fuse* has to do with electricity. Explain that if something is *mute*, it is silent. Have children repeat the words after you.

Phonics

5 Mins

Blend Words with Long *u*: *u_e*, *ue*

1 Model Display **Word-Building Cards** for *u, s, e*. Model how to blend the sounds. Say: *This is the letter* u. *It can stand for* /ū/. *This is the letter* s. *It stands for* /z/. *This is the letter* e. *It is silent. Listen as I blend these sounds together:* /ūūūzzz/. *The word is:* use.

Continue by modeling the words *huge, fuse,* and *mute*.

2 Guided Practice/Practice Repeat the routine with children with *fuel, amuse, hue,* and *cues*.

Guide practice until children can work independently. Provide corrective feedback as needed.

DIFFERENTIATED INSTRUCTION

TIER 2

Approaching Level If children are having difficulty blending words with /ū/ spelled *u_e* and *ue*:

I Do Display Word-Building Cards *f, u, m, e*. Say: *This is the letter* f. *It stands for* /f/. *This is the letter* u. *It stands for* /ū/ *in this word. This is the letter* m. *It stands for* /m/. *The letter* e *is silent. I'll blend all these sounds:* /fffūūūmmm/, fume. *I blended the word* fume.

We Do Guide children to blend the sounds and read: *mule, fuel, reuse, excuse*. Give corrective feedback if children need more support.

You Do Have children blend and decode: *huge, mute, cues, confuse*.

You may wish to review Phonics with **ELL** using this section.

Build Words with Long *u: u_e, ue*

Provide children with **Word-Building Cards** for the alphabet. Have children put the letters in order from *a* to *z*.

1 Display Word-Building Cards *c, u, b, e.* Blend: /k/ /ū/ /b/, *cube.*

- Replace *b* with *t* and repeat with *cute.*
- Replace *c* with *m* and repeat with *mute.*
- Replace *t* with *l* and repeat with *mule.*

2 **Guided** Continue with *hue, cue, cues, fuel, fuse, use, reuse, muse, amuse.* Guide children to build and blend each word.

Once children have built the words, dictate the words to children and have them write the words down. Children can work with a partner to check their spelling.

DIFFERENTIATED INSTRUCTION 》》

TIER 2

Approaching Level If children are having difficulty building words with /ū/ spelled *u_e, ue:*

I Do Display Word-Building Cards *u, s, e. The letters* u, s, *and* e *stand for /ūūū/ and /zzz/. Listen as I blend the sounds together: /ūūūzzz/,* use. *The word is* use.

We Do *Now, let's do one together. I will add the letter* f *to the beginning of* use. *Let's blend: /fff/ /ūūū/ /zzz/, /fffūūūzzz/,* fuse. *Now we'll add the letter* d *to the end of* fuse. *Let's blend and read the new word: /fūz/ /d/, /fffūūūzzzd/,* fused.

You Do Have children build the words: *cube, cute, mute, mule, fuel, cue, hue, hues.* Provide corrective feedback if needed.

You may wish to review Phonics with **ELL** using this section.

OBJECTIVES

- Identify and read words with comparative endings –er and –est.
- Know and apply grade-level phonics and word-analysis skills in decoding words.

HIGH-FREQUENCY WORDS REVIEW

America, beautiful, began, climbed, come, country, didn't, give, live, turned
Say the words and have children Read/Spell/Write them. List the words so children can self-correct.

Cumulative Review
Use the same routine. with last week's words.

Digital Tools

For more practice, have children use this activity.

Structural Analysis

Structural Analysis: page 245

🕔 5 Mins Structural Analysis

Comparative Endings -er, -est

1 **Model** Write the words *colder* and *coldest.* Underline the endings *-er* and *-est.* Explain to children that they can use adjectives to compare nouns. Tell children that you can add the ending *-er* to an adjective to compare two nouns. You can add the ending *-est* to an adjective to compare more than two nouns. Write these sentences: *This room is colder than that one. This room is the coldest one of all.* Read each sentence with children. Point out that the word *colder* compares two rooms and that the word *coldest* compares more than two rooms.

2 **Guided Practice/Practice** Write these words: *quick, kind, thick.* Have children add *-er* and *-est* to each word and then use each new word in a sentence. Give corrective feedback if children need further support.

Have children independently practice comparative endings *–er, -est* using **Practice Book** page 245.

DIFFERENTIATED INSTRUCTION

TIER 2 **Approaching Level** If children are having difficulty with comparative endings *-er, -est*:

I Do Write comparative endings *-er* and *-est.* Say: *Let's add these endings to the word* old. Write *older* and *oldest.* Say: *When I add* -er *to* old, *it means I am comparing two people, places, or things. Len is older than Kim. When I add* -est *to* old, *it means I am comparing more than two people, places, or things. I think my dad is the oldest man in the room.*

We Do Say: *Let's add* -er *to* long. Write *longer.* Say: *How many things do you compare using the word* longer? *The ending* -er *is used to compare two nouns. My pencil is longer than your pencil.* Repeat to form the words *longest, kinder, kindest, higher, highest.* Review the meanings of the words with children, and give corrective feedback if needed.

You Do Have children add endings *-er* and *-est* to adjectives. Say: *Now it's your turn. Add endings* -er *and* -est *to* low, few, dull. *With a partner, talk about the meanings.*

Repeat Have children add endings *-er* and *-est* to other adjectives. Ask them to tell the meaning of each word.

Decodable Reader: "Mules"

5 Mins

Focus on Foundational Skills

Review words with long *u* spelled *u_e* and *ue,* as well as the high-frequency words *beautiful* and *live* that children will find in the **Decodable Reader.**

Read the Decodable Reader

Guide children in reading "Mules." On page 63, have children point to each word, sounding out the decodable words and saying the high-frequency words quickly.

Mules

"As stubborn as a mule" means to argue and refuse to change your mind. But mules aren't really that stubborn!

61

Decodable Reader, Vol. 3

Check Comprehension

p. 61   *What does "as stubborn as a mule" mean?*

p. 62   *What can mules do because they are so huge and strong?*

p. 63   *What do mules like to eat?*

p. 64   *What animals are a mule's mom and dad?*

Remind children that they can ask themselves questions to make sure they understood what they have read. Have children use both text and photographs to answer their questions.

Retell Have partners use key ideas and details to retell "Mules."

Focus on Fluency

COLLABORATE

Have children practice reading from the Decodable Reader to a partner. Have them concentrate on both accuracy and appropriate rate. Remind them to raise their voice at the end of a question and to read with appropriate emphasis. Offer corrective feedback if necessary.

English Language Learners

ELL

Check Comprehension Provide sentence frames, as needed, to help children answer the questions:

p. 61   "As stubborn as a mule" means to <u>refuse to change your mind</u>.

p. 62   Mules can carry <u>heavy loads</u> and climb <u>steep hills</u>.

p. 63   Mules eat <u>grain, hay,</u> and <u>grasses</u>.

p. 64   A mule's dad is a <u>donkey</u>. Its mom is a <u>horse</u>.

OBJECTIVES

- Know and apply grade-level phonics and word-analysis skills in decoding words.
- Recognize and read grade-appropriate irregularly spelled words.
- Read on-level text with purpose and understanding.
- Read with sufficient accuracy and fluency to support comprehension.

✓ Check for Success

Rubric Use the online rubric to record children's progress.

Can children decode words with long *u* spelled *u_e* and *ue?*

Can children identify and read the high-frequency words?

Differentiate
SMALL GROUP INSTRUCTIONS

If No

| Approaching | pp. T387–T391 |

| ELL | pp. T387–T391 |

If Yes

| On | p. T414 |

| Beyond | p. T420 |

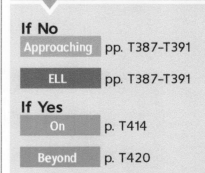

Daily Focus

Phonemic Awareness
• Phoneme Blending

Phonics
• Introduce Long *u: ew, u;*
  Blend and Build Words with
  Long *u: u_e, ue, ew, u*

Structural Analysis
• Comparative Endings *-er, -est*

High-Frequency Words

Read
• Decodable Reader, Vol. 3:
  "Growing Stew"

OBJECTIVES
• Blend phonemes to form words.

Phonemic Awareness

5 Mins

Phoneme Blending

1 Model Use the **Response Board** to show children how to orally blend phonemes. Say: *I will place a marker on the Response Board for each sound I say. Listen as I say the three sounds in a word: The beginning sound is /f/. The middle sound is /ū/. The ending sound is /l/. Now I'll blend the sounds together to say the word, /fffūūūlll/, fuel. I blended the word fuel.*

2 Guided Practice/Practice Have children practice blending phonemes to form words. Say: *Listen as I say one sound at a time. Then we will blend the sounds to say the word.* Do the first one together. Provide corrective feedback if necessary.

hue	cube	huge	pews	music
mule	unit	few	human	fumes

DIFFERENTIATED INSTRUCTION >>

TIER 2

Approaching Level If children are having difficulty blending phonemes in words with /ū/:

I Do Explain to children that they will be blending sounds to form words. Say: *Listen to three sounds: /h/ /ū/ /j/. Listen as I say the sounds again: /h/ /ū/ /j/. I will blend the three sounds: /h/ /ū/ /j/, /hūūūj/, huge. The word is huge.*

We Do *Listen as I say two sounds: /f/ /ū/. Repeat the sounds: /f/ /ū/. Let's blend the sounds: /f/ /ū/, /fffūūū/, few. We made one word: few.* Repeat the blending routine with these words:

cubes	mews	mule	fume	cue	fuel

Give corrective feedback as necessary until children can work on their own.

You Do Say: *It's your turn. Blend the sounds I say to form words: fume, use, cute, mule.*

Repeat the blending routine with additional /ū/ words.

You may wish to review Phonemic Awareness with **ELL** using this section.

Phonics

OBJECTIVES
• Know and apply grade-level phonics and word-analysis skills in decoding words.

Introduce Long *u: ew, u*

1 **Model** Display the *Cube* **Sound-Spelling Card.** Teach /ū/ spelled *ew* and *u*. Say: *This is the* Cube *Sound-Spelling Card. The vowel sound is /ū/. You know that the long* u *sound can be spelled* u_e *and* ue. *The long* u *sound can also be spelled* ew. *I'll say /ū/ as I write the letters* ew *several times.* Repeat with *u*.

Sound Spelling Card

2 **Guided Practice/Practice** Have children practice connecting the letters *ew* and *u* to the sound /ū/ by writing them. Say: *Say /ū/ as I write the letters* ew. *Now write the letters* ew *five times as you say the /ū/ sound.* Repeat with *u*. Then review /ū/ spelled *u_e* and *ue*. Offer corrective feedback as necessary if children need more support.

Have children independently practice long *u: u_e, ue, ew, u* using **Practice Book** page 244.

Digital Tools

For more practice, have children use this activity.

Phonemic Awareness

To differentiate instruction for key skills, use the results of this activity.

Phonics

DIFFERENTIATED INSTRUCTION

TIER 2

Approaching Level If children are having difficulty with long *u* spelled *ew* and *u*:

I Do Display the **Word-Building Card** *u*. *This is lowercase* u. *The letter* u *can stand for the /ū/ sound. I am going to trace the letter* u *while I say /ū/, the sound that the letter* u *can stand for.* Trace the letter *u* while saying /ū/ five times.

We Do Say: *Now do it with me.* Have children trace the lowercase *u* on the Word-Building Card with their finger while saying /ū/. Trace the letter *u* five times and say /ū/ with children. Repeat the routine with the Word-Building Cards for long *u* spelled *ew*. Give corrective feedback if needed for more support.

You Do Have children connect the letter *u* to the sound /ū/ by tracing lowercase *u* with their finger while saying /ū/ five to ten times. Write the letter *u* as you say /ū/. Have children write *u* while saying /ū/ five to ten times. Repeat the process with *ew*.

Repeat, connecting the letters *ew* and *u* to /ū/ through tracing and writing the letters throughout the week. Review /ū/ spelled *u_e* and *ue* as well.

You may wish to review Phonics with **ELL** using this section.

Phonics: page 244

OBJECTIVES

- Know and apply grade-level phonics and word-analysis skills in decoding words.

Phonics

OPTION 5 Mins

Blend Words with Long *u: u_e, ue, ew, u*

1 **Model** Display **Word-Building Cards** *m, e, w.* Model how to blend the sounds. Say: *This is the letter* m. *It stands for /m/. These are the letters* ew. *They stand for /ū/. Listen as I blend the two sounds together: /mmmūūū/. The word is* mew. Repeat with *unit* for /ū/u.

   Continue by modeling blending the words *pew* and *pupil* to emphasize the *ew* and *u* spellings of /ū/. Then review the *u_e* and *ue* spellings of /ū/ by modeling blending of the words *cute, huge,* and *cues.*

2 **Guided Practice/Practice** Display the Day 3 Phonics/Fluency Practice chart. Read each word in the first row, blending the sounds—for example, say: */fffūūū/. The word is* few. Have children blend each word with you. Ask children to read the connected text, sounding out the decodable words. Guide practice and give corrective feedback.

few	unit	pew	mews	music
hues	cute	cubic	humid	amuse
cue	dewy	fume	infuse	human
wee	niece	meal	theme	flow

I can play a few notes of the music.

Hugh and Sue are so amused!

It was hot and humid on Tuesday.

Day 3 Phonics/Fluency Practice

DIFFERENTIATED INSTRUCTION >

TIER 2

Approaching Level If children are having difficulty blending words:

I Do Display Word-Building Cards *c, u, t, e.* Say: *This is the letter* c. *It stands for /k/. This is the letter* u. *It stands for /ū/. This is the letter* t. *It stands for /t/. This is the letter* e. *It is silent. Listen as I blend these sounds: /kūūūt/,* cute.

We Do *Let's do some together. Let's blend and read these words:* cube, few, hue, menu. Offer corrective feedback if necessary.

You Do Display the following words: *fume, mute, crew, hue, music, humid.* Have children blend and read the words.

You may wish to review Phonics with **ELL** using this section.

Build Words with Long *u: u_e, ue, ew, u*

Provide children with **Word-Building Cards** *a* to *z*. Have children put the letters in alphabetical order as quickly as possible.

1 **Model** Display Word-Building Cards *b,l,e,w*. Blend the sounds /b/ /l/ /u/, /blllūūū/, *blew*.

- Replace *b* with *f* and repeat with *flew*.
- Take away *l* and repeat with *few*.

2 **Guided Practice/Practice** Continue having children blend and build words with *pew, mew, music, mule, mute, cute, cue, cues*. Guide children and provide corrective feedback as needed until they can work independently.

Once children have built the words, dictate the words to children and have them write the words. Children can work with a partner to check their spelling.

DIFFERENTIATED INSTRUCTION

TIER 2

Approaching Level If children need more support building words with /ū/:

I Do Display Word-Building Cards *u, s, e*. Say: *The letters* u, s, *and* e *stand for /ū/ and /z/. Listen as I blend the sounds together: /ūūū/ /zzz/, /ūūūzzz/,* use. *I blended the word* use.

We Do *Now, let's do one together.* Add the letter *m* to the beginning of *use. Let's blend the new word: /mmm/ /ūūū/ /zzz/, /mmmūūūzzz/,* muse. *Now let's add* d *to the end of* muse. *Let's blend the sounds and read the new word: /mmmūūūzzz/ /d/, /mmmūūūzzzd/,* mused. *Offer children corrective feedback as needed.*

You Do Have children build the words: *cube, cute; few, mew, chew; mule, mute, music; hue, cue, fuel.*

You may wish to review Phonics with **ELL** using this section.

ELL English Language Learners

Guided Practice After dictation, when partners are checking their spelling, provide sentence frames to help them discuss which spelling pattern they used in each word: How do you spell the word <u>mew</u>? I spell it <u>m-e-w</u>. Which letters stand for the long *u* sound in <u>mew</u>? The letters <u>e-w</u> stand for the long *u* sound in <u>mew</u>.

Digital Tools

To differentiate instruction for key skills, use the results of this activity.

Phonics

OBJECTIVES

- Identify and read words with comparative endings *-er* and *-est*.
- Know and apply grade-level phonics and word-analysis skills in decoding words.

Digital Tools

For more practice, have children use this activity.

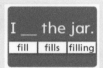

I __ the jar.

| fill | fills | filling |

Structural Analysis

OPTION 5 Mins

Structural Analysis

Comparative Endings *-er, -est*

1 **Model** Write the words *sweeter* and *sweetest* and underline the endings *-er* and *-est*. Remind children that you can add the ending *-er* or *-est* to an adjective to compare nouns. Review that the ending *-er* is added to an adjective to compare two nouns and the ending *-est* is added to an adjective to compare more than two nouns.

2 **Guided Practice/Practice** Write the following words and read them with children: *slow, high, fast.* Call on volunteers to add the endings *-er* and *-est* to each word, read the new words, and use each word in a sentence.

DIFFERENTIATED INSTRUCTION >>

TIER 2

Approaching Level If children are having difficulty with comparative endings *-er, -est*:

I Do Write comparative endings *-er* and *-est*. Say: *Let's add these endings to the word* kind. Write *kinder* and *kindest*. Say: *When I add* -er *to* kind, *it means I am comparing two people, places, or things. My friend Sue is kinder than Jim. When I add* -est *to* kind, *it means I am comparing more than two people, places, or things. My sister is the kindest lady in my family.*

We Do Say: *Let's add* -er *to* high. Write *higher*. Say: *How many things do you compare using the word* higher? *The ending* -er *is used to compare two nouns. The red kite is higher than the blue one. How many things do you compare using the word* highest? *The ending* -est *is used to compare more than two nouns. The yellow kite is the highest of all the kites.* Repeat to form the words *older, oldest, longer, longest.*

You Do Have children add endings *-er* and *-est* to adjectives. Say: *Now it's your turn. Add endings* -er *and* -est *to* slow, new, light. *With a partner, talk about the meanings.*

Repeat Have children add endings *-er* and *-est* to other adjectives.

High-Frequency Words

⏱ 5 Mins

America, beautiful, began, climbed, come, country, didn't, give, live, turned

1 **Model** Say each word and have children Read/Spell/Write it. Ask children to picture the word, and then write it the way they see it. Display the answers for children to self-correct.

2 **Guided Practice** Have children identify the high-frequency words in connected text and blend the decodable words. Encourage children to make up their own sentences for more practice.

1. I want to learn about **America**.
2. Jo chose some **beautiful** paints.
3. Their baby **began** to cry.
4. My cat **climbed** up the tree.
5. I will **come** in if it rains.

6. This is a great **country**!
7. She **didn't** know what to do.
8. Please **give** some time to help.
9. Do any pets **live** in your home?
10. We **turned** left and then right.

Point out any irregularities in sound-spellings; for example, the *i_e* spelling stands for the short *i* sound in *give* and *live*.

Have children independently practice the high-frequency words using **Practice Book** page 246.

Practice Add the high-frequency words to the cumulative word bank. Have children work in pairs to make up new sentences for each word.

Cumulative Review Review last week's words using the Read/Spell/Write routine. Repeat; mix the words and have children say each one.

DIFFERENTIATED INSTRUCTION

TIER 2

Approaching Level If children need support with high-frequency words:

I Do Use the **High-Frequency Word Cards**, one at a time. Follow this routine for each word: Display the word. Read the word. Spell the word.

We Do Ask children to state the word and spell the word with you. Model using the word in a sentence, and have children repeat.

You Do Display each word for children to say and spell. Flip through the card set as children chorally read the words. Give opportunities for children to use the words in conversation. Have children write each word in their writer's notebook.

OBJECTIVES

- Know and apply grade-level phonics and word-analysis skills in decoding words.

- Recognize and read grade-appropriate irregularly spelled words.

Digital Tools

For more practice, have children use this activity.

High-Frequency Words

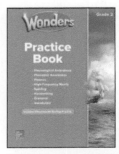

High-Frequency Words: page 246

Decodable Reader, Vol. 3

- Know and apply grade-level phonics and word-analysis skills in decoding words.
- Recognize and read grade-appropriate irregularly spelled words.
- Read on-level text with purpose and understanding.
- Read with sufficient accuracy and fluency to support comprehension.

Decodable Reader: "Growing Stew"

5 Mins

Focus on Foundational Skills

Review the words and letter-sounds that children will find in the **Decodable Reader**.

- Review with children the high-frequency words *beautiful, began,* and *give*.
- Review that *u_e, ue, ew,* and *u* can stand for the long *u* sound.

Preview and Predict Point to the title of the story and have children sound out each word with you as you run your finger under it. Ask: *What do you see in the illustration? What is the family doing together?*

Read the Decodable Reader

Begin guiding children to read the story "Growing Stew." On page 66, have children point to each word, sounding out the decodable words and saying the high-frequency words quickly. If children need support reading decodable words, model blending for them. If children are having difficulty with high-frequency words, reread the high-frequency word in isolation and then reread the word in context.

Check Comprehension

p. 66 *Where does this story start? What time of the year is it?*

p. 67 *What tells the reader that it was not quiet in the garden?*

pp. 68–69 *What did the family do to help the plants grow?*

p. 70 *What did the family pick from their garden? What happened after that?*

Retell Have partners use key ideas and details to retell "Growing Stew."

Focus on Fluency

With partners, have children read "Growing Stew" to focus on accuracy. Guide them to run their fingers under the text as they read. Children should note whether they are correctly reading the words on the page. As children read, they can monitor themselves and provide feedback to their partners.

Listen in: If children are having difficulty reading accurately, have them start again at the beginning of the page. If children are reading too quickly, suggest to them that they should slow down and read as they speak.

English Language Learners

Check Comprehension Provide sentence frames, as needed, to help children answer the questions:

p. 66 The story starts in a garden. It is the beginning of spring.

p. 67 The birds and bugs were making sounds like music.

pp. 68–69 The family kept feeding the baby plants. They pulled the weeds. They chased off harmful birds and bugs.

p. 70 The family picked carrots, peas, and beans from their garden. Then they ate a tasty veggie stew.

Focus on Fluency Before reading "Growing Stew," point out the potential pronunciation challenges in each section of the story so children can practice the words in isolation beforehand. Have children first echo read each section after you, then choral read with you.

Remember to model self-corrective techniques on a regular basis as you read aloud. For example, pretend to mispronounce a word, then self-correct. Encourage children to follow your example as they read.

✔ Check for Success

Rubric Use the online rubric to record children's progress.

Can children decode words with long *u* spelled *u_e, ue, ew, u?*

Can children identify and read the high-frequency words?

Differentiate
SMALL GROUP INSTRUCTIONS

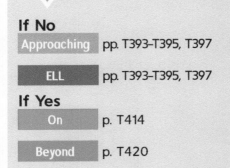

If No

| Approaching | pp. T393–T395, T397 |
| ELL | pp. T393–T395, T397 |

If Yes

| On | p. T414 |
| Beyond | p. T420 |

Daily Focus

Phonemic Awareness
• Phoneme Addition and Deletion

Phonics
• Blend and Build Words with Long *u: u_e, ue, ew, u*

Read
• Decodable Reader, Vol. 3: "Dan and Jen Made Music"

Dan and Jen Made Music

OBJECTIVES
• Add and delete phonemes in words.

OPTION 5 Mins

Phonemic Awareness

Phoneme Addition and Deletion

1 **Model** *Listen carefully to this word:* old. *I will add /h/ to the beginning of* old: /h/ old, hold. *The new word is* hold.

Now I will take away the last sound in date. Date *without /t/ is* day.

2 **Guided Practice/Practice** Have children add a phoneme to the beginning of the words in the first column and take away a phoneme from the words in the second column.

Add /m/ to *ice* (mice)   Take /n/ from *hunt* (hut)

Add /g/ to *ate* (gate)   Take /l/ from *belt* (bet)

> **DIFFERENTIATED INSTRUCTION** >>

TIER 2

Approaching Level If children are having difficulty with phoneme addition and deletion:

I Do Explain to children that they will be adding and deleting phonemes to make new words. *Listen as I say a word:* use. *I will add /m/ to the beginning of* use: /m/ /ūz/, muse. *The new word is:* muse.

Now listen for the first sound in flute: /f/. *Listen as I take away the first sound in* flute: lute. *When I took away the first sound in* flute, *I got a new word,* lute.

We Do *Listen as I say a word:* lend. *Say the word with me,* /lend/. *Let's add /b/ to the beginning of* lend: /b/, /lend/, blend. *Say it with me:* blend. Lend *with /b/ added is* blend. *Repeat with adding /s/ to* low, /f/ to *light,* /s/ to *no, and /t/ to* wig. *Now let's practice deleting sounds. Take away the first sound of a word I say, and say the new word. Do the first one together:* scold, plate, *and* clock.

You Do *It's your turn. Add the sound to the beginning of the words to form new words. Add /t/ to* rack, /g/ *to* rain, /k/ *to* oat, *and /g/ to* round. *Now take away the first sound, and say the new word. Take away /k/ from* cloud, /s/ *from* score, *and /p/ from* preach.

You may wish to review Phonemic Awareness with **ELL** using this section.

Phonics

5 Mins

Blend Words with Long *u: u_e, ue, ew, u*

1 **Model** Display **Word-Building Cards** *f, e, w*. Model how to blend the sounds. Say: *This is the letter* f. *It stands for /f/. These are the letters* ew. *Together, they stand for /ū/. Let's blend all the sounds together: /fffūūū/. The word is* few. Repeat with *mule*.

Continue by modeling the words *cube, huge, cue*, and *unit*.

2 **Guided Practice/Practice** Repeat the routine with *pew, mute, use, music, cube, pupil, cues*. Provide corrective feedback if necessary.

DIFFERENTIATED INSTRUCTION

TIER 2

Approaching Level If children are having difficulty blending words:

I Do Display Word-Building Cards *m, u, l, e, s*. Say: *This is the letter* m. *It stands for /m/. This is the letter* u. *It can stand for /ū/. This is the letter* l. *It stands for /l/. This is the letter* e. *It is silent. This is the letter* s. *It stands for /z/. Listen as I blend all these sounds: /mmmūūūlllzzz/,* mules.

We Do Say: *Let's do some together. Blend and read these words with me:* cute, menu, pew, hues. Offer corrective feedback if children need more support.

You Do Display the following words: *music, amuse, hue, fume, humid*. Have children blend and read the words.

Repeat, blending additional words with /ū/ spelled *u_e, ue, ew, u*.

You may wish to review Phonics with **ELL** using this section.

OBJECTIVES
• Know and apply grade-level phonics and word-analysis skills in decoding words.

SOUND-SPELLING REVIEW

Build Fluency
Display the Word-Building Cards *u, u_e, ew, ue, o, oa, ow, oe, i, igh, ie, y, e, ee, ea, y, ey, ie, a, ai, ay, ea, ei, eigh*. Have children say each sound. Repeat, and vary the pace.

Digital Tools

For more practice, have children use this activity.

Phonemic Awareness

To differentiate instruction for key skills, use the results of this activity.

Phonics

OBJECTIVES

- Know and apply grade-level phonics and word-analysis skills in decoding words.
- Build words.

5 Mins

Phonics

Build Words with Long *u: u_e, ue, ew, u*

1 Review Remind children that the letters *u_e, ew, ue,* and *u* can spell the long *u* sound. Tell them you will build words with long *u.* Display the Word-Building Cards *m, u, l, e* and blend the sounds to read the word.

- Replace the *l* with *t* and blend and read the new word, *mute.*
- Replace the *m* with *c* and blend and read the new word, *cute.*

2 Practice Have children continue building and blending with *cube, huge, hue, cue, fuel, fuse, fume, fumes, few, pew, pupil.*

Once children have built the words, dictate the words and have children write the words on a piece of paper. Children can work with a partner to check their words for spelling.

STRUCTURAL ANALYSIS REVIEW

Write *wilder* and *wildest.* Review that the ending *-er* can be added to an adjective to compare two nouns and the ending *-est* can be added to an adjective to compare more than two nouns. Then write the following: *soft + er, high + est, few + er, light + est.* Ask pairs to write each new word and use it in a sentence.

DIFFERENTIATED INSTRUCTION

On Level For more practice building words:

I Do Display **Word-Building Cards** *c, u, b, e.* Say: *This is the letter c. It stands for /k/. This is the letter u. It can stand for /ū/. This is the letter b. It stands for /b/. This is the letter e. It is silent. Listen as I blend these three sounds /kūūūb/. The word is* cube.

We Do Say: *Now, let's do one together. Make the word* cube *using your Word-Building Cards. Change the letter* b *in* cube *to the letter* t. *Let's blend: /k/ /ū/ /t/, /kūūūt/,* cute. *The new word is* cute. *Provide corrective feedback if needed.*

You Do Have children build and blend these words: *cue, hues, fueled; use, fuse, muses; chew, few, mew; mute, mule, music.*

Digital Tools

To differentiate instruction for key skills, use the results of this activity.

Phonics

OPTION
5
Mins

Decodable Reader: "Dan and Jen Made Music"

OBJECTIVES

• Know and apply grade-level phonics and word-analysis skills in decoding words.

• Recognize and read grade-appropriate irregularly spelled words.

• Read on-level text with purpose and understanding.

• Read with sufficient accuracy and fluency to support comprehension.

Focus on Foundational Skills

Review with children the words with long *u* spelled *u_e, ue, ew, u,* as well as the high-frequency words *beautiful, began,* and *live* that they will find in the **Decodable Reader**.

Dan and Jen Made Music

Dan and Jen both liked music. They played music each day. For Dan and Jen, any time was a great time to make music.
71

Decodable Reader, Vol. 3

Read the Decodable Reader

Guide children in reading "Dan and Jen Made Music." Point out the high-frequency words and the words with long *u* spelled *u_e, ue, ew, u.*

Read the Book On page 72, have children point to each word, sounding out the decodable words and saying the high-frequency words quickly.

Check Comprehension

p. 71 *What does the illustration show?*

p. 72 *How did Jen feel when Dan played his flute music?*

p. 73 *How did Dan feel when Jen played her drum music?*

p. 74 *What happened when Dan and Jen played music together?*

Remind children that they can ask themselves questions to make sure they understood what they have read. Have children use both text and illustrations to answer their questions.

Retell Have partners use key ideas and details to retell the story.

Focus on Fluency

COLLABORATE

Have children practice reading from the Decodable Reader to a partner. Have them concentrate on both accuracy and appropriate rate. Remind them to raise their voice at the end of a question and to read with appropriate emphasis and excitement. Offer corrective feedback as necessary.

ELL

English Language Learners

Check Comprehension Provide sentence frames, as needed, to help children answer the questions:

p. 71 The illustration shows Dan and Jen playing <u>music</u>.

p. 72 Jen <u>did not like</u> the tunes from Dan's flute.

p. 73 Dan <u>did not like</u> the sounds from Jen's drum.

p. 74 They <u>made new music</u>. Dan and Jen both think it is <u>great</u>!

HIGH-FREQUENCY WORDS REVIEW

America, beautiful, began, climbed, come, country, didn't, give, live, turned

Display **High-Frequency Word Cards**. Have children Read/Spell/Write each word.

✓ Check for Success

Rubric Use the online rubric to record children's progress

Can children decode words with long *u?*

Can children read the high-frequency words?

Differentiate
SMALL GROUP INSTRUCTION

If No

| Approaching | pp. T401–T403 |
| ELL | pp. T401–T403 |

If Yes

| On | p. T414 |
| Beyond | p. T420 |

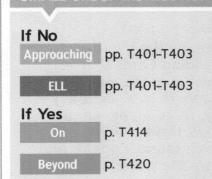

Daily Focus

Phonemic Awareness
• Phoneme Blending

Phonics
• Blend and Build Words with Long *u: u_e, ue, ew, u*

Structural Analysis
• Comparative Endings *-er, -est*

High-Frequency Words

OBJECTIVES

• Blend phonemes to form words.

• Identify letter-sound correspondence spelled long *u*.

• Decode words with long *u*.

• Identify and read words with comparative endings *-er* and *-est*.

• Know and apply grade-level phonics and word-analysis skills in decoding words.

• Recognize and read grade-appropriate irregularly spelled words.

SOUND-SPELLING REVIEW >>

Build Fluency
Display the Word-Building Cards *u, u_e, ew, ue, o, oa, ow, oe, i, igh, ie, y, e, ee, ea, y, ey, ie, a, ai, ay, ea, ei, eigh*. Have children say each sound. Repeat, and vary the pace.

 Phonemic Awareness

Phoneme Blending

Review Guide children to blend phonemes to form words. Say: *Listen as I say a group of sounds. Then blend those sounds to form a word.*

/k/ /ū/ /z/ (cues)	/p/ /ū/ (pew)	/m/ /ū/ /l/ (mule)
/m/ /e/ /n/ /ū/ (menu)	/f/ ū/ /z/ (fuse)	/ū/ /n/ /i/ /t/ (unit)

 Phonics

Blend and Build Words with Long *u: u_e, ue, ew, u*

Review Write the following words: *cute, few, music, hue,* and *humid.* Have children read and say the words. If children are having difficulty, remind them to segment the word and then blend the sounds together. Then have children follow the word-building routine with **Word-Building Cards** to build *mew, pew; menu, unit, music; fuse, use; cue, cube, cute, mute.* Once children have built the words, dictate the words to children and have them write the words. Children can work with a partner to check their spelling.

Word Automaticity Give children practice by displaying decodable words, pointing to each word as children chorally read it. Test how many words children can read in one minute. Model blending any words children miss.

DIFFERENTIATED INSTRUCTION >>

TIER 2

Approaching Level If children need extra support blending and building:

I Do Display Word-Building Cards *f, u, m, e, s. These letters stand for the sounds /fff/, /ūūū/, /mmm/, and /zzz/. Listen as I blend all four sounds: /fffūūūmmmzzz/,* fumes. *The word is* fumes.

We Do *Now let's do one together. Let's make the word* fuse *using Word-Building Cards. Let's blend: /fff/ /ūūū/ /zzz/, /fffūūūzzz/,* fuse. *Now we'll add the letter s at the end of* fuse. *Let's blend and read the new word: /fff/ /ūūū/ /zzz/ /əzzz/, /fffūūūzzəzzz/,* fuses. *Continue to build with:* refuses, refute, mute, mule, muse, amuse. *Offer corrective feedback if needed.*

You Do Have children blend and build these words: *few, pew, mew, hew, hue, cue, cube, cute, mute, mule, mules, muse, use, fuse, confuse.* Review the meanings of the words.

Repeat, blending and building additional words with long *u*.

You may wish to review Phonics with **ELL** using this section.

Structural Analysis

Comparative Endings *-er, -est*

Review Ask children to explain why the endings *-er* and *-est* are added to adjectives. Have them add each ending to these words, write the new words, and use them in a sentence: *great, rich, old.*

High-Frequency Words

America, beautiful, began, climbed, come, country, didn't, give, live, turned

Review Have children identify and read the high-frequency words. Display the **High-Frequency Word Cards** for each of the words. Have children Read/Spell/Write each word. Have partners use the words in conversation. Then have children write a sentence for each word.

DIFFERENTIATED INSTRUCTION

TIER 2

Approaching Level If children need further support with high-frequency words:

I Do Use the High-Frequency Word Cards. Display one word at a time, following the routine: Display the word. Read the word. Then spell the word.

We Do Ask children to state the word and spell the word with you. Model using the word in a sentence and have children repeat after you.

You Do Display the words in random order. Ask children to say the word and then spell it. When completed, quickly flip through the word card set as children chorally read the words. Provide opportunities for children to use the words in speaking and writing. For example, supply sentence starters, such as *On a beautiful day, we climbed up to ___ .* Ask children to write each word in their writer's notebook.

Digital Tools

To differentiate instruction for key skills, use the results of this activity.

Phonics

For more practice, have children use this activity.

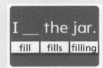

Structural Analysis

✔ Check for Success

Rubric Use the online rubric to record children's progress.

Can children decode words with long *u: u_e, ue, ew, u*?

Can children identify and read the high-frequency words?

Differentiate
SMALL GROUP INSTRUCTION

If No

Approaching | pp. T404–T405

ELL | pp. T404–T405

If Yes

On | p. T414

Beyond | p. T420

Lexile 410

OBJECTIVES

Know and use various text features to locate key facts or information in a text efficiently.

Identify the main purpose of a text, including what the author wants to answer, explain, or describe.

Participate in collaborative conversations with diverse partners about grade 2 topics and texts with peers and adults in small and larger groups.

ACADEMIC LANGUAGE

• *expository, main idea, key details, text features, prefix*
• Cognates: *expositivo, detalles, prefijo*

Approaching Level

Leveled Reader *The Sounds of Trash*

Preview and Predict

• Read the Essential Question: *How do you express yourself?*
• Have children preview the title, opening pages, and photographs. Prompt children to predict what the selection might be about.

Review Genre: Expository Text

Have children recall that an expository text gives facts and information about a topic. The author may include text features, such as photographs, captions, charts, and graphs, to help explain information.

Close Reading

Note Taking: Have children use a copy of the online Main Idea and Key Details **Graphic Organizer 51** as they read to record key ideas from the text.

Think Aloud: When I read, I'll look to the text, photos, and captions to find the key details, or the most important details. On pages 4-5, I read that you can express yourself by using a bottle with water as an instrument. This is one key detail. Let's add this to the Main Idea and Key Details chart. As we read, we'll continue to add our details to the chart. The key details will help us to determine the main idea, which we'll also add to the chart.

Pages 2–5 *Turn to a partner and take turns asking each other a question about ways to express yourself. Then answer each other's question.* (Possible response: How do you like to express yourself? I like to draw pictures. How can you use trash to express yourself? You can use trash to make instruments and play music to show how you feel.) *Look at the word "recycle" on page 5. What prefix does this word have?* (re-) *What do you think it means?* (back or again.)

Pages 6–7 *Turn to a partner and take turns asking each other a question about how to make and play a guitar. Then answer each other's question.* (Possible response: What do you need to make a guitar? You need a box, colored paper, a pencil, and rubber bands.)

Pages 8–13 *What text features on pages 8-13 tell you this selection is informational text?* (photos and captions, a chart, a graph) *How does the photo on page 9 help you understand how to make a trombone?* (It shows how the paper and tubes fit together. The arrows show how to slide the tube.)

Pages 14–15 *Turn to a partner and each take a turn asking the other a question about playing instruments. Then answer each other's questions.* (Possible response: What can you do with the instruments you make? You can play with other kids. What songs can you play with the instruments you make? (You can play along with your favorite song or make your own song.)

Retell Have children take turns retelling the selection using the retelling cards. Help children make a personal connection by asking: *Which instrument would you most like to make? Why?*

Respond to Reading Have children complete Respond to Reading questions on page 16 after reading.

 Write About Reading In children's responses to question 4 on page 16, check that they were able to describe how they can express themselves through music.

Fluency: Intonation and Accuracy

Model Fluency Read aloud page 4, one sentence at a time. Have children chorally repeat. Point out how your voice changes when reading the question.

Apply Have children practice reading pages 4–5 with partners. Provide feedback as needed.

Paired Read: "Talking Underwater"

 Make Connections: Write About It

Before reading, ask children to note that the genre of this text is also expository. Then discuss the Essential Question. After reading, ask children to make connections between the information they learned from "Talking Underwater" and *The Sounds of Trash.*

Leveled Reader

 Focus on Science

Children can extend their knowledge of homemade musical instruments and their sounds by completing the science activity on page 20.

Literature Circles

Lead children in conducting a literature circle using the Thinkmark questions to guide the discussion. You may wish to discuss what children have learned about expressing themselves from both selections in the leveled reader.

LEVEL UP

IF children read the Approaching Level fluently and answered the questions

THEN pair them with children who have proficiently read the On Level and have approaching children

- echo-read the On Level main selection.

- use self-stick notes to mark one key detail they would like to discuss in each section.

 **Access Complex Text**

The On Level challenges children by including more **specific vocabulary** and **complex sentence structures**.

"Musical Expression"
Lexile 480

OBJECTIVES

Know and use various text features to locate key facts or information in a text efficiently.

Identify the main purpose of a text, including what the author wants to answer, explain, or describe.

ACADEMIC LANGUAGE

- *expository, chart, key details, main idea, prefix, organize*
- Cognates: *prefijo, organizar*

Approaching Level

Genre Passage *"Musical Expression"*

Build Background

- Read aloud the Essential Question: *How do you express yourself?* Ask children how they like to express themselves, and how they feel when they do. Use the following sentence starters to help focus discussion:

  When I feel sad, I can express myself by . . .

  When I dance or make music, I feel . . .

- Let children know that the online **Differentiated Genre Passage** "Musical Expression" tells how some real musicians used their instruments to express feelings.

Review Genre: Expository Text

Remind children that expository text gives facts and information about a topic. Explain that it can include text features such as photographs, captions, diagrams, and charts.

Close Reading

Note Taking As children read the passage the first time, ask them to annotate the text. Have them note key ideas and details, unfamiliar words, and questions they have. Then have them read again. Use the following questions to help focus discussion. Encourage children to cite text evidence from the selection as they respond to the questions.

> **Read**

Genre: Expository Text Reread the first paragraph on page A1. *What does the author want readers to learn about in this selection?* (The author wants the readers to learn about how musicians used music to show their feelings.)

Main Idea and Key Details *Reread the second paragraph on page A1. What key details tell how Louis Armstrong played to show sadness?* (He would blow low or high notes slowly.) *What key details tell how Armstrong played to show happiness?* (He would make high notes fast.) *Reread the third paragraph on page A1. How did Marian McPartland use the piano to show her feelings?* (She would play low notes to show she was unhappy, and faster notes if she felt excited.) *Reread the first paragraph on page A2. How did Melba Liston use her trombone to express her feelings?* (She would play high notes lightly to show joy, and low notes loudly to show energy.)

Text Features *Look at the chart on page A2. What kinds of feelings can be expressed with high, fast sounds?* (excited, happy, love, nervous, surprised) *What kinds of feelings can be expressed with low, slow sounds?* (angry, careful, sad, scared, sneaky, tired)

Summarize Have children use their notes to summarize how the musicians used their instruments to express their feelings.

Reread

Use the questions on page A3 to guide children's rereading of the passage. Accept all possible answers.

Author's Purpose *What is the author's purpose for writing "Musical Expression"?* (The author wants to explain how musicians expressed their feelings with their instruments and music.)

Main Idea and Key Details *Reread the three sections about the musicians and their instruments on pages A1–A2. What is one way the musicians were alike?* (The musicians used their instruments to show how they felt.)

Text Features: Chart *Reread the chart on page A2. How does the chart add new information to the text?* (The chart adds information about how musical instruments can make different sounds to show different feelings.)

Integrate

Make Connections Guide children to understand the connections between "Musical Expression" and other selections they have read. Tell them to work with a partner to find text evidence and respond to this question: *How do the authors help you understand how music can be used to show feelings? How do they show you that you can make music?*

Compare Genres Use a copy of online Venn Diagram **Graphic Organizer 50**. Help children compare and contrast key details that show how we can express ourselves. Use information from all of the selections from the genre study.

Differentiate and Collaborate

Be Inspired Have children think about the selections they read. Ask: *What do the texts inspire you to do?* Use the following activities, or have partners think of a way to respond to the texts.

Express Musical Feelings Have partners play music to express feelings. First, have them find or make musical instruments. Then have them play their instruments together to show emotions. Have other pairs listen and guess the feelings being expressed.

Make a Poster Have children choose a musical instrument and research how it is played. Children can make a poster with a picture of the instrument and key details that explain how it is played.

Readers to Writers

Text Organization Remind children that authors use headings to organize text. Point out that the author of "Musical Expression" used a heading at the beginning of the second, third, and fourth paragraphs. Have children reread the passage. Ask: *Why do you think the author used the musicians' names as headings? How can headings help readers understand a text?*

LEVEL UP

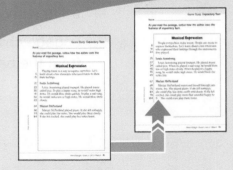

IF children read the Approaching Level fluently and answered the questions,

THEN pair them with children who have proficiently read the On Level. Have them

- partner-read the On Level passage.

- summarize how the musicians could express sad feelings.

Approaching Level

Vocabulary

REVIEW VOCABULARY WORDS

TIER
2

OBJECTIVES
Determine or clarify the meaning of unknown and multiple-meaning words and phrases based on grade 2 reading and content, choosing flexibly from an array of strategies.

I Do Display each **Visual Vocabulary Card** from this genre study and state the word. Explain how the photograph illustrates the word. State the example sentence and repeat the word.

We Do Point to the word on the card, and read the word with children. Ask them to repeat the word. Engage children in structured partner talk about the image as prompted on the back of the vocabulary card.

You Do Display each visual in random order, hiding the word. Have children match the definitions and context sentences of the words to the visuals displayed.

CUMULATIVE VOCABULARY REVIEW

TIER
2

OBJECTIVES
Use sentence-level context as a clue to the meaning of a word or phrase.

I Do Use **Visual Vocabulary Cards** from the previous genre study to review previously taught vocabulary. Display one card at a time. Read the definition and example sentence and repeat the word.

We Do Point to the word and read with children. Read the question on the back of the card or make up a new question. Ask children to answer the question using the vocabulary word. If a response is an incomplete sentence, restate using a complete sentence.

You Do Engage children in structured partner talk using a Partner Talk prompt from the back of the card.

IDENTIFY RELATED WORDS

OBJECTIVES

Determine or clarify the meaning of unknown and multiple-meaning words and phrases based on grade 2 reading and content, choosing flexibly from an array of strategies.

Use sentence-level context as a clue to the meaning of a word or phrase.

I Do Display the *sounds* **Visual Vocabulary Card** and say aloud the word set *sounds, tastes,* and *noises.*

Point out that *noises* means almost the same thing as *sounds.*

We Do Display the vocabulary card for *rhythm.* Say aloud the word set *rhythm, tune,* and *beat.* With children, identify the word that has almost the same meaning as *rhythm* and discuss why.

You Do Have children work in pairs to choose the word that means almost the same as the first word in each group.

movements, actions, thoughts

concert, practice, performance

understand, know, ask

Have children choose words from their writer's notebook and use an online thesaurus to find synonyms and a dictionary to check their pronunciation.

PREFIXES

OBJECTIVES

Read with sufficient accuracy and fluency to support comprehension

Decode words with common prefixes and suffixes.

I Do Remind children that a prefix is a word part added to the beginning of a word to change the meaning of the word. Tell children they can use prefixes to figure out the meaning of an unknown word. Read aloud the third paragraph on page A1 of "Musical Expression" from the Approaching Level online **Differentiated Genre Passages**.

Think Aloud *I want to know what the word* unhappy *means. I know the word* happy *means "feeling good." The prefix* un- *means "not." So, the word* unhappy *means "not happy, or not feeling good."*

We Do Point out the word *excited* in the same paragraph and discuss its meaning. Help children create a new word by adding the prefix *un-* to *excited.* Then ask: *How might Marian McPartland have played if she had felt unexcited?* (Possible responses: slowly, quietly)

You Do Have children work in pairs to find the word *safe* in the chart on page A2. Have them make a new word by adding the prefix *un-* to the word *safe.* Have them use the new word in a sentence and tell what it means. Ask them what kind of music they could play to express feeling *unsafe.*

Approaching Level

Fluency/Comprehension

FLUENCY

TIER 2

OBJECTIVES
Read with sufficient accuracy and fluency to support comprehension.

I Do Read the second paragraph on page A1 of "Musical Expression" in the Approaching Level online **Differentiated Genre Passages**. Model using correct intonation. Use a quick, happy tone as you read the third and fourth sentences. Use a slow, gloomy tone as you read the fifth and sixth sentences.

We Do Read the next paragraph and have children repeat each sentence after you. Point out how you change your intonation to match the meaning of the sentences.

You Do Have children read the last paragraph of the selection aloud. Remind them to read accurately, with correct intonation, and at an appropriate rate.

KEY DETAILS

TIER 2

OBJECTIVES
Ask and answer such questions as *who, what, where, when, why,* and *how* to demonstrate understanding of key details in a text.

Identify the main topic of a multiparagraph text as well as the focus of specific paragraphs within the text.

I Do Remind children that they have been reading expository text. Tell them that, when they read expository text, they should look for the key details. Say: *When we look for key details, we look for the most important facts in the text.* Remind children that finding key details will help them find the main idea.

We Do Read aloud the first two paragraphs on page A1 of "Musical Expression" in the Approaching Level online **Differentiated Genre Passages**. Pause to identify the key details, and discuss why they are important. *We read that Louis Armstrong played trumpet, and that he played jazz. We also read that he could play happy or sad songs. These are important details. They tell us what kind of music Louis Armstrong played.*

You Do Guide children to read the rest of the selection. As they read, prompt them to identify important details as they read. Help children explain why each detail is important.

REVIEW MAIN IDEA AND KEY DETAILS

OBJECTIVES

Ask and answer such questions as *who, what, where, when, why,* and *how* to demonstrate understanding of key details in a text.

Identify the main topic of a multiparagraph text as well as the focus of specific paragraphs within the text.

I Do Remind children that expository texts express a main idea. It is the most important point an author makes about a topic. Each key detail tells more information about the main idea.

We Do Read the last paragraph on page A1 of "Musical Expression" in the Approaching Level online **Differentiated Genre Passages** together. Pause to identify the key details. *We read that Marian McPartland could play low notes if she felt unhappy. These details help us understand how she uses the piano to express her feelings.*

You Do Read the paragraphs on page A2 and ask: *What important details are on this page?* Record each detail on a copy of online Main Idea and Key Details **Graphic Organizer 51**. Continue having children add details. Then guide children to determine the main idea.

SELF-SELECTED READING

OBJECTIVES

Read with sufficient accuracy and fluency to support comprehension.

Read on-level text with purpose and understanding.

Apply the strategy and skill to reread text.

Read Independently

Have children choose an expository text for sustained silent reading and set a purpose for reading that book. Children can check the online **Leveled Reader Database** for selections. Remind them that:

- they should look for the key details in the text and text features.
- the main idea is what all of the key details in the selection have in common.
- they can ask themselves questions as they read and then look for the answers in the text and images.

Read Purposefully

As they read independently, have children record the key details and the main idea on a copy of online Main Idea and Key Details **Graphic Organizer 51**. After reading, guide children to participate in a Book Talk about the selection they read. Guide children to:

- share the information they recorded on their Main Idea and Key Details graphic organizer.
- tell what interesting facts they learned from reading the selections.
- share what questions they asked themselves and how they found the answers.

Offer assistance and guidance with self-selected assignments.

Lexile 530

OBJECTIVES

Read with sufficient accuracy and fluency to support comprehension.

Use text features to locate key facts or information in a text.

Identify the main purpose of a text, including what the author wants to answer, explain, or describe.

Determine or clarify the meaning of unknown words based on grade 2 reading and content, choosing flexibly from an array of strategies.

ACADEMIC LANGUAGE

- *expository, main idea, key details, text features, prefix*
- Cognates: *expositivo, detalles, prefijo*

On Level

Leveled Reader *The Sounds of Trash*

Preview and Predict

- Have children read the Essential Question: *How do you express yourself?*
- Have children preview the title, opening pages, text features, and photos to make a prediction about the selection. Have children discuss their predictions.

Review Genre: Expository Text

Remind children that expository text gives facts and information about a topic. The author may include text features, such as photographs, captions, charts, and graphs, to help explain information. Have children identify features of expository text in *The Sounds of Trash*.

Close Reading

Note Taking: Ask children to use a copy of the online Main Idea and Key Details **Graphic Organizer 51** as they read to record the main idea of the selection and key details that support the main idea.

Pages 2–5: *Turn to a partner and discuss the main idea of Chapter 1. What key details do you learn?* (The main idea is that there are many ways to express yourself and be creative. Key details: You can make art, act, dance, sing, write, or play instruments to express yourself. You can recycle trash to make instruments.) *Which word has a prefix on page 5?* (recycle) *What is the prefix?* (re-) *What does the prefix* re- *mean?* (again) *What does the word* recycle *mean?* (to cause something to go through a cycle, or process, again)

Pages 6–9: *What questions can you ask to help you find key details on these pages? Find answers to your questions.* (Possible response: How does a homemade guitar make music? The rubber bands vibrate and make sound.) *What is the main idea of the boxed information at the bottom of page 7?* (Different sizes of rubber bands make different sounds.) *What text feature does the author use to introduce the text on page 9?* (a question printed in bold)

Pages 10–11: *How does the author organize information about making maracas?* (The author uses headings, a bulleted list of items needed, and numbered directions that tell steps in order.) *What key detail do you learn about maracas on page 11?* (Things inside maracas move around and hit the inside of the bottle to make sound.)

Pages 12–14: *What is the main idea of page 14?* (Express yourself by using your instruments to make music you can share with others.)

Retell Have children take turns retelling the selection using the retelling cards. Help children make a personal connection by asking: *What instrument would you most like to make? Why?*

Respond to Reading Have children complete the Respond to Reading questions on page 15.

 Write About Reading In children's responses to question 4 on page 15, check that they were able to describe how they can express themselves through music.

Fluency: Accuracy and Intonation

Model Model reading aloud pages 13 and 14 with accuracy and intonation. Have children chorally repeat. Point out how your voice goes up when reading the question and expresses excitement when reading the exclamations.

Apply Have children practice repeated reading with partners. Provide feedback as needed.

Paired Read: "Talking Underwater"

 Make Connections: Write About It

Before reading, ask children to note that the genre of this text is also expository. Then discuss the Essential Question. After reading, ask children to make connections between the information they learned from "Talking Underwater" and *The Sounds of Trash*.

Leveled Reader

Focus on Science

Children can extend their knowledge of homemade musical instruments and their sounds by completing the science activity on page 20.

Literature Circles

Lead children in conducting a literature circle using the Thinkmark questions to guide the discussion. You may wish to discuss what children have learned about expressing themselves from both selections in the leveled reader.

LEVEL UP

IF children read the On Level fluently and answered the questions

THEN pair them with children who have proficiently read the Beyond Level and have on-level children

- partner-read the Beyond Level main selection.

- discuss the key details and main idea with their partners.

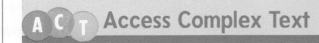 Access Complex Text

The Beyond Level challenges children by including more **specific vocabulary** and **complex sentence structures**.

"Musical Expression"
Lexile 590L

OBJECTIVES

Read with sufficient accuracy and fluency to support comprehension.

Use text features to locate key facts or information in a text.

Identify the main purpose of a text, including what the author wants to answer, explain, or describe.

ACADEMIC LANGUAGE

• *expository, chart, key details, main idea, prefix, organize*

• Cognates: *prefijo, organizar*

On Level

Genre Passage *"Musical Expression"*

Build Background

• Read aloud the Essential Question: *How do you express yourself?* Ask children how they like to express themselves when they feel happy or excited. Use the following sentence starters to help focus discussion:

> *When I feel excited, I can express myself by . . .*
>
> *Playing or listening to music is a way to . . .*

• Let children know that the online **Differentiated Genre Passage** "Musical Expression" tells how some real musicians used their instruments to express their feelings.

Review Genre: Expository Text

Review with children that expository text gives facts and information about a topic. Remind them that the author may give information through text features, such as photographs, captions, diagrams, and charts.

Close Reading

Note Taking As children read the passage the first time, ask them to annotate the text. Have them note key ideas and details, unfamiliar words, and questions they have. Then have them read it again and use the following questions. Encourage children to cite text evidence from the selection as they respond to the questions.

> **Read**

Genre: Expository Text *Reread the first paragraph on page O1. What do you think the author wants you to learn in this selection?* (The author wants to share information about how musicians used music to express their feelings.) *Reread the last paragraph on page O2. How does the author feel about music?* (The author thinks that music is a great way for people to express their feelings.)

Main Idea and Key Details Have partners talk about how the three musicians used their instruments to express their feelings.

Text Features *Reread page O2. What text feature do you see that is a feature of expository text?* (the chart at the top of the page) *What information does the chart give?* (It tells what feelings are expressed by different sounds and speeds when playing an instrument.)

Summarize Have children refer to their notes to summarize how the three musicians used their instruments to express their feelings.

Reread

Use the questions on page O3 to guide children's rereading of the passage. Accept all possible answers.

Author's Purpose *What is the author's purpose for writing "Musical Expression"?* (The author wants to explain how musicians expressed their feelings with their instruments and music.)

Main Idea and Key Details *Reread the three paragraphs about the musicians and their instruments on pages O1–O2. What is one way the musicians were alike?* (The musicians used their instruments to show how they felt.)

Text Features: Chart *Reread the chart on page O2. How does the chart add information to the text?* (The chart adds information about how musical instruments can make different sounds to show their feelings.)

Integrate

 Make Connections Guide children to understand the connections between "Musical Expression" and other selections they have read. Tell them to work with a partner to find text evidence and respond to this question: *How do the authors help you understand how musicians used their music to show feelings? How do they encourage you to make music to show your feelings?*

Compare Genres Draw a Venn Diagram. Help children compare or contrast key details that show how people use music to show their feelings.

Differentiate and Collaborate

 Be Inspired Have children think about "Musical Expression" and other selections they read. Ask: *What do the texts inspire you to do?* Use the following activities, or have partners think of a way to respond to the texts.

Perform a Song Have children work with a partner to find a song that they feel expresses a specific feeling. Have them perform the song for the class or play a recording of the song. Then have the class guess which emotion the song represents.

Make an Instrument Have children work with a partner to create a musical instrument. Have pairs demonstrate how to play their instrument for the class.

Readers to Writers

Text Organization Remind children that authors use headings to organize text. Point out that the author of "Musical Expression" used a heading at the beginning of second, third, or fourth paragraphs. Ask children to reread the passage. Ask: *Why do you think the author used the musicians' names as headings? How can headings help readers better understand a text?*

LEVEL UP

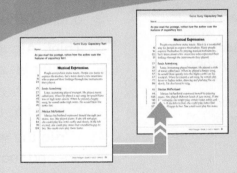

IF children read the On Level fluently and answered the questions

THEN pair them with children who have proficiently read the Beyond Level. Have them

- partner-read the Beyond Level passage.
- identify the key details and the main idea.

On Level

Vocabulary

REVIEW VOCABULARY WORDS

OBJECTIVES

Use context to confirm or self-correct word recognition and understanding, rereading as necessary.

Demonstrate understanding of word relationships and nuances in word meanings.

I Do Use the **Visual Vocabulary Cards** to review the key selection words *cheered, concert, instrument, movements, music, rhythm, sounds,* and *understand.* Point to each word, read it aloud, and have children chorally repeat it.

We Do Ask these questions and help children record and explain their answers:

- What *instrument* would you like to learn to play?
- When have you ever *cheered* for someone?
- What kind of *music* do you like to listen to?

You Do Have children work with a partner to write questions using each of the remaining vocabulary words. Have them exchange their questions with another pair, and answer the other pair's questions.

Have children choose words from their writer's notebook and use an online thesaurus to find synonyms.

PREFIXES

OBJECTIVES

Determine the meaning of the new word formed when a known prefix is added to a known word (e.g., *happy/ unhappy, tell/retell*).

Use a known root word as a clue to the meaning of an unknown word with the same root (e.g., *addition/ additional*).

I Do Read aloud the third paragraph of "Musical Expression" in the On Level online **Differentiated Genre Passages**, page O1.

Think Aloud *I want to find a word with a prefix in the third paragraph. I know that a prefix is a word part added to the beginning of a root word to make a new word. I see the word* unhappy. *I can use what I know about prefixes to figure out what* unhappy *means.*

We Do Write the word *unhappy* on the board. Guide children to identify the prefix *un-* and root word *happy.* Ask: *What does the prefix* un- *mean?* (not) *What does the word* unhappy *mean?* (not happy) Then have children find a word in the second paragraph that means the same as *unhappy.* (sad)

You Do Have children work in pairs to find the words *excited* and *safe* in the chart on page O2. Have them make new words by adding the prefix *un-.* Have them tell what the new words mean and use them in a sentence. Ask them what kind of music they could play to express feeling *unexcited* or *unsafe.*

Comprehension

REVIEW MAIN IDEA AND KEY DETAILS

OBJECTIVES

Identify the main topic of a multiparagraph text as well as the focus of specific paragraphs within the text.

Ask and answer such questions as *who, what, where, when, why,* and *how* to demonstrate understanding of key details in a text.

I Do Remind children that key details are important facts in expository texts. Say: *We can use the key details in the text and text features to figure out the main idea. The main idea of the selection is what all of the details have in common.*

We Do Read the last paragraph on page O1 of "Musical Expression" in the On Level online **Differentiated Genre Passages** together. Pause to identify the key details. *We read that Marian McPartland could play low notes if she felt unhappy. These details help us understand how she uses the piano to express her feelings.*

You Do Guide children to read the rest of the selection. Remind them to identify the key details as they read and record them on the online Main Idea and Key Details **Graphic Organizer 51**. Then have children use the details to determine the main idea.

SELF-SELECTED READING

OBJECTIVES

Read with sufficient accuracy and fluency to support comprehension.

Read on-level text with purpose and understanding.

Read Independently

Have children choose an expository text for sustained silent reading and set a purpose for reading that book. Children can check the online **Leveled Reader Database** for selections. Remind them to:

- use the key details to help them figure out the main idea.
- ask themselves questions about key details and then look for the answers in the text and text features.

Read Purposefully

Have children record the key details and the main idea on a copy of online Main Idea and Key Details **Graphic Organizer 51**. After reading, guide partners to:

- share what they recorded on their Main Idea and Key Details chart.
- tell what interesting facts they learned reading the selections.
- share the questions they asked themselves and how they found the answers.

 You may want to include **ELL** students in On Level vocabulary and comprehension lessons. Offer language support as needed.

Lexile 590L

OBJECTIVES

Read with sufficient accuracy and fluency to support comprehension.

Ask and answer such questions as *who, what, where, when, why,* and *how* to demonstrate understanding of key details in a text.

Identify the main topic of a multiparagraph text as well as the focus of specific paragraphs within the text.

ACADEMIC LANGUAGE

- *expository, main idea, key details, text features, prefix*
- *Cognates: expositivo, detalles, prefijo*

Beyond Level

Leveled Reader *The Sounds of Trash*

Preview and Predict

- Have children read the Essential Question: *How do you express yourself?*
- Next, have them preview the title, opening pages, text features, and photos to make a prediction about the selection. Have children discuss their predictions.

Review Genre: Expository Text

Remind children that expository text gives facts and information about a topic. Prompt children to name key characteristics of expository texts, such as photos, captions, charts, and diagrams. Tell them to look for these as they read *The Sounds of Trash*.

Close Reading

Note taking Ask children to use a copy of the online Main Idea and Key Details **Graphic Organizer 51** as they read to record the main idea of the selection and key details that support the main idea.

Pages 2–5: *Turn to a partner and discuss the main idea of Chapter 1. What key details do you learn? How are they connected?* (The main idea is that there are many ways to express yourself and be creative. Key details: you can make art, act, dance, do tricks, sing, write, or play instruments. You can recycle trash to make instruments. All these key details show ways to express yourself creatively.) *What word can you make if you add the prefix re- to the word* write *on page 2? What does it mean?* (rewrite; to write again)

Pages 6–9: *What questions can you ask to better understand key details? Find answers to your questions.* (Possible response: How does a homemade guitar make music? The rubber bands vibrate and make sound.) *What text feature does the author use to introduce the text on page 9?* (a question printed in bold)

Pages 10–11: *How does the author organize information about making maracas?* (The author uses headings, a bulleted list of items needed, and numbered directions that tell steps in order.) *What key detail do you learn about maracas on page 11?* (Things inside maracas move around and hit the inside of the bottle to make sound.)

Pages 12–14: *What key detail do you learn about guiros on page 13?* (You can make one from a coffee can.) *What is the main idea of page 14?* (Use your instruments to make music you can share with others.)

Retell Have children take turns telling what they learned from the selection. Help children make a personal connection by writing about making an instrument. Say: *Write about the instrument you would like to make. How would you use it to express yourself?*

Respond to Reading Have children complete the Respond to Reading questions on page 15.

 Write About Reading In children's responses to question 4 on page 15, check that children are able to share ideas about how they express themselves through music.

Fluency: Intonation and Accuracy

Model Read aloud pages 13 and 14. Have children chorally repeat. Point out how your voice goes up when reading the questions and how it expresses excitement when reading the exclamations.

Apply Have pairs practice reading the page together. Remind them to read with good intonation and accuracy.

Paired Read: "Talking Underwater"

 Make Connections: Write About It

Before reading "Talking Underwater," have children preview the title page and identify the genre. Then discuss the Essential Question. After reading, have partners discuss "Talking Underwater" and *The Sounds of Trash*. Ask children to make connections by comparing and contrasting the ways we use sound to communicate.

Leveled Reader

Prompt children to discuss what they learned about expressing themselves.

 ## Focus on Science

Children can extend their knowledge of homemade musical instruments and their sounds by completing the science activity on page 20.

 ## Literature Circles

Lead children in conducting a literature circle using the Thinkmark questions to guide the discussion. You may wish to discuss what children have learned about expressing themselves from both selections in the leveled reader.

 ## Gifted and Talented

SYNTHESIZE Challenge children to learn more about how an instrument from the selection makes sound. Children should make a diagram to show how the instrument makes sound and how the sound waves travel. Have children gather facts from the library and online resources.

"Musical Expression"
Lexile 690

OBJECTIVES

Ask and answer such questions as *who, what, where, when, why,* and *how* to demonstrate understanding of key details in a text.

Determine or clarify the meaning of unknown and multiple-meaning words and phrases based on grade 2 reading and content, choosing flexibly from an array of strategies.

ACADEMIC LANGUAGE

• *expository, chart, key details, main idea, prefix, organize*
• Cognates: *prefijo, organizar*

Beyond Level

Genre Passage *"Musical Expression"*

Build Background

• Read aloud the Essential Question: *How do you express yourself?* Ask children how they like to express themselves when they feel happy or sad. Use the following sentence starters to help focus discussion:

> *When I feel happy, I can express myself by . . .*
>
> *Playing or listening to music can help you . . .*

• Let children know that the online **Differentiated Genre Passage** "Musical Expression" tells how real musicians used their instruments to express their feelings.

Review Genre: Expository Text

Review with children that expository text gives facts and information about a topic. Remind them that the author may give information through text features such as photographs, captions, diagrams, and charts.

Close Reading

Note Taking As children read the passage the first time, ask them to annotate the text. Have them note key ideas and details, unfamiliar words, and questions they have. Then have them read it again and use the following questions. Encourage children to cite text evidence from the selection as they respond to the questions.

> **Read**

Author's Purpose *Reread the first and last paragraphs of this selection. Based on these two paragraphs, what does the author want the reader to learn from this text?* (The author wants readers to know that playing music and listening to music can provide them with opportunities to express their emotions.)

Main Idea and Details Have partners talk about the key details that show how the three musicians used their instruments to express their feelings.

Text Features *Reread page B2. What text feature do you see that is a feature of expository text?* (the chart) *What information does the chart give?* (It tells what feelings are expressed by different sounds and speeds when playing an instrument.) *Use the chart to tell how a musician could play an instrument to show that she felt sleepy.* (She could play high notes slow.) *Use the chart to tell how a musician could play an instrument to show that he felt scared.* (He could play low notes fast, or low notes slow.)

Summarize Have children use their notes to summarize how the three musicians used their instruments to express their emotions.

Reread

Use the questions on page B3 to guide children's rereading of the passage. Accept all possible answers.

Author's Purpose *What is the author's purpose for writing "Musical Expression"?* (The author wants to explain how musicians expressed their feelings with their instruments and music.)

Main Idea and Key Details *Reread the three paragraphs about the musicians and their instruments on pages B1–B2. What is one way the musicians were alike?* (The musicians used their instruments to show how they felt.)

Text Features: Chart *Reread the chart on page B2. What are some ways the chart adds information to the text?* (The chart adds information about how musical instruments can make different sounds to show feelings.)

Integrate

Make Connections Guide children to understand the connections between "Musical Expression" and the other selections they have read. Tell them to work with a partner to find text evidence and respond to this question: *How do the authors help you understand how music can be used to show feelings?*

Compare Genres Draw or use a Venn Diagram. Help children compare or contrast key details that show how people use music to show their feelings.

Differentiate and Collaborate

Be Inspired Have children think about "Musical Expression" and other selections they read. Ask: *"What do the texts inspire you to do?"* Use the following activities, or have partners think of a way to respond to the texts.

Write a Song Have partners work together to write an original song to express a specific emotion. Partners can choose a familiar tune, such as "Row, Row, Row Your Boat," and provide new lyrics to express an emotion. Encourage partners to rehearse their song and to use musical cues, such as high notes, low notes, fast notes, or slow notes to help convey their target emotion. Children can record their original song and then play it for the class, or they can choose to perform their song in front of the class.

Write a Journal Entry Ask children to write a journal entry about a time they used art or music to express themselves. Have them include details about how they felt before and after.

Readers to Writers

Text Organization Remind children that authors use headings to organize text. Point out that the author of "Musical Expression" used a heading at the beginning of the second, third, and fourth paragraphs. Have children reread the passage. Ask: *Why do you think the author used the musicians' names as headings? How can headings help readers better understand a text?*

Gifted and Talented

Synthesize Have groups of children listen to a jazz recording. Have them take notes as they listen, noting whether the music is fast or slow, loud or soft, high or low. Ask them to write about how the music makes them feel and what feelings they think the music expresses.

Extend Have children discuss their notes as a class. Point out that music can affect different people in different ways, so their notes may differ from those of other class members.

Beyond Level

Vocabulary

REVIEW DOMAIN-SPECIFIC WORDS

OBJECTIVES

Use context to confirm or self-correct word recognition and understanding, rereading as necessary.

Demonstrate understanding of word relationships and nuances in word meanings.

Model Use the **Visual Vocabulary Cards** to review the meaning of the words *music* and *sounds*. Have children create a Venn diagram comparing the meaning of the words *music* and *sounds*.

Write the words *collages, solo,* and *emotion* on the board, and discuss the meanings with children. Then help children describe orally how you can show emotion through art, such as collages, and performances, such as solo dances.

Apply Have children work in pairs to review the meanings of the words *concert* and *rhythm*. Have children prepare a brief report about an exciting concert attended and share it with the rest of the class.

PREFIXES

OBJECTIVES

Determine the meaning of the new word formed when a prefix is added to a known word (e.g., *happy/unhappy, tell/retell*)

Use a known root word as a clue to the meaning of an unknown word with the same root (e.g., *addition/additional*).

Model Read aloud the third paragraph of "Musical Expression" in the Beyond Level online **Differentiated Genre Passages**, page B1.

Think Aloud *I see a word with a prefix in the third paragraph:* unhappy. *I can use what I know about prefixes to figure out what* unhappy *means.*

Apply Write the word *unhappy* on the board. Have children identify the prefix *un-* and the root word *happy*. Ask: *What does the prefix* un- *mean?* (not) *What does the word* unhappy *mean?* (not happy) Then have children find a word in the second paragraph that means the same as *unhappy*. (sad)

Have children find the words *excited, safe,* and *surprised* in the chart on page B2. Have them make new words by adding the prefix *un-*. Have them tell what the new words mean and use them in a sentence. Ask them what kind of music they could play to express feeling *unexcited, unsafe,* or *unsurprised*.

Synthesize Have children select a root word from the activity. Have them add known prefixes, suffixes, and inflectional endings to the word. Ask partners to write an explanation of the differences between the words.

Have children repeat the activity by finding words in their writer's notebook and adding prefixes, suffixes, and inflectional endings to them, as appropriate.

Comprehension

REVIEW MAIN IDEA AND KEY DETAILS

OBJECTIVES

Identify the main topic of a multiparagraph text as well as the focus of specific paragraphs within the text.

Ask and answer such questions as *who, what, where, when, why,* and *how* to demonstrate understanding of key details in a text.

Model Discuss with children how they can use the key details to determine the main idea of an expository text. Say: *We can use the key details in the text and text features to figure out the main idea. The main idea of the selection is what all of the details have in common.*

Have children read page B1 of "Musical Expression" in the Beyond Level online **Differentiated Genre Passages**. Ask open-ended questions to facilitate discussion, such as "How did Marian McPartland express her feelings?" Children should support responses with details from the text.

Apply Have children read the rest of the selection independently. Remind them to identify key details as they read and record them on the online Main Idea and Key Details **Graphic Organizer 51**. Have children use the details to determine the main idea.

SELF-SELECTED READING

OBJECTIVES

Read with sufficient accuracy and fluency to support comprehension.

Read on-level text with purpose and understanding.

Read Independently

Have children choose an expository selection for sustained silent reading. They can check the online **On Level Reader Database** for selections.

- As children read, have them fill in a copy of the online Main Idea and Key Details **Graphic Organizer 51**.
- Remind them to ask themselves questions about key details and then to look for the answers in the text and text features.

Read Purposefully

Encourage children to keep a reading journal. Ask them to read different books in order to learn about a variety of subjects.

- Children can write summaries of the books in their journals.
- Ask children to share their reactions to the books with classmates.

 Gifted and Talented **Independent Study** Challenge children to discuss how their books relate to the weekly theme of how we express ourselves. Have children explain how they like to express themselves or give a demonstration.

Reading/ Writing Companion

Scaffolded Shared Read

OBJECTIVES

Ask and answer such questions as who, what, where, when, why, and how to demonstrate understanding of key details in a text.

Identify the main topic of a multiparagraph text as well as the focus of specific paragraphs within the text.

LANGUAGE OBJECTIVE

Children will analyze how key details support understanding of informational text.

ACADEMIC LANGUAGE

• ask and answer, detail, questions, main idea
• Cognate: *detalle*

Digital Tools

Have children listen to the selection to develop comprehension and practice fluency and pronunciation.

English Language Learners

"They've Got the Beat!"

Plan Your ELL Small Group Instruction for the Shared Read		
Beginning	**Intermediate**	**Advanced/Advanced High**
Use the online **Scaffolded Shared Read** to focus on comprehension of a sheltered version of "They've Got the Beat!" Then have all ELL levels participate together in the activities on pages T428-T429.	Use pages T426-T427 to support children's comprehension of the on-level text, reinforce skills and strategies, and develop oral language. Then have all ELL levels participate in the activities on pages T428-T429.	Use pages T426-T427 to support children's comprehension of the on-level text, reinforce skills and strategies, and develop oral language. Then have all ELL levels participate in the activities on pages T428-T429.

Prepare to Read

Build Background Point and say: *The children in the photo sing in a group called a chorus.* Invite children who have participated in a chorus, or who have seen a chorus perform, to share their experiences. Ask questions like the following and provide frames, as needed: *Where did you perform/watch a performance? I performed in/watched a chorus* at school. *What did you sing/hear? I sang/ heard* holiday songs. *How did it feel to sing in/watch a chorus? It was* exciting. *Are there different groups of voices in a chorus? Yes,* soprano, tenor, bass, and alto. Invite children to ask their peers other questions about performing in and watching a chorus to help develop their own background knowledge. Provide linguistic support, as needed.

Vocabulary Use the **Visual Vocabulary Cards** to review the vocabulary: *cheered, concert, instrument, movements, music, rhythm, sounds, understand* (Cognates: *concierto, instrumento, movimientos, música, ritmo*). Use the online **Visual Vocabulary Cards** to teach ELL Vocabulary from the Shared Read: *audience, beat, chorus, encourages, recalls, type* (Cognates: *audiencia, coro, tipo*).

Set Purpose *Today we will read "They've Got the Beat!" and focus on understanding the language in the text. As we read, think about the Essential Question:* How do you express yourself?

Interactive Question-Response Routine

After each paragraph, ask questions that help children understand the meaning of the text. Explain difficult or unfamiliar concepts and words. Provide sentence stems for **Intermediate** ELLs. Have **Advanced/Advanced High** ELLs retell the information. Reinforce the meaning of new vocabulary. Ask children questions that require them to use the vocabulary. Reinforce weekly strategies and skills through modeling and questions. Use the images and other text features to aid children's comprehension.

Page 65

Paragraphs 1–2 *The President of the United States lives in the White House. It's in our nation's capital, Washington, D.C. Where is the White House?* The White House is in <u>Washington, D.C.</u> *Talk with a partner about how it would feel to perform at the White House.*

Paragraph 3 *Who is the girl in the picture?* (a singer in the chorus) *How does she feel at first about singing for a big audience?* (She feels nervous) *How does she feel later?* (excited when she sees the joy on the faces of the audience)

Intermediate *Reread paragraph 3 and find three words that name feelings.* (nervous, joy, excited) *Ask and answer with a partner: When does Brianna feel <u>nervous</u>?* She feels <u>nervous</u> when <u>she sings for a big audience</u>.

Advanced High *Turn to a partner and discuss why the singers might feel nervous or excited. How do you think they feel when the audience cheers for them?*

Page 66

Paragraphs 1–2 *What are the names of the two groups in the chorus?* (sopranos and altos) *Which group sings the high notes?* (sopranos) *Which group sings the lower notes?* (altos) *How many groups are in most adult choruses?* (four) *After reading "Sounds Good," ask: What important **detail** did you learn about the different voices in a chorus?* (Answers should reflect the text.)

Paragraph 1 *Remember, you can **ask and answer questions** about the text as you read. Let's read the first sentence. I'm not sure what P.S. 22 means. Let's ask a question: What does P.S. 22 mean? To answer the question, look for a clue in paragraph 1 on page 65.* (Public School 22; it is the name of the school)

Intermediate *Look at the word* rhythm. *Which word from the paragraph is a clue to the meaning of* rhythm? (beat)

Advanced High *How does the drum help the chorus?* (The drum keeps the beat. This helps the two groups make the right sounds together.)

Paragraph 2 *How is an adult chorus different from the P.S. 22 chorus?* (It is made up of adults; it has four groups.)

Graph *There is an adult chorus in Pennsylvania. Look at the graph. It shows how many singers are in that chorus. How many sopranos are in the chorus?* (17) *Ask and answer with a partner: How many <u>tenors</u> are in the chorus?* There are <u>eight</u> <u>tenors</u>.

Page 67

Paragraph 1 *The author says being in the chorus is hard work. What **key detail** supports this idea?* (They practice for three hours each week.)

Intermediate *The prefix* dis- *means "not." What does the word* disagree *mean?* (not agree) *What does* won't *mean?* "Won't" *means will <u>not</u>. What does "won't disagree" mean?* "Won't disagree" *means "<u>will</u> agree." Have children choral read the first two sentences again. What will the chorus members agree about?* The chorus members agree that being part of the chorus <u>is hard work</u>.

Paragraphs 2–3 *Why do the children move their hands when they sing?* (to show how they feel)

Intermediate *Do the children all move the same way when they sing?* (No) *Why or why not?* Because the children feel the music in <u>different ways</u>.

Advanced/Advanced High *What does one student say about being in the chorus?* (We just want to give it our best!) *How do you give something your best? Use the words "good job" or "bad job" to answer.* When I give something my best, I <u>try to do a very good job</u>.

Advanced High *How do the children give it their best?* (Possible responses: The children go to every practice; the children pay attention to the music teacher; they try to sing well.)

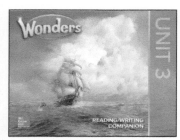

Reading/Writing Companion

OBJECTIVES

Recall information from experiences or gather information from provided sources to answer a question.

Demonstrate command of the conventions of standard English capitalization, punctuation, and spelling when writing.

Demonstrate understanding of word relationships and nuances in word meanings.

Ask and answer such questions as *who, what, where, when, why,* and *how* to demonstrate understanding of key details in a text.

LANGUAGE OBJECTIVE

Children will listen and take notes to identify key details in text that is read aloud.

ACADEMIC LANGUAGE

• *key details, main idea*

• Cognate: *detalles*

DIFFERENTIATED READING

ELL Have Beginning and Early-Intermediate ELLs use the **Scaffolded Shared Read** Glossary Activities during Vocabulary Building.

English Language Learners

"They've Got the Beat!"

 Text Reconstruction

Focus on a single chunk of text to support comprehension and language development across the four domains.

1. Read aloud paragraph 2 on page 67 while children just listen.

2. Write the following on the board, providing definitions as needed: *encourages, chorus, movements, music.* Instruct children to listen for these words as you read the paragraph a second time.

3. Read the paragraph a third time. Tell children to listen and take notes.

4. **COLLABORATE** Have children work in pairs to reconstruct the text from their notes. Help them write complete sentences as needed.

5. Have children look at the original text. Ask them to tell what the paragraph is mostly about. (It's about how the children move their hands to show how they feel while they sing.) Tell children they are going to look at how the key details support the main idea.

6. *What does the teacher encourage the children to do?* (use movements while they sing) *What key details tell how and why the children move?* (They move their hands to show how the songs make them feel.) *What key detail tells you that each child moves in a different way?* (The teacher says, "They have their own movements.") *What key detail tells you why each child moves in a different way?* (The teacher says, "Nobody feels music the same way.") Use the key details to tell the main idea of the paragraph. (Each child moves in a different way because they have different feelings about the music.)

7. Have children compare their text reconstructions to the original text. Have them check if they used their own words to state the main idea.

Beginning Have children follow along in the **Reading/Writing Companion** as you read the text aloud. Have them circle the words from Step 2 as they hear them.

Make Connections

 All Levels Combine children at different English proficiency levels to discuss how "They've Got the Beat!" relates to the Essential Question, *How do you express yourself?* and the Key Concept, *Express Yourself.*

Grammar in Context

Notice the Form Display sentences about the text. Have children underline the form of the verb *have* in each sentence.

> Most adult choruses <u>have</u> four groups of voices.
>
> The P.S. 22 chorus <u>has</u> two groups of voices.

Ask: *Why does the first sentence use* have? The first sentence uses *have* because the subject is <u>plural</u>. *Why does the second sentence use* has? The second sentence uses *has* because the subject is <u>singular</u>. Write sentences on the board and help children edit for subject-verb agreement by writing the correct form of *have*. (1) The singer <u>has</u> a good voice. (2) The band <u>has</u> four sections. (3) The sopranos <u>have</u> the highest voices. (4) The children <u>have</u> practice every day.

Apply and Extend Ask children to imagine that they are in the P.S.22 chorus. Have them write sentences about the chorus, using forms of the verb *have*. Invite partners to switch papers to edit their writing for subject-verb agreement.

Independent Time

Vocabulary Building Have children build their glossaries using a chart like the one below.

Beginning/Early Intermediate Children can also continue the Glossary Activities in the **Scaffolded Share Read**.

Intermediate/Advanced/Advanced High After children add the vocabulary from **Reading/Writing Companion** pages 68–69 to the chart, have them scan the text for self-selected words they would like to learn and add to the chart.

WORD/PHRASE	DEFINE	EXAMPLE	ASK
return	come back to a place	I like this park, so I will return next weekend.	What places will you return to?

Mixed Levels Combine children at different proficiency levels to teach each other new vocabulary. Beginning and Early-Intermediate ELLs will teach vocabulary from their Scaffolded Shared Read glossaries. Intermediate and Advanced/Advanced High ELLs will teach their self-selected words.

Write and Tell Have partners work together to summarize "They've Got the Beat!" orally and in writing. Ask partners to complete the online **Shared Read Writing Frame** and then take turns telling what the text is about. Have partners edit to confirm they used the correct forms of *have*.

OBJECTIVES
Demonstrate command of the conventions of standard English grammar and usage when writing or speaking.

LANGUAGE OBJECTIVE
Children will write sentences about the P.S. 22 chorus using the verb *have*.

ACADEMIC LANGUAGE
• *verb, present tense, past tense*
• Cognate: verbo

Language Transfers Handbook page 19 for the verb *have*

Digital Tools

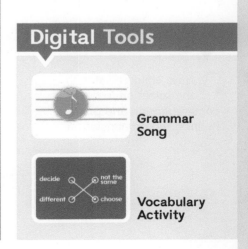

Grammar Song

Vocabulary Activity

Literature Anthology

Digital Tools

🎧 Have children listen to the selection to develop comprehension and practice fluency and pronunciation.

English Language Learners

Many Ways to Enjoy Music

Reread

Before focusing on Author's Craft, Author's Purpose, and Main Idea and Details in *Many Ways to Enjoy Music,* support children's basic comprehension of the text.

- Provide context and background information: People who are deaf are unable to hear. Some use sign language to communicate. Sign language uses body movements instead of sounds. In this selection, we will learn how some people who are deaf enjoy music.

- Use the **Visual Vocabulary Cards** to review vocabulary (*cheered, concert, instrument, movements, music, rhythm, sounds, understand*)

- Use the point-of-use Spotlight on Language tips on pages T357A–T357D to break down linguistic barriers to comprehension.

- Use the **Interactive Question-Response Routine** to help children access small chunks of text in the selection. (See page T426 for the complete routine.)

- Have **Advanced/Advanced High** ELLs work with native speakers to fill in a Main Idea and Key Details chart.

Page 263, Author's Craft: Word Choice

Remind children that authors are very careful in choosing their words to communicate a message or describe an experience. Invite children to read the title. *What kind of performance will you read about?* (music) *Are there different ways of enjoying music?* (yes) *What words give you the answer?* (many ways)

Beginning Have children read the first paragraph. *Where are people enjoying music?* (at a concert) *What instruments do the musicians play?* The musicians play guitars and drums. *What does the band do with their guitars?* (rock the guitars) *When people put their hands together at a concert, what are they doing?* (clapping) *What do people also do when they hear a song they like?* People sing along at a concert.

Intermediate *What word names people who go to concerts?* (fans) *What sounds do the drums make?* (pound, clash) Demonstrate the sounds and say the words. Have children repeat. *What words help you understand how loud the music is at the concert?* (ears buzzing) Explain that not everyone who goes to a concert can hear the music. Explain that fans who are deaf cannot hear the words but can understand them through an interpreter.

👥 **Advanced/Advanced High** *How does a fan who cannot hear feel* **COLLABORATE** *about the concert?* (excited, happy) *Which words show how the fans felt? Partner up to find the words.* (cheered; shaking her fist; big smile; really loved)

Page 264, Author's Purpose

Remind children that authors give their readers information in different ways. Authors can include information in the text and clarify it with photos, captions, and other features. Have children choral read the caption at the bottom of page 264. Explain that an *interpreter* is a person who helps people communicate by changing the words of one language into another language. Invite children to pretend to be interpreters from their native language to English.

Beginning *Look at the photo. Who are the people in the photo?* I see a singer and a woman who is moving her arms. *Read the caption. Who is the interpreter?* The woman is the interpreter. *What does she use to help people understand the words?* She uses sign language. *What does the photo show you about an interpreter?* The photo shows that the interpreter stands on stage, next to the person she interprets for.

Intermediate *Who is the woman in the photo?* The woman is an interpreter. *What is she doing?* The woman uses sign language to show the words of the song. *What do you learn about what an interpreter does from the photo?* I learn that an interpreter uses sign language next to the person she interprets for.

Advanced/Advanced High Have children study the photo and tell why the author may have included it. (Possible answer: It shows the reader how an interpreter works, moves, and stands at a concert.)

Page 265, Author's Purpose

Remind children that to understand the author's message, it's important to look for evidence in the text that supports the message.

Beginning *Work with a partner to answer this question. What does the special chair do?* The special chair moves with the music's rhythm. *Why does the author give details about this special chair?* The author gives details about this chair to show one way people who are deaf can enjoy music.

Intermediate *What kind of technology can help people who are deaf enjoy music?* (a special chair) *How does the chair work?* The chair moves with the music. *What does the fan have to do to feel the rhythm?* The fan sits on the chair to feel the rhythm. *Why does the author give details about this special chair?* The author gives details about this chair to show one way people who are deaf can enjoy music.

Advanced *Find sentences to answer this question: What makes the chair beat hard and then softer?* ("A loud, pounding sound makes the chair beat hard." "Low, quiet sounds make the chair beat softer.") *Why do you think the author tells about this chair?* (To let us know that there's an object that helps people who are deaf enjoy music.)

Advanced High Have children talk about the kind of music they enjoy. Invite them to tell how the author shows that people and technology can help people who are deaf enjoy the same music they enjoy.

Page 265, Main Idea and Key Details

Tell children that by finding the key details in a text, they can retell and summarize the main ideas. Invite children to work on their Main Idea and Details charts during small group time. Remind children that they should only put the most important details in their charts.

Beginning *This text tells how fans who are deaf enjoy music. Read the first sentence on page 264. Find the detail that tells who they can watch.* (an interpreter)

Intermediate *Think about the most important details in the text. What does an interpreter do at a concert?* An interpreter uses sign language to show what the band is singing. *How can a special chair help people who are deaf enjoy music?* They can use a special chair to feel the music.

Advanced/Advanced High *Think about the most important details in the text. How can technology help people who are deaf enjoy music?* (They can use a special chair to feel the music.)

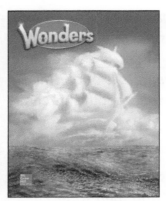

Literature Anthology

OBJECTIVES

Ask and answer such questions as who, what, where, when, why, and how to demonstrate understanding of key details in a text.

Identify the main topic of a multiparagraph text as well as the focus of specific paragraphs within the text.

Demonstrate command of the conventions of standard English grammar and usage when writing or speaking

LANGUAGE OBJECTIVE

Children take notes in order to identify key details and the main idea in a text that is read aloud.

ACADEMIC LANGUAGE

• *summarize, key details, main idea*
• Cognate: *detalles*

English Language Learners

Many Ways to Enjoy Music

Text Reconstruction

Focus on a single chunk of text to support comprehension and language development across the four domains.

1. Read aloud the section called "Watching the Signs" and the photo caption on page 264 of *Many Ways to Enjoy Music.*

2. Write the following key words and phrases on the board, providing definitions as needed: *concert, interpreter, movements, communicate, understand, sign language.* Instruct children to listen for these words as you read the text a second time.

3. Read the text a third time while children listen and take notes.

4. Have children work with a partner to reconstruct the text from their notes. Help them write complete sentences as needed.

5. Have children look at the original text. Ask them to tell what the text is mostly about. (Fans who are deaf can enjoy a concert by watching an interpreter.) Tell children they are going to look at how the key details support this idea.

6. *Which detail tells one way people who are deaf can enjoy a concert?* ("by watching an interpreter") *Which phrases give details about how interpreters communicate what is happening on stage?* ("use body movements, like swaying or jumping") *Which detail explains how an interpreter can show the words of a song?* ("uses sign language")

7. Have children compare their text reconstructions to the original text. Have them check if they included details that support the main idea.

Beginning Allow children to follow along in the **Literature Anthology** as you read the text aloud. Have them point to words from Step 2 as they hear them.

Apply Writer's Craft: Word Choice

Authors choose words to help readers understand what an experience is like. In Many Ways to Enjoy Music, *the author uses "shaking her fist in the air" to describe a fan at a concert. Imagine listening to a song you like. How do you show you are enjoying it?* Invite children to pantomime. Write words and phrases on the board, such as *hum, sway, nod heads, close eyes, clap, dance, jump, shake,* or *wave arms.* Have partners ask and answer: What do you do when you hear _____? I close my eyes and sway. After oral practice, have children write in their notebooks: When I hear _____, I close my eyes and sway.

Grammar in Context: Text Deconstruction

Write this sentence from page 265 of *Many Ways to Enjoy Music* on the board: *A loud, pounding sound makes the chair beat hard.*

- *What is the purpose of the words "loud and pounding"?* (They describe the word *sound*.)

- *The word "makes" is a verb. We sometimes use the word "makes" when one thing causes another.*

- *What is the subject of the verb "makes"?* (a loud, pounding sound) *What does <u>a loud, pounding sound</u> do? What does <u>it</u> do?* It makes the chair <u>beat hard</u>.

- *Say the sentence another way, in your own words.* (Possible: A loud, pounding sound causes the chair to beat hard.)

- *What kind of sentence is this: statement, question, exclamation, or command? How do you know? Discuss with a partner.* (It's a statement. It gives information. It does not ask a question/ tell someone what to do/ express strong emotions.)

Independent Time

Vocabulary Building Remind children that nouns name people, places, and things, and verbs name actions. Invite children to list some new words from the selection that they want to remember. Have partners decide if each word is a noun or a verb, then fill in a chart like the one below. Encourage them to write original sentences. Have children add new words to their glossaries.

Beginning/Intermediate Children can draw small pictures to help them remember difficult words.

Advanced/Advanced High Challenge children to identify verb tenses.

Noun	Sentence with Noun	Verb	Sentence with Verb
concert	I'm going to a <u>concert</u>.	pound	The drums <u>pound</u>.
sounds	<u>Sounds</u> make the chair move.	cheered	The fans <u>cheered</u>.
interpreter	The <u>interpreter</u> uses sign language.	watch	Deaf people <u>watch</u> the interpreter.

Make Connections Help children connect the Essential Question to their own lives. Provide sentence frames for partners to ask and answer about the Shared Read and the Anchor Text: How did the children in "They've Got the Beat" express themselves? They expressed themselves by <u>singing in a chorus</u>. How can people who are deaf express themselves? They can enjoy music using <u>interpreters</u> and <u>technology</u>. How do you like to express yourself? I like to <u>dance when I listen to music</u>.

The Sounds of Trash
Lexile 380L

OBJECTIVES

Identify the main purpose of a text, including what the author wants to answer, explain, or describe.

Identify the main topic of a multiparagraph text as well as the focus of specific paragraphs within the text.

Determine or clarify the meaning of unknown and multiple-meaning words and phrases based on grade 2 reading and content, choosing flexibly from an array of strategies.

LANGUAGE OBJECTIVES

Children will show comprehension of a nonfiction text by asking and answering questions about the content.

ACADEMIC LANGUAGE

• ask and answer, questions, intonatio

• Cognate: entonación

Digital Tools

🎧 Have children listen to the selections to develop comprehension and practice fluency and pronunciation.

English Language Learners

Leveled Reader: *The Sounds of Trash*

Build Background

• Read the Essential Question: *How do you express yourself?* Have children share ideas about how they express themselves.

• Choral read the title. Explain that *trash* is stuff we throw away. Tell children that sometimes we can use *trash* to make new things, like musical instruments. Ask: *What kind of trash is the boy using?* He is using an old bottle.

Vocabulary

Use the routine on the **Visual Vocabulary Cards** to pre-teach the ELL vocabulary: *act* and *feelings*. Use the glossary on page 19 to identify and model the use of other vocabulary in context.

Interactive Question-Response Routine

After each paragraph, use Interactive Question-Response prompts such as the following to provide language support and guide comprehension. Pause at the end of each paragraph and have partners **ask and answer questions** about what they just read.

Chapter 1

Beginning Have children circle the words *draw, paint, act, dance, write, sing,* and *play an instrument* on pages 2 and 3. Pair up children. Have partners take turns acting out each word while the other names the action.

Advanced *Read the caption on page 2. Which words help you understand what "express yourself" means?* (share your thoughts and feelings)

Advanced High *How is the water bottle being recycled?* (It is used to make music.) *What does the boy do to make music?* (he blows into the bottle)

Chapter 2

Beginning *What do you learn on page 6?* I learn how to make a guitar. *What do you do with scissors?* (cut) *What do you do with a pencil?* (draw, write)

Intermediate *What do you do with the scissors to make a guitar?* You cut a hole. *What do you do with the rubber bands?* You stretch them around the box.

Advanced/Advanced High *How do you make music with the guitar?* (you pluck the rubber bands) *What happens to the rubber bands?* (They vibrate.)

Chapter 3

Beginning *How do you put the tubes together?* One tube goes <u>inside</u> the other <u>tube</u>. Guide children to use their hands to explain the phrase *back and forth.*

Intermediate *Is cardboard* thick *or* thin*?* (thick) *Why use cardboard instead of a thin piece of paper for the body of the trombone?* We use cardboard because <u>thick</u> paper is stronger than <u>thin</u> paper.

Advanced/Advanced High *How can you change the sounds of the trombone?* (Use different tubes. Slide the tubes slower or faster.)

Chapter 4

Intermediate *How do you play the maracas?* (You shake them.) *How do you shake the maracas?* (slowly, quickly) Have children pantomime shaking maracas slowly, then quickly.

 Advanced/Advanced High *Tell a partner which instrument you would like to make. Talk about how you can use it to show feelings.*

 Respond to Reading Have partners discuss the questions on page 15.

Fluency: Intonation Read page 12 to model proper intonation for reading a list and directions. Have children echo read. Then have them record themselves and choose a version to play for you.

Paired Selection: "Talking Underwater"

 Make Connections: Write About It

Before children write, have partners use sentence frames to discuss the questions on page 18: We can play music that shows how <u>we feel</u>. The *Sounds of Trash* is about how to <u>make instruments</u>. *Talking Underwater* is about how <u>divers can talk when they are underwater</u>.

ELL Leveled Reader

Self-Selected Reading Have children choose an informational text from the online **Leveled Reader Library**.

Focus on Science

Have children complete the activity on page 20 to make their own instruments.

Literature Circles

Ask children to conduct a literature circle using the Thinkmark questions to guide the discussion. You may wish to use the Leveled Reader selections to discuss how children could use musical instruments to express feelings.

LEVEL UP

IF children read the ELL Level fluently and answered the questions

THEN pair them with children who have proficiently read the On Level and have children

- echo-read the On Level main selection with their partner
- list difficult words and phrases and discuss them with their partners.

Access Complex Text

The On Level challenges children by including more **domain-specific words** and **complex sentence structures**.

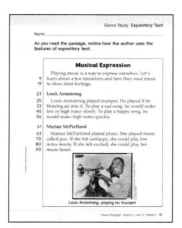

Musical Expression
Lexile 510L

OBJECTIVES

Determine the meaning of the new word formed when a known prefix is added to a known word (e.g., *happy/unhappy, tell/retell*).

Identify the main topic of a multiparagraph text as well as the focus of specific paragraphs within the text.

Identify the main purpose of a text, including what the author wants to answer, explain, or describe.

LANGUAGE OBJECTIVE

Show comprehension of a leveled selection by answering questions about details.

ACADEMIC LANGUAGE

- chart, key details, main idea, prefix
- Cognate: *prefijo*

Digital Tools

Have children listen to the selections to develop comprehension and practice fluency and pronunciation.

English Language Learners

Genre Passage: "Musical Expression"

Build Background

- Review with children that when we express ourselves, we show how we feel. Remind them that playing music is a way to show feelings. Tell children that they will be reading about how some musicians play different sounds to show different feelings.

Vocabulary

Use the **Define, Example, Ask** routine to pre-teach difficult words or unfamiliar concepts, such as *trumpet, blowing, low/high notes, jazz, emotion, trombone, energy*. Invite children to add new vocabulary to their glossaries.

Interactive Question-Response Routine

After each paragraph, use Interactive Question-Response prompts such as the following to provide language support and guide comprehension.

Page E1

Look at the photo of Louis Armstrong. What instrument is he playing? (trumpet)

Beginning *What do you call a person who plays music?* (a musician) *What musicians does the author write about on this page?* (Louis Armstrong and Marian McPartland) *What instruments do they play?* They play <u>trumpet</u> and <u>piano</u>.

Prefixes *Reread the last paragraph on page E1. Notice the word* unhappy. *The prefix* un- *means* not. *What does the word* unhappy *mean?* (not happy) *How did Marian McPartland play if she felt unhappy?* She played <u>low notes slowly.</u>

 Intermediate *Which word in the second paragraph means the same as* unhappy? (sad) *How was Armstrong's sad music like McPartland's sad music? How were they different?* Armstrong and McPartland both played <u>slowly</u> to show that they were <u>sad</u>. Armstrong played <u>low or high notes</u>, but McPartland only played <u>low notes</u>. Have children turn to a partner and talk about music that sounds sad and how it is different from happy music.

Advanced/Advanced High *With a partner, find words that have opposite meanings* (sad, happy, low, high, slowly, quickly)

Page E2, Chart

Discuss the emotion words in the **chart**, using body language, gestures, and examples to help clarify meanings. Then invite children to pantomime a feeling from the chart for others to guess.

Beginning *What does the chart show?* It shows how instruments can show feelings. *Which words describe the sound of music?* (high, low) *Which words describe the speed you can play music?* (fast, slow)

Intermediate *What is another word for feeling?* (emotion) Use your voice to demonstrate as you ask: *What feelings can you show if you play an instrument slowly but with a high sound?* (happy, love, sad, safe, sleepy, gentle) *What feelings can you show if you play an instrument fast but with a low sound?* (angry, excited, nervous, scared, sneaky)

Advanced/Advanced High *What emotions can you show if you play an instrument fast or slow, but with a high sound?* (happy, love) *What emotions can you show if you play an instrument fast or slow, but with a low sound?* (angry, scared, sneaky)

Page E2

Beginning Point out the sentence *This showed energy.* Guide children to understand that the word *this* refers to playing *low* and *loud* notes. Explain that in this context *energy* means *being lively, active.* Point out the sentence *This showed joy. What does the word* this *refer to in this sentence?* (playing high and light notes) Have partners discuss music they like to listen to when they feel energy or joy.

Intermediate *What kinds of notes was Melba Liston able to play?* Melba Liston was able to play low and high notes. *What emotions was Ms. Liston able to show through her notes?* (energy and joy)

Advanced/Advanced High *What key details tell how Melba Liston played to show energy?* (low notes loudly) *What words tell how she played to show joy?* (high notes lightly) *Based on these **details**, what is the **main idea** of this paragraph?* (Melba Liston could play different sounds to show different feelings.)

Respond to Reading

Use the following instruction to help children answer the questions on page E3.

1. Review the first paragraph. *What kind of people do we learn about?* (musicians) *How do musicians express their feelings?* (with instruments)

2. Have children review **key details** that tell how Louis Armstrong played to show feelings. Help them use those details to express the **main idea**. Repeat the process for Marian McPartland and Melba Liston. Then talk about how the musicians are the same.

3. Help children use information in the **chart** to answer these questions: *What speed can show an excited feeling?* (fast) *What speed can show gentle feeling?* (slow)

Fluency Have partners take turns reading the passage.

Make Connections

Remind children of the Essential Question: *How do you express yourself?* Ask children how they like to express themselves.

LEVEL UP

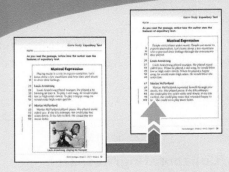

IF children read the **ELL Level** fluently and answered the questions,

THEN pair them with children who have proficiently read the **On Level**. Have them

- partner-read the On Level passage.
- identify the key details and main ideas of the passage.

 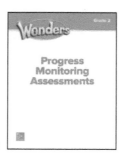  

GENRE STUDY: EXPOSITORY TEXT
Skills assessed in Progress Monitoring Assessment

FORMALLY ASSESSED SKILLS	INSTRUCTIONAL FOCUS
Main Idea and Key Details	Comprehension Skill
Prefixes	Vocabulary Strategy

Informal Assessment

INFORMALLY ASSESSED SKILLS	INSTRUCTIONAL FOCUS	HOW ASSESSED
Analytical Writing	• Comprehension Skill • Written Response • English Language Conventions	Reading/Writing Companion: Respond to Reading
Grammar, Mechanics, Usage	English Language Conventions	Practice Book, digital activities, writing activities
Spelling	English Language Conventions	Practice Book, word sorts, digital activities, writing activities
Phonics	Foundational Skills	Practice Book, digital activities
Listening/Collaborating/Research	• Listening • Speaking • Research	Checklists, rubrics
Oral Reading Fluency (ORF) Fluency Goal: 74–94 words correct per minute (WCPM) Accuracy Rate Goal: 95% or higher	• Reading Accuracy • Prosody	Fluency Assessment

 Assign practice pages online for auto-grading.

Making the Most of Assessment Results

Make data-based grouping decisions by using the following reports to verify assessment results. For additional support options for your students, refer to the reteaching and enrichment opportunities.

ONLINE ASSESSMENT CENTER

- *Item Analysis Report*
- *Standards Analysis Report*

DATA DASHBOARD

- *Recommendations Report*
- *Activity Report*
- *Skills Report*
- *Progress Report*

 RETEACHING OPPORTUNITIES with Intervention Online PDFs

IF CHILDREN SCORE . . .	THEN ASSIGN . . .
below 70% in **comprehension**	lessons 85–87 on Main Idea and Key Details in **Comprehension PDF**
below 70% in **vocabulary**	lessons 100–101 on Prefixes in **Vocabulary PDF**
below 2 on **constructed-response items**	lessons 85–87 on Main Idea and Key Details and/or Write About Reading from Section 13 in **Comprehension PDF**
65–73 WCPM in **fluency**	lesson from Sections 1, 9 or 10 of **Fluency PDF**
0–64 WCPM in **fluency**	lesson from Sections 2–8 of **Fluency PDF**

Use the **Phonemic Awareness** *and* **Phonics/Word Study PDFs** *for additional reteaching lessons.*

 ENRICHMENT OPPORTUNITIES for Gifted and Talented Students

Beyond Level small group lessons include suggestions for additional activities in the following areas to extend learning opportunities for gifted and talented students:

- *Leveled Readers*
- *Genre Passages*
- *Vocabulary Strategy*
- *Comprehension*
- *Leveled Readers Library Online*
- *Workstation Activities*

Review, Extend, and Assess

Reading

Reading Digitally

TIME FOR KIDS. "Antarctica-Bound!"
Genre: Online Article

Reader's Theater

I'll Be the Dragon
Genre: Play

ONLINE Writer's Notebook

PROCESS WRITING

| Expert Model > | Plan > | Draft > | Revise > | Edit and Proofread > | Publish |

WEEK 5   WEEK 6

Writing

Process Writing

- Revise an Expository Text
- Peer Conferences

- Edit and Proofread an Expository Text
- Publish, Present, and Evaluate

Presenting

Presentation Options

Research and Inquiry
- Project Presentations
- Presentation Rubric

Writing
- Student Choice
- Portfolio Choice

Reader's Theater
- Perform *I'll Be the Dragon*

Student Outcomes

Comprehension
- Review strategies and skills
- Track progress
- Cite relevant evidence from text
- Summarize the text
- Interpret information presented visually

Writing

Writing Process
- Complete an expository text
- Share writing and choose a portfolio piece

Analytical Writing
- Write an opinion
- Write a summary

Speaking and Listening
- Paraphrase information presented digitally
- Engage in collaborative discussions

Language Development

Vocabulary Acquisition
- Use context to determine the meaning of unfamiliar words
- Use prefixes to determine word meaning

Foundational Skills

Fluency
- Read grade-level text fluently with appropriate prosody, accuracy, rate

Research and Inquiry
- Conduct and present research
- Use Internet Browser Tools
- Gather relevant information from digital sources
- Navigate links

Content Area Learning

- Identify the order of historical events

 Scaffolded supports for English Language Learners are embedded throughout the instruction.

Assess

Unit Assessments

Unit 3 Test

Fluency

Unit Online Assessments

Evaluate Student Progress

 Use the *Wonders* online assessment reports to evaluate student progress and help you make decisions about small group instruction and assignments.

Suggested Lesson Plan

Teach It Your Way

Week 6 lessons review and extend previously taught skills. This week is meant to be used flexibly and to offer time for you to use your own resources.

KEY

✎ Writing activity

◀ Can be taught in small groups

CORE

DAY 1

Reading Digitally
Read "Antarctica-Bound!," T444–T445 TIME FOR KIDS ◀

Show What You Learned
"Landing the Eagle," T448–T449 ◀

Writing Revise, T458–T459 ✎ ◀

DAY 2

Show What You Learned
"A Shower in the Sky," T450–T451 ◀

Writing Peer Conferencing, T460–T461 ✎

OPTIONAL

DAY 1

Reader's Theater
"I'll Be the Dragon"
Read the Play and Model Fluency, T446 ◀

DAY 2

Reading Digitally
Reread "Antarctica-Bound!," T444–T445 TIME FOR KIDS ◀

Reader's Theater
"I'll Be the Dragon"
Assign Roles and Practice the Play, T446 ◀

SMALL GROUP ▶ INSTRUCTION

APPROACHING

Level Up to On Level
The Sounds of Trash, T474
"Talking Underwater," T474
Literature Circles, T474

ON LEVEL

Level Up to Beyond Level
The Sounds of Trash, T475
"Talking Underwater," T475
Literature Circles, T475

HOW TO DIFFERENTIATE

Take time this week to identify any gaps in students' understanding using the Data Dashboard. Use resources from the unit or your own resources.

Customize your own lesson plans
my.mheducation.com

DAY 3

Extend Your Learning
Focus on Genre, T452
Sequence of Events, T453

Writing
Edit and Proofread, T462–T463

Reader's Theater
"I'll Be the Dragon"
Practice the Play, Extend, T446–T447

DAY 4

Extend Your Learning
Prefixes, T454
Write a Personal Narrative, T455
Community Helpers Ad, T456
Musical Instrument Diagram T457

Writing Publish, Present, and Evaluate,
T464–T465

Reader's Theater
"I'll Be the Dragon"
Performance, Reread the Play, T447

DAY 5

Writing Publish, Present, and Evaluate,
T464–T465

Track Your Progress T466

Wrap Up the Unit T467

Summative Assessment T478–T479

Presentation Options
Speaking and Listening, T468–T469

Research and Inquiry
Presentations , T470

Inquiry Space
Review and Evaluate, T471

Writing
Student Choice, T472
Portfolio Choice, T473

BEYOND

**Level Up to Self-Selected
Trade Book** T477

Literature Circles, T477

ENGLISH LANGUAGE LEARNERS

Level Up to On Level
The Sounds of Trash, T476
"Talking Underwater," T476
Literature Circles, T476

OBJECTIVES

Recount or describe key ideas or details from a text read aloud or information presented orally or through other media.

Identify the main topic of a multiparagraph text as well as the focus of specific paragraphs within the text.

Know and use various text features (e.g., captions, bold print, subheadings, glossaries, indexes, electronic menus, icons) to locate key facts or information in a text efficiently.

Recall information from experiences or gather information from provided sources to answer a question.

Participate in shared research and writing projects (e.g., read a number of books on a single topic to produce a report; record science observations).

ACADEMIC LANGUAGE

• *summary, sequence, opinion*
• Cognates: *sumario, opinión*

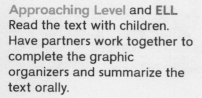

DIFFERENTIATED READING

Approaching Level and **ELL** Read the text with children. Have partners work together to complete the graphic organizers and summarize the text orally.

On Level and **Beyond Level** Have children read the text and access the interactive features independently. Complete the Reread activities during Small Group time.

Antarctica-Bound!

Before Reading

Introduce the Genre Scroll through the online article "Antarctica-Bound!" and have children identify text features. Clarify how to navigate through the article. Point out the interactive features, such as **hyperlinks** and **slideshows**. Explain that you will read the article together first, and then access these features.

Close Reading Online

Read

Take Notes Read the article aloud. As you read, ask children questions about the order in which the events of the narrative take place. Have children take notes using **Graphic Organizer 2**. After each section, have partners paraphrase the main ideas, giving text evidence. Make sure children understand phrasal verbs in the text, such as *got ready*.

Access Interactive Features Help children access the interactive features. Discuss what information these elements add to the text.

Summarize Review children's graphic organizers. Model using the information to summarize "Antarctica-Bound!" Ask children to write a brief summary of the article, retelling what the narrator experienced in the correct order of events. Partners should discuss their summaries.

Reread

Craft and Structure Have children reread parts of the article, paying attention to text structure and author's craft. Discuss these questions:

• What text structure does the author use to organize the information?

• What can you learn from the slide show that is not in the article?

Author's Purpose Tell children they will reread to answer this question: *What did Claire and her dad see in Antarctica?* Have children skim and scan to find details about the family's trip to Antarctica. Have partners discuss how the author helps readers understand the purpose of the article.

Make Connections

Text Connections Have children compare what they learned about Antarctica with what they have learned about other surprising places in texts they have read in this unit.

Research Online

Navigate Links to Information Point out that online texts may include **hyperlinks**. Hyperlinks provide a connection from the Web page you are on to another Web page with related information. Model how to use a hyperlink to jump to another Web page. Discuss any information on the new Web page related to the question *What are the animals that live in Antarctica like?* Before navigating back, demonstrate bookmarking the page so children can return to it another time. Model verifying one piece of information from the first website that you visited by checking it on another reliable Web page.

Using Internet Browser Tools Tell children that Internet browsers have tools to help users navigate the Web. Have children follow these three-step oral directions. First, help them find navigation buttons on a Web browser such as forward, back, and home buttons. Second, help them save a location of a reliable Web page to return to later by bookmarking it or making it a favorite site. Finally, help them return to the reliable Web page to find more information on a topic. You may decide to repeat this process, this time having children give you the oral directions. Help as necessary to clarify the process.

Inspire Action

Take a Stand Have children write a short paragraph about why it is important for people to learn about distant places. Remind children to clearly state their opinion and give good supporting reasons from their online research. Tell children to focus on including the main parts of an opinion argument, such as

- An opening that tells about the topic
- A clearly stated opinion and two or three facts that support it
- An ending sentence that retells the opinion using different words

Independent Study

Choose a Topic Children should brainstorm questions related to the article. For example, they might ask: *What is the weather like in Antarctica?* Then have children choose a question to research. Help them narrow their topic as needed.

Conduct Internet Research Help children use navigation features to visit different Web pages on their research topic. Model bookmarking a page. Then visit another Web page to check the information shown on the bookmarked page. Show children how to return to the original page using their bookmark.

Present Have groups present a round-table discussion on the topic of the animals in Antarctica.

English Language Learners

Craft and Structure
Focus on the question: *What text structure does the author use to organize the information?* Use prompts to help children answer. *How does the first paragraph look different from the rest of the article?* (the type is different) *Which sentence tells the reader what they will read, or introduces the topic of the article?* (Here, Claire tells about her experience...) *What do the words we, I, and us tell you about the point of view? Who is the author?* (It's written in first person; Claire is the author.) *With a partner, find all the time and sequence signal words and phrases you can.* (First, From there, for two days, once we arrived, On day three, After landing, Then we finally, First, Then, two days) Reinforce meaning, as needed, to help children understand that the author narrates her experience by telling the events in order. Finally have children retell the events using time signal words.

Readers to Writers

Encourage children to think about how they might use interactive features such as slide shows and hyperlinks in their own writing.

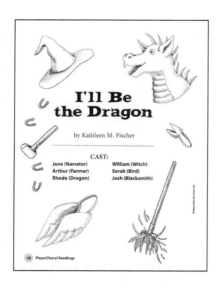

OBJECTIVES

Read with sufficient accuracy and fluency to support comprehension.

Read on-level text with purpose and understanding.

Read on-level text orally with accuracy, appropriate rate, and expression on successive readings.

Use context to confirm or self-correct word recognition and understanding, rereading as necessary.

TEACH IN SMALL GROUP

You may wish to teach the Reader's Theater lesson during Small Group time and then have groups present their work to the class.

I'll Be the Dragon

Introduce the Genre

Explain that *I'll Be the Dragon* is a play-within-a-play. At first, it's about children discussing performing a play, and then it's the actual play. Distribute the Elements of Drama handout pages 2-3 and scripts from the **Reader's Theater** pages 12-24.

- Review the features of a play.
- Review the list of characters. Explain that since this is a play-within-a-play, each character has two roles.
- Point out the stage directions. Point out that this play has two acts.

Read the Play and Model Fluency

Model reading the play as children follow along in their scripts. As you read each part, state the name of each character, and read the part emphasizing the appropriate phrasing and expression.

Focus on Vocabulary Stop and discuss any vocabulary words that children may not know. You may wish to teach:

- dragon
- speech
- magnificent
- harmless
- straw
- genuine

Monitor Comprehension As you read, check that children are understanding the characters, setting, and plot.

- After reading the part of Jane/Narrator, ask children to identify what information the narrator is giving about the play.
- After reading each character part, ask partners to note the character's main trait. Model how to find text evidence that tells them about the characters.

Assign Roles

You may wish to split the class into two groups. If necessary, you can assign the Narrator's role to more than one child.

Practice the Play

Each day, allow children time to practice their parts in the play. Pair fluent readers with less fluent readers. Pairs can echo-read or choral-read their parts. As needed, work with less fluent readers to mark pauses in their script using one slash for a short pause and two slashes for longer pauses.

Throughout the week, have children work on the **Reader's Theater Workstation Activity Card 26.**

Once children have practiced reading their parts several times, allow them time to practice performing the script. Remind them that non-verbal communication is an important part of portraying a character and provide examples.

Extend: Place to Place Settings

Review the settings of Act II of *I'll Be the Dragon* with children. Help them create a chart telling the various settings, and giving at least one detail to describe each place. Then split children into groups, one for each setting. Each group should create a prop, background illustration, or other item that will help explain to the audience the changing settings. Since Act II follows the dragon from place to place, you may wish to take this opportunity to discuss stage hands and prop management with children.

Perform the Reader's Theater

Remind children not to focus on the audience, but to continue to follow along word-by-word in the script, even if they are not in the scene.

- As a class, discuss how performing the play aloud is different from reading it silently. With a partner, have children list what they liked about performing the play and what they found difficult.

Reread the Play

Work with children to discuss times they've had to work with others, and encourage children to make decisions so everyone can be involved. Reread Act I of *I'll Be the Dragon* and have children point out places where the characters compromise or reach new decisions. Ask questions to help guide discussion:

1. Who are the characters in Act I? What are they arguing about?

2. Who makes the first decision? What is the decision?

3. How do the characters decide who will play the dragon?

4. What information do you learn about each part from listening to the characters talk about the play they're going to perform?

English Language Learners

Practice the Play Review the features of a play with Beginning ELLs: character, setting, dialogue, stage directions. Have all children read aloud the lines for their roles and record them. With each child, listen to the recording as you trace the dialogue with your finger. Ask: *Which words or phrases do you find difficult to pronounce?* Model pronouncing the words and phrases slowly and record them for children to use for practice. Then review details about the character and any stage directions that refer to their character. Ask children to think about whether they are saying the lines appropriately. *How can you say the dialogue to show _____?* Help children decide on the tone and record it for them to use for practice.

Reading/Writing Companion

OBJECTIVES

Determine the meaning of the new word formed when a known prefix is added to a known word (e.g., happy/unhappy, tell/retell).

Ask and answer such questions as who, what, where, when, why, and how to demonstrate understanding of key details in a text.

Identify the main purpose of a text, including what the author wants to answer, explain, or describe.

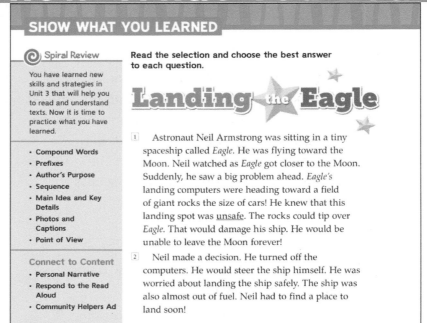

SHOW WHAT YOU LEARNED

Spiral Review

You have learned new skills and strategies in Unit 3 that will help you to read and understand texts. Now it is time to practice what you have learned.

- Compound Words
- Prefixes
- Author's Purpose
- Sequence
- Main Idea and Key Details
- Photos and Captions
- Point of View

Connect to Content

- Personal Narrative
- Respond to the Read Aloud
- Community Helpers Ad

94   Unit 3 • Show What You Learned

Read the selection and choose the best answer to each question.

Landing the Eagle

1   Astronaut Neil Armstrong was sitting in a tiny spaceship called *Eagle*. He was flying toward the Moon. Neil watched as *Eagle* got closer to the Moon. Suddenly, he saw a big problem ahead. *Eagle's* landing computers were heading toward a field of giant rocks the size of cars! He knew that this landing spot was <u>unsafe</u>. The rocks could tip over *Eagle*. That would damage his ship. He would be unable to leave the Moon forever!

2   Neil made a decision. He turned off the computers. He would steer the ship himself. He was worried about landing the ship safely. The ship was also almost out of fuel. Neil had to find a place to land soon!

Reading/Writing Companion, p. 94

TEACHER CHOICE

The test passages can be completed in Whole Group, Small Group, or independently.

- **Approaching/ELL Beginning and Intermediate**: Read each passage with children and work through the questions.

- **On Level** and **ELL Advanced/Advanced High**: Read the Second Passage. Guide children through the first question and have them complete the remaining questions and following passage and questions independently.

- **Beyond Level**: Have children work independently and provide assistance as needed.

Genre: Test Passages

Remind children that narrative nonfiction texts may have text features, including photos and captions, to give additional information about the topic. Have them pay attention to how the author organizes the information with text structure.

Have children note the numbers next to each paragraph as they read. They may wish to read the questions before they read the passage. After reading the passage, children should read each question twice and eliminate any obvious wrong answer choices. Children should remember that each answer they choose must be supported by text evidence.

Discuss the Questions

Test questions serve several purposes. By answering the questions, children demonstrate their mastery of the unit's skills and strategies. These questions also give children practice with the kinds of questions they may find on state tests.

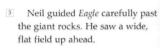 NARRATIVE NONFICTION

[3] Neil guided *Eagle* carefully past the giant rocks. He saw a wide, flat field up ahead.

[4] "That is the place!" he thought. Slowly, he lowered *Eagle* onto the field. But his rocket boosters blew a big cloud of dust into the air. Neil was blinded as he guided *Eagle* down.

[5] Finally, *Eagle's* small feet thumped onto the Moon. Neil breathed a sigh of relief. He clicked his radio and sent a happy message back home. "Houston . . . The Eagle has landed."

Neil Armstrong was the first person to walk on the Moon. He placed a flag on the Moon to show that America's astronauts reached it first.

Unit 3 • Show What You Learned   95

Reading/Writing Companion, p. 95

SHOW WHAT YOU LEARNED

1 In paragraph 1, the reader can use the prefix "un-" to know that the word <u>unsafe</u> means —
   A Very safe
   B Not safe
   C Somewhat safe
   D Able to be safe

> **Quick Tip**
> You can separate the root word from a prefix, such as *re-* or *un-* to help you figure out what the word means.

2 Which sentence from the article best helps the reader understand that *Eagle* is fragile?
   F *The rocks could tip over* Eagle.
   G *He would be unable to leave the Moon forever!*
   H *But his rocket boosters blew a big cloud of dust into the air.*
   J *"Houston . . . The Eagle has landed."*

3 Which idea from the article is supported by the photograph?
   A Neil Armstrong did great things for space travel.
   B *Eagle* is difficult to fly for an astronaut.
   C Neil Armstrong was worried about landing on the Moon.
   D *Eagle* is small and can be broken easily.

4 The author wrote the article most likely to —
   F convince the reader to become an astronaut
   G share information about an interesting space program
   H tell the reader about an important person in history
   J explain how to land a spaceship on the Moon

96   Unit 3 • Show What You Learned

Reading/Writing Companion, p. 96

Question 1: PREFIXES

In paragraph 1, the reader can use the prefix "un-" to know that the word <u>unsafe</u> *means –*

Remind children that knowing the meanings of prefixes will help them determine the meaning of potentially unfamiliar words. Review that the prefix "un-" means "not." Then have them look for the correct answer. (B)

Question 2: MAIN IDEA AND KEY DETAILS

Which sentence from the article best helps the reader understand that Eagle *is fragile?*

Have children look at paragraph 1 for details that explain why Armstrong knew that landing on rocks would be a problem. (F)

Question 3: GENRE/TEXT FEATURES

Which idea from the article is supported by the photograph?

Point out that readers can get information about a topic from the photographs and captions in a text. Ask them to think about what they learn from the photograph. (A)

Question 4: AUTHOR'S PURPOSE

The author wrote the article most likely to –

Children should scan the article for text evidence about Neil Armstrong to help them answer the question, "What does the author want me to know?" (H)

 English Language Learners

Genre: Test Passages Read each question and answer choice with children to help them determine the information they need to look for. As needed, review prefixes, main idea and details, text features, and author's purpose. Encourage children to ask questions about ideas, words, or phrases they don't understand. Help them clarify the meaning. For example, for Question 2: *Which phrase describes something Armstrong saw before he landed?* ("giant rocks the size of cars") *Which word means the area was dangerous?* ("unsafe") *What is an example of why the rocks were unsafe?* ("The rocks could tip over the Eagle.")

Show What You Learned

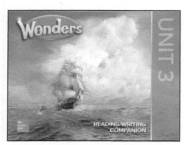

Reading/Writing Companion

OBJECTIVES

Determine or clarify the meaning of unknown and multiple-meaning words and phrases based on grade 2 reading and content, choosing flexibly from an array of strategies.

Acknowledge differences in the points of view of characters, including by speaking in a different voice for each character when reading dialogue aloud.

FICTION

Read the selection and choose the best answer to each question.

A Shower in the Sky

1   The sky grew dark. Rico was excited. Tonight was going to be the best meteor shower of the year. Rico had looked forward to this night for a long time. He and his father drove to the top of a dark hill. They lay two sleeping bags on a tarp in the grass. Then they watched the dark sky.

2   Suddenly Rico saw a bright streak in the sky. A meteor! It lasted less than a second. Then it was gone.

3   "I saw one!" he shouted.

Unit 3 · Show What You Learned   97

Reading/Writing Companion, p. 97

Review the Genre

Explain that this passage is fiction. It tells a story with a beginning, a middle, and an end which is called a sequence of events. Fiction has made-up characters and events. The story we will read is realistic fiction. This means that the events in the story could really happen. A fantasy story is a type of fiction that has events that could not happen in real life such as talking animals or people doing things against the laws of nature. Those types of things do not happen in this story. All types of fiction may include dialogue. Dialogue is the words characters say. Writers use quotation marks to show dialogue.

Question 1: SEQUENCE

Which detail from the story belongs in the empty box?

Have children think about the order of the events in the story. Have them think about what happens after Rico sees the first meteor, and before he goes to sleep. (C)

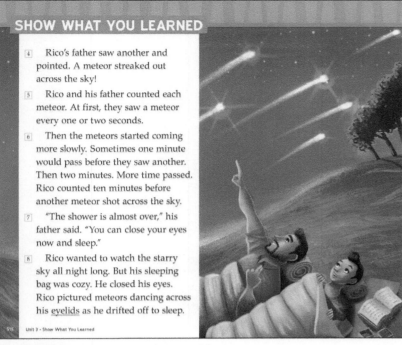

SHOW WHAT YOU LEARNED

4 Rico's father saw another and pointed. A meteor streaked out across the sky!

5 Rico and his father counted each meteor. At first, they saw a meteor every one or two seconds.

6 Then the meteors started coming more slowly. Sometimes one minute would pass before they saw another. Then two minutes. More time passed. Rico counted ten minutes before another meteor shot across the sky.

7 "The shower is almost over," his father said. "You can close your eyes now and sleep."

8 Rico wanted to watch the starry sky all night long. But his sleeping bag was cozy. He closed his eyes. Rico pictured meteors dancing across his <u>eyelids</u> as he drifted off to sleep.

Unit 3 • Show What You Learned

Reading/Writing Companion, p. 98

FICTION

1 Which detail belongs in the empty box in the chart?

A Rico looks forward to the meteor shower.

B Rico and his father lay out sleeping bags.

C Rico and his father count each meteor.

D Rico drifts off to sleep.

2 How do you know that the story is told in the third person point of view?

F The narrator is a character in the story.

G The narrator is quoted in the story.

H The narrator plays a big role in helping Rico and his father look at the sky.

J The narrator tells what the characters are doing but is not in the story.

3 Which words in paragraph 8 help you understand the meaning of <u>eyelids</u>?

A watch the starry sky

B all night long

C closed his eyes

D meteors dancing

| Rico and his father drive to a dark hilltop. |
| Rico sees the first meteor. |
| |
| Rico closes his eyes. |

Quick Tip

The third person point of view happens when a narrator tells a story about events that happened.

Unit 3 • Show What You Learned   99

Reading/Writing Companion, p. 99

Question 2: POINT OF VIEW

How do you know that the story is told in third person point of view?

Ask children to look for text evidence that helps them understand who is telling the story and whether the narrator is involved in the story or not . Have them reread paragraph one, and note that the person telling the story is using words like *he* and *they* to describe the characters. This helps them understand that the narrator is not a character in the story. (J)

Question 3: COMPOUND WORDS

Which words in paragraph 8 help the reader understand the meaning of eyelids?

Remind children that compound words are made up of two smaller words. The smaller words give clues to the meaning of the compound word. (C)

ELL English Language Learners

Genre: Test Passages Read each question and answer choice with children to help them determine the information they need to look for. As needed, review sequence, point of view, and compound words. Encourage children to ask questions about ideas, words, or phrases they don't understand. Help them clarify the meaning. For example, *Which phrase in paragraph 2 describes the first meteor?* (a bright streak in the sky) *Which clue helps you figure out what "drifted off to sleep" means?* (He closed his eyes.)

Extend Your Learning

Reading/Writing Companion

OBJECTIVES

Use information gained from the illustrations and words in a print or digital text to demonstrate understanding of its characters, setting, or plot.

Acknowledge differences in the points of view of characters, including by speaking in a different voice for each character when reading dialogue aloud.

ACADEMIC LANGUAGE

- personal narrative, first person, point of view

TEACH IN SMALL GROUP

You may wish to reteach characteristics of personal narratives during small group time.

Approaching Level Reteach the concepts before children begin the Spiral Review.

On Level and **Beyond Level** Focus discussion on the purpose, characteristics, and features of personal narratives.

ELL Help children complete sentence frames with examples of the characteristics, structures, and purpose of personal narratives.

EXTEND YOUR LEARNING

Focus on Genre

Reread the personal narrative "Landing on Your Feet" on pages 234-237.

- When you read the story, how can you tell it is a personal narrative? What words does the author use to show that the story is written in the first person point of view?

  It is a personal narrative because it tells a story with events that could be true.

  The author uses I, me, my, and we.

- What are the parts of the story that make you think it could really take place in the real world?

  The characters of the story, like Ryan, could be real people. The places are real

  places in this world.

Talk about how the author uses time-order words to tell events in order. Then use the Graphic Organizer to write down the parts of the story that happen in the beginning, middle, and end of the story.

Quick Tip
The first person point of view happens when someone tells their own story. A personal narrative is usually written in the first person.

100   Unit 3 · Extend Your Learning

Reading/Writing Companion, p. 100

Focus on Genre

Explain Review the author's purpose in *Landing on Your Feet. The author wants to tell a story about her dad, a gymnastics coach, who hurt his ankle.* Remind children that in this story, the girl tells about the events in the order in which they happened. This story is a personal narrative because the person who wrote it tells about an actual experience that is from her point of view.

PERSONAL NARRATIVE

- Is written in the first person point of view
- Uses words *I, me, my, we*
- Tells a story about real people, places, and events
- Uses time-order words to tell events in order

Guided Practice Have children reread *Landing on Your Feet*. Guide partners to identify the words *I, me, my, we*. Ask them why they think the author wrote this as a personal narrative. Then ask them to respond to the first question on page 100 of the **Reading/Writing Companion.**

Apply Have partners answer the second question and discuss with the class. Then have them discuss how the author used time-order words to tell events in order. Guide them to talk about what happened in the beginning, middle, and end of the story.

Beginning

One Friday, Ryan's father hurt his ankle while coaching gymnastics.

Middle

Over the weekend, Ryan took care of her father and helped him get better.

End

On Monday, Ryan's father was able to coach gymnastics.

Unit 3 · Extend Your Learning   101

Reading/Writing Companion, p. 101

English Language Learners

Guided Practice Use the chart on page 101 to discuss the sequence of events. Tell children you will call out some events from "Landing on Your Feet" and ask them to tell whether each one happened at the beginning, middle, or end. Use examples such as: *When Dad came home he went to the couch to lie down.* (beginning) *Ryan got books for her dad to read.* (middle) *It wasn't easy for Dad to walk, but he coached gymnastics.* (end)

Explain Have children read the sentence frames together and discuss their ideas about what happened in the beginning, middle, and end of the story. Then have partners work together to complete the chart on page 101 of the **Reading/Writing Companion.**

Guided Practice *What happened one Friday?* (One Friday, Ryan's father hurt his ankle while coaching gymnastics.) **Point out that the narrator of the story tells readers when the story events begin by stating** *One Friday.*

What happened over the weekend? (Over the weekend, Ryan took care of her father and helped him get better.) **The narrator wants readers to know what events took place after her Dad hurt his ankle, but before he was expected to coach again on Monday.**

Guide partners to discuss what happens at the end of the story. *What happened on Monday?* (On Monday, Ryan's father was able to coach gymnastics.) Continue to guide children as they add ideas to the chart.

Apply When children have completed their charts, have pairs share their work with the class to tell about the events in the order in which they happened.

Extend Your Learning

Reading/Writing Companion

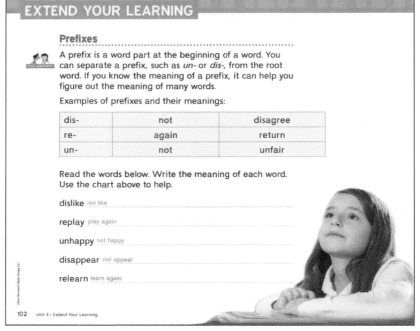

EXTEND YOUR LEARNING

Prefixes

A prefix is a word part at the beginning of a word. You can separate a prefix, such as *un-* or *dis-*, from the root word. If you know the meaning of a prefix, it can help you figure out the meaning of many words.

Examples of prefixes and their meanings:

dis-	not	disagree
re-	again	return
un-	not	unfair

Read the words below. Write the meaning of each word. Use the chart above to help.

dislike not like

replay play again

unhappy not happy

disappear not appear

relearn learn again

102   Unit 3 · Extend Your Learning

Reading/Writing Companion, p. 102

Prefixes

Explain After children read the introduction to the activity on the **Reading/Writing Companion** page 102, provide some examples of words with prefixes in sentences that include clues. For example: *I had to uncover my puppy who was hiding under the blanket.* Model how to separate the prefix from the root word to figure out the correct meaning of *uncover*. Say: *I think that* uncover *means the opposite of cover, so in this sentence* uncover *means taking the cover or blanket off the puppy.*

Guided Practice Guide partners or small groups to read and discuss the activity on **Reading/Writing Companion** page 102. Model reading each prefix, its meaning, and example of a word that has that prefix. Give an example of each word used in a sentence.

Apply Have children work with a partner to complete the activity. Make sure children use the chart to help them write the words' meanings. Have groups share their answers with the class.

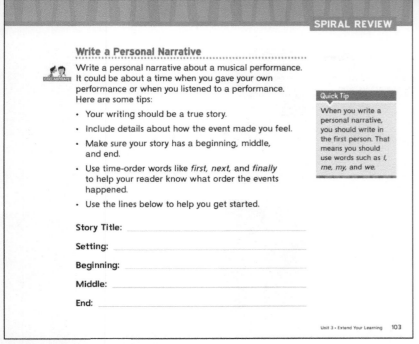

SPIRAL REVIEW

Write a Personal Narrative

Write a personal narrative about a musical performance. It could be about a time when you gave your own performance or when you listened to a performance. Here are some tips:

· Your writing should be a true story.

· Include details about how the event made you feel.

· Make sure your story has a beginning, middle, and end.

· Use time-order words like *first, next,* and *finally* to help your reader know what order the events happened.

· Use the lines below to help you get started.

Quick Tip

When you write a personal narrative, you should write in the first person. That means you should use words such as *I, me, my,* and *we.*

Story Title: _____

Setting: _____

Beginning: _____

Middle: _____

End: _____

Unit 3 · Extend Your Learning   103

Reading/Writing Companion, p. 103

Write a Personal Narrative

Explain Remind children that a personal narrative tells about a real life experience the writer has had. Explain that they may write about giving a musical performance or listening to a musical performance. Review the bulleted list of tips that will help them write their personal narratives.

Guided Practice Guide partners to work together to fill out the information for their personal narratives on **Reading/Writing Companion** page 103.

Apply Make sure children understand that they should write in the first person point of view, using the words *I, me, my, we.* Provide art supplies so that children can draw a picture that illustrates an idea from their personal narratives. Have children share their personal narratives with a partner or in front of the class.

 English Language Learners

Apply Explain that writers organize their personal narratives to make it easier for readers to understand when the events took place and the order in which they occurred. Help children make a list of time-order words they can use in their own personal narratives. Provide some sample sentences children can use as models to include time order words in their narratives.

You may wish to provide ELLs with additional support in editing for subject-verb agreement when writing in the first person.

Extend Your Learning

Reading/Writing Companion

OBJECTIVES

Recall information from experiences or gather information from provided sources to answer a question.

With guidance and support from adults, use a variety of digital tools to produce and publish writing, including in collaboration with peers.

ACADEMIC LANGUAGE

- *community, advertisement, diagram, label*
- Cognates: *comunidad, diagrama*

EXTEND YOUR LEARNING

Respond to the Read Aloud

The main events tell about what happens in the story in the beginning, middle, and end. The events help you to understand the order of the story, the characters, and the plot.

Listen to "The Hidden Sun."

Describe what happens in the story.

Write about three of the main events.

> **Quick Tip**
>
> Listen closely to understand how one important event can lead to another important event.

Event
Hollie and Mike decide to write a report about a solar eclipse.

Event
They are invited to an observatory to learn more about solar eclipses.

Event
Hollie and Mike wear special glasses that let them see a solar eclipse.

104   Unit 3 · Extend Your Learning

Reading/Writing Companion, p. 104

Respond to the Read Aloud

Explain Discuss the Graphic Organizer on **Reading/Writing companion** page 104 with children. Tell children that realistic fiction stories often have a beginning, middle, and end story structure. Authors often introduce the characters in the beginning, present a problem in the middle, and then solve the problem at the end of the story.

Guided Practice Guide children to summarize what happens at the beginning of "The Hidden Sun." Review the quick tip and explain that the events in the story are related to each other. After they have completed the Graphic Organizer, ask them to explain how the events are related.

Apply Have children work in pairs to tell what happens in the middle and end on the Graphic Organizer for "The Hidden Sun."

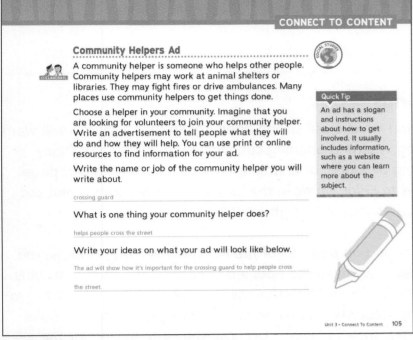

Reading/Writing Companion, p. 105

Community Helpers Ad

Explain/Guided Practice Guide partners or small groups to read and discuss the activity on **Reading/Writing Companion** page 105.

Make sure children understand the purpose of community helpers. Point out that community helpers help other people in many different ways. Help children name community helpers they know of in your community. Then have children choose one of these community helpers for this activity. Have them answer the questions on page 105.

Apply Have children make their advertisements and share with a partner. Invite volunteers to tell how the community helper will help others. Remind children to include specific details that tell what the helper will do and whom they will help.

English Language Learners

Community Helpers Ad, Guided Practice Help children brainstorm community helpers, such as police officers, firefighters, and librarians, and name some of the things these helpers do. Allow children to use strategies to express themselves in English, such as using gestures and pantomime to show different actions, or using circumlocution to describe a person or action using available English. Provide translation support and language clarification, as needed. After children learn some of this basic vocabulary, have partners work together to write answers to the questions on page 105.

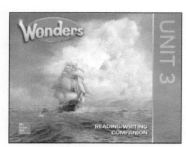

Reading/Writing Companion

OBJECTIVES

With guidance and support from adults and peers, focus on a topic and strengthen writing as needed by revising and editing.

ACADEMIC LANGUAGE

• *revise*

• Cognate: *revisar*

DIFFERENTIATED WRITING

Check student progress on revisions at this stage during Small Group Time.

Approaching Level Review drafts for Strong Openings.

On Level Partners can review each other's drafts.

Beyond Level Encourage children to describe their feelings about the music or instrument that they chose. *How does it make you feel?*

ELL Help children focus on each sentence in a paragraph during the Revise phase.

Revise

Strong Openings

Remind children that writers use strong openings so that a reader will want to continue reading. A strong opening can include an exciting or funny moment, interesting dialogue, or a striking description. Read aloud page 263 of *Many Ways to Enjoy Music* in the **Literature Anthology**. Point out how the writer creates excitement about the concert.

Read aloud the opening on page 65 of the **Reading/Writing Companion**. Model adding a detail to make the opening stronger. Say: *The writer gets your attention with the idiom "sing their hearts out.." Let's add a detail to tell more about the students.* Model adding a descriptive detail to make the opening stronger, such as "That's because they love to sing for the school chorus at Public School 22." Have children continue to add details to improve the opening.

Ask volunteers to share their revised versions. Discuss details children added. Then ask children to underline the words, phrases, or sentences in their revisions that made the opening stronger. Ask: *Does this opening make you want to continue reading the story?*

Revision

Allow time for children to review their drafts, focusing on their openings. Remind children that their opening should encourage the reader to continue reading.

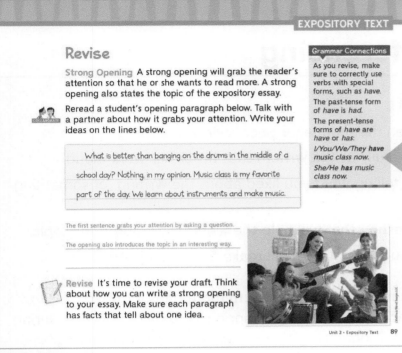

Reading/Writing Companion, p. 89

English Language Learners SCAFFOLD

Use the following scaffolds with **Revision.**

Beginning

Have children work in mixed proficiency groups to write strong openings. Have Beginning ELLs first read the openings of higher proficiency ELLs as models, and tell what they liked about them: I like the description of ___. I like the dialogue between ___ and ___. I like the part about ___. It sounds exciting/funny. I want to keep reading because ___.

Intermediate

Have partners discuss their openings using language like the following: *Are you going to write about something funny or exciting?* I am going to write something exciting. It was exciting to hear the audience. I'm going to write about the cheers from the audience. *Will you use dialogue?* Yes, I'm going to include the conversation between Mom and my teacher. Will you use a strong description? Yes, I'm going to use the phrase "louder than a thunderstorm."

Advanced/Advanced High

Have children brainstorm a few possible openings. Then have partners review their ideas and share their opinions about which is best. For example, *I really like the dialogue between the sisters. It makes me want to keep reading to see how they solve their problem.*

Digital Tools

Use these digital tools to enhance the lesson.

 Revised Student Model

 Revise Checklist

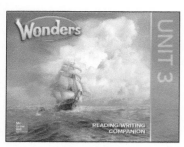

Reading/Writing Companion

OBJECTIVES

With guidance and support from adults and peers, focus on a topic and strenghen writing as needed by revising and editing.

Demonstrate command of the conventions of standard English grammar and usage when writing or speaking.

ACADEMIC LANGUAGE

- revise, suggestion
- Cognates: *revisar, sugerencia*

Digital Tools

 Children can view the Peer Conferencing Checklist and watch the Peer Conferencing Collaborative Conversation video.

Peer Conferencing

Review a Draft

Review with children the routine for peer review of writing.

- Step 1: Listen carefully as the writer reads his or her work aloud.
- Step 2: Begin by telling what you liked about the writing, or something you learned.
- Step 3: Ask a question that will help the writer think about the topic.
- Step 4: Make a suggestion that will make the writing stronger.

Anchor Chart You may wish to brainstorm more rules for peer conferencing and add them to your anchor chart. Display the rules during all peer conferences. Model using the sentence starters on **Reading/ Writing Companion** page 90. Say: *I was interested in that music because...* Discuss the steps of the routine for peer conferencing. Ask: *How can you show you are listening?* (I can keep my eyes on the reader.) *What ideas might you have about strengthening the text?* (Possible responses: making sure paragraphs are about one topic; making sure I have written a strong opening; adding more descriptive details)

Partner Feedback

Circulate to be sure children are following the peer conferencing rules. As needed, remind them to look directly at a partner as he or she reads aloud, with a friendly expression. Allow children time to think through the suggestions, choosing at least one to take action on as part of their revision routines.

Revision

Review the revising checklist on **Reading/Writing Companion** page 90. Allow children time to implement suggestions. Remind children that the rubric on page 93 can also help with revision. After children have completed their revisions, allow them time to share how their partners' feedback helped improve their writing.

WRITING

Revise: Peer Conferences

Review a Draft Listen carefully as a partner reads his or her work aloud. Begin by telling what you like about the draft. Make suggestions that you think will make the writing stronger.

Partner Feedback Write one of your partner's suggestions that you will use in the revision of your text.

Based on my partner's feedback, I will _____

_____

_____

After you finish giving each other feedback, reflect on the peer conference. What was helpful? What might you do differently next time?

_____

_____

Revision Use the Revising Checklist to help you figure out what text you may need to move, add to, or delete. Remember to use the rubric on page 93 to help you with your revision.

> **Quick Tip**
>
> Use these sentence starters to discuss your partner's work. *Where did you find the information about... Can you explain how... I think that it would be clearer to say...*

> **Revising Checklist**
> - [ ] Does my essay tell about the topic?
> - [ ] Does each paragraph tell about one idea?
> - [ ] Does it have a strong opening?
> - [ ] Does it have a conclusion?
> - [ ] Are the sources clearly cited?

90   Unit 3 • Expository Text

Reading/Writing Companion, p. 90

English Language Learners SCAFFOLD

Use the following scaffolds with **Review a Draft.**

Beginning

Pair children with more proficient speakers for peer review collaboration. Have children monitor their understanding as they listen to their partners read their drafts aloud, and use frames like the following to ask for clarification and provide feedback: *Will you read that sentence again? What does the word ___ mean? I liked ___.*

Intermediate

Remind children to monitor their understanding as they listen to their partners. Encourage partners to ask questions to clarify understanding before providing feedback. For example, *When you said ___ did you mean ___? Can you explain ___?* Then help them formulate feedback: I liked how you used dialogue. I think you should add more dialogue to this section.

Advanced/Advanced High

Remind children to monitor their understanding as they listen to their partners, and to ask for clarification using phrases, such as: *What did you mean by ___? I didn't understand the part where ___. Can you explain it?* Then have partners provide feedback. After they tell what they liked and make suggestions, help them ask questions to help the writer think about the topic.

Teacher Conferences

As students revise, hold teacher conferences with individual students.

Step 1: Talk About Strengths

Point out strengths in the expository essay. For example, say: *Your opening grabs my attention and states the topic.*

Step 2: Focus on Skills

Give feedback on how the student could improve on features of the essay. For example, say: *An expository essay develops the topic with facts and information. Try adding more facts and information.*

Step 3: Make Concrete Suggestions

Point out a section that needs to be revised. Have students use a specific strategy. For example, ask students to rewrite a paragraph so that it tells about one idea.

CLASSROOM CULTURE

We promote ownership of learning. Remind children what it means to be responsible for their own learning. While working with a group, children should do their best and learn from others. If they don't understand something, they should ask questions such as:

- How can I take ownership of my own learning?
- If I don't understand something, what steps can I take to get help?

Reading/Writing Companion

OBJECTIVES

With guidance and support from adults and peers, focus on a topic and strengthen writing as needed by revising and editing.

Demonstrate command of the conventions of standard English grammar and usage when writing or speaking.

ACADEMIC LANGUAGE

• correct, edit
• Cognates: *corregir, editar*

Edit and Proofread

Explain

Tell children that after they have finished their drafts, they must go back and edit and proofread. First comes editing, which is the step when writers focus on how clearly they have presented their ideas. For example, with expository text, you might decide to begin each paragraph with the main idea. Proofreading is a final step, the last opportunity to be sure there are no errors in grammar, usage, punctuation, and spelling. Look carefully at each sentence to make sure capitalization and punctuation are correct.

Correct Mistakes

Review the editing checklist on **Reading/Writing Companion** page 91 Write these sentences on the board:

I like country songs? They tell a story. the singers pla the guitar

Proofread and edit as a class using the Editing Checklist. (Replace question mark with a period; make lowercase "t" in "the" uppercase; change "pla" to "play; add a period after "guitar.") **Identify each mistake, and write the corrected sentences on the board. Ask volunteers to share mistakes they found when using the Editing Checklist for their own work.**

Using the Editing Checklist

Pair children to edit and proofread each other's drafts using the Editing Checklist as a guide. First, they should read their drafts aloud to each other. Then have them mark each other's texts to show problems that need to be corrected. Listening closely helps to identify areas that need editing attention. One helpful tip for effective proofreading is to focus on one sentence at a time. Remind children to be helpful and polite to each other. When they are done, have them write a reflection on how collaborating helped their writing.

Digital Tools

Children can view the Edited Student Model

Children can view the Edit Checklist and the Revise Checklist

EXPOSITORY TEXT

Edit and Proofread

When you **edit** and **proofread**, you look for and correct mistakes in your writing. Rereading a revised draft several times will help you catch any errors. Use the checklist below to edit your sentences.

Tech Tip

If you type your text, use the "Tab" key to indent each paragraph.

✓ Editing Checklist

☐ Do all sentences end with the correct punctuation mark?
☐ Does the verb agree with the subject in each sentence?
☐ Are the verbs used correctly in the past and future tenses?
☐ Is the word "have" used correctly?
☐ Are all of the words spelled correctly?

Grammar Connections

As you proofread, make sure you correctly used different types of nouns in sentences. Remember, a collective noun names a group that acts as one thing.
Our band practices on Monday.

List two mistakes you found as you proofread your text.

1 _____

_____

2 _____

_____

Unit 3 · Expository Text   91

Grammar Connections

Remind children that a noun is a person, place, or thing. When a noun refers to a group, it is called a collective noun.

Reading/Writing Companion, p. 91

English Language Learners SCAFFOLD

Use the following scaffolds with **Using the Editing Checklist.**

Beginning

Set up editing and proofreading sessions with mixed proficiency partners. Suggest that they read each sentence and check for one item on the checklist at a time. Display some examples of conjugated verbs for partners to refer to for subject-verb agreement during their review. Also display some examples of verbs in the past and future tense so children have a quick reference.

Intermediate

As children read each other's texts, they should work collaboratively to use the Editing Checklist. Allow them to use a dictionary to confirm spellings. Children can refer to samples of conjugated verbs and verbs used in the past and future tenses to confirm their work.

Advanced/Advanced High

After children use the Editing Checklist to check for punctuation, subject-verb agreement, verb tenses, and spelling, ask them to identify any collective nouns in their writing and double-check subject-verb agreement. For example, words like *band, family, team,* and *orchestra* are collective nouns that use the singular third-person verb form: *The band plays music. It plays music.*

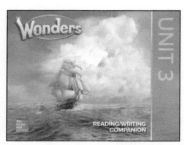

Reading/Writing Companion

OBJECTIVES

With guidance and support from adults, use a variety of digital tools to produce and publish writing, including in collaboration with peers.

Ask and answer questions about what a speaker says in order to clarify comprehension, gather additional information, or deepen understanding of a topic or issue.

ACADEMIC LANGUAGE

• details, publish, successful
• Cognates: *detalles, publicar*

Publish, Present, and Evaluate

Publishing

Once their drafts are final, children can prepare for publishing and presenting their work. Published work should be error-free with illustrations or photos in place.

Presentation

For the final presentation of their texts, have children choose a format for publishing: print or digital. They might want to include a visual. Allow time for children to record an audio/video presentation of their writing. Have children consult the Presenting Checklist before they present.

Evaluate

Explain that rubrics show what is expected from the assignment and how it will be evaluated. Ideally, children should look at rubrics before they begin writing in order to fulfill all the requirements. When they finish, they should evaluate their work. Direct them to the rubric in the **Reading/ Writing Companion** page 93 to check their work.

• Does the text focus on one topic?

• Are the facts reliable?

• Does the text have a strong opening?

• Does each paragraph have one main idea?

• Is the text free or almost free of errors?

If children answer "no" to any of these points, they should revisit their work. Make sure they note what they did successfully and what needs more work. After children have evaluated their texts using the rubric, have them exchange texts with a partner. Have them go through each point and give the partner a score. Remind them to read carefully and thoughtfully, and to word their comments respectfully. When they are finished, have children reflect on the effectiveness of the collaboration and on their progress as writers. Have them note where they need improvement and set writing goals.

Digital Tools

 Children can view the Anchor Papers

 Children can watch the How to Give a Presentation video

WRITING

Publish, Present, and Evaluate

Publishing Create a neat, clean final copy of your expository essay. Add illustrations or a diagram to make your published work more interesting.

Presentation Practice your presentation when you are ready to present your work. Use the Presenting Checklist to help you.

Evaluate After you publish and present your essay, use the rubric on the next page to evaluate your writing.

1 What did you do successfully? _____

_____

_____

_____

2 What needs more work? _____

_____

_____

_____

✔ Presenting Checklist
- ☐ Sit up or stand up straight.
- ☐ Look at different people in the audience.
- ☐ Speak slowly and clearly.
- ☐ Speak loudly so that everyone can hear you.
- ☐ Answer questions using facts from your text.

Reading/Writing Companion, p. 92

Listening When you listen actively, you pay close attention to what you hear. When you listen to other students' presentations, take notes to help you better understand their ideas.

What I learned from ....'s presentation:

_____

Questions I have about ....'s presentation:

_____

✔ Listening Checklist
- ☐ Make eye contact with the speaker.
- ☐ Use body language that shows you are listening.
- ☐ Listen for key words that relate to the topic.
- ☐ Identify what the speaker does well.
- ☐ Ask about any facts that are unclear.

4	3	2	1
• focuses on a topic related to music	• focuses mostly on one topic related to music	• lacks focus on a topic	• does not focus on a topic
• has a strong opening and a concluding statement or section	• introduces the topic in the opening and has a conclusion	• does not have a strong opening and lacks a conclusion	• does not have an opening or a conclusion
• each paragraph tells about an idea	• in each paragraph, most details relate to one idea	• attempts to write complete paragraphs	• does not organize ideas into paragraphs
• is free or almost free of errors	• has few errors	• has errors that distract from the meaning of the essay	• has many errors that make the essay hard to understand

Reading/Writing Companion, p. 93

English Language Learners SCAFFOLD

Use the following scaffolds with **Presentation.**

Beginning

Have partners practice together to build their confidence. Partners who are presenting should attend to the ideas on the Presenting Checklist on page 92 of the **Reading/Writing Companion**. Read this checklist aloud as needed. Provide several opportunities for children to practice presenting.

Intermediate

Have children tell you when they are ready for you to record their presentations. Play the recordings for children, and have them tell you what they like best about their presentations. Suggest one area of improvement they can focus on. Then videotape them again when they present and use this as a basis for evaluation.

Advanced/Advanced High

Have partners take turns presenting to each other and giving feedback. Check children's comprehension of the Presenting Checklist and the rubric. Have partners show specific examples where their writing meets the rubric standards.

Track Your Progress

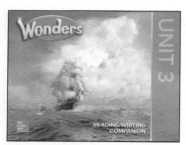

Reading/Writing Companion

OBJECTIVES

Recall information from experiences or gather information from provided sources to answer a question.

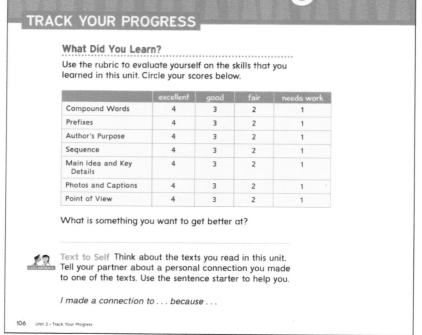

TRACK YOUR PROGRESS

What Did You Learn?

Use the rubric to evaluate yourself on the skills that you learned in this unit. Circle your scores below.

	excellent	good	fair	needs work
Compound Words	4	3	2	1
Prefixes	4	3	2	1
Author's Purpose	4	3	2	1
Sequence	4	3	2	1
Main Idea and Key Details	4	3	2	1
Photos and Captions	4	3	2	1
Point of View	4	3	2	1

What is something you want to get better at?

Text to Self Think about the texts you read in this unit. Tell your partner about a personal connection you made to one of the texts. Use the sentence starter to help you.

I made a connection to . . . because . . .

106 Unit 3 · Track Your Progress

Reading/Writing Companion, p. 106

HABITS OF LEARNING

I believe I can succeed.
During the unit, children have learned new things about the world around them. Guide a class discussion on the specific things they have learned in this unit. After the discussion, ask children: How does learning new things help you feel empowered to succeed? Ask children to support their answer.

What Did I Learn?

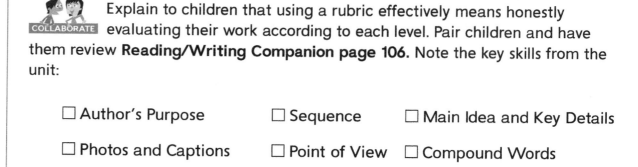

Explain to children that using a rubric effectively means honestly evaluating their work according to each level. Pair children and have them review **Reading/Writing Companion page 106.** Note the key skills from the unit:

- ☐ Author's Purpose
- ☐ Sequence
- ☐ Main Idea and Key Details
- ☐ Photos and Captions
- ☐ Point of View
- ☐ Compound Words
- ☐ Prefixes

Have children jot down notes on each skill. Then have each student review his or her unit work using the rubric scores. Have them score each skill in the box provided. Noting the lowest score, they should reflect on their progress, writing an honest evaluation of the lowest scoring skill.

Text to Self

Explain that a personal connection is when readers make a connection between what they read and their own personal experiences. Allow children to explore and express personal connections to one of the texts they have read in this unit. Have them describe their personal connections to a partner.

When all of the exercises on page 106 are done, have partners switch papers to get corroboration and reflect on their self-assessments.

Wrap Up the Unit

Make Connections

Connect to a Big Idea

Text to Text Write this Big Idea question on the board: *What have you learned about the world that surprises you?* Remind children that they have been reading selections about how we interact with the natural world. Divide the class into small groups. Tell children that each group will compare what they learned about people and our world in order to answer the Big Idea question. Model how to compare this information by using examples from the Leveled Readers and what they have read in this unit's selections.

Collaborative Conversations Have children review their class notes, writing assignments, and completed graphic organizers before they begin their discussions. Have children collaborate to take notes. Explain that each group will use an Accordion Foldable® to record their ideas. Model how to use an Accordion Foldable to record comparisons of texts.

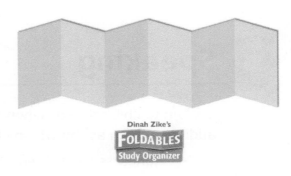

Dinah Zike's
FOLDABLES
Study Organizer

Present Ideas and Synthesize Information When children finish their discussions, ask for volunteers from each group to share their ideas aloud. After each group has presented, ask: *What interesting things have we learned about how we interact with the natural world? What did you learn that surprised you?* Lead a class discussion and list children's ideas on the board. Have children share any personal or emotional connections they felt to the texts they read and listened to over the course of the unit.

Building Knowledge Have children continue to build knowledge about the Big Idea. Display classroom or library sources and have children search for articles, books, journals and other resources that are related to the Big Idea. After each group has presented their ideas, ask: *What have you learned about the world that surprises you from these new resources?* Lead a class discussion asking children to use information from their charts to answer the Big Idea question.

Reflect At the end of the discussions, have groups reflect on their collaboration and acknowledge the contributions of one another.

OBJECTIVES

Ask and answer questions about what a speaker says in order to clarify comprehension, gather additional information, or deepen understanding of a topic or issue.

Participate in collaborative conversations with diverse partners about grade 2 topics and texts with peers and adults in small and larger groups.

Follow agreed-upon rules for discussions (e.g., gaining the floor in respectful ways, listening to others with care, speaking one at a time about the topics and texts under discussion).

SOCIAL EMOTIONAL LEARNING

Initiative, Curiosity, Creativity Encourage children to think about how these skills can help them learn more about the world around them. Have children think about these questions:

- How does learning about the world help you become more curious?
- What have you learned that surprised you?

Presentation Options

OBJECTIVES

Demonstrate command of the conventions of standard English grammar and usage when writing or speaking.

Follow agreed-upon rules for discussions (e.g., gaining the floor in respectful ways, listening to others with care, speaking one at a time about the topics and texts under discussion).

Digital Tools

Children can watch the How to Give a Presentation video online.

Collaborative Conversation Video

Presentation Checklist

TEACHER CHOICE

As you wrap up the unit, invite children to present their work to small groups, the class, or a larger audience. Choose from among these options:

✓ Have children perform the Reader's Theater play. See page T446.

✓ Small groups can share their completed Research and Inquiry projects, which they started in Genre Study 3. See page T470.

✓ Hold a Publishing Celebration and encourage children to self-select a piece of writing to present. See page T472.

Use the Speaking and Listening minilessons below to help children prepare.

OPTION
10 Mins

Speaking

Explain to children that when orally giving a formal presentation to a large audience, such as the whole class, they should remember these strategies:

- Rehearse the presentation in front of a friend and ask for feedback.

- Speak clearly, and with appropriate speaking rate, volume, enunciation, and conventions of language.

- Emphasize points so that the audience can follow important ideas.

- Make appropriate eye contact with people in the audience.

- Use hand gestures naturally when appropriate.

Remind children to time themselves during practice sessions to allow enough time for questions from the audience following the presentation.

Listening

Remind children that an effective listener

- listens for facts and key ideas about the topic
- stays focused on the speaker's presentation and ignores distractions
- listens without interruption but is prepared to ask questions and provide constructive feedback after the presentation is finished
- listens carefully to evaluate the speaker's point of view
- articulates thoughts clearly and builds upon the ideas of others

After the presentation, guide a discussion, asking some children to paraphrase or summarize the key ideas.

OBJECTIVES

Participate in collaborative conversations with diverse partners about grade 2 topics and texts with peers and adults in small and larger groups.

Follow agreed-upon rules for discussions (e.g., gaining the floor in respectful ways, listening to others with care, speaking one at a time about the topics and texts under discussion).

Presentation Rubric

4 Excellent	**3** Good	**2** Fair	**1** Unsatisfactory
• presents the information clearly • includes many facts and details • presents ideas in a logical sequence • may include sophisticated observations	• presents the information adequately • provides adequate facts and details • sequences ideas adequately • includes relevant observations	• attempts to present information • may offer few or vague facts and details • may struggle with sequencing ideas • may include few or irrelevant personal observations	• may show little grasp of the task • may present irrelevant information • may lack a logical sequence of ideas • may reflect extreme difficulty with research or presentation

Presentation Options

OBJECTIVES

Participate in collaborative conversations with diverse partners about grade 2 topics and texts with peers and adults in small and larger groups.

Follow agreed-upon rules for discussions (e.g., gaining the floor in respectful ways listening to others with care, speaking one at a time about the topics and texts under discussion).

ACADEMIC LANGUAGE

• *presentation, audience, collage, song*

• Cognates: *presentación, audiencia*

TEACH IN SMALL GROUP ◀◀

You may wish to teach the Research and Inquiry lesson during Small Group time and then have groups present their work to the class.

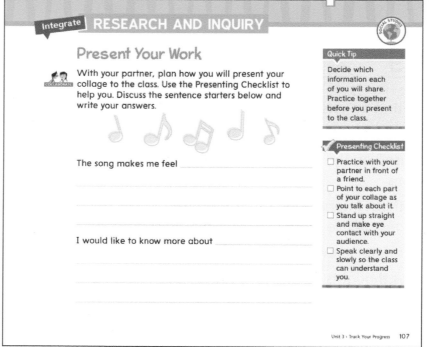

Reading/Writing Companion, p. 107

OPTION 10 Mins Present Research and Inquiry

Planning the Presentation

 Tell children that they will need to prepare in order to best present their work. Discuss each item on the Presenting checklist on **Reading/Writing Companion** page 107. Children can work with partners to complete the sentence frames on the page.

Discuss options for audio elements, such as recording their own voice-overs or including clips from experts to give the audience additional information. Model ways to emphasize the most important information. Allow partners and small groups time to rehearse.

Remind children that they will be part of the audience for their classmates' presentations, and listeners serve an important role. Review with and model for children the behaviors of an effective listener. You may want to show children the Listening Checklist from the **Resource Toolkit.**

During the Presentation

Tell children to write down any questions they have during the presentation. Explain that this will help them remember their questions when the speaker is finished. Guide a discussion of the presentation, asking some children to paraphrase or summarize its key ideas.

Review and Evaluate

To evaluate children's presentations, use the Informative Presentation Rubric from the Resource Toolkit or the Teacher Checklist and rubric below.

Student Checklist

Presenting

☑ Did you express your ideas clearly using the correct conventions of language?

☑ Did you support your topic with appropriate facts and details?

☑ Did you present your ideas in a logical sequence?

☑ Did you make appropriate eye contact with your audience?

☑ Did you speak with appropriate rate, volume, and enunciation?

☑ Did you use appropriate digital technology such as visuals and audio to enhance your presentation?

Teacher Checklist

Assess the Presentation

☑ Spoke clearly and at an appropriate pace and volume.

☑ Used appropriate and natural gestures.

☑ Maintained eye contact.

☑ Used appropriate visuals and technology.

Assess the Listener

☑ Listened quietly and politely.

☑ Made appropriate comments and asked clarifying questions.

☑ Responded with an open mind to different ideas.

OBJECTIVES

Participate in collaborative conversations with diverse partners about grade 2 topics and texts with peers and adults in small and larger groups.

Follow agreed-upon rules for discussions (e.g., gaining the floor in respectful ways listening to others with care, speaking one at a time about the topics and texts under discussion).

With guidance and support from adults, use a variety of digital tools to produce and publish writing, including in collaboration with peers.

OPTION
10
Mins

Writing
Student Choice

Select the Writing

Now is the time for children to share one of the pieces of writing that they have worked on through the unit. You may wish to invite parents or children from other classes to the Publishing Celebrations.

Preparing for Presentations

Tell children that they will present their writing and that preparing beforehand will help them best explain their writing to listeners.

Give children time to practice their presentations. Encourage them to reread their pieces a few times to become more familiar with the piece. Tell children that good speakers present their writing without just reading it word-for-word from the page.

Children should consider any props or digital elements that they may want to use to present their text. Discuss a few possible options with children.

- Would a poster or illustration relating to their writing help listeners understand their topic?
- Are there books, newspaper articles, or other materials that they can share with listeners?
- Is there a website related to their writing that they can project?

Children can practice presenting to a partner in the classroom. They can also practice with family members at home or in front of a mirror. Share this checklist with students to help them rehearse.

Speaking Checklist

Review the Speaking Checklist with children as they practice.

- ☐ Have all your notes and visuals ready.
- ☐ Show your visuals at the right time.
- ☐ Stand up straight.
- ☐ Make eye contact with people in the audience.
- ☐ Speak clearly and slowly.

- ☐ Speak loudly enough so everyone can hear.
- ☐ Emphasize important details that support your opinion.
- ☐ Use appropriate, natural gestures.
- ☐ Hold your visual aids so everyone can see them.
- ☐ Point to relevant features of the visual aids as you speak.

TEACH IN SMALL GROUP

You may wish to arrange groups of various abilities to complete their presentations, evaluate each other's work, and discuss portfolio choices.

Listening to Presentations

Remind children that they not only will take on the role of a presenter, but they will also be part of the audience for other children's presentations. As a listener, children have an important role. Review with children the following Listening Checklist.

Listening Checklist

DURING THE PRESENTATION

☐ Listen to the speaker carefully.

☐ Pay attention to how the speaker organizes information logically.

☐ Notice how the speaker supports the topic with relevant, descriptive details.

☐ Write one question or comment you have about the information presented.

AFTER THE PRESENTATION

☐ Summarize the speaker's main points.

☐ Tell why you liked the presentation.

☐ Ask a question or share a comment you have based on the information presented.

☐ Draw conclusions based on class discussion about the information.

Portfolio Choice

Ask children to select one finished piece of writing, as well as two revisions, to include in their writing portfolio. As children consider their choices, have them use the questions below.

PUBLISHED WRITING	WRITING ENTRY REVISIONS
Does your writing	**Do your revisions show**
• clearly describe your topic or main idea? • have enough details to support your ideas? • end with a strong conclusion? • have few or no spelling or conventions errors? • have a neat and clear final draft?	• varied sentence lengths to make the writing more interesting? • revised linking words that connect your ideas? • a good ending that restates your opinion?

Leveled Reader

OBJECTIVES

Explain how specific images (e.g., a diagram showing how a machine works) contribute to and clarify a text.

Identify the main purpose of a text, including what the author wants to answer, explain, or describe.

Read on-level text with purpose and understanding.

Approaching Level
to On Level

The Sounds of Trash

Preview Discuss what children remember about using "trash" to make musical instruments. Tell them they will be reading a more challenging version of *The Sounds of Trash*.

Vocabulary Use the Visual Vocabulary Cards and routine.

▶ **Genre** Explain that informational texts often have certain kinds of text features to help readers understand complicated information. Point out the procedural directions on pages 6, 8, 10, and 12. Explain that in this selection, the author is giving step-by-step instructions for how to make different kinds of musical instruments. Point out the parts of the instructional text, including the materials lists and the numbered steps. Discuss why the author chose to use numbers to write the steps in each process.

▶ **Connection of Ideas** Help children understand how the information in the caption on page 3 connects to the content on the page. With children, list the main idea and key details in the information on the page. Then find a key detail that connects to the information in the text feature.

▶ **Purpose** Help children understand that the author had two purposes for writing *The Sounds of Trash*: to explain how to use music to express feelings, and to explain how to make musical instruments using "trash." Have children discuss how effective the author was in achieving her purpose.

Have children complete the Respond to Reading on page 15 after they have finished reading. Then have them finish the Paired Read and hold Literature Circles.

On Level
to Beyond Level

The Sounds of Trash

Leveled Reader

Preview Discuss what children remember about using "trash" to make musical instruments. Tell them they will be reading a more challenging version of *The Sounds of Trash.*

Vocabulary Use the Visual Vocabulary Cards and routine.

▶ **Genre** Tell children that informational text often includes text features, such as photos, captions, and illustrations, that help the reader understand the text. Point out the illustrations of the guitar on page 7 and the trombone on page 9. Ask children how these illustrations can help them if they choose to make one of these instruments.

▶ **Connection of Ideas** Children may need help connecting and synthesizing ideas from page to page and section to section. After completing each paragraph, model for children how to make connections from the information in the paragraph they just read to the information from the previous paragraph. Then ask children to connect the text they read from section to section.

▶ **Specific Vocabulary** Review with children the following new music-related words that appear in this title. Model how to use context clues or the glossary to determine their meaning. *vibrate   pitch   guiro*

Have children complete the Respond to Reading on page 15 after they have finished reading. Then have them finish the Paired Read and hold Literature Circles.

OBJECTIVES

Determine or clarify the meaning of unknown and multiple-meaning words and phrases based on *grade 2 reading and content,* choosing flexibly from an array of strategies.

Explain how specific images (e.g., a diagram showing how a machine works) contribute to and clarify a text.

Leveled Reader

OBJECTIVES

Determine or clarify the meaning of unknown and multiple-meaning words and phrases based on *grade 2 reading and content,* choosing flexibly from an array of strategies.

Read with sufficient accuracy and fluency to support comprehension.

Read on-level text with purpose and understanding.

English Language Learners to On Level

The Sounds of Trash

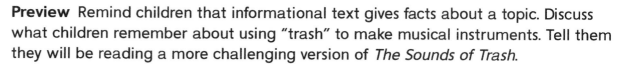

Preview Remind children that informational text gives facts about a topic. Discuss what children remember about using "trash" to make musical instruments. Tell them they will be reading a more challenging version of *The Sounds of Trash.*

Vocabulary Use the Visual Vocabulary Cards and routine.

▶ **Genre** Explain that informational texts often have certain kinds of text features to help readers understand complicated information. Point out the procedural directions on pages 6, 8, 10, and 12. Explain that in this selection, the author is giving step-by-step instructions for how to make different kinds of musical instruments. Point out the parts of the instructional text, including the materials lists and the numbered steps. Discuss why the author chose to use numbers to write the steps in each process.

▶ **Specific Vocabulary** Explain that some words have more than one meaning. Model using context clues to find the meanings of the word *can.* First, point out the words *cans* on in the second sentence on page 4. Explain that *can* has more than one meaning. Help children use context to determine each meaning of the word in this sentence. Then point out the word *bands* on page 6. Have partners work together to identify the meaning of *bands* as it is used in this context, and then discuss other meanings of *bands* that children know.

▶ **Connection of Ideas** Help children understand how the information in the caption on page 3 connects to the content on the page. With children, list the main idea and key details in the information on the page. Then find a key detail that connects to the information in the text feature.

Have children complete the Respond to Reading on page 15 after they have finished reading. Then have them finish the Paired Read and hold Literature Circles.

Beyond Level
to Self-Selected Trade Book

Independent Reading

| Leveled Reader | Advanced Level Trade Book |

Together with children, identify the particular focus of their reading, based on the text they choose. Children who have chosen the same title will work in groups to closely read the selection throughout the week.

Taking Notes Assign a graphic organizer for children to use to take notes as they read. Reinforce a specific comprehension focus from the unit by choosing one of the graphic organizers that best fits the book.

EXAMPLES	
Fiction	**Informational Text**
Plot: Sequence	Main Idea and Key Details
Graphic Organizer 2	Graphic Organizer 51

Ask and Answer Questions Remind children to ask questions as they read. As children meet, have them discuss the section that they have read. They can share the questions they noted and work together to find text evidence to support their answers. You may wish to have children write their responses to their questions.

EXAMPLES	
Fiction	**Informational Text**
What happens in the beginning, middle, and the end of the story? What is the problem? What steps are taken to solve the problem?	What is the main idea of this text, and what keys details support that idea?

Literature Circles Suggest that children hold Literature Circles and share interesting facts or favorite parts from the books they read.

OBJECTIVES

Participate in collaborative conversations with diverse partners about *grade 2 topics and texts* with peers and adults in small and larger groups.

Ask and answer such questions as *who, what, where, when, why,* and *how* to demonstrate understanding of key details in a text.

Read with sufficient accuracy and fluency to support comprehension.

Read on-level text with purpose and understanding.

 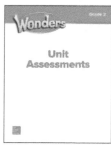  

UNIT 3 TESTED SKILLS

COMPREHENSION	VOCABULARY	GRAMMAR	WRITING
Author's Purpose	Synonyms	Action Verbs	Write About Text
Plot: Sequence	Compound Words	Present-, Past-, and Future-Tense Verbs	Writing Prompt
Main Idea and Key Details	Prefixes		
Text Evidence		Subject-Verb Agreement	
Third-Person Point of View	**PHONICS**	The Verb *Have*	
Photos and Captions	Long *a, i, o, e, u*		
Bar Graph			
Heads (Subheads)			
Graphic Features (Diagrams)			

ADDITIONAL ASSESSMENT OPTIONS

Fluency

Conduct assessments individually using the differentiated passages in **Fluency Assessment**. Children's expected fluency goal for this Unit is 74–94 WCPM with an accuracy rate of 95% or higher.

Running Records

Use the instructional reading level determined by the calculations for regrouping decisions. Children at Level 16 or below should be provided reteaching on specific Comprehension skills.

ELL Assessment

Assess children's English language proficiency and track children's progress using the **McGraw-Hill English Learner Benchmark Assessments**. This resource draws from a variety of contexts to evaluate social and academic language proficiency. These assessments also can be used for placement to achieve an optimal learning experience for new children.

Making the Most of Assessment Results

Review the assessments with children. Have them correct their errors. Then use available data to guide decisions about providing reteaching and enrichment opportunities for additional support options for your children.

ONLINE ASSESSMENT CENTER

- *Item Analysis Report*
- *Standards Analysis Report*

DATA DASHBOARD

- *Recommendations Report*
- *Activity Report*
- *Skills Report*
- *Progress Report*

 TIER 2 RETEACHING OPPORTUNITIES with Intervention Online PDFs

IF STUDENTS SCORE . . .	THEN RETEACH . . .
below 70% in **comprehension**	tested skills using the **Comprehension PDF**
below 70% in **vocabulary**	tested skills using the **Vocabulary PDF**
below 70% in **phonics**	tested skills using the **Phonics/Word Study PDF**
0–73 WCPM in **fluency**	tested skills using the **Fluency PDF**

Use the Phonemic Awareness PDF *and the* Foundational Skills Kit *for additional reteaching lessons.*

Gifted and Talented ENRICHMENT OPPORTUNITIES for Gifted and Talented Students

Beyond Level small group lessons include suggestions for additional activities in the following areas to extend learning opportunities for gifted and talented children:

- *Leveled Readers*
- *Genre Passages*
- *Vocabulary Strategy*
- *Comprehension Vocabulary*
- *Leveled Readers Library Online*
- *Workstation Activities*

Next Steps

Data Dashboard

NEXT STEPS FOR YOUR STUDENTS' PROGRESS . . .

Interpret the data you have collected from multiple sources throughout this unit, including formal and informal assessments.

Who ▶ Regrouping Decisions

- Check children's progress against your interpretation of the data, and regroup as needed.
- Determine how English Language Learners are progressing.
- Consider whether students are ready to Level Up or Accelerate.

What ▶ Target Instruction

- Decide whether to review and reinforce particular skills or concepts to reteach them.
- Target instruction to meet children's strengths/needs.
- Use Data Dashboard recommendations to help determine which lessons to provide to different groups of children.

Coach and Classroom Videos

Methodology

How ▶ Modify Instruction

- Vary materials and/or instructional strategies.
- Address children's social and emotional development.
- Provide children with opportunities for self-reflection and self-assessment.

AUTHOR INSIGHT

NEXT STEPS FOR YOU . . .

As you prepare children to move on to the next unit, don't forget to take advantage of the many opportunities available online for self-evaluation and professional development.

PROFESSIONAL DEVELOPMENT

"It's rare for students to benefit from lessons on what they already know, just as it is unusual for them to thrive when instruction flits from one not-quite-learned skill to another. Use assessment—including daily observations of kids' learning—to aim instruction at ensuring that they master essential reading skills."
—Dr. Timothy Shanahan

Learn to Use *Wonders*

Instructional Routines

Manage Assessments

Program Author Whitepapers

Research Base

Courtesy of Timothy Shanahan

Contents

Program Information

Additional Digital Resources   my.mheducation.com

- Unit Bibliography
- Word Lists
- Web Sites
- More Resources

Scope and Sequence

Genre Focus	Read Aloud	Shared Read	Literature Anthology	Leveled Readers	Vocabulary
Genre Study 1: Weeks 1 and 2 **Genre:** Realistic Fiction **Essential Question:** How are families around the world the same and different? **Literary Elements:** Beginning, Middle, End *Differentiated Genre Passages available*	**Interactive Read Aloud:** "Dinner at Alejandro's" **Genre:** Realistic Fiction	"Maria Celebrates Brazil" **Genre:** Realistic Fiction **Lexile:** 460L *ELL Scaffolded Shared Read available*	**Anchor Text** *Big Red Lollipop* **Genre:** Realistic Fiction **Lexile:** 410L **Paired Selection** "A Look at Families" **Genre:** Informational Text **Lexile:** 480L	**Main Selections** **Genre:** Realistic Fiction A: *Music in My Family* **Lexile:** 250L O: *Happy New Year!* **Lexile:** 350L ELL: Happy New Year! **Lexile:** 300L B: *I'm Down Under* **Lexile:** 560L **Paired Selections** **Genre:** Informational Text A: "Making Music" O: "New Year's Eve" ELL: "New Year's Eve" B: "Perfect Pavlova"	**Words:** *aside, culture, fair, invited, language, plead, scurries, share* **Strategy:** Inflectional Endings
Genre Study 2: Weeks 3 and 4 **Genre:** Fantasy **Essential Question:** How do friends depend on each other? **Literary Elements:** Use Illustrations *Differentiated Genre Passages available*	**Interactive Read Aloud:** "The New Kid" **Genre:** Fantasy	"Little Flap Learns to Fly" **Genre:** Fantasy **Lexile:** 390L *ELL Scaffolded Shared Read available*	**Anchor Text** *Help! A Story of Friendship* **Genre:** Fantasy **Lexile:** 410L **Paired Selection** "The Enormous Turnip" **Genre:** Folktale **Lexile:** 500L	**Main Selections** **Genre:** Fantasy A: *Cat and Dog* **Lexile:** 230L O: *The Quest* **Lexile:** 340L ELL: The Quest **Lexile:** 300L B: *Class Pets* **Lexile:** 500L **Paired Selections** **Genre:** Poetry A: "Uncle Max and I" O: "Together" ELL: "It Takes a Friend" B: "What Friends Do"	**Words:** *actions, afraid, depend, nervously, peered, perfectly, rescue, secret* **Strategy:** Root Words
Genre Study 3: Week 5 **Genre:** Expository: Informational Text **Essential Question:** What happens when families work together? **Text Features:** Charts *Differentiated Genre Passages available*	**Interactive Read Aloud:** "Families Today" **Genre:** Expository Text	"Families Work!" **Genre:** Expository Text **Lexile:** 500L *ELL Scaffolded Shared Read available*	**Anchor Text** "Families Working Together" **Genre:** Expository Text **Lexile:** 560L	**Main Selections** **Genre:** Informational Text A: *Families at Work* O: *Families at Work* ELL: *Families at Work* B: *Families at Work* **Paired Selections** **Genre:** Informational Text A: "A Family Sawmill" O: "A Family Sawmill" ELL: "A Family Sawmill" B: "A Family Sawmill"	**Words:** *check, choose, chores, cost, jobs, customers, spend, tools* **Strategy:** Synonyms

Week 6	Reading Digitally	Fluency	Show What You Learned	Extend Your Learning	Writing	Presentation Options
Review, Extend, and Assess	"Super Skiers" **Genre:** Online Article	**Reader's Theater:** *Room for More*	**Passage 1** "Community Heroes" **Genre:** Expository Text **Passage 2** "If Squirrels Were Rabbits" **Genre:** Fantasy	Focus on Genre Synonyms Write a Book Report Respond to the Read Aloud **Connect to Content:** Create a Technology Chart	**Writing Process** Expository Essay **Revise:** Descriptive Details **Peer Conferences; Edit and Proofread; Publish, Present, and Evaluate**	**Reader's Theater** **Research and Inquiry** **Writing**

Comprehension	Word Work	Fluency	Writing and Grammar	Research and Inquiry
Strategy: Visualize **Skill:** Character, Setting, Events **Author's Craft:** Captions	**Week 1** **Phonemic Awareness:** Blending, Categorization, Segmentation **Phonics/Spelling*:** short *a*; short *i* **Structural Analysis:** Plural Nouns with *-s, -es* **High-Frequency Words:** ball, blue, both, even, for, help, put, there, why, yellow **Handwriting:** Manuscript Review **Week 2** **Phonological Awareness:** Identify and Generate Rhyme **Phonemic Awareness:** Isolation, Blending **Phonics/Spelling*:** short *e*, short *o*, short *u* **Structural Analysis:** Inflectional Endings *-s, -es* (Nouns and Verbs) **High-Frequency Words:** could, find, funny, green, how, little, one, or, see, sounds **Handwriting:** Letter and Word Spacing	**Week 1:** Intonation **Week 2:** Expression	**Respond to Reading** **Writing Process** Realistic Fiction **Expert Model:** Realistic Fiction Story **Plan:** Sequence **Draft:** Descriptive Details **Grammar and Mechanics** **Week 1:** Statements and Questions; Sentence Capitalization/ Punctuation **Week 2:** Commands and Exclamations; Sentence Capitalization/ Punctuation	**Product:** Poster About Foods from Around the World **Study Skill:** Internet Search Using Keywords **Blast:** "Welcome to Our Home"
Strategy: Visualize **Skill:** Key Details **Author's Craft:** Theme	**Week 3** **Phonemic Awareness:** Categorization, Substitution, Blending **Phonics/Spelling*:** two-letter blends: *r*-blends (*br, cr, dr, fr, gr*); s-blends (*sc, sk, sl, sm, sn, sp, st, sw*); t-blends (*tr, tw, -nt*); *l*-blends (*bl, cl, fl, gl, pl, -lk, -lt*) **Structural Analysis:** Closed Syllables **High-Frequency Words:** boy, by, girl, he, here, she, small, want, were, what **Handwriting:** Manuscript to Cursive: Lowercase **Week 4** **Phonemic Awareness:** Segmentation, Categorization, Blending **Phonics/Spelling*:** short *a*; long *a*: a_e **Structural Analysis:** Inflectional Endings *-ed, -ing* **High-Frequency Words:** another, done, into, move, now, show, too, water, year, your **Handwriting:** Manuscript to Cursive: Uppercase	**Week 3:** Expression **Week 4:** Intonation	**Respond to Reading** **Writing Process** Realistic Fiction **Revise:** Strong Openings **Peer Conferences; Edit and Proofread; Publish, Present, and Evaluate** **Grammar and Mechanics** **Week 3:** Subjects; Quotation Marks with Dialogue **Week 4:** Predicates; Quotation Marks with Dialogue	**Product:** Illustrated list of How We Depend on Friends **Study Skill:** Ask Questions **Blast:** "We Celebrate Our Friends"
Strategy: Ask and Answer Questions **Skill:** Key Details **Author's Craft:** Photos and Captions	**Week 5** **Phonemic Awareness:** Isolation, Categorization, Blending **Phonics/Spelling*:** short *i*; long *i*: i_e **Structural Analysis:** Possessives **High-Frequency Words:** all, any, goes, new, number, other, right, says, understands, work **Handwriting:** Cursive Writing Position; Cursive Alphabet	**Week 5:** Phrasing	**Respond to Reading** **Writing Process** Expository Essay **Expert Model:** Expository Essay **Plan:** Develop Questions **Draft:** Sentence Types and Lengths **Grammar and Mechanics** **Week 5:** Expanding and Combining Sentences; Commas in a Series	**Product:** Create a Job Description Sheet **Study Skill:** Interview **Blast:** "A Job for Everyone"

*Differentiated Spelling Lists available

Scope and Sequence

Genre Focus	Read Aloud	Shared Read	Literature Anthology	Leveled Readers	Vocabulary
Genre Study 1: Weeks 1 and 2 **Genre:** Expository: Informational Text **Essential Question:** How are offspring like their parents? **Text Features:** Diagrams and Labels *Differentiated Genre Passages available*	**Interactive Read Aloud:** "Wild Animal Families" **Genre:** Expository Text	"Eagles and Eaglets" **Genre:** Expository Text **Lexile:** 520L *ELL Scaffolded Shared Read available*	**Anchor Text** *Baby Bears* **Genre:** Expository Text **Lexile:** 590L **Paired Selection** "From Caterpillar to Butterfly" **Genre:** Expository Text **Lexile:** 560L	**Main Selections** **Genre:** Expository Text A: *Animal Families* **Lexile:** 320L O: *Animal Families* **Lexile:** 490L ELL: *Animal Families* **Lexile:** 390L B: *Animal Families* **Lexile:** 600L **Paired Selections** **Genre:** Informational Text A: "Tadpoles Into Frogs" O: "Tadpoles Into Frogs" ELL: "Tadpoles Into Frogs" B: "Tadpoles Into Frogs"	**Words:** *adult, alive, covered, fur, giant, groom, mammal, offspring* **Strategy:** Homographs
Genre Study 2: Weeks 3 and 4 **Genre:** Fable **Essential Question:** What can animals in stories teach us? **Literary Elements:** Story Structure: Beginning, Middle, End *Differentiated Genre Passages available*	**Interactive Read Aloud:** "The Fox and the Crane" **Genre:** Fable	"The Boy Who Cried Wolf" **Genre:** Fable **Lexile:** 460L *ELL Scaffolded Shared Read available*	**Anchor Text** *Wolf! Wolf!* **Genre:** Fable **Lexile:** 580L **Paired Selection** "Cinderella and Friends" **Genre:** Expository Text **Lexile:** 520L	**Main Selections** **Genre:** Fable A: *The Cat and the Mice* **Lexile:** 200L O: *The Dog and the Bone* **Lexile:** 440L ELL: *The Dog and the Bone* **Lexile:** 320L B: *The Spider and the Honey Tree* **Lexile:** 590L **Paired Selections** **Genre:** Poetry A: "Beware of Tiger!" O: "The Dingo and His Shadow" ELL: "The Dingo and His Shadow" B: "The Girl and the Spider"	**Words:** *believe, delicious, feast, fond, lessons, remarkable, snatch, stories* **Strategy:** Antonyms
Genre Study 3: Week 5 **Genre:** Poetry **Essential Question:** What do we love about animals? **Literary Elements:** Rhyme *Differentiated Genre Passages available*	**Interactive Read Aloud:** "The Furry Alarm Clock," "Little Crocodile" **Genre:** Poetry	"Cats and Kittens," "Desert Camels," "A Bat is Not a Bird" **Genre:** Poetry **Lexile:** NP *ELL Scaffolded Shared Read available*	**Anchor Text** "Beetles," "The Little Turtle" **Genre:** Poetry **Lexile:** NP **Paired Selection** "Gray Goose" **Genre:** Poetry **Lexile:** NP	**Main Selections** **Genre:** Fiction A: *Amira's Petting Zoo* **Lexile:** 250L O: *Alice's New Pet* **Lexile:** 570L ELL: *Alice's New Pet* **Lexile:** 350L B: *Ava's Animals* **Lexile:** 570L **Paired Selections** **Genre:** Informational Text A: "Sheep Season" O: "Baby Joey" ELL: "Four Little Ducklings" B: "Nanook"	**Words:** *behave, express, feathers, flapping* **Strategy:** Suffixes *-ly, -y*

Week 6	Reading Digitally	Fluency	Show What You Learned	Extend Your Learning	Writing	Presentation Options
Review, Extend, and Assess	"Under the Sea" **Genre:** Online Article	**Reader's Theater:** "The Secret Song"	**Passage 1** "Monarch Butterflies on the Move" **Genre:** Expository Text **Passage 2** "The Fox and the Grapes" **Genre:** Fable	Focus on Genre Homographs **Connect to Content:** Write a Pet Owner Book Create a Habitat Poster "Under the Sea"	**Writing Process** Rhyming Poem **Revise:** Rhyme **Peer Conferences; Edit and Proofread; Publish, Present, and Evaluate**	**Reader's Theater** **Research and Inquiry** **Writing**

Comprehension	Word Work	Fluency	Writing and Grammar	Research and Inquiry
Strategy: Reread **Skill:** Main Topic and Key Details **Author's Craft:** Diagrams	**Week 1** **Phonemic Awareness:** Addition, Substitution, Blending **Phonics/Spelling*:** Short *o*, Long *o*: *o_e* **Structural Analysis:** Inflectional Endings *-ed, -ing* **High-Frequency Words:** because, cold, family, friends, have, know, off, picture, school, took **Handwriting:** Strokes that Curve Up: *e, l; i, t* **Week 2** **Phonemic Awareness:** Deletion, Segmentation, Blending **Phonics/Spelling*:** Short *u*, Long *u*: *u_e* **Structural Analysis:** CVCe Syllables **High-Frequency Words:** change, cheer, fall, five, look, open, should, their, won, yes **Handwriting:** Strokes that Curve Down: *o, a; c, d*	**Week 1:** Intonation **Week 2:** Phrasing	**Respond to Reading** **Writing Process** Expository Essay **Expert Model:** Expository Text **Plan:** Research: Generate Questions **Draft:** Organization: Order Ideas **Grammar and Mechanics** **Week 1:** Nouns; Commas in a Series **Week 2:** Singular and Plural Nouns; Abbreviations	**Product:** Diagram About an Insect's Life Cycle **Study Skill:** Identify and Gather Sources **Blast:** "Amazing Animal Parents"
Strategy: Make, Confirm, Revise Predictions **Skill:** Character, Setting, Plot: Problem and Solution **Author's Craft:** Text Structure: Compare and Contrast	**Week 3** **Phonemic Awareness:** Segmentation, Substitution, Blending **Phonics/Spelling*:** Words with Soft *c* and *g* **Structural Analysis:** Prefixes **High-Frequency Words:** almost, buy, food, out, pull, saw, sky, straight, under, wash **Handwriting:** Strokes that Curve Over: *m, n* **Week 4** **Phonological Awareness:** Identify and Generate Rhyme **Phonemic Awareness:** Segmentation, Blending **Phonics/Spelling*:** Digraphs and Trigraphs *ch, tch, sh, ph, th, ng, wh* **Structural Analysis:** Suffixes **High-Frequency Words:** baby, early, eight, isn't, learn, seven, start, these, try, walk **Handwriting:** Joining Letters	**Week 3:** Expression **Week 4:** Phrasing	**Respond to Reading** **Writing Process** Expository Essay **Revise:** Sentence Fluency **Peer Conferences; Edit and Proofread; Publish, Present, and Evaluate** **Grammar and Mechanics** **Week 3:** Kinds of Nouns: Common Nouns, Proper Nouns, Collective Nouns; Capital Letters **Week 4:** Irregular Plural Nouns; Quotation Marks with Dialogue	**Product:** Diagram About the Wolf Food Chain **Study Skill:** Cite Sources **Blast:** "Creatures as Teachers: Aesop's Fables"
Literary Elements: Rhythm **Skill:** Key Details **Author's Craft:** Structures and Patterns	**Week 5** **Phonological Awareness:** Identify and Generate Rhyme **Phonemic Awareness:** Substitution, Blending **Phonics/Spelling*:** Three-Letter Blends *scr, spr, str, thr, spl, shr* **Structural Analysis:** Compound Words **High-Frequency Words:** bird, far, field, flower, grow, leaves, light, orange, ready, until **Handwriting:** *u, w; b, f*	**Week 5:** Expression	**Respond to Reading** **Writing Process** Rhyming Poem **Expert Model:** Rhyming Poem **Plan:** Word Choice: Precise Language **Draft:** Ideas: Specific Details **Grammar and Mechanics** **Week 5:** Possessive Nouns; Apostrophes	**Product:** Animal Habitat Cards **Study Skill:** Generate Questions **Blast:** "Dogs on the Job"

*Differentiated Spelling Lists available

Scope and Sequence

Genre Focus	Read Aloud	Shared Read	Literature Anthology	Leveled Readers	Vocabulary
Genre Study 1: **Weeks 1 and 2** **Genre:** Narrative Nonfiction **Essential Question:** How can people help out their community? **Text Features:** Photos and Captions *Differentiated Genre Passages available*	**Interactive Read Aloud:** "Color Your Community" **Genre:** Nonfiction Narrative	"Lighting Lives" **Genre:** Informational Text **Lexile:** 650L *ELL Scaffolded Shared Read available*	**Anchor Text** *Biblioburro: A True Story from Columbia* **Genre:** Narrative Nonfiction **Lexile:** 700L **Paired Selection** "Landing on Your Feet" **Genre:** Personal Narrative **Lexile:** 610	**Main Selections** **Genre:** Narrative Nonfiction A: *City Communities* **Lexile:** 290L O: *City Communities* **Lexile:** 470L ELL: *City Communities* **Lexile:** 400L B: *City Communities* **Lexile:** 620L **Paired Selections** **Genre:** Folktale A: "Magic Anansi" O: "Magic Anansi" ELL: "Magic Anansi" B: "Magic Anansi"	**Words:** *across, borrow, countryside, ideas, insists, lonely, solution, villages* **Strategy:** Synonyms
Genre Study 2: **Weeks 3 and 4** **Genre:** Fiction **Essential Question:** What can we see in the sky? **Literary Elements:** Point of View (third person) *Differentiated Genre Passages available*	**Interactive Read Aloud:** "The Hidden Sun" **Genre:** Fiction	"Starry Night" **Genre:** Fiction **Lexile:** 540L *ELL Scaffolded Shared Read available*	**Anchor Text** *Mr. Putter and Tabby See the Stars* **Genre:** Fiction **Lexile:** 580L **Paired Selection** "Day to Night" **Genre:** Expository Text **Lexile:** 550L	**Main Selections** **Genre:** Fiction A: *A Special Sunset* **Lexile:** 200L O: *A Different Set of Stars* **Lexile:** 390L ELL: *A Different Set of Stars* **Lexile:** 330L B: *Shadows in the Sky* **Lexile:** 540L **Paired Selections** **Genre:** Expository Text A: "Shadows and Sundials" O: "Stars" ELL: "Stars" B: "Eclipses"	**Words:** *adventure, delighted, dreamed, enjoy, grumbled, moonlight, neighbor, nighttime* **Strategy:** Compound Words
Genre Study 3: **Week 5** **Genre:** Expository: Informational Text **Essential Question:** How do you express yourself? **Text Features:** Bar Graph *Differentiated Genre Passages available*	**Interactive Read Aloud:** "Why People Drum" **Genre:** Expository Text	"They've Got the Beat!" **Genre:** Expository Text **Lexile:** 620L *ELL Scaffolded Shared Read available*	**Anchor Text** "Many Ways to Enjoy Music" **Genre:** Expository Text **Lexile:** 680L **Paired Selection** "A Musical Museum" **Genre:** Expository Text **Lexile:** 640L	**Main Selection** **Genre:** Expository Text A: *The Sounds of Trash* **Lexile:** 410L O: *The Sounds of Trash* **Lexile:** 530L ELL: *The Sounds of Trash* **Lexile:** 380L B: *The Sounds of Trash* **Lexile:** 590L **Paired Selections** **Genre:** Expository Text A: "Talking Underwater" O: "Talking Underwater" ELL: "Talking Underwater" B: "Talking Underwater"	**Words:** *cheered, concert, instrument, movements, music, rhythm, sounds, understand* **Strategy:** Prefixes

Week 6	Reading Digitally	Fluency	Show What You Learned	Extend Your Learning	Writing	Presentation Options
Review, Extend, and Assess	"Antarctica Bound!" **Genre:** Online Article	**Reader's Theater:** "I'll Be the Dragon"	**Passage 1** "Landing the Eagle" **Genre:** Narrative Nonfiction **Passage 2** "A Shower in the Sky" **Genre:** Fiction	Focus on Genre Sequence of Events Prefixes Write a Personal Narrative Respond to the Read Aloud **Connect to Content:** Write an Ad for Community Helpers	**Writing Process** Expository Essay **Revise:** Strong Openings **Peer Conferences; Edit and Proofread; Publish, Present, and Evaluate**	**Reader's Theater** **Research and Inquiry** **Writing**

Comprehension	Word Work	Fluency	Writing and Grammar	Research and Inquiry
Strategy: Ask and Answer Questions **Skill:** Author's Purpose **Author's Craft:** Time Words	**Week 1** **Phonological Awareness:** Identify and Generate Rhyme **Phonemic Awareness:** Categorization, Blending **Phonics/Spelling*:** Long *a: a, ai, ay, ea, ei, eigh, ey* **Structural Analysis:** Contractions with *'s, 're, 'll, 've* **High-Frequency Words:** about, around, good, great, idea, often, part, second, two, world **Handwriting:** *h, k; g, q* **Week 2** **Phonemic Awareness:** Isolation, Substitution, Blending, Categorization **Phonics/Spelling*:** Long *i: i, y, igh, ie* **Structural Analysis:** Open Syllables **High-Frequency Words:** also, apart, begin, either, hundred, over, places, those, which, without **Handwriting:** *j, p; r, s*	**Week 1:** Expression **Week 2:** Phrasing	**Respond to Reading** **Writing Process** Personal Narrative **Expert Model:** Personal Narrative **Plan:** Organization: Sequence **Draft:** Focus on an Event **Grammar and Mechanics** **Week 1:** Action Verbs; Book Titles **Week 2:** Present-Tense Verbs; Commas in a Series	**Product:** History Picture Book **Study Skill:** Primary and Secondary Sources **Blast:** "Making Our Lives Better... Together"
Strategy: Reread **Skill:** Sequence **Author's Craft:** Heads	**Week 3** **Phonemic Awareness:** Deletion, Substitution, Addition, Blending **Phonics/Spelling*:** Long *o: o, oa, ow, oe* **Structural Analysis:** Contractions with *not* **High-Frequency Words:** better, group, long, more, only, our, started, three, who, won't **Handwriting:** *y, z, v, x* **Week 4** **Phonological Awareness:** Identify Syllables **Phonemic Awareness:** Categorization, Blending **Phonics/Spelling*:** Long *e: e, ee, ea, ie, y, ey, e_e* **Structural Analysis:** Plurals with *-s, -es* (change y to i) **High-Frequency Words:** after, before, every, few, first, hear, hurt, old, special, would **Handwriting:** Letter and Word Spacing	**Week 3:** Intonation **Week 4:** Expression	**Respond to Reading** **Writing Process** Personal Narrative **Revise:** Conclusion **Peer Conferences; Edit and Proofread; Publish, Present, and Evaluate** **Grammar and Mechanics** **Week 3:** Past- and Future-Tense Verbs; Letter Punctuation **Week 4:** Subject-Verb Agreement; Abbreviations	**Product:** Moon Phase Report **Study Skill:** Develop a Research Plan **Blast:** "When the Night Sky Dances"
Strategy: Ask and Answer Questions **Skill:** Main Idea and Key Details **Author's Craft:** Text Features: Diagrams	**Week 5** **Phonological Awareness:** Identify and Generate Alliteration **Phonemic Awareness:** Addition and Deletion, Blending **Phonics/Spelling*:** Long *u: u_e, ue, u, ew* **Structural Analysis:** Comparative Endings *-er, -est* **High-Frequency Words:** America, beautiful, began, climbed, come, country, didn't, give, live, turned **Handwriting:** Review lower case letters	**Week 5:** Intonation	**Respond to Reading** **Writing Process** Expository Essay **Expert Model:** Expository Essay **Plan:** Research: Choose and Evaluate Sources **Draft:** Paragraphs **Grammar and Mechanics** **Week 5:** The Verb *have*; Sentence Punctuation	**Product:** Patriotic Song Collage **Study Skill:** Relevant Information **Blast:** "Show Yourself Through Your Art"

*Differentiated Spelling Lists available

Scope and Sequence

Genre Focus	Read Aloud	Shared Read	Literature Anthology	Leveled Readers	Vocabulary
Genre Study 1: Weeks 1 and 2 **Genre:** Realistic Fiction **Essential Question:** How are kids around the world different? **Literary Elements:** Point of View *Differentiated Genre Passages available*	**Interactive Read Aloud:** "My New School" **Genre:** Realistic Fiction	"Happy New Year!" **Genre:** Realistic Fiction **Lexile:** 590L *ELL Scaffolded Shared Read available*	**Anchor Text** *Dear Primo: A Letter to My Cousin* **Genre:** Realistic Fiction **Lexile:** 610L **Paired Selection** "Games Around the World" **Genre:** Expository Text **Lexile:** 600L	**Main Selections** **Genre:** Realistic Fiction A: *Sharing Cultures* **Lexile:** 350L O: *A New Life in India* **Lexile:** 480L ELL: *A New Life in India* **Lexile:** 440L B: *Akita and Carlo* **Lexile:** 620L **Paired Selections** **Genre:** Expository Text A: "Music Around the World" O: "Dress Around the World" ELL: "Dress Around the World" B: "Food Around the World"	**Words:** *common, costume, customs, favorite, parade, surrounded, travels, wonder* **Strategy:** Similes
Genre Study 2: Weeks 3 and 4 **Genre:** Expository Text **Essential Question:** How does the Earth change? **Text Features:** Subheads and Bold Print *Differentiated Genre Passages available*	**Interactive Read Aloud:** "Earth Changes" **Genre:** Expository Text	"Into the Sea" **Genre:** Expository Text **Lexile:** 650L *ELL Scaffolded Shared Read available*	**Anchor Text** *Volcanoes* **Genre:** Expository Text **Lexile:** 680L **Paired Selection** "To The Rescue" **Genre:** Expository Text **Lexile:** 750L	**Main Selections** **Genre:** Expository Text A: *Earthquakes* **Lexile:** 350L O: *Earthquakes* **Lexile:** 530L ELL: *Earthquakes* **Lexile:** 430L B: *Earthquakes* **Lexile:** 630L **Paired Selections** **Genre:** Expository Text A: "Glaciers" O: "Glaciers" ELL: "Glaciers" B: "Glaciers"	**Words:** *active, Earth, explode, island, local, properties, solid, steep* **Strategy:** Sentence Clues
Genre Study 3: Week 5 **Genre:** Poetry **Essential Question:** What excites us about nature? **Literary Elements:** Free Verse, Repetition *Differentiated Genre Passages available*	**Interactive Read Aloud:** "Redwood National Forest," "The Amazing Meadow," "The Sahara Desert" **Genre:** Poetry	"Snow Shape," Nature Walk," "In the Sky" **Genre:** Poetry **Lexile:** NP *ELL Scaffolded Shared Read available*	**Anchor Text** "April Rain Song," "Rain Poem" **Genre:** Poetry **Lexile:** NP **Paired Selection** "Helicopters," "Windy Tree" **Genre:** Poetry **Lexile:** NP	**Main Selections** **Genre:** Fiction A: *A Hike in the Woods* **Lexile:** 340L O: *A Little World* **Lexile:** 500L ELL: *A Little World* **Lexile:** 400L B: *Star Party* **Lexile:** 590L **Paired Selections** **Genre:** Poem A: "The Woods" O: "See a Star" ELL: "By the Sea" B: "Moon"	**Words:** *drops, excite, outdoors, pale* **Strategy:** Antonyms

Week 6	Reading Digitally	Fluency	Show What You Learned	Extend Your Learning	Writing	Presentation Options
Review, Extend, and Assess	"Hope for the Everglades!" **Genre:** Online Article	**Reader's Theater:** *A Whale of a Story*	**Passage 1** "Rivers of Ice" **Genre:** Expository Text **Passage 2** "How to Wait," "Against the Wind" **Genre:** Free Verse Poems	Comparing Genres Antonyms Write a Thank You Letter **Connect to Content:** Game Guide Reading Digitally	**Writing Process** Free Verse Poem **Revise:** Word Choice **Peer Conferences; Edit and Proofread; Publish, Present, and Evaluate**	**Reader's Theater** **Research and Inquiry** **Writing**

Comprehension	Word Work	Fluency	Writing and Grammar	Research and Inquiry
Strategy: Visualize **Skill:** Compare and Contrast **Author's Craft:** Maps	**Week 1** **Phonemic Awareness:** Identity, Categorization, Blending **Phonics/Spelling*:** Silent Letters *wr, kn, gn, mb, sc* **Structural Analysis:** Prefixes *re-, un-, dis-*; Suffixes *-ful, -less* **High-Frequency Words:** below, colors, don't, down, eat, many, morning, sleep, through, very **Handwriting:** Strokes for Cursive Writing; Size and Shape **Week 2** **Phonemic Awareness:** Substitution, Blending, Addition **Phonics/Spelling*:** *r*-Controlled Vowel /ûr/: *er, ir, ur, or* **Structural Analysis:** Inflectional Endings **High-Frequency Words:** animal, away, building, found, from, Saturday, thought, today, toward, watch **Handwriting:** *A, O; C, E*	**Week 1:** Intonation **Week 2:** Expression	**Respond to Reading** **Writing Process** Realistic Fiction **Expert Model:** Realistic Fiction **Plan:** Ideas: Develop Details **Draft:** Compare and Contrast **Grammar and Mechanics** **Week 1:** Linking Verbs; Letter Punctuation **Week 2:** Helping Verbs; Book Titles	**Product:** Celebrations Chart **Study Skill:** Primary and Secondary Sources **Blast:** "What in the World is for Dinner?"
Strategy: Reread **Skill:** Text Structure: Cause and Effect **Author's Craft:** Text Structure	**Week 3** **Phonological Awareness:** Identify and Generate Rhyme **Phonemic Awareness:** Substitution, Blending **Phonics/Spelling*:** *r*-controlled vowels /ôr/: *or, ore, oar* and /är/: *ar* **Structural Analysis:** Plurals (irregular) **High-Frequency Words:** ago, carry, certain, everyone, heavy, outside, people, problem, together, warm **Handwriting:** *L, D; B, R* **Week 4** **Phonological Awareness:** Identify Syllables **Phonemic Awareness:** Blending **Phonics/Spelling*:** *r*-controlled vowel /îr/: *eer, ere, ear* **Structural Analysis:** Abbreviations **High-Frequency Words:** again, behind, eyes, gone, happened, house, inside, neither, stood, young **Handwriting:** *T, F; S, G*	**Week 3:** Phrasing **Week 4:** Intonation	**Respond to Reading** **Writing Process** Realistic Fiction **Revise:** Voice **Peer Conference; Edit and Proofread; Publish, Present, and Evaluate** **Grammar and Mechanics** **Week 3:** Irregular Verbs; Capitalization of Proper Nouns **Week 4:** Contractions with *not*; Apostrophes	**Product:** Drawing of Earth Changes **Study Skill:** Sequence Information **Blast:** "How Mountains Form"
Literary Elements: Repetition **Skill:** Theme **Author's Craft:** Figurative Language	**Week 5** **Phonological Awareness:** Identify Syllables **Phonemic Awareness:** Categorization, Blending **Phonics/Spelling*:** *r*-controlled vowel /âr/: *are, air, ear, ere* **Structural Analysis:** *r*-controlled vowel syllables **High-Frequency Words:** among, bought, knew, never, once, soon, sorry, talk, touch, upon **Handwriting:** *I, J;* Punctuation Marks (cursive)	**Week 5:** Phrasing	**Respond to Reading** **Writing Process** Free Verse Poem **Expert Model:** Free Verse Poem **Plan:** Word Choice: Sensory Words **Draft:** Visual Patterns **Grammar and Mechanics** **Week 5:** Using Conjunctions to Form Compound Subjects and Predicates; Sentence Punctuation	**Product:** Diagram Water Cycle **Study Skill:** Develop and Follow a Research Plan **Blast:** "From the Oceans to the Skies"

*Differentiated Spelling Lists available

Scope and Sequence

Genre Focus	Read Aloud	Shared Read	Literature Anthology	Leveled Readers	Vocabulary
Genre Study 1: Weeks 1 and 2 **Genre:** Biography **Essential Question:** What do heroes do? **Text Features:** Boldprint and Timeline *Differentiated Genre Passages Available*	**Interactive Read Aloud:** "A Hero On and Off Skis" **Genre:** Biography	"César Chávez" **Genre:** Biography **Lexile:** 600L *ELL Scaffolded Shared Read available*	**Anchor Text** *Brave Bessie* **Genre:** Biography **Lexile:** 650L **Paired Selection** "The Princess Frog" **Genre:** Fairy Tale **Lexile:** 610L	**Main Selections** **Genre:** Biography A: *Rudy Garcia-Tolson* **Lexile:** 420L O: *Rudy Garcia-Tolson* **Lexile:** 550L ELL: *Rudy Garcia-Tolson* **Lexile:** 490L B: *Rudy Garcia-Tolson* **Lexile:** 640L **Paired Selections** **Genre:** Biography A: "The Unsinkable Molly Brown" O: "The Unsinkable Molly Brown" ELL: "The Unsinkable Molly Brown" B: "The Unsinkable Molly Brown"	**Words:** *agree, challenging, discover, heroes, interest, perform, study, succeed* **Strategy:** Synonyms
Genre Study 2: Weeks 3 and 4 **Genre:** Realistic Fiction **Essential Question:** What do good citizens do? **Literary Elements:** Story Structure: First Person *Differentiated Genre Passages Available*	**Interactive Read Aloud:** "A Colorful Problem" **Genre:** Realistic Fiction	"A Difficult Decision" **Genre:** Realistic Fiction **Lexile:** 510L *ELL Scaffolded Shared Read available*	**Anchor Text** *Grace for President* **Genre:** Realistic Fiction **Lexile:** 580L **Paired Selection** "Helping to Make Smiles" **Genre:** Narrative Nonfiction **Lexile:** 520L	**Main Selections** **Genre:** Fantasy A: *Fixing the Playground* **Lexile:** 340L O: *The Food Crew* **Lexile:** 480L ELL: *The Food Crew* **Lexile:** 430L B: *How Many Greats* **Lexile:** 620L **Paired Selections** **Genre:** Narrative Nonfiction A: "Hero" O: "A School Feeds Others" ELL: "A School Feeds Others" B: "Freedom Walk"	**Words:** *champion, determined, issues, promises, responsibility, rights, volunteered, votes* **Strategy:** Suffixes -ful, -less
Genre Study 3: Week 5 **Genre:** Persuasive Text **Essential Question:** Why are rules important? **Text Features:** Chart *Differentiated Genre Passages Available*	**Interactive Read Aloud:** "Towns Need Rules!" **Genre:** Persuasive Text	"The Problem with Plastic Bags" **Genre:** Persuasive Article **Lexile:** 670L *ELL Scaffolded Shared Read available*	**Anchor Text** "A Call to Compost" **Genre:** Persuasive Text **Lexile:** 660L **Paired Selection** "American Symbols" **Genre:** Expository Text **Lexile:** 650L	**Main Selections** **Genre:** Persuasive Text A: *Do People Need Rules?* **Lexile:** 510L O: *Do People Need Rules?* **Lexile:** 620L ELL: *Do People Need Rules?* **Lexile:** 610L B: *Do People Need Rules?* **Lexile:** 710L **Paired Selections** **Genre:** Expository Text A: "Pool Rules" O: "Pool Rules" ELL: "Pool Rules" B: "Pool Rules"	**Words:** *exclaimed, finally, form, history, public, rules, united, writers* **Strategy:** Multiple-Meaning Words

Week 6	Reading Digitally	Fluency	Show What You Learned	Extend Your Learning	Writing	Presentation Options
Review, Extend, and Assess	"Good Deeds Add Up" **Genre:** Online Article	**Reader's Theater:** "The Search for the Magic Lake"	**Passage 1** "George Washington Carver" **Genre:** Biography **Passage 2** "Dad for Mayor!" **Genre:** Realistic Fiction	Comparing Genres Suffixes Write a persuasive letter Respond to the Read Aloud **Connect to Content:** Create a Timeline	**Writing Process:** Persuasive essay **Revise:** Voice **Peer Conferences; Edit and Proofread; Publish, Present, and Evaluate**	**Reader's Theater** **Research and Inquiry** **Writing**

Comprehension	Word Work	Fluency	Writing and Grammar	Research and Inquiry
Strategy: Summarize **Skill:** Connections Within a Text: Sequence **Author's Craft:** Third Person Point of View	**Week 1** **Phonemic Awareness:** Reversal, Substitution, Blending **Phonics/Spelling*:** diphthongs *ou, ow* **Structural Analysis:** Plurals (irregular) **High-Frequency Words:** answer, been, body, build, head [body part], heard, minutes, myself, pretty, pushed **Handwriting:** *N, M, H, K* **Week 2** **Phonemic Awareness:** Blending, Substitution, Segmentation, Deletion **Phonics/Spelling*:** diphthongs *oy, oi* **Structural Analysis:** consonant + *le* syllables (*el, al, tion, sion*) **High-Frequency Words:** brought, busy, else, happy, I'll, laugh, love, maybe, please, several **Handwriting:** *P, Q, V, U*	**Week 1** Phrasing **Week 2** Intonation	**Respond to Reading** **Writing Process** Biography **Expert Model:** Biography **Plan:** Identify Primary and Secondary Sources **Draft:** Sequence **Grammar and Mechanics** **Week 1:** Pronouns (singular, plural); Capitalizing the pronoun *I* **Week 2:** Subjective, Objective, Possessive Pronouns; Commas in Dates	**Product:** Poster About an American Hero **Study Skill:** Paraphrase and Understand Information **Blast:** "What Makes a Hero?"
Strategy: Make and Confirm Predictions **Skill:** Point of View **Author's Craft:** Graphic Features/Callouts	**Week 3** **Phonological Awareness:** Identify Syllables **Phonemic Awareness:** Categorization, Blending **Phonics/Spelling*:** variant vowel /ü/: *oo, u, u_e, ew, ue, ui*; Variant Vowel /ů/: *oo, ou, u* **Structural Analysis:** Contractions with *not* **High-Frequency Words:** air, along, always, draw, during, ever, meant, nothing, story, strong **Handwriting:** *W, X,Y, Z* **Week 4** **Phonological Awareness:** Identify Syllables **Phonemic Awareness:** Deletion, Blending, Addition **Phonics/Spelling*:** variant vowel /ô/: *a, aw, au, augh, al, ough* **Structural Analysis:** Vowel Team Syllables **High-Frequency Words:** city, father, mother, o'clock, own, questions, read, searching, sure, though **Handwriting:** Spacing: Letters and Words	**Week 3:** Phrasing **Week 4:** Expression	**Respond to Reading** **Writing Process** Realistic Fiction **Revise:** Strong Conclusion **Peer Conferences; Edit and Proofread; Publish, Present, and Evaluate** **Grammar and Mechanics** **Week 3:** Pronoun-Verb agreement; Capitalization of Proper Nouns **Week 4:** Possessive Pronouns & Reflexive Pronouns; Letter Punctuation	**Product:** Make a Pamphlet About What Good Leaders Do **Study Skill:** Ask and Answer Questions **Blast:** "I Can Be a Good Citizen, Too!"
Strategy: Summarize **Skill:** Author's Purpose **Author's Craft:** Print and Graphic Features	**Week 5** **Phonemic Awareness:** Deletion, Segmentation, Reversal, Blending **Phonics/Spelling*:** short vowel digraphs /e/*ea*; /u/*ou*; /i/*y* **Structural Analysis:** Alphabetical Order **High-Frequency Words:** anything, children, everybody, instead, paper [piece of paper], person, voice, whole, woman, words **Handwriting:** Review of Lowercase and Uppercase	**Week 5:** Intonation	**Respond to Reading** **Writing Process** Persuasive Essay **Expert Model:** Persuasive Text **Plan:** Voice: Persuasive Language **Draft:** Ideas: Develop a Topic **Grammar and Mechanics** **Week 5:** Contraction; Contractions with Pronouns/Possessive Pronouns	**Product:** Make a Recycling Chart **Study Skill:** Find and Gather Sources **Blast:** "Rules of Respect at School"

Differentiated Spelling Lists available

Scope and Sequence

Genre Focus	Read Aloud	Shared Reading	Literature Anthology	Leveled Readers	Vocabulary
Genre Study 1: Weeks 1 and 2 **Genre:** Expository Text **Essential Question:** How do we use money? **Text Features:** Subheads and Graphs *Differentiated Genre Passages available*	**Interactive Read Aloud:** "Keep the Change!" **Genre:** Expository Text	"The Life of a Dollar Bill" **Genre:** Expository Text **Lexile:** 660L *ELL Scaffolded Shared Read available*	**Anchor Text** *Money Madness* **Genre:** Expository Text **Lexile:** 780L **Paired Selection** "King Midas and the Golden Touch" **Genre:** Myth **Lexile:** 720L	**Main Selections** **Genre:** Expository Text A: *How to Be a Smart Shopper* **Lexile:** 450L O: *How to Be a Smart Shopper* **Lexile:** 540L ELL: *How to Be a Smart Shopper* **Lexile:** 500L B: *How to Be a Smart Shopper* **Lexile:** 680L **Paired Selections** **Genre:** Myth A: "The Golden Fleece" O: "The Golden Fleece" ELL: "The Golden Fleece" B: "The Golden Fleece"	**Words:** invented, money, prices, purchase, record, system, value, worth **Strategy:** Paragraph Clues
Genre Study 2: Weeks 3 and 4 **Genre:** Drama/Myth **Essential Question:** What do myths help us understand? **Literary Elements:** Elements of a Play *Differentiated Genre Passages available*	**Interactive Read Aloud:** "The Queen of Flowers" **Genre:** Myth	"The Starry Asters" **Genre:** Myth **Lexile:** NP *ELL Scaffolded Shared Read available*	**Anchor Text** *The Contest of Athena and Poseidon* **Genre:** Drama/Myth **Lexile:** NP **Paired Selection** "A Pumpkin Plant" **Genre:** Expository Text **Lexile:** 600L	**Main Selections** **Genre:** Drama/Myth A: *The Apples of Idun* **Lexile:** 400L O: *Hercules and the Golden Apples* **Lexile:** 550L ELL: *Hercules and the Golden Apples* **Lexile:** 440L B: *Demeter and Persephone* **Lexile:** 630L **Paired Selections** **Genre:** Expository Text A: "Tomatoes" O: "Apples" ELL: "Apples" B: "Pomegranates"	**Words:** appeared, crops, develop, edge, golden, rustled, shining, stages **Strategy:** Idioms
Genre Study 3: Week 5 **Genre:** Poetry **Essential Question:** Where can your imagination take you? **Text Features:** Stanza *Differentiated Genre Passages available*	**Interactive Read Aloud:** "Give Me a Brown Box," "Music Sends Me" **Genre:** Poetry	"A Box of Crayons," "What Story is This?," "The Ticket" **Genre:** Poetry **Lexile:** NP *ELL Scaffolded Shared Read available*	**Anchor Text** "Books to the Ceiling," "I've Got This Covered," "Eating While Reading" **Genre:** Poetry **Lexile:** NP **Paired Selection** "Clay Play," "Crayons" **Genre:** Poetry **Lexile:** NP	**Main Selections** **Genre:** Fiction A: *Matt's Journey* **Lexile:** 430L O: *A Fantastic Day!* **Lexile:** 560L ELL: *A Fantastic Day!* **Lexile:** 470L B: *A Day in Ancient Rome* **Lexile:** 640L **Paired Selections** **Genre:** Poetry A: "Autumn Leaves/The Orchestra" O: "A Butterfly Life/Circus Day" ELL: "Pablo and I/My Tiny Friend" B: "Lost and Found/My Magic Car"	**Words:** create, dazzling, imagination, seconds **Strategy:** Metaphors

Week 6	Reading Digitally	Fluency	Show What You Learned	Extend Your Learning	Writing	Presentation Options
Review, Extend, and Assess	"Whispering Whales" **Genre:** Online Article	**Reader's Theater:** "Mother Goose to the Rescue"	**Passage 1** "Building a Career" **Genre:** Expository Text **Passage 2** **Genre:** "The Thunder Goddess" **Genre:** Drama	Comparing Genres Idioms Write a How-To Guide **Connect to Content:** Write an online article **Reading Digitally:** "Whispering Whales"	**Poetry:** Rhyming Poem **Revise:** Rhythm **Peer Conferences; Edit and Proofread; Publish, Present, and Evaluate**	**Reader's Theater** **Research and Inquiry** **Writing**

Comprehension	Word Work	Fluency	Writing and Grammar	Research and Inquiry
Strategy: Summarize **Skill:** Text Structure: Problem and Solution **Author's Craft:** Word Choice	**Week 1** **Phonological Awareness:** Identify and Generate Rhyme **Phonemic Awareness:** Addition, Blending, Deletion **Phonics/Spelling*:** Closed and open syllables **Structural Analysis:** Compound words **High-Frequency Words:** door, front, order, probably, remember, someone, tomorrow, what's, worry, yesterday **Handwriting:** Abbreviations; Envelope **Week 2** **Phonemic Awareness:** Addition, Segmentation, Substitution, Blending **Phonics/Spelling*:** Words with CVCe Syllables **Structural Analysis:** review prefixes *re-, un-, dis-* and suffixes *-ful, -less* **High-Frequency Words:** alone, became, beside, four, hello, large, notice, round, suppose, surprised **Handwriting:** Letter punctuation marks; Letter format	**Week 1:** Intonation **Week 2:** Phrasing	**Respond to Reading** **Writing Process** Research Report **Expert Model:** Research Report **Plan:** Generate Questions for Research **Draft:** Paraphrase **Grammar and Mechanics** **Week 1:** Adjectives including articles; Abbreviations **Week 2:** Articles and *this, that, these, and those*; Commas in Dates	**Product:** Create a Flow Chart **Study Skill:** Visual Materials **Blast:** "Making Dollars and Cents"
Strategy: Reread **Skill:** Theme **Author's Craft:** Instructions	**Week 3** **Phonological Awareness:** Identify Syllables **Phonemic Awareness:** Segmentation and Blending, Addition and Deletion **Phonics/Spelling*:** Final stable syllables: words with consonant + *le el, al, tion, sion* **Structural Analysis:** Contractions, Possessives **High-Frequency Words:** above, brother, song, follow, listen, month, soft, something, who's, wind **Handwriting:** Form; Poster **Week 4** **Phonemic Awareness:** Segmentation, Substitution, Reversal, Blending **Phonics/Spelling*:** Vowel team syllables. **Structural Analysis:** Comparative endings **High-Frequency Words:** against, anymore, complete, enough, river, rough, sometimes, stranger, terrible, window **Handwriting:** Poem	**Week 3:** Expression **Week 4:** Intonation	**Respond to Reading** **Writing Process** Research Report **Revise:** Sentence Fluency **Peer Conferences; Edit and Proofread; Publish, Present, and Evaluate** **Grammar and Mechanics** **Week 3:** Adjectives that Compare; Apostrophes **Week 4:** Adverbs (including adverbs that convey time and adverbs that convey place); Names and Title	**Product:** Create a Diagram of a Plant **Study Skill:** Diagrams **Blast:** "Plants and Flowers That Grow into Myths"
Literary Elements: Rhyme **Skill:** Point of View **Author's Craft:** Rhythm and Rhyme	**Week 5** **Phonemic Awareness:** Addition, Substitution, Segmentation **Phonics/Spelling*:** Words with *r*-controlled vowel syllables. **Structural Analysis:** three (or more) syllable words **High-Frequency Words:** afternoon, ahead, anyone, everything, pretended, scientist, somehow, throughout, trouble, wherever **Handwriting:** Story	**Week 5:** Expression	**Respond to Reading** **Writing Process** Poetry **Expert Model:** Rhyming Poem **Plan:** Word Choice **Draft:** Rhyme and Rhythm **Grammar and Mechanics** **Week 5:** Prepositions and Prepositional Phrases; Sentence Punctuation	**Product:** Create an Oral Report **Study Skill:** Present Information **Blast:** "Set Your Imagination Free!"

Differentiated Spelling Lists available.

Social Emotional Development

Emotional Self Regulation
Manages feelings, emotions, and words with decreasing support from adults

As the child collaborates with a partner, the child uses appropriate words calmly when disagreeing.

Behavioral Self Regulation
Manages actions, behaviors, and words with decreasing support from adults

Rules and Routines
Follows classroom rules and routines with increasing independence

Transitioning from one activity to the next, the child follows established routines, such as putting away materials, without disrupting the class.

Working Memory
Maintains and manipulates distinct pieces of information over short periods of time

Focus Attention
Maintains focus and sustains attention with minimal adult supports

During Center Time, the child stays focused on the activity assigned and is able to stop working on the activity when it is time to move on to a different task.

Relationships and Prosocial Behaviors
Engages in and maintains positive relationships and interactions with familiar adults and children

Social Problem Solving
Uses basic problem solving skills to resolve conflicts with other children

Self Awareness
Recognizes self as a unique individual as well as belonging to a family, community, or other groups; expresses confidence in own skills

Creativity
Expresses creativity in thinking and communication

Initiative
Demonstrates initiative and independence

When working independently, the child understands when to ask for help and gets the help needed.

Task Persistence
Sets reasonable goals and persists to complete the task

Logic and Reasoning
Thinks critically to effectively solve a problem or make a decision

Planning and Problem Solving
Uses planning and problem solving strategies to achieve goals

Flexible Thinking
Demonstrates flexibility in thinking and behavior

GRADE 2 ⟫⟫⟫ GRADE 3 ⟫⟫⟫ GRADE 4 ⟫⟫⟫ GRADE 5

During class discussions, the child can wait until called upon to provide a response, without shouting out.

When responding to a text, the child can identify text evidence from notes previously recorded.

The child willingly works with any other child in the class on partner or group activities that are assigned.

When working on a project in a small group, the child negotiates roles and cooperates with others to complete the task.

In class discussion, the child is not fearful of sharing a unique perspective while respecting the opinions of others.

The child finds a creative way to gather information needed for a writing assignment.

When assigned to read a difficult text, the child applies routines or strategies learned to complete the reading.

Through logic and reasoning, the child is able to figure out how the author's choices of words and structures affect the communication of ideas.

When working on a long-term research project, the student can think through how to complete the different parts of the assignment over a period of time.

As the child struggles with an activity, she can determine a different way to complete the activity successfully.

(t) Terra Image/Shutterstock; (b) Patrick Foto/Shutterstock

Key 3 = Unit 3

Key 3 = Unit 3

Key 3 = Unit 3

U

Unit wrap up, Units 1–3: T467, Units 4–6: T463

V

Verbs. *See* **Grammar.**

Videos, 1: T205, T231, T305, T444, T464, T465, T472, 2: T464, T465, 3: T75, T218, T219, T464, T465, 4: T214, T287, T441, T453, T460, 5: T73, T214, T460, T468, 6: T46, T214, T452, T460, T468

See also **Digital Learning.**

Vocabulary development

academic vocabulary, Units 1–3: T72, T228, T374, Units 4–6: T70, T224, T370

cognates, Units 1–3: T24, T34, T36, T38, T44, T52, T54, T56, T58, T60, T62, T80, T86, T104, T112, T132, T134, T140, T142, T146, T148, T152, T154, T156, T158, T160, T162, T180, T190, T192, T194, T196, T198, T200, T202, T204, T206, T208, T210, T231, T288, T290, T296, T298, T302, T304, T308, T310, T312, T314, T316, T318, T334, T342, T344, T358, T360, T362, T364, T368, T377, T378, T388, T408, T414, T416, T426, T428, T432, T434, T436, T444, T452, T454, T456, T458, T460, T462, T464, T470, Units 4–6: T24, T32, T34, T36, T38, T40, T42, T44, T46, T48, T50, T52, T54, T56, T60, T74, T76, T78, T102, T106, T110, T130, T132, T138, T140, T144, T146, T150, T152, T154, T156, T158, T160, T178, T186, T188, T190, T192, T194, T196, T198, T200, T202, T204, T206, T208, T210, T212, T214, T228, T284, T286, T292, T294, T298, T300, T304, T306, T308, T310, T312, T314, T330, T338, T340, T342, T346, T350, T352, T354, T356, T358, T360, T402, T410, T416, T422, T424, T426, T432, T440, T448, T450, T452, T454, T456, T458, T460, T466

computer-related, 1: T48, T444, T445, 2: T444, T445, 3: T444, T445, 4: T444, T445, 5: T444, T445, 6: T53, T444–T445

domain-specific Units 1–3: T150, T306, T424, Units 4–6: T148, T302, T420

expanding, Units 1–3: T72–T73, T228–T229, T374–T375, Units 4–6: T70–T71, T224–T225, T370–T371

explain/model/practice routine, Units 1–3: T34, T190, T342, Units 4–6: T32, T186, T338

multiple-meaning words, 3: T81, T109, 5: T338–T339, T353B, T414, T420, T431, T446

oral vocabulary, Units 1–3: T26, T182, T336, Units 4–6: T26, T180, T332

reinforcing, Units 1–3: T72, T228, T374, Units 4–6: T70, T224, T370

selection words, Units 1–3: T144, T300, T418, Units 4–6: T142, T296, T414

sort words, Units 1–3: T68–T69, T70–T71, T224–T225, T226–T227, T372–T373, Units 4–6: T66–T67, T68–T69, T220–T221, T222–T223, T368–T369

words in context, Units 1–3: T34, T190, T342, Units 4–6: T32, T186, T338

sentence clues, 2: T188, 3: T31, T183, T339, 4: T31, T183, T184, T185, T302, 6: T201E

See also **Academic language; Vocabulary skills and strategies.**

Vocabulary skills and strategies

antonyms, 2: T33, T73, T186, T187, T188, T191, T207C, T229, T293, T300, T306, T451, 4: T69, T71, T181, T221, T223, T225, T296, T332, T335, T338–T339, T371, T405, T407, T412, T414, T418, T420, T433, T447, 5: T225

compound words, 3: T51B, T185, T186, T190–T191, T206G, T229, T288, T293, T296, T300, T302, T306, T318, T451, 4: T312, T337, 5: T201K, 6: T71

context clues, 1: T34, T72, T190, T339, T341, T342, T359A, 2: T34, T137, T144, T150, T183, T188, T190–T191, T341, T359A, 3: T144, T150, T189, T339, 4: T31, T47D, T47K, T183, T184, T185, T302, 5: T30, T33, T47D, T184, T187, T201D, T336, T337, 6: T32, T71, 158, T186, T201E

paragraph clues, 3: T31, T183, 4: T31, T183, 5: T30, T184, 6: T32, T71

sentence clues, 2: T188, 3: T31, T183, T339, 4: T31, T183, T184–T185, T302, 6: T201E

See also **Vocabulary development: words in context.**

contractions, 1: T49G, 3: T80, T88, T94, T103, T244, T250, T259, 4: T218–T219, 5: T232, T240, T246, T255, T366–T367, T425

explain/model/practice routine, Units 1–3: T34, T190, T342, Units 4–6: T32, T186, T338

dictionary, using, 1: T69, T71, T136, T225, T227, T229, T293, T373, T411, T454, T462, 2: T69, T71, T72–T73, T148, T225, T227, T293, T373, T411, 3: T69, T71, T73, T159, T225, T227, T293, T373, T411, T463, 4: T67, T69, T135, T157, T212, T221, T223, T289, T369, T407, T450, T454, 5: T67, T69, T70, T187, T212, T221, T223, T225, T337, T369, T470, T446, T458, 6: T67, T71, T135, T186, T212, T221, T223, T289, T370, T407

figurative language, 4: T29, T336, T342, T348, T343B, T353D, T354, T355B, T356–T357, T358, T362, T371, T404, T412, T418, T433, T446, T448, T449, 6: T338–T339, T358, T362, T410, T412, T413, T418

Greek and Latin roots, 6: T70, T224

homographs, 2: T34–T35, T49F, T73, T135, T137, T143, T144, T148, T150

homophones, 3: T69, T72, 5: T79, T221, T223, T379

idioms, 1: T33, T205K, 2: T57, T189, 3: T458, 4: T47J, T256, 5: T185, T195, T224, 6: T85, T186–T187, T225, T284, T315, T450

inflectional endings, 1: T30–T31, T33, T34–T35, T49D, T73, T116, T122, T131, T134, T137, T143, T144, T149, T150, T161, T264, T272, T278, T287, T451 2: T88, T94, T103, 4: T106, T114, T120, T129, 5: T135

metaphor, 4: T356, 6: T337, T338–T339, T371, T404, T407, T410, T412, T413, T414, T416, T418, T419, T420, T421, T423, T424, T426, T429

multiple-meaning words, 3: T81, T109, 5: T336–T337, T338–T339, T353B, T414, T420, T431, T446

possessives. *See* **Grammar: nouns; Grammar: pronouns.**

prefixes, 1: T73, T228, 2: T31, T250, T259, T457, 3: T342–T343, T406, T411, T414, T418, T420, T424, T434, T436, T449, T454, 4: T78, T86, T92, T101, T450, 5: T370–T371, T423, 6: T71, T106, T114, T120, T129, T447

root words, 1: T34, T72–T73, T137, T187, T190–T191, T205G, T229, T278, T288, T290, T293, T298, T302, T305, T306, 2: T229, T342, T343, T406, T411, T414, T418, T420, T424, 3: T72, T228, T342–T343, T374, T418, T424, T454, 4: T78, T86, T92, T120, T183, T224, T370, 5: T70, T186, T201C, T201F, T201H, T224, T284, T286, T289, T294, T296, T298, T301, T302, T370, T450, 6: T70, T106, T114, T222, T223, T224, T370

shades of meaning, Units 1–3: T72, T228, T374, Units 4–6: T70, T224, T370

similes, 1: T49F, T157, 2: T357B, T430, T432, 3: T459, 4: T30, T32–T33, T47C, T71, T132, T135, T140, T142, T146, T148, T160–T161, T336, T354, T355B, T356, T404, T410, T417, T418–T419, T446, 6: T185

suffixes, 1: T187, 2: T228–T229, T264, T272, T278, T287, T297, T302, T337, T340, T342–T343, T406, T411, T418, T420, T424, T450, 3: T73, 4: T70, T78, T86, T92, T101, T225, 5: T181, T183, T185, T186–T187, T201C, T201F, T201H, T225, T284, T286, T289, T292, T294, T296, T298, T301, T302, T305, T313, T315, T370, T447, T450, 6: T71, T106, T114, T120, T225

synonyms, 1: T339, T342, T406, T411, T414, T417, T418, T420, T424, T437, T449, T454, 3: T34–T35, T73, T137, T140, T142, T144, T146, T149, T150, T159, 4: T332, 5: T31, T32–T33, T71, T130, T132, T135, T138, T140, T142, T146, T148, T160, T225, T289, T295, T355B, T371, T407, T414, T445, 6: T32, T71, T142, T187, T225, T289, T296, T371, T407, T414

use reference sources, 1: T69, T71, T73, T136, T144, T225, T227, T229, T293, T300,

Key 3 = Unit 3